Andrea Schulte-Peevers &
Tom Parkinson

Berlin

The Top Five

1 Reichstag
Stand in awe of the weight of its history (p99)

2 Potsdamer Platz
Sample the vibrant scenes of Berlin's newest city quarter (p101)

3 Schloss Charlottenburg
Revel in royal pomposity and stroll in the fabulous gardens (p107)

4 Jüdisches Museum
Get ready for bold architecture and a journey through history (p122)

5 Museumsinsel
Feast your eyes on treasures from around the world (p86)

Contents

Published by Lonely Planet Publications Pty Ltd
ABN 36 005 607 983

Australia Head Office, Locked Bag 1, Footscray,
Victoria 3011, ☎ 03 8379 8000, fax 03 8379 8111,
talk2us@lonelyplanet.com.au

USA 150 Linden St, Oakland, CA 94607,
☎ 510 893 8555, toll free 800 275 8555,
fax 510 893 8572, info@lonelyplanet.com

UK 72–82 Rosebery Ave, Clerkenwell, London,
EC1R 4RW, ☎ 020 7841 9000, fax 020 7841 9001,
go@lonelyplanet.co.uk

France 1 rue du Dahomey, 75011 Paris,
☎ 01 55 25 33 00, fax 01 55 25 33 01,
bip@lonelyplanet.fr, www.lonelyplanet.fr

The Authors

ANDREA SCHULTE-PEEVERS

Andrea was born and raised in Germany, and educated in London and at the University of California at Los Angeles. She has made a career out of writing about her native country for the past 14 years, the last eight for Lonely Planet. Berlin – in all its complexity and frivolity – has captured her imagination since childhood. She's been back time and again to revisit old friends and favourite places, and to delve into new neighbourhoods and experiences. Along the way she's seen the city shed its division-era heaviness and blossom into a vibrant, sexy and increasingly cosmopolitan metropolis. If she were ever to move back to Germany, you'd find her name in the Berlin phone book.

TOM PARKINSON

Tom wrote the City Life, Arts, History, Entertainment and Excursions chapters. He first visited Berlin briefly on Interrail trips and didn't actually like the city much; luckily the city grew on him in absentia, and when he landed a job there as part of his German degree it seemed ideal. After a year of so-late-they're-early nights, outlandish music, free drinks and random encounters, Berlin was firmly established as Tom's favourite European city, and he regularly revisits old and new haunts, just to make sure they don't remember him.

PHOTOGRAPHER
RICHARD NEBESKY

Richard was not born with a camera in his hand; however, it wasn't long before his father, an avid photo enthusiast, gave him his first happy-snap unit. Ever since then, the camera has been by his side. Richard has written and photographed for numerous Lonely Planet guides as well as for various magazines and other travel guide book publishers. Being Prague based, Richard has a close affinity with all central European cities – Berlin included. The former division of the city makes Berlin a unique and exciting place – an exceptional experience for the photographer and visitor alike.

Introducing Berlin

The bear is a fitting symbol of Berlin – gruff, endlessly adaptable, aggressive, fiercely protective of its young, able to endure times that would spell doom to a lesser species and – at once – loveable and frightening in some of its aspects.

With a history that has disproportionately shaped Europe's destiny – for both good and ill – Berlin today is a galvanic force in German, European and world affairs, wielding great influence in the realms of technology, commerce and the arts, and the inner workings of democracy. The 'New World Order' – whatever *that* may be – has a well-tuned, roaring outpost here.

Berlin functions on a welcoming and exquisitely human scale. It's a city in which you can embrace and be embraced, relish and explore its endless charms and variety with total abandon and feel energised in ways that you'll feel in few other world-class cities. A simple *'Wie geht's?'* (how are you?) uttered in any pub or street-side café may well unleash a torrent of opinions and perceptions in perfect English. And, boy, do Berliners *ever* have their opinions! It's no exaggeration to say that your average cabbie can hold forth respectably on any subject from the best sausage in the city to the meanderings of Nietzsche to the likely outcome of elections anywhere in the world. Berliners are that broadly learned and curious about the world and its people.

Since reunification, Berlin has undergone a massive evolution in how it presents and regards itself. Throwing off its oppressive self-perception as a beleaguered and schizoid city existing under constant threat and the ominous presence of the Wall, its true spirit has been unleashed. The dancing in the streets that happened after Gorbachev gave his tacit nod has never really stopped: it just moved indoors. And if you don't party hearty, you just don't belong in Berlin. No matter your age, you won't be seeing the inside of your hotel room at weekends until 4am. Be warned and prepare yourself!

Your own 'movie' of time spent in Berlin – whether you're indulging your appetites, drinking in culture by the bucketful, or exploring pathways, parks and forests within the city – is going to star a huge international cast thronging with gusto into the streets. The sheer exuberance of post-Wall Berlin sweeps you along with its throbbing beat and hurls you – via one of the best transport systems in the world – into its pulsing club life, vibrant neighbourhoods, dining and arts scenes and close encounters with some of the greatest sights from all of European history.

Your time in the city will be spent rubbing shoulders with influence peddlers and politicos from every corner of the planet: government courtiers to fashion couturiers to the cultural illuminati. Berlin is one of their primary international playgrounds and you'll find them cruising the halls and labyrinths of the most elaborate and accomplished corporate 'temples' found anywhere. Flocks of diplomats – bedecked in their Armani and Versace – skate edgily over the thin ice of diplomacy in search of influence and power. Much of what the future holds for the nations of the European Union is being hammered out in the corridors and office suites of Berlin.

While Berlin's physical scars are distinctly healing, flesh and blood have proven less malleable than brick and mortar. The 'Wall' that lingers in the hearts and minds of Berliners

Lowdown

Population 3.39 million
Time zone Western European (GMT+1hr)
3-star double room €120
Cup of coffee €1.80
Glass of beer €2.50
U-Bahn ticket €2
Currywurst €1.50–2
Doner kebab €2–2.50
Pack of 20 cigarettes €3.30 (will increase to €3.90 by July 2005)

has proven harder to tear down than the one they once looked across with such longing. But behold! The teenage daughters of immigrant Anatolian shepherds have shirked their headscarves and now opt to display their legs in French silk. Yesterday's dour correspondent for Pravda now runs an ad agency with major contracts from Sony and Disney. A browbeaten teacher of the official communist line is now a real estate tycoon with a mobile phone screwed to her ear and a lovely villa in Capri, thank you very much! Divisions among Berliners may persist, but the edges are being blurred by new realities and the need to simply get on with it all.

If there's a single earmark of the Berlin mentality it would have to be that of tolerance. Some may not like what you do, how you look or what you eat, but most Berliners follow the motto of Frederick the Great: *'Jeder nach seiner Façon'*, which loosely translates as 'live and let live'. It's no coincidence that one in every 7.5 Berlin residents is an immigrant or that Europe's liveliest gay and lesbian scene flourishes here.

All these factors make Berlin a most 'un-German' city; one that is largely free of the rigid social structure so entrenched in much of the country at large. A trendsetter by nature and necessity, Berlin feeds on fledgling moods, trends and appetites and processes them into the new *Zeitgeist*, which is then exported to the rest of the country and beyond. The world has always looked to Berlin – sometimes in fascination, sometimes in horror and sometimes even in deep sympathy. At once repellent and seductive, light-hearted and brooding, Berlin continues to be a city of exhilarating extremes.

Coming to Berlin *demands* that you abandon yourself to its pleasures and forget about however you might behave at home. This is a larger-than-life city with a past, present, future and creative and youthful vibe that will, in short order, have you shouting, *'Ich bin ein Berliner!'* So join in and unleash your inner carnivore. Berlin is indeed a bear. But it's one that's learned how to dance and sing. And, above all else, *roar!*

ANDREA'S TOP BERLIN DAY

Bono is wailing *It's a Beautiful Day* on my alarm clock radio as I toss back the covers just after 9am. A quick shower and email check, then it's out the door to meet my friend Kerstin for a scrumptious breakfast at **Tomasa** (p183). We catch up on all the gossip, then hop on the U-Bahn to take in the latest art show at the **Neue Nationalgalerie** (p106). Kerstin's off to work, so I decide to see what all the buzz about the new embassy buildings in the nearby **Diplomatenviertel** (p103) is about. Suitably impressed, I make my way north through the **Tiergarten** (p101) – its greenery redolent with the sweet smell of summer – to the **Reichstag** (p99). With the sun hovering in a cerulean sky, I figure the views from the glass dome must be pretty stellar today. They are, but I can't linger too long because I need to pick out a new outfit for tonight's concert at the **Philharmonie** (p106) with a group of old friends. I get lucky browsing the boutiques of the **Scheunenviertel** (p93) and make it to the hall just in time for a preconcert drink. Energised by the brilliance of Bach and Beethoven, we decide to finish the night with tapas and cocktails at **Yosoy** (p167), our favourite Spanish restaurant. Olé!

Essential Berlin

- **Bar-hopping** (p194) – just pick a neighbourhood
- **Pergamon Museum** (p87) – stunners from antiquity
- **Pfaueninsel** (p144) – perfect for lovebirds
- **Reichstag dome** (p99) – Berlin from above
- **Scheunenviertel** (p93) – boutique and gallery hopping

City Life

City Life

BERLIN TODAY

Berlin just can't help having character. Somehow the continual changes and shifts in the city's fortunes and status have become part of its nature, creating a restless dynamism that makes even the most normal facet of urban life part of an insistent individuality. After all, this is the city where squatting became a national pastime, where a divided wasteland is now some of the most expensive development property in Europe, where any old building can transform itself into a cultural centre and where even Starbucks hosts live jazz – conventional is a hard word to apply to any aspect of life here.

Hot Conversation Topics

- What the Senate should be spending Berlin's money on.
- Student strikes – power to the people or pain in the posterior?
- What people in Friedrichshain feed their dogs.
- The GDR: those were the days.
- Does Berlin really need its Schloss back?
- Hot spots – where's in, where's out, where's closed down to make way for offices.
- Ooh, another Ikea.

It's equally hard to pin down the Berliners themselves; as with all things in Berlin, it's the mix that defines the whole, and you just need to step on the U-Bahn to see the extraordinary range of people who call the city home, with suits, punks, civil servants, anarchists and all stops in between. The city may be bankrupt, but the richness of its culture and social fabric transcends its often complicated politics, and once you've tapped into the pace of life here it's easy to see why it's a dominant force in so many aspects of German life.

Berlin is generally at the forefront of any trend that hits Germany, and with a young, mostly work-age population, lifestyle is a crucial concept, fuelled by the vast selection of leisure and cultural activities vying for the hearts, minds and cash of an up-and-coming generation.

The restoration of capital status marked a new era of pride in the city, which is finally returning to centre stage as an international capital in every respect.

Above all, life here is characterised by an endless capacity to surprise. History may not have been kind, but the future is a blank canvas – as the tourist office proudly proclaims, Berlin is 'different every hour', and its constant reinvention of itself is without a doubt the city's finest feature.

Berlin street café

CITY CALENDAR

Berlin is very much a party town, and almost every weekend there is some form of event, anniversary or celebration; the arts scene is particularly active, and the ICC Messe centre (☎ 303 80; www.icc-berlin.de; Messedamm 22, Charlottenburg) holds a wide-ranging programme of trade fairs throughout the year, many of which are open to the public. High points of the year are the Berlinale, Germany's high-profile February film festival; the techno institution of the Love Parade in July; and the Day of German Unity on 3 October, when Berliners do their best to re-create the scenes of jubilation that marked the fall of the Wall. See the Directory (p285) for a full list of public holidays.

JANUARY

BERLINER SECHSTAGERENNEN
Almost 100 years old, this is Berlin's premier international cycling event (p216).

INTERNATIONALE GRÜNE WOCHE
☎ 303 80; ICC Messe
International Green Week, officially a week-long consumer fair for food, agriculture and gardening, is actually more like an excuse for gorging on exotic morsels from around the world.

LANGE NACHT DER MUSEEN
☎ 283 973; www.lange-nacht-der-museen.de
On the last Saturday of January, 150,000 visitors take the opportunity to wander round Berlin's museums at night, with most doors staying open until at least midnight. It can be surprisingly sociable, and the whole thing is repeated in August on the last Saturday of the month.

MAULHELDEN
☎ 3087 85685; www.maulhelden.de; Tempodrom
The 'Mouth Heroes' are not superhuman dentists but the diverse stars of Berlin's new international comedy and spoken word festival, held for the third time in 2004.

TRENDVISION
Kunstraum Kreuzberg/Bethanian, Mariannenplatz 2
Held from late January into February, this unusual crossover event brings aspiring fashionistas and artists together to create themed installations.

UNTERBROCHENE KARRIEREN
☎ 615 3031; Neue Gesellschaft für Bildende Kunst, Oranienstrasse 25
An occasional exhibition showing the work of artists who have died prematurely of cancer or AIDS, 'Interrupted Careers' was initiated by the NGBK in 1997.

FEBRUARY

BERLINALE
☎ 259 200; www.berlinale.de
The *Internationale Filmfestspiele Berlin* (Berlin International Film Festival), better known as the Berlinale, is Germany's answer to the Cannes and Venice film festivals and no less prestigious. Stars, starlets, directors, critics and the world's A-to-Z-list celebrities faithfully turn out to catch the two-week event, with about 750 films screened at various theatres around town. Many screenings are quickly sold out, so check the schedule early and call the cinema for ticket availability. As well as awarding the Golden and Silver Bears, the festival also sees the award ceremony for the Teddy, a gay and lesbian film prize.

MARCH

INTERNATIONALE TOURISMUS BÖRSE
☎ 303 80; www.itb-berlin.de; ICC Messe
Reportedly the world's largest travel show, the ITB (International Tourism Fair) rounds up exhibitors from everywhere under the sun. It's open to the public at the weekend.

MAERZMUSIK
☎ 2548 9128; www.maerzmusik.de
Founded in 1967 under the GDR regime as the biannual Muzik-Biennale, Berlin's principal forum for new and experimental music has been held yearly under the new name 'March Music' since 2002.

APRIL

FESTTAGE
☎ 2035 4555; www.staatsoper-berlin.org; Philharmonie/Staatsoper Unter den Linden
The Festival Days are an annual 10-day festival of high-profile gala concerts and operas, bringing renowned conductors, soloists and orchestras to Berlin.

MAY

1 MAY

Absolutely not for those of a nervous disposition, on this day Berlin's central districts are the regular rendezvous for large-scale anti-capitalist demonstrations. Traditionally, right-wing groups schedule their marches for the same day, the police turn out in force and within a couple of hours there'll be chaos. That means violence, vandalism and burning vehicles – we only mention it at all so you can stay out of the way.

BRITSPOTTING

www.britspotting.de

It's hard to imagine the Brits returning the compliment, but this small festival of British films that never made it into the multiplexes is a surprising hit with the Berlin arthouse buffs. Participating screens include the Acud (p205), Central (see Babylon p214) and fsk (p215).

GAY & LESBIAN RUN

☎ 445 7561; glrinfo@gmx.de

Formerly held exclusively in Berlin, this highly unorthodox fun run has become nomadic and only returns to the capital every couple of years. It's worth catching when it does; after all, what better way to show solidarity than by donning a garish tracksuit and pounding the streets with your queer peers?

KARNEVAL DER KULTUREN

☎ 622 2024; www.karneval-berlin.de

This is a lively street festival with a parade of flamboyantly costumed people dancing and playing music on floats.

LADIES' GERMAN OPEN

The only German stop on the international tennis circuit, this is always a big event (p217).

SEHSÜCHTE

www.sehsuechte.de

Berlin's International Student Film Festival provides six days of the most random, experimental, alternative and occasionally pretentious film making around. Sure, they're not all future Fassbinders, but there aren't many Ed Woods in there either.

THEATERTREFFEN BERLIN

☎ 2548 9233; www.theatertreffen-berlin.de

The Berlin Theatre Meeting stages three weeks of new productions by emerging and

---

Top Five Quirky Holidays & Events

- **Britspotting** A UK filmfest, because clearly everyone comes to Berlin to catch the latest British films.
- **Christopher Street Day Parade** The country's biggest gay and lesbian street party. Think big, think colourful, think raucous, think drag as far as the eye can see.
- **Fuckparade** Join the hardcore anti-capitalists and ageing techno-hippies to bemoan the state of the Love Parade.
- **Berliner Gauklerfest** Annual circus festival, providing aversion therapy for those terrified of clowns. Or jugglers, mimes, trapeze artists...
- **Nikolaus (St Nicholas' Day)** Apparently Berliners are never too old to believe in Santa Claus, especially if there's chocolate involved.

---

established German-language ensembles from Germany, Austria and Switzerland. They are held in venues around town.

JUNE

ALL NATIONS FESTIVAL

☎ 863 9160; www.allnationsfestival.de

For one day in June or July, Berlin's foreign embassies open their doors to promote their respective countries, with food, drink, music and talks. A shuttle bus ferries visitors around.

BACH TAGE BERLIN

☎ 301 5518

This is an annual one-week festival featuring music by Bach and his contemporaries.

CHRISTOPHER STREET DAY

☎ 0177-277 3176; www.csd-berlin.de

Commemorating the anniversary of the 1969 Stonewall riots in New York, this is Berlin's biggest gay parade, with over 400,000 people coming out to play on the city streets. Outrageous costumes, rainbow flags, techno music and naked torsos are guaranteed.

FÊTE DE LA MUSIQUE

☎ 0190-581 058; www.lafetedelamusique.com

This unique festival of free concerts, held worldwide on 21 June, is the brainchild of former French culture minister Jack Lang, who first managed to persuade international musicians to play without pay in 1982. Up to 500 bands now turn up for the Berlin event alone.

MOZART FESTIVAL
☎ 254 880
This festival is sponsored by the Berliner Philharmonie and is held over Whitsun/Pentecost.

JULY

CLASSIC OPEN AIR GENDARMENMARKT
☎ 843 7350; www.classic-openair.ch
A prestigious series of classical concerts held al fresco on the Gendarmenmarkt in early July.

FOTOMARATHON
☎ 4434 2254; www.fotomarathon.de
Putting art photography firmly in the public domain, this inspired event calls on keen snappers to take 24 pictures in twelve hours on 24 separate themes, and turns the result into an exhibition.

FUCKPARADE
☎ 069-9435 9090; www.fuckparade.org
Uncompromising as ever, several thousand hardcore anti-capitalist, anti-globalisation, anti-fascist protesters turn out every year for this contentious political street party, originally conceived to highlight the commercialisation of the Love Parade. Tellingly, the FP was declared a demonstration by the Senate in 2001, whereas the LP is considered a 'fun event'.

LOVE PARADE
☎ 284 620; www.loveparade.de
The original and, in a good year, still the best – Berlin's top annual techno parade sees at least half a million ravers following the floats towards the Brandenburg Gate, followed by nonstop partying in clubs and bars all over town. There's no denying that it's sold out, with brand advertising everywhere, but no one seems to care as long as they can keep dancing.

AUGUST

BERLINER GAUKLERFEST
www.gauklerfest.de
In the first week of August this lively circus festival, now in its 14th year, occupies the eastern end of Unter den Linden with a colourful array of performers.

HANFPARADE
www.hanfparade.de
Germany's contribution to the ongoing debate on the legalisation of the hemp plant – you'll hear a lot about its industrial applications (yeah, like that's why 10,000 slightly dazed people parade through the streets every year). Local shops do a roaring trade in hemp cookies, hemp shakes, hemp falafel etc etc.

INTERNATIONALE FUNKAUSSTELLUNG
☎ 303 38; ICC Messe
The huge International Consumer Electronics Fair is open to the public, demonstrating gadgets everyone will be wanting for Christmas.

INTERNATIONALES TANZFEST BERLIN
☎ 2590 0427; www.tanzfest.de; Hebbel Am Ufer
The top date in the Berlin dance calendar, attracting loose-limbed talent and highly experimental choreography from around the globe.

SEPTEMBER

ART FORUM BERLIN
☎ 303 80; www.art-forum-berlin.com
An international contemporary art fair hosted by Berlin's leading galleries.

BERLIN MARATHON
The best street race in the country, with a route that takes it past a lot of people's front doors.

INTERNATIONALES LITERATURFESTIVAL
☎ 2787 8620; www.literaturfestival.com
Founded in 2001, this growing international literature festival puts on readings and events under a different country theme each year, and managed to attract 15,000 visitors in only its second year.

OCTOBER

AAA – DIE HAUPTSTADT AUTO-SHOW
☎ 303 80; ICC Messe
This international car exhibition is held from late October to early November. Heaven for petrolheads.

LESBIAN FILM FESTIVAL
☎ 7871 8109; www.lesbenfilmfestival.de
One of the longest-running events of its kind, Berlin's LFF celebrated its 20th anniversary in

good and a stone if they've been bad. Eventually this tradition developed into Father Christmas' yearly rounds, but in Germany they seem pretty attached to the original – an astounding number of clubs hold Nikolaus parties, complete with footwear-invading St Nicks.

TAG DER DEUTSCHEN EINHEIT

The 3 October has been declared the national Day of German Unity, and Berlin takes it particularly seriously, with street parties from the Brandenburg Gate to the Roten Rathaus and all kinds of other celebrations around town.

NOVEMBER

JAZZFEST BERLIN

☎ 2548 9279; www.jazzfest-berlin.de

Top-rated jazz festival with performances held at venues throughout the city.

SPIELZEITEUROPA

www.festwochen.de

This new festival replaces the theatrical element of the old Berliner Festwochen from 2004, staging up to 15 plays on a national theme (eg the Netherlands, the Balkans) between November and January.

DECEMBER

BERLIN BIENNALE

Presenting new art at unusual sites around town, this biennial exhibition of contemporary art (last held in 2003) was founded by the Kunst-Werke centre (p94).

NIKOLAUS

St Nicholas' day is on 6 December, when children who leave their shoes out before they go to bed receive sweets if they've been

SILVESTER

This is the German name for the New Year's Eve celebrations, and the only place to be at midnight is out with the crowds on Unter den Linden, cooing at the fireworks, trying to ignore the dismal chart music from the speakers all along the road, quaffing cheap *Sekt* (sparkling wine) from street stalls, hugging strangers and generally enjoying the abnormally sociable atmosphere. If you're at a club nearby, they'll happily let you out for an hour to catch the festivities before the indoor party kicks off.

VERZAUBERT INTERNATIONAL QUEER FILM FESTIVAL

www.verzaubertfilmfest.com

The Berlin leg of the 'Enchanted' festival takes over the Hackesche Höfe Filmtheater in early December, at the end of a tour taking in Munich, Frankfurt and Cologne. The scope and range of the films included is generally huge.

WEIHNACHTSMÄRKTE

Christmas markets of all shapes and sizes are held from late November to around 21 December at locations around Berlin, including Breitscheidplatz, Winterfeldtplatz, Unter den Linden, Alexanderplatz and the Marktplatz in Spandau. The outlying district of Köpenick sets up stalls from mid-December around the town hall.

CULTURE
IDENTITY

With just under 3.4 million inhabitants, Berlin is Germany's largest city. Statistically the average denizen of the city is politically liberal, nominally Protestant (though probably not practising) and educated to degree level with an excellent grasp of English. They drink, smoke, recycle and use public transport, though they may have a car in town; chances are they're also young, professional and well travelled, with the USA and UK favourite destinations. For Berliners, identity is predominantly defined by district, and every *Bezirk* has its own unique character, reflecting the nature of its 'typical' inhabitants. Charlottenburg, Wilmersdorf and Tiergarten are reliably affluent areas, attracting bourgeois bachelors, suited business types and local celebrities; Schöneberg, too, is relatively upscale, but is most noted for its prominent gay population, thanks to the concentration of bars around Nollendorfplatz. Kreuzberg is divided into the smarter western section along Bergmannstrasse and the old alternative patch around Kottbusser Tor, now home

Ostalgie

The fall of the Wall in 1989 is still recent enough to be fresh in people's minds, but for many the demise of the GDR is just not a straightforward issue – after all, large numbers of older Berliners lived under the East German regime for a significant part of their lives, and while certain aspects of the police state can hardly be defended, conditions for many ex-citizens have not improved enough for them to write off the period entirely.

Perhaps because of this perceived ambivalence, Westerners have become obsessed with the idea of the old East, and there has been huge recent interest in a form of '80s GDR 'revival' in popular culture, harking back almost fondly to less controversial features of life behind the Iron Curtain. Known as *Ostalgie* (from *Ost*, 'east', and *Nostalgie*, 'nostalgia'), the most notable example has been the hit film *Good Bye Lenin!*, which was a surprise international success in 2003, building on previous GDR comedies such as *Sonnenallee*.

Satirical but generally benign, the focus of the *Ostalgie* wave is fixed on the everyday, romanticising everything from long-vanished cleaning products to state-controlled television, and there are plenty of museums in Berlin and elsewhere displaying these unlikely relics. Books on the subject cover everything from Communist domestic politics to classic *Ossi* jokes, often using the era as a selling point for tourists; to cap it all, there are even plans to build a GDR theme park in Köpenick so visitors can experience *Ost*-life for themselves! However much real Easterners may miss their Trabant cars and Vita-Cola, this may well prove a memory too far.

of much of Berlin's Turkish population. A similar split characterises Mitte, separating the very wealthy Friedrichstrasse/Unter den Linden area from the more rundown, studenty area to the north.

Prenzlauer Berg and Friedrichshain start where Mitte leaves off. 'F'hain' has largely assumed Kreuzberg's alternative mantle and is known for its nonconformist punk and squatter communities (and for the staggering amount of dog crap on its streets), whereas 'Prenzlberg' is more on the arty side of experimental, with large gay and student contingents. Of the outer districts, Wedding and Lichtenberg enjoy the worst reputations, known for right-wing undercurrents and an unhappy mix of immigrants and disgruntled old-school working class families. East-West divisions, too, are still an issue for many people, though with demographics shifting, incomes gradually balancing out and rivalries fading, few of the old *Ossi/Wessi* (Easterner/Westerner) stereotypes still apply. The main difference you'll notice is that fewer older people from East Berlin speak English, as they will have learnt Russian in school instead.

As the country's most multicultural city, Berlin is also heavily influenced by its minorities, with an amazing patchwork of people from 185 nations making up 13% of the total population. The vast majority of immigrants live in the western districts, with Kreuzberg having the highest concentration (32%), followed by Wedding and Tiergarten. The largest groups are those of Turkish descent and eastern Europeans from Poland, the former states of Yugoslavia and the old Soviet republics; sizeable communities of Italians, Greeks, Vietnamese and Americans are also present. The steady growth in foreign nationals since reunification has, however, been offset by a decline in the indigenous population, due in part to the exodus of young families from the capital to the surrounding countryside, and the overall population of the city has actually fallen since 1993. There is also an increasing trend towards insularity on the part of the various minorities, and despite the city's legendary tolerance, few groups mix on a day-to-day basis. The Senate even has a member for integration and migration matters, a post currently held by Green senator Günter Piening, who is responsible for keeping track of developments and trying to encourage better relationships between communities. Racial tensions are rare but increasing, particularly in the outer eastern districts. Neo-Nazi and other right-wing groups are still vastly outnumbered by antifascist activists, but there has been a sharp increase in violent incidents involving young Muslims. Fuelled by the international climate and controversial 'secular' legislation in France, many conservatives have called for anti-Islam measures such as banning headscarves in schools, which would effectively alienate immigrant communities even further.

Berlin is also an extremely 'young' city. More than half of its people are under 35 years in age; by contrast, only 14% are over 65 (with women over 75 vastly outnumbering men because of wartime losses). However, the actual number of children residing in the city is declining, and birth rates are going down – the immigrant birth rate has even halved since 1991, suggesting that many people are now coming to Berlin to work and returning to their home country to raise their families. And Berlin's diversity extends further than its ethnic mix. It's estimated that 500,000 gays and lesbians currently call the city home; by electing Klaus Wowereit as governing mayor, Berlin became only the second European city (after Paris) to be led by an openly gay

Kisses & Make-up

An interesting side-product of the gay scene, though by no means exclusively limited to gay men, is the huge popularity of drag artists in Berlin and in Germany as a whole – glamorous trannies such as Edith Superstar, Lilo Wanders and Nina Queer pop up to present everything from cabaret parties to national TV shows, and the **Black Girls Coalition** (p203) in Friedrichshain holds some of the country's wildest drag parties.

politician. With an active scene and a real sense of community, it's widely considered second only to Amsterdam as Europe's gay capital. However, friction does exist, particularly between homosexuals and extreme Muslim groups, and assaults on gay men are a growing problem (the gay AIDS project Café PositHIV has effectively been forced to move after frequent attacks).

The student population, too, amounts to a sizeable minority presence, with three major universities, the Freie Universität (FU), Technische Universität (TU) and Humboldt Universität (HU), attracting students from all over the country. Recent protests over proposed funding cuts demonstrated the impact the student body can have on city life, and their inventive nonviolent actions are a good illustration of the creative buzz of the capital: participants occupied Ikea demanding 'educational asylum' in Sweden, swam in the freezing Spree, streaked through Alexanderplatz and even started building their own cafeteria at the FU!

LIFESTYLE

Lifestyle here is defined by activity, and Berliners are invariably busy people; with an average 40-hour working week, they're either on their way to the office, the gym, the shops, the pub, the cinema, the theatre or all of the above. Many average-earning people have cleaners, usually Polish women without work permits, and when Berliners are not eating out, dinner will be something quick and easy (if the microwave didn't exist, Berlin would have paid someone to invent it). Staying in and watching TV is a last resort for locals here, and even if they specifically want to watch a programme they'll probably be doing something else at the same time.

Professional salaries in Berlin range from around €2000 to €4000 a month before tax, allowing for some very reasonable disposable incomes. Full-time work is the norm for both

Berlin Living

The typical Berlin dwelling is a spacious rented 1½ bedroom apartment on at least the first floor of a large postwar house (no-one wants to live at street level), probably facing onto a *Hinterhof* (courtyard) full of coloured bins. The apartment itself has very high ceilings, large windows and, as often as not, polished wood floors; the kitchen will almost invariably be the smallest room in the house, used mainly for stacking crates of beer and sparkling mineral water. Many homes still have the traditional tiled heating stoves in place, though no-one actually uses them.

Berlin flats are usually nicely turned-out, whatever the style favoured by the occupant, and a lot of attention is paid to design, though comfort is also considered. At least one item of furniture will come from Ikea – the Swedish store recently opened its third branch here, near Tempelhof airport. Depending on income, the rest may come from the Stilwerk centre, Polish craftsmen, a flea market or eBay, as long as it fits the look of the room.

Rent is calculated according to space, starting at around €360 a month for 40 sq metres (depending on the area). Any conversation about costs with a Berlin tenant will inevitably lead to them asking you how many square metres your place is – do some sums before you leave home!

sexes and in general male and female employees earn roughly the same, but as ever there are far fewer women than men at the very top of the wage scale.

Perhaps because of their frantic schedules, family is less of a priority for many Berlin-dwellers, and in the central districts the vast majority of households are single-occupancy. There is also an increasing trend towards single parenthood: as many first-born children now live with one parent as with two.

Berliners tend to be serious but very opinionated, and conversations may touch on many subjects, from international politics to local curiosities. It is OK to mention 'the War', if done with tact and relevance; after all, history is still current affairs here, and a lot of people you meet will have grown up demanding explanations for all the events of the last 60 years. What will cause offence is a 'victor' mentality, which is perceived as self-righteous and gloating, or the suggestion that fascist ideas are intrinsically German, which is downright bigoted.

Overall, locals are accommodating and fairly helpful towards visitors, and many will volunteer assistance if you look lost. This politeness does not necessarily extend to friendliness, however, and in public, people usually maintain a degree of reserve towards strangers – you won't find many conversations striking up on the U-Bahn, for example, and Berlin bus drivers have a reputation for being the rudest in Europe.

On the other hand, in younger company it's easy to talk to just about anyone, particularly around the many student hangouts (remember German students are generally older than elsewhere, often graduating at 28 rather than 21), and if you start frequenting a place you'll quickly get to know staff and regulars. You'll also probably find people very open after a relatively short time, discussing sex, relationships and life with equal candour.

Another key feature of Berlin lifestyle is the concept of the *Szene*, the indefinable 'scene' that determines where the fashionable young set go out and what they wear, drink or talk about. As an outsider it can be pretty tricky keeping track of what's in, and as soon as anything becomes too popular the real scene people go elsewhere.

Of course, much of the above applies mainly to *Neu-Berliner* (New Berliners), people who have moved here rather than being born in the city; in fact, much like in London you'll seldom run across a real native unless you happen to know them already. Some of the most 'authentic' denizens of the city are the working-class mullet-sporting *Ossis* you'll see in the dingiest *Kneipen* in districts like Wedding and Lichtenberg, and unlike the newbies they tend not to welcome visitors.

FOOD & DRINK

Most sophisticated Berliners now opt for Thai or one of the many international options on offer, but traditional Berlin cuisine still exists and forms the basis of the menu at most ordinary *Kneipen*. Overall, it tends to be high-calorie, hearty and heavy on the meat; pork is a staple, prepared in umpteen ways, including *Kasseler Rippen* (smoked chops) and *Eisbein* (knuckles). Minced meat often comes in the form of a *Boulette*, a cross between a meatball and a hamburger. Other regulars are roast chicken, schnitzel and *Sauerbraten* (marinated beef), usually with sauerkraut and potatoes on the side.

The true Berlin classic, however, is *Currywurst*, a spicy sausage in tangy curried ketchup, usually served with chips; stalls all over town sell them in the millions. Thanks to the large Turkish population, the doner (or döner) kebabs here are also a fast-food highlight, far superior to the limp imitations elsewhere. Locals inevitably have their favourite spots for both delicacies, and will argue incessantly about which *Imbiss* (snack stall or outlet) serves the best concoction.

Eating is predominantly a communal activity, and most people eat out with colleagues at lunchtime or with friends in the evening; mid-afternoon coffee and cake is *de rigeur* at weekends, as is a cheeky döner on your way home after a night out (central kebab shops are busiest between 3am and 5am midweek, when the U-Bahn isn't running). Cooking, on the whole, is something you only do on very special occasions.

Sunday brunch is a social institution in its own right, lasting a couple of hours and providing the ideal excuse to meet up with friends and discuss the weekend's events over a leisurely bite to eat. Almost every café, bistro, restaurant, bar and lounge that opens before dinner time will have some kind of all-you-can-eat buffet on offer from morning until the afternoon, and they're always popular affairs, especially in student areas.

This being Germany, beer is the drink of choice for both sexes, although many would argue it's actually a food group, and you'll find a variety of local, national and import brews on offer. *Fassbier* (draught beer) is generally limited to one or two brands of local lager or Pils, usually served in 0.3l glasses. Berlin's particular speciality is *Berliner Weisse*, a light, sour beer served with a shot of raspberry (red) or woodruff (green) syrup. Be warned, though, by drinking this stuff you're advertising yourself as a tourist.

All places stock at least one variety of *Weizenbier* (wheat beer), which comes in 0.5l bottles with a choice of *Hefe* (yeasty) and *Kristall* (filtered); this is most Berliners' preference for afternoon or early evening drinking. Other options may include *Schwarzbier* (black beer, like porter), *Dunkelbier* (dark ale), *Bock* (strong seasonal beer) and *Kölsch* (Cologne Pils). Non-alcoholic Clausthaler and Becks are common, and you can also drink your lager as a *Radler* (shandy), an *Alster* (with sparkling water) or a *Diesel* (with orangeade), or you can even drink it with coke.

Wine is mainly popular in restaurants, with widely varying German and international selections available. The best German bottles are dry Riesling, Müller-Thurgau and Silvaner whites. Champagne, too, has lost none of its exalted status in Berlin's swisher bars; for less special occasions or a break from the Cristal, local *Sekt* and Italian *prosecco* (sometimes served on ice) are well-tried and often excellent alternatives.

Cocktails have also undergone a major renaissance over the last few years, and the majority of new pubs opening in Berlin are cocktail bars; as a result you can now get fruity mixed drinks at just about any hostelry in town as the old guard try to compete with the flash new arrivals. Thanks to the ongoing Latin craze, the '*caipi*' (*caipirinha* – made with lime, sugar and overproof *cachaça* cane spirit) is now Berlin's drink of choice.

For daytime stimulation most people go for coffee, often in huge cups with lots of milk. There's nothing wrong with the tap water, but you'd never catch anyone drinking it – sparkling mineral water is the norm, and still versions are also available. Fruit juices, shakes and smoothies have all caught on in a big way, and the ubiquitous German *Apfelschorle* (apple juice with sparkling water) remains a refreshing favourite.

FASHION

In everyday terms, Berlin is a very casual city. Except for formal gourmet restaurants, there's no need to dress up for dinner or a theatre or opera performance (unless you particularly want to). Some of the more exclusive nightclubs do have dress codes, but it's generally originality they're looking for rather than expense. On a day-to-day basis most people aren't overly concerned about what they wear, and with the ongoing retro craze you're just as likely to see Berlin's bright young things blowing their cash in second-hand stores, which abound in Kreuzberg and Prenzlauer Berg, as in designer outlets.

Of course, designer fashion is hardly ignored, and the moneyed shoppers who patronise the big houses have no shortage of choice in the flash boutiques around the Ku'damm and

Berlin En Vogue

Mayor Klaus Wowereit got some strange looks on a visit to London in 2003 when he proclaimed Berlin to be a 'fashion city' – for an international capital, the city has shown a remarkably lackadaisical attitude towards international fashion in the past, perhaps because of its overwhelmingly casual ethos. As in the arts, experimentation is the order of the day here, and with the latest streetwear boom, Berlin has come to be a fertile spot for innovative young talent, finally showing the potential to return to the forefront of global fashion.

Wowereit's boast was inspired by the success of Bread & Butter, the fashion industry trade fair inaugurated in Spandau in 2000, where over 400 brands congregate to exhibit their products to retailers and the press. The event has put the Berlin scene firmly on the fashion map, providing an ideal forum for the many talented young designers working in the city. Following the fair, summer is the time when eagerly awaited new ranges from independent labels such as Hafenstadt, Hartbo & L'wig, FIRMA, Irie Daily, Hasipop, Butterfly Soulfire and Urban Speed should hit the market.

along Friedrichstrasse. However, individuality ranks above all else, and Europe's most tolerant city has no time for clones – different scenes have their own styles, but there's never a single 'uniform' to follow. It's quite possible to be fashionable without spending a fortune, but personal style is essential whether you're a glamour girl or a grunge boy, and the real hipsters are the ones who know how to work it.

Accessories are equally important, and just about anything can be used to put the finishing touches on a Berlin outfit: glasses from IC!Berlin, hats from Fiona Bennett, jewellery and bags from such local labels as IchIchIch. Hair and make-up are more a matter of taste, though a certain amount of styling can be expected from both sexes on a night out; men tend to grow their hair out a bit, though thankfully mullets and rats' tails are now largely restricted to the very young and the tragically '80s. Piercings and tattoos are entirely everyday occurrences among younger people, especially women, and the more alternative the scene the more extreme the decoration.

In the pragmatic German mind, PDAs (personal digital assistants), mobile phones and other devices simply don't count as fashion accessories, so don't bother comparing phone fascias!

SPORT

Sport is no exception to the Berlin rule of variety in all things – there are teams representing just about every recognised sport you can think of, from beach volleyball and water polo to handball and American football. Spectators at even the smaller events tend to be fanatical about their club, and atmosphere is guaranteed, especially when big-name opponents come to town.

Of course the dominant sport here is and always will be football. Hertha BSC, Berlin's *Bundesliga* (national league) soccer team, is famed for the dramatic ups and downs of its fortunes; after a particularly heartbreaking end to the 2003 autumn period, it's best not to mention departed Dutch coach Huub Stevens' name anywhere near the Olympiastadion faithful. Croatian Fredi Bobic, on the other hand, was recently voted fifth most popular player in Germany. The season runs from September until May or June, with a winter break.

Lower-league football is also popular. In the *Bundesliga's* second division, FC Union Berlin is the former East's team, though its performance is consistently miserable. Another 15 local leagues pit teams from the various districts against each other and against sides from other national cities, playing on tiny pitches around town with lively support based on an entirely impenetrable mesh of rivalries and old scores; if you know a couple of people this can be great fun to watch!

Ice hockey is another Berlin obsession, with hordes of fans in scarves and baggy shirts turning out on winter weekends to watch the Berlin Capitals or their eastern counterparts the Eisbären. Like American football, many of the star players (such as Eisbären darling Sven Felski) are enlisted from professional clubs in the USA and Canada, but supporters adopt them wholeheartedly, and a foreign player who 'defects' to a rival side will receive just as hostile a reception as any local star who does the same. The hockey season is September to April.

Other well-supported games include basketball, with Alba Berlin putting in solid wins for the capital (season October to April), and American football, where Berlin Thunder is one of the leading teams (season May to October). Athletics, tennis and horse racing are the most popular of the individual competitions. See Sport, Health & Fitness (p216) for full details on clubs, events and other sports facilities.

MEDIA

The newspaper with the largest circulation in Berlin is the *BZ*, which is borderline sensationalist and practically devoid of meaningful content. It is, believe it or not, a step up from identikit rival the *Berliner Kurier* and national über-rag *Bild*, the pride of media tycoon Axel Springer's publishing empire (see the boxed text, p18), which woos readers with headlines like 'Sex Waves From Space' and photographs of scantily clad young women. *BZ* is not to be confused with the respected *Berliner Zeitung*, a left-leaning daily newspaper that is most widely read in the eastern districts.

The *Berliner Morgenpost* is especially noted for its vast classified section; its Sunday edition is where to look first for cars, flats, second-hand appliances etc. *Der Tagesspiegel* has a centre-right political orientation, a solid news and foreign section and decent cultural coverage. At the left end of the spectrum is the alternative *tageszeitung* or *taz*, which appeals to an intellectual crowd with its news analysis and thorough reporting; a *taz-Leser* ('*taz* reader', sometimes used as a slightly derogatory term) is essentially the Berlin equivalent of a *Guardian* reader in the UK.

Early editions of some dailies are available after 9pm from newspaper vendors passing through pubs and restaurants or outside theatres and U-Bahn stations.

Die Zeit is a highbrow national weekly newspaper with in-depth reporting on every-thing from politics to fashion. Germany's most widely read weekly news magazines are *Der Spiegel* and the much lighter *Focus*. Both offer hard-hitting investigative journalism and a certain degree of government criticism, despite frequent 'exposés' on swinger clubs and covers often featuring scantily-clad models. *Stern* bites harder on the popular nerve (think regular Michael Jackson features) and recently launched *Neon* is attempting to latch onto the youth market. *Zitty* and *tip* are Berlin's best what's-on magazines (p193).

English-language newspapers and magazines, mostly from the UK and the USA, are readily available in bookstores and at international newsagents, especially those at the larger train stations. *Spotlight* is a monthly publication for Germans who want to learn English, with good feature articles and travel pieces, while the *Ex-Berliner* is aimed primarily at the Anglophone ex-pat community, providing a very readable perspective on the city.

Germany has two national public TV channels, the ARD (Allgemeiner Rundfunk Deutschlands, commonly known as Erstes Deutsches Fernsehen) and the ZDF (Zweites Deutsches Fernsehen). B1, BRIII and RBB (Rundfunk Berlin Brandenburg) are regional public stations; local cable stations include TVB and FAB.

Generally, programming is relatively highbrow, featuring political coverage, discussion forums and foreign films. Advertising is limited to the two hours between 6pm and 8pm.

King of the Springers

Hamburg-born publisher Axel Springer (1912–85) was essentially the German answer to Rupert Murdoch, a colourful and often controversial figure who did much to shape the current state of the German media. Having taken over the family firm from his father after WWII, Springer created *Bild* in 1952, based on the model of British tabloid newspapers, and went on to build a huge portfolio of magazines and papers including *Die Welt*, the *Berliner Morgenpost* and pioneer-ing teen mag *Bravo*.

The first wave of controversy came in 1967, when students and the Gruppe 47 forum of liberal authors protested that Springer's virtual monopoly was a threat to press freedom. *Bild*, too, became notorious for its vocal criticism of student demonstrations and for supposedly aggressive investigative tactics on the part of reporters, and was one of the bomb targets of the Red Army Faction in 1972. In 1977 journalist Günter Wallraff went undercover at *Bild* offices and later published a book alleging serious breaches of ethics among its staff (tapping subjects' phones, for example); the following year the paper was sued for erroneously labelling student Eleonore Poensgen a terrorist. Ironically, author Heinrich Böll had already invented a very similar case in 1974, for his famous novella *Die verlorene Ehre der Katharina Blum* (The Lost Honour of Katharina Blum).

Amid all this attention, Springer managed to maintain a dual existence, often reviled in public, but highly respected for his commitment to German-Jewish reconciliation, a personal project that he pursued for most of his life. By the time he died he had received countless awards, citations and honorary doctorates from Jewish institutions in Germany and Israel, as well as the American Friendship Medal.

Springer also considered himself a German patriot and was a staunch proponent of reunification from the very first days of division – in 1958 he even visited Moscow to outline his plans to Khrushchev in person. When this somehow failed to work, he made support for reunification editorial policy in all his titles and refused to recognise the legitimacy of the East German state; to hammer home the point, any mention of the GDR was put in inverted commas. Ironically, he died just four years before his vision was realised, missing out on what would doubtless have been publishing's biggest ever 'I told you so'.

Even after his death, Springer managed to make his presence felt: his will left the Axel-Springer-Verlag to his fifth wife and his two children, stipulating that they couldn't sell any of it for 30 years. The man may have gone, but his name will live on – at least until 2015.

Private cable TV offers up the familiar array of sitcoms, soap operas, chat and game shows, feature films and drama, overwhelmingly dominated by dubbed US imports. ProSieben, Sat1 and Vox generally have the best selection; Kabel1 shows some real archive sitcoms, and RTLII has many of the latest US shows, though it's often mocked for the gratuitous nudity in its factual programming (something both private and public channels are frequently guilty of). The French/German shared channel arte provides slightly more serious fare.

Top Five Berlin Websites

- www.berlin.de – official city site
- www.berlin-online.de – more city info
- www.berlin.gay-web.de – gay information and listings
- www.tip-berlin.de – listings, ads etc
- www.wir-in-berlin.de – for children and schools

German news station ntv is a recent addition to the airwaves. DSF and EuroSport are dedicated sports channels; MTV (in German, with presenters such as Charlotte Roche and Markus Kavka) and its local equivalent VIVA can also be received. Several Turkish-language channels cater for Germany's large population with roots in Turkey. Commercial breaks are frequent on all these stations; after 11pm roughly twice a week (usually Wednesday and Saturday), a handful of the private cable channels switch entirely to erotic content, interspersed with incessant 10-second sex hotline ads.

Virtually all hotel rooms have a television set, and most will be hooked up to a cable connection or satellite dish, providing access to at least 15 channels. English-language channels broadcast within Germany include CNN, BBC World, CNBC and MSNBC. The quality of the reception, though, depends on the location, on whether the TV is hooked up to cable or to a satellite dish and on the quality of the television set.

Berlin has a bewildering choice of radio stations, many modelled on the US format of contemporary chart music and oldies interspersed with inane banter and adverts. If you like that kind of thing, check out the youth-oriented Fritz at 102.6 FM, the techno-driven Kiss at 98.8 or Energy at 103.4. The BBC broadcasts at 90.2. Among the more sophisticated stations are Radio Eins (95.8), which has lots of high-quality programming with topical information and political and social themes, and SFB4 (106.8), aka Radio Multikulti, an excellent multicultural station with music and event information about various ethnic groups, occasionally in the relevant languages. Jazz fiends should check out Jazzradio at 101.9, while classical music rules Klassik-Radio at 101.3. InfoRadio at 93.1 has an all-news format, including live interviews.

Internet radio is also on the verge of becoming mainstream in Berlin, and you can already tune in to hundreds of private and part-time programmes, with many clubs and record companies such as !K7 getting in on the act. A simple search should bring up more possibilities than you can shake your tailfeather at, though you'll generally need to download a player such as RealOne to listen in.

LANGUAGE

Only a small number of Berliners speak the pure Berlinisch dialect, but the regional accent is also very distinctive and often impenetrable to visitors. Listen out for *ge* pronounced as a soft *je*, the soft *ch* as a hard *ck*, or *das* as *det*; reading the phonetic spelling in Berlin cartoons will give you an idea of how it works. Slang words abound for just about anything (*Olle* is a woman, *Molle* a beer, *Stampe* a pub) and almost all the public buildings in the city have nicknames – only a true Berliner would think to call the Haus der Kulturen der Welt the 'Pregnant Oyster', for example.

In 1998 Berlin, along with the rest of Germany, had to adapt to a thorough spelling reform, standardising some of the quirks and inconsistencies in the German language. Surprisingly for such an opinionated bunch, most Berliners took the changes in their stride, but many other states organised citizens' petitions in protest, and things were uncertain for a while. In the end, though, the reform prevailed, and both old and new ways of spelling are correct until 2005, when new orthography becomes standard usage. For more information about the spelling changes visit www.neue-rechtschreibung.de.

See the Language chapter (p294) for useful phrases.

ECONOMY & COSTS

Germany is the world's third largest economic power behind the USA and Japan, is a committed member of the EU, and has been a member of the G8 (formerly G7) group of industrial nations since 1974. In recent years, however, the German economy has weakened, in part due to pressure from foreign competition, antiquated machinery, technophobia, and high wages and social-security overheads. Berlin has been hit along with the rest of the country, with its own spending crisis to boot.

For the time being, Berlin is still in the process of painful economic restructuring, moving away from manufacturing and towards service industries. More than half the workforce is now in the service sector, including state and federal government agencies. In fact, Berlin has more than twice as many civil servants as any other big city in Germany – one in 10 people holds a government job in eastern Berlin.

Reunification initially generated a growth spurt, but it took only a couple of years to fizzle. Unemployment figures are at record highs with around 295,000 people out of work in December 2003 (17.4%). The statistics would probably be even worse if entrepreneurship – especially in the service sector and among young people – hadn't picked up some of the slack. Around 158,000 people are now self-employed, especially in the fields of finance, corporate services, construction, commerce and tourism.

Tourism is one sector that has clocked tangible growth. In 2003 over 4.5 million visitors came to Berlin, up 1.5 million since 1992. Another driving force is information and communication technology, serving an increasingly computer-literate population; growth areas also include software development, marketing, advertising, law and financial services.

How Much?

Public transport Day Pass €5.60
Cup of coffee €1.80
Tabloid newspaper €0.50
Glass of beer €2.50
Currywurst €1.50-2
Midweek cinema ticket €5.50
Caipirinha €5
Nightclub entry €8
Doner kebab €2-2.50
Taxi home €8 (eg from Mitte to Friedrichshain)

Flea market, Brandenburg Gate (p80)

In terms of costs, Berlin is on a par with many European capitals and is still considerably cheaper than London or Paris, with the cost of living rising roughly 1% every year. Hotel accommodation is comparatively low as well, along with plenty of excellent hostels catering for less demanding travellers. Electronic goods, clothes, CDs and other purchases are unlikely to be less than you'd pay at home. Snackers and self-caterers will find food reassuringly cost-effective here, and while top-flight restaurants charge exactly what you'd expect for international *haute cuisine*, there's no shortage of smaller cafés and bistros where a meal needn't be an investment.

There are also plenty of opportunities to save a few euros on various activities during your stay. Many museums are free on one particular day every week or month; cinemas are almost half price before 5pm Monday to Wednesday; and most restaurants offer a range of set menus and special meals for children, seniors, theatregoers and other thrifty types. Sunday brunch buffets, available almost everywhere, are generally a dead-set bargain. Families are also well catered for, with many attractions offering good-value *Familienkarten*, which usually cover two adults and two (or more) children.

On average you can reckon on spending around €80 to €120 a day for a short stay in three-star accommodation and three ample meals a day; luxury-lovers could easily double or treble that figure to get the finest the city has to offer, and budget travellers could probably subsist on as little as €30 a day if they're really easy-going.

GOVERNMENT & POLITICS

Along with Hamburg and Bremen, Berlin is a German city-state. Its government consists of the *Abgeordnetenhaus* (parliament, or legislative body) and the *Senat* (Senate, or executive body). Members of parliament are voted for directly by the electorate for a five-year term. Their primary function is to pass legislation and to elect and supervise the Senate.

The Senate consists of the *Regierender Bürgermeister* (governing mayor) and eight senators. The mayor sets policy and represents Berlin internationally and nationally; senators have similar roles to cabinet ministers, with each in charge of a particular department. The seat of government of both the mayor and the Senate is the Rotes Rathaus (Red Town Hall; p92). Parliament meets in the Abgeordnetenhaus (p120) on Niederkirchnerstrasse, opposite the Martin-Gropius-Bau.

After reunification, Berlin also became the official seat of the national government once again, with parliament returning to Sir Norman Foster's Reichstag in 1999 and the *Bundesrat* (upper house) moving into the restored Preussisches Herrenhaus building in 2000. Some ministries, such as Defence and Education, still maintain headquarters in Bonn, partly to stop the former West German capital from sinking into political oblivion, but also partly to placate a school of thought that felt that, given its history, Berlin should not be given too much power for symbolic reasons. To all extents and purposes, however, Berlin has resumed its rightful role as capital of the united Germany, and few people now give Bonn a second thought.

From 1984 the dominant party in Berlin, as in Germany, was the centre-right Christliche Demokratische Union (CDU; Christian Democratic Union), led by governing mayor Eberhard Diepgen. In elections held in October 2001, however, a large number of voters turned away from the CDU as apparent payback for plunging the city into its

Berlin Districts

In January 2001, Berlin's 23 *Bezirke* (districts) were reduced to 12 in an effort to curb bureaucracy. Most of the 'new' districts were created by merging existing ones so that each now has a population of roughly 300,000. The current divisions are: Mitte, Friedrichshain-Kreuzberg, Pankow (incorporating Prenzlauer Berg), Charlottenburg-Wilmersdorf, Spandau, Steglitz-Zehlendorf, Tempelhof-Schöneberg, Neukölln, Treptow-Köpenick, Marzahn-Hellersdorf, Lichtenberg and Reinickendorf.

As the old district names are still used, the move hasn't made much difference to visitors, but locals in some areas have complained bitterly at being lumped together with their neighbours. The merging of Kreuzberg and Friedrichshain must have particularly rankled – even in 2003 'activists' were still organising mass district-wide water fights to protest!

most severe postwar financial crisis. The party, which commanded 41% of the vote in 1999, dropped to just 24%, and the opposition Sozialdemokratische Partei Deutschlands (SPD; Social Democratic Party of Germany), under interim mayor Klaus Wowereit, overtook with 30%. Another major winner was the Partei des Demokratischen Sozialismus (PDS; Party of Democratic Socialism), the successor to the GDR's communist Sozialistische Einheitspartei Deutschland (SED; Socialist Unity Party of Germany), which got 23% of the overall vote, expanding its appeal beyond the eastern districts for the first time since reunification.

Since no single party obtained an absolute majority, a coalition government formed, bringing together the SPD and the PDS for the first time. Surprisingly, the socialist politics of the latter don't seem to have translated into any markedly leftist shift in city policy on major issues, perhaps because so far attentions have been concentrated on sorting out the mess left behind by the previous incumbents.

Despite the high-profile kerfuffle surrounding the city's financial status, local politics is not necessarily a primary concern for the people who live here. In fact, Berliners seem more interested in national politics – voter turnout for city elections in 2001 was just 68%, compared with up to 85% in some areas for the 2002 national elections, and you won't meet many people who can name all nine members of the Senate, let alone explain what any of them actually do.

ENVIRONMENT

THE LAND

The year 1920 saw the amalgamation of seven cities and countless communities into Gross-Berlin (Greater Berlin), making it one of the largest cities in the world, with an area of 87,000 hectares and a population of nearly 4 million. Today Berlin is still Germany's largest city, both in terms of population (just under 3.4 million) and area, though it's been overtaken by other European and North American cities several times over.

Berlin now covers a total of 889 sq km; its north–south length measures 38km, while from east to west it stretches for 45km. Most visitors never stray outside the central districts to see the full extent of the city, but just try walking from Zoo station to Alexanderplatz and you'll realise it's a lot bigger than the transport system makes it feel.

The city lies in the heart of the vast north German plains and, apart from rivers and lakes, lacks distinctive geographical features; as such, the city's development can be almost entirely credited to its architects. Some of the rare hills in the area, like the Teufelsberg in the Grunewald forest, are actually *Trümmerberge*, made from rubble gathered during the post-WWII clean-up.

Berlin's historical importance as a trade centre stems from the two rivers that cross here. These are the 343km-long Havel, which has its headwaters in Mecklenburg about 110km

---

Pig Ignorance

You wouldn't think of Berlin as a pigsty, but the city's leafy outer suburbs have become a paradise for wild boar in recent years. The districts most affected are Grunewald, Zehlendorf, Wilmersdorf, Reinickendorf and Spandau, and many is the resident who's woken up to find their gardens trashed by porcine marauders.

The population explosion is said to have been caused by mild winters and an abundance of acorns and other foods, driving the swine to scavenge human habitats. Many have developed a taste for lawns, flower beds and scraps scavenged from compost heaps and garbage cans. According to a report in the *Berliner Morgenpost*, wild pigs even wait regularly on the steps of one school to beg for food at break times.

Reactions to the problem are mixed; even the most green-minded Berliners start screaming 'cull' the moment they see their lovingly tended geraniums massacred by careless trotters. In response to complaints, the Senate recently published an information pamphlet on city boars, giving information on their diet and habits and encouraging people to be more tolerant of their piggy visitors. Failing that, of course, the pigs are fair game outside populated areas, and licensed hunters bag around 1000 hapless porkers a year.

northwest of Berlin, and its tributary the Spree, which joins it in Spandau. On its course, the Havel travels through several canals and lakes, including the Wannsee; these are some of the city's most popular summertime spots, with beaches around the lakes and beer gardens overlooking the canals throughout town.

GREEN BERLIN

Berlin is a relatively green city, with parks, forests, lakes and rivers taking up about one-third of its space. Nearly every neighbourhood has its own park, and a ring of forests encircles the urban sprawl, a result of a successful tree-planting campaign during the last two decades. Of the city's 411,000 urban trees most are linden (lime) and maple trees; others are oak, plane and chestnut. The eastern district of Hohenschönhausen has the most trees: 134 per kilometre of road, compared to a city average of 78.

Animal life overall has declined dramatically since WWII. Construction and a growing population have about halved the number of existing species, and low ground-water levels have dried up biotopes, threatening the survival of reptiles, amphibians and fish. Only about 33 fish species still inhabit the city's rivers and lakes, the most common being perch, pike, roach and bream. Sparrows and pigeons are the most prevalent bird species.

At the same time, a different development has taken place in the leafy forest belt surrounding Berlin, where the population of wild rabbits, foxes, martens and even boar has increased enormously (see the boxed text opposite).

On the down side, Berlin has some of the highest air pollution levels in Germany – higher than any other big city in the former West Germany, though still lower than in some eastern cities such as Dresden, Halle or Chemnitz. Pollution and acid rain are increasingly doing damage to Berlin's surrounding forests, and the most recent survey in 2000 showed less than one in five trees remained healthy. In 1991, Berlin joined the International Climate Convention, pledging to reduce total CO_2 emissions by a quarter before 2010; by 1998 emissions were already down by 18%.

Berlin's drinking water is fine, though the water quality of its lakes and rivers is not. The Havel lakes, including the Wannsee, are prone to excessive algae growth; the Spree River and the Landwehr Canal that flow right through the city are badly polluted. Only the lakes in the Grunewald forest are relatively clean.

Pariser Platz (p82)

Despite such problems Berlin is, in many ways, a very ecologically minded city. The state government has a strong record of investing in ambitious initiatives such as the Programme for the Protection of Land and Endangered Species, which seeks to balance the objectives of nature and conservation with urban development; industry has been given particularly strict emission-reducing targets, a state-wide energy-saving campaign was launched in 1994, and solar power has been adopted on a massive scale.

Awareness also happens on a smaller scale, and the success of the city's energy-saving programmes is largely due to people's willingness to contribute on an individual level. Bicycle lanes abound, there are solar-powered parking voucher dispensers and recycling is the norm – even U-Bahn and S-Bahn stations have colour-coded *Trennmüll* (sorted rubbish) bins. The city has a comprehensive and efficient public transport system, which the majority of people use regularly; by the same token, it tries to discourage drivers through restricted parking, and expensive parking meters and garages.

Greenpeace (www.greenpeace-berlin.de) is very active in Germany; another important and similarly radical environmental group is the **Grüne Liga** (www.grueneliga.de). The Green Party has also traditionally been strong in Berlin, but won only 9% of the local vote in the most recent elections in 2001, compared to 15% in 1995. One reason for voters' disenchantment may have been the support for military involvement in Afghanistan that this once thoroughly pacifist party has shown on the national level, a miscalculation that in light of opposition to the subsequent Iraq war may prove terminally costly.

URBAN PLANNING & DEVELOPMENT

Berlin is essentially a work in progress. Cranes have been an everyday sight on the skyline virtually since the end of WWII, but it was reunification that signalled the start of the large-scale building and reconstruction programmes that are still going on today. You just need to look at photos of Potsdamer Platz over the last 10 years to see how much has changed, and the process is far from finished, with projects continuing apace all over the city.

So far, the dramatic Friedrichstadtpassagen have breathed new life into languishing Friedrichstrasse; the New Synagogue on Oranienburger Strasse is a fervent symbol of the rebirth of Jewish culture in Berlin; and around Zoo station, the architectural sins of the 1950s are being replaced with dramatic new structures. The most prominent development, though, has emerged around Potsdamer Platz, whose ballet of cranes was a symbol of the 1990s. Here, a new urban district has sprung up, anchored by DaimlerCity, the Sony Center and the new Potsdamer Platz rail station.

Further prestige projects are planned for the area around Potsdamer Platz, with international companies vying for office space around Leipziger Platz and along Ebertstrasse; Pariser Platz, in front of the Brandenburg Gate, has already been snapped up by embassies, the big banks and the Academy of Arts, and is once again becoming Berlin's 'reception room'.

In housing terms, however, all this development has made it much harder to find affordable lodgings in the centre of town; families in particular almost invariably live in the outlying districts, particularly Marzahn. As buildings are increasingly subdivided, many more people are living in single apartments, and the German tradition of the *Wohngemeinschaft* (shared house, or WG) is becoming a relative rarity in the inner city. Some long-term squatted houses still survive in Friedrichshain and Kreuzberg, the old favourite haunts of the squat scene, but with gentrification marching on it's anyone's guess how long they'll last.

Arts

Arts

Berlin is the cultural hub of the country. Nowhere else can touch the dynamism and international clout of the Berlin arts scene. The city itself provides an iconic setting for any number of books, films, paintings and songs, its unmistakeable presence imposing on local and international artists just as it does on residents. Above all the eternal reinventions of Berlin are reflected in the relentless diversity of the styles, forms and ideas that spring from its creative communities.

For a comprehensive guide to everything that goes on in the city, buy the annual *Berlin Kultur(ver)führer* handbook (Helmut Metz Verlag; €10.50), a conversational but detailed rundown of all things cultural in Berlin.

VISUAL ARTS

Berlin is one of Europe's great art cities, with dozens of fine exhibition spaces and a particular reputation for encouraging contemporary and alternative art. Besides the main museums, the best spots are the gallery quarters which are around the Hackesche Höfe and Auguststrasse in Mitte, around Zimmerstrasse near the former Checkpoint Charlie, and the established Charlottenburg scene around Ku'damm, Uhlandstrasse and Fasanenstrasse. High points of the art year include the Berlin Biennale (p12) and Art Forum Berlin (p11).

Top Five Museums & Galleries

- **Neue Nationalgalerie** (p106) The best cutting-edge modern art.
- **Käthe-Kollwitz-Museum** (p113) Celebrating Germany's best-known female artist.
- **Kunsthaus Tacheles** (p94) Blanket graffiti, antimainstream workshops and studios.
- **Das Verborgene Museum** (p114) Rediscovering work by forgotten 1920s women.
- **Alte Nationalgalerie** (p86) A healthy dose of classic Romanticism.

Despite its current prominence, fine arts only really began to flourish in Berlin in the late 17th and early 18th centuries, largely because self-crowned King Friedrich I felt the need to surround himself with sophistication and grandeur. At the instigation of sculptor Andreas Schlüter (1660–1714), he founded the Academy of the Arts in 1696. Schlüter was also responsible for several outstanding sculptures, including the *Great Elector on Horseback* (1699), now in front of Schloss Charlottenburg (p107), and the haunting *Masks of Dying Warriors* in the courtyard of the Zeughaus (p81) on Unter den Linden.

During this period, the allegorical fresco re-emerged as an established art form and came to adorn the ceilings of various palaces. This endeavour kept German painters such as Johann Friedrich Wentzel and Friedrich Wilhelm Weidemann busy, but Antoine Pesne (1683–1757) was the acknowledged master of the craft, satisfying Friedrich I's taste for the French rococo style.

The arts languished again under his successor, Soldier King Friedrich Wilhelm I, but took a turn towards greatness when his son, Friedrich II (Frederick the Great), ascended the throne in 1740. Friedrich drew heavily on the artistic, architectural and decorative expertise of Georg Wenzeslaus von Knobelsdorff (1699–1753), a student of Pesne. Knobelsdorff gave the world Schloss Rheinsberg (p265), though he's most famous for designing the Staatsoper Unter den Linden (p83) and Schloss Sanssouci (p258) in Potsdam.

The 19th century saw a proliferation of styles, which in some ways reflected the socio-political undercurrents rumbling through Europe at this time. New political and economic ideas coming to Germany from England and France resonated especially with the educated middle classes and found expression in neoclassicism, a style which brought a formal shift to both line and body and an emphasis on Roman and Greek mythology. One major artist of the period was Johann Gottfried Schadow (1764–1850), whose most famous work is the *Quadriga*, the horse-drawn chariot that crowns the Brandenburger Tor (p80). While basing his work on classic Greek sculpture, Schadow also imbued it with great naturalness and sensuousness.

Another important neoclassical sculptor was Christian Daniel Rauch (1777–1857), a student of Schadow. Rauch had a talent for representing idealised, classical beauty in a realistic fashion. He created the sarcophagi of Friedrich Wilhelm III and Queen Luise (both on view in the Mausoleum at Schloss Charlottenburg). His most famous work, though, is the monument of Friedrich II on horseback (1851), which stands outside the **Humboldt Universität** (p81).

A student of Rauch, the sculptor Reinhold Begas (1831–1911) developed a neobaroque, theatrical style that was so ostentatiously counter-neoclassical that he met with a fair amount of controversy, even in his lifetime. The Neptune fountain (1891) outside the Marienkirche is a Begas work, as is the Schiller monument on Gendarmenmarkt.

In painting, Romanticism gradually overtook neoclassicism in popularity. A reason for this was the awakening of a nationalist spirit in Germany – spurred by the Napoleonic Wars – during the reign of Friedrich Wilhelm III (1797–1840). Romanticism was the perfect form of expression for the idealism and emotion that characterised the period. The genre's leading light was Caspar David Friedrich (1774–1840), whose evocative works are on display at the Alte Nationalgalerie. Also here are paintings by Karl Friedrich Schinkel, Berlin's dominant neoclassical architect (p43), who, early in his career, created a series of moody landscapes and fantastic depictions of Gothic architecture. Other Romantic painters, like Wilhelm Schadow and Karl Wilhelm Wach, represent a group of intensely religious artists called the Nazarener (Nazareths).

A parallel development during the period of 1815 to 1848 was the so-called Berliner Biedermeier, a more conservative and painstakingly detailed style. The most successful artist of this period was Franz Krüger (1797–1857), whose best-known works are meticulous depictions of public parades. There was also an early interest in paintings that chronicled Berlin's constantly evolving cityscape, which sold especially well among the middle classes; important artists of the genre include Eduard Gaertner and Wilhelm Brücke.

In 1892 the first tendrils of modernity reached Berlin. Conservative groups opposed to nontraditional art forced the closure of an exhibition displaying pictures by Edvard Munch, prompting a group of young artists to band together in protest. Initially calling themselves the Gruppe der XI (Group of 11), they became better known under the name Berlin Secession, adopted in 1898. Led by Max Liebermann (1847–1935) and Walter Leistikow (1865–1908), member artists were not linked by a common artistic style, but by a

Alte Nationalgalerie (p86)

rejection of reactionary attitudes towards the arts that stifled new forms of expression. They preferred scenes from daily life to historical and religious themes, shunned studios in favour of natural outdoor light, and were hugely influential in inspiring new styles.

Liebermann himself evolved from a painter of gloomy naturalist scenes to one of the most important representatives of 'Berlin impressionism'. In the early 1900s, Lovis Corinth (1858–1925) and Max Slevogt (1868–1932) joined the group, as did Käthe Kollwitz (1867–1945). Kollwitz was a veritable 'Renaissance woman', active in virtually all fields of visual art. Her keen social and political awareness lent a tortured power to her work, and she is still regarded as Germany's finest female artist, with exhibitions dedicated to her all over the country.

After WWI, this liberal tradition allowed Berlin to evolve into the centre of contemporary German and international art. Radical movements proliferated as a veritable Who's Who of artists flocked to the city, and Dadaism, cofounded by George Grosz (1893–1959), emerged as a prevalent form. Dadaists rejected traditional art in favour of collage and montage, and considered chance and spontaneity to be determining artistic elements; the first Dada evening in 1917 was by all accounts a chaotic affair, with Grosz urinating on the pictures, Richard Huelsenbeck declaring that too few people had been killed for art, and the police trying to close the whole thing down. The works were outrageous, provocative and much debated.

Totally Grosz

In this age of stuffed sharks, performance piercing and plastified corpses, it's hard to imagine the furore that a straightforward painting could cause in the 1920s. With the work of native Berliner George Grosz, however, the leap of imagination required is pretty small – the ferocious satire of his paintings still has the power to shock, if not offend. Just look at the steaming turd filling the brainpan of the fat capitalist in the famous *Pillars of Society* (1926) in the Neue Nationalgalerie and it's easy to see why Germany was scandalised!

Parallel movements had expressionist artists like Max Beckmann (1884–1950) and Otto Dix (1891–1969), who examined the threats posed to humanity by urbanisation, while Wassily Kandinsky, Paul Klee, Lyonel Feininger and Alexej Jawlensky formed the 'The Blue Four' (the successor to the Munich-based Blaue Reiter group) in 1924 and went on to work and teach at the Bauhaus art school.

The impact on the Berlin arts scene after the Nazi takeover was devastating. Many artists left the country; others ended up in prison or concentration camps, their works classified as 'degenerate' and often confiscated and destroyed. As a rule the kind of art promoted by the regime was pretty terrible, favouring straightforward forms and epic styles. Propaganda artist Mjölnir defined the typical look of the time with instantly recognisable Gothic scripts and idealised figures of Aryan soldiers, women and Hitler himself – much of his work is displayed in Berlin's historical museums such as the **Deutsches Historisches Museum** (p81).

After WWII, Berlin's art scene was as fragmented as the city itself. In the east, artists were forced to toe the 'socialist-realist' line, which Otto Nagel and Max Lingner frequently managed to leap over by feigning conformity while maintaining aesthetic and experimental aspects in their work. In the late '60s, East Berlin established itself as an arts centre in the German Democratic Republic (GDR) with the formation of the Berliner Schule (Berlin School). Main members such as Manfred Böttcher and Harald Metzkes succeeded at freeing themselves from the confines of officially sanctioned socialist art in order to embrace a more multifaceted realism. In the '70s, when conflicts of the individual in society became a prominent theme, underground galleries flourished in Prenzlauer Berg and art became a collective endeavour.

In postwar West Berlin, artists eagerly absorbed abstract influences from France and the USA. Pioneers included Zone 5, which revolved around Hans Thiemann, and surrealists Heinz Trökes and Mac Zimmermann. At the same time, returning veteran expressionists Max Pechstein and Karl Schmidt-Rottluff provided a more 'traditional' counterweight. In the 1960s, politics was a primary concern and a new style called 'critical realism' emerged, propagated by artists like Ulrich Baehr, Hans-Jürgen Diehl and Wolfgang Petrick. The 1973 movement called Schule der Neuen Prächtigkeit (School of New Magnificence) had a similar approach and involved artists like Manfred Bluth, Matthias Koeppel and Johannes Grützke. In the 1980s, expressionism found its way back onto the canvasses of painters like Salomé, Helmut Middendorf and Rainer Fetting, a group known as the Junge Wilde (Young Wild Ones).

After the Wende (the turning point that led to the collapse of the GDR), fuelled by the sense of change, Berlin's arts scene developed into one of the most exciting and dynamic in Europe, and today the city is considered an international centre of contemporary art. The **Neue Nationalgalerie** (p106) in particular hosts excellent thematic exhibitions by major local and international artists. Other pioneering galleries include **Galerie Wohnmaschine** (p227) and **Galerie Eigen+Art** (p227); the **Kunsthaus Tacheles** (p94) is home to numerous smaller-scale artists' studios. On the international stage, look out for Italian-German rising star and Berlin resident Monica Bonvicini, whose installations examine the nature of space and destruction and have already received widespread critical acclaim.

Arts – Film

FILM

In 1895 Germany's first commercial film projection took place in Berlin. The city soon became synonymous with film making in Germany, at least until the outbreak of WWII. With filming having resumed in Babelsberg in 1992, Berlin has become the second-most important film centre in Germany behind Munich, with a prolific experimental scene lurking in the shadows of the big names.

Berlin also plays host to most German premieres of international movies, and stages the single most important event in Germany's annual film calendar, the **International Film Festival** (p9). Better known as the Berlinale, it was founded in 1951 on the initiative of the western Allies and features screenings of around 750 films, with some of them competing for the prestigious Golden and Silver Bear trophies. In 2000 the Berlinale moved to new digs at Potsdamer Platz, also home of the Filmmuseum Berlin. Since 1971 the International Forum of New Cinema, which showcases more radical and alternative films, has taken place alongside the more traditional competition.

Berlin's pioneering role in movie history is undeniable. America had Edison, France the Lumière brothers, and Berlin had Max Skladanowsky, a former fairground showman whose 1895 invention – the bioscope, a prototype film projector – paved the way for others to improve on his technological achievement and ring in the era of film making in Germany. By 1910, Berlin had 139 *Kinematographentheater* (hence the German word for cinema, *Kino*) showing mostly slapstick, melodramas and short documentaries. The city now has more cinemas than ever (around 265), including numerous multiplexes as well as smaller screens showing movies in their original language.

The 1920s and early '30s were boom time for Berlin cinema, with Marlene Dietrich seducing the world, and the mighty UFA studio (originally founded to produce WWI propaganda) producing virtually the whole of Germany's celluloid output. The two dominant

Top Five Berlin Films

Berlin itself has 'starred' in many films, providing an iconic and evocative backdrop for everything from historical dramas to modern thrillers (and of course *Cabaret*). If you're feeling lazy, a video night can be a great way to explore!

- *Berlin: Sinfonie einer Grosstadt* (Berlin: Symphony of a City; Walter Ruttmann; 1927) – ambitious for its time, this fascinating silent documentary captures a day in the life of '20s Berlin, with some telling juxtaposed images
- *Good Bye Lenin!* (Wolfgang Becker; 2003) – a witty story of a young East Berliner replicating the GDR for his mother after the fall of the Wall. Unexpectedly, this very German film was a huge hit worldwide, with nominations at both the Golden Globes and the Oscars.
- *Herr Lehmann* (Berlin Blues; Leander Haussmann; 2003) – the Weltrestaurant Markthalle, the World Time Clock and the Berlin Wall itself are just some of the landmarks featured in this cult novel adaptation
- *Der Himmel über Berlin* (Wings of Desire; Wim Wenders; 1987) – this angelic love story swoops around the old, bare no-man's-land of Potsdamer Platz. Under no circumstances rent the Nicolas Cage/Meg Ryan remake, *City of Angels*.
- *Lola rennt* (Run Lola Run; Tom Tykwer; 1997) – the geography's largely fictional but the city's unmistakeable in this inventive, energetic MTV-generation movie

29

directors of the time were Georg Wilhelm Papst, whose use of montage and characterisation defined the Neue Sachlichkeit (New Objectivity) movement, and Fritz Lang, whose seminal works *Metropolis* (1926) and *M* (1931) brought him international fame. After 1933, however, film makers found their artistic freedom, not to mention funding, increasingly curtailed, and by 1939 practically the entire industry had fled abroad.

Like most of the arts, the film industry has generally been well funded in Berlin since 1945, and particularly large subsidies were offered in the 1970s to lure film makers back to the city. It worked, and the leading lights of the Junge Deutsche Film (Young German Film), directors such as Rainer Werner Fassbinder, Volker Schlöndorf, Wim Wenders and Werner Herzog, magically reappeared from Munich at the promise of more cash.

Fassbinder, perhaps the most talented and challenging of the group, died in an accident in 1982, but the other three have remained at the forefront of German cinema. Herzog, best known for his work with psychotic actor Klaus Kinski, is still an active documentary director and produce. Wenders has been highly acclaimed for USA-based films such as *Paris, Texas* (1984), *Buena Vista Social Club* (1999) and *The Million Dollar Hotel* (2000). Schlöndorf, with consistent foreign and domestic successes under his belt, now runs the show at Potsdam's Babelsberg complex, once the domain of the great UFA studios.

With its fundamentally commercial infrastructure and a series of recent hits, the Berlin film community has not been as badly affected as some by the city's financial crisis, though there are frequent complaints that not enough money finds its way down to the truly independent small-time film makers. This doesn't seem to have much impact on the really alternative scene, which like the antimainstream art movement has thrived for years, putting on its own seasons and events in the various cultural centres around town. The first Anti-Globalisation Film Festival was held in 2003 in the **Acud** (p205) and **Eiszeit** (p215) cinemas, showcasing all kinds of local and international talent under its broad political umbrella.

As befits a city with such a chequered past, recent history has always been an issue for Berlin film makers, from the early postwar *Trümmerfilme* ('rubble films') to the latest wave

Documenting Evil

I filmed the truth as it was then. Nothing more.
Leni Riefenstahl

Films made during the Nazi period bring their own historical dilemma, none more so than the works of brilliant Berlin director Leni Riefenstahl (1902–2003).

A former actress and resident of the northern district of Wedding, Riefenstahl caught the regime's attention with her first feature as director, *Das blaue Licht* (The Blue Light; 1932), and was recruited to make 'informational' films. Considered a vital part of the Third Reich propaganda machine, Riefenstahl's epics depicted Nazi events such as the 1936 Olympics. Her visually stunning *Triumph des Willens* (Triumph of the Will; 1934), a documentary about Hitler that centres on the Nuremberg rallies, is one of the most controversial pieces in cinematic history.

After the war, shocked by the atrocities exposed, Riefenstahl maintained that she had held no fascist sympathies, protesting both her right as a film maker to record such events and her lack of choice in the matter under the Nazis. Demonised by the Allies and the industry, she spent four years in a French prison. In 1954, in an attempt to clear her reputation, she completed *Tiefland*, an allegorical, supposedly anti fascist fairy tale she had started work on in 1944; however, with no distributor willing to touch it, her cinematic career was effectively over.

From then on Riefenstahl concentrated mainly on photography. Between 1972 and 1997 she published several books about the Sudanese people, based on her own experiences and frequent visits, which went some way towards refuting accusations of racism. In 1992 she published her autobiography, and subsequently found herself the subject of a number of documentaries, including *Leni Riefenstahl: Die Macht der Bilder* (The Power of the Image; 1993) and *The Wonderful Horrible Life of Leni Riefenstahl* (2003). Despite a consistently high public profile in Germany and abroad she made only one more film, an underwater documentary called *Impressionen unter Wasser* (Impressions under Water), in 2002.

In September 2003 Leni Riefenstahl died in Germany, aged 101, leaving no real answers in the ongoing debate over art and complicity. In the USA, at least, she has succeeded in regaining some public sympathy – Jodie Foster is mooted to direct and star in a forthcoming biopic.

of post-Wende *Ostalgie* (GDR nostalgia). Some of the best films about the Nazi era include East Germany's first postwar film, *Die Mörder sind unter uns* (The Murderers Are Among Us; 1946); *Jakob der Lügner* (Jacob the Liar; 1974), later remade with Robin Williams; Fassbinder's *Die Ehe von Maria Braun* (Maria Braun's Marriage; 1979); *Aimée & Jaguar* (1999), the true story of a Jewish woman and a soldier's wife who fell in love during the war; and Margaretha von Trotta's latest film *Rosenstrasse* (2003), about a group of women fighting for the release of their Jewish husbands.

Since reunification, however, few serious critical feature films have dealt with the GDR era, perhaps because of the proximity of the events and a reluctance to engage with their implications. Movies that do deal with the divide tend to be light-hearted comedy-dramas, and have garnered considerable success recently: *Sonnenallee* (1999) and *Herr Lehmann* (Berlin Blues; 2003) played well to Berlin audiences, while *Good Bye Lenin!* (2003), about a son trying to re-create GDR life to reassure his sick mother, was a major international hit, quite an achievement for a German-language production.

In Berlin as in Germany, women have taken an unusually active role in the film industry, a trend that can be traced back as far as the heyday of Marlene Dietrich. Many of the most ground-breaking and challenging films have been driven by women: directors Jutta Brückner, Sylke Enders and Doris Dörrie, and producer Ewa Karlstrom are all active in Berlin, as is legendary director Margarethe von Trotta, who has been an influential figure since the early days of the Junge Deutsche Film, tackling a range of historical and political issues. Karlstrom's former colleague Katja von Garnier has also taken the mantle to America, where she caused a stir in 2003 with the forthright women's suffrage TV movie *Iron Jawed Angels* (she also briefly dated Brad Pitt in 1997).

Modern male directors, on the other hand, seem more concerned with the private sphere, particularly the theme of male friendship, which recurs time and again in mainstream German films – *Sonnenallee*, *Crazy* (Hans-Christian Schmid; 2000), *Herr Lehmann* and *Fremde Freund* (Christopher Hein; 1982) are just a few examples. In the context of Berlin, this could suggest the last gasp of the Love Parade boys, struggling to redefine their relationships with each other in the broke and disillusioned post-Ecstasy capital.

The most significant exception to this trend has been Fatih Akin's powerful drama *Gegen die Wand* (Against the Wall; 2003), an incisive and unflinching look at the pressures facing Turkish Germans, which won the Golden Bear prize at the 2004 Berlinale against stiff international competition. The film's success shows that, as with so many aspects of Berlin culture, the city's strength lies in its diversity, and right now the possibilities for minority film makers seem limitless.

THEATRE & DANCE

Since the Wende, major artistic, structural and personnel changes have swept Berlin's theatrical landscape on a regular basis. The major stages have traditionally been very well subsidised (although funding has dropped dramatically with the recent fiscal problems), with the result that theatre has risked lapsing into staid complacency. However, the current directors of the city's leading venues are, for the most part, presiding over a boom period, for young audiences and innovative ensembles in particular, with a lively fringe scene flourishing around them.

Enfant terrible Frank Castorf is the man behind much of this new wave, igniting a creative firestorm at the Volksbühne. Meanwhile, Claus Peymann has restored greatness to the Berliner Ensemble. Bernd Wilms, who made the Maxim Gorki Theater into one of the most respected theatres in town, moved to the Deutsches Theater in 2001, while young gun Volker Hesse has taken over at the Gorki. Also part of the new generation is Thomas Ostermeier, codirector of the Schaubühne am Lehniner Platz. For information on venues see the Entertainment chapter (p211).

Dance, too, is alive and kicking up its heels in Berlin, which has three state-sponsored ballet troupes (attached to the three opera houses) as well as a thriving independent scene. Ballet arrived under Friedrich II, who brought Italian star Barberina to the city in 1744; the first royal company was formed in 1811; and eccentric American dancer Isadora Duncan

Toller & Piscator

The names of playwright Ernst Toller (1893–1939) and producer Erwin Piscator (1893–1966) no longer mean much to the average theatregoer, but they were two of the most interesting figures of their time, and their single collaboration, the Berlin premiere of Toller's play *Hoppla, wir leben!* (Whoops, We're Alive!), was arguably the biggest theatrical event of the 1920s.

From the start the two men clashed. Toller was a committed socialist with humanist leanings, traumatised by WWI and the years he spent in prison after the short-lived 1919 Munich revolution, and the play was based on his experience of postwar society and the problems of political activism. Piscator, on the other hand, was a radical communist aiming to create a spectacle and establish 'total theatre' as an extreme, agitatory form of political engagement – the premiere was also the opening night of his new Piscatorbühne theatre on Nollendorfplatz, carefully timed to coincide with the 10th anniversary of the Russian Revolution.

Piscator's revolutionary production methods, using elaborate multisectioned sets, revolving stages, music and film clips, were actually ideally suited to Toller's vision of a world swamped in new technology, and had a profound influence on modern documentary theatre. However, the play's indeterminate ending was not the radical statement Piscator wanted to make; he rewrote it to have the lead character commit suicide, a crass stroke that undermined Toller's thoughtful attempt to examine the issues of political commitment and progress. The two never spoke again, and Toller reinstated his original ending for every subsequent run of the play.

opened her own school here in 1904. Today new and innovative groups attract a growing audience, with performances often staged in unconventional settings. Leading venues are the TanzWerkstatt Berlin and Hebbel m Ufer, while Sascha Waltz is the latest female star to make her mark on the dance community, sharing the directorship of the Schaubühne with Thomas Ostermeier.

Surprisingly, Berlin's theatre scene had rather modest beginnings. The first quality productions weren't staged until the arrival of such stellar dramatists as Gotthold Ephraim Lessing and Johann Wolfgang von Goethe in the middle of the 18th century. One of the first impresarios was August Wilhelm Iffland (1759–1814), who took over the helm of the Royal National Theatre in 1796. Iffland was noted for his natural yet sophisticated productions, especially of Schiller plays, and for cultivating a talented ensemble.

Iffland's act proved hard to follow: when he died in 1814, Berlin theatre languished for 80 years until Otto Brahm became director of the Deutsches Theater in 1894. Dedicated to the naturalistic style, Brahm is considered a pioneer of modern dramatic theatre. He coaxed psychological dimensions out of the characters and sought to make their language and situations mirror real life. The critical works of Gerhart Hauptmann and Henrik Ibsen were staples on his stage throughout the 1890s.

In 1894, Brahm hired a young actor named Max Reinhardt (1873–1943), who became perhaps the most famous and influential director ever in the German theatre. Born in Vienna, Reinhardt quickly moved from acting to producing, founding Berlin's first literary cabaret, running the Kleines Theater and Neues Theater simultaneously, and eventually inheriting the reins of the Deutsches Theater from Brahm himself. Stylistically, Reinhardt completely broke the naturalist mould favoured by his old mentor and became known for his lavish productions, using light effects, music and other devices to enhance the illusionary effects of the theatre. In 1919 he opened the Grosse Schauspielhaus, now the **Friedrichstadtpalast** (p210).

Reinhardt's path later crossed that of another seminal theatre figure, Bertolt Brecht (1898–1956), who moved to Berlin in 1924. The two worked together briefly at the Deutsches Theater until Brecht developed his own unique style, so-called 'epic theatre', which, unlike 'dramatic theatre', forces its audience to detach themselves emotionally from the play and its characters and to reason intellectually.

Over the next decade Brecht developed this theory and its 'alienation techniques' in plays like *Die Dreigroschenoper* (The Threepenny Opera; 1928). A staunch Marxist, he went into exile during the Nazi years, surfaced in Hollywood as a scriptwriter, then left the USA during the communist witch hunts of the McCarthy era. He wrote most of his best plays during his years in exile: *Mutter Courage und ihre Kinder* (Mother Courage and Her

Children; 1941), *Leben des Galilei* (The Life of Galileo; 1943), *Der gute Mensch von Sezuan* (The Good Woman of Sezuan; 1943) and *Der kaukasische Kreidekreis* (The Caucasian Chalk Circle; 1948) are considered among the finest examples of his extraordinary style.

Brecht returned to East Berlin in 1949 and founded the Berliner Ensemble with his wife, Helene Weigel, who directed it until her death in 1971. *Mother Courage and Her Children* premiered successfully in 1949 at the Deutsches Theater, but for much of the rest of his lifetime the great playwright was both suspected in the East for his unorthodox aesthetic theories and scorned (and often boycotted) in the West for his communist principles.

At the same time as Brecht was experimenting in prewar Berlin, new expressionistic approaches to musical theatre came from classically trained composers including Hanns Eisler and Kurt Weill, who collaborated with Brecht on *The Threepenny Opera* and *The Rise and Fall of the City of Mahagony*. On the more mainstream variety circuit, champagne, cancan and long-legged showgirls were all the rage, and Mischa Spoliansky was among the leading lights of the cabaret stages.

The 1920s were also an active time for dance. Berlin even gave birth to a new form, so-called 'grotesque dance'. Influenced by Dadaism, it was characterised by excessive, and often comical, expressiveness. One of its prime practitioners was Valeska Gert, but even more influential was Mary Wigman, who regarded body and movement as tools to express the universal experience of life. Her style inspired some of today's leading German choreographers, including Pina Bausch and Reinhild Hoffmann.

After WWII, artistic stagnation spread across German theatre for more than two decades. In West Berlin the first breath of recovery came in 1970 with the opening of the Schaubühne am Halleschen Ufer under Peter Stein. The theatre, which later moved to the Ku'damm and became the Schaubühne am Lehniner Platz, rapidly developed into one of Germany's leading stages. In East Berlin the Volksbühne grew to be a highly innovative venue, along with the Deutsches Theater. Taking advantage of relative political and artistic freedom granted by the government, they provided platforms for political exchange and contributed to the peaceful revolution of 1989. One of the driving forces was prolific and outspoken dramatist Heiner Müller.

Ballet, too, experienced a postwar renaissance under the Russian immigrant Tatjana Gsovsky, though it came and went quicker than the theatre revival. Initially working without a permanent stage, Gsovsky choreographed a number of memorable productions, including *Hamlet* (1953) and *The Idiot* (1954), at the Theater des Westens before becoming ballet director at the Deutsche Oper. Sadly her impetus hasn't lasted, and today's ballet troupes concentrate on audience-pleasing classical repertoire such as *Swan Lake* and *The Nutcracker*.

MUSIC

Germany's contemporary music scene has many centres, but Berlin is still the big one for most of today's multifarious styles and genres. It boasts at least 2000 active bands, countless DJs and the country's leading orchestras, not to mention the three great state-funded opera houses. Like the city itself, music here is constantly evolving, changing shape and redefining itself, and Berlin continues to be a fertile breeding ground for new musical trends. For information on venues see the Entertainment chapter (p206).

For centuries, Berlin was largely eclipsed by Vienna, Leipzig and other European cities when it came to music. In 1882, however, the Berliner Philharmonisches Orchester was established, gaining international stature under Hans von Bülow and Arthur Nikisch. In 1923, Wilhelm Furtwängler became artistic director, a post he held, with interruptions during and shortly after the Nazi years, until 1954. His successor, the legendary Herbert von Karajan, was an autocratic figure who established a position of real dominance on the world stage and remained director until 1989. He was followed by Claudio Abbado and, in 2002, flamboyant British conductor Sir Simon Rattle, who won a Grammy with the orchestra before he had even officially started in the post.

The pulsating 1920s drew numerous musicians to Berlin, including Arnold Schönberg and Paul Hindemith, who taught at the Academie der Künste and the Berliner Hochschule, respectively. Schönberg's atonal compositions found a following here, as did his

Gig advertisements, Bar jeder Vernunft (p210)

experimentation with noise and sound effects. Hindemith explored the new medium of radio and taught a seminar on film music.

Today the classical scene is considerably less high profile; look out for composer Wolfgang Rihm, tenor Peter Schreier's oratorio performances and director Andreas Homoki's fresh productions at the Komische Oper. To get a taste of the latest pieces from the capital's composers, try Rainer Rubbert's weekly Unerhörte Musik (Unheard-of Music) concerts at the BKA Theatre.

Jazz and popular music formed another key feature of the '20s, providing the staple diet of the city's clubs, cabarets and drinking dens. Modern singer Max Raabe has carved out a niche for himself by recreating the typical sounds of the period with his Palast Orchestra, and is a regular fixture in Berlin.

The 1920s also generated the Berlin *Schlager*, silly but entertaining songs with titles like *Mein Papagei frisst keine harten Eier* (My Parrot Doesn't Eat Hard-boiled Eggs) and *Veronika, der Lenz ist da* (Veronica, Spring Is Here). Singing groups such as the Comedian Harmonists built their success on this music, and it still survives today with Funny van Dannen. Our personal *Schlager* favourite is young Kabarett regular Marco Tschirpke, whose mock-melancholy 30-second 'astronaut songs' strike a wonderful balance between absurdity and observation. Look him up before he sells out.

With modernity ever at the forefront, Berlin has spearheaded most of Germany's popular music revolutions. In the late '60s, Tangerine Dream helped to propagate the psychedelic sound with albums such as *Zeit* (1972), *Atem* (1973) and *Stratosfear* (1976). A decade later, East Berlin–born Nina Hagen followed her adopted father, writer Wolf Biermann, to West Germany and soon became the diva of German punk, a role she still occupies today. Hagen also laid the groundwork for the major musical movement of the '80s, NDW or Neue Deutsche Welle (German New Wave), which gave the stage to Berlin bands like Ideal, the Neonbabies and UKW, and now provides the raw materials for dozens of weekly '80s revival nights.

Back in the GDR, where access to Western rock and other popular music was restricted, bands such as Die Puhdys and Rockhaus kept alive a vibrant underground scene. With no constraints, West Berlin also attracted a slew of international talent: David Bowie and Iggy Pop both spent stints living at Hauptstrasse 152, while Nick Cave owned a club here and

U2's classic albums *Achtung Baby* (recorded in Berlin) and *Zooropa* both use Zoo station as a central motif.

Coinciding with the Wende, another essentially home-grown music form took over Berlin. Techno may have its roots in Detroit-based house music, but it was from Berlin that it conquered the world, tapping into the simultaneous explosion of the UK rave scene and the popularity of ecstasy. Pioneering clubs included Ufo, Planet, E-Werk and still-surviving Tresor; the scene also spawned the famous **Love Parade** (p11), which packs the central city streets every July. What began as a three-car procession in 1989 quickly turned into a weekend-long phenomenon that topped 1.5 million ravers in 1999; recently, though, figures have dropped to a mere half million.

The most important proponents of the Berlin techno sound include Dr Motte, cofounder of the Love Parade and 'godfather of techno'; Westbam, who has also had considerable commercial success with housier sounds and as half of big-beat duo Mr X and Mr Y; Ellen Allien, star act of the bpitch control record label; and Tanith, another Love Parade stalwart. The Tresor record label, a spin-off of the club's success, has become an international brand with a full range of merchandising.

Pure techno is, however, being slightly sidelined as more and more successive splinter genres of electronic music percolate into the club scene. House is not as ubiquitous here as it is in the rest of Europe and the USA, but does dominate hipper spaces such as the Sage Club, with more commercial trance playing to younger clubbers and certain gay crowds. The biggest name here is local boy and international superstar Paul van Dyk ('Powl fan Dook' in German), one of the earliest propagators of the euphoric trance sound – his *For an Angel* is a solid-gold club classic. Ironically, his brand of dance music is far more popular in southern Germany than in über-cool Berlin. PvD still DJs here regularly, but names you'll see slightly more often include Clé, Highfish, Djoker Daan, ED 2000 and André Galluzzi, former resident at the sadly defunct Ostgut club.

Unsurprisingly, given Berliners' love of hardcore beats, drum and bass also commands a dedicated following, with clubs such as Icon and Watergate thundering away every weekend. Indigenous DJs such as Bleed, Metro, Appollo and N'Dee are all well in touch with the music and their audience, and MCs Mace, Santana and White MC keep the mic rocked, but the real highlights are the frequent special guests, who come from as far away as London and San Francisco to play here. Goldie, DJ Storm, Grooverider, Alley Cat, Frankfurt's Kabuki and Cologne's X-plorer are all regular faces.

On the other side of the equation, some of the finest exports of Berlin come from a jazz/breaks angle (an electrojazz or breakbeat angle, favouring lush grooves, obscure samples and chilled rhythms) – offbeat producers and remix masters Jazzanova, part of the loose Sonarkollektiv group of musicians, are the undisputed champions of a downtempo scene encompassing DJs and bands such as Micatone, Andre Langenfeld, Terranova and

Designer Label

It's a law of nature – where musicians lead, record companies follow. In Berlin, however, there are a staggering number of independent record labels doing exactly the opposite, creating sounds, setting trends and 'collecting' artists to fit their vibe. Compost, Kitty-Yo and Bungalow are all names to watch, but foremost among the trailblazers is !K7 Records, founded in the mid-'80s as Studio !K7 by 'the mighty' Horst Weidenmüller.

Originally started as Studio !K7 to produce videos about punk, !K7 branched out with the 3Lux and X-Mix series of coordinated digital film clips and DJ mixes, but then abandoned the less popular visual element to concentrate on the music. The defining moment came in 1995 with the launch of the DJ Kicks series, eclectic compilations mixed by DJs according to their own tastes rather than a prescribed brief; the signing of Austrian duo Kruder and Dorfmeister also marked the label's transition from Detroit-based tech-house to a broader embracing of the underground scene.

Since then the label has been a byword for musical innovation, reaching its 150th release in 2003; DJ Kicks now reaches a large international audience, !K7 Flavour explores Internet broadcasting and the new !K7 Records brand is putting out actual artist albums (as distinct from compilations) for the first time. The ambition, scope and antimainstream ethos of !K7 makes it one of the best and most challenging independent companies around, and its resolutely leftfield vision is as varied and changeable as Berlin itself.

Fauna Flash. Head to WMF or pick up the Berlin Lounge compilation CD (2001, Wagram Music) for a glimpse of this particular corner of Berlin nightlife. The charmingly named German-Scandinavian label Shitkatapult is one of the top outfits for full-on breakbeat, with local boy T.raumschmiere a regular name on Berlin flyers. Maria am Ufer is the number one address for a piece of this action.

More experimental, laptop-driven electronica is another growth area. Sampling everything from skipping CDs to kitchen noises, artists like Funkstörung, Pole and Thomas Fehlmann create tracks from next to nothing, a technique which has also developed its own spin-off genre, the minimalist sound known as 'click house'.

As elsewhere, soul, R&B and black music of all shades are very much in vogue, though few other European cities can offer such a thriving reggae-dancehall scene. Dozens of sound systems put on nights all over Berlin. Such a Sound is among the longest-running, while summer band of 2003 Seeed look like being the next big thing. Homegrown hip hop is also a growing feature of the musical landscape, but unlike in Cologne and other German cities, the rivalries between crews have apparently often distracted them from actually getting their music out there to be heard.

Of course, even amid the beeps and beats good old guitar music never went away, and there are plenty of indie, punk and alternative bands gigging to appreciative audiences, as well as the resolutely grim Gothic and darkcore fringe. Berliner group Rosenstolz has enjoyed considerable commercial success thanks to some radio-friendly rock ballads, and is currently one of Germany's top names. Electronic crossover is a growing by-product of the two scenes: raucous riot girls and former art school 'fake band' (as they describe themselves) Chicks on Speed are firmly in the ascendant, while Stereo Total have attracted a cult following with their punky tunes.

Sadly, prefab bands, singing soap stars and public vote shows such as *Deutschland sucht den Superstar* (the German equivalent of *Pop Idol* and *American Idol*) and *Popstars – Die Rivals* are just as big in Berlin as elsewhere in Germany and the rest of the world. The only vaguely bearable specimen is Jeanette Biedermann, formerly of teen TV favourite *Gute Zeiten schlechte Zeiten*, who is at least enough of a Berlinerin to proclaim her love of *Currywurst* on MTV.

LITERATURE

Since its beginnings, Berlin's literary scene has reflected a peculiar blend of provincialism and worldliness. As with the other arts, Berlin didn't emerge as a centre of literature until relatively late, reaching its zenith during the dynamic 1920s. Overall, the city was not so much a place that generated influential writers as where they came to meet each other, exchange ideas and be intellectually stimulated.

Today there are several literary organisations and author forums serving the same purpose, including the **Literaturforum im Brechthaus** (☎ 282 2003; Chausseestrasse 125), which awards bursaries and prizes such as the Alfred-Döblin-Preis for unpublished work; the **Literarisches Colloquium Berlin** (☎ 816 9960; Am Sandwerder 5); and **literaturWERKstatt** (Map pp322-4; ☎ 485 2450; Kulturbrauerei), which organises regular large events such as the 2000 'literature train' from Portugal to Russia.

Berlin's literary history began during the Enlightenment in the late 18th century, an epoch dominated by humanistic ideals. A major author was Gotthold Ephraim Lessing (1729–81) who is noted for his critical works, fables and tragedies. In Berlin he wrote the play *Minna von Barnhelm* (1763), though his best-known dramatic works are *Miss Sara Samson* (1755), *Emilia Galotti* (1772) and especially *Nathan der Weise* (Nathan the Wise; 1779).

The Romantic period, which grew out of the Enlightenment, was marked by a proliferation of literary salons, usually sponsored by women such as Rahel Levin (later Rahel Varnhagen), an author best known for her correspondence and essays. Men and women from all walks of life came together to discuss philosophy, politics, art and other subjects. Literary greats working in Berlin in this era included Friedrich and August Wilhelm von Schlegel and the Romantic poets Achim von Arnim, Clemens Brentano and Heinrich von Kleist.

Top Five Berlin Books

- *Berlin Alexanderplatz* (Alfred Döblin; 1929) – with quotations displayed on office buildings on Alexanderplatz itself, this stylised meander through the seamy 1920s is still a definitive Berlin text
- *Goodbye to Berlin* (Christopher Isherwood; 1939) – another brilliant, semiautobiographical perspective on Berlin's 'golden age', seen through the eyes of gay Anglo-American journalist Isherwood. The book formed the basis of *Cabaret.*
- *Der geteilte Himmel* (Divided Heaven; Christa Wolf; 1964) – set against an industrial backdrop, this is the powerful story of a woman's love for a man who fled to the West
- *Herr Lehmann* (Berlin Blues; Sven Regener; 2001) – it's hard to imagine a Berlin novel where the fall of the Wall is almost incidental to the plot, but this cult story of Kreuzberg nights pulls it off nicely
- *Russendisko* (Russian Disco; Wladimir Kaminer; 2000) – this collection of stranger-than-fiction stories presents a whole host of unusual characters, adding up to an entertaining and unsentimental portrait of the present-day city from the perspective of a Russian immigrant

During the realist movement in the mid-19th century, novels and novellas gained in popularity, thanks to increased interest from the newly established middle class. Historical novels and works critical of society also caught on, such as those by Wilhelm Raabe (1831–1910), who examines various aspects of Berlin life in *Chronik der Sperlingsgasse* (Chronicle of Sperling Lane; 1857). The Berlin society novel was raised to an art form under the pen of Theodor Fontane (1819–98). Most of his works are set around the March of Brandenburg and in Berlin, and show both the nobility and the middle class mired in their societal confinements.

Naturalism, a spin-off of realism, took things a step further after 1880, painstakingly recreating the milieu of entire social classes, right down to the local dialect. In Berlin, Gerhart Hauptmann (1862–1946) was a key practitioner of the genre. Many of his plays and novels focus on social injustice and the harsh life of workers – subjects so provocative that several of his premieres ended in riots. An 1892 production of *Die Weber* (The Weavers), depicting the misery of Silesian weavers, even prompted the Kaiser to cancel his subscription at the Deutsche Theater. The play, however, was a smashing success. In 1912, Hauptmann won the Nobel Prize for Literature.

In the 1920s, renowned as a period of experimentation and innovation, Berlin became a magnet for writers from around the world. Alfred Döblin's (1878–1957) *Berlin Alexanderplatz* provided a dose of big-city lights and the underworld during the Weimar Republic. Other notables from this era included political satirists Kurt Tucholsky (1890–1935) and Erich Kästner (1899–1974), as well as Egon Erwin Kisch, a journalist and critical essayist. Also a dominant force, primarily in drama, was Bertolt Brecht, who was among the artists who left Germany after the Nazis came to power. Many of those who stayed went into 'inner emigration', keeping their mouths shut and working underground, if at all.

In the mid-1970s, a segment of the East Berlin literary scene began to detach itself slowly from the party grip. Authors such as Christa Wolf (1929–) and Heiner Müller (1929–95) belonged to loose literary circles that regularly met in private houses. Wolf is one of the best and most controversial East German writers; Müller, meanwhile, had the distinction of being unpalatable in both Germanies. It is said that he worked for the Stasi, but that his messages were so ambiguous as to be worthless. His dense, difficult works include *Der Lohndrücker* (The Man Who Kept Down Wages) and the *Germania* trilogy of plays.

In West Berlin the postwar literary scene didn't revive until the arrival of Günter Grass in the late 1950s. His famous *Die Blechtrommel* (The Tin Drum; 1958) humorously traces recent German history through the eyes of Oskar, a child who refuses to grow up; written in a variety of styles, the book is an enjoyable but significant retrospective of the Nazi years and the postwar period, and quickly made Grass a household name. He has followed up with an impressive body of novels, plays and poetry, becoming the ninth German to win the Nobel Prize for Literature in 1999. In Berlin he lived and worked as part of a writers' colony that also included Hans-Magnus Enzensberger, Ingeborg Bachmann and the Swiss writer Max Frisch. Together they paved the way for the political and critical literature that has been dominant since the 1960s.

Literary achievement stagnated at first after the Wende, as writers from the east and west began a process of self-examination. Only Heiner Müller and Botho Strauss stood out amid the creative void. In the late 1990s Berlin's literary scene finally picked up steam. New books dealing with the past are characterised not by analytical introspection but by emotionally distanced, nearly grotesque, imagery. Examples here include Thomas Brussig's *Helden wie wir* (Heroes like us; 1995) and Ingo Schulze's *Simple Stories* (1998). Bernhard Schlink, a former Berliner now living in the USA, caused perhaps the biggest furore with his novel *Der Vorleser* (The Reader; 1995), which approaches issues of collective and individual responsibility through the unusual relationship between a teenage boy and a woman accused of war crimes.

Since 2000 several cult authors have come to the forefront of the literary scene with novels about Berlin itself. Sven Regener's *Herr Lehmann* (2001) has already been made into a film, and Russian-born Wladimir Kaminer's *Russendisko* (2000) and *Schönhauser Allee* (2003) established both the author and his Russian parties as a firm part of the Berlin scenescape. *Wedding* (2003), by comedy writer Horst Evers, is an entertaining and slightly surreal collection of humorous texts centred on Berlin's least popular residential district.

To catch the latest underground and unpublished authors, look out for readings by individuals and groups such as the Surfpoeten (Surf Poets), a collective of young Berlin writers; Kaffee Burger, Kalkscheune, Podewil and the Acud arts centre are favourite locations. See the Entertainment chapter (p205) for venue information.

Architecture

Architecture

The soul of a city and its people, its origins, ambitions, history and cultural geography; all are defined and revealed in the palimpsest of its structures, concepts of urban order and the desire to impose itself – for good or ill – on those who dwell within it. The soul of a city is made manifest most tellingly by its architecture. And perhaps it's in Berlin, as in no other modern city in the world, that the story of a city and its people finds expression in its skylines, historic and modern buildings and the thought given to how people might interact with their environs.

After visiting Berlin in 1891, Mark Twain remarked, 'Berlin is the newest city I've ever seen'. He would probably be astonished to gaze upon what Berlin has become since his time. What was new to Twain then was an energetic colossus thrust into greatness by the waves of construction that followed the founding of the German empire in 1871. While still preserving the grandeur of the palaces and regal estates of the Prussian emperors and warlords, this new Berlin was built to foment revolutions in technology and learning, and to exploit the overwhelming successes of its middle class, merchants and manufacturers. From a hotchpotch of loosely affiliated villages, Berlin became, almost overnight in terms of its long history, *the* powerhouse of European endeavour and expression.

Then came WWII, near obliteration and the horrifying bifurcation into East and West. What had so quickly been laid to waste beneath the 'counter-blitzkrieg' of the Allies was (not quite as quickly) rebuilt from the ashes and rubble, with little else then in mind than to restore the hopes of Berliners and once again to provide them with a sense of civility. This massive reconstruction, naturally, took on decidedly different forms of expression in the Allied zones and in the 'worker's paradise' being touted in the Socialist East. The contrasts between European sensibilities and Moscow's penchant for bombast could not have been made more evident.

Then, following yet another 'unification', Berlin hurled its prodigious energies into a veritable orgy of new construction to signal to the world that the city was once again the centre of European commerce, thought and creativity. It has become a virtual laboratory of the architecturally possible with the enormity of the Potsdamer Platz undertaking and the return of diplomatic courtiers and corporate headquarters. Berlin indeed became an overnight showcase for the best efforts of the world's master architects, IM Pei, Frank Gehry and Renzo Piano among them. Their corporate palaces and governmental centres rose to announce that Berlin was once again the heart, soul and primary engine of the thinking, planning, creativity and commercial instincts of the German nation and its people.

Top Five Buildings

- **IM Pei Bau** (German Historical Museum; p81)
- **Jüdisches Museum** (p120)
- **Nordic embassies** (p50)
- **Philharmonie** (p106)
- **Reichstag** (p99)

IM Pei Bau (p81)

MODEST BEGINNINGS

Berlin, as Mark Twain implies, is essentially a creation of modern times, although it is in fact much older than it first looks. Very little survives from the days of its founding in the early 13th century, although the **Nikolaikirche** (p133), Berlin's oldest church, offers a good introduction to medieval building techniques. Excavations revealed late Romanesque basilica foundations but later generations apparently fancied the Gothic style and converted it into a three-nave hall church topped by a pair of slender twin spires.

Not far behind in age are the **Marienkirche** (p91), first mentioned in 1294, and the **Franziskaner Klosterkirche** (p90), although the latter only survives as a picturesque ruin. All three of Berlin's surviving medieval structures are built in a style called *Backsteingotik* (Brick Gothic) in reference to the red bricks used in their construction, a building material prevalent throughout northern Germany.

The Renaissance, which reached Berlin in the early 16th century, did not leave many traces. Alas, the single most important structure from that period, the Berliner Stadtschloss (1540), was torn down by the GDR government in 1951. Renaissance survivors include the **Jagdschloss Grunewald** (p143), the **Zitadelle Spandau** (p135) and the ornately gabled **Ribbeckhaus** (p88), a late Renaissance work and the oldest extant residential building in Berlin.

GOING FOR BAROQUE

Berlin's first architectural heyday arrived in the mid-17th century. This was the age of baroque, a style merging architecture, sculpture, ornamentation and painting into a single *Gesamtkunstwerk* (complete work of art). In northern Germany, it retained a formal and precise bent, never quite reaching the exuberance achieved in the southern part of the country.

The emergence of baroque architecture is linked to the period of absolutism following the Thirty Years' War (1618–48), when feudal rulers asserted their power by building grand residences. In Berlin this role fell to the Great Elector Friedrich Wilhelm, who brought in an army of architects, engineers and artists to systematically expand the city. By the time they were done, the elector's residence had grown three new quarters – the Dorotheenstadt, Friedrichstadt and Friedrichswerder – a fortified town wall and a grand, tree-lined boulevard known as **Unter den Linden** (p80).

His father may have laid the groundwork but Berlin didn't truly acquire the stature of an exalted residence until Friedrich III came to power in 1688. His representative needs only increased after he had himself crowned *King* Friedrich I in 1701. During his reign, Berlin gained two major baroque buildings that are still tourist magnets. In 1695, shortly before his death, Johann Arnold Nering began construction of the Zeughaus (armoury), which now houses the **Deutsches Historisches Museum** (German Historical Museum; p81); and of Schloss Lietzenburg, a pleasure palace for Friedrich's wife, Sophie Charlotte, which was renamed **Schloss Charlottenburg** (p107) after her death in 1705. Johann Friedrich Eosander expanded the structure into a three-wing palace inspired by Versailles, topping it with a domed central tower.

Across town, construction of the Zeughaus proved to be fraught with obstacles. After Nering's death, Martin Grünberg took over but he resigned in 1699, passing the baton to Andreas Schlüter, who apparently was more of a sculptor than an architect. Schlüter added the masks of dying warriors to the central courtyard with remarkable effect but had to hand the whole project over to Jean de Bodt after part of the structure collapsed. Accomplished art, it seems, is not necessarily the soundest of foundations. The square, two-storey structure was finally completed in 1706.

At the time of research the Zeughaus was nearing completion of a top-to-bottom restoration that will leave its famous courtyard sheltered by a glass-and-steel roof. It was designed by Chinese-American architect IM Pei (famous for his Louvre addition), who also built the sleek new exhibition hall, the **IM Pei Bau** (p81), behind the Zeughaus. Fronted by a transparent, spiralling staircase shaped like a snail shell, it was Pei's first German commission and is an excellent example of his softened modernist approach.

Meanwhile, back in the early 18th century, two formidable churches were taking shape south of the Zeughaus on Gendarmenmarkt, the central square of Friedrichstadt, which had been settled by immigrant Huguenots. These were the **Deutscher Dom** (German Cathedral; p84) by Martin Grünberg and the **Französischer Dom** (French Cathedral; p84) by Louis Cayart, modelled after the Huguenots' destroyed mother church in Charenton.

A minor 'author' of Berlin's skyline was Friedrich Wilhelm I, the son of Friedrich I. He was a pragmatic fellow who loved soldiers more than art and architecture. His introduction of the military draft launched a veritable exodus among the local population. Those who stayed didn't much care for his conversion of parts of the **Tiergarten** (p97) and the **Lustgarten** (Pleasure Garden; p87) into military exercise grounds.

The king's expansion of the Friedrichstadt quarter created a surplus of housing, at least until people dared return to Berlin after the draft's abolition in 1730. Friedrich Wilhelm's most lasting architectural legacy was the construction of a new city wall, which defined Berlin's boundaries until 1860.

Deutscher Dom (p84)

Under the rule of his son, Friedrich II – better known as Frederick the Great – Berlin finally became a true cultural and political capital. Friedrich fought for two decades to wrest Silesia from Austria and Saxony. When not busy on the battlefield, 'Old Fritz' (or 'Old Freddy', as he was also called, sought greatness through building and embracing the ideals of the Enlightenment.

The king's dream was to build his 'Forum Fridericianum', a cluster of cultural venues in the heart of town. Together with his childhood friend, the master architect Georg Wenzeslaus von Knobelsdorff, he hatched plans for the master design, which blended late baroque and neoclassical elements in a style called 'Frederician Rococo'.

Although never completed, the beautiful ensemble included the **Staatsoper Unter den Linden** (State Opera House; p83), an elegant early neoclassical design; the **Sankt-Hedwigs-Kathedrale** (p82), inspired by Rome's Pantheon; the **Alte Königliche Bibliothek** (Old Royal Library; p80), an exuberant baroque confection; and the **Humboldt Universität** (Humboldt University; p81), originally a palace for the king's brother Heinrich. Knobelsdorff also added the **Neuer Flügel** (New Wing; p109) to Schloss Charlottenburg, although **Schloss Sanssouci** in Potsdam (p258) is widely considered his crowning achievement.

After Knobelsdorff's death in 1753, two architects continued in his tradition: Philipp Daniel Boumann, who designed **Schloss Bellevue** (p100) as a gift to Frederick's youngest brother, August Ferdinand; and Carl von Gontard, who added the domed towers to the Deutscher Dom and Französischer Dom the same year.

THE SCHINKEL TOUCH

If Frederick the Great had already begun to dabble in neoclassicism, the style would reach its pinnacle during the long reign of his great-nephew, Friedrich Wilhelm III. A reaction against baroque flamboyance, it brought a return to classical design elements such as columns, pediments, domes and restrained ornamentation that had been popular throughout antiquity.

No single style has had a more lasting effect on Berlin's cityscape than neoclassicism, thanks in large part to one man: Karl Friedrich Schinkel, Prussia's greatest architect (see the boxed text opposite). Schinkel's first commission was the **Mausoleum** (p108), built for Queen Luise in Schloss Charlottenburg's park, although he didn't really make his mark until 1818 with the **Neue Wache** (p82), originally an army guardhouse and now a war memorial.

Prussia's Building Master: Karl Friedrich Schinkel

No single architect stamped his imprimatur on the face of Berlin more than Karl Friedrich Schinkel (1781–1841). The most prominent and mature architect of German neoclassicism, Schinkel was born in Neuruppin in Prussia and studied architecture under Friedrich Gilly and his father David at the Building Academy in Berlin. He continued his education with a two-year trip to Italy (1803–05) to study the classics up close, but returned to a Prussia hamstrung by Napoleonic occupation. Unable to practise his art, he scraped by as a romantic painter, and furniture and set designer.

Schinkel's career took off as soon as the French left Berlin. He steadily rose through the ranks of the Prussian civil service, starting as surveyor to the Prussian Building Commission and ending as chief building director for the entire state. He travelled tirelessly through the land, designing buildings, supervising construction and even developing principles for the protection of historical monuments.

His travels in Italy notwithstanding, Schinkel actually drew greater inspiration from classic Greek architecture. From 1810 to 1840 his vision very much defined Prussian architecture and Berlin even came to be known as 'Athens on the Spree'. In his buildings he strove for the perfect balance between functionality and beauty, achieved through clear lines, symmetry and an impeccable sense for aesthetics. Driven to the end, Schinkel fell into a coma in 1840 and died one year later in Berlin.

Nearby, the **Altes Museum** (Old Museum; p86), with its colonnaded front, is considered Schinkel's most mature work. Other neoclassical masterpieces include the magnificent **Schauspielhaus** (now the Konzerthaus; p85) on Gendarmenmarkt and the small **Neuer Pavillon** (New Pavilion; p109), also in the palace garden of Schloss Charlottenburg. For the **Friedrichswerdersche Kirche** (p83), however, Schinkel drew inspiration from the Gothic Revival style popular in early-19th-century England.

After Schinkel's death several of his disciples kept his legacy alive, most notably Friedrich August Stüler who built the **Neues Museum** (New Museum; p87), the Greek-temple-style **Alte Nationalgalerie** (Old National Gallery; p86) and the **Matthäuskirche** (p105).

THE HOBRECHT PLAN

The onset of industrialisation in the middle of the 19th century brought fundamental changes to Berlin as thousands flocked to the capital city in hope of improving their lot in the factories. Between 1850 and 1900 the city's population surged from 511,000 to 2.7 million.

To keep pace with this development, an 1862 commission helmed by chief city planner James Hobrecht drew up plans for an expanded city layout. It called for two circular ring roads bisected by diagonal roads radiating in all directions from the centre, much like the spokes of a wheel. The areas between the roads were divided into large lots and sold to speculators and developers. In a move uncharacteristic of Prussian bureaucracy, the commission imposed practically no building codes to regulate construction. The only restrictions called for building heights not to exceed 22m and for courtyards to measure at least 5.34 sq metres so that fire trucks could turn around.

Ruthless developers pounced on such lax regulations faster than a lion on a wounded hyena. The result of the Hobrecht plan was the uncontrolled proliferation of *Mietskasernen*, huge tenements four or five storeys high wrapped around as many as five inner courtyards. Behind fancy street-side façades reined nothing less than squalor in dark and dank flats, many consisting of little more than a single room and kitchen shared by up to six people. Many tenements even contained small factories, workshops and other businesses. Thanks to the Hobrecht plan, a ring of working-class districts (eg Prenzlauer Berg, Kreuzberg, Friedrichshain) with inhumane and high-density housing almost encircled central Berlin by the end of the 19th century.

THE GRÜNDERZEIT

The founding of the German empire in 1871 under Kaiser Wilhelm I ushered in the so-called Gründerzeit (Foundation Time), which architecturally went hand in hand with Historism (also called Wilhelminismus). This retro approach to architecture merely recycled earlier styles, sometimes even blending several together in an aesthetic hotchpatch. Public buildings from this period reflect the confidence of the new Germany and are a bit ostentatious. The most prominent examples of Historism are the **Reichstag** (p99) by Paul Wallot and the **Berliner Dom** (Berlin Cathedral; p86) by Julius Raschdorff, both in neo-Renaissance style; Franz Schwechten's **Anhalter Bahnhof** (p120) and the **Kaiser-Wilhelm-Gedächtniskirche** (p113), both examples of the neo-Romanesque; and the neobaroque **Staatsbibliothek zu Berlin** (State Library; p83) and **Bodemuseum** (p87) by Ernst von Ihne.

It was Otto von Bismarck who turned his attention to the residential development of the western city and Charlottenburg in particular. He widened the **Kurfürstendamm** (p111), lining it and its side streets with attractive townhouses for the middle class. Like the *Mietskasernen*, they were four or five storeys high and wrapped around a central courtyard, but there similarities ended. Courtyards were large, allowing light to enter the flats, some of which had as many as 10 rooms. These days, some harbour charming Old Berlin–style B&Bs (see Sleeping, p240).

Bismarck also instigated the development of the Grunewald villa colony at the western end of Kurfürstendamm. It quickly evolved into the Beverly Hills of Berlin, its villa-studded, leafy lanes popular with bankers, academics, scientists, rich entrepreneurs and plenty of famous folk, including writers Gerhart Hauptmann and Lion Feuchtwanger.

THE BIRTH OF MODERNISM

The Gründerzeit was not a time of experimentation but a few progressive architects still managed to make their mark, mostly in industrial and commercial design. On Leipziger Platz, Alfred Messel created a prototype of the department store in 1906 with the Waren-haus Wertheim (destroyed in WWII). Then the largest such store in Europe, it had huge display windows, classical lines and a spacious interior layout.

The main pre-WWI trailblazer, though, was Peter Behrens (1868–1940) who is often called the 'father of modern architecture'. Le Corbusier, Walter Gropius and Ludwig Mies van der Rohe all worked in his office at one time or another. Behrens also cofounded the Deutscher Werkbund, a group that sought to develop a synergetic relationship between architects and industry. From 1907 to 1914, he worked as artistic consultant for the AEG electrical company in Berlin. His most famous building is the 1909 **AEG Turbinenhalle** (Map pp320-1; AEG Turbine Factory; Huttenstrasse 12-16, Tiergarten), an airy, functional and light-flooded 'industrial cathedral' with lofty ceilings and exposed structural beams. Behrens essentially reinterpreted Schinkel's classical lines, replacing stone columns with steel trusses, and a sculpture-studded triangular gable with an unadorned polygonal one. It is considered an icon of early industrial design.

THE WEIMAR YEARS

WWI put creativity on hold but it flourished all the more during the years of the Weimar Republic, a dizzying era of unbridled experimentation in nearly all areas of society. This climate of creativity brought some of the finest minds in avant-garde architecture to Berlin, including Bruno and Max Taut, Le Corbusier, Mies van der Rohe, Erich Mendelsohn, Hans Poelzig and Hans Scharoun. Although each had his own vision, all shared a wholesale rejection of traditional architecture, especially the backward-looking Historism of the Gründerzeit.

Various styles developed in the 1920s. Mendelsohn was one of the leading exponents of architectural expressionism, following an organic, sculptural approach to design. Among his finest works is a solar observatory, the **Einsteinturm** (Einstein Tower; 1924) in Potsdam with its dynamic, flowing structure. Mendelsohn's other major Berlin commission, the **Universum Kino** (Universum Cinema; 1928), today's Schaubühne Theater (p212), marked his transition to the more linear forms of the New Objectivity that emerged in the mid-1920s.

Other good examples of this latter style include Hans Poelzig's masterpiece, the 1931 **Haus des Rundfunks** (Masurenallee 8-14, Charlottenburg) and Emil Fahrenkamp's **Shell-Haus** (p106). Also working in Berlin was Alfred Grenander, who, as head architect of the Berlin U-Bahn system, designed many of the city's beautiful stations, including the ones at **Krumme Lanke** (1929) and **Onkel-Toms-Hütte** (1929), both in Zehlendorf.

Onkel-Toms-Hütte is not only an U-Bahn station but one of four *Siedlungen* (large-scale residential estates) that also sprung up in the 1920s in response to a critical housing shortage in Germany after WWI. Berlin's progressive chief city planner, Martin Wagner, encouraged the city's leading architects to come up with an economical but humanised approach to mass housing in contrast to the dreary *Mietkasernen*. Together with Bruno Taut, Wagner himself designed the famous **Hufeisensiedlung** (p139), a horseshoe-shaped development in southern Neukölln. This innovative model community featured many of the elements typical of these mod-

Shell-Haus (p106)

ern colonies, including height limits of four stories and plenty of open green spaces.

Together with Hugo Häring and Otto Rudolf Salvisberg, Taut also designed the garden-like colony **Onkel-Toms-Hütte** (1926–32), on Argentinische Allee, Zehlendorf, near the Grunewald forest. It consists of 1100 flats and 800 single-family homes arranged in rows of various lengths and enlivened by colourful and structured façades. The two other major estates are **Siemensstadt** (1929–31), near Spandau, designed by a team including Gropius, Hans Scharoun and Häring, and the **Weisse Stadt** (1929–30), in the northwestern district of Reinickendorf, created by a team led by Salvisberg. Taut's smaller **Flamensiedlung** (p130), in Prenzlauer Berg, is also an outgrowth of this new approach to residential living.

NAZI MONUMENTALISM

Progressive architecture came to an abrupt end as soon as Adolf Hitler came to power in 1933. The new regime immediately closed down the Bauhaus School, one of the most influential forces in 20th-century architecture. Founded by Walter Gropius in 1919, it had moved to Berlin from Dessau only in 1932. Many of its visionary teachers, including Gropius, Mies van der Rohe, Wagner and Mendelsohn, went into exile but found a welcoming climate for their ideas in the United States.

Back in Berlin, Hitler's rise to power ushered in a period of architectural monumentalism. In 1937, he appointed Albert Speer chief architect and put him in charge of redesigning Berlin into the 'Welthauptstadt Germania', the future capital of the Reich. At its core would be two major intersecting thoroughfares, the North–South axis stretching from the Reichstag to Tempelhof, and the East–West axis connecting the Brandenburger Tor (Brandenburg Gate) with Theodor-Heuss-Platz (then Adolf-Hitler-Platz) in Charlottenburg. At the top of the North–South axis, near today's Reichstag, Speer planned the Grosse Halle des Volkes (Great Hall of the People), which would have accommodated 150,000 people and been topped by a dome measuring 250m in diameter.

The axes and the hall were never realised but a number of Nazi-era buildings have survived and offer a hint of what Berlin might look like had history taken a different turn. One of the most prominent Third Reich relics is the Olympic area in western Charlottenburg. Walter and Werner March designed the coliseum-like **Olympia Stadion** (p115), along with the adjacent **Maifeld** (1936). Another major Third Reich architect was Ernst Sagebiel, whose legacy survives in the chunky **Reichsluftfahrtsministerium** (Air Force Ministry; p121), now home to the Federal Ministry of Finance, and the **Flughafen Tempelhof** (p121), at the time the largest airport in Europe. Heinrich Wolff designed the **Reichsbankgebäude**, which, along with a modern extension by the young design team of Thomas Müller and Ivan Reimann, now houses the Federal Foreign Office. The again-burgeoning **Diplomatenviertel** (Diplomatic Quarter; p103) south of the Tiergarten park was another Speer idea; the giant embassies of Nazi allies Japan and Italy still reflect the pompous grandeur in vogue at the time.

The bombing raids and street fighting of WWII destroyed or damaged about half of all buildings, leaving around 25 million cubic metres of rubble, most of which was cleared by the so-called *Trümmerfrauen* (rubble women). A memorial in their honour stands in front of the **Rotes Rathaus** (p92). Many of Berlin's modest hills are in fact *Trümmerberge* (rubble mountains), piled up from the wartime debris and then reborn as parks and recreational areas. The best-known ones are **Teufelsberg** (p116) in Wilmersdorf and Mont Klamott in the **Volkspark Friedrichshain** (p126). The first new structure after the end of the war was the **Sowjetisches Ehrenmal** (Soviet War Memorial; p140) in Tiergarten park, built with red marble reputedly scavenged from Hitler's destroyed Reichskanzlei on Vossstrasse.

THE DIVIDED CITY

With the division of Germany, Berlin developed into two separate cities, even long before being physically separated by the Wall. The clash of ideologies and economic systems also transferred into the architectural arena. East German architecture was to reflect that country's new Moscow-oriented, socialist political order, in stark contrast to the modernist aspirations of the democratic West.

Built between 1952 and 1965, **Karl-Marx-Allee** (called Stalinallee until 1961; p126) became the GDR's first 'socialist boulevard'. For inspiration its team of architects – led by Hermann Henselmann – looked to Moscow and Leningrad (today's St Petersburg) to copy the backward-looking, monumental *Zuckerbäckerstil* (wedding-cake style) of which Stalin was such a fan. The **Russische Botschaft** (Russian Embassy; p82) on Unter den Linden is another example of this peculiar brand of 'neo-neoclassicism'.

After Stalin's death in 1961 even East Berlin slowly began embracing modern architecture, most notably on **Alexanderplatz** (p89), which had been devastated in WWII. Based on a carefully crafted 'socialist master plan', the square was enlarged, turned into a pedestrian zone and developed into East Berlin's commercial hub and architectural showcase. The only prewar buildings that were restored rather than demolished were Peter Behrens' 1930 **Berolinahaus** and the 1932 **Alexanderhaus**, just north of the railway tracks.

Other significant buildings orbiting Alexanderplatz include Henselmann's **Haus des Lehrers** (House of Teachers; p89) and the **Kongresshalle** (Congress Hall; 1964), which are currently being converted into the Berlin Congress Centre. Henselmann also designed the landmark **Fernsehturm** (TV Tower; p90).

The behemoth paralleling the square's northeastern flank is the 220m-long 1970 **Haus der Elektroindustrie** (Map pp328-9; House of the Electrical Industry), by Heinz Mehlan, Emil Leibold and Peter Skujin. Completely renovated, it now serves as the Berlin seat of the Federal Ministry for the Environment, Nature Conservation and Nuclear Safety. Patches of colour and large letters spelling out a quote from Alfred Döblin's novel *Berlin Alexanderplatz* enliven the façade.

In West Berlin, by contrast, urban planners sought to eradicate any hint of the monumentalism so closely associated with the Nazi period. Instead, the goal was to rebuild the city in a modern, rhythmic and organic manner and to open up landscapes as a metaphor for a free society.

A good example of this approach is the 1954–57 **Hansaviertel** (Map pp320-1; Hansa Quarter) in an area northwest of Tiergarten park that had been obliterated by wartime bombing. It's a loosely structured, leafy neighbourhood for 3500 residents with a mix of high-rises and single-family homes. The Hansaviertel U-Bahn station anchors the area's commercial centre with a church, school and library. The Hansaviertel was the product of an architectural exposition, the Internationale Bauausstellung, or Interbau, held in 1957. Attracting 54 renowned architects from 13 countries – including Gropius, Luciano Baldessari, Alvar Aalto and Le Corbusier – it represents the pinnacle of architectural vision in the 1950s.

Interbau also produced several interesting structures outside the Hansaviertel. They include the **Haus der Kulturen der Welt** (House of World Cultures; p98), originally a congress hall designed by Hugh A Stubbins as the American contribution to the exposition; and the **Le Corbusier Haus** (p115), a giant apartment complex of uncompromisingly rectangular geometry by the French architect who thought of a house as a 'machine for living'.

Meanwhile, in another wartime wasteland southeast of Tiergarten park, a further major development was beginning to take shape: the **Kulturforum** (p103). This cluster of cultural institutions was part of Hans Scharoun's vision of a cultural belt stretching from Museumsinsel to Schloss Charlottenburg. But the construction of the Berlin Wall in 1961 put an end to such wishful thinking. Rather than being a central link between the eastern and western cities, the Kulturforum found itself up against the concrete barrier.

Construction proceeded nevertheless, with Scharoun's **Philharmonie** (p106) the first piece in the Kulturforum puzzle to be completed, in 1963. This amazing concert hall is considered a masterpiece of sculptural, expressionistic modernism. Like many of Scharoun's buildings it was essentially designed from the inside out, adapting the façade to the shape of the hall rather than the other way around. Scharoun also drew up the plans for the **Staatsbibliothek zu Berlin** (State Library; p83) on Potsdamer Strasse and the **Kammermusiksaal** (Chamber Music Hall; p106) but didn't live to see their completion.

Plattenbauten, Marzahn (below)

Mies van der Rohe's **Neue Nationalgalerie** (New National Gallery; p106) is another outstanding presence within the Kulturforum. This temple-like art museum takes the shape of a 50m-long glass-and-steel cube perching on a raised granite podium. Its coffered rib-steel roof seems to defy gravity with the help of eight steel pillars and a floor-to-ceiling glass front.

Alexanderplatz and the Kulturforum may have been celebrated prestige projects, but both Berlins also had to deal with the more prosaic need of creating inexpensive, modern housing for their growing populations. This led to several urban planning mistakes on both sides of the Wall in the 1960s, most notably the birth of soulless, monotonous satellite cities that could accommodate tens of thousands of people.

In West Berlin, Gropius drew up the plans for the Grosssiedlung Berlin-Buckow in southern Neukölln, which was renamed **Gropiusstadt** (p138) after his death. The **Märkisches Viertel** in Reinickendorf in northwest Berlin is another such development. On the other side of the border, **Marzahn, Hohenschönhausen** and **Hellersdorf** became three new city districts made up entirely of high-rise *Plattenbauten*. This fast and inexpensive building technique involving precast concrete slabs was much favoured throughout East Germany. Although equipped with modern conveniences such as private baths and lifts, these giant developments suffered from a paucity of open space, green areas and leisure facilities. They were indeed the ultimate 'machines for living'.

INTERBAU 1987

While giant housing developments mushroomed on the peripheries, much of the central city was suffering from decades of decay and neglect. This was especially true of neighbourhoods languishing in the shadow of the Berlin Wall, and no more so than in Kreuzberg. To remedy this situation the Berlin Senate decided, in 1978, to hold another building exposition and competition – the Internationale Bauausstellung (Interbau) – with a dual mission: 'critical reconstruction' and 'careful urban renewal'. The goal was to usher in a return to urban architecture and to move away from the modernist monoliths so popular in previous decades.

Josef Paul Kleihues was put in charge of critical reconstruction, a phrase he coined to describe the process of filling in the gaps left in a neighbourhood – through wartime destruction or subsequent demolition – by harmoniously integrating existing and new structures. Much of the effort focused on the southern parts of Friedrichstadt in northern Kreuzberg, an area roughly bounded by Checkpoint Charlie in the north and the Hallesches Tor in the south. In the early 1980s attractive – and, above all, smaller and more human-scale – housing blocks with more than 2500 new flats were created along such streets as Ritterstrasse, Dessauer Strasse and Alte Jakobstrasse. These were supported by such infrastructure as new schools, kindergartens and parks, and the blending of existing historical structures such as the **Martin-Gropius-Bau** (p124) and the building housing the entrance to the **Jüdisches Museum** (Jewish Museum; p122) into the neighbourhood.

Hardt-Waltherr Hämer was the coordinator of the 'careful urban renewal' project, which sought to restore and modernise historical structures without undermining the integrity of their design. This approach turned about 7000 flats, mostly in eastern Kreuzberg (eg along the Landwehrkanal), into attractive, fully modernised living spaces. Other areas singled out for restoration included the **Chamissoplatz** (p120) in western Kreuzberg and the **Klausenerplatz** in Charlottenburg.

Once again, the finest minds in international architecture took up the challenges of Interbau, including Rob Krier, James Stirling, Rem Koolhaas, Charles Moore, Aldo Rossi and Arata Isozaki, as well as Germans such as OM Ungers, Gottfried Böhm, Axel Schultes and Hans Kollhoff. Collectively, they introduced a new aesthetic to Berlin, moving away from the harsh and repetitive modernist look and replacing it with a more diverse, decorative and innovative postmodernist approach.

Interestingly, reconstruction and restoration were also a major focus in East Berlin. In Prenzlauer Berg, which had been as neglected as Kreuzberg, **Husemannstrasse** (p128) looked better than ever in newly sparkling, late-19th-century glory. Around the same time, construction began of the **Nikolaiviertel** (Nikolai Quarter; p92), a small medieval 'theme park' cobbled together from original and reconstructed historical buildings anchored by the Nikolaikirche. All this activity – in both city halves – was at least in part motivated by Berlin's 750th birthday celebrations in 1987.

THE NEW BERLIN

Reunification presented Berlin with both the challenge and the opportunity to redefine itself architecturally at the dawn of the new millennium. As major building sites mushroomed throughout the city, Berlin's physical evolution became as much a tourist magnet as its prized museum collections.

As the guiding approach to rebuilding the city, urban planners decided to subscribe to the principles of critical reconstruction, rejecting anything too bold, avant-garde or monumental. Development was to forge a link with history by following traditional urban street patterns – especially the typical Berlin city block – rather than emulating loosely structured modernist colonies such as the Hansaviertel or Gropiusstadt. Regulations prescribed many design details such as building height and façade materials.

This approach has not always been entirely successful. On Friedrichstrasse, for instance, the **Friedrichstadtpassagen** (p84), a trio of luxurious shopping complexes, was supposed to restore bustling street life to the boulevard that had been a nexus of urban vitality until WWII. Instead, they are like jewel boxes, their rather bland postmodern exteriors hiding the sparkling treasures within, such as Jean Nouvel's shimmering glass funnel at the **Galeries Lafayette** (p227) or the Henry Cobb/IM Pei marble extravaganza at **Quartier 206** (p228).

Pariser Platz (p82) experienced a similar fate. Reconstructed from the ground up, it is framed by bank buildings and embassies with homogeneous and rather nondescript façades. At least two of the architects building here, though, had the last laugh by putting all their outrageous creativity on the inside. The **DG Bank** (2000), by California-based deconstructivist Frank Gehry, for instance, hides a vast atrium as bizarre as a sci-fi movie behind a vanilla-coloured façade. At its centre floats an enormous free-form stainless-steel sculpture – a fish?

Quartier 206 (p228)

a horse's head? – harbouring a conference room. Daylight streams in through the curving glass roof with steel girders as intricate as a spider's web.

Most of the other buildings around here cannot match Gehry's whimsy, although Michael Wolford's **British Embassy** (2000) – in its historic location with the main entrance facing Wilhelmstrasse – comes close. Wolford breaks up the monotony of the sandstone façade by cutting out a giant chunk from the middle and inserting a jutting blue cube and a purple cylinder in its stead. Lit from within, it looks especially attractive at night.

By comparison, the **French Embassy** (2002), in Pariser Platz's northeastern corner, surprisingly lacks *joie de vivre*. Its cool and functional façade borrows from its baroque predecessor, which was demolished in 1960. On the inside, architect Christian de Portzamparc has made maximum use of open space, natural light and greenery, including a large roof garden and a birch-lined promenade on the 4th floor.

Flanking the Brandenburger Tor, the **Liebermann Haus** and **Haus Sommer** by Kleihues closely resemble Stüler's original 19th-century structures.

The biggest and grandest of the post-1990 Berlin developments is **Potsdamer Platz** (p101), a complete reinterpretation of the famous historic square that was the bustling heart of the city until WWII. Images of the ballet of cranes hovering above what was Europe's largest building site went around the world in the 1990s, a symbol of the rebirth of united Berlin. From an ugly wasteland created by the Wall's death strip has sprung a dynamic urban quarter swarming with shoppers, revellers, movie fans, hotel guests, restaurant patrons, office workers and residents.

An international team of renowned contemporary architects collaborated on Potsdamer Platz, which is divided into **DaimlerCity** (p101), the **Sony Center** (p102) and the still-emerging **Beisheim Center** (p101). In keeping with critical reconstruction, the master plan follows the layout of a 'European city', complete with a dense, irregular street grid, squares and medium-height structures. An exception is the trio of high-rises facing the intersection of Potsdamer Strasse and Ebertstrasse, which form a kind of visual gateway. The result is pleasant, if not the kind of cutting-edge, 'new millennium' architecture that many had expected.

The most successful structure is the **Kollhoff-Haus**, the middle of the three skyscrapers. Clad in a mantle of reddish-brown clinker bricks on a greyish-green granite base, its height descends in two steps away from the intersection. The attractive, if quite conservative, exterior stands in stark contrast to the svelte, curved-glass skin of Helmut Jahn's futuristic Sony Tower across the street.

Other architects working on Potsdamer Platz included Arata Isozaki, who created the waffle-patterned, coffee-coloured **Berliner Volksbank** (1998); Rafael Moneo, who conceived the sleek, minimalist **Grand Hyatt Hotel** (p245); and Richard Rogers (best known for the Centre Pompidou in Paris), who planned the **Potsdamer Platz Arkaden** (p229), a three-storey shopping mall. Engulfed by all these modern structures stands the sole survivor from the original Potsdamer Platz, the **Weinhaus Huth** (p103).

Some of Berlin's most exciting new architecture can be found a short walk west of here in the revitalised **Diplomatenviertel** (Diplomatic Quarter; p103), which rubs up against the southern edge of Tiergarten park. Many countries rebuilt their embassies in the same locations as their historic predecessors, which had been damaged or destroyed in WWII.

One of the most extravagant new structures is the 2000 **Austrian Embassy** (Map p334; Stauffenbergstrasse 1, Tiergarten) by Viennese architect Hans Hollein. It consists of three linked, but visually very different, components: a curved front building, clad in patina-green copper, containing a festival hall; an orange terracotta central entrance section with an overhanging roof; and a grey concrete cube housing the consular division. Next door, the 2001 **Egyptian Embassy** (Map p334; Stauffenbergstrasse 6-7), with its shiny, reddish-brown façade ornamented with scenes from ancient Egypt, exudes an almost temple-like dignity.

West of here, the 1942 **Italian Embassy** (Map p334; Hiroshimastrasse 1) occupies its restored historical digs built by Friedrich Hetzelt, Hermann Göring's favourite architect. Inspired by the Palazzo della Consulta in Rome, it is a Nazi-era interpretation of a Renaissance palace whose bombast is only slightly tempered by the flamingo-pink paint job.

Across the street, the 1940 **Japanese Embassy** (Map p334; Tiergartenstrasse 24-27) looks very much like a foreboding fortress. It is an almost exact replica of the Nazi-era original by Ludwig Moshamer. Only the elliptical structure along Hiroshimastrasse, which houses a conference room, is a nod to modern architecture. The golden sun above the main entrance symbolises imperial Japan.

The retro look of the Italian and Japanese embassies contrasts sharply with two new embassies located a little further west. The 2000 **Mexican Embassy** (Map pp330–1; Klingelhöferstrasse 3) is an avant-garde work by Teodoro Gonźalez de Léon and Francisco Serrano. Two soaring, slanted curtains of slender concrete pillars protect the glass front and main entrance. The building doubles as a cultural institute.

Just north of here, the 1999 **Nordic Embassies** (Map pp330–1; Rauchstrasse 1) is one of the most exciting architectural contributions to the New Berlin. It's a compact compound uniting the representative offices of Denmark, Sweden, Finland, Iceland and Norway behind one dramatic turquoise façade made of copper lamellas. Although forming a harmonious whole, each country occupies its own building designed to reflect its cultural identity. The complex is entered through the Felleshus, the only building shared by all embassies, which is also used for cultural events.

More cutting-edge architecture awaits in the northeastern corner of the Tiergarten, where Germany's political power concentrates in its new **Regierungsviertel** (federal government district; p98). Arranged in linear east–west fashion are the **Bundeskanzleramt** (Federal Chancellery; p98), the **Paul-Löbe-Haus** (p99) and the **Marie-Elisabeth-Lüders-Haus** (p99). Together with the chancellor's garden, they form the Band des Bundes (Ribbon of the Federation), which represents a symbolic linking of the formerly divided city halves.

Overlooking all these shiny new structures is the venerable **Reichstag** (p99), which received a complete makeover courtesy of Norman Foster. Its crowning glory is the giant glass dome filled with a ramp spiralling up around a central mirrored cone. It is one of Berlin's most beloved new landmarks.

North of here, workers are putting in long hours to complete the **Lehrter Zentralbahnhof** (Map pp320–1; Lehrter Central Train Station; Invalidenstrasse, Tiergarten) in time for the 2006 soccer World Cup. Designed by Meinhard von Gerkan, it will be one of the largest and most modern railway stations in Europe. A glass-and-steel roof will cover the main hall, and local, regional and international trains will travel in all directions from four underground levels. It will be Berlin's first ever central railway station.

Although the most spectacular new building projects cluster in Mitte and Tiergarten, other districts are not completely devoid of up-to-the-minute architectural fame. In Kreuzberg, the **Jüdisches Museum** (p122) was a career-making commission for Daniel Libeskind who, in 2003, got the nod to rebuild the World Trade Center in New York City. With its irregular, zigzagging floor plan and shiny zinc skin pierced by gash-like windows, the museum is the most daring and provocative structure in the New Berlin. A bold deconstructivist space, it is not merely a place to shelter an exhibit but also a powerful visual metaphor for the troubled history of the Jewish people.

Across town, in Charlottenburg, a few new structures are slowly adding some spice to the rather drab postwar architecture south of Berlin-Zoo train station and along the Ku'damm. The **Ludwig-Erhard-Haus** (p113), home of the stock market, is a great example of the organic architecture of Nicholas Grimshaw. A row of 15 arched steel girders form the building's skeleton, which has garnered it the nickname 'armadillo'.

Nearby, Kleihues' **Kantdreieck** (p113) establishes a visual accent on Kantstrasse by virtue of its rooftop metal 'sail'. According to the architect, the design was inspired by Josephine Baker, who performed in the Theater des Westens across the street in the 1920s.

Other buildings worthy of a look here include Jahn's **Neues Kranzler Eck** (p114) and the 2001 **Ku'damm-Eck** (Map pp332–3; Kurfürstenstrasse 227), a corner building with a gradated and rounded façade. Housing a clothing store and a hotel, it also features an exterior electronic billboard and sculptures by Markus Lüppertz.

Although much has been accomplished since reunification, Berlin clearly remains a work in progress. Major projects soon to be completed include the **Leipziger Platz** (p102), an octagonal square just east of Potsdamer Platz, and the **Holocaust Memorial** (p81) a bit north of there. The possible reconstruction of the Berliner Stadtschloss (Berlin City Palace) and a complete revamping of Alexanderplatz are also exciting possibilities in a distant future. One thing's for sure: Berlin, with its constantly evolving cityscape offering ever-new angles of discovery, will remain a 'new' city for some time to come.

History

History

THE RECENT PAST

Berlin has not had an easy start to the 21st century. In 2001 the city finally plunged into the deep financial crisis that had been threatening it for years. Accused of mismanagement, excessive spending and corruption during his 15-year period in office, Christliche Demokratische Union (CDU or Christian Democratic Union) mayor Eberhard Diepgen was forced to resign. Klaus Wowereit (Social Democrat Party) was confirmed as his successor at the October elections, but has so far made little headway in combating the economic problems. In 2003 an appeal to the national Constitutional Court for federal help was accepted, but only under stringent conditions of financial performance.

The year 2003 was also tough for Wowereit on the streets. Early in the year Berlin was at the forefront of German protests against the US-led Iraq war. Just a few months later it was the turn of the city's student population to make a point, organising a long and disruptive campaign of demonstrations against huge proposed funding cuts for universities and social schemes. With Chancellor Gerhard Schröder bent on country-wide cuts and tax reforms, Berlin may be in for a hard time over the next few years.

FROM THE BEGINNING

MEDIEVAL BERLIN

Berlin's 'modern' history began in the 13th century with the founding of the trading posts of Cölln and Berlin by itinerant merchants in the area of today's Nikolaiviertel. Thanks to their strategic location at the crossroads of medieval trading routes, the settlements soon developed into *Handelsstädte* (trade centres). In 1307 they merged into the double city of Berlin-Cölln, thus formalising the loose cooperation that had existed since their establishment.

In the 1440s, under Elector Friedrich II (ruled 1440–70), Berlin and Cölln gradually lost their independence. Their administrative council was dissolved and the foundation for a

---

Top Five Books on Berlin's History

- *Berlin Rising: Biography of a City* by Anthony Read and David Fisher (1994) – an excellent social history tracing the life of the city from its beginnings to post-Wall times
- *Voluptuous Panic: The Erotic World of Weimar Berlin* by Mel Gordon (2000) – sounds lurid but it's actually a relevant and fascinating account of the sex industry between the wars. An equally serious companion volume, *Hot Girls of Weimar Berlin* (2002), examines women's roles in the liberal pre-Nazi capital.
- *Berlin Diary: Journal of a Foreign Correspondent 1934–41* by William Shirer (1941) – one of the most powerful works of reportage ever written, Shirer's portrait of the city he loved, grew to fear and eventually fled is a giant of the genre
- *The Last Division: Berlin and the Wall* by Ann Tusa (1996) – a saga of the events, trials and triumphs of the Cold War, the building of the Wall and its effects on the people and the city
- *The File* by Timothy Garton Ash (1997) – having done his doctoral research in 1980s East Berlin, Garton Ash applied to see his own Stasi dossier when the files were released. This compelling book recounts his confrontations with the former friends who informed on him.

TIMELINE	3000 BC	AD 1307
	First agricultural settlements	Trading posts Berlin and Cölln join to form a city

Statue of the Great Elector, Schloss Charlottenburg (p107)

History – The Phoenix Rises

city palace, the future Berliner Schloss, was laid. By the time Friedrich II's nephew Johann inherited the realm in 1486, Berlin-Cölln had become a residential city and the capital of the March of Brandenburg.

Under the electors Berlin grew into a powerful and civilised city; however, the Thirty Years' War (1618–48) put paid to further expansion. An outgrowth of the Reformation, the war began as a religious conflict between Protestant and Catholic leagues and soon degenerated into one of Europe's bloodiest dynastic wars. Over the period of hostilities the entire Holy Roman Empire, including Berlin, was ravaged.

THE PHOENIX RISES

By 1648 Berlin's prewar population of 12,000 had been slashed to a mere 6000 people, with more than one-third of the city's houses in ruins. Replenishing the population was foremost in the mind of Elector Friedrich Wilhelm (the Great Elector, ruled 1640–88), which he shrewdly accomplished by inviting foreigners to settle in Berlin. In 1671, for instance, he asked 50 Jewish families who had been expelled from Vienna to come to the city – on the proviso that they bring their enormous fortunes.

The bulk of new settlers, though, were Huguenot refugees from France, fleeing from Louis XIV's anti-Protestant regime. Between 1685 and 1700 Berlin's population swelled by 25%, and the French language superseded German in some districts. By 1700, one in five inhabitants was of French descent; the Französischer Dom on Gendarmenmarkt (p84) serves as a tangible reminder of the Huguenots' influence.

Berlin continued to grow in leaps and bounds throughout the 18th century, in no small part because it was known for its religious tolerance. The population catapulted from 29,000 in 1700 to 172,000 a century later, making Berlin the second-largest city in the Holy Roman Empire.

1618	1685
Start of the Thirty Years War	Large numbers of French Huguenot refugees arrive in Berlin

Jews in Berlin

Elector Friedrich Wilhelm's ploy of inviting wealthy Jews to his city to exploit their capital may seem cynical, but it was typical of the way the Jewish community was regarded during the 17th century. In fact, the policy was distinctly enlightened in comparison with treatment meted out in the Middle Ages.

Jewish families resided in Berlin-Cölln from its early trading days, but their position depended on a religious technicality that allowed them to charge interest on money lent, a practice forbidden to Christians. As a result the corrupt Brandenburg nobility relied on local Jews to prop up their extravagant lifestyles, spawning massive resentment towards a people they regarded as inferior to themselves. Of course, it was easy enough to find an outlet for this hostility – any time their debts climbed too high, the rulers could find a pretext to expel the entire Jewish community from the city, inviting them back later on payment of substantial *Schützgeld* (protection money).

Expulsion was common practice, but with anti-Semitism the status quo, there were many far worse incidents. Untold numbers of Berlin Jews were subjected to brutally inventive torture and execution, often for the flimsiest of reasons. In 1510, for example, 38 Jews were tortured and burned for stealing the host from a church, simply because the real (Christian) perpetrator's confession was deemed too straightforward to be true. Pogroms were also regular occurrences, as the Jews were scapegoated for everything from food shortages to the plague.

Disturbingly, Berlin was by no means an isolated example, with states all over Europe following similar practices. By 1700 the city was even regarded as relatively liberal due to its high number of foreigners, and the long-suffering Brandenburg Jews can have found no better alternative – large Jewish communities remained in the region right up until 1935.

THE AGE OF PRUSSIA

The Great Elector's son, Elector Friedrich III, was a man with great ambition and a penchant for the arts and sciences. Joined by his beloved wife, Sophie Charlotte, he presided over a lively and intellectual court, founding the Academy of Arts in 1696 and the Academy of Sciences in 1700. One year later, he advanced his career by promoting himself to King Friedrich I (elector 1688–1701, king 1701–13) of Prussia, making Berlin a royal residence and the capital of the new state of Brandenburg-Prussia.

His son, Friedrich Wilhelm I (ruled 1713–40), was quite a different leader. Frugal and militaristic, his obsession was to build an army of 80,000 men, earning him the nickname *Soldatenkönig* (Soldier King). In the early years of his reign, around 17,000 men left Berlin to avoid being drafted. Friedrich Wilhelm responded by enclosing the city with a wall in 1734. It's Berlin's most mordant historic irony that almost 230 years later a rather different government would use this very same idea.

Everyone breathed a sigh of relief when Friedrich II (ruled 1740–86) – better known to English speakers as Frederick the Great and to his subjects as *der alte Fritz* (Old Freddy) – came to the throne. He sought greatness through developing the city architecturally and was known for his political and military savvy. Berlin flourished as a great cultural centre and became known as Spree-Athen (Athens on the Spree).

Friedrich's cultural side was counterbalanced by a thirst for military exploits and, in particular, a desire for the territory of Silesia in today's Poland. After a series of battles stretching over two decades, victory was his: with the Peace of Hubertusburg in 1763, Austria and Saxony agreed to sign Silesia officially over to Prussia.

THE ENLIGHTENMENT & NAPOLEONIC OCCUPATION

During Friedrich II's reign, the Enlightenment arrived in Berlin with some authority. The playwright Gotthold Ephraim Lessing, the thinker and publisher Christophe Friedrich Nicolai and the philosopher Moses Mendelssohn (grandfather of composer Felix Mendelssohn-Bartholdy) all helped make Berlin a truly international city. After 1780,

1740	1806
Friedrich II – Frederick the Great – succeeds his father Friedrich Wilhelm I	Napoleon occupies Berlin and stays for seven years

intellectual salons, organised by women such as Henriette Herz and Rahel Levin, provided an open forum of discussion for anybody regardless of social standing or religious background.

Around 1800 another wave of scientists, philosophers and literary greats descended on the capital. The group included Heinrich von Kleist, Clemens von Brentano, Achim von Arnim, Novalis, Johann Gottlieb Fichte and the brothers Alexander and Wilhelm von Humboldt.

Politically, though, Prussia went into a downward spiral after the death of Friedrich II, culminating in defeat by Napoleon's forces at Jena, around 400km southwest of Berlin, in 1806. On 27 October Napoleon marched through the Brandenburg Gate, beginning an occupation of Berlin that lasted seven years. The French troops finally left in 1813 in exchange for a tidy sum in reparations, leaving behind a humiliated city mired in debt that would take 53 years to pay off.

REFORMS & NATIONALISM

The first half of the 19th century was a crucial period in the development of both Germany and Europe, when a self-made class of public servants, academics and merchants questioned the right of the nobility to rule. Brandenburg-Prussia was caught up in the maelstrom of reforms: restrictive guild regulations were lifted, allowing anyone to take up any profession; agricultural reforms abolished bonded labour, providing the basis for industrialisation; and Jews won civic equality in 1812.

The decay of feudal structures, the redistribution of wealth and the rise of industry changed the socioeconomic ground rules, eventually leading to nationalist calls for a centralised state. All this ferment brought relatively little change from the top, however, and in March 1848 Berlin joined other German cities in a bourgeois revolution demanding freedom of the press, formation of a parliament, withdrawal of the military from politics and other basic democratic rights. Government troops quickly suppressed the riots, and stagnation set in for the next eight years under the reactionary Friedrich Wilhelm IV (ruled 1840–61).

THE INDUSTRIAL AGE

With manufacturing trades already well established by the 18th century, Berlin developed into a centre of technology and industry right from the dawn of the Industrial Age. The building of the German railway system (the first Berlin to Potsdam track opened in 1838) led to the foundation of more than 1000 factories, including electrical giants AEG and Siemens.

The abundance of factory jobs created a new class in Berlin – the proletariat – as workers flocked to the city from throughout Germany. From 1850 to 1870, the population more than tripled to 870,000. Housing shortages were solved by building countless *Mietskasernen* (literally 'rental barracks'), labyrinthine tenements built around successive courtyards, where entire families subsisted in tiny, poorly ventilated flats without indoor plumbing.

New political parties formed to give a voice to the proletariat, including the Sozialdemokratische Partei Deutschland (SPD, Social Democratic Party). Founded in 1875 as the Socialist Workers' Party, it took its present name in 1890 and grew steadily in influence. At the height of its popularity in 1912, the SPD garnered 75% of the Berlin vote.

ROAD TO THE GERMAN EMPIRE

When Friedrich Wilhelm IV suffered a stroke in 1857, his brother Wilhelm became regent and, in 1861, King Wilhelm I. Unlike his brother, Wilhelm was a man who recognised more clearly the signs of the times and was not averse to progress. Besides appointing a number of liberal ministers, he made Otto von Bismarck Prussian prime minister in 1862.

1810	1812
Founding of the Humboldt Universität	Civic equality is granted to Jews

Bismarck's grand ambition was to create a Prussian-led unified Germany, and his methods were old-fashioned and effective: domination, manipulation and war. Bismarck began by winning Schleswig-Holstein province in a war with Denmark in 1864 (with Austria as his ally), then fought and beat Austria itself in 1866 and formed the North German Confederation the following year.

With northern Germany under his control, Bismarck turned his attention to the south. Through skilful diplomacy, he isolated France and manoeuvred it into declaring war on Prussia in 1870. He then surprised Napoleon III by winning the backing of most southern German states. The war with France ended with Prussia's annexation of Alsace-Lorraine.

Most importantly, though, with the southern German princes no longer opposed to him, Bismarck's grand plan could finally come to fruition: Germany was unified, with Berlin as its capital. On 18 January 1871 King Wilhelm I was crowned Kaiser Wilhelm I at Versailles (the ultimate humiliation for the French), with Bismarck as his 'Iron Chancellor'. The German empire was born.

With French reparations pouring in and Berlin the dynamic centre of its empire, Germany was now a wealthy, unified country, thanks largely to Bismarck's force and vision. The conservative chancellor made considerable concessions to progress, even providing health and accident benefits and retirement pensions, but his deep-rooted aversion to real reform was his downfall. When Wilhelm II became Kaiser in 1888 (Friedrich, the son of Wilhelm I, ruled for only 99 days), divisions arose between the emperor, who wanted to extend the social security system, and Bismarck, who enacted ever-stricter antisocialist laws. In 1890 the Kaiser finally sacked his renegade chancellor, excising Bismarck from the political scene.

WWI & REVOLUTION

On 28 June 1914 the heir to the Austrian throne, Archduke Franz Ferdinand, and his wife were assassinated in Sarajevo, triggering a war between Austria-Hungary and Serbia. Russia mobilised as part of its alliance with Serbia; Germany, allied with Austria-Hungary since 1879, promptly declared war on Russia, then two days later declared war on France (which had taken the Russian side). The Reichstag (German parliament) immediately granted the necessary war credits. Among the general population, initial euphoria and belief in a quick victory soon gave way to disillusionment, exacerbated by the increasing hardship of food shortages in Berlin and elsewhere.

When peace came with defeat in 1918, it meant an end to fighting but also an end to domestic stability. The Treaty of Versailles forced Germany to relinquish Alsace-Lorraine, western Poland and its colonies in Africa, and to pay cripplingly high punitive reparations. Furthermore, the treaty made Germany responsible for all losses incurred by its enemies. The humiliation was huge.

The loss of the war also caused the collapse of the monarchy. Kaiser Wilhelm II abdicated on 9 November 1918, ending more than 500 years of Hohenzollern rule and paving the way for a power struggle between socialist and democratic parties. In the early afternoon of the same day, from a window of the Reichstag, Philipp Scheidemann of the SPD proclaimed the birth of the German Republic. Hours later Karl Liebknecht, founder of the German Communist Party (then known as the Spartacus League) proclaimed the Free Socialist Republic of Germany from a balcony of the Berliner Schloss.

Founded by Rosa Luxemburg and Karl Liebknecht, the Spartacus League sought to establish a republic based on Karl Marx's theories of proletarian revolution. Opposed by moderate socialists, it merged with other groups to form the Kommunistische Partei Deutschland (KPD, or German Communist Party) in the final days of 1918. Rivalry between the SPD and the Spartacists led to the so-called Spartacus Revolt in Berlin in January 1919. Following the bloody suppression of this uprising, Luxemburg and Liebknecht were

1848	1862
Democratic reform riots are suppressed by troops	Bismarck becomes Prussian prime minister

murdered by right-wing Freikorps soldiers and their bodies unceremoniously dumped in Berlin's Landwehrkanal.

THE WEIMAR REPUBLIC

The federalist constitution of the fledgling republic, Germany's first serious experiment with democracy, was adopted in July 1919 in the town of Weimar, where the constituent assembly had sought refuge from the chaos of Berlin. It gave women the vote and established basic human rights but also, crucially, gave too much power to the president, who could rule by decree in times of emergency.

A broad centre-left coalition government formed, led by President Friedrich Ebert of the SPD, which remained Germany's largest party until 1932. Too many forces in Germany rejected the republic, however, and the government satisfied neither communists nor monarchists. Trouble erupted in 1920 when the Freikorps brigades staged the so-called Kapp Putsch, occupying the government quarter in Berlin with the support of other right-wing military elements. Called on by the government to act, workers and unions went on strike, and the coup collapsed.

THE 'GOLDEN' TWENTIES

The 1920s began as anything but golden, marked by the humiliation of a lost war, social and political instability, hyperinflation, hunger and disease. Around 235,000 Berliners were unemployed and strikes, demonstrations and riots became nearly everyday occurrences. The introduction of a new currency, the rentenmark, brought some relief but things only really started to turn around after cash, in the form of loans under the Dawes Plan, flowed into Germany after 1924. Berlin was on the rise once again.

For the next few years, the city experienced a cultural heyday that exceeded anything that had come before. It gained a reputation as a centre for both tolerance and indulgence, and outsiders flocked to a city bursting with the exciting new forms of cabaret, Dada and jazz.

In 1923 Germany's first radio broadcast hit the airwaves over Berlin, and in 1931 TV had its world premiere here. In the field of science, Berliners Albert Einstein, Carl Bosch and Werner Heisenberg were awarded Nobel Prizes, and some of Europe's biggest names in architecture (including Bruno Taut, Martin Wagner, Hans Scharoun and Walter Gropius), fine arts (George Grosz, Max Beckmann and Lovis Corinth) and literature (Bertolt Brecht, Kurt Tucholsky, WH Auden and Christopher Isherwood) contributed to Berlin's reputation as the artistic centre of the world.

The end of the decade, however, put the whole country back to square one when the stock market crashed on 25 October 1929, 'Black Friday'. Within weeks about 500,000 Berliners were jobless, and riots and demonstrations again ruled the streets. The ensuing Depression undermined an already fragile German democracy and bred support for extremist parties.

In response to the chaos, Field Marshal Paul von Hindenburg, who had succeeded Ebert as president in 1925, used the constitution's ill-conceived emergency powers to circumvent parliament and appoint the Catholic Centre Party's Heinrich Brüning as chancellor. Brüning immediately deflated the economy, forced down wages and destroyed whatever savings – and faith – the middle classes had built up since the last economic debacle. It earned him the epitaph 'the hunger chancellor'.

The volatile, increasingly polarised political climate led to frequent confrontations between communists and members of a party that had only just begun to gain momentum – the Nationalsozialistische Deutsche Arbeiterpartei (National Socialist German Workers' Party, or NSDAP), led by a failed Austrian artist named Adolf Hitler.

1870	1871
Franco-Prussian War; Prussia annexes Alsace-Lorraine	German states unified under Kaiser Wilhelm I

HITLER'S RISE TO POWER

In 1930 the NSDAP made astounding gains, winning 18% of the national vote. Hitler set his sights on the presidency in 1932, running against Hindenburg; he received 37% of the second-round vote. In the ensuing national elections, the Nazis became the largest party in the Reichstag, with 230 seats. Berliners, though, remained comparatively sceptical, and only one in four voted for Hitler.

Shortly thereafter, Brüning was replaced as chancellor by Franz von Papen, a hardcore monarchist associated with a right-wing club for industrialists and gentry in Berlin. Von Papen called two Reichstag elections, hoping to build a parliamentary base, but Hindenburg soon replaced him with Kurt von Schleicher, a military old boy.

Schleicher's attempt to prime the economy with public money – a policy begun by von Papen – alienated industrialists and landowners. Finally on 30 January 1933, won over by the right and following Papen's advice, Hindenburg dismissed Schleicher and appointed Hitler as chancellor, with a coalition cabinet consisting of National Socialists (Nazis) and von Papen's Nationalists. The NSDAP was now by far the largest single party but was still short of an absolute majority.

In March 1933, without a clear majority, Hitler called Germany's last 'officially' free prewar election. Even with the help of his intimidating party militia, the Sturmabteilung, or SA, and the staged Reichstag fire, which gave him an excuse to use emergency laws to arrest opponents, he still failed to win an absolute majority. Berliners, who perhaps caught more of what was going on, were even less convinced, with only 31% voting for the NSDAP.

With democracy already crumbling, the Enabling Law provided the last piece of the puzzle, giving Hitler the power to decree laws and change the constitution without consulting parliament. By June 1933 the SPD had been banned and all other parties disbanded. Hitler's Nazi Party governed alone.

THE ROAD TO WWII

The totalitarian Nazi ethos brought immediate, far-reaching consequences for the entire population. Loudspeakers sprang up in cafés and on street corners, blaring out 'patriotic' messages and martial music, and encouraging people to denounce their neighbours. Unions were swiftly banned. Propaganda Minister Joseph Goebbels' crack-down on intellectuals and artists sent many of them into exile. On 10 May 1933, students burned 'un-German' books on Bebelplatz. Freedom of the press was nonexistent as the NSDAP took over publishing houses. With great emphasis placed on physical perfection and early indoctrination,

Albert Speer

A crucial part of the Nazis' agenda was their extensive construction programme in Berlin, creating monumental buildings that were to reinforce the restored pride of the German nation. The man responsible for planning it all was Albert Speer (1905–81), a brilliant architect who worked closely with Hitler and eventually became his armaments minister in 1942, orchestrating forced labour from concentration camps.

Hitler and Speer's ultimate vision was to transform Berlin into a fitting world capital for the new Nazi empire. 'Germania' was to be centred on the Great Hall, a proposed assembly hall in a domed structure that would have dwarfed the Reichstag. Sizeable tracts of land around Tiergarten and central Berlin were bulldozed to make room for these ambitious architectural projects; Speer got as far as building the huge Reichskanzlei, but WWII quickly put paid to his efforts.

Having survived to see his work bombed to the ground, Speer served 20 years in Spandau prison; on his release, he wrote *Inside the Third Reich* (1970), a detailed account of the day-to-day operations of Hitler's inner circle. Read it alongside Gitta Sereny's biography *Albert Speer: His Battle with Truth* (1996) for an insight into the complicated life of this controversial and oddly tragic Nazi figure.

1875	1888
Foundation of the Socialist Workers' Party – later the SPD	Wilhelm II becomes kaiser

membership of the Hitlerjugend (Hitler Youth) became compulsory for boys aged 10 to 18, while girls had to join the Bund Deutscher Mädchen (League of German Girls).

Amazingly, the situation in Germany largely eluded the attention of the international community, in part because many leaders were happy to see a single party taking control after all the political upheavals. Further reassurance came from Hitler's extensive program of public works and industrial nationalisation, which ostensibly succeeded in eradicating unemployment (largely by using forced labour) and stabilising the shaky economy. Even the 1936 Berlin Olympics was a PR triumph, serving to legitimise the Nazi government and distract the world from the everyday terror of the regime.

Originally formed to guard public meetings, the SA had become a powerful force of 4.5 million men by 1934, capable of challenging and undermining Hitler's authority. With rumours of revolt circulating, on 30 June 1934 the elite SS troops (Hitler's personal guard) rounded up and executed more than 1000 high-ranking SA officers, including leader Ernst Röhm, in what came to be known as the 'Night of the Long Knives'. In Berlin, Hermann Göring led the death squads, with executions taking place in the SS barracks in Lichtenberg.

In the same year, the death of Hindenburg allowed Hitler to take the final step and merge the positions of president and chancellor, giving himself absolute power and *Führer* (leader) status.

WWII

On 1 September 1939 Germany attacked Poland, kicking off the century's second pan-European conflict. The war was not greeted with pleasure in Berlin, whose people still remembered the hunger years of WWI and the early 1920s. Again war brought food shortages and even greater political oppression.

Belgium and the Netherlands fell quickly to Germany, as did France. In June 1941 Hitler attacked the USSR, opening up a new front. Delays in staging what was called 'Operation Barbarossa' would contribute to Germany's downfall as lines of supply were overextended. Bogged down and ill-prepared for the bitter Russian winter of 1941–42, Hitler's troops were forced into retreat. With the defeat of the German 6th Army at Stalingrad (then called Volgograd) the following winter, morale flagged both at home and on the fronts.

In 1941 the USA signed the Lend-Lease Agreement with Britain to provide and finance badly needed military equipment. In December of the same year, the Japanese attack on the American fleet at Pearl Harbor finally prompted the USA to officially enter the war.

The 'Final Solution'

By the time WWII broke out, Jews had long been the main target of persecution in Nazi Germany. In April 1933 Goebbels organised boycotts of Jewish businesses and medical and legal practices. Jews were expelled from public service and prohibited from engaging in many professions, trades and industries. The Nuremberg Laws of 1935 deprived all non-Aryans of German citizenship and prohibited their marriage with Aryans.

On the night of 9 November 1938 the terror escalated with the Reichspogromnacht (meaning Purge Night, also known as Kristallnacht, or Night of Broken Glass). The windows of thousands of Jewish businesses and shops throughout Berlin and all of Germany were shattered, the premises looted and set alight. Jews had started to emigrate after 1933, but this terror set off a new wave, with boatloads of frightened refugees fleeing towards Britain and the USA in particular. Very few of those who remained in Berlin – about 60,000 – were still alive in 1945.

The fate of Jews deteriorated after the outbreak of war. Heinrich Himmler's SS troops systematically terrorised and executed local populations in occupied areas, and war with the USSR was portrayed as a fight against 'subhuman' Jews and Bolsheviks. At Hitler's behest, Göring commissioned his functionaries to find an Endlösung (Final Solution) to the 'Jewish

1918	1919
End of WWI; Wilhelm II abdicates; SPD declares the German Republic	Communist Spartacus Revolt is violently suppressed; declaration of the Weimar Republic

question'. A conference, held in January 1942 on the shores of Berlin's Wannsee lake, laid the basis for the Holocaust, the efficient, systematic and bureaucratic murder of millions.

Concentration camps, though not a Nazi invention, reached a new level of efficiency. Besides Jews, the main target groups were Gypsies, political dissidents, priests (especially Jesuits), homosexuals and resistance fighters. In the end there were 22 concentration camps, mostly in Eastern Europe, and another 165 work camps. Altogether, about seven million people were sent to the camps; only 500,000 survived to be freed by Soviet and Allied soldiers.

The Battle of Berlin

With the Normandy invasion of June 1944, Allied troops arrived in formidable force on the European mainland, supported by systematic air raids on Berlin and most other German cities. In the last days of the war Hitler, broken and paranoid, ordered the destruction of all remaining German industry and infrastructure, a decree that was largely ignored.

The final Battle of Berlin began on 16 April 1945. More than 1.5 million Soviet soldiers approached the capital from the east, reaching Berlin on 21 April and encircling it on 25 April. Two days later they were in the city centre, fighting running street battles with the remaining handful of loyal SS troops. On 30 April the fighting reached the government quarter where Hitler was ensconced in his bunker behind the Chancellery with his long-time mistress Eva Braun, whom he'd married just a day earlier. That afternoon, they committed suicide.

Berlin fell two days later, and on 7 May 1945 Germany capitulated. The signing of the armistice took place at the US military headquarters in Reims (France) and at the Soviet military headquarters in Berlin-Karlshorst.

The Aftermath

The war took an enormous toll on Berlin and its people. The civilian population had borne the brunt of the bombings. Entire neighbourhoods had been reduced to rubble, with more than half of all buildings and one-third of industry destroyed or damaged. With around

Sowjetisches Ehrenmal (p140), Treptower Park

1920	1929
City limits extended, forming Greater Berlin	'Black Friday' stock market crash signals the return of economic depression

The Berlin Airlift

The ruined city of Berlin was still digging itself out from the rubble of WWII when the Soviets made their bid for total domination on 24 June 1948. The military leadership ordered a complete blockade of all rail and road traffic into the city. Berlin would be completely cut off; everyone assumed it would be a matter of days before the city submitted to the Soviets.

Faced with such provocation, many in the Allied camp urged responses that would have been the opening barrages of WWIII. In the end wiser heads prevailed, and a mere day after the blockade began the US Air Force launched 'Operation Vittles'. The British followed suit on 28 June with 'Operation Plane Fare'. (France did not participate because its planes were tied up with rather less humanitarian missions in Indochina.)

For about 11 months Allied planes supplied the entire city, bringing in coal, food and machinery. Every day, around the clock, determined pilots made treacherous landings at Berlin's airports, sometimes as frequently as one per minute. On one day alone – the 'Easter Parade' of 16 April 1949 – they flew 1400 sorties, delivering 13,000 tons of supplies. By the end of the airlift they had flown a total of 125 million miles in 278,000 flights and delivered cargo totalling 2.5 million tons. The operation cost the lives of 79 people, commemorated by the Airlift Memorial at Tempelhof and Cologne airports.

Given the ever-escalating Allied effort and increasing international condemnation, the Soviets backed down in May 1949, and Berlin's western sectors were free once again. The whole debacle had only strengthened the relationship between Germany and the Allies – Berliners now regarded them not as occupational forces but as *Schutzmächte* (protective powers).

one million women and children evacuated, only 2.4 million people were left in the city in May 1945 (compared to 4.3 million in 1939), two-thirds of them women. About 125,000 Berliners had lost their lives.

In Soviet-occupied Berlin it was the women who did much of the initial clean-up, earning them the name *Trümmerfrauen* (rubble women). Over the following years, enormous amounts of debris were piled up into so-called *Trümmerberge* (rubble mountains), artificial hills such as the Teufelsberg in the Grunewald.

Some small recoveries did come quickly after the armistice. The first U-Bahn train ran on 14 May 1945, the first newspaper was published on 15 May, and on 26 May the Berliner Philharmonie gave its first postwar concert.

THE POLITICS OF PROVOCATION

In line with agreements reached at the Yalta Conference in February 1945, Germany was divided into four zones of occupation. Berlin was carved up into 12 administrative areas under British, French and US control and another eight under Soviet control. At the Potsdam Conference in July and August 1945, regions east of the Oder and Neisse Rivers were transferred to Poland as compensation for earlier territorial losses to the Soviet Union.

Friction quickly built between the occupying powers. Soviet demands for high reparations were rejected by the Allies, leading to a breakdown in cooperation; frustrated by this refusal, the Russians exacted compensation by brutalising their own zones of occupation. Factory production was requisitioned and able-bodied men and POWs were put to work in labour camps in the Soviet Union. Due to foot-dragging by the Soviets, American and British troops didn't actually occupy their Berlin sectors until 4 July; the French arrived on 12 August. The Soviets also forcibly fused the communist KPD party and the SPD into the Sozialistische Einheitspartei Deutschland (Socialist Unity Party of Germany, or SED) on 22 April 1946, with Walter Ulbricht as general secretary.

The coalition of the Western Allies and the USSR eventually collapsed in June 1948 with the Berlin Blockade. Proposed currency reform in the Allied zones not only prompted the USSR to issue its own currency, the ostmark, but was also used as a pretext for an economic

1933	1936
Hitler is appointed chancellor; the Reichstag burns; by June the National Socialists are the only political party in Germany	Berlin Olympics showcase Nazi power

blockade of West Berlin, intended to bring the entire city under its control. The Allies responded with the Berlin Airlift (see the boxed text on p61).

TWO GERMAN STATES

With the Cold War on the horizon, the Allies went ahead with establishing government institutions and, in 1949, the Federal Republic of Germany (FRG, or BRD by its German initials). Konrad Adenauer, a former mayor of Cologne during the Weimar years, became West Germany's first chancellor at the age of 73, and Bonn was chosen as the provisional capital. Berlin remained an isolated island in the Soviet sector, dependent on help from the West.

Meanwhile, the Soviet zone evolved in 1949 into the German Democratic Republic (GDR, or DDR in German), with Berlin its capital. Nominally a parliamentary democracy, the dominance of the SED meant that party boss Walter Ulbricht called the shots. The early years saw a party takeover of economic, judicial and security functions, including the establishment of the Ministry for State Security, or Stasi, which was intended to neutralise opposition to the SED and quickly became notorious.

In 1952 the GDR began to cut off relations with the West. West Berliners were no longer allowed to travel to East Germany, and their real estate and property was expropriated. At the same time, political and moral pressure was exerted on East Berliners to participate in the Nationale Aufbauwerk (National Reconstruction Project), which effectively meant rebuilding the country in their spare time – for no pay. On 27 May 1952, all phone connections between the GDR and West Germany were cut.

UPRISING IN EAST BERLIN

By 1953 the first signs of discontent had appeared in the GDR. Production bottlenecks stifled industrial output, heavy industry was given priority over consumer goods, and increased demands on industrial workers bred bitterness. Furthermore, the death of Stalin that year had raised hopes of reform but brought little in the way of real change. Under pressure from Moscow, the government backed down on a decision to raise prices, but it refused to budge on tougher production goals.

Strikes and calls for reform turned to unrest in urban and industrial centres, culminating in demonstrations and riots on 17 June 1953. Triggered by construction workers on Berlin's Karl-Marx-Allee, the unrest soon involved about 10% of the country's workers. When the GDR government proved incapable of containing the situation, Soviet troops stationed in East Germany quashed the uprising, with scores of deaths and the arrest of about 4000 people.

BRICKS IN THE WALL

As the GDR government continued to restrict the freedom of its citizens, the flow of refugees to the West increased. In 1953 alone about 330,000 East Germans fled to the West, most of them well educated and young, thus amplifying the strain on East Germany's already brittle economy. The exodus reached such a level that on the night of 12 August 1961, with the approval of Warsaw Pact countries, fences and ditches were erected between East and West Berlin. Three days later, construction of the Berlin Wall began, creating a physical manifestation of the Iron Curtain and the Cold War's most potent symbol.

Formal protests from the Western Allies, as well as demonstrations by more than 500,000 people in West Berlin, went unheeded. Tension rose further on 25 October 1961 as US and Soviet tanks faced off at Checkpoint Charlie, sparked by the GDR's refusal to grant free passage to some members of the US forces. Soon, the entire FRG–GDR border was fenced off and mined, and the guards given the order to shoot to kill anybody trying to escape. By

1938	1945
Kristallnacht – Jewish businesses and institutions all over Berlin are attacked	Battle of Berlin devastates the city; Hitler commits suicide; the Yalta conference divides Berlin between the Allies

Graffiti showing the former Berlin Wall, East Side Gallery (p125)

the time the Wall collapsed on 9 November 1989, more than 80 people had died in such attempts in Berlin alone.

The building of the Wall marked a new low in East–West relations worldwide, and tense times were to follow. In 1963, nine months after the Cuban Missile Crisis, US president John F Kennedy made a flying visit to West Berlin, praising locals for their pro-freedom stance in his famous *'Ich bin ein Berliner'* speech and putting the city firmly on the front line of the Cold War.

RAPPROCHEMENT

Restrictions that had prevented anybody from entering the GDR eased temporarily in 1963 with the Passagierscheinabkommen (Pass Agreement). It permitted Westerners to visit relatives in East Berlin between 19 December 1963 and 5 January 1964. About 1.2 million visits were recorded in this period. From 1964 to 1966 the GDR opened up its borders three more times for short periods.

In 1971, after Erich Honecker replaced Walter Ulbricht as SED party head, the Vier-Mächte-Abkommen (Four Powers Agreement) set up permanent regulations for visits from west to east, including a transit route to Berlin from West Germany through GDR territory. Except for senior citizens, however, no-one was allowed to leave the GDR and visitors were saddled with a compulsory exchange from Deutschmarks to the weak ostmark (based on a 1:1 exchange rate).

In December 1972 the two Germanies signed the Basic Treaty. This guaranteed sovereignty in international and domestic affairs, normalised East–West relations and paved the way for both countries to join the United Nations.

1949	1961
Formation of the German Democratic Republic (GDR)	Construction of the Berlin Wall begins

ECONOMY & IMMIGRATION

During a period of economic stabilisation in the 1960s, the standard of living in the GDR rose to the highest in the Eastern bloc and the country became its second-largest industrial power (behind the USSR).

Meanwhile, West Germany strengthened its ties to the US and Western Europe and embarked on a policy of welfare-state capitalism. An economic boom known as the *Wirtschaftswunder* (economic miracle) lasted throughout the 1950s and most of the 1960s. Its architect, Ludwig Erhard, oversaw policies that encouraged investment and capital formation, aided by the Marshall Plan and a trend towards European economic integration. *Gastarbeiter* (guest workers) were called in from southern Europe (mainly Turkey, Yugoslavia and Italy) to solve a labour shortage, creating many of the ethnic communities that characterise Berlin and other German cities.

In 1958 West Germany was one of the five countries to sign the Treaty of Rome, which created the European Economic Community, now the expanded European Union.

STUDENT UNREST & TERRORISM

In West Germany the two major parties, the CDU and the SPD, formed a broad coalition in 1966. The absence of parliamentary opposition fuelled an increasingly radical student movement with Berlin at its centre. At sit-ins and protests, students demanded an end to the Vietnam War and reform of Germany's dated university system and teaching programs. By 1970 the movement had fizzled but not without having shaken up the country and brought about some changes, including women's emancipation, university reforms and a politicisation of the student body.

A few radicals, though, didn't think that enough had been achieved and went underground. Berlin became the germ cell of the terrorist Red Army Faction (RAF), led by Ulrike Meinhof, Andreas Baader and Gudrun Ensslin. Throughout the 1970s the RAF abducted and assassinated prominent business and political figures. By 1976, however, Meinhof and Baader had committed suicide (both in prison). Remaining members found themselves in jail, in hiding or seeking refuge in the GDR. Eventually that country's demise would expose them to West German attempts to bring them to justice.

COLLAPSE OF THE GDR

The rise of hardline communist and former Nazi prisoner Erich Honecker to the position of state secretary in 1971 rang in an era of changes to the East German constitution. Hopeful reunification clauses were struck out in 1974 and replaced by one declaring East Germany's irrevocable alliance with the USSR. Honecker fell comfortably in line with Soviet policies, rode out a world recession and an oil crisis in the early 1970s, and oversaw a period of housing construction, pension increases and help for working mothers.

In the mid-1980s, however, prices for consumer goods rose sharply and, with East Germany struggling to keep pace with technological innovations elsewhere in the world, stagnation set in. Reforms in Poland and Hungary, and especially Soviet leader Mikhail Gorbachev's new open foreign policy, put pressure on an increasingly recalcitrant SED leadership to introduce reforms.

The *Wende* (turning point) began in May 1989, when Hungary announced it would suspend the travel agreement preventing East Germans from entering the West via Hungary. The SED responded by tightening travel restrictions. Meanwhile more and more East Germans filled West German consulates and embassies in East Berlin, Warsaw, Prague and Budapest, seeking to emigrate. On 10 September 1989 Hungary's foreign minister, Gyula Horn, officially opened the Hungarian border to Austria, allowing refugees to cross legally to the West.

1971	1989
Staunch communist Erich Honecker succeeds Walter Ulbricht as East German leader	Hungary opens its borders, throwing the GDR into crisis; in November the Berlin Wall finally opens

Supported by church leaders, the *Neues Forum* (New Forum) of opposition groups emerged and led calls for human rights and an end to the SED political monopoly. This sparked a leadership crisis in the SED, resulting in the replacement of Honecker by Egon Krenz. On 4 November 1989, about 500,000 demonstrators gathered on Berlin's Alexanderplatz demanding political reform. By this time East Germany was losing about 10,000 citizens a day.

The day of reckoning came on 9 November 1989, when the GDR Politbüro tried to turn events around by approving direct travel to the West. The announcement was made in a televised press conference by leading Politbüro member Günter Schabowsky. Asked by one reporter when this would come into effect, Schabowsky searched his notes uncomfortably and, at a loss, mistakenly said 'right away'. After a momentary double take, tens of thousands rushed through border points in Berlin, watched by perplexed guards, who, though they knew nothing about this new regulation, did not intervene. West Berliners went into the streets to greet the visitors; tears and champagne flowed. Amid scenes of wild partying, mile-long queues of Trabants (cars manufactured in the GDR) and even David Hasselhoff singing astride the broken Wall, the two Berlins came together again.

REUNIFICATION

Opposition groups and government representatives soon met to hammer out a course of action. In March 1990 the first free elections since 1949 took place in East Germany and an alliance headed by the CDU's Lothar de Maizière won convincingly. The SPD, which took an equivocal view of reunification, was accordingly punished by voters. The old SED administrative regions were abolished and the *Länder* (states) revived. Currency and economic union became a reality in July 1990.

In September 1990 the two Germanies, the USSR and the Allied powers signed the Two-Plus-Four Treaty, ending postwar occupation zones. One month later the East German state was dissolved and Germany's first unified post-WWII elections were held. Berlin once again became the German capital when, in 1991, a small majority (338 to 320) of members in the Bundestag (German parliament) voted in favour of moving the government to Berlin. On 8 September 1994 the last Allied troops stationed in Berlin left the city after a festive ceremony.

What's in a Date?

The public holiday to mark German reunification was originally proposed for 9 November, the day the Berlin Wall fell, as it was felt this would have the most resonance with the public. Unfortunately this also happened to be the date of both Hitler's 1923 Munich coup and the infamous Kristallnacht (Night of Broken Glass) attacks on Jews in 1938, making it a potential rallying day for neo-Nazis and a PR disaster waiting to happen. In the end the holiday was set for the less evocative but much more tactful date of administrative reunification in 1990: 3 October.

THE BERLIN REPUBLIC

In 1999 the German parliament moved from Bonn to Berlin, convening its first session in the restored Reichstag building on 19 April. The ministries have since followed, as have diplomats, government agencies, industrial associations, lobbyists and others – an estimated total of 15,000 people. A new government district around the Reichstag has sprung up, with new offices for parliamentarians, sleek embassies and, most notably, the striking Chancellery, which opened in 2001.

Elsewhere, too, the face of Berlin has been greatly changed since reunification. An architectural frenzy has rejuvenated most of the central areas, restoring the Mitte district to its rightful place as the city's heart. The cultural vibrancy of the 1920s has returned with a vengeance, transforming Berlin from a political curiosity to a vital presence among European capitals. The city exudes a new sophistication and a greater internationalism

1994	1999
The last Allied troops leave Berlin	German parliament returns from Bonn to take its place in the restored Reichstag

Glass dome of the Reichstag (p99)

than ever before, and signs of creative energy, construction and modernisation abound wherever you look.

In part because of its geopolitical location, Berlin is also increasingly positioning itself as a conduit between East and West in all arenas, including politics, culture, business and finance, communication and science. Immigration has increased significantly since 1989, particularly from the former Eastern bloc. This trend is likely to continue with the European Union's expansion into Poland and the Czech Republic.

But not everything is rosy in Berlin or the new Germany. Scandals surrounding the financial dealings of former chancellor Helmut Kohl and his unification government rocked the political establishment in 2000 and shook many people's faith in politicians, while the Berlin Senate's overenthusiastic investment has effectively bankrupted the city. Whatever its domestic problems, however, Berlin seems to have its worst days firmly behind it, and looks destined to thrive as a European force well into the 21st century.

2001	2003
Financial crisis and political pressure force mayor Diepgen to resign	Iraq war and proposed funding cuts provoke marches and demonstrations

1 Roof of the Sony Center (p102), Potsdamer Platz *2* Sculpture, Potsdamer Platz (p101) *3* Display, Ampelmann Galerie Shop (p225), Mitte *4* Courtyard, Neues Kranzler Eck (p114), Charlottenburg

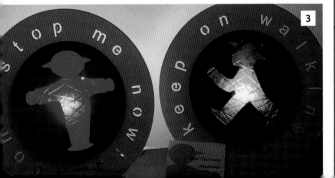

1 Austrian Embassy (p49), Tiergarten 2 Philharmonie (p106), Tiergarten 3 Neue Nationalgalerie (p106), Tiergarten 4 Brandenburg Gate (p80)

1 *Schlossgarten Charlottenburg (p109)* 2 *Erotik Museum (p111), Charlottenburg* 3 *Theater des Westens (p210), Charlottenburg* 4 *Kaiser-Wilhelm-Gedächtnis-kirche (p113), Charlottenburg*

HANC DOMVM ARTIS COLENDAE CAVSA CONDIDIT.
ANNO MDCCCLXXXXVI BERNHARD SEHRING.

1 Haus der Kulturen der Welt (p98), Tiergarten 2 Staatsbibliothek Zu Berlin (p106), Tiergarten 3 Filmmuseum Berlin (p102), Potsdamer Platz 4 Siegessäule (p100), Tiergarten

1 *Reiterdenkmal Friedrich des Grossen (p82), Unter den Linden*
2 *Museum für Kommunikation (p85), Mitte* 3 *Alte Nationalgalerie (p86), Museumsinsel*
4 *Fernsehturm (p90), Alexanderplatz*

1 *Checkpoint Charlie (p120)*
2 *Chapati (p234), Kreuzberg*
3 *Café Achteck (p159)*
4 *Deutsches Technikmuseum Berlin (p121), Kreuzberg*

1 *Oberbaumbrücke (p126),
Friedrichshain* 2 *Rathaus
Schöneberg (p119)* 3 *Topographie
des Terrors (p124), Kreuzberg*
4 *Grave of Marlene Dietrich
(p117), Schöneberg*

1 *Freilichtmuseum Domäne Dahlem (p142), Zehlendorf*
2 *Berlin Wall, Gedenkstätte Berliner Mauer (p132), Wedding*
3 *Statue, Versöhnungskapelle (p132), near Gedenkstätte Berliner Mauer* 4 *Botanischer Garten (p141), Zehlendorf*

Districts

Districts

Berlin is a German city-state surrounded by a region known from medieval times as the Mark (March) of Brandenburg, now the *Bundesland* (federal state) of Brandenburg. In 2001, Berlin's previous 23 administrative *Bezirke* (districts) were reduced to 12 in an effort to curb bureaucracy (see the boxed text p21). In most cases this has meant merging existing districts, a behind-the-scenes move with no impact on visitors as the old district names – Mitte, Charlottenburg, Kreuzberg etc – continue to be used by locals. The old district names are also the divisions we've used in organising this book.

We start out by profiling the eight central districts, beginning with **Mitte**, the city's historic core, and then moving in an anticlockwise direction. Next up is **Tiergarten** – with its giant park, government quarter and Potsdamer Platz. **Charlottenburg**, the heart of the western city, is up next, with its fun shopping and magnificent Schloss Charlottenburg. From here it's south to **Wilmersdorf**, a residential district anchored by the sprawling Grunewald forest. East of here is **Schöneberg**, known for its throbbing gay quarter and great farmers market, and **Kreuzberg**, where Checkpoint Charlie and the Jewish Museum are major attractions. We then cross the Spree back into former East Berlin and the emerging district of **Friedrichshain** with its bubbly nightlife and monumental GDR architecture. The central loop concludes with **Prenzlauer Berg**, a newly gentrified district centred on Kollwitzplatz.

The outer districts have been grouped together by compass direction, starting with the **Northern Districts** (Pankow and Wedding), then again moving anticlockwise to the **Western Districts** (Spandau), the **Southern Districts** (Köpenick, Neukölln, Treptow and Zehlendorf) and finally the **Eastern Districts** (Lichtenberg-Hohenschönhausen and Marzahn-Hellersdorf).

ITINERARIES
One Day
Get up early to beat the crowds to the dome of the **Reichstag** (p99), then head south to the **Brandenburg Gate** (p80) and a lavish breakfast at the **Hotel Adlon** (p82). Walk south on Ebert-

Great Hall, Gemäldegalerie (p104)

strasse past the **Holocaust Memorial** (p81) to **Potsdamer Platz** (p101), Berlin's showcase of urban renewal. Make a stop at the **Filmmuseum** (p102), then hop on the U-Bahn to Stadtmitte. This puts you right onto classy Friedrichstrasse, where you should have a look inside the **Friedrichstadtpassagen** (p84) to see their amazing design. Grab a quick bite, then wander over to beautiful **Gendarmenmarkt** (p84) and north to **Unter den Linden** (p80). Head east along this classic boulevard and have a quick peek inside the **Berliner Dom** (p86) before being awed by the antiquities at the **Pergamon Museum** (p87). Conclude the day exploring the narrow lanes of the **Scheunenviertel** (p93), where you'll have no trouble finding happening spots for dinner, drinks and dancing.

Three Days

Follow the one-day itinerary, then revisit Cold War history at **Checkpoint Charlie** (p120) and the nearby **Haus am Checkpoint Charlie** (p122) museum before spending the rest of the morning at the amazing **Jüdisches Museum** (Jewish Museum; p122). After lunch at the museum, make a beeline to the **Gemäldegalerie** (p104) and the **Neue Nationalgalerie** (p106) at the Kulturforum. Freshen up and have an early dinner before catching a concert or cabaret show, then wrap up the day sampling the bars of **Prenzlauer Berg** (p127).

There's plenty more to do in Berlin proper on your third day, but we wouldn't want you to leave without a visit to **Schloss Sanssouci** (Sanssouci Palace; p258) in Potsdam, the German version of Versailles; it's just a quick and easy S-Bahn ride away.

One Week

After the beauty of Sanssouci, it's time to explore Berlin's sinister past on day four with visits to such places as the **East Side Gallery** (p125), the **Topographie des Terrors** (Topography of Terror; p124), the **Gedenkstätte Normannenstrasse** (Stasi Museum; p146), the **Alliierten Museum** (Allied Museum; p141) or the **Gedenkstätte Deutscher Widerstand** (German Resistance Memorial; p104). Make **Schloss Charlottenburg** (p107) and the nearby museums, especially the **Ägyptisches Museum** (Egyptian Museum; p110), the focus of your fifth day before taking a break from culture on day six by heading to Wannsee. Take a dip in the lake at **Strandbad Wannsee** (p219), then find your perfect picnic spot on the enchanting **Pfaueninsel** (p144) nearby, followed by a digestive one-hour stroll south along the Havel to **Schloss Glienicke** (p145).

Shop till you drop on your last day. Hit the Ku'damm and the **KaDeWe** (p232) in the morning, then pick up some unique Berlin-designed duds and accessories in the boutiques around the Scheunenviertel and along Kastanienallee. For your farewell dinner, indulge in fine gourmet fare, for instance at **Margaux** (p165) or **Maxwell** (p165) in Mitte.

ORGANISED TOURS
Walking Tours

Three companies offer scheduled guided English-language tours of Berlin, all of them excellent with well-informed and affable guides who provide lively commentary and are eager to answer your questions. Look for their flyers in hostels, hotels and the tourist offices.

BREWER'S BEST OF BERLIN
www.brewersberlin.de; tours €10
For an all-day immersion, put on your most comfortable walking shoes and sign up for Brewer's Total Berlin tour, which runs from six to 11 hours, depending on your group's stamina. Brewer's four-hour Classic Berlin focuses on the main sights only.

INSIDER TOUR
☎ 692 3149; www.insidertour.com; tours €10-12, bike tour (including bicycle) €20, discounts for students, under 26, seniors and WelcomeCard holders
This popular company's daily Famous Insider Tour offers an insightful and entertaining overview of all the main sites. Its extended summer repertory includes the always intriguing Third Reich Insider and Red Star (GDR-era Berlin) tours, as well as the spot-on Insider Bar & Pub Crawl and Berlin by Night. If you like to combine your sightseeing with a little exercise, try its Berlin by Bike tour.

ORIGINAL BERLIN WALKING TOURS
☎ 301 9194; www.berlinwalks.de; tours €10-15, discounts if under 26 or with WelcomeCard
This well-established outfit runs a daily (twice daily April to October) Discover Berlin Walk,

which gives a thorough general introduction to Berlin's must-see sights. Its equally fascinating Infamous Third Reich Sites and Jewish Life in Berlin tours are offered on a limited schedule.

Bus Tours

Most city sightseeing tours work on the 'hop on, hop off' principle and there's very little difference between operators. Buses navigate central Berlin on routes designed to pass all the major attractions, including Kurfürstendamm, Brandenburg Gate, Schloss Charlottenburg, Unter den Linden and Potsdamer Platz. The entire loop takes about two hours without getting off. Unless noted, taped commentary comes in – count 'em – eight languages.

Buses depart roughly every 15 minutes and make their merry rounds from about 10am until 5pm or 6pm every day. Besides the main departure points that are mentioned below, you can start your journey at any of the other stops around town. Except where noted, tickets cost between €15 and €18 (50% discount for children under 13) and are sold on the bus.

Most companies also run one or two traditional city tours daily where you see the sights without getting off the bus; the cost of these is between €20 and €25. Combination boat and bus tours as well as organised trips to Potsdam and the Spreewald are also available.

For full details, call or look for company flyers in hotel lobbies and at the tourist offices.

BBS Berliner Bären Stadtrundfahrt (Map pp332-3; ☎ 3519 5270; www.bbsberlin.de; Kurfürstendamm, cnr of Rankestrasse)

Berolina Sightseeing (Map pp332-3; ☎ 8856 8030; www.berolina-berlin.com; Kurfürstendamm 220)

BVB (Map pp332-3; ☎ 683 8910; www.bvb.net; Kurfürstendamm 225)

BVG Top Tour (Map pp332-3; ☎ 2562 6570; www.bvg.de; Kurfürstendamm 18; adult/child 6-14 €20/15; tours mid-Apr–Oct) Open-top double-decker with live German and English commentary.

Severin & Kühn (Map pp332-3; ☎ 880 4190; www.severin-kuehn-berlin.de; Kurfürstendamm 216)

Tempelhofer Reisen (Map pp328-9; ☎ 752 4057; www.tempelhofer.de; Unter den Linden 14)

Boat Tours

A lovely way to experience Berlin on a warm summer day is from the deck of a boat cruising the city's rivers, canals and lakes. Tours range from one-hour spins around Museumsinsel taking in the historic sights (from €4) to leisurely three-hour trips into the green suburbs (from €10) and dinner cruises. Narration is in English and German. Food and drink are sold on board, or bring along a picnic. Small children usually travel for free, while those under 14 and seniors can expect a 50% discount. The season runs roughly from April to October.

Berliner Wassertaxi (Map pp328-9; ☎ 6588 0203; www.berliner-wassertaxi.de)

Reederei Bruno Winkler (☎ 3499 5933; www.reederei winkler.de)

Reederei Riedel (☎ 691 3782; www.reederei-riedel.de)

Stern und Kreisschiffahrt (☎ 536 3600; www.sternund kreis.de)

Speciality Tours
BERLINER UNTERWELTEN Map pp322-4
☎ 4991 0518; www.berliner-unterwelten.de; adult/ concession €9/7, under 12 free; tours noon, 2pm, 4pm & 6pm Sat

Dive into Berlin's underbelly on this tour of two WWII-era underground bunkers built around U-Bahn station Gesundbrunnen. One was renovated in the 1980s as shelter in case of civil disaster or atomic attack. You'll see hospital beds, bathrooms, filter systems and cases filled with war detritus, from helmets to buttons to condoms. Tours are in German only (for now) but tours in English may be arranged. Tours meet at Badstrasse at the corner of Hochstrasse right by U-Bahn station Gesundbrunnen.

TRABI SAFARI Map pp328-9
☎ 2759 2273; www.trabi-safari.de; Gendarmenmarkt, cnr Markgrafenstrasse; 2/3/4 passengers per person €30/25/20

The tinny Trabant (Trabi for short) was the archetypal GDR-made automobile. This company gives you a shot at exploring Berlin behind the wheel – or as a passenger – of this venerable relic. Choose from the Classic tour covering major Berlin sights or come face to face with eastern Berlin's socialist flair on the Wild East tour. You'll be following your guide who delivers live commentary (in English by prior arrangement) that's piped into your car. Tours last 90 minutes.

MITTE

Eating pp164–8; Shopping pp225–9; Sleeping pp241–5

Mitte (literally 'Middle') is Berlin's birthplace and, throughout its history, has always been a nexus of politics, culture and commerce. Packed with blockbuster sights, museums, entertainment and hotel options, this is where Berlin visitors spend most of their time.

You'll be spoiled for choice on what to do in Mitte. You could start at the landmark **Brandenburg Gate** and make your way east along **Unter den Linden**, the city's grandest boulevard. Throughout history, great architects – Schinkel, Langhans, IM Pei and Frank Gehry among them – have left their mark here and also on and around the glamorous **Gendarmenmarkt**.

You can also squeeze in a spot of shopping along the elegant **Friedrichstrasse** or in the warren of lanes that make up the delightful **Scheunenviertel**, which has one of Berlin's hottest after-dark scenes. The world-class collections of **Museumsinsel** (Museum Island), currently being preened to become the Berlin equivalent of Paris's Louvre, can easily keep you busy for an entire day.

You can plunge into the city's medieval origins at the **Nikolaiviertel** or explore GDR aesthetics on **Alexanderplatz**, which, despite its obvious charisma deficit, is still an interesting testament to that former country's inflated sense of self-importance. And if all goes according to plan, the brand-new **Holocaust Memorial** will finally have been unveiled by the time you're reading this.

Orientation

Mitte, formerly in East Berlin, forms an administrative unit with Tiergarten, seat of the federal government, to the west and working-class Wedding to the northwest. It's small and compact and eminently walkable, although bus 100 and 200 are also great ways to get around.

Mitte's biggest sights line up like Prussian soldiers for inspection along Unter den Linden, which stretches west–east from the Brandenburg Gate to Museumsinsel whence it continues as Karl-Liebknecht-Strasse to just beyond Alexanderplatz.

Friedrichstrasse, flanked by shops, hotels and restaurants, is the main north–south route. South of Unter den Linden it leads to the Gendarmenmarkt area and onward to Checkpoint Charlie and Kreuzberg. Following it north takes you to the historic theatre district around U/S-Bahn Friedrichstrasse, with easy access to post-performance drinks in the Scheunenviertel anchored by the Hackesche Höfe. The Prenzlauer Berg district is just north of here, while Alexanderplatz is the gateway to eastern districts including Friedrichshain, just down Karl-Marx-Allee. Berlin's first settlement once stood southwest of here in the Nikolaiviertel and the southern half of Museumsinsel.

Transport

Bus Nos 100 and 200 run along Unter den Linden to Alexanderplatz; No 240 runs along Torstrasse to Scheunenviertel; JetExpressBus TXL for Tegel airport has stops including Alexanderplatz, Französische Strasse, Unter den Linden and Friedrichstrasse.

S-Bahn S5, S7 and S9 from Zoo station serve Friedrichstrasse, Hackescher Markt (for Scheunenviertel) and Alexanderplatz; S1 and S2 also stop at Friedrichstrasse.

Tram 52 and 53 connect northern Museumsinsel with Scheunenviertel and Prenzlauer Berg; 1 goes north from Hackescher Markt along Prenzlauer Allee.

U-Bahn Weinmeisterstrasse (U8), Rosa-Luxemburg-Platz (U2) or Oranienburger Tor (U6) for Scheunenviertel; Stadtmitte (U2, U6) for Gendarmenmarkt; Friedrichstrasse or Französische Strasse (U6) for Unter den Linden; U2, U5 or U8 for Alexanderplatz.

ALONG UNTER DEN LINDEN

Berlin's most splendid boulevard extends for about 1.5km from the Brandenburg Gate to the Schlossbrücke. Before being developed into a showpiece road, Unter den Linden was merely a riding path connecting the Berliner Stadtschloss with the Tiergarten, once the royal hunting grounds. Under Elector Friedrich Wilhelm (ruled 1640–88), the eponymous linden trees were planted, but it took another century to complete the harmonious ensemble of baroque, neoclassical and rococo structures. Wartime brought especially heavy destruction, but restoration has, for the most part, been sensitive and authentic.

ALTE KÖNIGLICHE BIBLIOTHEK
Map pp328-9
Bebelplatz; U-Bahn Hausvogteiplatz, bus 100, 200
The Alte Königliche Bibliothek (Old Royal Library) is a handsome 1775 baroque building whose elegantly curved façade has garnered it the nickname *Kommode* (chest of drawers). Now part of the **Humboldt Universität** (p81), it originally housed the royal library before the fast-growing collection migrated across Unter den Linden to the much larger **Staatsbibliothek** (p83) in 1914.

BEBELPLATZ Map pp328-9
U-Bahn Hausvogteiplatz, bus 100, 200
Bebelplatz is best known as the square where the Nazis organised their first official book burning on 10 May 1933, torching the works of authors they considered subversive, including Bertolt Brecht, Heinrich and Thomas Mann and Karl Marx. It was a portentous event that signalled the death of the cultural greatness Berlin had achieved over the previous two

Mitte Top Five

- Stand in awe of the artistry of ancient civilisations at the **Pergamon Museum** (p87).
- Walk in the footsteps of history along **Unter den Linden** (p80).
- Relax to the sound and majesty of a classic opera at the **Staatsoper Unter den Linden** (p83).
- Put together the ultimate Berlin look while browsing the **Scheunenviertel** (p93) boutiques.
- Let the sights drift by you while sipping a cool drink on the deck of a **canal cruiser** (p78).

centuries. A poignant **memorial** by Micha Ullmann, consisting of an underground library with empty shelves, keeps the memory of this event alive.

The square was planned as the focal point of Frederick the Great's pet project, the Forum Fridericianum, an intellectual and artistic centre inspired by ancient Rome. Alas, the king's costly war exploits left his coffers too strained to fully realise such grandiose visions but several buildings still got built, including the **Alte Königliche Bibliothek** (p80) on the square's western side with the **Staatsoper Unter den Linden** (p83) opposite and **St-Hedwigs-Kathedrale** (p82) in the southeast corner.

It was the State Opera House that gave the square its original name, Opernplatz. In 1947 it was renamed after August Bebel, the cofounder and leader of the Social Democratic Party (SPD).

BRANDENBURG GATE Map pp328-9
Pariser Platz; Raum der Stille; admission free;
⏰ **11am-6pm Apr-Oct, 11am-5pm Nov & Jan-Mar, 11am-4pm Dec; S-Bahn Unter den Linden, bus 100, 200**
The recently restored landmark Brandenburger Tor (Brandenburg Gate), a symbol of division during the Cold War, now epitomises German reunification. It was against this backdrop in 1987 that then-US president Ronald Reagan uttered the now famous words: 'Mr Gorbachev – tear down this wall.' Two years later, the Wall was history.

The gate's history, however, began a couple of centuries earlier. Designed by Carl Gotthard Langhans, it was widely considered the most beautiful of Berlin's 18 city gates. Johann Gottfried Schadow's **Quadriga**, a sculpture of the winged goddess of victory piloting a horse-drawn chariot, proudly perches atop the curtain of Doric columns. During Napoleon's occupation of Berlin after 1806, the statue Victoria was kidnapped and held hostage in Paris for years, but she returned triumphantly in 1814, freed from the French by a gallant Prussian general.

The gate's northern wing contains the **Raum der Stille** (Room of Silence), where the weary and frenzied can sit and contemplate peace. In the south wing is a **BTM tourist office** (p291).

The Brandenburg Gate's main side overlooks **Pariser Platz** (p82), while on the west it borders the newly named **Platz des 18. März**, which commemorates the bloody quashing of a demonstration in favour of democratic rights on 18 March 1848.

DEUTSCHE GUGGENHEIM BERLIN

Map pp328-9

☎ 202 0930; www.deutsche-guggenheim.de; Unter den Linden 13-15; adult/concession €3/2, free Mon; ⊙ 11am-8pm Fri-Wed, 11am-10pm Thu; U-Bahn Französische Strasse, bus 100, 200

If you've been to any of the other Guggenheim museums, especially those in New York and Bilbao, this small, minimalist gallery space – a joint venture between Deutsche Bank and the Guggenheim Foundation – might be a tad disappointing. Curators mount several exhibits a year featuring international contemporary artists of some renown, such as Tom Sachs, Richard Artschwager and Gerhard Richter. Free tours are held at 6pm daily and there's a nice shop and even better café on site.

DEUTSCHES HISTORISCHES MUSEUM & IM PEI BAU Map pp328-9

☎ 203 040; www.dhm.de; Museum Unter den Linden 2, IM Pei Bau Hinter dem Giesshaus 3; admission €2, more for special exhibits, under 18 free; ⊙ 10am-6pm Tue-Sun; U-Bahn Hausvogteiplatz or bus 100 and 200 stop outside

The pink building opposite the **Kronprinzenpalais** (p81) is the baroque **Zeughaus**, a former armoury completed in 1706. It usually houses the German Historical Museum, which is supposed to reopen in late 2004 following a complete restoration. Meanwhile, exhibits take place at its brand-new extension, the **IM Pei Bau** by the 'Mandarin of Modernism' IM Pei. It's a truly awesome space, starkly geometric, yet imbued with a sense of lightness achieved through an airy atrium and generous use of glass.

HOLOCAUST MEMORIAL Map pp328-9

Along Ebertstrasse; www.holocaust-mahnmal.de; S-Bahn Unter den Linden

Just south of the Brandenburg Gate, behind the future US Embassy, construction finally began in August 2003 of the Memorial to the Murdered Jews of Europe, colloquially known as Holocaust Memorial. You can watch its progress from viewing platforms along Ebertstrasse.

New York architect Peter Eisenman's vision consists of a vast grid of concrete pillars of varying heights positioned on a gently wavy ground, sort of an abstract interpretation of a field of wheat in the wind. Visitors will be able to access this maze at any point and make their individual journey through it. An **underground information centre** will provide historical background and personalise the memorial

---

Top Five Historic Buildings

- Reichstag (p99)
- Brandenburg Gate (opposite)
- Schloss Charlottenburg (p107)
- Altes Museum (p86)
- Olympia Stadion (p115)

---

with life stories of some of the victims. Its inauguration is planned for 8 May 2005, the 60th anniversary of the end of WWII.

HUMBOLDT UNIVERSITÄT Map pp328-9

☎ 209 30; Unter den Linden 6; U-Bahn Friedrichstrasse, bus 100, 200

The students and faculty of the Humboldt Universität, Berlin's oldest university, are up against it to uphold their alma mater's illustrious legacy. Marx and Engels both studied here and the long list of famous professors includes the Brothers Grimm and such Nobel Prize winners as Albert Einstein, Max Planck and the nuclear scientist Otto Hahn.

The university was founded in 1810 by the lawyer and politician Wilhelm von Humboldt in this former palace of Frederick the Great's brother Heinrich. Renamed in Humboldt's honour in 1949, it became the top academic institution in the GDR. Statues of the man and his famous explorer brother Alexander flank the main entrance.

KOMISCHE OPER Map pp328-9

☎ 4799 7400; Unter den Linden 41; S-Bahn Unter den Linden, bus 100, 200

The Komische Oper (Light Opera) is one of Berlin's three opera houses. A theatre has stood in this spot since 1764, but the core of the structure dates only to 1892. After WWII, the original interior – a richly festooned baroque extravaganza – was largely restored, clashing with the decidedly functional '60s façade.

KRONPRINZENPALAIS Map pp328-9

Unter den Linden 3; bus 100, 200

The Kronprinzenpalais (Crown Princes' Palace) was merely a townhouse until Philipp Gerlach got his hands on it in 1732 and converted it into a residence for crown prince and future king Frederick the Great. Various other royals resided here until the demise of the monarchy in 1918.

Soon after Prussia's former first family moved out, the National Gallery happily moved in.

Crowds flocked to see works by the finest artists of the day – Lovis Corinth, Otto Dix and Paul Klee among them – until the Nazis closed the show in 1937. 'Degenerate art', they sneered, while secretly stashing much of it away in their own collections.

The building was bombed to bits in WWII but faithfully re-created in the late 1960s to serve as the GDR's guesthouse for visiting dignitaries. Yes, Indira Gandhi slept here. On 31 August 1990 the palais captured the headlines again when the agreement paving the way to German unification was signed here.

The Crown Princes' Palace is connected to what used to be the **Crown Princesses' Palace**, built for the three daughters of Friedrich Wilhelm III in 1811. In its current incarnation as the **Opernpalais**, it houses a restaurant-café famous for its cake selection, as well as a pub and cocktail bar. It's great in summer when the beer garden is in full swing but pretty stuffy otherwise.

NEUE WACHE Map pp328-9
Unter den Linden 4; admission free; ☉ 10am-6pm; bus 100, 200

Built in 1818 by Schinkel, the Neue Wache was originally a royal guardhouse and is now a memorial to the 'victims of war and tyranny.' It was Schinkel's first major Berlin commission and is an excellent example of neoclassical architecture. Inspired by a classic Roman fortress, it's the double row of Doric columns supporting a tympanum embellished with allegorical war scenes that gives the building a certain gravitas.

The original inner courtyard was covered in 1931 leaving only a skylight, which now lasers in on Käthe Kollwitz's heart-wrenching sculpture *Mother and her Dead Son*, also known as *Pietà*. Buried below the austere room are the remains of an unknown soldier and a resistance fighter as well as soil from nine European battlefields and concentration camps.

PARISER PLATZ Map pp328-9
S-Bahn Unter den Linden, bus 100, 200

Once nothing but an empty field languishing in the shadow of the Berlin Wall, Pariser Platz is again poised to be the city's 'reception parlour', just as it was during its glorious 19th-century heyday. The French and British embassies have already returned to their historical locations and, eventually, so will the US embassy with its prime spot next to the Brandenburg Gate.

Some of the world's finest architects have left their mark on the 'new' Pariser Platz, including the Brit Michael Wolford, the Frenchman Christian de Portzamparc and Los Angeles–

based Frank Gehry. The latter designed the square's most spectacular structure, the **DG Bank** on its south side. Although he gave city planners the rather subdued façade they demanded, Gehry did have the last laugh with the interior, which is a perfect reflection of his warped and boundary-pushing talents. See the Architecture chapter for more details about the new Pariser Platz buildings (p48).

In the southeastern corner, the **Hotel Adlon** (now called the Adlon Kempinski, p243) was the first building to return to Pariser Platz in 1997. In its earlier incarnation, the former grande dame of Berlin caravanseries gave shelter to such celebs as Charlie Chaplin, Greta Garbo and Thomas Mann. Architecture critics have scoffed at this fairly faithful replica of the 1907 original but this doesn't seem to bother the presidents, diplomats, actors and merely rich, who regularly shack up here these days. Remember Michael Jackson dangling his baby out the window? It happened at the Adlon.

REITERDENKMAL FRIEDRICH DES GROSSEN Map pp328-9
Unter den Linden; bus 100, 200

Seemingly surveying his domain, Frederick the Great cuts an imposing figure on horseback in this famous 1850 monument, which kept Christian Daniel Rauch busy for a dozen years. The plinth features a who's who of famous German military men, scientists, artists and thinkers as well as scenes from the king's life. The early GDR leaders didn't think much of the man and exiled the statue to Potsdam until Honecker restored it to its rightful place in 1980.

RUSSISCHE BOTSCHAFT Map pp328-9
☎ 226 6320; Unter den Linden 63-65; S-Bahn Unter den Linden, bus 100, 200

The hulking Russische Botschaft (Russian Embassy) is a white marble behemoth built in Stalin-era *Zuckerbäckerstil* (wedding-cake style). A tall wall allows glimpses of the compound, but if you are interested in this type of building, swing by Karl-Marx-Allee in Friedrichshain, which is lined with them (p126).

SANKT-HEDWIGS-KATHEDRALE
Map pp328-9
☎ 203 4810; Behrenstrasse 39; admission free; ☉ 10am-5pm Mon-Sat, 11am-5pm Sun; U-Bahn Hausvogteiplatz, bus 100, 200

Nothing less than the Pantheon in Rome provided the inspiration for St-Hedwig-Cathedral

Sankt-Hedwigs-Kathedrale (opposite)

Works by all of the period's heavyweights, including Johann Gottfried Schadow, Christian Daniel Rauch and Christian Friedrich Tieck, fill the softly lit nave. Upstairs the spotlight is firmly trained on Schinkel himself with a comprehensive exhibit about his life and his accomplishments.

The chunky structure southeast of here, by the way, housed the Reichsbank during the Third Reich and the central committee of the Sozialistische Einheitspartei Deutschland (SED; Socialist Unity Party of Germany) in GDR times. In united Germany, the building with its modern extension is home of the **Auswärtiges Amt** (Federal Foreign Office).

STAATSBIBLIOTHEK ZU BERLIN
Map pp328-9

☎ 2660; www.sbb.spk-berlin.de; Unter den Linden 8; day-use fee €0.50; 🕘 9am-9pm Mon-Fri, 9am-7pm Sat; U-Bahn Friedrichstrasse, bus 100, 200
The original sheet music of Beethoven's 9th Symphony, medieval maps drawn by Nicolas von Kues, poems penned by the Persian writer Hafez – this is just a tiny sampling of the amazing archive of over 10 million books, periodicals and other printed matter amassed by the Staatsbibliothek (State Library). Founded in 1661 by the Great Elector Friedrich Wilhelm, the collection outgrew even its mammoth current quarters built in 1914 by Ernst von Ihne. In fact, all books published after 1955 are housed in the library's second Hans Scharoun–designed branch (p106) near Potsdamer Platz which opened in 1978. The Unter den Linden branch has an especially pretty inner courtyard with a café. Free 90-minute tours run at 10.30am every first Saturday of the month.

STAATSOPER UNTER DEN LINDEN
Map pp328-9

☎ 203 540; www.staatsoper-berlin.org; Unter den Linden 7; U-Bahn Hausvogteiplatz, bus 100, 200
The Staatsoper (State Opera House) on Bebelplatz is one of Berlin's earliest neoclassical structures, completed in 1743 as Frederick the Great's court opera to plans by Georg Wenzeslaus von Knobelsdorff. It's hard to imagine that this beautiful building, fronted by a curtain of Corinthian columns, has been completely destroyed three times, the first time by a major fire in 1843 and twice during WWII. Today it is the most prestigious of Berlin's three opera houses and well respected throughout Europe (also see p210).

(1773) whose giant copper dome overlooks Bebelplatz. Frederick the Great named the church in honour of the patron saint of Silesia, which he just happened to have conquered.

St Hedwig was Berlin's only Catholic house of worship until 1854 and has been the mother church of the Berlin archdiocese since 1929. During WWII, it was a centre of Catholic resistance under Father Bernard Lichtenberg (1875–1943), who died in a cattle car en route to the Dachau concentration camp. Like so many buildings around here, the church was more or less flattened during WWII and now features a rather modern interior.

SCHINKELMUSEUM/ FRIEDRICHSWERDERSCHE KIRCHE
(SMB) Map pp328-9

☎ 208 1323; www.smpk.de; Werderscher Markt; admission free; 🕘 10am-6pm; U-Bahn Hausvogteiplatz
With its twin square towers and phalanx of slender turrets punctuating the roofline, the neogothic Friedrichswerdersche Kirche (1830) is a perky presence on the Werderscher Markt, a short stroll southeast of Bebelplatz. Inspired by English churches, Karl Friedrich Schinkel dreamt up this playful design, which has housed a showcase of 19th-century sculpture since 1987.

GENDARMENMARKT & AROUND

Once a thriving marketplace, graceful Gendarmenmarkt is Berlin's most beautiful square. The twin structures of Französischer Dom (French Cathedral) and Deutscher Dom (German Cathedral) frame Schinkel's Schauspielhaus (now Konzerthaus) to form a superbly harmonious architectural trio. In recent years, several luxury hotels and fancy restaurants have sprouted around the square, giving it an increasingly metropolitan flair.

Gendarmenmarkt was created in 1700 as the centrepiece of Friedrichstadt by Elector Friedrich III, later King Friedrich I. The new quarter was primarily settled by Huguenots, who had fled to Berlin after their expulsion from France in 1685. Gendarmenmarkt derives its name from the Gens D'arms – a Prussian regiment of Huguenot soldiers – stationed here in the 18th century.

A magnificent **statue of Friedrich Schiller** anchors the square. Squirreled away by the Nazis, it ended up in West Berlin, from where it returned across the Wall in 1988 following an exchange of artworks between the two German states.

DEUTSCHER DOM Map pp328-9

☎ 2273 0431; Gendarmenmarkt 1; admission & tours free; ☼ 10am-10pm Tue year round, 10am-6pm Wed-Sun Sep-May, 10am-7pm Wed-Sun Jun-Aug, tours 11am & 1pm; U-Bahn Französische Strasse, Stadtmitte

One in the trio of Gendarmenmarkt beauties, the Deutscher Dom (German Cathedral) – a 1708 work of Martin Grünberg – wasn't much of a looker until getting its dazzling galleried dome courtesy of Carl von Gontard in 1785. Since 1996 it's been used for exhibitions organised by the *Bundestag*, the German parliament. The current one is a hopelessly academic historical survey of German parliamentarism that regularly bores groups of German teenaged school children to tears.

FRANZÖSISCHER DOM Map pp328-9

☎ 229 1760; www.franzoesischer-dom-berlin.de; Gendarmenmarkt 5; adult/concession museum €2/1, tower €3/2; ☼ museum noon-5pm Tue-Sat, 11am-5pm Sun, tower 9am-7pm; U-Bahn Französische Strasse, Stadtmitte

A near mirror image of the Deutscher Dom, the Französischer Dom (French Cathedral) was built as a place of worship for the Huguenots who settled in Berlin in the late 17th century. Completed in 1705, it was modelled on the group's main church in Charenton, which had been destroyed in 1688. By 1785 it too had acquired its landmark Gontard-designed domed tower, matching that of the Deutscher Dom.

On the ground floor, the **Hugenottenmuseum** (Huguenots Museum) chronicles their story with descriptions in French and German. If you're not vertigo-prone it's worth climbing the spiralling staircase to the top of the **tower**. Also here is the **carillon**, which plays its merry tune several times daily.

FRIEDRICHSTADTPASSAGEN Map pp328-9

Friedrichstrasse btwn Französische Strasse & Mohrenstrasse; U-Bahn Französische Strasse, Stadtmitte

If you're going to drop your hard-earned cash, it might as well be in stunning surroundings.

The Stasi – Fear and Loathing in the GDR

The walls had ears. Modelled after the Soviet KGB, the GDR's Ministerium für Staatssicherheit (Ministry for State Security, 'Stasi' for short) was founded in 1950. It was secret police, central intelligence agency and bureau of criminal investigation, all rolled into one. Called the 'shield and sword' of the paranoid SED leadership – which used it as an instrument of fear and oppression to secure its power base – the Stasi grew steadily in power and size over the four decades of its existence. By the end, it had 91,000 official full-time employees plus 173,000 IMs (*inoffizielle Mitarbeiter*; unofficial informants) recruited among regular people to spy and snitch on their co-workers, friends, family and neighbours. By the time the system collapsed, there were files on six million people.

The Stasi's all-pervasiveness is unimaginable. Its methods knew no limits with wire-tapping, video-tape observation and opening of private mail being the more conventional techniques. Perhaps the most bizarre form of Stasi terror was the conservation of a suspected 'enemy's' body odour. Samples taken during interrogations – usually by wiping the unfortunate victim's crotch with a cotton cloth – were stored in hermetic glass jars. If a person needed to be identified, specially trained groin-sniffing dogs – euphemistically known as 'smell differentiation dogs' – sprang into action.

Learn more about the subject at **Stasi – Die Ausstellung** (p85), the **Gedenkstätte Normannstrasse** (p146) and the **Gedenkstätte Hohenschönhausen** (p146).

This instantly qualifies this trio of shopping complexes (called Quartiers) linked by an underground passageway. When the Friedrichstadtpassagen opened in the mid-90s, they ushered in the revival of Friedrichstrasse as one of Berlin's most elegant boulevards, a long-time tradition interrupted by WWII and communism.

Quartier 207 is home to the French department store Galeries Lafayette. Parisian architect Jean Nouvel designed its spectacular centrepiece, a translucent glass funnel that reflects light with the intensity of a hologram. At **Quartier 206**, the work of a team helmed by Henry Cobb, light streaming through a tented glass roof illuminates the stunning Art Deco–inspired décor, including its amazing patterned coloured marble floors. Cologne-based OM Ungers came up with **Quartier 205**, whose lofty light court is anchored by an installation by John Chamberlain. For more details, see the Shopping chapter (p225).

KONZERTHAUS Map pp328-9

☎ 203 090; www.konzerthaus.de; Gendarmenmarkt 2; U-Bahn Französische Strasse, Stadtmitte

One of Schinkel's finest accomplishments, the Konzerthaus (1821), originally called the Schauspielhaus, rose up from the ashes of Carl Gotthard Langhans' National Theater. It is the unifying element of Gendarmenmarkt, visually linking the German and French Cathedrals. Schinkel kept the few remaining

Konzerthaus (above)

outside walls and columns that hadn't been consumed by flames but added the grand staircase leading to a raised Ionic portico. World War II, of course, took its toll, but since its reopening in 1984 the Konzerthaus has once again been a shining beacon of Berlin culture. It's truly a fabulous building, both inside and out, and it's well worth attending a concert or taking a guided tour (€5 per person; usually offered at 1pm Saturdays). Also see p207.

MUSEUM FÜR KOMMUNIKATION

Map pp328-9

☎ 202 940; www.museumsstiftung.de; Leipziger Strasse 16; admission free; ☒ 9am-5pm Tue-Fri, 11am-7pm Sat & Sun; U-Bahn Mohrenstrasse

The famous Red and Blue Mauritius stamps, the world's first telephone and three cheeky robots are among the main draws of the Museum für Kommunikation (Museum of Communication). Founded in 1898, it is considered to be the world's oldest postal museum. The most precious exhibits are in the 'treasure chamber' in the basement. Upstairs, themed exhibits look at how media and telecommunications have changed human activity. Side galleries present great collections of telephones, answering machines, TVs and other communication devices.

At least as interesting as the exhibits is the museum's sumptuous architecture, especially its galleried and heavily ornamented light court. At night, clever illumination makes the building glow like a blue crystal. A café, shop and free Internet access are also available.

STASI – DIE AUSSTELLUNG Map pp328-9

☎ 2324 7951; www.bstu.de; Mauerstrasse 38; admission free; ☒ 10am-6pm; U-Bahn Französische Strasse, Mohrenstrasse

They hid tiny cameras in watering cans and flowerpots, stole keys from school children to install listening devices in their homes and collected body odour samples from suspects' groins. Stasi – Die Ausstellung (Stasi – The Exhibit) engagingly reveals the GDR's Ministry for State Security as an all-pervasive power with an all-out zeal and twisted imagination when it came to controlling, manipulating and repressing its own people.

Unfortunately it's all in German only, but a comprehensive English-language booklet is available free for the asking (so far) at the reception desk.

MUSEUMSINSEL

The sculpture-studded **Schlossbrücke** (Palace Bridge) leads to the little island in the Spree where Berlin's settlement began in the 13th century. On its northern half is Museumsinsel (Museum Island), a fabulous treasure-trove of art, sculpture and objects spread across five grand old museums. Only three of them are open for business right now while the complex, which was named a Unesco World Heritage Site in 1999, undergoes a complete overhaul expected to last until at least 2010.

Museumsinsel is the result of a late-18th-century fad among European royalty to open up their collections to the public. The Louvre in Paris, the British Museum in London, the Prado in Madrid and the Glyptothek in Munich all date back to this time. Back in Berlin, not to be outdone, Friedrich Wilhelm III and his successors followed suit, thereby creating one of the world's great museum-going experiences.

ALTE NATIONALGALERIE (SMB)

Map pp328-9

☎ 2090 5801; www.smpk.de; Bodestrasse 1-3; adult/ concession €8/4, under 16 free, free for everyone last 4hrs Thu, incl same-day admission to Altes Museum, Pergamon Museum; ☺ 10am-6pm Tue-Sun, 10am-10pm Thu; bus 100, 200

The Alte Nationalgalerie (Old National Gallery), a sensitively restored Greek-temple building by Friedrich August Stüler, is a stylish setting for this exquisite collection of 19th-century European art. The wall-sized paintings by Franz Krüger and Adolf Menzel glorifying Prussia's military might are hard to miss, but there are also sensitive portraits by Max Liebermann and Wilhelm Leibl. On the top floor, the mysterious landscapes of Caspar David Friedrich and Arnold Böcklin fill two of the rooms. Elsewhere you'll find French Impressionists, including Auguste Renoir, and sculpture by Johann Gottfried Schadow and Christian Daniel Rauch. The gorgeously restored upstairs

Top Five Views

- Berliner Dom (this page)
- Fernsehturm (p90)
- Panorama Observation Deck (p101)
- Reichstag (p99)
- Siegessäule (p100)

rotunda showcases the emotional sculptures of Reinhold Begas, while the marble stairwell is decorated with a frieze of German greats by Otto Geyers.

ALTES MUSEUM (SMB) Map pp328-9

☎ 2090 5254; www.smpk.de; Am Lustgarten; adult/concession €8/4, under 16 free, free for everyone last 4hrs Thu, incl same-day admission to Alte National-galerie, Pergamon Museum; ☺ 10am-6pm Tue-Sun; bus 100, 200

Schinkel's imposing neoclassical Altes Museum (Old Museum, 1830) was the first exhibition space to be built on Museumsinsel. It's a monumental work fronted by a phalanx of Ionic columns that gives way to a rotunda festooned with sculptures of Zeus and his celestial entourage. For now, art and sculpture from ancient Greece dominates the galleries on the main floor, although you'll also find a few Roman pieces thrown into the mix, including portraits of Caesar and Cleopatra. The upper floor is reserved for special exhibits. In August 2005, the bust of Nefertiti and other treasures from the Egyptian Museum currently in Charlottenburg (p110) are scheduled to move to the museum's upper floor.

BERLINER DOM Map pp328-9

☎ 202 690; www.berliner-dom.de; Am Lustgarten; adult/concession €5/3, under 14 free; ☺ church 9am-8pm Mon-Sat, noon-8pm Sun Apr-Sep, closes at 7pm Oct-Mar, viewing gallery 9am-8pm Apr-Sep, 9am-5pm Oct-Mar, crypt 9am-6pm Mon-Sat, noon-6pm Sun, last admission 1hr before closing; bus 100, 200

A church has occupied the spot of the Berliner Dom (Berlin Cathedral) since 1750 but the current version was only completed in 1905. Built in a magnificent if rather pompous Italian Renaissance style, this was where the royal Hohenzollerns – the Prussian royal family – came to worship and be buried; their city palace stood just across the street on Schlossplatz. Wartime destruction kept the Dom closed until 1993 and restoration is still ongoing.

A catalogue of top Prussian artists' work embellishes the cathedral's interior. Look for the baptismal font by Christian Daniel Rauch, the Petrus mosaic by Guido Reni and the altar table by Friedrich August Stüler. The organ, a 1904 work by Wilhelm Sauer, has over 7200 pipes, making it one of the largest in Germany.

The niches in the northern and southern apses hold the ornate sarcophagi of members of the Hohenzollern clan, including those carved by Andreas Schlüter for Friedrich I and his second wife Sophie Charlotte.

A central copper dome tops the colossal structure whose dimensions are best appreciated by climbing the 270 steps to the **viewing gallery**. Besides giving you nice views over Mitte, you'll also enjoy close-ups of the intricate church décor and design.

Concerts, guided tours and readings take place throughout the year. Ask at the box office or check the website or listings magazines for details.

BODEMUSEUM Map pp328-9
Am Kupfergraben; U-Bahn Hackescher Markt
On the northern tip of Museumsinsel, the Bodemuseum is closed to the public while it undergoes a complete overhaul, expected to last until at least 2006. A neobaroque work by Ernst von Ihne, who also designed the **Staatsbibliothek zu Berlin** (p83) on Unter den Linden, it was originally called Kaiser-Wilhelm-Museum before being renamed in 1956. Upon reopening it will house the Collection of Antique Sculpture, the Museum of Byzantine Art and the Coin Cabinet.

LUSTGARTEN Map pp328-9
Am Lustgarten; bus 100, 200
The Lustgarten (Pleasure Garden) fronting the Altes Museum looks like a peaceful little patch of green, but it has actually seen quite a few ups and downs in its career. Its life began rather innocently as a garden that supplied the nearby palace kitchen with fruit and vegetables, including Berlin's first-ever potatoes. Things got more interesting after the Thirty Years' War (1648), when the Great Elector had it turned into a real pleasure garden with statues, grottoes and fountains among which to frolic. Such 'frivolity' was not tolerated by his austere grandson, Friedrich Wilhelm I (aka the Soldier King) who, naturally, turned the little park into an exercise ground for his beloved troops. It fell to Schinkel to completely redesign the grounds in 1830 in order to create a worthy complement to his then brand-new Altes Museum. Alas, the Nazis paved it over one more time but in the late 1990s, after much debate, the garden was restored to its Schinkel-era appearance.

NEUES MUSEUM Map pp328-9
Bodestrasse; bus 100, 200
With space getting tight in the Altes Museum, Friedrich August Stüler got the nod to build a second gallery, which opened in 1859 as the prosaically named Neues Museum (New Museum). World War II reduced it to rubble but it is now being painstakingly rebuilt. This immense undertaking is expected to take until 2009 whereupon Queen Nefertiti and her entourage from the Egyptian Museum (currently in Charlottenburg, p110, from August 2005 in the Altes Museum, p86) will be moving into their new permanent digs.

PERGAMON MUSEUM (SMB)
Map pp328-9

☎ 2090 5555; www.smpk.de; Am Kupfergraben; adult/concession €8/4, under 16 free, free for everyone last 4hrs Thu, incl audio-guide & same-day admission to Altes Museum, Alte Nationalgalerie; ☺ 10am-6pm Tue-Sun, 10am-10pm Thu; bus 100, 200

If you only have time for one museum while in Berlin, make it the Pergamon. It's a veritable feast of classical Greek, Babylonian, Roman, Islamic and Middle Eastern art and architecture excavated by German archaeologists at the turn of the 20th century.

The giant complex, which was only completed in 1930, actually harbours three important collections under one roof: the Collection of Classical Antiquities, the Museum of Near Eastern Antiquities and the Museum of Islamic Art. Each one is worth seeing at leisure, but if you're pressed for time, make a beeline to the following highlights.

Pergamon Altar, Pergamon Museum (above)

The museum's namesake and main draw is, of course, the **Pergamon Altar** (165 BC) from Asia Minor (in today's Turkey). It's a gargantuan raised marble shrine surrounded by an amazingly vivid frieze of the gods doing battle with the giants. Behind the altar, and reached by walking up its steps, is the Telephos Frieze, which depicts the life story of the legendary founder of Pergamon.

The next room presents another key exhibit: the immense Market Gate of Miletus (AD 2nd century), a masterpiece of Roman architecture. As you enter the gate, you'll travel back in time and to another culture: Babylon during the reign of King Nebuchadnezzar II (604–562 BC).

It's impossible not to be awed by reconstructions of amazing Babylonian monuments such as the Ishtar Gate, the Processional Way leading up to it and the façade of the king's throne hall. All are sheathed in glazed bricks glistening in a luminous cobalt blue and ochre. The striding lions, horses and dragons, which represent major Babylonian gods, are so striking that you can almost hear the roaring and fanfare. Another highlight in the Museum of Near Eastern Antiquities is the intricate temple façades from Uruk decorated with colourful clay inlays and detailed brick reliefs.

Finally, in the Museum of Islamic Art, keep an eye out for the fortress-like 8th-century Caliph's palace from Mshatta in today's Jordan. Crowds also gather by the 17th-century Aleppo Room, taken from the house of a Syrian merchant, whose walls are entirely covered in intricately painted wood panelling.

Budget at least two hours for this amazing museum.

SCHLOSSPLATZ

Nothing of today's Schlossplatz, renamed Marx-Engels-Platz in GDR times, evokes memory of the magnificent edifice that stood here from 1451 to 1951: the Berliner Stadtschloss (Berlin City Palace), for centuries the primary residence of the ruling Hohenzollern family. Despite international protests, the GDR government demolished the barely war-damaged structure, which it considered a 'symbol of Prussian militarism', in 1951. In its stead was put the country's political nerve centre, anchored by the Palast der Republik, the Staatsratsgebäude and the Marx Engels Forum. It was a decision even some East Berlin political honchos later admitted regretting.

MARSTALL & RIBBECKHAUS Map pp328-9
Breite Strasse; U-Bahn Spittelmarkt, Klosterstrasse

Southeast of Schlossplatz, the neobaroque **Neuer Marstall** (New Stables) is a 1901 work by Ernst von Ihne that once sheltered the royal horses and carriages. During the 1918 November Revolution, the building became the home base of the revolutionary leaders. The bronze reliefs on its northern façade recall this period in history. One panel shows Karl Liebknecht's famous proclamation of the German socialist republic from the balcony of the City Palace.

The Neuer Marstall is an extension of the **Alter Marstall** (Old Stables), built by Michael Matthias Smids in 1670, making it Berlin's oldest baroque building. It rubs shoulders with the **Ribbeckhaus**, a rare Renaissance structure with four pretty gables and a highly ornate sandstone portal. The latter two buildings now house public libraries.

PALAST DER REPUBLIK Map pp328-9
Schlossplatz; bus 100, 200

By the time you're reading this, there may well be a huge empty lot in the spot where the Palast der Republik (Palace of the Republic) once stood. Or maybe it'll still be there in all its preposterous concrete, steel and orange glass glory. After years of debate about the fate of the GDR's main parliamentary building, it now looks as though an encounter with the wrecking ball will be inevitable. However, nobody's willing to say when, so don't hold your breath.

The GDR's 'palace' stands (or stood) indeed on the site of the historical royal Berliner Stadtschloss (Berlin City Palace), demolished in 1951 by the East German government despite an international outcry (p88). It was built in the early 1970s at the initiative of Erich Honecker and even garnered the nickname 'Erich's Lampenladen' (Erich's lamp shop) for the many ceiling lamps dangling in the foyer.

The multipurpose building, which could accommodate up to 5000 people, quickly became an anchor of cultural life in East Berlin. The GDR parliament (the Volkskammer) met in the Kleiner Saal (Small Hall) but the other sections were open to the public. Stars like Harry Belafonte performed in the Grosse Halle (Big Hall), also used for congresses and balls. The sweeping foyer contained a gallery showcasing the works of contemporary GDR artists, a variety theatre and restaurants.

After reunification the place was immediately boarded up after the discovery of major asbestos contamination. In 1993, one step ahead of Christo and his wrapped Reichstag (see p99), a French artist covered the structure with cloth painted like the old Schloss façade, sparking a movement to rebuild the historical landmark. The idea gathered steam for a while, but for now a prohibitive price tag has put those lofty plans on ice. Stay tuned.

STAATSRATSGEBÄUDE Map pp328-9
Schlossplatz 1; admission free; ⏰ 9am-7.30pm; U-Bahn Hausvogteiplatz, bus 100, 200

The only piece of the Berlin City Palace spared demolition was the arched portal from which Karl Liebknecht proclaimed a German socialist republic in 1918. In honour of the Marxist martyr, the GDR politicos had the section incorporated into the Staatsratsgebäude (State Council Building, 1964) on the south side of Schlossplatz.

If the doors are open, sneak a peek into the foyer with its three-storey tall painted glass windows depicting scenes from the GDR's worker's movement. From 1999 until 2001, Chancellor Gerhard Schröder kept his offices here, while his new Chancellery was taking shape (p98).

ALEXANDERPLATZ & AROUND

Formerly East Berlin's main commercial hub, Alexanderplatz – 'Alex' for short – was first called Ochsenmarkt (ox market) and renamed in honour of Tsar Alexander I, who visited Berlin in 1805. Today it is a mere shadow of the low-life district Alfred Döblin called 'the quivering heart of a cosmopolitan city' in his 1929 novel *Berlin Alexanderplatz*.

Badly bombed in WWII, it got its current socialist look in the 1960s courtesy of GDR city planners. The TV tower, the 123m-high **Interhotel** (now Park Inn) and the **Centrum Warenhaus** (now Kaufhof), once the GDR's largest department store, all date back to those days. Other landmark relics include the **Brunnen der Völkerfreundschaft** (Fountain of Friendship among the Peoples) and the **Weltzeituhr** (World Time Clock). Off to the side is the **Haus des Lehrers** (House of Teachers) with a frieze by Walter Womacka, which was being restored to become part of the **Berlin Congress Centre**.

Alexanderplatz also played a role in the downfall of the GDR. On 4 November 1989 some 700,000 people gathered here to rally against the GDR regime. They were vociferous but peaceful and they were heard: five days later, the Berlin Wall came tumbling down.

AQUADOM & SEALIFE BERLIN
Map pp328-9

☎ 992 800; Spandauer Strasse 3; adult/student/child €13.50/12.60/10; ⏰ from 10am, closing times vary but 6pm earliest; S-Bahn Hackescher Markt, bus 100

One of Berlin's newest attractions, this small but entertaining aquarium takes you on a virtual journey along the Spree, Havel and Elbe Rivers into the frigid waters of the North Atlantic. Along the way you'll meet the aquatic denizens living in the various habitats, which have been re-created in 30 tanks, including a 360° aquarium where a giant school of mackerel make its merry rounds. Other crowd favourites include smile-inducing sea horses, the otherworldly jellyfish and a big tank with manta rays and small sharks. Kids can test their knowledge by answering quiz questions throughout. All labelling is in English and German.

Visits conclude with what is billed as the big highlight: a very slow lift ride through a 16m-tall cylindrical aquarium teeming with tropical fish. It's effectively in the lobby of the spanking new Radisson SAS Hotel, allowing you to sneak a free preview.

Aquadom & Sealife Berlin (above)

EPHRAIM-PALAIS Map pp328-9

☎ 2400 2121; www.stadtmuseum.de; Poststrasse 16; adult/concession €3/1.50, free Wed, combination ticket with Museum Knoblauchhaus & Museum Nikolaikirche adult/concession €5/3; ⏱ 10am-6pm Tue-Sun; U-Bahn Klosterstrasse

The 1762 Ephraim-Palais, on the southern edge of the Nikolaiviertel (p92), was originally the home of the court jeweller and coin minter Veitel Heine Ephraim. It is considered one of Berlin's most beautiful buildings, primarily because of its elegantly curving rococo façade decorated with frolicking cherubs and gilded wrought-iron balconies.

The present structure is in fact a complete replica of the original, torn down in 1936 to make room for the widening of Mühlendamm. Fortunately, sections of the precious façade survived in storage in West Berlin until given to the eastern city in 1984 to be used in the construction of the Nikolaiviertel.

These days, the palais presents changing exhibits focusing on aspects of art and the cultural history of Berlin as well as the graphics collection of the Stadtmuseum (City Museum). Architectural highlights include the oval staircase and the Schlüterdecke, an ornate ceiling, on the 1st floor.

Ephraim-Palais (above)

FERNSEHTURM Map pp328-9

☎ 242 3333; www.berlinerfernsehturm; Panoramastrasse 1a; adult/child under 16 €6.50/3; ⏱ 9-1am Mar-Oct, 10am-midnight Nov-Feb; U/S-Bahn Alexanderplatz

The Fernsehturm (TV Tower) is Berlin's tallest structure, soaring skyward for 368m. From the panorama platform at a lofty 203m, you'll be able to pinpoint the city's major landmarks, marvel at the size of the Tiergarten park and compare the layout of the former eastern and western city halves. Upstairs, the Telecafé serves coffee, snacks and full meals (€6 or €13).

Built in 1969, the tower was intended to demonstrate the technological superiority of the GDR, but ironically it became a source of embarrassment. In sunlight, the steel sphere below the antenna produces the reflection of a giant cross – not a welcome sight in a secular land where crosses had been removed from church roofs. West Berliners gleefully dubbed the phenomenon 'the Pope's revenge'.

FRANZISKANER KLOSTERKIRCHE
Map pp328-9

☎ 636 1213; Klosterstrasse; admission free; ⏱ during construction noon-6pm Sat & Sun; U-Bahn Klosterstrasse

The husk of its ancient church is all that is left of the medieval Franciscan monastery that once stood on Klosterstrasse. In 1534 it was converted into a prestigious grammar school where pupils such as Karl Friedrich Schinkel and Otto von Bismarck prepared for their illustrious careers.

Destroyed in the final days of WWII, the ruins offered silent testimony against war and fascism in GDR days. Currently under restoration, it is one of the few examples of Gothic architecture left in Berlin and will again be used as a cultural venue once the scaffolding disappears, scheduled for October 2004 at the time of writing.

Behind the ruins, at Littenstrasse 12–17, looms a branch of the **Landgericht Berlin** (state courthouse), which is worth a look for its handsome Art Nouveau staircases.

HISTORISCHER HAFEN BERLIN
Map pp328-9

☎ 2147 3257; www.historischer-hafen-berlin.de; Märkisches Ufer; exhibit adult/concession €2/1, under 10 free; ⏱ 2-6pm Tue-Fri, 11am-6pm Sat & Sun May-Oct; U-Bahn Märkisches Museum

With its many rivers, canals and lakes, it's not surprising that Berlin has a long tradition in inland navigation and in fact had the busiest river port in Germany until WWII. The Historischer Hafen (Historical Harbour), at the southern tip of Museumsinsel, is an outdoor museum with over 20 boats, barges and tugboats, many still operational. One boat has a café in summer while another contains a small exhibit documenting 250 years of river shipping on the Spree and Havel.

MARIENKIRCHE Map pp328-9

☎ 242 4467; Karl-Liebknecht-Strasse 8; admission free; ⏰ 10am-4pm Mon-Thu, noon-4pm Sat & Sun; U/S-Bahn Alexanderplatz, Hackescher Markt

Dwarfed by the TV Tower, the Marienkirche (St Mary's Church) was first established in the late 13th century and is considered Berlin's second-oldest church after the Nikolaikirche (p92). It's a three-nave hall construction (meaning all naves are of equal height) filled with art treasures, the oldest being the bronze baptismal font from 1437. Other eye-catchers are the baroque alabaster pulpit by Andreas Schlüter (1703) and the badly faded Dance of Death wall fresco in the vestibule, created after the plague epidemic of 1484. Call about English-language tours usually offered at 1pm on Saturday and Sunday.

MÄRKISCHES MUSEUM Map pp328-9

☎ 308 660; www.stadtmuseum.de; Am Köllnischen Park 5; adult/concession €4/2, free Wed; ⏰ 10am-6pm Tue-Sun; U-Bahn Märkisches Museum

'Peoples of the world, look upon this city!' exclaimed Berlin mayor Ernst Reuter in 1948, appealing to the international community for help during the Berlin Airlift (p61). 'Look upon this city!' is also the motto of the permanent exhibit of this sprawling museum designed to help you understand how the tiny trading village of Berlin-Cölln evolved into today's modern metropolis.

Rooms are organised by theme rather than chronology. An armoury, a magnificent Guild Hall and a collection of religious sculptures, for instance, represent medieval times. Exhibits on industrialisation take care to point out both advances in science and technology and the subhuman living conditions in the working-class tenements that underpinned such progress.

A highlight is the wonderful Kaiserpanorama (literally, emperor's panorama), basically a three-dimensional slide show that was a form of mass entertainment in the early 20th century. If you happen to visit on a Sunday, don't miss the quirky automatophones, historic mechanical musical instruments that are wound up and launched on their cacophonous journey at 3pm (separate admission, €2/1).

The red-brick building complex that houses the museum (1908) is interesting as well. Designed by Ludwig Hoffmann, it's an intentional hotchpotch of other actual buildings found throughout Brandenburg. The tower, for instance, is modelled after that of the bishop's palace in Wittstock, while St Catherine's Church in the town of Brandenburg inspired the Gothic gables. A copy of the Roland statue from the same town guards the museum entrance.

MARX-ENGELS-FORUM Map pp328-9

Bounded by Karl-Liebknecht-Strasse, Spandauer Strasse, Rathausstrasse & the Spree River; U/S-Bahn Alexanderplatz, Hackescher Markt

When Erich Honecker inaugurated this sterile square in 1986 he dedicated the 'artistic ensemble' to the 'greatest sons of the German people': Karl Marx and Friedrich Engels. A twice life-size sculpture anchoring the grounds shows the 'fathers of socialism' staring out towards the TV Tower. Reliefs showing people living happily under socialism and others deploring the inhumanity of capitalism supply additional artistic accents.

MOLKENMARKT Map pp328-9

Intersection of Mühlendamm, Stralauer Strasse & Spandauer Strasse; U-Bahn Klosterstrasse

It's hard to imagine that Berlin's oldest market square, the Molkenmarkt, once occupied the area southeast of the Nikolaiviertel that is now so thoroughly engulfed in roaring traffic. There's not much left to see around here, a minor exception being the baroque **Palais Schwerin** (1704) on the south side of Mühlendamm. The only redeeming value of the next-door building, the **Münze** (1935), where coins were minted by both the Nazis and the GDR, is a decorative frieze depicting the evolution of metallurgy and coin minting. The original by Johann Gottfried Schadow and Friedrich Gilly once graced the old mint on Werderscher Markt west of here.

Looming above it all is the **Altes Stadthaus** with its elegant domed tower. Built in 1911 as an extension of the Red Town Hall and later used by the GDR's Ministerrat (council of ministers), it's been undergoing restoration for years.

MUSEUM KNOBLAUCHHAUS

Map pp328-9

☎ 2345 9991; www.stadtmuseum.de; Poststrasse 23; admission €1.50, free Wed, combination ticket with Museum Nikolaikirche & Ephraim-Palais adult/concession €5/3; ⏱ 10am-6pm Tue-Sun; U-Bahn Klosterstrasse

The 1761 Knoblauchhaus is the oldest residential building in the Nikolaiviertel. It was the home of the prominent Knoblauch family, which included politicians, the founder of a first aid society and the architect of the original synagogue on Oranienburger Strasse (p95). As patrons of the arts, the Knoblauchs enjoyed tea and talk with people such as Schinkel, Schadow and Begas in this very house.

Today, four period rooms on the 1st floor offer glimpses into the life of the Berlin bourgeoisie in the Biedermeier period (early 19th century). The upper floor has changing exhibits and the basement a wine restaurant.

MUSEUM NIKOLAIKIRCHE Map pp328-9

☎ 2472 4529; www.stadtmuseum.de; Nikolaikirchplatz; admission €1.50, free Wed, combination ticket with Museum Knoblauchhaus & Ephraim-Palais adult/concession €5/3; ⏱ 10am-6pm Tue-Sun; U-Bahn Klosterstrasse

Lording it over the Nikolaiviertel are the twin spires of the late-Gothic Nikolaikirche (1230), Berlin's oldest church. One of the few buildings that was restored rather than built after WWII, it contains a moderately interesting exhibit about the church's role in local history. Of greater interest, perhaps, are baroque epitaphs of prominent Berliners on its walls and pillars.

NEPTUNBRUNNEN Map pp328-9

Spandauer Strasse, btwn Marienkirche & Rotes Rathaus; U/S-Bahn Alexanderplatz, Hackescher Markt

This fountain, now the visual focus of the vast open space outside the Rotes Rathaus (p92), was designed by Reinhold Begas in 1891 and originally stood on Schlossplatz between the palace and the Marstall. It shows Neptune holding court over a quartet of buxom beauties symbolising major rivers: the Rhine, Elbe, Oder and Vistula.

NIKOLAIVIERTEL Map pp328-9

Bounded by Rathausstrasse, Spandauer Strasse, Mühlendamm & the Spree River; U-Bahn Klosterstrasse

Just behind the Rotes Rathaus, the twee Nicholai Quarter occupies the area of Berlin's first settlement dating back to the early 13th century. Despite its Disney-esque patina, it is a fairly successful attempt by GDR architects to re-create Berlin's medieval core, a prestige project undertaken in celebration of the city's 750th anniversary in 1987. The result is a maze of narrow, cobbled lanes lined with historic buildings, some original, most reconstructed. The Knoblauchhaus, Ephraim-Palais and Nikolaikirche all contain small museums (also described in this section).

It's a nice place for strolling but you won't find too many Berliners patronising the pricey cafés, restaurants and cutesy shops. One of the more ambience-laden places is the restaurant-pub called **Zum Nussbaum** (p167), a favourite watering hole of humorist and local legend Heinrich Zille (1858-1929).

ROTES RATHAUS Map pp328-9

☎ 902 60; Rathausstrasse 15; admission free; ⏱ 9am-6pm Mon-Fri; U-Bahn Klosterstrasse

Dominating the skyline west of Alexanderplatz, the hulking Rotes Rathaus (Red Town Hall) with its jutting clock tower has been Berlin's political nexus since 1860. The neo-Renaissance structure, where the governing mayor and his Senate keep their offices, gets its 'red' suffix from the colour of the bricks used in its construction (not the political leanings of its occupants). Note the terracotta frieze (1879) running along the building's length, which depicts scenes from the city's history. The two bronze sculptures outside the main façade are called *Trümmerfrauen* and *Aufbauhelfer* and honour the men and women who helped rebuild the city – literally with their hands – after WWII.

SAMMLUNG KINDHEIT & JUGEND

Map pp328-9

☎ 275 0383; Wallstrasse 32; adult/concession € 2/1, free on Wed; ⏱ 9am-5pm Tue-Fri, 10am-6pm Sat & Sun; U-Bahn Märkisches Museum, Spittelmarkt

This museum offers a sometimes entertaining, sometimes tedious journey through the history of growing up in Germany, Berlin in particular. You can squeeze behind the wooden desks of a re-created 1912 classroom or discover the purpose of an *Eselskappe* (donkey hat) that had to be worn by undisciplined kids. In the Scriptorium you'll be able to test your penmanship using quill and ink and other antiquated writing tools. There's also a big collection of toys from the past two centuries.

SCHEUNENVIERTEL

North of Alexanderplatz, the Scheunenviertel (Barn Quarter) is one of the city's liveliest spots, teeming with restaurants, bars and nightclubs, especially around the Hackescher Markt, along Oranienburger Strasse and in such restored courtyard complexes as the Hackesche Höfe. Alte Schönhauser Strasse and Neue Schönhauser Strasse are hip shopping streets, lined with dozens of über-trendy boutiques filled with fun fashions by hot Berlin designers. Auguststrasse has become a famous art mile with leading galleries like Eigen + Art (p227) and the Kunst-Werke Berlin (p94) being major art scene hubs. Since reunification, the Scheunenviertel has also reprised its historic role as Berlin's Jewish quarter.

GROSSE HAMBURGER STRASSE
Map pp328–9
S-Bahn Hackescher Markt

The Grosse Hamburger Strasse is a key street in Berlin's Jewish history. The city's first Jewish Cemetery, the **Alter Jüdischer Friedhof**, once occupied the grassy area near the corner with Hackescher Markt. Over 12,000 people were buried here between 1672 and 1827, including Veitel Heine Ephraim (see Ephraim-Palais, p90) and the Enlightenment philosopher Moses Mendelssohn. The latter is honoured with a memorial tombstone (not the original one), which stands solitary and silent as a reminder of the destruction wreaked upon the sacred grounds by the Gestapo in 1943.

Nearby, in what would be Grosse Hamburger Strasse 26, a plaque marks the site of the city's first **Jewish seniors' home**. In 1942 the Nazis

turned the building into a detention centre for Jews scheduled for deportation. A haunting sculpture by Will Lammert shows a group of fatigued women standing in abject resignation to their fate. Bombs flattened the building and it was never rebuilt. Every year, the names of all 55,696 Berlin Jews who perished at the hands of the Nazis are read out aloud here on Holocaust Memorial Day (27 January).

The building at Grosse Hamburger Strasse 27 originally housed a **Jewish boys' school** founded in 1788 at the instigation of Moses Mendelssohn; he's honoured by a plaque. The Nazis closed the school but it survived the war intact. Today, both boys and girls – Jewish or not – once again hit the books in its hallowed rooms.

On the opposite side of the street is the **Missing House** (1990), an installation and memorial by French artist Christian Boltanski. The 'missing house' in question was a neobaroque apartment building that stood at Grosse Hamburger Strasse 15/16 until it was destroyed by a direct bomb hit.

HACKESCHE HÖFE Map pp328–9
www.hackesche-hoefe.com; S-Bahn Hackescher Markt

One of Berlin's biggest tourist magnets, the Hackesche Höfe (1907) is a warren of eight beautifully restored courtyards filled with cafés, galleries, boutiques and entertainment venues. The nicest one is Hof 1 (enter from Rosenthaler Strasse), whose façades are emblazoned with intricately patterned Art Nouveau tiles designed by August Endell. Also here is the **Chamäleon Varieté** (p210), which occupies the ballroom of the former and fashionably famous wine-restaurant Neumann.

In the next courtyard, **Hackesches Hoftheater** (☎ 283 2587; www.hackesches-hof theater.de;

Scheunenviertel through the Ages

The Scheunenviertel's tumultuous history goes back to 1672 when the Great Elector ordered all flammable crops to be stored outside the city walls. Around 30 barns quickly sprang up around what is today Rosa-Luxemburg-Platz and surrounding streets.

The quarter wasn't settled until 1737 when the Great Elector's grandson, Friedrich Wilhelm I (the Soldier King), forced Jews who didn't own property to live among the barns. In the early 20th century, the Scheunenviertel absorbed huge numbers of new Jewish immigrants from Eastern Europe, and its streets and shops soon rang with the sound of Yiddish. Most newcomers were Hasidic Jews who had trouble assimilating with the existing and more liberal Jewish community living along Grosse Hamburger Strasse in the Spandauer Vorstadt a few blocks west.

The Scheunenviertel quickly became a poor people's quarter. Prostitution, petty and not-so-petty crime, and revolutionary rumbling flourished here from the late 19th century until Hitler assumed power in 1933. It was the Nazis who first applied the name Scheunenviertel – by then a derogatory term – to the entire Jewish quarter, including the much more upmarket Spandauer Vorstadt around Oranienburger Strasse.

Rosenthaler Strasse 40/41) popularly keeps alive Yiddish culture with a busy programme of theatre and music. The Yiddish Music Summer festival draws major crowds here every year.

Court VII offers access to the whimsical **Rosenhöfe**, a smaller set of courtyards with a sunken rose garden and sculpted filigree metal balustrades intended to resemble flowers and botanical tendrils. It can also be entered from Rosenthaler Strasse.

HANDWERKERVEREINSHAUS (SOPHIENSAELE) Map pp328-9

☎ 2859 9360; Sophienstrasse 18; U-Bahn Weinmeisterstrasse

This handsome building, now a performance venue called **Sophiensaele** (p214), looms large in the history of Berlin's workers' movement. It was built in 1905 as the clubhouse of the Handwerkerverein, the city's first workers' association, which became a germ cell of the labour movement. Its large assembly halls hosted numerous political gatherings, especially in the aftermath of WWI when members of the Spartacus League, including Karl Liebknecht and Wilhelm Pieck, rallied the troops in support of a socialist revolution. This, of course, failed. Liebknecht was soon murdered; but Pieck went on to become the GDR's first president.

HECKMANNHÖFE Map pp328-9

www.heckmann-hoefe.de; Oranienburger Strasse 32; S-Bahn Oranienburger Strasse

For our money, this is the nicest of the Scheunenviertel courtyard complexes. A total restoration has morphed this former machine factory into an elegant, open space with great brick buildings housing upmarket shops and restaurants. It's anchored by a peaceful little park whose benches and pretty fountain invite you to linger.

KUNSTHAUS TACHELES Map pp328-9

☎ 282 6185; www.tacheles.de; Oranienburger Strasse 54-56; U-Bahn Oranienburger Tor

'What's *that* crumbling thing doing here in pretty Mitte?' you might be thinking as you wander along Oranienburger Strasse. But what may *look* like something only days away from demolition is in fact one of Berlin's most cherished treasures: the Tacheles, one of the liveliest and most creative art and cultural spaces in town.

It was originally built in 1909 as the Passage-Kaufhaus department store, but was flattened in WWII and languished behind the Iron Curtain until reunification. In early 1990, some 50 artists occupied the ruin and tried to have it declared a protected building. Miraculously, the Berlin Senate gave its thumbs up in 1992, giving birth to the vast alternative art centre it still is today.

Over the years, the Tacheles has lost some of its anarchic edge but it's still a chaotic, graffiti-covered warren of artists' studios and galleries, including a cinema, café and beer garden. There's always something going on here: theatre, readings, happenings, parties – just check the listings mags, *Zitty* or *Tip*, or the website. How long this underground feel will survive is anybody's guess. The writing may be on the wall, though: in an apparent nod to gentrification, the Tacheles now also houses a very establishment-looking restaurant, the **Milagro** (p165).

KUNST-WERKE BERLIN Map pp328-9

☎ 243 4590; www.kw-berlin.de; Auguststrasse 69; adult/concession €4/2.50, under 12 free; ☽ noon-6pm Tue-Sun; S-Bahn Oranienburger Strasse

Housed in a converted margarine factory, this nonprofit institution is one of the most dynamic contemporary art spaces in Berlin. Founded in 1990, it propelled the Scheunenviertel's development into one of the city's main artistic centres. An international cast of artists presents cutting-edge works in all media during several exhibits annually. The integrated Café Bravo, inside a double-cube installation by US artist Dan Graham, is a nice place for a respite.

MUSEUM BLINDENWERKSTATT OTTO WEIDT Map pp328-9

☎ 2859 9407; www.blindes-vertrauen.de; Rosenthaler Strasse 39; admission €1.50; ☽ noon-8pm Mon-Fri, 11am-8pm Sat & Sun; S-Bahn Hackescher Markt

This small museum, an affiliate of the **Jüdisches Museum** (p122) in Kreuzberg, tells the story of Otto Weidt, a broom and brush maker who was able to protect many of his blind and deaf Jewish workers from the Nazis until 1943. Weidt provided food, hiding space and false papers, and even bribed Gestapo officials into releasing Jews awaiting deportation. The exhibit, which occupies three rooms of the original workshop, is suitably called 'Blind Trust – Life in Hiding at the Hackescher Markt, 1941–1943'.

NEUE SYNAGOGUE & CENTRUM
JUDAICUM Map pp328-9

☎ 2840 1250; www.cjudaicum.de; Oranienburger
Strasse 28-30; adult/concession €3/2, tours €1.50/1;
⌚ 10am-8pm Sun & Mon, 10am-6pm Tue-Thu, 10am-
5pm Fri May-Aug & 10am-6pm Sun-Thu, 10am-2pm Fri
Sep-Apr, cupola closed Oct-Mar, tours 4pm Wed & Sun,
2pm Sun; S-Bahn Oranienburger Strasse

The gleaming gold dome of the rebuilt New
Synagogue stands as a beacon of the revitalised Jewish community in Berlin. Designed in
Moorish-Byzantine style by Eduard Knoblauch,
this was Germany's largest synagogue, with
seating for more than 3200. Bismarck and
other Prussian dignitaries attended its opening in 1866 and, thanks to its beauty and
rich decoration, the synagogue became an
instant landmark and attracted visits even
from non-Jews.

During the 1938 Kristallnacht pogroms, a
local police chief prevented SA thugs from
setting it on fire, an act of courage commemorated by a plaque. The Nazis still managed
to desecrate it, although services continued
until 1940 when the Wehrmacht (the German
armed forces during the Third Reich) appropri-
ated it for storage. It wasn't severely damaged
until hit by bombs in 1943.

With the consent of East Berlin's small
Jewish community, the GDR government demolished the ruins in 1958, keeping only the
main façade as a memorial. On the occasion
of the 50th anniversary of Kristallnacht in 1988,
Honecker announced the decision to rebuild
the synagogue, a project that didn't get off the
ground until after reunification. The New Synagogue was finally opened in May 1995.

Today it contains a community and research
centre called the Centrum Judaicum, with a
permanent exhibit about the history and architecture of the synagogue and its role in the
lives of the people who worshipped here. The
first room, a beautiful 12-sided hall underneath
the dome, contains a model of the synagogue,
a Torah scroll and an eternal lamp from the
original structure, which was discovered during excavations in 1989.

A few steps lead to the main exhibition hall
with photographs, documents and other objects retrieved during the restoration. There's
also a good view from this room of the adjacent empty lot where the magnificent main
hall once stood. A stone band traces its dimensions like a scar. Upstairs is a space for special
exhibits and a small room where Jewish prayer
services are held.

The Women of Rosenstrasse

Rosenstrasse has carved out its spot in the history
books for being the site of a famous women's protest
that took place in 1943. On 27 February, the SS arrested about 7000 Berlin Jews at their factory jobs
and corralled them in a former Jewish welfare office
at Rosenstrasse 2–4 for deportation to Auschwitz.
All had one thing in common: they were married to
Christian spouses, a status that had given them some
degree of protection until that day.

Outraged and desperate, their wives and mothers
soon gathered in protest by the hundreds outside the
building, quietly, peacefully but strongly demanding
the release of their men. They stayed through night
and day, braving rain and subzero temperatures, and
miraculously they were heard: on 11 March, Goebbels
ordered the release of every single prisoner.

Today a red sandstone sculpture by Inge Hunzinger called *Block der Frauen* (Block of the Women,
1994) honours this great act of courage. There are
also two information pillars offering historical background. In 2003, renowned filmmaker Margarethe
von Trotta turned the event into a feature film called
Rosenstrasse.

SOPHIE-GIPS-HÖFE & SAMMLUNG
HOFFMANN Map pp328-9

☎ 2849 9121; Sophienstrasse 21; tours €6;
⌚ 10am-4pm Sat by appointment only; U-Bahn
Weinmeisterstrasse

Just past the **Handwerkervereinshaus** (p94), a
tunnel-like entrance spills out into the quiet
and dignified Sophie-Gips-Höfe whose trio of
courtyards contain galleries and the popular
Barcomi's (☎ 2859 8363; Sophienstrasse 21, 2nd
courtyard; snacks €2-5; ⌚ 9am-10pm) café. In
its former life, this handsome 19th-century
brick complex housed a sewing machine
factory; in GDR days, medical equipment was
produced here. Take note of the neon-light
installation by Gunda Förster which lines the
connecting walkways.

One of the complex's main draws is the
Sammlung Hoffmann, a showcase of contemporary art gathered by Erika and Rolf Hoffmann
in 30 years of collecting. Every Saturday the
Hoffmans open their private two-storey apart-
ment/gallery for guided tours, complete with
felt slippers. Actual displays change once a
year but may include works by Frank Stella,
Lucio Fontana and scores of lesser-known
artists from around the world.

SOPHIENKIRCHE Map pp328-9

☎ 282 5877; www.sophien.de; Grosse Hamburger Strasse 29; admission free; 3-6pm Wed, 3-5pm Sat May-Sep; U-Bahn Weinmeisterstrasse

The baroque Sophienkirche is a simple single-nave, galleried confection with a delicate stucco ceiling and an ornate tower with a copper hood. This was the first parish church in the Spandauer Vorstadt, completed in 1713 with funds provided by Sophie Luise, the third wife of King Friedrich I. The queen, however, was sadly missing from its inaugural service, having been banished from Berlin by her step-son and newly crowned Friedrich Wilhelm I. The enchanting churchyard has some fine-looking tombstones from the 18th century.

ORANIENBURGER TOR & AROUND

BERLINER MEDIZINHISTORISCHES MUSEUM Map pp320-1

☎ 450 536 156; www.bmm.charite.de; Charité Hospital, Schumannstrasse 20-21; adult/concession €4/2; 10am-5pm Tue-Sun, 10am-7pm Wed; U-Bahn Oranienburger Tor

'Not suitable for children under 16' reads the warning on the door to the Medizinhistorisches Museum (Medical History Museum) on the campus of the Charité Hospital. And it's no joke.

Exhibits start off innocently enough with a dental office from the 1920s and the desk of the famous doctor, researcher and professor, Rudolf Virchow (1821–1902). It's Virchow's pathology collection – essentially a three-dimensional medical textbook – in the next room that requires a stronger stomach.

Crammed into glass cases are hundreds of organs showing the havoc various diseases can wreak on them: inflamed appendices, cancer-stricken lungs, broccoli-like skin tumours, a colon the size of an elephant trunk. If you think this is bad, skip the last row, which features two-headed babies and deformed fetuses not even the makers of *Alien* could imagine.

Virchow first displayed his amazing collection in 1899 in the same building, an adjunct to his Institute of Pathology. It integrates his lecture hall – a preserved ruin – and rooms used for special exhibits. A future presentation on the history of medicine from 1700 to today is in the planning stages. The museum is in the campus' northwestern corner, which is accessible from Schumannstrasse, Luisenstrasse and Invalidenstrasse.

BRECHT-WEIGEL GEDENKSTÄTTE
Map pp322-4

☎ 283 057 044; Chausseestrasse 125; tours adult/concession €3/1.50; tours half-hourly 10-11.30am Tue-Fri, also 5-6.30pm Thu, 9.30am-1.30pm Sat, hourly 11am-6pm Sun; U-Bahn Oranienburger Tor

Bertolt Brecht, one of Germany's seminal 20th-century playwrights, lived in this house not far from his theatre, the Berliner Ensemble, from 1953 until his death in 1956. You'll see Brecht's office, his large library with everything from classics to crime stories, and the tiny bedroom where he died. Decorated with Chinese artwork, it's been left as though he'd just stepped out for a moment, leaving his hat and woollen cap hanging on the door.

Downstairs are the cluttered living quarters of his actress wife Helene Weigel, who continued to live here until her death in 1971. The couple are buried at the **Dorotheenstädtischer Friedhof** (see below) next door.

Call ahead to find out about the English-language tours. The basement restaurant serves Austrian food prepared from Weigel's recipes (mains €9 to €14).

DOROTHEENSTÄDTISCHER FRIEDHOF Map pp328-9

Chausseestrasse 126; U-Bahn Oranienburger Tor, Zinnowitzer Strasse

This cemetery wins, hands down, the award for the most celebrity corpses in Berlin. A veritable pantheon of German greats lies buried here, including architects Schadow and Schinkel (who designed his own tombstone), composers Paul Dessau and Hanns Eisler, and writers Heinrich Mann and Bertolt Brecht plus his wife Helene Weigel. Brecht lived in a house just north of here (see above), allegedly to be close to his idols, the philosophers Hegel and Fichte, who are also interred here.

HAMBURGER BAHNHOF (SMB)
Map pp320-1

☎ 3978 3412; www.hamburgerbahnhof.de; Invalidenstrasse 50-51; adult/ concession €6/3, under 16 free, free for everyone last 4hrs Thu, incl same-day admission to Kunstgewerbemuseum, Gemäldegalerie, Kupferstichkabinett & Neue Nationalgalerie, ticket also includes admission to Musikinstrumenten-Museum and the Kunstgewerbemuseum in Schloss Köpenick; 10am-6pm Tue-Fri, 11am-6pm Sat & Sun; S-Bahn Lehrter Stadtbahnhof

Andy Warhol's smiling *Mao*, Cy Twombly's luminous abstractions, Joseph Beuys' provocative installations – they're all part of the collection at Berlin's premier contemporary art museum, which picks up where the **Neue Nationalgalerie** (p106) at the Kulturforum leaves off (about 1950). Fans of Beuys will get their fill as the entire western wing is dedicated to the enfant terrible of German late-20th-century art. Robert Rauschenberg, Roy Lichtenstein, Anselm Kiefer and Keith Haring are among the artists represented in the east wing. There are also visiting exhibits, an evening programme of concerts, lectures, films and meet-the-artist sessions.

At least as interesting as the art (and to some, perhaps even more so) is the architecture of the building, a former late-neoclassical train station converted by Josef Paul Kleinhues into a gallery space. The main hall, a lofty affair with iron girders decoratively exposed, is a perfect setting for megasized canvases, installations and sculptures. The gleaming white façade exudes great elegance and surprising dignity, especially at night when a light installation by the late Dan Flavin bathes the building in mystical blues and greens.

MUSEUM FÜR NATURKUNDE

Map pp322-4

☎ 2093 8591; www.museum.hu-berlin.de; Invalidenstrasse 43; adult/concession €3.50/2; 🕙 9.30am-5pm Tue-Fri, 10am-6pm Sat & Sun; U-Bahn Zinnowitzer Strasse

With over 25 million items, the collection of the Humboldt University–affiliated Museum für Naturkunde (Natural History Museum) is one of the largest in the world. Only a fraction can be displayed but it includes some showstoppers. The **Dinosaur Hall** contains the museum's star, a 23m-long and 12m-tall brachiosaurus. The world's largest exhibited dinosaur skeleton has a place of honour in the museum's prettiest room. Also here is a specimen of a fossilised archaeopteryx, the species that forms the evolutionary link between reptiles and birds.

There's plenty more including the largest piece of amber ever found, meteorites from Mars and a spectacular dioramas. Children are delighted by 'Bobby' (1925–35), a stuffed gorilla that was the first such animal raised in captivity to adulthood.

TIERGARTEN

Eating pp168–9; Shopping p229; Sleeping pp245–6

Named for the sprawling urban park, the Tiergarten district languished for decades on the edge of western Berlin, but is now once again a vital link between the city's western and eastern halves. Newly revitalised and, for the most part, upmarket, it received the lion's share of new construction and is home to two of Berlin's most exciting and important megadevelopments: the **Regierungsviertel** (Government Quarter) and

Potsdamer Platz, both tourist magnets of the first rank. More architectural treasures await in the quiet streets south of the park, which have resumed their historic role as the **Diplomatenviertel** (Diplomatic Quarter). East of here, the museums and galleries of the **Kulturforum** continue to delight art lovers with their world-class collections.

Tiergarten park itself started out as the private hunting grounds of the Great Elector, Friedrich Wilhelm (r 1640–88) and became a park, masterfully landscaped by Peter Lenné, in the 18th century. During the frigid winter of 1946–47, Berliners chopped down virtually all the trees for firewood.

ORIENTATION

Most of the Tiergarten district is taken up by the park, which extends from Zoo station to the Brandenburg Gate, bisected by Strasse des 17 Juni. Germany is governed from the new Regierungsviertel to the northeast, and the Kulturforum and Potsdamer Platz are off its southeastern corner. The Diplomatenviertel is west of here. Moabit and the Lehrter Zentralbahnhof are outside the northern park boundaries.

REGIERUNGSVIERTEL & AROUND

Berlin's new government quarter has sprung up in a horseshoe-shaped bend of the Spree River. Called the Band des Bundes (literally 'Ribbon of the Federation'), it comprises several buildings running in an east–west direction and symbolically joining the two city halves across the Spree.

BUNDESKANZLERAMT Map pp320-1

☎ 01888-400 2526; Willy-Brandt-Strasse 1; closed to the public; S-Bahn Lehrter Stadtbahnhof

The huge Bundeskanzleramt (Federal Chancellery), a sparkling, modern design by Axel Schultes and Charlotte Frank, is the most prominent building in the Band des Bundes. The complex revolves around a nine-storey-high white cube with circular openings that quickly inspired Berliners to nickname the place 'washing machine'. Views from the upper floors, which contain the chancellor's offices and private residence, are reportedly stupendous. Also here are the cabinet meeting room and a super-secure, special-access only floor.

Two lower elongated blocks housing the staff offices flank the cube, giving the compound an 'H' shape if viewed from above. The **Kanzlergarten** (Chancellor's Garden) is west of here, across the river.

The Chancellery generated a storm of controversy even before its occupants had sharpened their pencils. Much of the debate centred on its size (too big) and the design (too modern). Even Chancellor Gerhard Schröder at first distanced himself from the design, which had been, after all, a pet project of his predecessor Helmut Kohl.

The Chancellery is closed to the public but you'll get fine views of the exterior from Moltkebrücke and the northern Spree bank.

HAUS DER KULTUREN DER WELT
Map pp320-1

☎ 397 870; www.hkw.de; John-Foster-Dulles-Allee 10; admission varies; ⏱ 10am-9pm Tue-Sun; bus 100

The extravagant Haus der Kulturen der Welt (House of World Culture) by Hugh Stubbins was the American contribution to the 1957 Interbau, an architecture exhibition that brought top international talent to Berlin. Originally a congress hall, its most striking design element is the gravity-defying parabolic roof, which flops upon the top of the building like a giant manta

Tiergarten Top Five

- Get an eyeful of cutting-edge architecture at **Potsdamer Platz** (p101).
- Pack a picnic for a mellow afternoon beneath the rhododendrons of **Tiergarten Park** (p101).
- Bravely fight vertigo from the top of the sleek **Reichstag** (p99) cupola.
- Study the finer points of Renaissance painting at the **Gemäldegalerie** (p104).
- Treat your ears and eyes to a concert at the otherworldly **Philharmonie** (p106).

ray. Berliners have nicknamed it the 'pregnant oyster'. Alas, the architect's vision outdistanced the technology of the time, causing the roof to partly collapse in 1980. It was faithfully rebuilt and, in 1989, the building was reincarnated as a cultural centre with a busy programme of art exhibits, lectures, seminars, concerts and other performances from around the world.

Chime concerts ring out at noon and 6pm daily from the 68-bell, black marble and bronze **Carillon** – the largest in Europe – just east of here.

MOABIT Map pp320-1

Around U-Bahn station Turmstrasse, along Alt-Moabit

Originally settled by French Huguenots, Moabit is slowly transitioning from blue-collar neighbourhood to trendy new district for government employees. The **Bundesinnenministerium** (Federal Ministry of the Interior) occupies futuristic riverfront digs at Alt-Moabit 98, and such residential developments as **'The Snake'** (p100) are attracting scores of government desk jockeys. Changes are likely to be even more dramatic once the **Lehrter Zentralbahnhof**, Berlin's futuristic central train station, starts operating, perhaps even in time for the soccer World Cup in 2006.

For now Moabit's few charms can be explored on an easy stroll. From U-Bahn station Turmstrasse, the area's commercial heart, head north to the **Arminius Markthalle** (Bremer Strasse 9), the nicest of Berlin's turn-of-the-20th-century market halls. South of here, along the road called Alt-Moabit, is the **Spree-Bogen Complex**, with the Ministry of the Interior, and the **St Johanniskirche** (1835), an early work by Schinkel fronted by an arcaded Italianate portico. Farther east lays the vast **Justizzentrum** (Centre of Justice), which incorporates courts and a fortress-like prison that has hosted such top crooks as Red Army Faction (RAF) terrorists, Erich Honecker and Stasi director Erich Mielke.

PAUL-LÖBE-HAUS & MARIE-ELISA-BETH-LÜDERS-HAUS Map pp320-1

☎ 2270; Konrad-Adenauer-Strasse & Schiffbauer-damm; S-Bahn Lehrter Stadtbahnhof, Friedrichstrasse

This pair of brand-new buildings facing each other on the Spree north of the Reichstag houses conference rooms and offices for the members of parliament and their staff. A double bridge connects the two across the river in a visual symbol of reunification.

Designed by Stefan Braunfels, both structures echo the design themes of the Bundeskanzleramt (Federal Chancellery; p98) just to the west. The seven-storey Paul-Löbe-Haus has the shape of a double-sided comb. Like a bowling alley built for giants, an atrium extends across the entire 200m length of the building.

The equally striking Marie-Elisabeth-Lüders-Haus houses the parliamentary library and other government-related institutions. Its most eye-catching design elements include a massive tapered stairway, a flat roofline jutting out like a springboard over a plaza, and a cube with giant circular windows containing the library reading room.

Underground tunnels connect both structures to the Bundestag inside the Reichstag. The whimsical-looking building just north of the Paul-Löbe-Haus houses the government day-care centre.

Paul Löbe and Marie-Elisabeth Lüders, by the way, were both strong voices of democracy before and after WWII; both were imprisoned by the Nazis.

Tours of the Paul-Löbe-Haus take place at 2pm and 4pm on Saturday and Sunday but registration is required. Call ☎ 2273 0027 for details or check www.bundestag.de.

REICHSTAG Map pp320-1

☎ 2273 2152; www.bundestag.de; Platz der Republik 1; admission free; ☽ lift to cupola 8am-midnight, last entry 10pm; S-Bahn Unter den Linden, bus 100

Just north of the Brandenburg Gate, the Reichstag has been the seat of the Bundestag, the German parliament, since 1999 following a complete renovation by Lord Norman Foster. The British star architect turned the 1894 building by Paul Wallot into a state-of-the-art parliamentary facility, preserving only the historical shell and adding its most striking contemporary feature: the glistening glass dome.

The quick lift ride to the top is one of the highlights of any Berlin visit, as much for the views of the city as for the mind-bending close-ups of the mirror-clad funnel at the dome's centre. The lift drops you at an outdoor viewing platform at the foot of the dome where there's also a pricey **restaurant** (☽ 9am-midnight). From here you can climb the spiralling ramp inside the dome itself, which, by the way, sits right above the Plenary Hall. There's always a queue for the lift, so prepare for a wait. Note that the dome is closed for cleaning for several days four times a year.

The Reichstag has been at the heart of momentous events in German history. After WWI, Philipp Scheidemann proclaimed the German republic from one of its windows. The Reichstag fire on 27 February 1933 allowed Hitler to blame the communists and seize power. A dozen years later, the victorious Soviets nearly obliterated the building. Restoration – without the dome – wasn't finished until 1972. At midnight on 2 October 1990 the reunification of Germany was enacted here. In the summer of 1995, the Reichstag again made worldwide headlines when Christo (a Bulgarian artist famous for wrapping public places like the Pont Neuf in Paris or an island off the coast of Miami) and his wife, Jeanne-Claude, wrapped

Visiting the Reichstag

Getting to the Reichstag cupola is easy and free and doesn't require reservations. The interior, though, including the Plenary Hall, can only be visited by prior arrangement. Last-minute tickets are occasionally available from the Besucherdienst (Visitor Services) located in the left entrance on the west (main) side of the building.

General guided tours (in German) are offered at 10.30am, 1.30pm, 3.30pm and 7.30pm on Sunday, Monday and holidays. There's also an art and architecture tour at 11.30am on Saturday, Sunday and holidays.

You can also attend a 45-minute lecture about parliament, and the building and its history given on the hour between 9am and 5pm (until 6pm April to October) on weekdays and 10am and 4pm (until 6pm April to October) at weekends. English lectures take place at noon on Tuesdays. It's also possible to attend a plenary session.

All tours and lectures are free but they need to be prebooked. To make arrangements, write to Deutscher Bundestag, Besucherdienst, Platz der Republik 1, 11011 Berlin, or send a fax to 2273 0027. See www.bundestag.de for full details.

the edifice in fabric for two weeks. Lord Norman set to work shortly thereafter

SCHLOSS BELLEVUE & BUNDESPRÄSIDIALAMT Map pp320-1

☎ 200 00; www.bundespraesident.de; Spreeweg 1; closed to the public; S-Bahn Bellevue, bus 100

This chalk-white neoclassical palace built by Philipp Daniel Boumann in 1785 for the youngest brother of Frederick the Great is the Berlin residence of the German president. Kaiser Wilhelm II demoted it to a school, whereas the Nazis moved their Museum of German Ethnology inside. It's right on the Spree, about 1km southwest of the Chancellery.

The president and his staff have their offices in the 1998 **Bundespräsidialamt** just south the palace. This is essentially Germany's version of the 'oval office', which in this case refers to the shape of the entire building: a sleek, beautifully proportioned ellipsis mantled in glass and shiny black granite.

Northeast of the palace across the Spree, in the area east of Paulstrasse, a rather unusual housing development with 718 flats for government employees has sprung up. Most are inside a single 300m-long structure that follows a winding ground plan, which is why it's known as **'The Snake'**.

SIEGESSÄULE Map pp320-1

☎ 391 2961; www.monument-tales.de; Grosser Stern; adult/concession €2.20/1.50, under 8 free; ☼ 9.30am-6.30pm Mon-Fri, 9.30am-7pm Sat & Sun Apr-Oct & 10am-5pm Mon-Fri, 10am-5.30pm Sat & Sun Nov-Mar; bus 100

Like arms of a starfish, five large roads merge into the roundabout called Grosser Stern at the heart of the Tiergarten. At its centre is the landmark Siegessäule (Victory Column), a triumphal column commemorating successful 19th-century Prussian military exploits, notably over Denmark (1864), Austria (1866) and France (1871). The large gilded lady on top (she stands 8.3m tall) predictably represents the goddess of Victory, although locals simply call her 'Gold-Else'. The Nazis moved her here from her previous perch in front of the Reichstag in 1938 and also added a level to the column, which now soars to an impressive 67m. And yes, you can climb to the top. Tickets also entitle you to admission to the small museum and discounts at the adjacent café and beer garden.

The Siegessäule has become a symbol of Berlin's gay community (the city's largest gay publication is named for it) and marks the terminus of the annual Christopher Street Parade. The park around here is a popular cruising spot for gay men, especially around the Löwenbrücke.

Also in the immediate vicinity are a few more **monuments to Prussian glory**, notably the one of Otto von Bismarck designed by Reinhold Begas northeast of the column.

SOWJETISCHES EHRENMAL Map pp320-1

Strasse des 17 Juni; S-Bahn Unter den Linden, bus 100

Just west of the Brandenburg Gate, the Soviet War Memorial commemorates the Red Army soldiers who died fighting in the epic Battle of Berlin. Two Russian tanks said to have been the first to enter the city in 1945 flank the monument. The reddish marble was allegedly scavenged from the ruins of Hitler's chancellery on Wilhelmstrasse. (More of this recycled marble was used in building the Soviet War Memorial in Treptower Park; p140.)

Schloss Bellevue (above)

STRASSE DES 17 JUNI Map pp320-1
S-Bahn Unter den Linden, Tiergarten, bus 100

This broad boulevard originally connected the Berlin City Palace on Unter den Linden with Schloss Charlottenburg and was called Charlottenburger Chaussee. In 1937 Hitler doubled its width and turned it into a triumphal road called, rather mundanely, East-West Axis. Its present name commemorates the 1953 workers' uprising in eastern Berlin (p62), which brought the GDR to the brink of collapse.

TIERGARTEN PARK Map pp320-1
S-Bahn Tiergarten, Bellevue, bus 100

Berlin's 'green lung' bristles with huge shady trees, groomed paths, woodsy groves, lakes and meadows, and is a great place for a jog, picnic or stroll. At 167 hectares, it is one of the world's largest city parks, bisected by the **Strasse des 17 Juni** (see above). In spring, when the rhododendrons erupt in full bloom, the area around Rousseau Island is an oasis from city stresses. On sunny summer weekends, the park becomes a giant grilling party as friends and families gather on the lawns for all day picnics.

POTSDAMER PLATZ & AROUND

A showcase of urban renewal, Potsdamer Platz is perhaps the most visible symbol of the 'New Berlin' and a major tourist attraction. The historical Potsdamer Platz was a busy traffic hub that became synonymous with metropolitan life and entertainment in the early 20th century. In 1924, Europe's first (hand-operated) traffic light was installed here, a replica of which was recently hoisted in the same spot. World War II sucked all life out of Potsdamer Platz and the area soon plunged into a coma, bisected by the Wall until reunification.

In the 1990s, the city tapped an international cast of the finest talents in contemporary architecture, including Arata Isozaki, Rafael Moneo, Richard Rogers and Helmut Jahn, to design 'Potsdamer Platz – The Sequel' based on a master plan by Renzo Piano. Hamstrung by city-imposed building guidelines, the final product, while certainly far from avant-garde, is nevertheless a pleasant and above all human-scale cityscape.

Berliners and visitors have by and large embraced the development, which consists of three sections: DaimlerCity, completed

in 1998; the Sony Center, inaugurated in 2000; and the Beisheim Center, only partly finished at press time. For more information see the Architecture chapter (p48).

For a birds-eye view of the area, you can take what is billed as the world's fastest elevator to the **Panorama Observation Deck** (Map p334; Potsdamer Platz 1; adult/concession €3/2; 11am-8pm Tue-Sun) or sway 150m above ground in a hot-air balloon – tethered safely to the ground – with **Berlin Hi-Flyer** (Map p334; cnr Ebertstrasse & Vossstrasse; adult/concession €19/10; 10am-6pm, weather permitting).

BEISHEIM CENTER Map p334
U/S-Bahn Potsdamer Platz

The final phase in the reconstruction of Potsdamer Platz is the triangular area framed by Lenné-, Bellevue- and Ebertstrasse, the so-called Lennédreieck (Lenné Triangle). Here, Otto Beisheim, one of the wealthiest men in Europe, has put €460 million towards immortalising himself in steel and stone. The five-building Beisheim Center is a complex of luxury apartments, offices and top-end hotels, the Ritz-Carlton and the Marriott. The complex was inspired by classic American skyscraper design; the Ritz-Carlton, for instance, conceived by Hilmer & Sattler and Albrecht, is modelled on the Rockefeller Center in New York.

DAIMLERCHRYSLER CONTEMPORARY
Map p334

2594 1420; Weinhaus Huth, Alte Potsdamer Strasse 5; admission free; 11am-6pm; U/S-Bahn Potsdamer Platz

Fans of 20th-century abstract, conceptual and minimalist art should pop into this loft-like gallery, a quiet and elegant space on the 4th floor of the historic **Weinhaus Huth** (p103). Ring the bell and someone will answer. Changing exhibits show off new acquisitions or selections from the DaimlerChrysler corporation's permanent collection, which ranges from Bauhaus artists like Oscar Schlemmer and Max Bill to international hot shots such as Andy Warhol and Jeff Koons.

DAIMLERCITY Map p334
Btwn Potsdamer Strasse, Landwehrkanal & Linkstrasse; U/S-Bahn Potsdamer Platz

DaimlerCity, which stretches south of Potsdamer Strasse, was the first of the three Potsdamer Platz mega-developments to be completed.

The Ghosts of Vossstrasse

You'd never know it today, but Vossstrasse, just northeast of Potsdamer Platz, was once the political nerve centre of Nazi Germany. Hitler's Neue Reichskanzlei (New Chancellery; 1938) ran for over 400m along almost the entire length of the street. Hitler's head architect, Albert Speer, worked some 4000 people through a gruelling 24-hour schedule, completing the massive structure in only 11 months, two days ahead of schedule.

Only the best building materials would do for the Führer: by all accounts the interior was a lavish mix of marble, bronze, glass and mosaics. After the war, the Russians stripped out all that marble and creatively recycled it in their war memorials in Treptower Park and on Strasse des 17 Juni.

The legendary Führerbunker, where Hitler, Eva Braun and the Goebbels family committed suicide on 30 April 1945, stood just a bit further west. Hitler had the bunker built in 1943 but only spent his last six weeks in it. It was entered through an earlier shelter from 1935, known as the Vorbunker, and was extremely deep. The ceiling plate was 1m below ground, and the roof alone consisted of 30cm-thick concrete topped by 20cm of soil.

After the war, the Soviets tried to blow up the whole thing but the concrete proved impervious to explosives and so they burned and flooded it. The ceiling was reportedly blown up bit by bit until the whole thing caved in. It was filled with rubble during construction of the adjacent apartment building in 1988.

Inaugurated in 1998, it's an attractive space with an open plaza, the **Marlene-Dietrich-Platz**, and interesting architecture by, among others, Rafael Moneo, Arata Isozaki and Renzo Piano. The large pond on its southern end is great for dipping one's toes on a hot summer day.

DaimlerCity is home to a large shopping mall, the **Potsdamer Platz Arkaden** (p229), and packed with entertainment options, including a musical theatre, a casino, several nightclubs, cinemas and scores of restaurants and bars.

Also here is the historic **Weinhaus Huth** (p103) with the **DaimlerChrysler Contemporary** (p101) art gallery.

DaimlerChrysler also sponsored the eight **sculptures** dotted around DaimlerCity. These include Keith Haring's The Boxers on Eichhornstrasse, Jeff Koons' Balloon Flower on Marlene-Dietrich-Platz, Mark Di Suvero's Galileo within the pond, Auke de Vries's Gelandet (Landed) on Schellingstrasse and Robert Rauschenberg's The Riding Bikes on Fontaneplatz.

Three more sculptures are in the atrium of the DaimlerChrysler Building: Jean Tinguely's Méta Maxi, François Morellet's Light Blue and Nam June Paik's Nam Sat.

FILMMUSEUM BERLIN Map p334

☎ 300 9030; www.filmmuseum-berlin.de; Potsdamer Strasse 2; adults/concession € 6/4; ☾ 10am-6pm Tue-Sun, 10am-8pm Thu; U/S-Bahn Potsdamer Strasse

A multimedia journey through German film history and a behind-the-scenes look at special effects are what await visitors to the Filmmuseum Berlin. The museum kicks off with appropriate theatricality as it sends you through a warped mirror room straight from The Cabinet of Dr Caligari.

Major themes include pioneers and early divas, Fritz Lang's silent epic Metropolis, Leni Riefenstahl's awe-inspiring Nazi-era Olympia (also see the boxed text, p30) and post-WWII movies. As she did in real life, though, it is femme fatale Marlene Dietrich who steals the show with selections from her private collection of costumes, personal finery, photographs and documents.

The museum is part of the **Filmhaus**, which also harbours a film school, the terrific **Arsenal** cinemas (p214), a library, a museum shop and the Billy Wilder bistro on the street level.

LEIPZIGER PLATZ Map p334
U/S-Bahn Potsdamer Platz

Just as with Potsdamer Platz, this historical square also being resurrected from the former wasteland of the GDR death strip. Leipziger Platz traces its origin to 1734; it became one of Berlin's most beautiful squares courtesy of the urban planning dream team Schinkel & Lenné. The new incarnation will replicate the original octagonal outline and will be lined with modern buildings adhering to the historical 35m-height limit. Architects include Axel Schultes, creator of the **Bundeskanzleramt** (Federal Chancellery; p98), and Jan Kleihues, son of Josef Paul Kleihues. Buildings will house high-end flats, offices, restaurants, shops and the Canadian Embassy.

SONY CENTER Map p334
www.sonycenter.de; Btwn Potsdamer Strasse, Entlastungsstrasse & Bellevuestrasse; U/S-Bahn Potsdamer Platz

Designed by Helmut Jahn, the Sony Center is one of the most spectacular new developments in Berlin. At its core is a central plaza canopied by a dramatic tentlike glass roof supported by steel beams emanating like the spokes of a bicycle wheel. After dark it is illuminated in constantly changing colours.

With plenty of sitting areas and a fun fountain, the plaza has become a popular place for hanging out and people watching. The buildings orbiting it contain restaurants, stores, a multiplex cinema, the **Filmmuseum** (opposite) and Sony's European headquarters.

Also integrated into the complex is the opulent **Kaisersaal**, the only surviving room of the prewar Hotel Esplanade, the erstwhile belle of Bellevuestrasse. It was moved 75m to its current location with the help of some wizardly technology and completely restored as a gourmet restaurant (p168).

WEINHAUS HUTH Map p334
Alte Potsdamer Strasse 5; U/S-Bahn Potsdamer Platz
This dignified structure, dwarfed by its postmodern neighbours, is the only eyewitness to the original incarnation of Potsdamer Platz. Designed in 1912 by Conrad Heidenreich and Paul Michel, it was one of the first steel frame buildings in town and miraculously survived both WWII and the Berlin Wall. Behind the

Bicycle statue outside Weinhaus Huth (above)

shell-limestone façade is once again a restaurant, **Dieckmann im Weinhaus Huth** (p168) and, on the 4th floor, the breezy galleries of the **DaimlerChrysler Contemporary** (p101).

KULTURFORUM & AROUND
This cluster of top-notch museums and concert venues off the southeastern edge of the Tiergarten was master-planned in the 1950s by Hans Scharoun, one of the era's premier architects. Most of the buildings weren't completed until the 1980s.

BAUHAUS ARCHIV/MUSEUM FÜR GESTALTUNG Map pp330-1
☎ 254 0020; www.bauhaus.de; Klingelhöferstrasse 14; adult/concession €4/2; ☉ 10am-5pm Wed-Mon; U-Bahn Nollendorfplatz; bus 100
From a distance the parallel rows of gleaming white shed roofs look a bit like the smokestacks of an ocean liner. The striking silhouette of the Bauhaus Archive/Museum of Design has been a firm fixture on Berlin's cultural landscape since opening day in 1979. Walter Gropius himself, the founder of the Bauhaus school (1919–33), came up with this avant-garde design, even though he didn't live long enough to witness its completion.

Behind the warped walls, exhibits document the enormous influence the Bauhaus exerted on all aspects of modern architecture and design. The collection includes everything from study notes to workshop pieces to photographs, models, blueprints and documents by such Bauhaus members as Klee, Kandinsky, Schlemmer, Feininger and many others. Prized collection highlights include the original model of the 1925 Bauhaus building in Dessau by Gropius and a reconstruction of Lázló Moholy-Nagy's *Licht-Raum-Modulator* (Light-Space-Modulator), a unique kinetic sculpture that combines colour, light and movement.

DIPLOMATENVIERTEL Map pp330-1
South of Tiergarten btwn Stauffenberg- & Klingelhöferstrasse & Landwehrkanal; bus 200
After WWI several embassies began moving into the quiet, villa-studded colony south of the Tiergarten, which had long been popular with Berlin's cultural elite; the Brothers Grimm and the poet Hoffman von Fallersleben were among those residing here in the 19th century. It was Hitler's chief architect Albert Speer who first coined the term Diplomatenviertel and arranged for other countries, including Italy and

Top Five WWII Sites

- Gedenkstätte Deutscher Widerstand (this page)
- Holocaust Memorial (p81)
- Museum Berlin-Karlshorst (p146)
- Sowjetisches Ehrenmal (Soviet War Memorial; p140)
- Topographie des Terrors (p124)

Japan, to move to the district. WWII practically obliterated the area, which was left in a state of quiet decay while the embassies all set up in Bonn. Reunification sparked a construction boom and the quarter has become a showcase of great contemporary architecture. For details, see the Architecture chapter, p48.

GEDENKSTÄTTE DEUTSCHER WIDERSTAND Map p334

☎ 2699 5000; Stauffenbergstrasse 13-14; admission free; ☷ 9am-6pm Mon-Fri, 9am-8pm Thu, 10am-6pm Sat & Sun; U-Bahn Mendelssohn-Bartholdy-Park, bus 200

The German Resistance Memorial Exhibit addresses an important (and often neglected) facet of the Third Reich: homegrown resistance against the Nazi terror regime. Photographs, documents and explanatory panels show how both ordinary and prominent Germans risked their life and livelihood to thwart Hitler's mob. Among them were artists such as Ernst Barlach and Käthe Kollwitz, scientists such as Carl von Ossietzsky, theologians such as Dietrich Bonhoeffer, exiles such as Thomas Mann, and university students such as Hans and Sophie Scholl, to name just a few.

The exhibit is in the Bendlerblock, a vast complex that housed the Wehrmacht headquarters from 1935 to 1945, now the German Defense Ministry. In this building a group of officers, led by Claus Schenk Graf von Stauffenberg, plotted the bold but failed assassination attempt on Hitler in 1944. Stauffenberg and his main co-conspirators were shot that night in the building's courtyard. A memorial now honours their legacy. In the aftermath of the foiled coup, over 600 people were arrested and 110 executed, many at Plötzensee Prison, now the Gedenkstätte Plötzensee memorial site (p132). Their photographs cover an entire wall.

All panelling is in German only, but a free English-language audio-guide with excellent information about each of the rooms may be borrowed by leaving some ID or a deposit.

GEMÄLDEGALERIE (SMB) Map p334

☎ 266 2951; www.smpk.de; Matthäikirchplatz 8; adult/concession €6/3, under 16 free, free for everyone last 4hrs Thu, incl same-day admission to Kunstgewerbemuseum, Kupferstichkabinett, Neue Nationalgalerie & Hamburger Bahnhof, Musikinstrumenten-Museum & Kunstgewerbemuseum at Schloss Köpenick; ☷ 10am-6pm Tue-Sun, 10am-10pm Thu; U/S-Bahn Potsdamer Platz

If you only have time for one Kulturforum museum, it should be the Gemäldegalerie (Picture Gallery), a spectacular showcase of European painting from the 13th to the 18th centuries with more than 1300 works on view. It opened in June 1998 in a glorious building designed by contemporary architects Hilmer & Sattler.

The collection is famous for its exceptional quality and breadth. Highlights come from Flemish/Dutch masters including Van Dyk and Rubens; Germans such as Cranach, Dürer and Holbein; Botticelli, Raffael, Titian and other Italians; Frenchmen such as Watteau and de la Tour; Brits including Gainsborough and Reynolds; and Spaniards such as Goya and Velázquez. The museum has one of the world's largest Rembrandt collections, with 16 paintings on display, including the famous *The Man with the Golden Helmet*.

The galleries are accessed from the lofty Great Hall, the building's centrepiece, which has the size and solemnity of a cathedral. Two rows of white columns divide it into three aisles bathed in diffused daylight filtering through circular skylights. It's a suitably elegant setting for the sculptures displayed here until the completion of the **Bodemuseum** (p87) on Museumsinsel.

Admission includes audio-guides with commentary (German or English) on selected paintings. Budget at least two hours.

KUNSTGEWERBEMUSEUM (SMB) Map p334

☎ 266 2951; www.smpk.de; Tiergartenstrasse 6; adult/concession €6/3, under 16 free, free for everyone last 4hrs Thu, incl same-day admission to Gemäldegalerie, Kupferstichkabinett, Neue Nationalgalerie, Hamburger Bahnhof, Musikinstrumenten-Museum & Kunstgewerbemuseum at Schloss Köpenick; ☷ 10am-6pm Tue-Fri, 11am-6pm Sat & Sun; U/S-Bahn Potsdamer Platz

The cavernous Kunstgewerbemuseum (Museum of Applied Arts) brims with decorative objects from the Middle Ages to the present. The vast collections here range from gem-encrusted reliquaries to Art Deco ceramics and modern appliances.

If you want to explore the museum chronologically, start in the medieval section on the ground floor, where church riches dominate. Here, the most precious items include the famous Guelph treasure, with a domed reliquary said to have contained the head of St George, and the baptismal font of Emperor Friedrich Barbarossa. Also keep an eye out for the amazingly ornate silver collection that once belonged to the rich town councillors of Lüneburg in northern Germany.

On the same floor, the Renaissance is represented with delicate Venetian glass, brightly pigmented earthenware called majolica, rich tapestries, elegant furniture and other objects reflective of the exalted lifestyle at court or in a patrician household.

From there it's off to the upper floor, which has a few more Renaissance items but also covers the baroque, neoclassical, Art Nouveau and Art Deco periods. It's an eclectic collection that includes historical board games, amazing works in ivory and porcelain from such famous manufacturers as Meissen, KPM and Nymphenburg. The Chinese Room from the Graneri Palace in Turin, Italy, is another highlight.

The basement houses the so-called New Collection, showcasing international 20th- and 21st-century glass, ceramics, jewellery and utilitarian products, including furniture by Michael Thonet, Charles Eames, Philippe Starck and other top practitioners.

KUPFERSTICHKABINETT (SMB)

Map p334

☎ 266 2951; www.smpk.de; Matthäikirchplatz 8; adult/concession €6/3, under 16 free, free for everyone last 4hrs on Thu, incl same-day admission to Kunstgewerbemuseum, Gemäldegalerie, Neue Nationalgaleri, Hamburger Bahnhof, Musikinstrumenten-Museum & Kunstgewerbemuseum at Schloss Köpenick; ☉ 10am-6pm Tue-Fri, 11am-6pm Sat & Sun; U/S-Bahn Potsdamer Platz

The Kupferstichkabinett (Museum of Prints & Drawings) has one of the world's finest and largest collections of graphics, including hand-illustrated books, illuminated manuscripts, drawings and prints produced in all major European countries from the 14th century onward. All the household names are represented, from Dürer to Botticelli, Rembrandt to Schinkel, Picasso to Giacometti.

Because of the light-sensitive nature of these works, only a tiny fraction of the collection can be shown in special exhibits at any given time. This is also the reason for the protective glass casings and muted lighting.

MATTHÄUSKIRCHE Map p334

☎ 261 3676; Matthäikirchplatz; tower admission €1; ☉ noon-6pm Tue-Sun; U/S-Bahn Potsdamer Platz

Standing a bit lost and forlorn within the Kulturforum, the Matthäuskirche is a neo-Romanesque confection designed by Friedrich August Stüler in 1846. Its attractive façade features alternating bands of red brick and ochre tiles. During the Third Reich, it was supposed to be dismantled and transplanted to Spandau to make room for Albert Speer's Germania (see the boxed text, p58). Fortunately the war – and history – took a different turn. Climb the tower for good views of the Kulturforum and Potsdamer Platz.

MUSIKINSTRUMENTEN-MUSEUM
Map p334

☎ 2548 1178; www.mim-berlin.de; Tiergartenstrasse 1; adult/concession €3/1.50, under 16 free, free for everyone last 4hrs Thu, incl admission to Kunstgewerbemuseum, Gemäldegalerie, Neue Nationalgalerie, Kupferstichkabinett, Hamburger Bahnhof, Kunstgewerbemuseum at Schloss Köpenick; ☉ 9am-5pm Mon-Fri, 10am-5pm Sat & Sun; U-Bahn Potsdamer Platz

Harpsichords, medieval trumpets, shepherds' bagpipes and other historical instruments may not start a stampede for tickets. But what about the flute Frederick the Great played to entertain his guests? Or the piano on which Carl Maria von Weber composed Der Freischütz? Or Johann Sebastian Bach's cembalo?

The superb collection of Berlin's Musikinstrumenten-Museum (Musical Instrument Museum) includes all these plus hundreds more treasures from the 16th century to today. There are historical paintings and porcelain figurines, Steinway pianos and curiosities such as a musical walking stick. At several listening stations you can hear what some of the more obscure or antiquated instruments sound like.

A crowd favourite is the Mighty Wurlitzer (1929), an organ with more buttons and keys than a troop of beefeater guards. Demonstrations take place at noon on Saturday. Also on Saturday, at 11am, the museum offers guided tours (€2). Classical concerts, many free, take place throughout the year (ask for a free schedule or check the website).

NEUE NATIONALGALERIE (SMB)

Map p334

☎ 266 2651; www.smpk.de; Potsdamer Strasse 50; adult/concession €6/3, under 16 free, free for everyone last 4hrs Thu, incl same-day admission to Kunstgewerbemuseum, Kupferstichkabinett, Gemäldegalerie, Hamburger Bahnhof, Musikinstrumenten-Museum & Kunstgewerbemuseum at Schloss Köpenick; ☺ 10am-6pm Tue-Fri, 10am-10pm Thu, 11am-6pm Sat & Sun; U/S-Bahn Potsdamer Platz

The first of the Kulturforum museums, the Neue Nationalgalerie (New National Gallery) opened in 1968 as Berlin's main repository of visual art by 20th-century European artists working until 1960. All major genres are represented: cubism (Picasso, Gris Leger), surrealism (Dalì, Miró, Max Ernst), new objectivity (Otto Dix, George Grosz), Bauhaus (Klee, Kandinsky) and, above all, German expressionism (Kirchner, Schmitt-Rottluff, Heckel and other members of *Die Brücke*, an early 20th-century artist's group).

Among many highlights are the warped works of Otto Dix (eg *Old Couple*; 1923), the wonderful 'egghead' figures of George Grosz, and Kirchner's chaotic *Potsdamer Platz* (1914) peopled by a demimonde of prostitutes and revellers. The 11 paintings by Max Beckmann offer a good overview of the artist's work between 1906 and 1942.

While the galleries in the basement present the permanent collection, the ground level – encased in a skin of glass – usually hosts special exhibitions. The sculpture garden out back is a veritable oasis of calm.

The museum building itself is also a work of art. It was designed by Ludwig Mies van der Rohe shortly before his death and is typical of his style, which favoured simple, geometric shapes in solitary settings.

PHILHARMONIE & KAMMERMUSIKSAAL Map p334

☎ 2548 8132; www.berliner-philharmoniker.de; Herbert-von-Karajan-Strasse 1; tours free; ☺ tours 1pm daily (in German); U/S-Bahn Potsdamer Platz

Berlin's premier classical concert venue, the Hans Scharoun–designed Philharmonie boasts almost otherworldly acoustics. This is achieved through a complicated floor plan of three pentagonal levels twisting and angling upward around a central orchestra pit. The audience sits in terraced blocks with perfect views and sound from every angle. From the outside, the 1963 structure with its upward-turning corners looks a bit like a postmodern

Chinese teahouse. In 1981 the honey-coloured aluminium façade was added. It is the permanent base of the Berliner Philharmoniker, one of the world's leading orchestras (p206).

Next door, the **Kammermusiksaal** (Chamber Music Hall), also based on a design by Scharoun, is essentially a smaller version of the Philharmonie to which it is connected by a foyer. It opened in 1987.

SHELL-HAUS Map p334

Reichspietschufer 60; U-Bahn Mendelssohn-Bartholdy-Park

Looking like a giant upright staircase, the eye-catching Shell-Haus is one of the most famous office buildings created during the Weimar Republic. Designed by Emil Fahrenkamp in 1931, it was one of Berlin's earliest steel-frame structures that is concealed beneath a skin of travertine. Its extravagant silhouette is best appreciated from the southern bank of the Landwehrkanal. Recently renovated, it's now the headquarters of Berlin's gas company GASAG.

Shell-Haus (above)

STAATSBIBLIOTHEK ZU BERLIN

Map p334

☎ 2660; www.sbb.spk-berlin.de; Potsdamer Strasse 33; day-use fee €0.50; ☺ 9am-9pm Mon-Fri, to 7pm Sat; free 90-minute tours 10.30am 3rd Sat of the month; U/S-Bahn Potsdamer Platz

The rambling building between Kulturforum and Potsdamer Platz houses part two of the State Library with books published after 1955, ie picking up where the collection at the main branch on Unter den Linden (p83) leaves off. Called 'Stabi' for short, the building was designed by Hans Scharoun and has been open since 1978. It's an academic lending and research library with huge reading rooms.

CHARLOTTENBURG

Eating pp169–80; Shopping pp229–32; Sleeping pp246–9

To anyone travelling to Berlin before the collapse of the Wall, Charlottenburg was the place to go. This was where hotels, restaurants, shops and nightlife clustered. In the 1990s, as all attention turned to Mitte and Prenzlauer Berg, Charlottenburg gradually lost its popularity, but this is not to say that it is no longer worth a visit. Hotels here, although older, offer good value. There's also good shopping and even some exciting new architecture to spice up the bland postwar cityscape.

Charlottenburg was born out of the tragic early death of a beloved queen. When Sophie-Charlotte, wife of King Friedrich I, died in 1705, the king gave town rights to the little settlement that had sprung up around the queen's summer palace and named it in her honour.

The early 20th century saw the founding of the Technische Universität (1884) and the Hochschule der Künste (University of the Arts, 1902). During the Weimar years, Charlottenburg became Berlin's cultural epicentre, with theatres, cabarets, jazz clubs and literary cafés lining its main artery, the fashionable Kurfürstendamm. In fact, much of the unbridled creativity – and decadence – of the Golden Twenties had its roots here. Although considerably tamer these days, Charlottenburg remains a vibrant and interesting part of the city.

ORIENTATION

Charlottenburg, which forms an administrative unit with Wilmersdorf just to the south, is a huge district stretching all the way from the Olympic Stadium in the west to Zoo station in the east. It is bordered by Spandau in the west and Tiergarten and Schöneberg in the east. Tegel Airport is just beyond its northern boundaries. Main arteries include Kurfürstendamm, the famous shopping and entertainment mile; Kantstrasse, which culminates at the Funkturm and trade show grounds; and Hardenbergstrasse and its continuation Otto-Suhr-Allee, which lead straight to Schloss Charlottenburg in northern Charlottenburg. The Olympic Stadium area is in the district's far west, about 6km from Zoo station.

Transport

Bus Zoo station is the main hub for sightseeing favourites Nos 100 and 200 (p281); Nos 109, 110, 119, 129 and 219 travel along Kurfürstendamm; No 145 and X9 for Schloss Charlottenburg; No 149 for the Funkturm and trade fair grounds (via Kantstrasse).

S-Bahn S5, S7 and S9 serve Zoo station from Friedrichshain, Alexanderplatz and Scheunenviertel.

U-Bahn Zoo station is the main hub served by the U2 from Mitte, Tiergarten, Schöneberg, Schloss Charlottenburg and Olympic Stadium; U2 and U7 from Spandau and Kreuzberg/Schöneberg bisect at Bismarckstrasse; U9 to Hansaplatz for northern Tiergarten park.

SCHLOSS CHARLOTTENBURG

Schloss Charlottenburg is an exquisite baroque palace and one of the few remaining sites in Berlin still reflecting the former splendour of the royal Hohenzollern clan. The grand structure you see today has rather modest origins as a petite summer residence built for Sophie-Charlotte, wife of Elector Friedrich III. Originally called Schloss Lietzenburg, it was designed by Arnold Nering and expanded in the vein of Versailles by Johann Friedrich Eosander after the Elector became King Friedrich I in 1701. Later royals dabbled with the

palace, most notably Frederick the Great who hired Georg Wenzeslaus von Knobelsdorff to build the spectacular Neuer Flügel (New Wing, 1746). In the 1780s, Carl Gotthard Langhans added the Schlosstheater (Palace Theatre), which now houses the Museum of Pre- and Early History.

Reconstruction became a priority after WWII and when it was finished in 1966, the restored **equestrian statue of the Great Elector** (1699) by Andreas Schlüter also returned to the courtyard outside the main entrance.

Schloss Charlottenburg is about 3km northwest of Zoo station, backed by a

Charlottenburg Top Five

- Fancy yourself king or queen for a day while roaming around **Schloss Charlottenburg** (p107).
- Discover that history can be fun at the **Story of Berlin** (p114).
- Fall in love with the graceful Nefertiti at the **Ägyptisches Museum** (p110).
- Plunge headlong into the shopping madness of **Kurfürstendamm** (p111).
- Take an inventory of Picasso's genius at the **Sammlung Berggruen** (p111).

lavish park and surrounded by several excellent museums (see Around Schloss Charlottenburg, p110). Each of the palace buildings charges separate admission, but the **Kombinationskarte Charlottenburg** (adult/concession one day €7/5, two days €12/9) is good for all except the lower floor of the Altes Schloss. Seeing the entire complex takes at least a day. Crowds often get huge on weekends and during summer holidays, so show up as early as possible.

ALTES SCHLOSS Map pp320-1
☎ 320 911; Spandauer Damm; www.spsg.de; adult/concession incl guided tour and upper floors € 8/5, upper floors only €2/1.50; ☉ 9am-5pm Tue-Fri, 10am-5pm Sat & Sun, last tour at 4pm; U-Bahn Sophie-Charlotte-Platz, Richard-Wagner-Platz, bus 109, 210, 145

Also known as the Nering-Eosander Building after its two architects, this is the central – and oldest – section of the palace. On the lower floor are the baroque living quarters of Friedrich I and Sophie-Charlotte, which must be visited on a 50-minute tour (in German only, but free English pamphlets are available).

Each room is an extravaganza in stucco, brocade and overall opulence. Highlights include the Oak Gallery (Room 120), a festival hall whose walls are clad in floor-to-ceiling wainscoting and family portraits; the lovely Oval Hall (Room 116), with views of the French gardens and the **Belvedere** (p108); the Audience Chamber (Room 101), filled with Belgian tapestries; Friedrich I's bedchamber, with the first-ever bathroom in a baroque palace (Room 96); the fabulous Porcelain Chamber (Room 95), smothered in Chinese and Japanese blueware from floor to ceiling; and the Eosander Chapel (Room 94), with its trompe l'oeil arches.

Before or after the tour, you are free to explore the upper floor, once the apartment of Friedrich Wilhelm IV. It's filled with paintings,

vases, tapestries, weapons, Meissen porcelain and other items essential to a royal lifestyle. A highlight here is the Silberkammern (Silver Chambers) featuring a sampling of a 2600-piece silver table setting, a wedding gift for Crown Prince Wilhelm. Completed in 1914, WWI and the demise of the monarchy ensured that no royal would ever use it.

BELVEDERE Map pp318-19
☎ 3209 1285; Spandauer Damm; www.spsg.de; adult/concession € 2/1.50; ☉ 10am-5pm Tue-Sun Apr-Oct, noon-4pm Tue-Fri, noon-5pm Sat & Sun Nov-Mar; U-Bahn Sophie-Charlotte-Platz, Richard-Wagner-Platz, bus 109, 210, 145

This pint-size palace in the far northeastern corner of the Schloss gardens got its start in 1788 as a teahouse for Friedrich Wilhelm II. Here he enjoyed reading, listening to chamber music and holding spiritual sessions with fellow members of the mystical Order of the Rosicrucians. These days, the late-rococo vision by Carl Gotthard Langhans makes an elegant backdrop for a prized collection of historic porcelain – tea cups to table settings to vases – by the royal manufacturer KPM.

MAUSOLEUM Map pp318-19
☎ 3209 1280; Spandauer Damm; www.spsg.de; admission €1; ☉ 10am-5pm Tue-Sun Apr-Oct, closed noon-1pm; U-Bahn Sophie-Charlotte-Platz, Richard-Wagner-Platz, bus 109, 210, 145

Framed by trees, near the palace garden's carp pond, the neoclassical Mausoleum (1810) serves as the final resting place of Queen Luise, for whom Christian Daniel Rauch conceived an especially ornate marble sarcophagus.

The temple-like structure was twice expanded to make room for other royals, including Luise's husband, Friedrich Wilhelm III who's in another Rauch tomb. Kaiser Wilhelm I and his second wife Auguste are among those buried in the crypt.

MUSEUM FÜR VOR- UND FRÜHGESCHICHTE (SMB) Map pp318-19
☎ 3267 4811; Spandauer Damm; www.smpk.de; adult/concession € 6/3, under 16 free, free for everyone last 4hrs Thu, ticket also valid for same-day admission to Sammlung Berggruen & Ägyptisches Museum; ☉ 9am-5pm Tue-Fri, 10am-5pm Sat & Sun; U-Bahn Sophie-Charlotte-Platz, Richard-Wagner-Platz, bus 109, 210, 145

The pride and joy of the Museum für Vor- und Frühgeschichte (Museum of Pre- and Early

History) are the antiquities unearthed in 1870 by Heinrich Schliemann in the ancient city of Troy in today's Turkey. After WWII, the Red Army raided the museum, spiriting anything made of gold or silver to Russia where it remains today. The Berliners made replicas of the most important items, which are displayed alongside the many remarkably well-preserved original clay vessels, weapons, jewellery, tools and other objects the Russians left behind.

Elsewhere in the newly revamped museum, which occupies the former palace theatre (Langhans Building), excellent finds from throughout the 'Old World' illustrate the region's cultural evolution from the early Stone Age to the Middle Ages.

NEUER FLÜGEL Map pp320-1

☎ 320 911; Spandauer Damm; www.spsg.de; adult/concession including audio-guide € 5/4; ☻ 10am-6pm Tue-Fri, 11am-6pm Sat & Sun; U-Bahn Sophie-Charlotte-Platz, Richard-Wagner-Platz, bus 109, 210, 145

The reign of Fredrick the Great saw the addition, in 1746, of the Neuer Flügel (New Wing) designed by Knobelsdorff. Here you'll find some of the palace's most beautiful rooms, including the confection-like White Hall, a former banquet room; the Golden Gallery, a rococo fantasy of pale apple-green walls, golden filigree ornamentation and mirrors; and the Concert Room filled with 18th-century paintings by French masters such as Watteau, Boucher and Pesne.

To the right of the staircase are the Winterkammern (Winter Chambers) of Friedrich Wilhelm II in a comparatively austere early neoclassical style. Noteworthy here are the Gobelin tapestries and the Schinkel-designed bedroom of Queen Luise.

You're free to explore on your own, but it's worth following the two audio-tours included in the admission price.

NEUER PAVILLON (SCHINKEL PAVILLON) Map pp320-1

☎ 3209 1212; Spandauer Damm; www.spsg.de; adult/concession with guided tour (summer only) € 2/1.50, without guided tour (winter only) € 1.50/1; ☻ 10am-5pm Tue-Sun; U-Bahn Sophie-Charlotte-Platz, Richard-Wagner-Platz, bus 109, 210, 145

Considered modest as far as Prussian kings go, Friedrich Wilhelm III (r 1797–1848) hired Schinkel to design this small summer palace inspired by a Neapolitan villa. It now houses works by early-19th-century Berlin artists, including Carl Blechen, Eduard Gaertner and Schinkel himself, alongside furnishings, porcelain and sculpture from the same period.

SCHLOSSGARTEN CHARLOTTENBURG Map pp318-19

Spandauer Damm; admission free; U-Bahn Sophie-Charlotte-Platz, Richard-Wagner-Platz, bus 109, 210, 145

The sprawling park behind Schloss Charlottenburg is a favourite spot with Berliners and visitors for strolling, jogging or whiling away a lazy summer afternoon. It was originally laid out in French baroque style, but this was changed when natural English gardens became all the rage at the turn of the 18th century. After WWII, a compromise was struck: the area adjacent to the palace is in the French style and the English park is behind the carp pond. The palace outbuildings – the Belvedere, Mausoleum and Neuer Pavillon – are described earlier in this section.

Schlossgarten Charlottenburg (above)

AROUND SCHLOSS CHARLOTTENBURG

Besides the dazzling splendour of Schloss Charlottenburg, there are five museums in the immediate vicinity, including a couple of definite must-sees.

ABGUSS-SAMMLUNG ANTIKER PLASTIK BERLIN Map pp320-1

☎ 342 4054; www.abguss-sammlung-berlin.de; Schlossstrasse 69b; admission free; ⏰ 2-5pm Thu-Sun; U-Bahn Sophie-Charlotte-Platz, Richard-Wagner-Platz, bus 109, 210, 145

If you are a fan of classical sculpture or simply enjoy the sight of naked guys without noses or other pertinent body parts, make this small collection a definite stopover. With works spanning 3500 years and societies from Minoan to Roman to Byzantine, you will be able to trace the evolution of this ancient art form.

ÄGYPTISCHES MUSEUM (SMB)

Map pp320-1

☎ 3435 7311; www.smpk.de; Schlossstrasse 70; adult/concession € 6/3, under 16 free, free for everyone last 4hrs Thu, tickets also valid for same-day admission to Sammlung Berggruen & Museum of Pre- and Early History; ⏰ 10am-6pm; U-Bahn Sophie-Charlotte-Platz, Richard-Wagner-Platz, bus 109, 210, 145

The undisputed star of Berlin's famous Ägyptisches Museum (Egyptian Museum) – and what everyone comes to see – is the **bust of Queen Nefertiti**, she of the long graceful neck and stunning looks (even after all these years – about 3300, give or take a century or two).

The bust was part of the treasure trove German archaeologists unearthed between 1911 and 1914 while sifting through the dirt around the Nile city of Armana. This was a one-time royal residence founded by Nefertiti's husband Ikhnaton (r 1353–1336 BC) in honour of the sun god Aton. A sculpture of the king himself is a main attention grabber in the darkened and intimately lit main exhibition room. He's surrounded by totemic animal figures, stone reliefs from ancient temples, statues of gods and more busts of royal family members. Objects from everyday life offer glimpses into the cult and culture of this ancient civilisation.

Highlights from later periods include the so-called Berlin Green Head (500 BC), which

Top Five Berlin Freebies

- Enjoy fine views of the city and the warped mirror funnel of the **Reichstag** (p99) dome.
- Grab a picnic for a mellow afternoon by the carp pond of the **Schlossgarten Charlottenburg** (p109).
- Visit the epicentre of the Cold War: **Checkpoint Charlie** (p120).
- See the best of contemporary architecture on a stroll around the **Tiergarten** (p154) district.
- Go museum-hopping from the **Museum für Kommunikation** (p85) to **Stasi – Die Ausstellung** (p85) and the **Haus der Wannsee-Konferenz** (p142).

is an almost expressionistic sculpture carved from green stone, and also the monumental Kalabsha Gate (dated around 20 BC). At press time, the Egyptian Museum was scheduled to move to the upper floor of the Altes Museum on Museumsinsel in Mitte (p86) in August 2005.

BRÖHAN MUSEUM Map pp318-19

☎ 3269 0600; www.broehan-museum.de; Schlossstrasse 1a; adult/concession € 4/2; ⏰ 10am-6pm Tue-Sun; U-Bahn Sophie-Charlotte-Platz, Richard-Wagner-Platz, bus 109, 210, 145

Karl Bröhan (1921–2000) was a man with a passion for furniture and furnishings from the Art Nouveau, Art Deco and functionalism periods. These decorative styles were very much in vogue during the period from 1889 to 1939 and are thus considered the mid-wives of modern design. Bröhan was also an extremely generous man: on his 60th birthday, he donated his entire prized collection to the city of Berlin.

On the ground floor you can wander past outstanding period rooms, each fully furnished and decorated with lamps, porcelain, glass, silver, carpets and other items by such famous designers as Hector Guimard, Émile Ruhlmann and Peter Behrens.

Upstairs, the museum's picture gallery has great works by Berlin Secession painters, including Hans Baluschek, Willy Jaeckel and Walter Leistikow. See Arts for more on the Berliner Secession (p26).

Henry van de Velde (1863–1957), the multi-talented Belgian Art Nouveau artist, gets his own room on the top floor, which is also used for special exhibitions.

HEIMATMUSEUM CHARLOTTENBURG-WILMERSDORF Map pp320-1

☎ 902 913 201; www.heimatmuseum-charlottenburg
-wilmersdorf.de; Schlossstrasse 69; admission free;
🕑 10am-5pm Tue-Fri, 11am-5pm Sat & Sun; U-Bahn
Sophie-Charlotte-Platz, Richard-Wagner-Platz, bus 109,
210, 145

More dynamic than most, this local history
museum mounts as many as 10 changing
exhibits annually, highlighting the traditions,
buildings and people that shaped this district.
The biggest crowds turn out for its Easter and
Christmas shows.

SAMMLUNG BERGGRUEN (SMB)
Map pp318-19

☎ 3269 5811; www.smpk.de; Schlossstrasse 1; adult/
concession €6/3, under 16 free, free for everyone last
4hrs Thu, ticket also valid for same-day admission to
Ägyptisches Museum & Museum of Pre- & Early History;
🕑 10am-6pm Tue-Sun; U-Bahn Sophie-Charlotte-
Platz, Richard-Wagner-Platz, bus 109, 145, 210

A delicacy for fans of Pablo Picasso, the small
but exquisite Berggruen Collection showcases
paintings, drawings and sculpture from all
major creative phases of this Catalán artist.
The early Blue and Rose periods (eg *Seated
Harlequin*, 1905) give way to his bold cubist
canvases (eg the portrait of George Braque,
1910) and the mellow creations of his later
years (eg *The Yellow Pullover*, 1939).

Upstairs it's off to the delicate and emotional world of Paul Klee, with a selection of
works created between 1917 and 1940. There's
also a sprinkling of Cézannes and Van Goghs
alongside African art, which inspired both
Klee and Picasso. Braque and Giacometti are
among the two artists' contemporaries also
represented here.

An excellent 50-minute audio tour is available for hire, although, unfortunately, it's in
German only (€ 3.50/2.50).

KURFÜRSTENDAMM & AROUND

Charlottenburg's main artery, this 3.5km-
long ribbon of commerce started out as a
riding path leading to the royal hunting
palace in the Grunewald forest. Known
as Ku'damm for short, this boulevard got
its current look in the 1880s courtesy of
Bismarck who had it widened, paved and
lined with fancy residential buildings. The
1920s added the luxury hotels and shops,
art galleries, restaurants, theatres and other
entertainment venues that still characterise
the Ku'damm today. Recent updates have
brought some striking new architecture, including Helmut Jahn's Neues Kranzler Eck.

BAHNHOF ZOO Map pp332-3
U/S-Bahn Zoologischer Garten

Gone are the days when Berlin's biggest train
station was the haunt of drug pushers and
child prostitutes, an era graphically portrayed
in *Wir Kinder from Bahnhof Zoo* (The Children
of Bahnhof Zoo), the 1981 biography of the
teenager Christiane F. A few years later, the
train station provided the band U2 inspiration
for the song 'Zoo Station', featured on *Achtung
Baby*. A few seedy characters notwithstanding,
Bahnhof Zoo has seriously cleaned up its act
and is now filled with cafés and shops, many of
which are open late and on Sundays.

BERLINER ZOO & AQUARIUM
Map pp332-3

☎ 254 010; adult/student/child zoo or aquarium €9/7/
4.50, both €14/11/7; U/S-Bahn Zoologischer Garten

An exotic Elephant Gate marks the gateway
to the **Berlin Zoo** (www.zoo-berlin.de; Hardenbergplatz 8; 🕑 9am-6.30pm Apr-Sep, to 6pm
Oct, to 5pm Nov-Feb, 5.30pm Mar), Germany's
oldest animal park and home to some 14,000
furry and feathered denizens from around the
world. Founded by King Friedrich Wilhelm IV
in 1844, its original cast of critters, including
bears and kangaroos, hailed from the royal
family's private zoo on the **Pfaueninsel** (see
p144). These days, perennial crowd pleasers
include cheeky orang-utans, endangered
rhinos, playful penguins and such classics as
giraffes, zebras and elephants. Bao Bao, a rare
giant panda donated by China, enjoys celebrity status among zoo connoisseurs.

Also worth a visit is the adjacent **Aquarium**
(www.aquarium-berlin.de; Budapester Strasse
32; 🕑 9am-6pm year round), which has three
floors of fish, amphibians, insects and reptiles,
including the famous crocodile hall. Elsewhere
you can commune with poison frogs, watch
slithering octopus or meet a real-life 'Nemo'
in the clownfish tank.

EROTIK MUSEUM Map pp332-3

☎ 886 06 66; Joachimstaler Strasse 4; adult/
concession € 5/4, over-18 only; 🕑 9am-midnight;
U/S-Bahn Zoologischer Garten

Relax, it's just sex. Berlin's Erotik Museum
is the brainchild of Beate Uhse, Germany's

Erotik Museum (p111)

late sex-toy marketing queen. Well-lit and sophisticated displays tell the story of human sexuality through the ages. On view are meerschaum-smoking devices engraved with time-honoured themes, extremely funny scrolls from 19th-century Japan, Balinese fertility demons, 'pillow books' and hilarious erotic films from the very early days of cinema. The selection of 17th-century chastity belts elicits lots of giggles, especially from women. Other exhibits focus on the work of gay movement pioneer Magnus Hirschfeld and of Frau Uhse herself.

EUROPA-CENTER Map pp332-3
Breitscheidplatz; U-Bahn Kurfürstendamm

The Europa-Center, a soaring shopping, restaurant and office complex, was Berlin's first high-rise when it opened in 1965. This temple of commerce stands on the site of the Romanisches Café, a legendary hangout of artists and intellectuals – Brecht to Sinclair Lewis to George Grosz – during the heady Golden Twenties. Step inside for a look at the vaguely psychedelic **Flow of Time Clock** by Bernard Gitton, which measures time via a series of vials and spheres filled with vile-looking phosphorous liquid. There's a **BTM tourist office** (p291) on the ground floor of the centre's Budapester Strasse (north) side.

The complex flanks bustling **Breitscheidplatz**, where everyone from footsore tourists to seasoned street performers gathers around the quirky **Weltbrunnen** (World Fountain, 1983) by

Joachim Schmettau. Made from reddish granite it shows a world split open with sculptures of humans and animals clustering in various scenes. Naturally, Berliners have found a nickname for it: Wasserklops (water meatball).

FASANENSTRASSE Map pp332-3
U-Bahn Uhlandstrasse

Galleries, haute couture boutiques and fancy restaurants line Fasanenstrasse, one of Berlin's most fashionable streets, especially between Kurfürstendamm and Lietzenburger Strasse. Nowhere does the aura of Charlottenburg's late 19th-century bourgeois grandeur survive better than on this quiet, leafy avenue lined by palatial townhouses. Sneak a peek into some of their foyers to discover stucco ceilings, romantic murals, marble fireplaces, and creaky wrought-iron or brass lifts resembling giant birdcages.

At Fasanenstrasse 23 is the **Literaturhaus**, where you can attend readings, check out the gallery, browse the bookstore or enjoy some fine café food at the **Café Wintergarten** (p169). Not to be missed is the **Käthe-Kollwitz-Museum** next door (opposite).

JÜDISCHES GEMEINDEHAUS
Map pp332-3

☎ 880 280; Fasanenstrasse 79-80; U-Bahn
Uhlandstrasse

The Jüdisches Gemeindehaus (Jewish Community Centre) has been a Berlin fixture since

1959, drawing visitors with its extensive cultural calendar that includes lectures, readings, concerts and even a Jewish Film Festival held in June. You can leaf through German and international Jewish periodicals in the library, surf the Web in the Internet café and indulge in kosher cuisine at the upstairs **Arche Noah** restaurant (p169).

The centre stands on the site of a once majestic Moorish synagogue destroyed by Nazi thugs during the Kristallnacht pogroms of 9 November 1938. Only the portal has survived. A memorial in the courtyard honours the Holocaust victims.

KAISER-WILHELM-GEDÄCHTNIS-KIRCHE Map pp332-3

☎ 218 5023; Breitscheidplatz; admission free;
🕙 Memorial Hall 10am-4pm or 5pm Mon-Sat, Hall of Worship 9am-7.30pm; U/S-Bahn Kurfürstendamm, Zoologischer Garten

The Kaiser Wilhelm Memorial Church (1895) stands quiet and dignified amid the commercialism engulfing Breitscheidplatz and Kurfürstendamm. Destroyed in 1943 by Allied bombs, the husk of the neo-Romanesque church's west tower is one of Berlin's most haunting and enduring landmarks. It is now home to a **Gedenkhalle** (Memorial Hall), whose mosaics, marble reliefs, liturgical objects and photos from before and after the bombing hint at the church's one-time opulence.

The adjacent octagonal **hall of worship**, added in 1961, has intensely midnight-blue windows and a giant golden Jesus figure 'floating' above the altar.

KANTDREIECK Map pp332-3

Kantstrasse 155; U-Bahn Uhlandstrasse

The award-winning 1994 'Kant Triangle' is Josef Paul Kleihues' most famous Berlin commission. The attractive office building combines a five-storey triangular glass-and-slate base with a 36m-high square tower. At the top is the landmark triangular 'sail' which shifts in the wind like a giant metal weather vane.

KÄTHE-KOLLWITZ-MUSEUM

Map pp332-3

☎ 882 5210; www.kaethe-kollwitz.de; Fasanenstrasse 24; adult/concession € 5/2.50; 🕙 11am-6pm Wed-Mon; U-Bahn Uhlandstrasse

This exquisite small museum is dedicated to Käthe Kollwitz (1867–1945), one of Germany's greatest woman artists (see boxed text p114). Lithographs, graphics, woodcuts, sculptures and drawings are the core of this private collection. Amassed by the late painter and gallery owner Hans Pels-Leusden, it shows the socialist artist's work in all its haunting complexity. Highlights include the antihunger lithography *Brot* (Bread; 1924) and the woodcut series *Krieg* (War; 1922–23). Among her favourite themes were motherhood and death; sometimes the two are strangely intertwined as in works that show death as a nurturing figure, cradling its victims. The collection also includes sculpture, self-portraits and a copy of the Kollwitz memorial by Gustav Seitz, also seen on **Kollwitzplatz** (p129). Two or three special exhibits annually supplement the permanent collection.

Audio-guides (in English, French and German) are available for an additional €3.

LUDWIG-ERHARD-HAUS Map pp332-3

Fasanenstrasse 83-84; U/S-Bahn Zoologischer Garten

Structure, space, skin – the building philosophy of British architect Nicholas Grimshaw is perfectly illustrated in his 1997 Ludwig-Erhard-Haus, a prime example of 'organic' architecture. The armadillo inspired the high-tech design, with its 'rib cage' of steel girders clad in a 'skin' of glass. It houses the Berlin Stock Exchange and the Chamber of Commerce and Industry.

MUSEUM FÜR FOTOGRAFIE

Map pp332-3

Jebensstrasse 2; U/S-Bahn Zoologischer Garten

Helmut Newton, widely regarded as one of the world's finest fashion photographers, donated

Ludwig-Erhard-Haus (above)

Käthe Kollwitz

Käthe Kollwitz (1867–1945) created deeply moving, often heart-wrenching works that capture the depth of human hardship, suffering and sorrow. Through her sculpture and graphic works she expressed a deep commitment to and concern for the suppressed and poor in a timeless and emotional fashion.

Kollwitz was born Käthe Schmidt in Königsberg (today's Kaliningrad, Russia) and, encouraged by her father, attended art schools in Berlin, Munich, Florence and Paris. Upon her return to Berlin in 1891, she married Karl Kollwitz, a physician with a practice on Weissenburger Strasse (today's Kollwitzstrasse), right in the heart of the Prenzlauer Berg working-class slums.

Kollwitz's outlook on life and approach to art were greatly influenced by the misery and poverty she observed daily while walking the streets or helping her husband. This was compounded by personal tragedies, most notably the death of her son in the battlefields of WWI and her grandson in WWII.

Kollwitz became a member of the Berlin Secession (p27) and, in 1919, joined the faculty of the prestigious Academy of Arts. The Nazis forced her resignation in 1933 only to go on to use some of her work for propaganda purposes. Despite being a staunch pacifist and committed socialist, she remained in Berlin until evacuated to the Harz Mountains in May 1943. She died in 1945, shortly before the end of WWII.

a sizeable collection of his works to the city of Berlin shortly before his deadly car accident in January 2004. They will form the core exhibit of the brand-new Museum of Photography scheduled to open in June 2004 in a former art library near Zoo Station. Newton was born in Berlin in 1920 and studied photography with famed fashion photographer YVA before fleeing from the Nazis in 1938. Hours and admission were not available at press time. Check with the tourist offices for updates (see p291).

NEUES KRANZLER ECK Map pp332-3
Cnr Kurfürstendamm & Joachimstaler Strasse; U-Bahn Kurfürstendamm

Helmut Jahn, architect of the Sony Center (p102), also dreamed up this office-and-retail complex (2000), a soaring glass palace with a cool, angular geometry. It's traversed by a pedestrian walkway linking Ku'damm and Kantstrasse that also leads to a courtyard with two giant birdcages. Only the rotunda remains of the historic Café Kranzler that once stood here.

STORY OF BERLIN Map pp332-3
☎ 8872 0100; www.story-of-berlin.de; Kurfürstendamm 207-208; adult/student/child €9.30/7.50/3.50; ❂ 10am-8pm, last admission 6pm; U-Bahn Uhlandstrasse

Inside the Ku'damm Karree shopping mall, the Story of Berlin is a local history museum with a 21st-century high-tech twist. You'll be outfitted with headsets whose narration (in English or German and backed by sound effects) magically activates as you enter each

of the 25 exhibition rooms. Each encapsulates a different epoch in the city's fascinating history, from its founding in 1237 to its days as the Prussian capital, the Golden Twenties and WWII. The Cold War period comes creepily to life during a tour of a still fully functional atomic bunker beneath the building. You'll want to budget at least two hours to experience this multimedia exhibit.

DAS VERBORGENE MUSEUM
Map pp332-3
☎ 313 3464; Schlüterstrasse 70; adult/concession €1.50/0.50; ❂ 3-7pm Thu & Fri, noon-4pm Sat & Sun during exhibits only; S-Bahn Savignyplatz

Founded by a pair of feminist artists and art historians, the small Verborgene Museum (Hidden Museum) gets its name not from having an obscure location but from its artistic focus: the largely forgotten works by early-20th-century Berlin women artists forced into retirement, exile or death by the Nazis. Past exhibits have highlighted the photography of Helmut Newton mentor YVA (her real name was decidedly less glam: Else Ernestine Neuland) and the works of Bauhaus artist Gertrud Arndt and the architect Lucy Hillebrand. Call or check the listings magazines for current shows.

WESTERN CHARLOTTENBURG
FUNKTURM
☎ 3038 2996; Hammarskjöldplatz; ❂ 10am-11pm Tue-Sun, 11am-9pm Mon; adult/concession: €3.60/1.80; U-Bahn Kaiserdamm

The Funkturm (radio tower), nicknamed 'Langer Lulatsch' by Berliners, is by far the most visible structure in western Charlottenburg. Its filigree outline, which bears an uncanny resemblance to Paris' Eiffel Tower, soars 138m into the Berlin sky and has been transmitting signals since 1926. From the viewing platform at 125m or the restaurant at 55m you can enjoy sweeping views of the Grunewald and the western city, as well as the **AVUS**, Germany's first car-racing track, which opened in 1921; AVUS stands for Automobil-, Verkehrs- und Übungsstrecke (auto, traffic and practice track). The Nazis made it part of the autobahn system, which it still is today.

GEORG KOLBE MUSEUM

☎ 304 2144; Sensburger Allee 25; www.georg-kolbe -museum.de; 🕑 10am-5pm Tue-Sun; adult/concession €4/2.50, under 12 free; S-Bahn Heerstrasse

Georg Kolbe (1877–1947) was one of Germany's most influential sculptors in the first half of the 20th century. A member of the Berlin Secession, he distanced himself from traditional sculpture and became a chief exponent of the idealised nude.

After his wife's death in 1927, Kolbe's figures took on a more solemn and emotional air, whereas his later works focus on the athletic male, an approach that found favour with the Nazis.

The attractive museum, in Kolbe's former studio, shows sculptures from all phases of the artist's life alongside temporary exhibits often drawn from his rich personal collection of 20th-century sculpture and paintings. The sculpture garden is an oasis of tranquillity and there's a nice museum café as well.

LE CORBUSIER HAUS

Flatowallee 16; U-Bahn Theodor-Heuss-Platz, then bus 149

Now looking like a typically soulless housing development, this humongous honeycomb was once considered the pinnacle of modern architecture. Some 575 flats are crammed into the 17-storey structure standing on stilts, its monotonous exterior brightened only by a few colour accents.

This was French architect Le Corbusier's (1887–1965) contribution to the 1957 International Building Exhibition (Interbau), and a new type of communal housing that would help remedy the post-WWII housing shortage across Europe. It was the third in a series of complexes he called 'unité d'habitation' (housing unit); the others are in Marseille and Nantes.

Le Corbusier's original plan called for the complex to be an autonomous vertical village, complete with a post office, shops, a school and other infrastructure. In Berlin, though, this vision never came to fruition because of the lack of funding, and the architect later distanced himself from the project.

OLYMPIA STADION

☎ 301 1100; Olympischer Platz 3; exhibit 🕑 10am-6pm Wed & Sun, Glockenturm 9am-6pm Apr-Oct & in good weather otherwise (call ☎ 305 8123 for details); stadium tours €5, adult/concession exhibit €2.50/1.50, Glockenturm €2.50/1; U-Bahn Olympia-Stadion

The Olympic Stadium, built for the 1936 Olympic Games, is one of the best examples of Nazi-era monumentalist architecture. African-American runner Jesse Owens won four gold medals here, shattering Hitler's theory that Aryans were all-powerful *Übermenschen* (a super race). Designed by the brothers Walter and Werner March, the coliseum-like structure replaced an earlier stadium completed by their father Otto in 1913.

Today the stadium is still very much in use for soccer, track and other sporting events. Sections of it remain closed while it is being preened and modernised for the soccer World Cup in 2006. Plans call for a new translucent roof to cover the 76,000 seats. For a preview, visit **Olympia-Stadion – Die Ausstellung**, a multimedia exhibit with cool computer-animated panoramas. There's also a small section documenting the stadium's often turbulent history. You can arrange stadium tours by appointment; they have a 10-person minimum.

The **Maifeld**, a vast field west of the stadium, was used for Nazi mass rallies (it holds more than half a million people) and later became the drilling ground for occupying British forces, which, until 1994, had their headquarters nearby. Today it is used for large-scale pop concerts. On its western edge, the 77m **Glockenturm** (Clock Tower), offers good views over the stadium, the city and the Havel. Check out the Nazi-era bell; it weighs 2.5 tonnes and was rung only twice – to signal the start and the finish of the Olympic Games.

Northwest of here, on the corner of Glockenturmstrasse and Passenheimer Strasse, the **Waldbühne** is a lovely outdoor amphitheatre which was originally built for the Olympic gymnastics competition. It's now a beloved summer venue for concerts, films and other cultural events (see p209).

WILMERSDORF

Eating pp180–1; Sleeping pp249–50

Wilmersdorf does not have much to offer in terms of traditional tourist sights but redeems itself with the vast Grunewald. The former royal hunting terrain is now a sprawling forest and formidable outdoor playground bordered by the Havel River. Freezing Berliners felled about 70% of all the trees to survive harsh winters during WWII and the Berlin Blockade, so what you see today is mostly new-growth forest.

Orientation

Wilmersdorf is a sprawling district bounded by Charlottenburg to the north and Zehlendorf to the south. The Grunewald forest takes up about half of its area. Hotels, restaurants and cafés abound in the eastern reaches where Wilmersdorf meets Charlottenburg and Schöneberg.

Transport

Bus No 218 travels through the Grunewald forest between S-Bahn stations Heerstrasse and Wannsee.

S-Bahn S7 connects Charlottenburg and Wannsee stations via the Grunewald forest; the circular S41 and S42 stops at Halensee and Hohenzollerndamm.

U-Bahn Served by U1 from Friedrichshain, Kreuzberg and Schöneberg; U9 from Zoo station; U7 from Spandau, Kreuzberg and Schöneberg.

GRUNEWALDTURM

☎ 304 1203; Havelchaussee 61; tower ascent €0.50; ☼ 10am–dusk, in summer sometimes to midnight; S-Bahn to Wannsee, then bus 218

With its turrets and ornate details, the 56m neo-gothic Grunewaldturm, near the Havel River, has a dreamy 'Rapunzel' quality, even if it was originally dedicated to a decidedly unromantic Kaiser Wilhelm I. It was designed in 1899 by Franz Schwechter to mark what would have been the emperor's 100th birthday; that's him immortalised in marble in the domed hall in the upper part of the tower. It's worth climbing the 204 steps to the top for views over the river, the suburbs of Gatow and Kladow, and all the way to the **Pfaueninsel** (p144). If the tummy rumbles, the restaurant in the base of the tower serves pretty decent food.

TEUFELSBERG

Teufelsseechaussee; S-Bahn Kaiserdamm

It may have a terrifying name, but at 115m high, the Teufelsberg (Devil's Mountain) in the northern Grunewald forest isn't the Matterhorn. Nonetheless, it is the tallest of Berlin's 20 'rubble mountains' built by Berliners, most of them women, during the cleanup of their bomb-ravaged city after WWII. It took 20 years to pile up 25 million cubic metres of debris.

The hill that was borne from destruction is now a fun zone, especially in snowy winters when you'll find hordes of squealing kids tobogganing or skiing down the slopes. Older ones try their climbing skills or explore the terrain on mountain bikes, while in autumn colourful kites flutter through the air like swarms of butterflies. The little lake at the bottom of the hill is the **Teufelssee** (not suitable for swimming). Just north of the lake is the moor, Teufelsfenn.

Kammergericht with Königskolonnaden in the foreground, Schöneberg (p118)

SCHÖNEBERG

Eating pp181–4; Shopping pp232–3; Sleeping pp250–1

Schöneberg is a comfortable transition zone between the sedateness of its western neighbour, Wilmersdorf, and the wackiness of Kreuzberg to the east. Tastefully restored 19th-century apartment buildings line residential streets, many of them packed with pubs, cafés and global-village restaurants. Much of the action centres on and around Winterfeldtplatz, which attracts young and old, bohemians and the bourgeois to its farmers market on Wednesdays and Saturdays.

It's hard to imagine that Schöneberg – especially the area around Winterfeldtplatz – was a squatter's stronghold in the 1980s. Pushed out by aggressive gentrification, they've been replaced by upwardly mobile thirtysomethings, including many families. Schöneberg is trendy and moderately chic, its people having the necessary money and education to appreciate the finer things in life.

Schöneberg has also been an active centre of the gay scene since the 1920s, a period vividly chronicled by one-time area resident Christopher Isherwood in *Goodbye to Berlin*. There are plenty of gay haunts around Nollendorfplatz and along Motzstrasse and Fuggerstrasse with all scenes catered for.

Schöneberg's most famous daughter is Marlene Dietrich who grew up on Leberstrasse and is buried in Friedhof Stubenrauchstrasse. Another famous name associated with this district is John F Kennedy. It was at Schöneberg's town hall where he told the world: '*Ich bin ein Berliner*' – I am a Berliner.

ORIENTATION

Schöneberg is framed by Charlottenburg and Wilmersdorf to the west, Tiergarten to the north, Steglitz to the south and Kreuzberg to the east. Key U-Bahn stations are Wittenbergplatz, with the shopping magnet KaDeWe, and Nollendorfplatz, which spills out into the restaurant and entertainment zone around Winterfeldtplatz as well as the 'gay triangle' between Eisenacher- Motz- and Fuggerstrasse. The major roads, Potsdamer Strasse and Hauptstrasse, have a multicultural and slightly seedy flair.

ALTER ST MATTHÄUS-KIRCHHOF

Map pp330-1

☎ 781 1297; Grossgörschenstrasse 12; ☉ 8am-7pm; S-Bahn Yorckstrasse

This pretty cemetery, created in 1856, was a favourite among Berlin's late 19th-century bourgeoisie and is filled with opulent gravestones and memorials. Famous people buried here include the Brothers Grimm and the physician and politician Rudolf Virchow. A tombstone honours Claus Schenk Graf von Stauffenberg and his fellow conspirators executed by the Nazis after their failed assassination attempt on Hitler in 1944. Their bodies were initially buried here, but members of the SS had them exhumed, cremated and their ashes scattered.

Transport

Bus No 119 and 219 travel from the Ku'damm to the KaDeWe; 119 continues to western Kreuzberg, including Tempelhof airport.

S-Bahn S41 and S42 stop at Schöneberg and Innsbrucker Platz stations.

U-Bahn Nollendorfplatz is the main hub served by U1 from Wilmersdorf and Friedrichshain/Kreuzberg, U2 from Charlottenburg and Prenzlauer Berg/Mitte, and the short intra-Schöneberg U4.

Ask at the cemetery office for a pamphlet with names and grave locations of these and other famous Berliners.

GRAVE OF MARLENE DIETRICH

Map pp318-19

☎ 7560 6898; Stubenrauchstrasse 43-45; U-Bahn Friedrich-Wilhelm-Platz

To pay homage to Marlene Dietrich (1901–92), you have to travel to the little **Friedhof Stubenrauchstrasse** in southern Schöneberg. This is where the 'Blue Angel' makes her final home in a not terribly glamorous plot not far from her mother's. Her tombstone says simply 'Marlene' along with the inscription: 'Here I stand on the marker of my days.' Look for the map

Schöneberg Top Three

- Enjoy breakfast and people-watching on market day on **Winterfeldtplatz** (p233).
- Pay homage to the first lady of German cinema: **Marlene Dietrich** (p117).
- Max out your credit card at the **KaDeWe** (p232) department store.

inside the cemetery entrance to locate the grave, which is near the Fehlerstrasse (north) side of the grounds. From the U-Bahn station, walk about 400m northwest on Görresstrasse, cross to Südwestkorso, then continue north on Stubenrauchstrasse; the entrance is on the west side of the street.

KAMMERGERICHT Map pp330-1

☎ 901 50; www.kammergericht.de; Elssholzstrasse 30-33; U-Bahn Kleistpark

West of Kleistpark, the imposing 1913 Kammergericht (Courts of Justice) was the site of the notorious show trials of the Nazi Volksgerichtshof (People's Court) against the participants – real and alleged – in the July 1944 assassination attempt on Hitler. Led by the fanatical judge Roland Freisler, hundreds of people were handed their death sentences here before being executed at Plötzensee prison, now the **Gedenkstätte Plötzensee memorial site** (p132). Freisler, alas, was crushed to death by a falling beam in the court building during an air raid in February 1945, thereby avoiding what would undoubtedly have been a starring role at the Nuremberg Trials.

After the war, the Allies confiscated the building and used it first as the seat of the Allied Control Council, and then, until 1990, as the headquarters of the Allied Air Control. Since 1997, after extensive renovations, it is once again being used as a courthouse.

KÖNIGSKOLONNADEN Map pp330-1

Potsdamer Strasse; U-Bahn Kleistpark

Just north of the U-Bahn station Kleistpark, the graceful sandstone Königskolonnaden (Royal Colonnades) are an incongruously elegant sight on this decidedly utilitarian stretch of Potsdamer Strasse. Richly ornamented with sculptures of angels and gods, they were designed in 1780 by Carl von Gontard (who is famous for the domes atop the Gendarmenmarkt churches, p84) and originally stood on Königsstrasse, now Rathausstrasse, between

today's Rotes Rathaus and Alexanderplatz. In 1910, road construction made it necessary to move them to Schöneberg where they became part of what used to be a botanical garden and now is simply the Kleistpark.

NOLLENDORFPLATZ Map pp330-1

U-Bahn Nollendorfplatz

Paintings and photographs from the early 20th century show Nollendorfplatz as a bustling urban square filled with cafés, theatres and people on parade. It was just this kind of liberal and libertine flair that drew British author Christopher Isherwood, whose writings inspired the movie *Cabaret*, to this area in the 1920s. The apartment building where he rented his modest room still stands nearby at Nollendorfstrasse 17.

To Isherwood, 'Berlin meant boys' and boys he could find aplenty in such famous bars as the Eldorado, haunt of a demimonde that even included Marlene Dietrich and chanteuse Claire Waldorff. The Nazis, of course, put an end to the fun, but not for good. Although the Eldorado never made a comeback, the area south of Nollendorfplatz quickly reprised its role as Berlin's gay mecca after the war and continues to be a major gay nightlife hub today.

Since 1989, a **pink granite triangle plaque** at the south entrance of Nollendorfplatz U-Bahn station commemorates the gay and lesbian victims of the Third Reich. Although rarely talked about, homosexuals suffered tremendously under the Nazis. They were socially ostracised and had to wear pink triangles on their clothing. Many were imprisoned, deported to concentration camps, tortured and murdered.

One of the few buildings on Nollendorfplatz to survive since the Roaring Twenties is the **Metropol Theater**, which started life in 1906 as the Neue Schauspielhaus (New Theatre) and was later taken over by Erwin Piscator (p32). Note the ornate frieze gracing its façade, which is best viewed after dark when it's sensuously lit. The theatre has most recently been used as a party venue (p202).

From Nollendorfplatz, it's only a short walk south on Maassenstrasse to **Winterfeldtplatz**, the site of a popular farmers market on Wednesdays and Saturdays. There are plenty of cafés and restaurants around the square and along its side streets, along with an eclectic assortment of small boutiques. See the Eating (p181) and Shopping (p232) chapters for suggestions. The **St-Matthias-Kirche** overlooks the square.

RATHAUS SCHÖNEBERG Map pp330-1
John-F-Kennedy-Platz; U-Bahn Rathaus Schöneberg

From 1948 to 1990, the Rathaus Schöneberg (Town Hall) was the seat of the West Berlin government, but it is a single day in 1963 for which the building is best remembered. John F Kennedy, the 35th president of the United States, was in town and he was going to speak. From the steps of the Rathaus, the silver-tongued orator flayed the forces of darkness to the east and applauded the powers of light in the west, concluding with the now famous words: 'All free men, wherever they live, are citizens of Berlin. And therefore, as a free man, I take pride in the words: Ich bin ein Berliner.' The adoring crowd of half a million cheered his words all the way into the history books.

There's an even earlier connection between the town hall and the US. In 1950, General Lucius D Clay, commander of the US army in Germany, presented the city with a copy of

the **Liberty Bell** to be installed in the Rathaus clock tower. More than seven million Americans had donated money towards this replica of the Philadelphia original.

A popular **flea market** takes place at weekends outside the town hall (p225).

Berlin's Top Five for Children

- Talk to Bao Bao the panda bear and other beloved critters at the **Berlin Zoo** (p111).
- Push buttons, pull knobs and watch experiments at the **Deutsches Technikmuseum** (p121).
- Splash around the pools and slippery slides of the **Blub Badeparadies** (p222) indoor water park.
- Turn back the hands of time at the farm-themed **Freilichtmuseum Domäne Dahlem** (p142).
- Meet the exotic cast of characters on strings at the **Puppentheater-Museum Berlin** (p139).

KREUZBERG

Eating pp184–6; Shopping pp233–5; Sleeping pp251–2

In many people's minds Kreuzberg is synonymous with chaos, a wild Berlin enclave of militant squatters, violent punks sporting rainbow-coloured Mohicans and anarchic artists. Clichés may be hard to eradicate but a reality check reveals that the radicals now hang out in Friedrichshain, the artists in Mitte and the punks, well, they've been a dying breed for quite some time.

It was reunification that ushered in dramatic change and turned Kreuzberg into the mostly peaceful outpost it is today. No longer a neglected border district, the disappearance of the Berlin Wall positioned Kreuzberg back at the heart of the city. Gentrification was all but inevitable even if it hasn't yet reached all corners of the district. The western half around the Viktoriapark has gone pretty upmarket in recent years. Its nicely restored flats in attractive 19th-century townhouses are popular with middle-class families and young professionals who've outgrown their alternative or even radical youth.

Rents are cheaper and houses less attractive in eastern Kreuzberg, a multicultural mosaic where Turks make up about a third of residents. The area around Kottbusser Tor is practically Berlin's 'Little Istanbul', a bubbling cauldron of Turkish cafés, doner stands and shops that keep their own hours. Whatever is left of Kreuzberg's alternative scene is in this part of town, especially on Oranienstrasse, a major nightlife strip, and its side streets.

ORIENTATION

Kreuzberg forms an administrative unit with Friedrichshain across the Spree, which once separated West and East Berlin. Other surrounding districts are Mitte to the north, Schöneberg to the west and Tempelhof and Neukölln to the south. Two of Berlin's blockbuster attractions, Checkpoint Charlie and the Jewish Museum, are in northern Kreuzberg, close to its border with Mitte.

Transport

Bus No 129 from Potsdamer Platz for Checkpoint Charlie and Oranienstrasse; 143 for the Jüdisches Museum from Alexanderplatz.

S-Bahn S1 and S2 stop at Yorckstrasse in western Kreuzberg.

U-Bahn Served by U1 from Wilmersdorf, Schöneberg and Friedrichshain; U6 and U8 from Mitte; U7 from Schöneberg.

Districts – Kreuzberg

The district is bisected by the Landwehrkanal, which makes for some pleasant strolling, as do the residential streets south of U-Bahn station Mehringdamm. The Viktoriapark area, Bergmannstrasse and Chamissoplatz are especially great for soaking up the local vibe of western Kreuzberg. Kottbusser Damm, by contrast, is the hub of Turkish Kreuzberg in the eastern part of the district. Just north of here, Oranienstrasse is lined with night-time diversions that haven't completely lost their alternative edge.

Kreuzberg Top Five

- Brace for the visual and emotional impact of the extraordinary **Jüdisches Museum** (p122).
- Revisit Cold War history at **Checkpoint Charlie** (this page).
- Discover Berlin's exotic side at the **Türkenmarkt** (Turkish Market; p235).
- Dig up unique treasures at the vintage boutiques on **Bergmannstrasse** (this page).
- Soak up the underwater sounds at the **Liquidrom** (p221).

Districts – Kreuzberg

ABGEORDNETENHAUS Map pp325-7

☎ 2325 2325; www.parlament-berlin.de; Niederkirchner Strasse 5; admission free; 🕑 9am-3pm Mon-Fri; U/S-Bahn Potsdamer Strasse

The stately neo-Renaissance structure across from the **Martin-Gropius-Bau** (p124), technically placing it in Mitte, has been a political power nexus since its late-19th-century days as the house of the Prussian Parliament. Under the Nazis, it went through a stint as a courthouse before being turned into an air force officers' club by Göring, whose ministry was only steps away (see former Reichsluftfahrtsministerium, p121). After reunification, it became the seat of Berlin's state parliament. Free changing exhibits, often featuring the work of emerging Berlin-based artists, are held in the foyer and on the mezzanine level.

ANHALTER BAHNHOF Map pp325-7

Askanischer Platz; S-Bahn Anhalter Bahnhof

Only a forlorn fragment of the entrance portal is left of the Anhalter Bahnhof, once Berlin's finest and busiest railway station, surrounded by luxury hotels and bustling cafés. Marlene Dietrich departed from here for Hollywood, and the king of Italy and the tsar of Russia were among the official visitors arriving at this station. Although badly bombed in WWII, Anhalter Bahnhof remained operational for years but was eventually eclipsed by Ostbahnhof. Not even vociferous protests by Berliners could halt its demolition in 1960.

BERGMANNSTRASSE Map pp325-7

U-Bahn Platz der Luftbrücke, Gneisenaustrasse, Südstern

Bergmannstrasse, which runs from Mehringdamm to Südstern, is a fun road teeming with funky second-hand stores, boutiques, bookshops, restaurants and cafés. A stroll along here is an afternoon well spent. Be sure to swing by **Chamissoplatz** (p120) before continuing on to Marheinekeplatz where the **Marheineke Markthalle** (p235), one of Berlin's few surviving historic market halls, is a main attraction. The red-brick **Passionskirche**, also on the square, often hosts classical and jazz concerts.

Further east you'll pass a cluster of **cemeteries** from the 18th and 19th centuries. Among the notable buried here, Gustav Stresemann, chancellor during the Weimar Republic, is one of the better known. Also here are the architect Martin Gropius, the sculptor Adolf Menzel and Schiller's girlfriend, Charlotte von Kalb.

CHAMISSOPLATZ Map pp325-7

U-Bahn Platz der Luftbrücke

This gorgeous square, with its park and stately 19th-century buildings, was almost unscathed by WWII. Walking around here will warp you right back to another era, an effect that hasn't been lost on film directors who often use these streets as backdrops for films. A restored **Café Achteck** pissoir, an ornate public men's toilet, octagonal in shape and painted poison-frog green, adds another layer of old-time authenticity. On Saturdays the entire neighbourhood turns up for the organic farmers market held on the square from 8am to 2pm.

CHECKPOINT CHARLIE Map pp325-7

Intersection of Friedrichstrasse & Zimmerstrasse; U-Bahn Kochstrasse

Alpha, Bravo, Charlie… The American phonetic alphabet inspired the name of the third Allied checkpoint in post-WWII Berlin. A symbol of the Cold War, Checkpoint Charlie was the main gateway for Allies, other non-Germans and diplomats between the two Berlins from 1961 to 1990. It was here where US and Soviet tanks faced off in October 1961, bringing the world to the brink of WWIII.

To commemorate this historical spot, Checkpoint Charlie has been partially reconstructed. There's a US Army guardhouse (the original is in the Alliierten Museum, p141) and a copy of the famous sign warning 'You are now leaving the American sector' in English, Russian, French and German. Also here are huge photos of an American soldier looking east and a Russian soldier looking west. To learn more about the place and the period, visit the **Haus am Checkpoint Charlie Museum** (p122).

A new office district, with buildings designed by Philip Johnson and other international architects, has sprouted up all around this former death strip.

DEUTSCHES TECHNIKMUSEUM BERLIN Map pp330-1

☎ 902 540; www.dtmb.de; Trebbiner Strasse 9; adult/concession €3/1.50; 9am-5.30pm Tue-Fri, 10am-6pm Sat & Sun; U-Bahn Möckernbrücke, Gleisdreieck

The giant German Museum of Technology is a fantastic place to keep kids entertained for hours. Its 14 departments are loaded with interactive stations, demonstrations and exhibits that examine technology through the ages. There's an entire hall of vintage locomotives and rooms crammed with historic printing presses, early film projectors, old TVs and telephones and lots more. A highlight is the reconstruction of the world's first computer, the Z1 (1938) by Konrad Zuse. All throughout, you'll have plenty of opportunity to push buttons and pull knobs or to watch the friendly museum staff explaining and demonstrating various machines. You may even get to print business cards, make paper, grind corn or step behind the microphone of a mock TV studio.

A wing shaped like a ship, which opened in December 2003, makes a fitting setting for the museum's vast navigational collection. Downstairs there are displays about inland shipping, but if you're pushed for time, head straight upstairs where it's off to the high seas.

Top Five Cold War Sites

- Alliierten Museum (p141)
- Checkpoint Charlie (opposite)
- East Side Gallery (p125)
- Gedenkstätte Hohenschönhausen (Stasi Prison; p146)
- Gedenkstätte Normannenstrasse (Stasi Museum; p146)

Early sea explorations and even controversial subjects such as whaling and the slave trade are all dealt with engagingly. There are plenty of ship models and original vessels, including a WWII-era 'Biber', a one-man U-Boat used to attack anchoring ships, which was effectively a suicide mission: 70% of the soldiers died in their vessels.

Outside, in the sprawling **Museumspark**, you can explore working windmills, a waterwheel, an engine shed and an historical brewery.

Be sure to save some time and energy for the adjacent **Spectrum** (enter from Möckernstrasse 26; admission included). At this fabulous science centre, you can participate in around 250 experiments that playfully explain the laws of physics and other scientific principles. If you ever wondered why the sky's blue or how a battery works, this is the place to get the low-down.

FLUGHAFEN TEMPELHOF Map pp325-7

Tempelhofer Damm & Columbiadamm; U-Bahn Platz der Luftbrücke

When it finally closes in 2005, Flughafen Tempelhof (Airport Tempelhof) can look back on a long and fascinating history. Aircraft have taken to the skies above Tempelhof since aviation pioneer Orville Wright came to town in 1909. The first commercial airport opened in 1923 and by the 1930s Tempelhof had become one of Europe's most important landing strips. The humongous building you see today is the work of Nazi architect Ernst Sagebiel, who also designed Göring's Aviation Ministry (p121).

Tempelhof had its finest hour during the Berlin Airlift when Allied planes took off and landed here every few minutes (also see Luftbrückendenkmal, p123, and the boxed text 'The Berlin Airlift', p61).

FORMER REICHSLUFTFAHRTSMINISTERIUM

Map pp325-7
Leipziger Strasse 5-7; U-Bahn Kochstrasse

A short walk west of Checkpoint Charlie (and technically in Mitte) looms the giant building that was once Hermann's Göring's Reich Aviation Ministry. Designed by Ernst Sagebiel, it is one of the few architectural relics from the Third Reich that – quite ironically – got through the Allied pounding relatively unscathed. It took less than a year to build this huge beehive-like complex honeycombed with over 2000 offices. After the war, the building housed several GDR ministries and in 1990 became headquarters of the Treuhand-Anstalt, the agency charged with privatising East German companies and property. It is now the home of the Federal Finance Ministry.

FRIEDHÖFE VOR DEM HALLESCHEN TOR Map pp325-7

☎ 622 1063; bounded by Mehringdamm, Blücherstrasse, Zossener Strasse & Baruther Strasse; admission free; ⏰ 8am-sunset; U-Bahn Mehringdamm

Founded in 1735, this is Berlin's oldest continuously used cemetery complex. It is also one of the most picturesque and filled with beautiful tombstones, many of artistic merit. Famous Berliners buried here include the architect Georg Wenzeslaus von Knobelsdorff, the painter Antoine Pesne, the writer and literary salon patron Henriette Herz, the poet and painter ETA Hoffmann and the composer Felix Mendelssohn-Bartholdy.

GRUSELKABINETT BERLIN Map pp325-7

☎ 2655 5546; www.gruselkabinett-berlin.de; Schöneberger Strasse 23a; adult/child €7/5; ⏰ 10am-7pm Sun-Tue & Thu, 10am-8pm Fri, noon-8pm Sat; U-Bahn Gleisdreieck, Mendelssohn-Bartoldy-Park, S-Bahn Anhalter Bahnhof

This 'Chamber of Horrors' is housed within a WWII air-raid shelter, once part of a network of bunkers, including Hitler's, which extended for miles beneath the city. A small exhibit in the basement focuses on the shelter's history with a smattering of actual belongings left behind by those once holed up here during the bombing raids. A broken-through section of the wall reveals its 2.13m thickness.

Other exhibits are more hokey than historical. On the ground floor, groaning dummies demonstrate the niceties of medieval surgery techniques, and upstairs you'll be encountering creepy characters while exploring a dark and dank maze. Little kids might find it all a bit too intense.

HAUS AM CHECKPOINT CHARLIE

Map pp325-7

☎ 253 7250; www.mauer-museum.de; Friedrichstrasse 43-45; adult/concession €9.50/5.50; ⏰ 9am-10pm; U-Bahn Kochstrasse

The Cold War years are engagingly chronicled in this private museum, with a strong emphasis on the history and horror of the Berlin Wall. The exhibit is strongest when documenting the courage and ingenuity some GDR citizens displayed in their escapes to the West using hot-

air balloons, tunnels, concealed compartments in cars and even a one-man submarine.

Elsewhere the focus is on major Berlin milestones, including the Berlin Airlift, the 1953 workers' uprising, the construction of the Wall and reunification. You'll also learn about events involving Checkpoint Charlie in particular, such as the stand-off between US and Soviet tanks and the death of would-be escapee Peter Fechtner, who was shot and left to bleed to death in full sight of GDR border guards. Displays are in various languages, including English, and a café is on site as well.

JÜDISCHES MUSEUM Map pp325-7

☎ 2599 3300; www.jmberlin.de; Lindenstrasse 9-14; adult/concession € 5.50/2.50; ⏰ 10am-10pm Mon, 10am-8pm Tue-Sun, last admission 1hr before closing; U-Bahn Hallesches Tor

One of Berlin's must-do sights, the Jüdisches Museum (Jewish Museum) is the largest in Europe. It offers a chronicle of 2000 years of Jewish history in Germany and the community's contributions to culture, art, science and other fields. It's all engagingly presented with listening stations, videos, documents 'hidden' in drawers and other multimedia devices.

The 14 divisions cover every major period from the Roman days to the Middle Ages, the Enlightenment and Emancipation to the Holocaust and, ultimately, to the re-emergence of a new Jewish community in Germany. There are exhibits about individuals, such as the philosopher Moses Mendelssohn, and others about Jewish family and holiday traditions.

Only one section directly deals with the Holocaust, but its horrors are poignantly reflected by the architecture. Designed by Daniel Libeskind, its design is a metaphor for the torturous history of the Jewish people. Zinc-clad walls rise skyward in a sharply angled zigzag ground plan that's an abstract interpretation of a star. Instead of windows, irregular gashes pierce the building's gleaming skin.

The visual symbolism continues on the inside. There's no direct entrance to the museum, which instead is reached through the adjoining baroque building. A steep staircase descends to a trio of stark, intersecting walkways, each so-called 'axis'. The Axis of Exile leads to the **Garden of Exile & Emigration**, a disorienting field of tilted concrete columns. The Axis of the Holocaust leads to the **Holocaust-Tower**, one of the museum's several 'voids' – tomblike empty spaces that symbolise the loss of humanity, culture and life. Only the Axis of Continuity leads to the actual exhibit, but it too is a cumbersome journey along an upward sloping walkway and several steep flights of stairs. Libeskind's architecture is a powerful language indeed.

Tickets include admission to the **Museum Blindenwerkstatt Otto Weidt** in Mitte (p94). Enquire about guided tours in English (€3). There's a café-restaurant in the main building and the museum is wheelchair accessible.

KREUZBERG & VIKTORIAPARK
Map pp325-7
Btwn Kreuzbergstrasse, Methfesselstrasse, Duden-strasse & Katzbachstrasse; U-Bahn Platz der Luftbrücke
Many people know Karl Friedrich Schinkel as one of Berlin's most influential architects but few realise that he's also responsible – at least indirectly – for giving Kreuzberg its name. After Napoleon's defeat by the Prussians in 1815, he was asked to commemorate this triumph with the **Kreuzberg Memorial**, to be installed atop a hill called Tempelhofer Berg. He came up with a pompous cast-iron spire standing taller than a giraffe, which is dramatically decorated with battle scenes and buttressed by a cross-shaped base. 'Kreuz' is the German word for 'cross' and so this is what actually inspired the renaming of the hill and thus the district.

Kreuzberg Memorial (above)

Since the late 19th century, most of the Kreuzberg, which rises 66m, has been given over to the rambling Viktoriapark. Its most distinctive feature is an artificial **waterfall**, which tumbles down a narrow, rock-lined canal on the park's northern side. It empties into a pool anchored by a **fountain** with a statue of Neptune and an ocean nymphet. In these times of empty city coffers, the water spectacle is rarely on. The rather decrepit green gazebo nearby, by the way, is one of the few surviving public *pissoirs* (ornate men's toilets) from the late 19th century. Berliners have nicknamed them **Café Achteck** (Café Octagon) for their shape.

In fine weather, the park is a great place for lounging, taking the kids to the playground or relaxing in the **Golgatha beer garden** (p197). On New Year's Eve, the entire hill becomes party-central with thousands of revellers watching the fireworks and partying till dawn.

KREUZBERG MUSEUM Map pp325-7
☎ 5058 5233; Adalbertstrasse 95a; www.kreuzbergmuseum.de; admission free; ⏰ noon-6pm Wed-Sun; U-Bahn Kottbusser Tor, bus 129, 140, 141
Still a work in progress, this museum chronicles the ups and downs of one of Berlin's most colourful districts, although, for now, through temporary exhibits only. Recent shows have focused on Kreuzberg's gay and lesbian community and on the district's legacy as a hotbed of protest. There's also a small permanent exhibit on the local printing industry, built around an actual historical print shop, although you must call ahead to see it.

KÜNSTLERHAUS BETHANIEN
Map pp325-7
☎ 616 9030; www.bethanien.de; Mariannenplatz 2; admission varies, often free; ⏰ 2-7pm Wed-Sun; U-Bahn Görlitzer Bahnhof
This beautiful building, designed by a trio of Schinkel students, began life in 1847 as a hospital and even employed the later writer and poet Theodor Fontane as a pharmacist. Today it's both a sanctuary and creative laboratory for emerging artists from around the globe, with 25 studios and three exhibition spaces. Check the listings magazines for upcoming shows and events.

LUFTBRÜCKENDENKMAL Map pp325-7
Platz der Luftbrücke; U-Bahn Platz der Luftbrücke
Hunkerharke (hunger rake) is what Berliners – never at a loss for a clever phrase – call the

Luftbrückendenkmal, the memorial that honours all those who participated in keeping the city fed and free during the 1948 Berlin Airlift (see the boxed text, p61). It stands outside Tempelhof Airport, which played a pivotal role in the effort. The trio of spikes represents the three Allied air corridors, while the names of the 79 airmen and other personnel who died during this amazing effort are engraved in the plinth.

MARTIN-GROPIUS-BAU Map pp325-7

☎ 254 860; Niederkirchner Strasse 7; admission & hours vary; U/S-Bahn Potsdamer Platz

One of the most beautiful exhibition spaces in Berlin, the Martin-Gropius-Bau began life in 1881 as a museum of arts and crafts and is now a fitting venue for large-scale travelling shows of international stature. Designed by the great-uncle of Bauhaus founder Walter Gropius, it's a three-storey cube inspired by the elegance and symmetry of Italian Renaissance palaces. A light-filled atrium and façades richly adorned with mosaics and terracotta reliefs are among the distinctive design features. Badly damaged during WWII, the building languished in the shadow of the Wall (there's still a short stretch of the Wall running east along Niederkirchner Strasse) until restored just in time for its 100th anniversary.

Martin-Gropius-Bau (above)

SCHWULES MUSEUM Map pp325-7

☎ 693 1172; www.schwulesmuseum.de; Mehringdamm 61; adult/concession €5/3; ⏰ 2-6pm Wed-Mon, 2-7pm Sat; U-Bahn Mehringdamm

The nonprofit Gay Museum is exhibition space, research centre and community hub rolled into one. Since 1985 volunteers have collected, catalogued and displayed materials on gay history, art and culture. A permanent exhibit is in still in its infancy but the temporary shows are often excellent and hopscotch from serious topics like the Nazi persecution of homosexuals to celebrations of famous gays (eg Oscar Wilde, Rainer Werner Fassbinder). The museum's archive and library upstairs include plenty of English-language publications. Check the listings magazines for upcoming lectures, literary salons and other events.

The museum is in the back courtyard; enter to the left of the Café Melitta Sundström.

TOPOGRAPHIE DES TERRORS

Map pp325-7

☎ 2548 6703; www.topographie.de; Niederkirchner Strasse 8; admission free; ⏰ 10am-8pm May-Sep, 10am-dusk Oct-Apr; U-Bahn Potsdamer Platz, Kochstrasse

West of Checkpoint Charlie, along Niederkirchner Strasse, there once stood some of the most feared institutions of the Third Reich: the Gestapo headquarters, the SS central command, the SS Security Service and, after 1939, the Reich Security Main Office. From their desks, Nazi thugs hatched Holocaust plans and issued arrest orders for political opponents; many of them suffered torture and death in the notorious on-site Gestapo prison. Today the buildings are gone and a ghostly air hangs over the bleak, abandoned grounds, whose creepiness is furthered by a short stretch of Berlin Wall along Niederkirchner Strasse.

Since 1997, this has been the setting for a harrowing open-air exhibit called Topographie des Terrors (Topography of Terror), which is essentially a primer on the Third Reich with particular focus on the historical importance of the site and the brutal institutions that occupied it. Displays are in German, but you can borrow a free audio-guide in English from the information kiosk, which also sells an excellent catalogue (€3). Note that some of the exhibit's photographs may be too graphic for children.

A permanent exhibit space has been planned for many years and is currently projected to open in 2005, but we're not placing any bets.

FRIEDRICHSHAIN

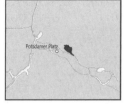

Eating pp186–8; Shopping pp235–6; Sleeping pp252–3

Friedrichshain is today what Mitte and Prenzlauer Berg were in the early to mid-1990s: a gentrification frontier. Rents are low, buildings are still awaiting their face-lifts, and restaurants, bars and clubs retain a pleasingly unpolished edge. Traditionally a working-class quarter, the district is now in vogue with students, artists and other bohemian types without fat bank accounts.

But even Friedrichshain has seen some recent upgrades. The 'workers' palaces' along Karl-Marx-Allee have been restored, the squatters along Rigaer Strasse are mostly gone and new urban development has sprung up along the Spree. Universal Music Germany definitely added a layer of hipness when it moved its headquarters from Hamburg to a converted old warehouse by the Oberbaumbrücke in 2002. And just north of here, a former light bulb factory shines again as the Oberbaumcity, with fancy office space and stylish lofts.

Still, Friedrichshain is unlikely to ever fully emulate Mitte or Prenzlauer Berg. It simply lacks the architectural splendour and historical substance of those districts. Sights are few, but you'll undoubtedly find your way to Simon-Dach-Strasse, the epicentre of the vibrant nightlife scene that gradually extends east as far as the S-Bahn station Ostkreuz. Ostalgie buffs won't want to miss the Karl-Marx-Allee, the GDR's showcase of socialist architecture, and the longest stretch of Berlin Wall, the East Side Gallery.

ORIENTATION

Friedrichshain is the smallest of Berlin's districts. It is bounded to the south by the Spree River, across which it is administratively paired with Kreuzberg. The Volkspark Friedrichshain is on its northern border with Prenzlauer Berg, while the main thoroughfare, the monumental Karl-Marx-Allee, links it with the districts of Mitte to the northwest and Lichtenberg further east.

The main entertainment district, centred on Simon-Dach-Strasse, lays east of Warschauer Strasse, a major north–south route that culminates at the Oberbaumbrücke leading to Kreuzberg. The Oberbaumcity is northeast of the bridge, while on the other side the East Side Gallery parallels the Spree.

Transport

Bus No 140 from Volkspark Friedrichshain to Kreuzberg via Ostbahnhof and Strausberger Platz; No 240 for Simon-Dach-Strasse from Ostbahnhof.

S-Bahn S3, S5, S7 and S9 stop at Ostbahnhof, Warschauer Strasse and Ostkreuz; S8, S41 and S42 stop at Frankfurter Allee and Ostkreuz.

Tram Served by Nos 6 and 7 from Alexanderplatz via Mollstrasse and Landsberger Allee; No 8 from Scheunenviertel; No 20 from Prenzlauer Berg; take No 23 from U/S Warschauer Strasse for Boxhagener Platz.

U-Bahn Served by U1 from Wilmersdorf, Schöneberg and Kreuzberg; U5 from Alexanderplatz along Karl-Marx-Allee.

CAFÉ SYBILLE Map pp322-4

☎ 2935 2203; Karl-Marx-Allee 72; ⏰ 10am-8pm; admission free; U-Bahn Weberwiese

One of the most popular cafés in East Berlin until the fall of the Wall, Café Sybille closed in 1997, but was given a new lease on life in 2001 when it was taken over by the Förderverein Karl-Marx-Allee (Friends of Karl-Marx-Allee). Not merely a spot for coffee and cake, it now functions as an information centre about Karl-Marx-Allee, with an exhibit about its history. The group has installed 39 information markers chronicling milestones on both sides of the street between Strausberger Platz and Proskauer Strasse. Some have been vandalised, but they're great tools for a self-guided tour of this historic boulevard. Nearby, the **Karl-Marx-Buchhandlung** (p236) has books about the GDR, the workers' movement and architecture.

EAST SIDE GALLERY Map pp325-7

Mühlenstrasse; U/S-Bahn Warschauer Strasse

The East Side Gallery is the longest, best-preserved and most interesting stretch of the

Berlin Wall and the one to see if you have little time. Paralleling the Spree, the 1300m-section is an open-air gallery originally created by international artists in 1990. Although partially restored in 2000, the Wall is in trouble thanks to vandals, weather and time. It's still worth a look for its eclectic hotchpotch of political statements, surreal imagery and truly artistic visions. Famous paintings include Birgit Kinder's *Test the Best*, showing a Trabi bursting through the Wall, and *The Mortal Kiss* by Dimitrij Vrubel, showing Erich Honecker and Leonid Brezhnev kissing.

KARL-MARX-ALLEE Map pp322-4
Btwn Alexanderplatz & Frankfurter Tor; U-Bahn Alexanderplatz, Schillingstrasse, Strausberger Platz, Weberwiese, Frankfurter Tor

The monumental Karl-Marx-Allee, leading southeast from Alexanderplatz, is one of the most impressive vestiges of the former East Berlin. This was the GDR's 'first socialist boulevard' and a source of considerable national pride. It provided modern flats for thousands of people and also served as a backdrop for military parades. Until the early 1970s, this was also the 'Ku'damm of the East', lined with shops, cafés, restaurants and even the glamorous, 1000-seat **Kino Kosmos** (p215).

Now newly restored and protected as a historic monument, Karl-Marx-Allee is undergoing a moderate renaissance with bars and businesses bringing new life to the giant boulevard. Its greater importance, though, lies in being a unique open-air showcase of GDR architecture and a perfect metaphor for the inflated sense of importance and grandeur of that country's regime (p127).

It may seem like a long walk, but the best way to appreciate this unique boulevard is on foot. If you're pushed for time, walk 1km or so east of Strausberger Platz. En route, information markers provide excellent historical background in both German and English. **Café Sybille** (p125) is another good place to learn more about this street.

Friedrichshain Top Three

- Walk along the fading glory of the **East Side Gallery** (p125).
- Marvel at socialist monumentalism on the **Karl-Marx-Allee** (this page).
- Greet the sunrise after a night of bar hopping and clubbing (p191).

OBERBAUMBRÜCKE Map pp325-7
U-Bahn Schlesisches Tor, U/S-Bahn Warschauer Strasse

One of Berlin's prettiest bridges, Oberbaumbrücke (1896) links Kreuzberg and Friedrichshain across the Spree. With its jaunty towers and turrets, crenellated walls and arched walkways, it looks very much like a medieval drawbridge leading up to a fortified castle. On the Friedrichshain side is the **East Side Gallery** (p125), the longest stretch of surviving Wall. Rising from the river south of the bridge is a giant aluminium sculpture called **Molecule Man** by American artist Jonathan Borofsky (p139).

OBERBAUMCITY Map pp325-7
Along Rotherstrasse btwn Warschauer Platz & Ehrenbergstrasse; U/S-Bahn Warschauer Strasse

Looking east from the Oberbaumbrücke, it's hard to miss the landmark tower topped by a glass cube, which at night glows in bright colours like a giant Rubik's Cube. The tower is the anchor of the Oberbaumcity, a high-tech office complex recycled from the once derelict buildings of a light bulb factory. Founded in 1906, it was originally called Osram but renamed NARVA in GDR times; over 5000 workers kept the lights on in that country until the factory was closed down in the wake of reunification. As a service centre, the Oberbaumcity hasn't quite taken off as much as developers had hoped and many of the luxurious offices remain empty for now. Still, the complex with its arcades, ornate brick façades and interior courtyards is still worth a quick look.

VOLKSPARK FRIEDRICHSHAIN
Map pp322-4
Am Friedrichshain & Friedenstrasse; bus 100, 200

Berlin's oldest public park was created in the 1840s for the Friedrichshain proletariat by Gustav Meyer, a student of master landscaper Peter Joseph Lenné. It's still a classic neighbourhood park with several playgrounds, tennis courts, a half-pipe for skaters and fun events including a summer outdoor film series.

The park's most attractive feature is the lovely 1913 **Märchenbrunnen** (Fairytale Fountain). It's a neobaroque fantasy in stone with several water basins and over 100 sandstone figures of turtles, frogs and other animals, many inspired by the Brothers Grimm fairytales. In the warmer months, the fountain is a popular cruising spot for gay men.

After WWII the park's landscape changed forever with the creation of a pair of **Bunkerberge** (rubble mountains) made from 2 million

Life in a GDR 'Palace'

When the GDR government decided to build its showpiece road, they didn't pick prestigious Mitte but humble working-class Friedrichshain for its setting. The reasons were both historical and practical. It was along today's Karl-Marx-Allee that the Red Army had snarled its way into Berlin at the end of WWII, almost completely destroying the road in the process.

Karl-Marx-Allee, or rather Stalinallee as it was called until 1961, was built in two phases between 1952 and 1965. A team of six architects led by Hermann Henselmann designed the first and architecturally more interesting section between Strausberger Platz and Frankfurter Tor. Following the diktat of the GDR honchos, they emulated a style called 'national tradition', which blended the so-called Zuckerbäckerstil (wedding-cake style) – then all the rage in Moscow and Leningrad – with more classical, Schinkel-inspired elements.

The result was a 90m-wide boulevard flanked by *Volkspaläste* (people's palaces), concrete behemoths up to 300m long and honeycombed with flats boasting hot water and central heating at a time when many people were still living in postwar squalor. Fancy tiles made in Meissen covered the façades, which would have been more impressive if they didn't keep falling off all the time. The first residents, who moved in on 7 January 1953, were SED party faithful along with a few token workers who'd helped build the palaces.

Phase 2 of Karl-Marx-Allee (1959–65) – between Strausberger Platz and Alexanderplatz – has a decidedly more modern look and marks the first large-scale use of Plattenbau construction using prefab building blocks that would become an epidemic throughout the GDR.

cubic metres of wartime debris piled atop two demolished flak towers. Berliners have nicknamed the taller one (78m) Mont Klamott; it seems at 48m the other one wasn't big enough to inspire its own moniker.

On the park's southern edge is the **Friedhof der Märzgefallenen**, a cemetery for the 183 victims of the revolutionary riots in March 1848, a tumultuous time now also commemorated on the square west of the Brandenburg Gate (p80).

The park's two GDR-era memorials have also survived reunification. Southeast of the fountain, along Friedenstrasse, the **Denkmal der Spanienkämpfer** (Memorial to the Spain Fighters) commemorates the German soldiers who lost their lives fighting fascism in the Spanish Civil War (1936–39). In the northeastern corner, the **Deutsch-Polnisches Ehrenmal** (German-Polish Memorial) honours the joint fight of Polish soldiers and the German resistance against the Nazis during WWII.

PRENZLAUER BERG

Eating pp188–90; Shopping pp236–8; Sleeping pp253–4

Prenzlauer Berg has, in recent years, evolved from a working-class backwater to one of the hippest and prettiest of Berlin's neighbourhoods. The façades that once bore the scars of war have been restored at a furious pace. At the same time, a wonderfully diverse café and pub scene has sprouted. Eager young entrepreneurs have opened up shops, studios, galleries and offices, bringing with them energy, ideas and optimism needed to inject new life and colour into this district.

Even during GDR days, Prenz'lberg – as Berliners refer to it – was a special district. In many ways it was the mirror image of Kreuzberg. Both were frontier districts, wedged against the Wall, neglected and brimming with old, claustrophobic tenements. Both attracted people in search of an alternative lifestyle: avant-garde artists, writers, homosexuals and political activists. Even squatting was prevalent here.

Today, Prenzlauer Berg retains some of its experimental edge, although the area around Kollwitzplatz has been gentrified almost too much for its own good. For a look at a less polished neighbourhood (at least for now), head to Helmholtzplatz north of Danziger Strasse. The currently trendiest strip is along Kastanienallee and its side street Oderberger Strasse, both lined with bohemian cafés and the boutiques of Berlin designers. The area around Schönhauser Allee U-Bahn station is also up-and-coming.

ORIENTATION

Prenzlauer Berg, which was absorbed into the Pankow administrative district in 2001, borders Mitte and Friedrichshain to the south and Wedding to the west. There are three main roads: Greifswalder Strasse, Prenzlauer Allee and Schönhauser Allee. The latter is not only the most interesting but also provides access to most sights, including the Kollwitzplatz area, the Kulturbrauerei and Kastanienallee.

Transport

Bus No 143 connects U-Bahn station Senefelderplatz a with Alexanderplatz, the Nikolaiviertel and the Jüdisches Museum.

S-Bahn S8, S41 and S42 stop at Schönhauser Allee, Prenzlauer Allee, Greifswalder Strasse, Landsberger Allee and Storkower Strasse.

Tram Served by 1 from Scheunenviertel via Prenzlauer Allee; 13 from Scheunenviertel via Kastanienallee; 20 from Friedrichshain.

U-Bahn U2 to/from Charlottenburg, Schöneberg and Mitte stops at Senefelderplatz, Eberswalder Strasse and Schönhauser Allee.

BERLINER PRATER Map pp322-4

☎ 247 6772; Kastanienallee 7-9; U-Bahn Eberswalder Strasse

The Berliner Prater has been serving beer and entertainment since 1852 when it was a popular stopover for people heading out for a day in the countryside. In the early 20th century, the Prater became a hot spot of the local workers' movement. August Bebel and Rosa Luxemburg were among those who fired up the crowds with rousing speeches here. Today, the Prater serves as a secondary stage of the Volksbühne theatre, with its provocative, offbeat productions. In summer, the beer garden is one of the finest in town (p198).

GETHSEMANEKIRCHE Map pp322-4

☎ 445 7745; Stargarder Strasse 77; U-Bahn Schönhauser Allee

This statuesque red-brick church is an 1893 neo-gothic work by August Orth, one of the most important church architects of the late 19th century. It was one of 53 churches financed by the Prussian government in those days in the hopes of creating a 'bulwark against social democracy', especially in such working-class districts as Prenzlauer Berg.

At least in the case of the Gethsemane church their intentions didn't meet with much success. Its congregation has a proud tradition of dissent, both during the Third Reich as well as in GDR times. The church made headlines in 1989 when a peaceful gathering of regime opponents was brutally quashed by the Stasi.

Today, it is at the centre of an increasingly lively section of Prenzlauer Berg and is surrounded by boutiques, cafés and speciality stores.

HUSEMANNSTRASSE Map pp322-4
U-Bahn Eberswalder Strasse

Nostalgia for the 'good old days' spurred the East Berlin government to have this entire street restored into a living museum of 19th-century Berlin, complete with cutesy shops, an old-time post office and atmospheric pubs. The project's completion was timed to coincide with the city's 750th anniversary in 1987. Although it was deemed a success, the sparkling reconstruction only highlighted the dismal condition of the surrounding streets. Husemannstrasse, which was named for a Nazi resistance fighter, still makes for a nice stroll today, even if most shops along here have that commercial, tourist-oriented feel.

JÜDISCHER FRIEDHOF Map pp322-4

☎ 441 9824; Schönhauser Allee 23-25; admission free; ☼ 10am-4pm Mon-Thu, 10am-1pm Fri; U-Bahn Senefelderplatz

This historic, triangular Jewish cemetery hides its leafy grounds behind a thick wall along Schönhauser Allee. It was created in 1827 as Berlin's second Jewish cemetery after the one in Grosse Hamburger Strasse (p93) had been filled to capacity; the last burial here took place in 1976. Many prominent Berliners are interred here, including the composer Giacomo Meyerbeer and the artist Max Liebermann. The Nazis vandalised the place and bombs did additional damage but it has been carefully restored and is dotted with exemplary tombstones and memorials.

Also restored was the so-called **Judengang**, a 10m-wide ritual pathway through which funerary processions originally entered the grounds. It runs for 400m between Kollwitzplatz and Senefelder Platz along the cemetery's eastern wall (enter from Kollwitzplatz).

KOLLWITZPLATZ Map pp322-4
U-Bahn Senefelderplatz

Orbited by trendy bars and restaurants, this leafy square was named for the artist Käthe Kollwitz who lived in the neighbourhood for over 40 years (see boxed text, p113). A 1958 bronze sculpture by Gustav Seitz of the artist anchors the square's little park. It's not terribly flattering, showing Kollwitz as an elderly woman, tired but dignified. Children often leave the excellent nearby playground to clamber around this larger-than-life sculpture or sit in her maternal lap. Kollwitz, who produced an entire series of mother and child drawings, would probably have liked this.

KULTURBRAUEREI Map pp322-4
www.kulturbrauerei-berlin.de; Knaackstrasse 97; U-Bahn Eberswalder Strasse

Towers and turrets, gables and arches; these design features are not usually the stuff of industrial sites. But when, in 1889, renowned architect Franz Schwechten (who also built the Anhalter Bahnhof in Kreuzberg, p120, and the Kaiser Wilhelm Memorial Church in Charlottenburg, p113) got the commission for a new brewery, he pulled out all the stops. The result was a vast complex of 20 ornate red and yellow brick buildings that is nothing short of lovely.

The last bottle of beer was filled in 1967 and the place more or less lingered until 1991 when it was reborn as the Kulturbrauerei (literally 'cultural brewery'), a happening cultural and entertainment centre. After a complete restoration, you'll now find a motley mix of theatre, concert and dance venues, galleries, a nightclub, restaurants, a multiplex cinema and even a supermarket.

The **Sammlung Industrielle Gestaltung** (Collection of Industrial Design; ☎ 4431 7868; adult/concession €2/1; ☺ 1-8pm), near the main entrance on Knaackstrasse, near Danziger Strasse, showcases East German product design dating back to the early days of the '50s.

Prenzlauer Berg Top Four

- Sink your teeth into the city's best *Currywurst* at **Konnopke Imbiss** (p190).
- See a show, eat dinner, do anything at the **Kulturbrauerei** (p129).
- Enjoy a spot of 'urban archaeology' at the **Flohmarkt am Arkonaplatz** (p225).
- Blend in with the Berlin hipsters along **Kastanienallee** (p236).

MAUERPARK & BERNAUER STRASSE
Map pp322-4

Btwn Eberswalder Strasse, Schwedter Strasse, Gleimstrasse & Malmöer Strasse; admission free; ☺ 24hr; U-Bahn Eberswalder Strasse

Not your usual urban oasis, the Mauerpark (Wall Park) occupies a spot right on the former border between East and West Berlin. A small section of the Wall has become the preferred canvas of graffiti artists, although the park's benches and trashcans prove to be pretty popular too. Behind the mound on the southern end is the **Friedrich-Jahn-Stadion**, where Stasi chief Erich Mielke used to cheer on his beloved Dynamo Berlin soccer team. Just north of here, the new **Max-Schmeling-Halle** is the home base of Berlin's hugely successful men's basketball team Alba Berlin.

The Wall ran along Schwedter Strasse, then continued west on Bernauer Strasse. Some of the most spectacular escape attempts took place right along here. Success stories include the day when 57 people burrowed their way to freedom in 1964. Others were less lucky: it was here where a despondent Ida Siekmann leapt to her death from a 3rd-floor window. Multilingual panels set up along the street recall these and other historical moments. For more about the Wall, it's well worth visiting the Gedenkstätte Berliner Mauer (p132) about 1km west of the Mauerpark.

PRENZLAUER BERG MUSEUM
Map pp322-4

☎ 4240 1097; Prenzlauer Allee 227; U-Bahn Senefelderplatz

This local history museum was under restoration at press time but it was expected to reopen in 2004. Call or check with the tourist office for updates.

SYNAGOGE RYKESTRASSE Map pp322-4

☎ 880 280; Rykestrasse 53; ☺ during services only, 6pm Fri winter, 7pm summer & 9.30am Sat; U-Bahn Senefelderplatz

This stately synagogue, built in 1904 in neo-Romanesque style, is the largest in Germany, with seating for around 2000 worshippers. It was the only Jewish house of worship in Berlin to survive both the 1938 Kristallnacht pogroms and Allied bombing, most likely thanks to its off-street location in a back courtyard.

Storm troopers still managed to thoroughly vandalise the interior and later converted the rooms into horse stables. Restored after the war, it served as the sole synagogue of East

Berlin's tiny congregation. The building is open only by appointment and during services, but you can get a peek at the exterior through the wrought-iron gates.

VITRA DESIGN MUSEUM Map pp322-4
www.design-museum.de/berlin
This cutting-edge design museum closed its doors on Kopenhagener Strasse in January 2004. But if all goes according to plan, it will reopen sometime in 2005 as part of the Pfefferberg cultural complex at Schönhauser Allee 176 in southern Prenzlauer Berg. Check with the tourist offices or the website.

WASSERTURM Map pp322-4
Cnr Knaackstrasse & Rykestrasse; U-Bahn Senefelder Platz
Locals affectionately call this handsome brick water tower 'Dicker Hermann' (fat Hermann), but the beloved 1873 landmark also went through a dark spell in its history. Soon after Hitler came to power, the SA turned the tower and the adjacent machine house into an improvised concentration camp where they imprisoned and tortured communists, Jews and other regime opponents. A plaque commemorates this period of unspeakable terror. After the war, the complex was converted into flats; the machine house is now a children's day-care centre.

ZEISS GROSSPLANETARIUM & AROUND Map pp322-4
☎ 4218 4512; www.astw.de; Prenzlauer Allee 80; adult/concession €5/4; show times vary; S-Bahn Prenzlauer Allee
The people of East Berlin were not allowed to see what was across the Wall, but at least they could gaze at the entire universe at this state-of-the-art planetarium. At its 1987 opening, the Zeiss Grossplanetarium was one of the most modern and largest star theatres in Europe. Today, it presents an imaginative schedule of traditional narrated shows (in German), classical music 'under the stars' and children's programming.

The planetarium is near a pair of interesting housing developments. East of its landmark silvery dome, **Ernst-Thälmann-Park** is not only a park but also a model of a high-rise housing development built for the GDR elite in the mid-80s. North of here, between Sültstrasse and Sodtkestrasse, is the 1930 **Flamensiedlung** (Flemish Colony). Inspired by Dutch architecture, Bruno Taut and Franz Hillinger sought to create mass housing without the suffocating density and dreariness that typified the tenement blocks. They added green courtyards, balconies and other features to the designs to help break the monotony and create much needed open spaces.

NORTHERN DISTRICTS

PANKOW
Pankow, Berlin's northernmost district, was once the centre of the East German government elite. Since 2001 it has also incorporated the old districts of Prenzlauer Berg (p127) and Weissensee. Pankow itself has preserved a pleasant, small-town atmosphere but is modest in terms of visitor attractions. Part of its appeal lies in the forests and parks that blanket more than one-third of its area.

Orientation
Pankow's Jewish cemetery is in Weissensee, right on the border with Prenzlauer Berg at the terminus of bus 100. Niederschönhausen is towards the northern end of Pankow about 6km north of Alexanderplatz.

JÜDISCHER FRIEDHOF WEISSENSEE
Map pp318-19
☎ 925 0833; Herbert-Baum-Strasse 45; ☷ 8am-5pm Sun-Thu May-Oct, 8am-4pm Sun-Thu Nov-Apr, 8am-3pm Fri year-round; bus 100
First laid out in 1880, Europe's largest Jewish cemetery is now the final resting place of more than 115,000 people, many of them killed during the Third Reich. Near the main entrance, past the yellow-brick wall, a monument honours victims of the Holocaust. A chart indicates the locations of some of the more prominent cemetery residents, including painter Lesser Ury and publisher Samuel Fischer.

Transport

Bus No 143 goes from Wedding to Kreuzberg via Alexanderplatz and the Jewish Museum; 245 connects Zoo station with Bernauer Strasse.

S-Bahn S8 connects Pankow and Schönefeld airport via Prenzlauer Berg and Friedrichshain; S2 connects Pankow with Mitte and Kreuzberg.

Tram 50 and 52 connect Pankow with Prenzlauer Berg and Mitte; main lines through Wedding are 23 and 24 to Rudolf-Virchow-Klinikum.

U-Bahn Pankow is the northern terminus of the U2; Wedding is served by the U8.

MAJAKOWSKIRING

In GDR-days, this oval ring road, southwest of **Schloss Niederschönhausen** (below), was where the SED party top brass lived side by side with prominent artists, scientists and writers, including Christa Wolf, Arnold Zweig and Hanns Eisler. Nicknamed the 'Städtchen' (little town), it was completely sealed off from the public, lest anyone saw the lavish villas and overall luxury in which their rulers wallowed while denying almost everyone else basic amenities such as a car or telephone. The GDR's first president, Wilhelm Pieck, lived at No 29.

SCHLOSS NIEDERSCHÖNHAUSEN

Ossietzkystrasse; Schloss closed; park ⏲ 8am-sunset; U/S-Bahn Pankow, then tram 52 or 53 to Tschaikowskystrasse

If you could peel away the many layers of alterations and expansions that have been made to Niederschönhausen Palace, you'd get to a modest, two-storey country home built in the 17th century. Elector Friedrich III (later to be King Friedrich I), acquired it in 1691 and had it enlarged by the same architectural team of Nering and Eosander who would later build his Schloss Charlottenburg. An audition, perhaps?

From 1740 to 1797, Frederick the Great's estranged wife Elisabeth Christine lived here and, some 150 years later it became the residence of Wilhelm Pieck, the GDR's first president. Its last official role was as a state guesthouse for visiting dignitaries: yes, Mikhail and Fidel slept here. After the GDR's demise, several so-called Round Table discussions, paving the way to reunification, took place here.

So all in all it's quite a historic site but unfortunately, at least for now, the Schloss remains closed to the public. You can see it from the outside – though it looks pretty dreary and forlorn – and at least enjoy a stroll through the Peter Lennè–designed Schlosspark where the little Panke River flows. Some of the trees here are reportedly over 1000 years old.

Part of the former Berlin Wall, Gedenkstätte Berliner Mauer (p132)

Northern Districts Top Two

- Explore dank and dark WWII bunkers on a tour with **Berliner Unterwelten** (p78).
- Enter a time warp back to the day the Berlin Wall was built at the **Gedenkstätte Berliner Mauer** (p132).

The Berlin Wall

Shortly after midnight on 13 August, 1961 construction began on a barrier that would divide Berlin for 28 years. The Berlin Wall was a desperate measure by a GDR government on the verge of economic and political collapse to stem the exodus of its own people: 2.6 million of them had already left for the west since 1949.

Euphemistically called the 'Anti-Fascist Protection Barrier', this grim symbol of oppression stretched for 160km, turning West Berlin into an island of democracy within a sea of socialism. Continually reinforced and refined over time, its cold concrete slabs – which you could touch or paint on the western side – ultimately backed up against a dangerous no-man's land of barbed wire, mines, attack dogs and watchtowers staffed by loyal border guards ready to gun down anyone trying to escape.

More than 5000 people attempted escape but only about 1600 made it across; most were captured, and 191 were killed – the first only a few days after 13 August. The full extent of the cruelty of the system became blatantly clear on 17 August 1962 when 18-year-old Peter Fechtner was shot during his attempt to flee and was then left to bleed to death while the East German guards looked on.

At the end of the Cold War this potent symbol was eagerly dismantled. Memento seekers chiselled away much of it and entire sections ended up in museums around the world. Most of it, though, was unceremoniously recycled for use in road construction. Today little more than 1.5km of the Wall is left.

WEDDING

When Wedding teamed up with Tiergarten and Mitte during the 2001 district reorganisation, it was a rather mismatched marriage, so to speak. Unlike its southern neighbours, gentrification has largely bypassed this working-class district, which has no grand historic buildings or happening nightlife to brag about. Still, those with an interest in the Wall, which ran right through here, or WWII will find a couple of worthwhile sights to visit.

Orientation

The Berlin Wall ran along Bernauer Strasse, which now separates Wedding from Mitte and continues east into Prenzlauer Berg. Plötzensee is about 4.5km northwest of here.

ANTI-KRIEGS-MUSEUM Map pp320-1

☎ 4549 0110; www.anti-kriegs-museum.de; Brüsseler Strasse 21; admission free; ☺ 4-8pm; U-Bahn Amrumer Strasse

The Anti-War-Museum may be small but it has a big – and timely – message. Erich Friedrich, who founded it in 1925, was an avowed peacenik and author of the book *War against War* (1924). After Nazis destroyed his museum in 1933, he emigrated to Belgium and later joined the French resistance. His grandson, Tommy Spree, reopened the museum in 1982 with objects from both world wars. A staircase descends to an air-raid shelter equipped with bunk beds, gas masks and a 'gas bed' for babies. The Peace Gallery presents changing exhibits.

GEDENKSTÄTTE BERLINER MAUER

Map pp322-4

☎ 464 1030; www.berliner-mauer-dokumentation szentrum.de; Bernauer Strasse 111; admission free; ☺ 10am-5pm Wed-Sun; U-Bahn Bernauer Strasse

The Berlin Wall Memorial combines a documentation centre, an original section of the Wall and a chapel to commemorate the city's division and to honour its victims. The small but high-tech exhibit in the **documentation centre** uses archival material and listening stations to chronicle the events leading up to 13 August 1961 and the early days of the barrier's construction.

Across the street, the **memorial** itself is an artistic rendition of the death strip built against a section of the Wall and falls short of conveying the complete inhumanity of the border. A short walk east on Bernauer Strasse is the **Versöhnungskapelle** (Reconciliation Chapel), noteworthy for its simple but radiant design. It stands on the place of an earlier church, which was destroyed in 1985 to make room for an expansion of the death strip.

GEDENKSTÄTTE PLÖTZENSEE

Map pp320-1

☎ 344 3226; www.gedenkstaette-ploetzensee.de; Hüttigpfad; admission free; ☺ 9am-5pm Mar-Oct, 9am-4pm Nov-Feb; U-Bahn Turmstrasse, then bus TXL

Nearly 3000 people were executed at Plötzensee prison during the Third Reich. The room where the beheadings and hangings took place is now a hauntingly simple memorial. Housed in a plain brick shed, only a steel bar with eight hooks pierces its emptiness. Next door, an exhibit documents the Nazis' perverted justice system, which gleefully handed out death sentences like candy at a parade. Some of the original prison is now a juvenile detention centre.

The cruelty of the prison guards (who received bonuses for each execution) knew no bounds: in a single night in 1943, following an air raid, 186 prisoners were hanged only to prevent them from escaping the partly destroyed prison. A year later, many of the conspirators of the failed assassination attempt on Hitler on 20 July 1944 – and their (mostly uninvolved) relatives and friends, a total of 86 people – were also hanged here, a process the Führer had allegedly captured on film.

An excellent, free, English brochure is available at the desk.

ZUCKER MUSEUM Map pp320-1

☎ 3142 7574; www.dtmb.de/zucker-museum; Amrumer Strasse 32; adult/concession €2.30/1; ☻ 9am-4.30pm Mon-Thu, 11am-6pm Sun; U-Bahn Amrumer Strasse

Those with a 'sweet tooth' might like to check out the quirky Zucker Museum (Sugar Museum), which celebrated its 100th birthday in 2004, making it the world's oldest exhibit of its kind. You'll learn all about the origin of sugar and its chemistry; find out about its uses in the production of vinegar, pesticides and even interior car panelling; and also discover its surprising role in the slave trade.

WESTERN DISTRICTS

SPANDAU

The far west of Berlin is taken up by a single, vast district called Spandau. Its medieval origins are still evident in the well-preserved Altstadt (old town) complete with cobblestone lanes, a traditional market square and medieval church

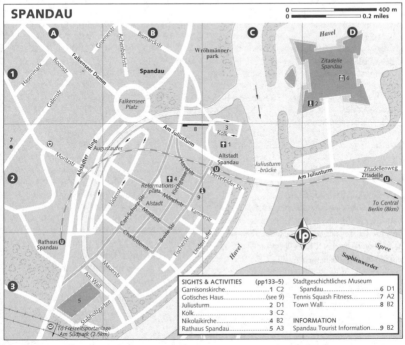

SPANDAU

0 — 400 m
0 — 0.2 miles

SIGHTS & ACTIVITIES	(pp133–5)
Garnisonskirche	1 C2
Gotisches Haus	(see 9)
Juliusturm	2 D1
Kolk	3 C2
Nikolaikirche	4 B2
Rathaus Spandau	5 A3

Stadtgeschichtliches Museum	
Spandau	6 D1
Tennis Squash Fitness	7 A2
Town Wall	8 B2
INFORMATION	
Spandau Tourist Information	9 B2

133

and, the pièce de résistance, an almost entirely intact 16th-century citadel. For nearly 800 years, Spandau thrived as an independent city until being absorbed into Greater Berlin in 1920. Its people, though, remain a fiercely independent bunch who, to this day, talk about 'going to Berlin' when travelling outside their district.

Orientation

Central Spandau is about 10km northwest of Zoo station. Nearly all its sights cluster in the cute Altstadt, which is easily reached by U-Bahn. The Luftwaffenmuseum is about 9km south of here in the suburb of Gatow.

GOTISCHES HAUS Map p133

☎ 333 9388; Breite Strasse 32; admission free; ☯ 10am-5pm Mon-Fri, 10am-1pm Sat; U-Bahn **Altstadt Spandau**

An Altstadt gem, the beautifully restored Gothic House is a rare example of a medieval townhouse made entirely from brick (instead of wood). Considered to be the oldest residential building in Berlin, it houses the Spandau tourist office and changing exhibits. Look for the ornate, Gothic, net-vaulted ceiling.

KOLK Map p133

U-Bahn Altstadt Spandau

The oldest section of Spandau's Altstadt lies north of the busy Strasse am Juliusturm. Toy-sized houses, including several handsome half-timbered ones, line this web of quiet, winding lanes. The **Garnisonskirche** (Garrison Church), also known as Marienkirche, dates from 1848 but was destroyed in WWII and rebuilt in 1964. West of here stands a 78m-long remnant of the medieval **town wall**.

LUFTWAFFENMUSEUM

☎ 3687 2604; www.luftwaffenmuseum.de; Flugplatz Gatow, Gross Glienicker Weg; admission free; ☯ 9am-5pm Tue-Sun, last admission 4pm; U-Bahn Rathaus Spandau, then bus 134 to Gross Glienicker Weg, then bus 334 to Luftwaffenmuseum

About 9km south of Altstadt Spandau, the German Airforce Museum occupies the grounds of the former military airport Berlin-Gatow. Built in 1934–35 as a Nazi air-force academy, it fell under British control after the war, becoming an important lifeline during the 1948 Ber-

Western Districts Top Two

- Play knight and damsel amid the imposing bulwark of the **Zitadelle Spandau** (opposite).
- Take a survey of West German, Allied, Soviet and GDR military planes at the **Luftwaffenmuseum** (this page).

lin Airlift (see the boxed text, p61). When the Army Air Corps left in 1994, the Bundeswehr took over, turning most of the airport into a museum.

An old hangar houses the core of the exhibition, which chronicles the evolution of the Luftwaffe from its inception until the present. Other rooms focus on the history of the airport itself, or house changing themed exhibits. Uniforms and miscellaneous memorabilia are on display in the nearby tower.

Plane buffs will have a field day here with over 100 craft from all eras and various countries on display inside the hangar and on the runways. Biplanes from WWI, a Russian-made MiG-21, the Messerschmidt ME-163 Komet and an Antonov An-14 used by the GDR airforce are just some of the highlights.

NIKOLAIKIRCHE Map p133

☎ 333 5639; Reformationsplatz; admission free, tower €1; ☯ 10am-4pm Wed, 10am-5pm Thu, 2-6pm Fri, 11am-3pm Sat, 2-4pm Sun; U-Bahn Altstadt **Spandau**

The graceful Nikolaikirche (Church of St Nicholas) in the heart of the Altstadt played a pivotal role during the Reformation. In 1539, it hosted the first public Protestant worship service in Brandenburg whose ruler, Elector Joachim II, had adopted the faith. That's him immortalised in bronze outside the church.

The Nikolaikirche was first mentioned in a record of 1240 but the structure you see today dates from the 15th century. The walls of the west tower, which doubled as fortress and watchtower, are up to 3m thick. Guided tower tours are sometimes offered at weekends. You can also climb to the top for impressive views.

The church itself is a three-nave Gothic hall design filled with important treasures, including the bronze **baptismal font** (1398) and the **baroque pulpit** (1714). Pride of place, though, goes to the late-Renaissance **altar** (1582) whose centre panel depicts the Last Supper. During WWII, a wall erected around the altar protected it from the firestorm of 1944.

ZITADELLE SPANDAU Map p133

☎ 354 944 200; www.zitadelle-spandau.de; Strasse am Juliusturm; adult/concession €2.50/1.50, incl museum & tower; ⏲ 9am-5pm Tue-Fri, 10am-5pm Sat & Sun; U-Bahn Zitadelle

The Zitadelle Spandau (Spandau Citadel, 1594), on a little island in the Havel River, is one of the most important and best-preserved Renaissance fortresses in the world. A moat protects it on three sides, while a fourth side opens up to the river. Its layout is classic textbook: a square with each corner protected by an arrowhead-shaped bastion. Its dramatic outline is best appreciated in winter when you can see it through the leafless trees of the surrounding park.

The citadel's most prominent – and oldest – feature is the 13th-century Juliusturm, the crenellated tower in the southwest corner.

The Last Prisoner

Outside of Germany, Spandau is perhaps best known for the Allied War Criminal Prison where several Nazis sentenced at the Nuremberg Trials were jailed. It was a custom-designed prison jointly administered by all four Allies with responsibility rotating between them every month. A flag would show who was in charge at any given time. Despite going to all this trouble, Spandau Prison had only seven inmates, including Karl von Dönitz, Albert Speer and Rudolf Hess. After Speer's release in 1966, Hess was the only remaining prisoner but the operation continued until his death at age 91 in 1987. To prevent it from becoming a neo-Nazi shrine, the building was demolished soon thereafter.

You can climb to the top for decent views over the Havel and Spree Rivers and the Altstadt. From 1873 to 1919 the tower sheltered part of the 'imperial war treasure', ie the reparation payments France had to make to Prussia after losing the war of 1870–81.

History buffs eager to learn more about Spandau should drop into the **Stadtgeschichtliches Museum Spandau** (Spandau City History Museum) in the New Armoury. The fortress also harbours numerous artist studios and creative workshops. Two galleries, one in the **Bastion Kronprinz**, the other in the **Palas** (once the residential wing), present changing art exhibits throughout the year.

The citadel is also hugely popular with **bats**, thousands of which spend the freezing Berlin winters hanging out in its catacombs. The Berliner Artenschutz Team, an organisation dedicated to protecting endangered species, offers guided tours in summer. Registration is mandatory (☎ 3675 0061).

SOUTHERN DISTRICTS
KÖPENICK

At the far southeastern tip of Berlin, Köpenick was administratively merged with Treptow (p139) in 2001 and is exceptionally green with forests and lakes covering about two-thirds of the land. Köpenick has Berlin's largest lake (Müggelsee), largest forest (Köpenicker Stadtforst) and highest natural elevation (Müggelberge, 115m). There's lots of boating, swimming, sailing, windsurfing, rowing and hiking.

Köpenick, the area's third medieval settlement besides Spandau and Berlin, was granted town rights in 1232, a full 30 years before Berlin, from which it remained independent until 1920. Culture and architecture fans have a protected Altstadt, baroque palace and the former fishing village, the Kietz, to look forward to.

Easily reached on the S3 from all major central Berlin S-Bahn stations, Köpenick makes an excellent half-day or day break from the big-city bustle of Berlin. For more information, stop by the **tourist office** (☎ 6548 4340; www.berlin-tourismus-online.de; Alt-Köpenick 34; ☉ 9am-6pm Mon-Fri). Guided one-hour Altstadt tours take place at 10am on Saturday (€5).

Orientation

Köpenick's Altstadt is a tiny area at the convergence of the Spree, Dahme and Müggelspree Rivers. It's about 1.5km south of S-Bahn station Köpenick along Bahnhofstrasse and Lindenstrasse and served by tram 62 or 68. Schloss Köpenick is nearby on a little island in the Dahme, with the Kietz fishing quarter visible across the water looking east. Friedrichshagen and the Müggelsee are about another 3.5km east of the Altstadt.

Transport

Bus In Neukölln, 171 serves Gropiusstadt from Hermannplatz; 104 serves Treptow from Charlottenburg, Schöneberg and Kreuzberg; in Zehlendorf, 115 along Clayallee, 116 for Schloss Glienicke, 218 for Pfaueninsel.

S-Bahn S3 for Köpenick; S8, S9, S41, S42 for Treptow; S1 for Zehlendorf.

Tram From S-Bahn station Köpenick: 62 and 68 for Altstadt; 60 and 61 for Müggelsee; 62 continues to Mahlsdorf.

U-Bahn U7 for Neukölln, U1 for Zehlendorf.

ALTSTADT

Rathaus: ☎ 6172 3351; Alt-Köpenick 21; admission free; ☉ 8am-6pm Mon-Fri, 10am-6pm Sat; S-Bahn Köpenick, then tram 62, 68

Much of Köpenick's Altstadt has recently been restored but many of its ancient cobblestone streets still follow their original, medieval lay-

Rathaus, Köpenick (above)

out. The oldest street is Böttcherstrasse but for the best parade of historic houses go to Strasse Alt-Köpenick which is lined with newly restored 18th-century beauties.

On the same street you'll come across the **Rathaus** (1904, Town Hall), a red-brick, neo-Gothic jumble with frilly turrets and a jutting 54m tower. Also note the step-gabled mock façade typical of northern German architecture. A statue of the legendary Hauptmann von Köpenick guards the main entrance and there's a small exhibit inside telling his story. Further south, Alt-Köpenick runs straight into the Schloss (p138).

GEDENKSTÄTTE KÖPENICKER BLUTWOCHE

☎ 657 1467; Puchanstrasse 12; admission free; ☉ 10am-4.30pm Tue-Wed, 10am-6pm Thu, 2-6pm Sat; S-Bahn Köpenick

In the early 20th century, Köpenick was a traditional stronghold of communists and social democrats. When Hitler rose to power, local workers defiantly flew the red (communist) flag. The Nazis naturally didn't let such provocation pass unpunished. In the week of 21–26 June 1933, the SA arrested and tortured hundreds of workers, killing around 90, the youngest just 18, the oldest 65. Several more died later as a result of their injuries.

The atrocities went down in history as the *Köpenicker Blutwoche* (Köpenick's Bloody Week). Most of the violence took place in the prison of the **Amtsgericht Köpenick** (Courthouse Köpenick), which today houses a small memorial exhibit, including a reconstructed cell. A GDR-era **monument** (1969), showing a raised clenched fist in typical socialist-realist style, honours the victims of the Blutwoche; it's on Platz des 23 April, a square located a quick stroll south of here.

The clenched fist, by the way, has given rise to much debate in the local government, with some members urging its removal. In late 2003 it was finally decided to keep the fist but to redesign the monument in such a way that it is de-emphasised.

The square, by the way, commemorates the date in 1945 when the Red Army arrived in Köpenick.

GROSSER MÜGGELSEE & AROUND

Stern und Kreis Schiffahrt ☎ 536 3600; S-Bahn Friedrichshagen, then tram 60, 61

The Müggelsee is aptly named 'Grosser' (big) for good reason. Measuring 4km in length and 2.5km in width, it's Berlin's largest lake. **Friedrichshagen**, the suburb on the north shore, dates back to 1753 when Frederick the Great brought 100 Bohemian families to the area to grow mulberry trees to feed the silkworms that supplied silk for weaving. At the end of the 19th century, a circle of poets and writers including Gerhart Hauptmann gathered here as well.

From May to October, cruise boats operated by Stern und Kreis Schiffahrt leave from landing docks at the confluence of the Spree and the lake. Several boats daily make the half-hour trip to the forested southern shore with lots of hiking trails.

In summer, there's swimming in the lake at two public pools: **Seebad Friedrichshagen**, just east of the north shore landing docks, and **Strandbad Müggelsee** on the eastern shore in the medieval fishing village of Rahnsdorf.

Southern Districts Top Five

- Give in to the romance and enchantment of the **Pfaueninsel** (p144).
- Look deep into the Russian soul at the **Soviet War Memorial** (p140).
- Learn how the Allies went from occupiers to friends at the **Allied Museum** (p141).
- Take a journey around the world and back in time at the **Museen Dahlem** (p143).
- Escape the city bustle with a day on Berlin's largest lake, the **Müggelsee** (p137).

GRÜNAUER WASSERSPORTMUSEUM

☎ 674 4002; Regattastrasse 191; admission free; ☽ 2-4.30pm Sat; S-Bahn Grünau, then tram 68 to Wassersportallee

The Water Sports Museum is in the Köpenick suburb of **Grünau**, a handsome colony founded in 1749 on the western bank of the Dahme River, about 4km south of the Altstadt. This section of the river, called **Langer See**, was the site of the Olympic regattas in 1936, which is a major focus of the museum's exhibits. Through its hotchpotch collection of flags, medals, clothing, newspaper articles, photos, boats and boat accessories the museum also tells the general history of water sports in the region.

HEIMATMUSEUM KÖPENICK

☎ 6172 3351; www.heimatmuseum-koepenick.de; Alter Markt 1; admission free; ☽ 10am-4pm Tue-Wed, 10am-6pm Thu, 2-6pm Sat; S-Bahn Köpenick, then tram 62, 68

The Heimatmuseum Köpenick occupies a 17th-century half-timbered house that has weathered time surprisingly well in the eastern Altstadt. The museum tracks momentous events in the town's history and also displays archaeological findings unearthed during recent construction.

KIETZ

Wäschereimuseum: ☎ 651 6424; www.omas -waschkueche.de; Luisenstrasse 23; tours adult/ concession €1.60/0.60; ☽ tours 3-6pm 1st Fri of the month only; S-Bahn Köpenick, then tram 62

A short walk southeast of the Altstadt, on the eastern shore of the Dahme River, the Kietz is Köpenick's traditional fishing village with origins in the Middle Ages. Its little lanes are lined with nicely restored but modest homes where the fisherfolk lived as far back as the 18th century.

The Kietz is home to the unique **Wäscherei-museum** (Laundry Museum) which commemorates the period in the early 20th century when Köpenick was Berlin's 'laundrette' with as many as 400 companies in operation at its peak in 1914. The museum's eclectic collection ranges from washboards and gas-fuelled irons to ancient mangles and steam-powered washing machines.

Guided tours (in German) are delivered with lots of humour but unfortunately only once a month (or by appointment for groups of six or more).

SCHLOSS KÖPENICK (SMB)

☎ 266 2951; www.smpk.de; Schlossinsel; adult/
concession €6/3, under 16 free, free for everyone last
4hrs Thu, incl same-day admission to Gemäldegalerie,
Kupferstichkabinett, Neue Nationalgalerie, Hamburger
Bahnhof, Musikinstrumenten-Museum & Kunstgewerbemuseum at Kulturforum; ⏱ 10am-6pm Tue-Fri,
11am-6pm Sat & Sun; S-Bahn Köpenick, then tram
62, 68

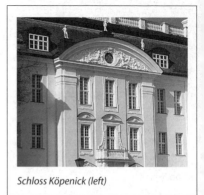

Schloss Köpenick (left)

The simple but graceful Köpenick Palace
stands on the Schlossinsel, an island in the
Dahme, and was built in Dutch baroque style
between 1677 and 1682. It served as a residence for Friedrich III, the later King Friedrich
I, and went through periods as a prison and
a teaching seminary before becoming a museum in 1963. Since 1990, it has been a subsid-
iary of the Kunstgewerbemuseum (Museum of
Applied Arts) at the Kulturforum (p104). After a
multi-year restoration, it reopened in May 2004
with an exhibit that takes visitors on a journey through three centuries of home design
spanning the Renaissance, baroque and rococo
periods. Displays include tapestries, leather wall
coverings, porcelain, silverware and glass as well
as the furniture.

Another highlight is the restored **Wappensaal**
(Coat of Arms Hall), a lavishly decorated 2nd-
floor hall. It was in this very room that, in 1730,
a military court meted out questionable justice
against two soldiers accused of attempted de-
sertion. The verdict(s)? The guillotine for Captain Hans and the throne for Captain Friedrich,
who just happened to have the good fortune
to be the son of King Friedrich Wilhelm I!

NEUKÖLLN

Neukölln, Berlin's most densely populated district, has a split personality. The north, bor-
dering Kreuzberg, has traditionally been a stronghold of the proletariat and continues to
be dominated by poor and immigrant folk. The main drag, Karl-Marx-Strasse, is a busy
high street peopled by the pale and downtrodden and lined by cheap import stores and
low-end chains.

The southern suburbs of Britz, Buckow and Rudow, on the other hand, have preserved
a tranquil small-town character, with tree-lined avenues, single-family homes and a largely
middle-class population. An exception is Gropiusstadt, a massive high-rise housing development that grew out of the urgent need for housing in western Berlin after the building
of the Berlin Wall.

Orientation

Northern Neukölln is basically an extension of Kreuzberg's 'Little Istanbul' with Hermannplatz at its centre. Southwest of here is the Volkspark Hasenheide, a large expanse of green
and a popular spot for recreation, picnics and barbeques. Karl-Marx-Strasse, the main
drag, heads south from here and changes its name a couple of times before reaching the
skyscrapers of Gropiusstadt after about 4.5km. Northeast of here is the considerably more
human-scale suburb of Britz.

GROPIUSSTADT

U-Bahn Johannisthaler Chaussee, Lipschitzallee,
Wutzkyallee, Zwickauer Damm

Gropiusstadt, in southern Neukölln, was the
largest new construction site in West Berlin
after WWII. Built from 1963 to 1973, it is a
glass and concrete jungle with 17,000 flats
for 50,000 people. Bauhaus guru Walter Gropius envisioned a model city with plenty of
green and open spaces. But then came the
Berlin Wall, creating an instant need for more
housing.

By the time the Berlin Senate approved the
blueprints, Gropius barely recognised them.
His pedestrian-friendly community with green,
open spaces and up to four-storey tall build-

ings was turned into a forest of high-rises –
some with as many as 31 floors – that stood
close enough together that residents could
see the neighbours brush their teeth.

There are no real attractions here for visitors,
but if you just want to get a feel for the place,
get off at any of the four U-Bahn stations south
of Johannisthaler Chaussee with its popular
mega-mall called Gropius Passagen.

HUFEISENSIEDLUNG
Lowise-Reuter-Ring; U-Bahn Parchimer Allee, then
250m walk north

A delicacy for modern architecture fans, the
Horseshoe Colony is an innovative housing
community from the late 1920s in the southern Neukölln suburb of Britz. Its architects,
Bruno Taut and Martin Wagner, were among
the first to do the seemingly impossible: hu-
manise high-density housing.

Individual three-storey-high housing blocks
arranged in the shape of a horseshoe enclose
a nicely landscaped park with a little pond.
The 1000 or so flats are small but all of them
have balconies facing the park and each section has its own small garden for growing
vegetables. It all looks clean, neat and quite
handsome.

While here, also check out the street called
Hüsung just west of Lowise-Reuter-Ring. Here
you'll find uninterrupted rows of narrow,
two-storey, single-family homes that follow
the diamond-shaped outline of the street.
Their tiny front lawns are separated from the
pavement with hedges of identical height;
trees are evenly spaced, about 10m apart. The
amazing symmetry and homogeneity of this
development is both a tad oppressive and
visually interesting.

PUPPENTHEATER-MUSEUM BERLIN
Map pp325-7
☎ 687 8132; www.puppentheater-museum.de; Karl-
Marx-Strasse 135, rear bldg; adult/child €2.60/2.10;
🕑 9am-4pm Mon-Fri, 11am-5pm Sun; shows €5;
U-Bahn Karl-Marx-Strasse

A wonderful diversion, not only for tots, the
Puppet Theater Museum transports you to a
fantasy world inhabited by an international
cast of hand puppets, marionettes, shadow
puppets, stick figures and all manner of dolls,
dragons and devils. Many of them get to perform during regular shows geared towards
both kids and adults.

SCHLOSS BRITZ
☎ 6097 9230; www.schloss-britz.de; Alt-Britz 73;
adult/concession €2/1; 🕑 tours 2-5.30pm Wed, park
9am-dusk; U-Bahn Parchimer Allee, then walk west
about 500m

Not really a palace but a large country estate,
Schloss Britz has become a cultural focal
point of this part of town. It frequently hosts
concerts and exhibits in its historical rooms,
the former horse barn or the park. Tours of
the interior offer a look at the lifestyle of a
wealthy family in the late 19th century. In fine
weather, the park is a relaxing place for a stroll
or a picnic.

The estate has a history going back to the
16th century and for centuries it was the country home of the Britzke family. It has survived
numerous alterations, the last of which was in
1880 when it was given a French Renaissance
makeover.

After WWII it was used as an orphanage but
a thorough renovation in the 1980s restored its
refined late-19th-century glamour.

Districts – Southern Districts

TREPTOW

To many people Treptow, which parallels the Spree's western bank, is synonymous with the
Treptower Park, a vast recreational area that segues into the Plänterwald further south. It's
a lovely patch of green with lots of trees, shady paths for strolling, lawns for picnicking as
well as the incongruously monumental Soviet War Memorial. Boats operated by Stern und
Kreis (p78) leave from landing docks on the Spree, and at weekends a popular flea market
(p225) takes place in an old warehouse.

Once a manufacturing stronghold, Treptow is staking its future on high-tech. TV and
film production have resumed in the former GDR television studios in the southern suburb of **Adlershof**, which is also home to a successful science and technology centre. Back
north, where the Landwehrkanal meets the Spree, the **Treptowers** is a new office complex
with Berlin's tallest office building, the 30-storey Allianz Tower.

American artist Jonathan Borowsky designed the soaring sculpture called **Molecule Man**
seemingly afloat in the river here. The sculpture shows the outline of three bodies in embrace, a symbol of the joining together of the three districts of Kreuzberg, Friedrichshain
and Treptow.

Orientation

The vast expanse of the Treptower Park and Plänterwald dominates northern Treptow. The leafy grounds stretch south for several kilometres passing the Soviet War Memorial and the Archenhold Observatory. A walk along the Spree passes by the Treptowers, the traditional Zenner restaurant and the Insel der Jugend (Island of Youth) connected to the mainland by a little bridge. Adlershof is about 6.5km south of the S-Bahn station Treptower Park.

Districts – Southern Districts

ANNA SEGHERS GEDENKSTÄTTE

☎ 677 4725; Anna-Seghers-Strasse 81; adult/concession €2/1; ☽ 10am-4pm Tue-Wed, 10am-6pm Thu; S-Bahn Adlershof

Fans of the writer Anna Seghers (1900–83) will be interested in making a pilgrimage to the small memorial exhibit inside her former flat. The original cramped living room and office with her precious library are still there, as is an exhibit documenting her life and work. A committed communist, Seghers (whose real name was Netty Radvanyi, nee Reiling) spent WWII in Mexico before choosing East Berlin as her domicile upon her return from exile. Her most famous work is *The Seventh Cross* (1941), a chilling account of the horrors of the Nazi regime.

ARCHENHOLD-STERNWARTE

☎ 534 8080; www.astw.de; Alt-Treptow 1; museum adult/concession €2.50/2, tours €4/2; ☽ 2-4.30pm Wed-Sun, tours 8pm Thu, 3pm Sat & Sun; S-Bahn Plänterwald

Germany's oldest astronomical observatory, in the southeastern corner of Treptower Park, is well known as the place where Albert Einstein first introduced his theory of relativity in 1915. But the observatory's true claim to fame is its 21m-long **refracting telescope**, the longest in the world. Built in 1896 by astronomer Friedrich Simon Archenhold (1861–1939) for a trade exhibition, it was such a tremendous success that a permanent space was created for it, thus giving birth to the observatory. The telescope is still the main attraction today, especially on the second Friday of the month when it's open for stargazers (weather permitting). Exhibits in the foyer focus on astronomy-related subjects and the history of the observatory.

GRENZWACHTURM Map pp325-7

Im Schlesischen Busch, cnr Pushkinallee & Schlesische Strasse; U-Bahn Schlesisches Tor

This is the only original GDR border watchtower still in its original spot next to where the Berlin Wall once stood. It has been preserved as a memorial. The little park surrounding it has been reclaimed from its previous function as the border 'death strip'.

SOWJETISCHES EHRENMAL Map pp318-19

Treptower Park; admission free; ☽ 24 hr; S-Bahn Treptower Park

Treptow's main sight is the monumental Soviet War Memorial (1949) right at the heart of Treptower Park. It's a gargantuan complex attesting both to the immensity of the losses of WWII and to the overblown self-importance of the Stalinist state. Some 5000 soldiers who fell in the Battle of Berlin lie buried beneath the memorial. An epic statue of Mother Russia grieving for her dead children is the first thing visitors see when approaching the monument.

Two mighty walls fronted by kneeling soldiers flank the main entrance; the red marble used here was supposedly scavenged from Hitler's ruined chancellery. This gives way to a wide plaza lined by sarcophagi representing the then 16 Soviet republics. Each features reliefs portraying scenes from the war and quotes from Stalin (in Russian and German). At the far end, on a mound, is a mausoleum topped by a 13m-high statue of a Russian soldier clutching a child, his great sword resting on a shattered swastika. The socialist-realism mosaic inside the plinth shows grateful Soviets – including workers, peasants and some Central Asian minorities – honouring the fallen.

To reach the monument from the S-Bahn station, head south for 750m on Puschkinallee, then enter the park through the stone gate.

USSR emblem, Sowjetisches Ehrenmal (above)

ZEHLENDORF

Zehlendorf is one of Berlin's greenest districts (only Köpenick is greener), with about half of its land covered by forest, rivers and lakes. The elegant suburbs of Dahlem and Wannsee with their villas and estates contribute greatly to Zehlendorf's small-town character. To visitors and locals, the district has much to offer. The southern half of Grunewald forest and Wannsee lake are great areas for outdoor activities, while several museums provide intellectual stimulation. A couple of palaces, important historical sites, a university and lovely gardens further add to its appeal.

Orientation

Zehlendorf is a vast district but most of its major sights, including several museums and the Botanical Gardens, concentrate in the northern suburb of Dahlem, which borders Wilmersdorf in the north and also embraces the southeastern reaches of the Grunewald forest. In the far southwestern corner, already on the border with Potsdam, is the suburb of Wannsee right on the Havel and the lake by the same name where the Pfaueninsel is a major attraction.

ALLIIERTEN MUSEUM

☎ 818 1990; www.alliiertenmuseum.de; Clayallee 135; admission free; ⓨ 10am-6pm Thu-Tue; U-Bahn Oskar-Helene-Heim, then any bus or 10-minute walk north on Clayallee

The Alliierten Museum (Allied Museum) documents the history and challenges faced by the Western Allies in Berlin after WWII and during the Cold War. Exhibits are presented chronologically in two buildings and the central yard. Start a tour in the former **Outpost cinema** for US troops, where the 1948 Berlin Airlift (see the boxed text, p61) is a major focus. Then it's off to the Cold War years, presented in all their drama at the nearby **Nicholson Memorial Library**. A highlight here is the partial reconstruction of the Berlin Spy Tunnel, built in 1953–54 by US and British intelligence services to tap into the central Soviet phone telephone system. The original was 2m wide and 450m long and recorded half a million calls until a double agent blabbed to the Soviets. The museum concludes with an overview of the events leading to the collapse of communism and the fall of the Berlin Wall.

Some of the most interesting objects are in the museum yard. They include the original guard cabin from Checkpoint Charlie, a 'Hastings' plane used during the Berlin Airlift, the restaurant car of a French military train, a small section of the Wall and a GDR guard tower.

All explanatory panelling is in German, English and French. Disabled access is good.

BOTANISCHER GARTEN & MUSEUM

☎ 8385 0100, 8385 0027 for recorded message (in German); www.bgbm.org; Königin-Luise-Strasse 6-8, enter from Unter den Eichen or Königin-Luise-Platz; adult/concession gardens & museum €5/2.50, museum only €2/1; ⓨ garden 9am-dusk, latest 9pm; museum 10am-6pm; S-Bahn Botanischer Garten

Berlin's stunning botanical garden is a symphony of perfume and colour. Over a 100 years old, it boasts more than 22,000 plant species from around the world beautifully arranged on 43 hectares. Highlights include a large pond framed by swamp plants and the 16 greenhouses filled with orchids, bamboo, cacti and other exotic plant life. Sight-impaired visitors can visit a special smell and touch garden.

Near the entrance on Königin-Luise-Platz, the **Botanisches Museum** (Botanical Museum) complements the garden by providing scientific background information about plants.

Both the garden and museum are part of the **Freie Universität Berlin** (p142).

BRÜCKE MUSEUM

☎ 831 2029; www.bruecke-museum.de; Bussardsteig 9; adult/concession €4/2; ⓨ 11am-5pm Wed-Mon; U-Bahn Oskar-Helene-Heim, then bus 115 to Pücklerstrasse

In 1905 Karl Schmidt-Rottluff, Erich Heckel and Ernst Ludwig Kirchner founded an artist group that sought to break away from the staid traditions that were taught at conventional

Top Five Escapes

- Botanischer Garten (this page)
- Müggelsee (p137)
- Pfaueninsel (p144)
- Potsdam (p258)
- Tiergarten Park (p101)

art academies. Calling itself Die Brücke (The Bridge, 1905–13), the group was soon joined by Emil Nolde, Max Pechstein and others in developing a ground-breaking approach that paved the way for German expressionism.

Shapes and figures that teeter on the abstract – without ever quite getting there – bright, emotional colours and unusual perspective characterise the style of Die Brücke. The Nazis, predictably, called this work subversive and destroyed much of it. Fortunately, plenty survived, including the 400 or so paintings and thousands of sketches and watercolours by all major Brücke members from which this museum's changing exhibits are drawn.

It's on the eastern edge of the Grunewald forest in an elegant Bauhaus-inspired building designed in 1967 by Werner Düttmann.

FREIE UNIVERSITÄT BERLIN
☎ 8381; www.fu-berlin.de; Kaiserwerther Strasse 16-18 (administration), Garystrasse 35-39 (Henry-Ford-Bau); U-Bahn Dahlem-Dorf, Thielplatz

The Free University is Berlin's largest and youngest major learning institution. It was founded in 1948 in reaction to the growing restrictions on academic freedoms imposed at the Humboldt University in the Soviet sector. Students and faculty were increasingly pressured to adopt a Marxist-Leninist world view. Those who resisted, risked harassment, dismissal, and even arrest.

With the consent of US military commander General Lucius Clay, a 'free' university began holding lectures in the spring of 1949, initially in empty villas throughout Dahlem, then in its first permanent structure donated in 1955 by the Henry Ford Foundation. Today, the campus consists of over 200 buildings scattered throughout Dahlem.

The fledgling university, freethinking and reform-minded, rejected many elements of Germany's antiquated educational system. It had one of the country's first student councils and abolished such reactionary organisations as sabre duelling fraternities. In the 1960s, it played a leading role in the country's student movement, which sparked major nationwide academic and political reforms (p64).

FREILICHTMUSEUM DOMÄNE DAHLEM
☎ 666 3000; www.domaene-dahlem.de; Königin-Luise-Strasse 49; adult/concession €2/1, free on Wed & to age 14; ☉ 10am-6pm Wed-Mon; U-Bahn Dahlem-Dorf

A favourite with children, this large farming estate turned open-air museum transports you back to preindustrial Berlin. It's a big, historical complex attached to an actual working farm whose organic products – vegetables, flowers, eggs, meats, etc – are sold in a little shop on site. The main exhibits occupy a restored 1560 manor, one of Berlin's oldest buildings, and focus on the region's agricultural history, rural handicrafts and beekeeping.

Elsewhere you'll find workshops where volunteers demonstrate spinning, weaving, pottery making, furniture painting and other ancient crafts. An organic farmers market takes place from noon to 6pm on Wednesday and 8am to 1pm Saturday. The museum also hosts hugely popular festivals. Check the website or call for upcoming events.

GLIENICKER BRÜCKE
www.glienicker-bruecke.de; S-Bahn Wannsee, then bus 116

It spans the Havel River over a length of 125m and connects Berlin with Potsdam. But the Glienicke Bridge is world famous mostly for being the setting of secret agent exchanges between the Soviets and the US during the Cold War. Despite its lead role in countless spy novels and feature films, only three exchanges actually took place: in 1962, 1985 and 1986.

GRAVE OF HEINRICH VON KLEIST
Bismarckstrasse btwn No 2 and 4; S-Bahn Wannsee

The Romantic poet Heinrich von Kleist (1777–1811) and his mistress Henriette Vogel (1780–1811) committed murder-suicide on 21 November 1811 in a spot on the southern shore of the Kleiner Wannsee, just south of Wannseebrücke. Kleist's grave is on a rise about halfway between the road and the lake.

Kleist, now one of Germany's most revered literary figures, never enjoyed success in his lifetime. At the time of his death, he was penniless and estranged from his family who had hoped he would pursue a military career. Henriette, who was married to a Prussian civil servant, suffered from advanced stages of cancer.

HAUS DER WANNSEE KONFERENZ
☎ 805 0010; www.ghwk.de; Am Grossen Wannsee 56-58; admission free; ☉ 10am-6pm Mon-Fri, 2-6pm Sat & Sun; S-Bahn Wannsee, then bus 114

In January 1942 a group of elite Nazi officials met in a stately villa on Lake Wannsee to discuss the so-called 'Final Solution', the systematic deportation and annihilation of the European Jews. The same building now houses the haunting Wannsee Conference Memorial Exhibit.

You can stand in that fateful room where discussions took place, study the minutes of the conference (taken by Adolf Eichmann) and look at photographs of the Nazi thugs, many of whom lived to a ripe old age. The other rooms chronicle, in a thorough and graphic fashion, the horrors leading up to and perpetrated during the Holocaust. English-language pamphlets may be borrowed from the desk, which also sells various books and booklets about the subject.

JAGDSCHLOSS GLIENICKE

☎ 805 010; Königstrasse 36b; S-Bahn Wannsee, then bus 116

As the name implies, the Jagdschloss was originally a hunting palace built by the Great Elector in 1684 but was later demoted to army hospital and even a wallpaper factory. Prince Carl, who lived in nearby **Schloss Glienicke** (p145), had it restored in French neobaroque style in 1859. Since 1962 it has served as an international conference and education centre.

JAGDSCHLOSS GRUNEWALD

☎ 969 4202, 813 3442; Hüttenweg 10; adult/concession €2/1.50; 🕙 10am-5pm Tue-Sun mid-May–mid-Oct; tours 11am, 1pm & 3pm Sun mid-Oct–mid-May; U-Bahn Fehrbelliner Platz, then bus 115 to Pücklerstrasse, then walk west

The Grunewald was the favourite hunting ground of the Prussian rulers until as late as the early 20th century. It was a tradition begun by Elector Joachim II who had this Renaissance palace built in 1542, making it the oldest existing royal abode in town. It has an attractive location near the Grunewaldsee shore. Originally called simply 'Haus am Grünen Walde' (House in the Green Woods), it also gave the entire forest its name.

Since 1932 the palace has housed a collection of German and Dutch paintings from the 15th to the 18th centuries. Exquisite works include oils by Lucas Cranach the Elder, an early-15th-century altar and *Venus and Armor* by the Dutchman Jan Lievens. Also on display are hunting-related items, antlers, and paintings depicting hunting scenes.

While you're here, you might like a stroll around the Grunewaldsee (swimming allowed). You'll soon notice, though, that this is also 'doggie paradise' and since pooper-

scoopers haven't exactly caught on in Berlin, we can only recommend you keep an eye on the trail. Sadly, it renders the place basically unsuitable for small children.

LIEBERMANN-VILLA AM WANNSEE

☎ 8058 3830; www.im-netz.de/liebermann; Colomierstrasse 3; adult/concession €3/2; 🕙 11am-5pm Sat & Sun; S-Bahn Wannsee, then bus 114

From 1910 until his death in 1935, the painter Max Liebermann spent his summers in this wonderful house with its large and lush garden overlooking the Wannsee. The garden especially, with its teahouse, benches, flower boxes, sundial and other elements, inspired some 400 oil paintings, pastels and prints. Both villa and garden are being restored and are open to the public on a limited schedule until the official opening in 2004. Call or check the website for updates. Exhibits will focus on Liebermann's work as an artist, politician and prominent figure in Berlin's Jewish community.

MUSEEN DAHLEM (SMB)

☎ 830 1438; www.smpk.de; Lansstrasse 8; adult/concession €4/2, under 16 free, free for everyone last 4hrs Thu, incl same-day admission to Museum Europäischer Kulturen; 🕙 10am-6pm Tue-Fri, 11am-6pm Sat & Sun; U-Bahn Dahlem Dorf

The huge museum complex combines three extraordinary collections under one roof. The **Ethnologisches Museum** (Museum of Ethnology) has one of the world's largest, most prestigious collections of pre-industrial non-European art and objects. It's impossible to describe fully the museum's extraordinary collection. Budget at least two hours to walk through its labyrinth of halls – it's an eye-opening journey of discovery that'll fly by in no time. Note that some sections may be closed while this museum is receiving a gradual overhaul.

The Africa exhibit is particularly impressive with its wealth of masks, ornaments, vases, musical instruments and other objects of ceremonial and everyday life, most hailing from Cameroun, Nigeria and Benin. Note the high level of artisanship, for instance, of the beaded throne given to Kaiser Wilhelm II by King Njoya of Cameroun. Another crowd-pleaser is the South Seas hall with cult objects, outriggers and other boats from such islands as New Guinea and Tonga.

The **Museum für Indische Kunst** (Museum of Indian Art) presents fine and applied art from India, Southeast Asia and Central Asia from the 2nd century BC to the present. Keep an eye out for exquisite terracottas, stone sculptures and bronzes as well as wall paintings and sculptures scavenged from Buddhist cave temples along the Silk Route.

Also here is the **Museum für Ostasiatische Kunst** (Museum of East Asian Art), which features ceramics, bronzes, lacquerware, jade objects, and graphics from China, Japan and Korea. A full-size Japanese tearoom is just one of the many highlights.

The entire museum complex is wheelchair-accessible.

MUSEUM EUROPÄISCHER KULTUREN (SMB)

☎ 8390 1295; www.smpk.de; Im Winkel 6-8; adult/concession €4/2, under 16 free, free for everyone last 4hrs Thu, incl same-day admission to Museum Dahlem; ☷ 10am-6pm Tue-Fri, 11am-6pm Sat & Sun; U-Bahn Dahlem Dorf

'Cultural Contacts in Europe: The Fascination of Pictures' is the name of the permanent exhibit at the Museum Europäischer Kulturen (Museum of European Cultures). Or perhaps more simply put: 'A picture tells a thousand words.'

The museum seeks to show how images have been a major factor in shaping the heritage and identity of the Old World countries. Pictures, rather than words, transcend time, borders and language barriers and bring people together.

The museum's collection combines the holdings of the former Museum of Folklore and the European section of the Museum of Ethnology to document the cross-cultural influence images have had within Europe. This translates into a moderately interesting and rather eclectic display that includes painted furniture and tiles, photographs, film and TV, Madonna statues, architectural blueprints and advertisements.

MUSEUMSDORF DÜPPEL

☎ 802 6671; Clauertstrasse 11; adult/concession €2/1; ☷ 3-7pm Thu, 10am-5pm Sun Apr-early Oct, admission until 1hr before closing; S-Bahn Zehlendorf, then bus 115

Find out what a Berlin village might have looked like in the Middle Ages when visiting the Museumsdorf Düppel (Düppel Museum Village). Over a dozen reed-thatched buildings have been re-created on the grounds of an actual 12th-century settlement surrounded by fields and woods. Museum volunteers grow threatened plant species like the Düppel rye and breed such endangered animals as the Skudde (a type of sheep) and the Düppeler Weidesch-

Schloss Glienicke (opposite)

wein (Düppel pasture pig). Demonstrations of various old-time crafts such as blacksmithing and pottery take place on Sunday.

PFAUENINSEL

☎ 805 3042; www.spsg.de; adult/concession incl palace & ferry €3/2.50, ferry-only €1; ☷ 8am-8pm May-Aug, 8am-6pm Apr & Sep, 9am-5pm Oct, 10am-4pm Nov-Mar; mock-medieval palace ☷ 10am-5pm Tue-Sun Apr-Oct; S-Bahn Wannsee, then hourly bus 216

As if lifted from a fairytale, the dreamy Pfaueninsel (Peacock Island) in the Havel River is one of the most enchanting places in Berlin and one of the best destinations for escaping the city. The island was the romantic fantasy of King Friedrich Wilhelm II who, in 1797, hired court architect Johann Gottlieb Brendel to build a **mock-medieval palace**, perfect for frolicking with his mistress away from the curious eyes of the court. The exotic exterior continues inside the snowy white building, which may be toured.

Definitely make time to explore the wonderful **park** with its ancient trees and lovely trails. It was designed by the prolific Peter Lenné around 1822 and originally teemed with tamed animals. These later went on to become the first denizens of the new Berlin Zoo, also created by Lenné on the edge of the Tiergarten in Charlottenburg (p111). Fortunately, the beautiful peacocks that gave the island its name still proudly strut their stuff here.

On your strolls you're likely to bump into a clutch of other buildings. A standout is the **Kavaliershaus**, more or less in the centre of the island, which provided living space for the royals and their visitors. In 1824, Schinkel added the Gothic façade that had previously graced a patrician house in Gdansk. A highlight on the island's north end is the **Meierei** (dairy), a Gothic-style artificial ruin.

Since the entire place is a nature preserve, the *verboten* list is rather long and includes smoking, cycling, swimming, animals and radios. Picnicking, though, remains legal and this is a nice place to do it. There are no cafés or restaurants on the island.

SCHLOSS GLIENICKE

☎ 805 3041; www.spsg.de; Königstrasse 36; adult/ concession incl tour €3/2.50, without tour €2/1.50, casino €1; ☺ 10am-5pm Sat & Sun mid-May–mid-Oct; S-Bahn Wannsee, then bus 116

Glienicke Palace, at the far southwestern tip of Berlin, is what happens when a rich, royal kid goes to Italy and falls in love with the country. Prince Carl of Prussia (1801–1883), a son of Friedrich Wilhelm III, was only 22 when he returned to Berlin wanting nothing more than to build his dream Italian villa. He bought an existing estate and hired Schinkel to turn it into an elegant compound inspired by classical architecture. It's embedded in a rambling, romantic park landscaped by Peter Joseph Lenné that is considered a classic of 19th-century garden design.

Schinkel expanded the existing mansion into a small palace decorated with coloured marble, rich woods and fine furniture. He also converted the former billiard house into the **Kasino**, an Italian villa with a double pergola. In the southwestern corner of the garden he built the **Grosse Neugierde** (literally 'Big Curiosity') a gazebo-like structure inspired by the monument to Lysicrates in Athens. It's in an especially scenic spot overlooking the Havel, Schloss Babelsberg and the outskirts of Potsdam.

A stroll through the park is a true delight, as beautiful vistas open up at every bend in the path. Prince Carl was an avid collector of antiquities and much of what you see today he personally brought to Berlin (some might say, stole) from such places as Pompeii and Carthage.

The Schloss itself is open for tours at summer weekends and also hosts changing exhibits and concerts. There's also a restaurant with a lovely terrace.

EASTERN DISTRICTS
LICHTENBERG-HOHENSCHÖNHAUSEN

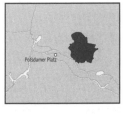

Since 2001, Lichtenberg has also incorporated Hohenschönhausen to the north. Although small and nondescript, this district should be a prime destination for anyone interested in the dark side of GDR history. It was from its headquarters in Lichtenberg that the Ministry for State Security, the all-pervasive Stasi, extended its tentacles across the country and beyond. And it was nearby in Hohenschönhausen where the Stasi operated one of its most fearsome prisons, torturing and incarcerating thousands. Both places have been preserved and offer chilling evidence of the machinations of the ultimate 'Big Brother' state (p84).

These days, life's still tough in Lichtenberg-Hohenschönhausen, where high unemployment and pessimism about the future have proven strong breeding grounds for both neo-Nazis and PDS supporters (the PDS is the successor party to the GDR's communist SED). Giant high-rise ghettos in classic GDR prefab characterise vast stretches of the district, especially in Hohenschönhausen. Pockets of delight include the sprawling animal park, which is bigger than the Zoo in Charlottenburg but with fewer animals, and a tidy little baroque palace on the same grounds.

Orientation

Lichtenberg is west of Friedrichshain and linked to Hohenschönhausen to the north. The Stasi headquarters are just off Frankfurter Allee, which eventually leads to the Tierpark Friedrichsfelde and Karlshorst in southern Lichtenberg. Further north, Landsberger Allee cuts straight through Hohenschönhausen.

Transport

Bus No 195 for Erholungspark Marzahn and Mahlsdorf.

S-Bahn S5 for Hellersdorf; S5, S7, S75 for Lichtenberg; S7 for Marzahn.

Tram Nos 6, 7 from Mitte to Hohenschönhausen and Marzahn via Landsberger Allee; No 8 to Lichtenberg and Alt-Marzahn via Herzbergstrasse and Allee der Kosmonauten.

U-Bahn U5 for Lichtenberg; U5 for Hellersdorf.

GEDENKSTÄTTE HOHENSCHÖN-HAUSEN (STASI PRISON)

☎ 9860 8230; www.stiftung-hsh.de; Genslerstrasse 66; adult/concession tours €3/1.50, free on Wed, exhibit admission free; ☺ 9am-6pm, tours (in German) 11am & 1pm Mon-Fri, hourly 10am-4pm Sat & Sun; S-Bahn Landsberger Allee, then tram 6 or 7 to Genslerstrasse

This memorial site in a feared former Stasi prison commemorates the suffering of thousands of victims of political persecution in eastern Germany after WWII. Tours of the complex, led by former prisoners, reveal the full extent of the unspeakable terror and cruelty perpetrated here on thousands of people, many of whom were completely innocent.

You'll learn all about the prison's three frightening incarnations. Right after the war, the Soviets used the place to process prisoners destined for the Gulag. More than 3000 of the men, women and children interned here died – usually by freezing to death in their unheated cells – until the Western Allies intervened in October 1946.

The Soviets then made it a regular prison, mostly dreaded for its 'U-Boat', a tract of damp, windowless, subterranean cells outfitted only with a wooden bench and a bucket. Prisoners were subjected to endless interrogations, beatings, sleep deprivation and water torture. *Everybody* signed a confession sooner or later.

In 1951, the Soviets handed over the prison to the folks at the GDR Ministry for State Security (Stasi), who happily adopted their mentors' methods. Suspected enemies of the regime, including participants in the 1953 workers' uprising, were locked up in the U-Boat until a new, much bigger cell block was built, with prison labour, in the late '50s. Psycho-terror now replaced physical torture: inmates had no idea of their whereabouts and suffered total isolation and sensory deprivation. Only the collapse of the GDR in 1989 and the demise of the Stasi put an end to the horror.

GEDENKSTÄTTE NORMANNEN-STRASSE (STASI MUSEUM)

☎ 553 6854; www.stasimuseum.de; Ruschestrasse 103, House 1; adult/concession €3.50/2.50; ☺ 11am-6pm Mon-Fri, 2-6pm Sat & Sun; U-Bahn Magdalenenstrasse

Anyone interested in GDR history, and the Stasi in particular, will find a visit to this museum – housed in the actual headquarters of the Ministry for State Security – very rewarding. Most interesting here is the 'lion's den', the offices

Eastern Districts Top Four

- Explore the 'Wild East' behind the wheel of a **Trabi** (p78).
- Sense the sinister presence of the Stasi on visits to the **Stasi Museum** (this page) and the **Stasi Prison** (this page).
- Meet the baby elephants of the **Tierpark Friedrichsfelde** (opposite).
- Explore the curious collection of the **Gründerzeit Museum** (p148).

from which Erich Mielke, who headed the Stasi from 1957 to 1989, wielded his power. Mielke knew not only the dirt about every GDR citizen, but he also had secret files of all the GDR government honchos, including Honecker, which explains his longevity in office. All the furniture is simple, functional and, above all, original.

Rooms downstairs are filled with Stasi memorabilia, including cunning surveillance devices, and exhibits explaining the GDR's political system and the extent of its repressiveness. Truly chilling is an original prisoner transport van, with five tiny, lightless cells, displayed in the foyer.

MUSEUM BERLIN-KARLSHORST

☎ 5015 0810; www.museum-karlshorst.de; Zwieseler Strasse 4, cnr Rheinsteinstrasse; admission free; ☺ 10am-6pm Tue-Sun; S-Bahn Karlshorst

On 8 May 1945, German commanders signed unconditional surrender of the Wehrmacht in the building now housing the Museum Berlin-Karlshorst. In doing so, they ratified the unconditional surrender of the Wehrmacht, thereby ratifying the capitulation agreement made a day earlier at General Eisenhower's headquarters in Reims, France. WWII was over.

From 1945 to 1949, the building was the seat of the Soviet Military Administration. The offices of Marshal Zhukov, the Soviet supreme commander, are still here, as is the Great Hall where the surrender was signed. Another important moment came in 1949 when the Soviets gave statehood to the GDR here.

The other rooms house an intriguing exhibit about every stage of the German-Soviet relationship from 1917 to reunification. Documents, photographs, uniforms and the usual eclectic assortment of items address such topics as the Hitler-Stalin Pact, the daily grind of life as a WWII soldier and the fate of Soviet civilians during wartime. Outside is a battery of

Soviet weapons, including a Howitzer canon and the devastating *Katjuscha* multiple rocket launcher, also known as the 'Stalin organ'.

The museum is about a 10- to 15-minute walk from the S-Bahn station; take the Treskowallee exit, then turn right onto Rheinsteinstrasse.

TIERPARK & SCHLOSS FRIEDRICHSFELDE

Tierpark: ☎ 515 310; www.tierpark-berlin.de; adult/student/child €9/7/4.50; ⏲ 9am-5pm Nov-Feb, 9am-6pm Mar, 9am-8pm Apr-Sep, 9am-7pm Oct, ticket office closes 1hr earlier

Schloss: ☎ 6663 5035; www.stadtmuseum.de; Am Tierpark 125; admission €0.50 on top of Tierpark fees; ⏲ 10am-6pm Tue-Sun; U-Bahn Tierpark

Tierpark Friedrichsfelde opened in 1955 and at last count had almost 10,000 animals representing over 1000 species, most of them living in open-moated habitats. Star residents include such rare, hoofed animals as wild horses, oryx antelopes and Vietnamese sika stags, all of which are extinct in the wild. Be sure to visit the **Alfred-Brehm-Haus** with its tigers and lions; the **Dickhäuterhaus** where the elephants (including some little ones born in the zoo) and rhinos reside; and the **Schlangenfarm**, which has more slithering, poisonous snakes than even Harry Potter could handle.

Before becoming a zoo, the Tierpark was the Peter Lenné-designed park of **Schloss Friedrichsfelde**. This little pleasure palace was the fancy of Benjamin Raulé and was completed in 1695 in late-baroque style and altered and expanded numerous times by subsequent owners. In 2003, following a complete restoration, the doors again opened to the public. The exhibits inside are still a work in progress, with period furniture and paintings filling rooms sheathed in historical wallpaper. There's also a hotchpotch collection of arts and crafts items, including baroque glass, hand-painted porcelain, silverware and other items that might once have been belonged to the palace residents.

Note that it's not possible to see the palace without paying admission to the Tierpark.

MARZAHN-HELLERSDORF

Marzahn and Hellersdorf are veritable test-tube cities that sprung up in the 1970s and early '80s to combat an acute housing shortage in East Berlin. Their most distinctive feature is row upon row of gigantic prefab housing developments – so-called *Plattenbauten* – rushing skyward for up to 21 storeys like concrete stalagmites. Marzahn alone boasted 62,000 flats for 160,000 people. These *Arbeiterschliessfächer* (workers' lockers), as the warrens of small flats were nicknamed, were actually in hot demand. Too great was the lure of private baths, central heating, lifts and parking aplenty.

After reunification anyone who could escape these high-rises did, leaving behind the old and socially weak. In recent years, the city of Berlin has made major investments into improving the appeal of Marzahn-Hellersdorf. Buildings have been renovated, retrofitted with balconies and spruced up with a bucket or two of paint. New public parks and cultural venues are dotted throughout the districts as well, but Marzahn still has a long way to go.

Orientation

Marzahn-Hellersdorf is on the far eastern edge of Berlin surrounded by Brandenburg in the east, Köpenick in the south, Lichtenberg in the west and Hohenschönhausen in the north. It's about 9km east of Alexanderplatz via Landsberger Allee. The Erholungspark Marzahn is smack-dab in the middle and the only large patch of green in the district.

Plattenbauten (above)

Charlotte von Mahldorf – The Grande 'Dame' of the GDR

Perhaps more interesting than the exhibits of the Gründerzeit Museum is the history of its eccentric founder, Charlotte von Mahlsdorf, the most famous gay figure in the GDR. As a small child, Charlotte already had a passion for dresses and bric-a-brac, and was a source of embarrassment for her Nazi father, who tried disciplining her into being a man. She responded at age 15 by bludgeoning him to death with his own revolver.

Having spent the final years of WWII in prison, Charlotte fully indulged in her passion for collecting furniture and *objets d'art* after the war, opening her first museum in 1960 in two rooms of the manor house. This eventually grew to 23 rooms but, under investigation by the East German tax authorities, Charlotte gave much of it away to friends in the early '70s, rather than risk it being confiscated.

Major recognition came in 1992 when Rosa von Praunheim made her the subject of a feature film and she was awarded the Cross of the Order of Merit by the German government. That same year, though, neo-Nazi attacks on her estate prompted Charlotte to flee to Sweden. Her final years were tainted by revelations that she had been a Stasi informant. She died of a heart attack during a visit to Berlin, two days after completing the recording of her autobiography, which was published in 2002 under the title, *I am my Own Woman*.

ERHOLUNGSPARK MARZAHN

☎ 546 980; www.erholungspark-marzahn.de; Eisenacher Strasse 98; adult/concession €2/1; ☼ park: 9am-4pm Nov-Feb, 9am-5pm Mar & Oct, 9am-7pm Apr, 9am-8pm May-Sep; Japanese Garden: from 1pm Mon-Fri, from 9am Sat & Sun mid-Apr–Oct, closing times same as main park; S-Bahn Marzahn, then bus 195 direction Mahlsdorf

This sprawling park, which opened in 1987 in celebration of Berlin's 750th anniversary, offers a breath of fresh air in densely populated eastern Berlin suburbia. You can wander among the rhododendrons and take the kids to the playground or animal preserve, but the biggest draw here is a trio of exotic gardens.

The **Chinese Garden** is the largest of its kind in Europe (2.7 hectares) and a collaboration between Berlin and its sister city Beijing. Designed by Chinese landscape artists, it centres on a big lake embedded in a hilly landscape. At the authentic teahouse you can sample green tea or participate in a traditional tea ceremony (reservations required; ☎ 0179-394 5564).

The **Japanese Garden**, designed by Yokohama-based priest and professor Shunmyo Masuno, uses water, rocks and plants to create an oasis of tranquillity and spirituality.

The newest in the trio is the **Balinese Garden** inside a greenhouse, which recreates a traditional family home in a jungle setting complete with ferns, orchids and frangipani tree.

GRÜNDERZEIT MUSEUM

☎ 567 8329; www.gruenderzeitmuseum.de; Hultschiner Damm 333; adult/concession €4.10/3.10; ☼ 10am-6pm Wed & Sun; S-Bahn Mahlsdorf, then tram 62 for 2 stops

Housed in the 18th-century Mahlsdorfer Gutshaus, this museum features a series of late 19th-century period rooms that offer a glimpse of the lifestyle during the early years of the German empire, ie the Gründerzeit (roughly 1870 to 1890). It's the brainchild of Charlotte von Mahlsdorf (1928–2002), born Lothar Berfelde, the GDR's most famous transvestite and gay icon (see the boxed text). Besides six fully furnished living rooms, there's also a kitchen, servant's quarters and, a true highlight, the Mulackritze, a famous gay bar that originally stood at Mulackstrasse 15 in the Scheunenviertel.

HANDWERKSMUSEUM & FRISEURMUSEUM

☎ 541 0231; www.stadtmuseum.de; Alt-Marzahn 31; adult/concession €2/1; ☼ 10am-6pm Tue, Wed, Sat & Sun; S-Bahn Springpfuhl, then tram 8, 18

These small and quirky museums are ensconced in an old farmhouse in Alt-Marzahn, a reconstructed medieval village complete with cobblestone lanes, a church and a wooden windmill. Although it stands on the grounds of an actual 13th-century settlement, it's a rather strange sight amid Marzahn's modern high-rises.

In the main building, the **Friseurmuseum** (Hairdressing Museum) displays an assortment of scissors, haircutting machines, crimping shears, dryers and other tools of the trade. A separate exhibit offers a keen introduction into the mysteries of wig making, while fans of Art Nouveau artist Henry van de Velde will delight in the furniture he designed for a Berlin hair salon.

The former stables now harbour the **Handwerksmuseum** (Crafts Museum) with its collection of tools, workshops and ceremonial guild sceptres and flags. Special pride of place goes to a huge collection of locks and keys, including some from the demolished Berlin City Palace.

Walking Berlin

Walking Berlin

Berlin is a great city for walking as it's reasonably compact and divided into clearly defined districts, each sprinkled with an intriguing cluster of sights and attractions. This chapter outlines six self-guided tour options (for Organised Tours, see p77). 'Essential Berlin' is perfect for first-time Berlin visitors as it introduces you to most of the city's 'must-see' sights. 'Jewish Life in the Scheunenviertel' is a fascinating exploration of historic and contemporary places associated with Berlin's Jewish community. If you want to see how the cityscape has evolved since reunification, follow the 'Contemporary Architecture' tour. Finally, there's a trio of tours taking you into the heart of Berlin's most appealing and interesting neighbourhoods – Charlottenburg, Kreuzberg and Prenzlauer Berg – covering the main attractions plus a few less obvious surprises. Happy trails!

ESSENTIAL BERLIN

Berlin in a nutshell: this walk covers all of Mitte's blockbuster sights, starting with the Reichstag, then following Unter den Linden east to Museumsinsel and ending in the heart of the Scheunenviertel. Along the way, you'll be treated to great views, fabulous architecture and plenty of places you might know from the history books.

Start at the hulking **Reichstag 1** (p99), where it's well worth joining the inevitable queue for the lift ride to the famous rooftop glass cupola. Back on solid ground, take a quick spin around the spanking new government buildings before heading east on Scheidemannstrasse, then south on Ebert-

Walk Facts

Start Reichstag (S-Bahn Unter den Linden)
Finish Hackesche Höfe (S-Bahn Hackescher Markt)
Distance 5km
Duration 2–3 hours, without museums

Gendarmenmarkt (p84)

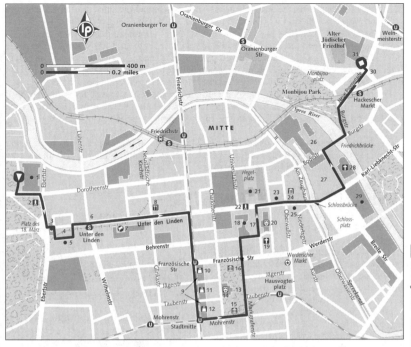

strasse. This takes you past the moving **Wall Victims Memorial 2**, which honours those who died trying to escape the sinister clutches of the GDR. A few more steps and you'd better get your camera ready for the majestic **Brandenburg Gate 3** (p80), the ultimate symbol of German reunification. It anchors the newly reconstructed **Pariser Platz 4** (p82), where you should pop into the **DG Bank 5** (p82) and ask nicely for permission to gawk at Frank Gehry's stunning atrium.

Pariser Platz gives way to **Unter den Linden 6** (p80), Berlin's grandest boulevard. On your right you soon spy the **Russian Embassy 7** (p82), a monumental confection in white marble. Nearby, the elegant **Café Einstein 8** (p181) makes for some stylish refuelling. A short walk south on Friedrichstrasse takes you to the ultradeluxe **Friedrichstadtpassagen 9** (p84), where you should check out Jean Nouvel's shimmering cone inside the **Galeries Lafayette 10** (p227), and Henry Cobb and IM Pei's coloured marble fantasy in **Quartier 206 11** (p228). The food court in **Quartier 205 12** (p228) offers plenty more options for fighting off hunger pangs.

Proceed by turning left on Mohrenstrasse to the **Gendarmenmarkt 13** (p84), Berlin's most beautiful square, which is anchored by Schinkel's **Konzerthaus 14** (p85) and the soaring towers of the **Deutscher Dom 15** (p84) and the **Französischer Dom 16** (p84).

Walk north on Markgrafenstrasse, then east on Behrenstrasse to **Bebelplatz 17** (p80), site of the infamous Nazi book burnings in 1933. A trio of stately 18th-century buildings orbits this handsome square: the **Alte Königliche Bibliothek 18** (p80), the **Sankt-Hedwigs-Kathedrale 19** (p82) and the **Staatsoper Unter den Linden 20** (p83).

Bebelplatz spills out onto Unter den Linden, which here is lined by a parade of gorgeous historic buildings, including **Humboldt Universität 21** (p81) and Schinkel's **Neue Wache 22** (p82). Also take a peak at Christian Daniel Rauch's epic **Reiterdenkmal Friedrich des Grossen 23** (statue of King Frederick the Great; p82). The pink building further east is the Zeughaus, an armoury converted into the **Deutsches Historisches Museum 24** (set to reopen in late 2004; p81). Its new wing by IM Pei, behind the main building, opened to great fanfare in 2003. Opposite, on the south side of Unter den Linden, is the ornate **Kronprinzenpalais 25** (p81).

Just past the Zeughaus, the Schlossbrücke – with its Schinkel-designed marble sculptures of gods and warriors – crosses a little canal to the **Museumsinsel 26** (p86), a cluster of world-class repositories of art, sculpture, classical antiquities and other amazing finds from around the world. Before getting to the museums, you'll spot a domed cathedral across the green expanse of the **Lustgarten 27** (p87): the **Berliner Dom 28** (p86), which has great city views from the gallery level. The royal city palace once stood just south of here on Schlossplatz, right where the GDR built its hideous **Palast der Republik 29** (p88), scheduled for demolition at press time.

For nice views of the back of Berliner Dom, follow Bodestrasse east across the Spree to Burgstrasse, then head north to get to the **Scheunenviertel 30** (p93), Berlin's historic Jewish quarter and now one of the hippest and most vibrant parts of town, with great eating, shopping and nightlife. A highlight here is the **Hackesche Höfe 31** (p93), reached by following Neue Promenade east to Hackescher Markt. This is a good place to end this tour. If you can muster the energy, you can continue with a detailed exploration of the Scheunenviertel by taking the **Jewish Life in the Scheunenviertel** tour.

JEWISH LIFE IN THE SCHEUNENVIERTEL

Like a phoenix rising from the ashes of WWII, Jewish life is again thriving in Berlin and nowhere is it more concentrated than in the Scheunenviertel, the city's traditional Jewish quarter.

The tour's departure point is the beautiful **Neue Synagogue 1** (p95), the most visible symbol of the city's Jewish renaissance, which houses a small museum called the Centrum Judaicum. The synagogue is flanked to the south by the stylish **Oren 2** (p166), which is a good spot for lunch or dinner, and to the north by the **Jüdische Galerie 3** (p227), which presents works by contemporary Jewish artists.

Walk Facts

Start Neue Synagogue (S-Bahn Oranienburger Strasse)
Finish Hackesche Höfe (S-Bahn Hackescher Markt)
Distance 2.25km
Duration 1½ hours, without museums

Walk northwest, then turn left on Tuch-olskystrasse where, at No 9, stands the **Leo-Baeck-Haus 4**. Originally a rabbinical training college, the 1907 building is now home to the Central Council of Jews in Germany as well as

Hackesche Höfe (p93)

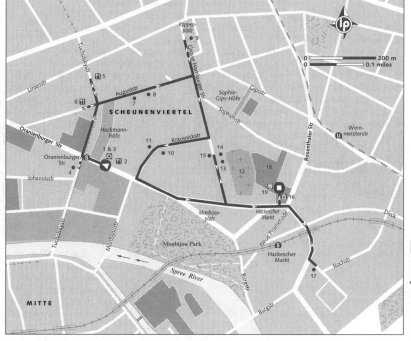

the editorial offices of a Jewish weekly newspaper. It is named for the college's last director, who survived the Theresienstadt concentration camp and died in London in 1956.

Turn back north on Tucholskystrasse to No 40, which houses the headquarters of the Berlin orthodox Jewish congregation, Adass Jisroel. It also operates the certified kosher **Beth Café 5** (p167) on the building's ground floor, as well as **Kolbo 6**, a small store selling kosher groceries, Israeli cosmetics, Menorahs and other items of Judaica. To reach Kolbo, backtrack to Auguststrasse, turn right and it'll be almost immediately there at No 77.

The tour continues east along Auguststrasse, which was once home to several Jewish institutions. The building at No 11/13 housed a **Jewish girls' school 7** from 1930 to 1942, while the one at No 14/16 was originally the **Jewish Hospital 8** and later harboured various Jewish institutions, including a kindergarten and a dental clinic. The Gestapo used it as a detention centre for old and sick Jews earmarked for extermination.

Follow Auguststrasse to Grosse Hamburger Strasse and turn north to Koppenplatz, where you see a table and two chairs, one knocked over, on a bronze floor made to look like wooden parquet. It's an installation called **Der verlassene Raum 9** (The Deserted Room) by Karl Biedermann. The quotes chiselled into a band framing the 'floor' are excerpted from a collection of poems published in 1947 by Nobel prize winner Nelly Sachs.

Walk south on Grosse Hamburger Strasse, then turn right on Krausnickstrasse where, at No 6, a **plaque 10** marks the home of the world's first female rabbi – Regina Jonas – who died in Auschwitz in 1944. Across the street, the **Tabularium 11** (☎ 280 8203; Krausnickstrasse 23; ☺ 11am-8pm Mon-Sat) stocks all manner of Judaica, including books, Klezmer music and kosher wine.

Follow Krausnickstrasse to Oranienburger Strasse, then turn left and left again on Grosse Hamburger Strasse to pay homage to Moses Mendelssohn and the 12,000 other Jews originally buried on the **Alter Jüdischer Friedhof 12** (p93). The Gestapo completely desecrated what was Berlin's first Jewish cemetery in 1943. A single memorial tombstone stands where Mendelssohn is believed to have been buried. Also here are a plaque and

153

a sculpture marking the spot of the city's first **Jewish seniors' home 13** (p93). The building at No 27, originally a **Jewish boys' school 14** (p93), has reopened as a co-ed high school for children of all faiths. Across the street you will see the **Missing House 15** (p93) installation by Christian Boltanski.

Work your way back south, then turn left on Rosenthaler Strasse where the **Museum Blindenwerkstatt Otto Weidt 16** (p94) tells the story of a courageous man who saved the lives of many of his Jewish workers. Another act of courage is commemorated in Rosenstrasse, reached by heading south along An-der-Spandauer-Brücke. Here, a sculpture by Inge Hunzinger called **Block der Frauen 17** (p95) recalls the protest of non-Jewish wives against the arrest of their Jewish husbands in 1943. End your tour by heading back north to the **Hackesche Höfe 18** (p93) where you could conclude the day with a show at the **Hackesches Hoftheater 19** (p93).

CONTEMPORARY ARCHITECTURE

The postreunification building boom has forever changed Berlin's cityscape and put it at the frontier of modern architecture. Nowhere is this trend more evident than in the Tiergarten district. This tour covers three major areas: the government quarter, the diplomatic quarter and Potsdamer Platz.

Start at the **Reichstag 1** (p99) the historic anchor of the Band des Bundes (Ribbon of the Federation), as the new federal-government quarter is called. Just north of the venerable building is the ultramodern **Paul-Löbe-Haus 2** (p99), which is connected by a double bridge across the Spree to the even more dramatic **Marie-Elisabeth-Lüders-Haus 3** (p99). West of this complex is the humungous **Bundeskanzleramt 4** (p98), where the chancellor and his cabinet hatch their plans for the future of the country. North of here, at Otto-von-Bismarck-Allee 4, the **Swiss Embassy 5** has linked its original historic wing to a jarringly postmodern extension.

Make your way south to John-Foster-Dulles-Allee, passing the **Haus der Kulturen der Welt 6** (p98), with its bizarre roof line that made headlines in 1957. There's a café inside. As you continue west, look across the Spree at the new megahousing development for government employees, called 'The Snake' 7 (p100) on account of its wavy outline. Turn left on Spreeweg, past **Schloss Bellevue 8** (p100), the home of the German president, to his office building, the distinctly oval **Bundespräsidialamt 9** (p100).

Make your way south to the Grosser Stern roundabout with the **Siegessäule 10** (p100) at its centre, then continue south along Hofjägerallee, where you'll soon spy the

Bauhaus Archiv (p103)

Walk Facts

Start Reichstag (S-Bahn Unter den Linden)
Finish Potsdamer Platz (U/S-Bahn Potsdamer Platz)
Distance 5.5km
Duration 2½ hours, without museums

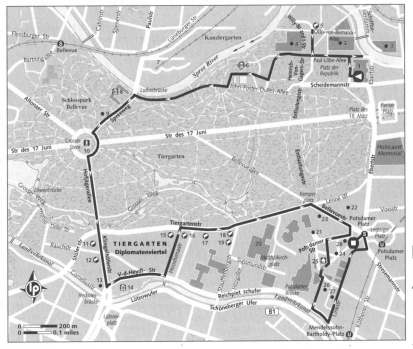

turquoise-panelled façade of the **Nordic Embassies 11** (p50). The complex looks stunning at night when it's lit like a giant crystal. Next door is the equally impressive **Mexican Embassy 12** (p50), fronted by a curtain of slanted concrete columns. It is followed by the new **national headquarters of the CDU 13**, one of Germany's main political parties. The extravagant building resembles an ocean liner encased in a wedge-shaped glass hall.

Across the street is the **Bauhaus Archiv 14** (p103), designed by the 'godfather' of modern architecture, Walter Gropius. It's worth taking a look inside the museum or maybe grabbing a quick cuppa in its cafeteria before continuing east on Von-der-Heydt-Strasse. Turn north on Hiroshimastrasse, which is punctuated by a pair of embassies, the beige **Japanese Embassy 15** (p49) and the pink **Italian Embassy 16** (p49). Both originally date to the Nazi era, which may explain their monumental proportions.

Continue east on Tiergartenstrasse past the new **South African Embassy 17** at No 18 to Stauffenbergstrasse and the **Austrian Embassy 18** (p49). Its immediate southern neighbour is the **Egyptian Embassy 19** (p49), easily recognised by the Pharaonic encryptions decorating its reddish-brown tile façade.

Beyond here, the diplomatic quarter gives way to the **Kulturforum 20** (p103), an architectural showcase created between 1961 and 1987. The tour, however, moves on to **Potsdamer Platz 21** (p101), a veritable treasure trove of contemporary architecture. Enter via Bellevue Avenue where the **Beisheim Center 22** (p101), inspired by American midcentury high-rise architecture, is taking shape on your left. On your right is the **Sony Center 23** (p102), with its dramatic, tented plaza and Helmut Jahn's soaring glass skyscraper. South of Potsdamer Strasse, the **DaimlerCity 24** (p101) complex is a reflection of the creative talents of several world-renowned architects, including Rafael Moneo, who designed the sleek **Grand Hyatt 25** (p245); Renzo Piano, who created the **DaimlerChrysler Building 26**; Arata Isozaki, who's responsible for the **Berliner Volksbank 27** building; and Hans Kollhoff's towering **Kollhoff-Haus 28** (p49), with its distinctive reddish-brown brick mantle. Potsdamer Platz is filled with eateries and cafés in case hunger strikes.

155

CHARLOTTENBURG

This walking tour meanders through the core of the western city centre. It's intended to give you a flavour of the district's commercial and residential areas and will take you past historic landmarks, museums, shopping areas and the design district.

Zoo station 1 (p111) takes its name from the **Berlin Zoo 2** (p111), a wonderful animal park a short walk east along Budapester Strasse. En route you pass the **Zoo-Palast 3**, the cinema that used to host the Berlin International Film Festival, and the ruined **Kaiser-Wilhelm-Gedächtniskirche 4** (p113), a haunting symbol of the destructiveness of WWII.

The Gedächtniskirche looks out over **Breitscheidplatz 5** (p112), a lively square where

the quirky **Weltbrunnen 6** (p112) is a popular people-watching spot. A modern counterpoint to the church is the **Europa-Center 7** (p112), a soaring shopping and restaurant complex that was Berlin's first high-rise when it opened in 1965. Inside is a **BTM tourist office 8** (p291) and the **First Floor 9** (p170) gourmet restaurant, which has reasonably priced business lunches.

Breitscheidplatz is the eastern terminus of Berlin's major shopping street, the **Kurfürstendamm 10** (p111) – better known as Ku'damm. Follow it west to the corner of Joachimstaler Strasse where Helmut Jahn's **Neues Kranzler Eck 11** (p114) soars skyward in all its shiny glass glory. This retail and office complex replaced the venerable Café Kranzler, one of the western city's most traditional coffee houses, of which only the rooftop rotunda remains.

Continue on Ku'damm, then hook south into fashionable **Fasanenstrasse 12** (p112), lined with fancy galleries and *haute couture* boutiques as well as a stately trio of proud villas collectively known as the Wintergarten Ensemble. The Literaturhaus, at No 23, hosts readings and literary discussions and also houses a gallery, a book store and the sophisticated

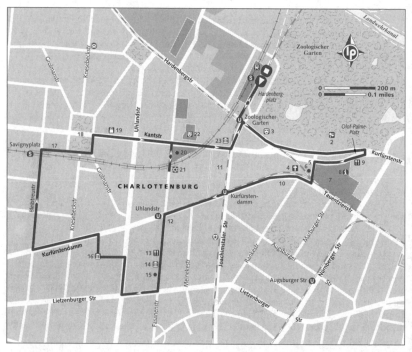

Neues Kranzler Eck (p114)

Café Wintergarten 13 (p169). Next door is the **Käthe-Kollwitz-Museum 14** (p113), followed by the Villa Grisebach, home of the prestigious **Galerie Pels-Leusden 15** and an auction house. Note the frilly iron grill work and witch's hat slate turret on this building.

Continue south to Lietzenburger Strasse, then west one block and north onto Uhlandstrasse where, on the left side of the street, is an entrance to the Ku'damm Karree. The main point of interest of this otherwise nondescript shopping mall is the excellent **Story of Berlin 16** (p114), which takes an 'edutaining' multimedia approach to presenting city history.

Take the Ku'damm exit out of the mall and stroll another two blocks west before cutting north along Bleibtreustrasse to the **Savignypassage 17**. In the 1980s this became the very first place in Berlin where the support archways of the elevated S-Bahn tracks were converted into galleries, stores and restaurants, a concept since copied throughout the city, especially in Mitte. Follow the pedestrian-only passageway past a good stretch of restaurants, cafés and shops to the southern end of **Savignyplatz 18**. This green expanse, bisected by roaring Kantstrasse, has been Charlottenburg's eating and nightlife hub since long before the Wall collapsed. Just east of here, on Kantstrasse, is a small interior design district anchored by **Stilwerk 19** (p231), a multilevel atrium-style mall filled with upmarket design companies as well as a restaurant and jazz club.

Continue east on Kantstrasse where you can soon spy Josef Paul Kleihues landmark **Kantdreieck 20** (p113), with its unmistakeable metal 'sail'. A quick detour south on Fasanenstrasse takes you to the **Jüdisches Gemeindehaus 21** (p112), built on the site of a synagogue destroyed during the 1938 Kristallnacht pogroms. Back on Kantstrasse, stroll past the 1896 **Theater des Westens 22** (p210), which looks majestic despite being an architectural jumble of baroque, neoclassical and Art Nouveau elements. If you're over 18 you're free to visit the exhibits of Berlin's **Erotik Museum 23** (p111), a little further east. From here it's just one block north back to Zoo station and the end of the tour.

KREUZBERG

Though devoid of major conventional sights, this tour introduces you to Kreuzberg's many intriguing facets. It starts in the western part of the district, the charming, middle-class neighbourhood around the Kreuzberg hill, and travels via Südstern into the heart of eastern Kreuzberg, the epicentre of Turkish Berlin. It ends on Oranienstrasse, a lively, multicultural strip that puts the 'fun' in funky.

From Mehringdamm U-Bahn station head south, then west on Yorckstrasse past the spiky twin towers of the **Bonifatiuskirche 1**, a neogothic church wedged between a row of apartment buildings. Next up, look for the two giants buttressing a balcony above an ornate iron gate. These belong to the attractive **Hotel Riehmers Hofgarten 2** (p251), a vast block-sized complex wrapped around a leafy sculpture-studded courtyard. A home for the well-heeled in the early 20th century, it now contains a lovely hotel. For a closer look, enter the courtyard through the iron gate. Exit on

Walk Facts

Start U-Bahn station Mehringdamm
Finish Oranienstrasse (U-Bahn Görlitzer Bahnhof)
Distance 6km
Duration 2½–3 hours

the other (south) side on Hagelberger Strasse, turn right, then left on Grossbeerenstrasse (if the gate's closed, walk to the corner of Grossbeerenstrasse and Yorckstrasse, then turn left).

A few more steps and you're at the foot of the Kreuzberg, the hill for which the district is named and which is covered by the rather unruly, rambling **Viktoriapark 3** (p123). Hike to the top for close-ups of the Schinkel-designed **Kreuzberg memorial 4** (p123) and nice views over the city (better in winter when the trees are leafless). Descend on the eastern side and take Methfesselstrasse south to Dudenstrasse, then turn left to arrive at the Platz der Luftbrücke, easily recognised by the **Luftbrückendenkmal 5** (p123), which commemorates the Berlin Airlift of 1948–49 and those who died making it happen. The Nazi-built **Tempelhof airport 6** (p121) behind the memorial served as a pivotal landing site for Allied planes during the airlift. It is scheduled for closure in 2005.

Walk north on Mehringdamm, then turn right on Fidicinstrasse, past the home of the English-language theatre **Friends of Italian Opera 7** (p213) and the windowless, brick **Wasserturm 8** (Water Tower). Looking very much like Rapunzel's tower, it is now a neighbourhood cultural centre.

Turn left on Kopischstrasse and follow it to **Chamissoplatz 9** (p120), a gorgeous square anchored by a peaceful little park and framed by stately 19th-century buildings with wrought-iron balconies. One block north, **Bergmannstrasse 10** (p120) is the lively main artery of western Kreuzberg. It's a fun road teeming with restaurants, cafés, and funky second-hand book and clothing shops, and culminating in Marheinekeplatz. Here be sure to drop into the bustling **Marheineke Markthalle 11** (p235), one of Berlin's few surviving late-19th-century market halls.

Continue east on Bergmannstrasse past a cluster of **cemeteries 12**. Among the many notables buried here, Weimar Republic chancellor Gustav Stresemann is one of the better known. From Südstern, follow Körtestrasse, then Grimmstrasse to the Planufer, which parallels a particularly scenic stretch of the Landwehrkanal. Both banks are lined by handsomely reno-

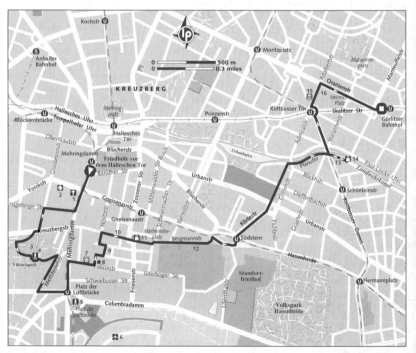

vated early-20th-century buildings and, in good weather, throngs of very happy folk gather by the canal and in nearby cafés and restaurants.

Following Planufer east quickly gets you to **Kottbusser Damm 13**, the bustling main thoroughfare of Turkish Kreuzberg. All along here, grocers, bakeries, supermarkets, shops, department stores and cafés have a distinctive oriental flair. On Tuesday and Friday, the canal banks of the Maybachufer come alive during the colourful **Türkenmarkt 14** (p235).

From the Kottbusser Tor U-Bahn station, head north on Adalbertstrasse, past the **Kreuzberg Museum 15** (p123) to **Oranienstrasse 16**, Kreuzberg's (in)famous nightlife drag which is also a major expanse of cafés, doner kebab takeaways and second-hand boutiques. End your tour here with a stroll, taking in the ambience and maybe staying for a bite to eat.

Marheineke Markthalle (p235)

PRENZLAUER BERG

This tour takes you through one of Berlin's prettiest neighbourhoods, its origins as a 19th-century workers' slum little more than a memory. You'll get an idea of its history, visit sights and places that define the lifestyle of the local population and encounter plenty of opportunities to grab a cuppa or a bite.

Start on **Senefelderplatz 1** (take the southern U-Bahn exit), a triangular patch of green named for the inventor of lithography, Aloys Senefelder (1771–1834); there's a monument to the man in the square's little park. Also here is one of Berlin's few remaining late-19th-century *pissoirs* (urinals), nicknamed Café Achteck for their octagonal shape.

Make a quick detour north on Schönhauser Allee to the **Jüdischer Friedhof 2** (p128), created in 1827 as the second cemetery of Berlin's Jewish community. Double back and turn east on Metzer Strasse, then north on Kollwitzstrasse. Soon on your left, at No 35, is the rather unusual **adventure playground 3**, which engages children in creative play under the supervision of a social worker. Open since 1990, this progressive project was the first such playground in eastern Berlin after reunification.

Continue north to **Kollwitzplatz 4** (p129), the heart of Prenzlauer Berg. This square, which until a few years ago was still framed

> ## Walk Facts
>
> **Start** U-Bahn station Senefelderplatz
> **Finish** U-Bahn station Eberwalder Strasse
> **Distance** 7km
> **Duration** 3 hours

by dilapidated buildings pockmarked with war wounds, has been thoroughly gentrified. Tourist buses plough through here and trendy restaurants, cafés and bars have popped up all over. A **bronze sculpture 5** depicting the square's namesake, the artist Käthe Kollwitz, anchors the square's little park.

Walk east on Knaackstrasse, where you soon come across a row of cafés overlooking the statuesque **Wasserturm 6** (p130), a local landmark that's been converted into flats. To learn more about the district's history, follow Knaackstrasse to Prenzlauer Allee and the **Prenzlauer Berg Museum 7** (p129). Otherwise, turn north on Rykestrasse, strolling past the **Synagoge Rykestrasse 8** (p129), Germany's largest Jewish house of worship. Turn left on Wörther Strasse to get back to Kollwitzplatz, then make your way north on **Husemannstrasse 9** (p128), which

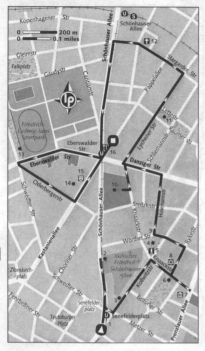

was thoroughly spruced up by the East German government in the late 1980s and is lined with cutesy shops and restaurants.

Following Husemannstrasse to Danziger Strasse and turning left takes you to the **Kulturbrauerei 10** (p129). This enormous 19th-century ex-brewery has become the most exciting cultural venue in Prenzlauer Berg, boasting an eclectic mix of stages, a museum, a restaurant and a multiplex cinema.

Cross Danziger Strasse and follow Lychener Strasse north to **Helmholtzplatz 11**, a parklike square shared by families (at one end) and a group of down-and-outers (at the other). The surrounding streets teem with hip bars and restaurants.

Continue north on Lychener Strasse, then turn left on Stargarder Strasse, a lovely street lined with nice boutiques, cafés and benches inviting a rest. It runs past the **Gethsemanekirche 12** (p128), a beautiful red-brick church framed by magnificent restored 19th-century buildings. In the late 1980s, it was one of the centres of the dissident movement that led to the collapse of the East German government.

A short walk west soon takes you to Schönhauser Allee, a bustling thoroughfare and shopping strip. Follow it south, then turn right on Eberswalder Strasse, which leads to the **Mauerpark 13** (p129), a small park containing one of the few remaining original sections of the Berlin Wall. Continue southeast on Oderberger Strasse, another fun street lined with boutiques selling locally made knickknacks, clothing and accessories. It runs into Kastanienallee, offering more of the same. If the door at Kastanienallee 12 is open, sneak a peek into the **Hirschhof 14**, a miniature park and playground 'guarded' by a bizarre stag sculpture assembled from recycled materials. It's in the third of three successive courtyards. Just north is the **Berliner Prater 15** (p128), a theatre venue with a superb beer garden in summer. Finish up at U-Bahn station Eberswalder Strasse with a famous Currywurst from **Konnopke Imbiss 16** (p190).

Eating

Eating

Berlin's traditional reputation as a culinary wasteland is no longer deserved, with a new generation of chefs, many with international experience, giving fresh impetus to the cuisine scene. Dishes have become lighter, healthier and more interesting. Fresh ingredients, low-fat cooking techniques and seasonal menus are increasingly commonplace.

Asian restaurants especially have proliferated and although spice levels and ingredients are usually calibrated to match conservative local tastes, there's still a decent pad Thai, Madras curry or tuna roll to be found. Vegetarians will be glad to discover that tofu, tempeh and seitan have finally entered the local culinary vernacular. And even those finicky Michelin testers have awarded precious stars to several establishments.

One of life's little luxuries is a leisurely breakfast and Berliners have just about perfected the art, especially on Sundays when many cafés dish out lavish buffets where you can seriously pig out. Speaking of pig...as elsewhere in Germany, it's a staple of traditional Berlin cooking and you may not want to leave town without having sunk your teeth into *Eisbein mit Sauerkraut* (pork knuckle with sauerkraut) or at least a classic *Currywurst* (sausage slices doused in a tangy curried sauce) or *Boulette* (meat patties) at the local *Imbiss* (snack bar). Berlin's most popular fast food, though, is the *döner* (doner kebab) invented here around 20 years ago by a Turkish immigrant (see the boxed text opposite).

German-reading foodies might like to pick up the annual restaurant guides published by *Zitty* and *Tip*, available at newsstands for around €5.

Opening Hours

Cafés and restaurants are usually open seven days a week, although some may observe a *Ruhetag* (closing day), usually Sunday or Monday, when business is slowest. Most restaurants serve lunch and dinner, except for gourmet temples, which are more likely to be dinner-only affairs. Typical lunch hours are noon to 3pm, with dinner between 7.30pm and 10pm. Kitchens stay open until at least 9.30pm and often longer, especially at weekends. Even after midnight, you'll usually find a *döner* or falafel shop feeding flocks of starving

Yosoy (p167)

night owls. Unless noted otherwise, eateries mentioned in this chapter serve lunch and dinner and stay open until at least midnight.

Cafés are best for breakfast. Hotels usually stop serving breakfast at 10am but don't worry if you've overslept: breakfast at a Berlin café is a time-honoured tradition that can be indulged in until well into the afternoon.

How Much?

In this chapter we've included eating options to match all tastes and budgets, with an emphasis on mid-range places where a hot meal and a drink will cost between €15 and €25. At Berlin's top restaurants you can expect to pay upward of €25 for a main course or from €60 for a three- or four-course tasting menu, wine excluded. Budget eateries, including *Imbisse*, *döner* shops and takeaways, where you can fill up for €10 or less, are listed under Cheap Eats in each neighbourhood section.

Booking Tables

Most restaurants take reservations for both lunch and dinner, so call ahead if you want to ensure a table. We've included reservation recommendations for the restaurants most likely to fill fast.

Tipping

Restaurant bills include a service charge and tipping is not compulsory. If you're satisfied with the service, add about 5% to 10%. It's customary to tip as you're handing over the money rather than leaving money on the table. For example say '30, *bitte*' if your bill comes to €28 and you want to give a €2 tip. If you have the exact amount, just say '*Stimmt so*' ('that's fine').

Self Catering

About half a dozen major supermarket chains vie for shoppers throughout Berlin. Kaiser's and especially Reichelt have fresh meat, cheese and deli counters and usually an attached bakery. Discount chains include Aldi, Lidl, Plus and Penny Markt, which offer good quality and a decent assortment in an often helter-skelter warehouse setting. For the ultimate selection, the food hall of the KaDeWe department store (p232) is simply unbeatable but prices are high. Farmers' markets and small Turkish corner stores are also good sources for fresh fruit, olives, breads, cheese spreads and other tasty goodies.

Try these places for stocking up after hours and on Sundays.

Edeka (Map pp328-9; S-Bahnhof Friedrichstrasse; ☺ 6am-10pm Mon-Sat, 8am-10pm Sun)

Lidl (Map pp330-1; U-Bahn station Innsbrucker Platz; ☺ 8am-9pm)

Minimal (Map pp325-7; Ostbahnhof; ☺ 7am-9pm)

Ullrich (Map pp332-3; Hardenbergstrasse 25; ☺ 9am-10pm Mon-Sat, 11am-7pm Sun; U/S-Bahn Zoologischer Garten)

Turkish Delights

The most popular fast food in Berlin is not the hamburger, nor the sausage. It's the doughty doner kebab. Throughout the city you'll find takeaways where giant cones of spiced meat rotate on an upright grill, waiting to be shaved into thin slivers, which are then stuffed into lightly toasted pita bread along with fresh salad and a garlicky yogurt sauce. It's a complete meal usually costing no more than €2.50.

In Turkey, meat has been put through its paces in this fashion for nearly two centuries but the idea of serving it sandwich-style was born in Berlin. Although nobody can really be sure, credit for the creation is usually given to Mehmed Aygün, an enterprising Turkish emigrant who, at the tender age of 16, opened the first *döner* stand in Neukölln in 1971. The success of Aygün's savvy sandwich pole-vaulted him to the helm of the small Hasir chain of eateries.

More than 30 years later, an estimated 1500 eateries sell doner kebab throughout Berlin, collectively doling out about 100 million portions annually. Our favourites are:

- **Grill & Schlemmerbuffet Zach** (p167)
- **Hasir** (p164)
- **Hisar** (p183)
- **Sesam** (p186)
- **Turkiyem Imbiss** (p186)

MITTE

Mitte's culinary scene will spoil you for choice with its international cast of restaurants, cafés and fast-food options. A handful of sizzling young chefs helm kitchens at the dining shrines around the Gendarmenmarkt and along the western end of Unter den Linden. The Scheunenviertel is filled with fun, lively and low-key spots, whereas the Nikolaiviertel attracts a more sedate audience with its Old Berlin flair and hearty German cuisine. Although tourists outnumber locals in most Mitte restaurants, competition keeps the overall quality pleasantly high.

BOCCA DI BACCO Map pp328-9 *Italian*
☎ 2067 2828; Friedrichstrasse 167; mains €17-25; ✕ closed Sun lunch; U-Bahn Französische Strasse
The mother ship in **Charlottenburg** (Map pp332-3; ☎ 211 8687; Marburger Strasse 5; U-Bahn Wittenbergplatz) has been drawing in the faithful for 35 years and this new branch has quickly garnered its own fan club. Champion chef Lorenzo Pizzetti's menu revolves around tender meats, handmade pasta, complex sauces and crisp vegetables. The elegant dining room with its vivid canvases is a feast for the eyes. Reservations recommended.

BORCHARDT Map pp328-9 *Franco-German*
☎ 2039 7117; Französische Strasse 47; mains €10-20; U-Bahn Französische Strasse
Attracting a power crowd of politicians, actors and other newsmakers, Borchardt is like a slice of Beverly Hills in the heart of Berlin. Fortunately, the dining room, with ceilings as lofty as the chef's ambitions, offers fairly unobstructed views of the action. Given the buzz, you may find it hard to focus on the food, but that would truly be a pity. Reservations recommended.

CAFÉ NÖ Map pp328-9 *Wine Café*
☎ 201 0871; Glinkastrasse 23; mains €6-12; ✕ closed Sat lunch & Sun; U-Bahn Mohrenstrasse
There's nothing trendy about this cosily cluttered wine bar and that's exactly why people

---

Top Five Mitte Eats

- **Margaux** (p165)
- **Maxwell** (p165)
- **Monsieur Vuong** (p168)
- **Pan Asia** (p166)
- **Vau** (p167)

---

regularly throng the place. Come for great wines, perfectly matured cheeses and hearty French fare. The wine tasting – five wines, cheese and baguette – is a steal at €14. At lunch time, bureaucrats from the nearby government offices invade the €7 special.

CANTAMAGGIO Map pp328-9 *Italian*
☎ 283 1895; Alte Schönhauser Strasse 4; mains €11-20; ✕ dinner Mon-Sat; U-Bahn Rosa-Luxemburg-Platz
The rather Spartan décor does little to distract diners from the delicious, homemade pasta and more substantial market-fresh mains at this convivial trattoria. Well established since long before tourists 'discovered' the Scheunenviertel, tables here are always crowded, sometimes with actors and directors from the nearby Volksbühne. Reservations advised.

ENGELBRECHT Map pp328-9 *French*
☎ 2859 8585; Schiffbauerdamm 6/7; mains €15-25; ✕ Mon-Sat; U-Bahn Friedrichstrasse
Bertolt Brecht used to be a regular when this was still the legendary Trichter restaurant and he probably would have liked its new incarnation just as well. Ebony furniture, ivory walls and brightly pigmented paintings form a classic setting for Wolfgang Petri's unpretentious yet highly competent cuisine. The focus is on French flavours with occasional excursions into Italy and even Asia.

GOOD TIME Map pp322-4 *Thai*
☎ 2804 6015; Chausseestrasse 1; mains €8-18; U-Bahn Oranienburger Tor
Take a trip to Thailand without packing your bags at this convivial restaurant with its winning mix of traditional yet tantalising food, décor that invites dreams of faraway places and unobtrusive yet efficient staff. Some dishes have Indonesian inflections (satay chicken and the like) but it's the fragrant coconut-based curries that steal the show.

HASIR Map pp328-9 *Turkish*
☎ 2804 1616; Oranienburger Strasse 4; mains €19-28; S-Bahn Hackescher Markt
The flagship branch of this small, family-run chain is a glamorous bazaar tucked into a courtyard around the corner from the Hackesche Höfe. The kitchen produces fireworks of flavours, from feta-filled artichoke hearts to clay-pot braised leg of lamb and loaves of *kuver*, a sesame flat bread served hot from the oven.

Smaller, more casual branches are in **Wilmersdorf** (Map pp332-3; ☎ 217 7774; Nürn-

berger Strasse 46; U-Bahn Augsburger Strasse),
Schöneberg (Map pp330-1; ☎ 215 6060; Maassenstrasse 10; U-Bahn Nollendorfplatz) and
Kreuzberg (Map pp325-7; ☎ 614 2373; Adalbertstrasse 10; U-Bahn Kottbusser Tor).

HONIGMOND
Map pp322-4   *Central European*
☎ 2844 5512; Borsigstrasse 28; lunch buffet €6,
mains €7-12.50; ☾ lunch Mon-Sun; breakfast Sat-Sun;
U-Bahn Oranienburger Tor
This charming restaurant, in business since the
1920s, was packed with dissidents nightly in
GDR times until the Stasi put an end to the
fun in 1987. Revived in 1995, it's now hugely
popular for its inexpensive lunch buffet and is
also good for dinner when *Königsberger Klopse*
(meat balls in caper sauce) and Swiss cheese
fondue top the list of favourites.

KASBAH
Map pp328-9   *Moroccan*
☎ 2759 4361; Gipsstrasse 2; mains €8-15; ☾ dinner;
U-Bahn Weinmeisterstrasse
A tantalising melange of cumin, coriander,
cinnamon and other spices wafts through the
flatteringly lit dining room as you lounge on
fluffy pillows orbiting low round tables. Order a
palate-cleansing mint tea to prepare your taste
buds for such traditional offerings as *tajine*, an
aromatic stew pairing meat, vegetables and
dried fruit, or *b'stilla* (filo filled with almond,
chicken and herbs).

KOKEBE
Map pp322-4   *Ethiopian*
☎ 4849 3578; Anklamer Strasse 38; mains €6.50-12;
☾ dinner; U-Bahn Bernauer Strasse
'Wat's' the matter? Pardon the pun. Wat is,
after all, a classic Ethiopian dish, a robust stew
featuring chunks of chicken or beef floating in
a spicy sauce and served with *injera*, a spongy
flat bread. Don't sulk if you're not a meat eater –
there's plenty of vegetable-based choices as
well. It's in the second courtyard of the Weiberwirtschaft, a complex of women-owned
businesses.

KUCHI
Map pp328-9   *Sushi & Asian*
☎ 2838 6622; Gipsstrasse 3; mains €7-23; U-Bahn
Weinmeisterstrasse
Sushi purists might shudder at the 'extreme'
creations at Kuchi, but the scenesters who
regularly invade the place for their protein
fix gobble 'em up like M&Ms. (How about the
one with deep-fried rice, hot sauce, cucumber and salmon?) Fortunately the menu also

makes forays into more traditional territory
with *yakitori*, tempura, stir-fries, *donburi* and
savoury noodle soups. Also in **Charlottenburg**
(Map pp332-3; ☎ 3150 7815; Kantstrasse 30;
S-Bahn Savignyplatz).

MALETE
Map pp328-9   *Turkish*
☎ 280 7759; Chausseestrasse 131; mains €6-13;
U-Bahn Oranienburger Tor
This cheerful little restaurant, whose name
translates as 'our home', serves delicious Turkish food that goes far beyond the usual *döner*
fare. Meat lovers should try anything with
lamb, whereas vegetarians can pick from such
inspired choices as *soslu enginar*, a medley of
sautéed artichokes with mushrooms, peppers
and other vegetables bathed in a herbed
cream sauce (€8.50).

MARGAUX
Map pp328-9   *French*
☎ 2265 2611; Unter den Linden 78; mains €24-40;
☾ closed Sun lunch; S-Bahn Unter den Linden
It took culinary wunderkind Michael Hoffman only one year to wrest a star from the
notoriously pedantic Michelin testers. With
that, Margaux instantly became the place
in which to be seen. And Hoffmann's avantgarde interpretations of classic French cuisine
are tasty. Meanwhile, the sensuous setting –
picture back-lit onyx walls, marble floors
and burgundy banquettes – offers serious involvement for the eyes.

MAXWELL
Map pp322-4   *International*
☎ 280 7121; Bergstrasse 22; mains €16-20;
☾ dinner; U-Bahn Rosenthaler Platz
Lou Reed, Oliver Stone and art-world *enfant
terrible* Damien Hirst (who's a friend of the
owner) are among the celebrity patrons of
this gorgeously restored 1895 red-brick exbrewery. It was Hirst's artwork featuring two
ducks encased in blue Plexiglas (on the wall
leading to the upper floor) that inspired the
signature dish: duck breast and confit with
black pepper sauce. In summer, the idyllic
courtyard is the place to sit.

MILAGRO
Map pp328-9   *Mediterranean*
☎ 2758 2330; Oranienburger Strasse 54-56, inside
Tacheles; mains €7-15; ☾ 10-2am; U-Bahn
Oranienburger Tor
Those who remember the Tacheles as an
anarchic artists' squat will do a double take
at this street-level restaurant with its nifty
green leather banquettes, oversized mirrors

and gilded ceiling. The food's mostly Mediterranean with modern German touches, and there's even a good breakfast selection. Nice garden, too.

The original **Kreuzberg** branch is more casual (Map pp325-7; ☎ 692 2303; Bergmannstrasse 12; U-Bahn Gneisenaustrasse).

NOLA'S AM WEINBERG

Map pp322-4   *International*
☎ 440 40766; Veteranenstrasse 9; mains €8-15;
U-Bahn Rosenthaler Platz

Location, location, location. Just north of the Scheunenviertel hubbub, this classy restaurant in a 1950s pavilion is an island of quiet afloat in an idyllic little park. In summer the terrace beckons but even if the weather gods are sinister you'll get to enjoy the same creative flavour pairings in the stylish retro ambience inside.

OREN Map pp328-9   *Jewish & Middle Eastern*
☎ 282 8228; Oranienburger Strasse 28; mains €6-15;
S-Bahn Oranienburger Strasse

Fuse cool moderne design with an eclectic crowd and you get this swank stop right next to the New Synagogue. Although this well-established place has lost some of its buzz quotient, the Orient-Express appetiser platter (€10) still offers an excellent sampling of tastes and textures. Other choices, all of them meatless, include casseroles, pickled fish and pastas. Menus come in Hebrew, English and German.

PAN ASIA Map pp328-9   *Asian*
☎ 2790 8811; Rosenthaler Strasse 38; mains €6-13;
S-Bahn Hackescher Markt

Manga films, video installations and long communal tables account for the high hipster quotient at this courtyard restaurant (outdoor seating in summer) next to the Hackesche Höfe. As the name suggests, the menu hopscotches from Thailand to China to Japan to Vietnam and back, mostly with convincing results. Spices are calibrated for German tastes but the chef's happy to turn up the heat on request.

RESTAURANT KÜRBIS

Map pp322-4   *Austrian*
☎ 5365 5960; Ackerstrasse 155; mains €12-18;
☾ dinner; U-Bahn Rosenthaler Platz

With pumpkins on the menu and the tables, you don't need German skills to figure out the meaning of *Kürbis*. Part of the charming An-

dechser Hof hotel (p241), this rustically elegant restaurant makes a classic Wiener schnitzel alongside more current creations such as, yes, pumpkin risotto. Wash it down with the excellent Andechser beer from Bavaria.

ROSMINI PASTA-MANUFAKTUR

Map pp322-4   *Italian*
☎ 2809 6844; Invalidenstrasse 151; mains €9-16;
☾ lunch Mon-Fri, dinner daily; U-Bahn Rosenthaler Platz

From linguine to rigatoni and fusilli; they're all handmade and fresh at this easy-going trattoria with its almost monastic furnishings. Chef Massimo finds endless way to pair his product with vegetables, meats, fish and sauces, which is why there's a new menu daily. Be sure to try the superb Teresianer beer imported from Italy.

SCHWARZENRABEN Map pp328-9   *Italian*
☎ 2839 1698; Neue Schönhauser Strasse 13; mains €19-23; ☾ 10-2am; U-Bahn Weinmeisterstrasse

This humming place is a darling of the see-and-be-seen crowd. The food is only so-so and the service even worse, but there's no denying that the historic hall (originally a late-19th-century soup kitchen), with its big arched windows and contemporary décor, is a winner in the looks department.

STÄV Map pp328-9   *German*
☎ 282 3965; Schiffbauerdamm 8; mains €6-12;
U-Bahn Friedrichstrasse

This place began as an island of Rhenish *joie de vivre* for homesick Bonn politicians and their entourages. Both Rhineland and Berlin specialities are served. The strange name, by the way, is an acronym for *Ständige Vertretung*, the euphemism used for the West German embassy in the former GDR.

THEODOR TUCHER Map pp320-1   *German*
☎ 2294 9464; Pariser Platz 6a; mains €6.50-16;
☾ 9-1am; S-Bahn Unter den Linden

The only eatery right on Pariser Platz unites a restaurant, café and literary salon beneath one roof supported by shiny copper-coloured columns. Chef Deff Haupt turns such ordinary dishes as pork knuckle and chicken fricassee into gourmet affairs, reportedly delighting even George W Bush on his 2002 state visit. The upstairs café, with its library looks and comfy armchairs, is the perfect sightseeing break.

Theodor Tucher (opposite)

UNSICHT-BAR Map pp322-4 *International*
☎ 2434 2500; Gormannstrasse 14; 3-/4-course menu
€40/45; ☾ dinner; U-Bahn Weinmeisterstrasse
Dinner at this boundary-pushing restaurant is a delicious treat for all the senses but one: sight. The dining room is bathed in pitch-black, can't-see-the-end-of-your-nose darkness. Mobile phones, cigarettes and any light source, however small, are banished. After choosing from several menus in the (lighted) reception area, you'll be led to your table by a sight-impaired server. Also see p213.

VAU Map pp328-9 *International*
☎ 202 9730; Jägerstrasse 54; lunch €12 per course; dinner mains €35, prix fixe menu from €75; ☾ noon-2.30pm & 7-10.30pm Mon-Sat; U-Bahn Hausvogteiplatz
In the same locale where Rahel Varnhagen held her literary salons a couple of centuries ago, Michelin-starred chef Kolja Kleeberg now pampers a Rolls-Royce crowd of diners with his fanciful gourmet creations. Hand-selected, seasonal ingredients find their destiny in such dishes as dove breast with polenta, or scallops with red beets. For the ultimate indulgence, order the degustation menu.

YOSOY Map pp328-9 *Spanish*
☎ 2839 1213; Rosenthaler Strasse 37; tapas €2-5, mains €7.50-15; S-Bahn Hackescher Markt
This lovely tapas bar transports you straight to Andalusia with its sunny walls, Moorish tiles and buzzing mix of tourists, Spanish expats and Iberophile Berliners. There's a fine menu of mains, including *filete de toro* (bull fillet), but regulars prefer sipping their sherry while grazing on classic tapas such as Serrano ham, tuna-stuffed peppers and potato tortilla.

ZUM NUSSBAUM
Map pp328-9 *German*
☎ 242 3095; Am Nussbaum 3; mains €6-9; U/S-Bahn Alexanderplatz
For old-time Berlin flair, this no-nonsense pub in the Nikolaiviertel has got the goods. It's an exact replica of the 1571 original, which stood on nearby Fischerinsel until WWII bombs put an end to it. Low ceilings, walls sheathed in shiny mahogany and a simple, stick-to-the-ribs menu perfectly re-create the times of yore. Touristy but still comfortingly authentic.

CHEAP EATS
BAGELS & BIALYS Map pp328-9 *Deli*
☎ 283 6546; Rosenthaler Strasse 46-48; dishes €2-5; ☾ until 5am; S-Bahn Hackescher Markt
This hole-in-the-wall has demonstrated impressive staying power in an area where yesterday's hot spot can go cold overnight. Office workers, tourists and night owls flock here to fuel up on bagels, salads, soups, *shwarma* and other pick-me-ups. Most offerings are made to order so expect a wait.

BETH CAFÉ Map pp328-9 *Kosher*
☎ 281 3135; Tucholskystrasse 40; mains €2-9; ☾ noon-8pm Sun-Thu, U-Bahn Oranienburger Strasse
This is a good-value café-bistro with a smoking ban and a pretty inner courtyard perfect for enjoying a leisurely lunch of lox on toast, various salads, gefilte fish or other staples of Jewish cuisine. It's affiliated with the congregation of Adass Jisroel, which also operates **Kolbo** (Map pp328-9; Auguststrasse 77-78), a small kosher market.

GRILL & SCHLEMMERBUFFET ZACH
Map pp322-4 *Middle Eastern*
☎ 283 2153; Torstrasse 125; dishes €1.10-5; ☾ 24hr; U-Bahn Rosenthaler Platz
This tiny takeaway gets our vote for best doner kebab in town. Portions are huge, the meat (veal or chicken) is light and shaved into thin slivers, the bread is toasted to perfection, the

Eating – Mitte

Top Five German Restaurants
- Alte Meierei (p168)
- Altes Zollhaus (p184)
- Fritz Fischer (p187)
- Offenbach Stuben (p189)
- Stäv (p166)

salads are fresh and the yogurt sauce has just the right garlic kick. A favourite with clubbers, cabbies and neighbours.

MONSIEUR VUONG Map pp328-9 *Asian*
☎ 3087 2643; Alte Schönhauser Strasse 46; mains €6.40; U-Bahn Rosa-Luxemburg-Platz
Despite the pepper-red walls, good-looking clientele and beautiful dishware, this bustling eatery only looks expensive. The Vietnamese fare – soups and two or three main courses daily – is made to order and is uniformly delicious, as are the fruit cocktails and exotic teas. No reservations, so be prepared to queue.

PICCOLA ITALIA Map pp328-9 *Italian*
☎ 283 5843; Oranienburger Strasse 6; dishes €3-7; ☾ until 1am Sun-Thu, until 3am Fri-Sat; S-Bahn Hackescher Markt
This takeout-only pizzeria around the corner from the Hackesche Höfe is always packed with snackers hungry for tasty, toothsome food. Mini-pizzas start at €1.50.

TIERGARTEN

Most of Tiergarten's eating options are as exalted as you'd expect from a neighbourhood teeming with diplomats, politicians and business executives. The quality, alas, doesn't always justify the steep price tags, a dictum especially true of the Potsdamer Platz establishments. Fortunately, there are a few real gems to be found, some just slightly away from the glitz.

ALTE MEIEREI Map pp320-1 *Modern German*
☎ 399 200; Alt-Moabit 99; mains €14-17; ☾ 11am-3pm; U-Bahn Turmstrasse
It's lunch time or no time if you want to sample the cut-above cuisine of German TV chef Rainer Strobel. The setting alone, in the stables of a historic dairy, offers eye-candy galore, with a neatly scalloped red-brick ceiling supported by inky cast-iron columns. It's a stylish backdrop for the delicious dishes revolving around light, healthy and local ingredients. The Sunday jazz brunch draws big crowds.

Top Three Tiergarten Eats
- Angkor Wat (this page)
- Edd's (this page)
- Kaisersaal (this page)

ANGKOR WAT Map pp320-1 *Cambodian*
☎ 393 3922; Paulstrasse 22; mains €10-16; ☾ dinner; S-Bahn Bellevue
This exotic, cavernous place serves Cambodian fondue, which involves cooking your own meat and fresh vegetables in a steaming cauldron right at your table (€35 for two). The other dishes, many of them coconut-milk-based, offer an intriguing cocktail of flavours. Service is unhurried and generous with the smiles.

CAFÉ AM NEUEN SEE Map pp330-1 *Café*
☎ 254 4930; Lichtensteinallee 2; mains €7-12; ☾ daily Mar-Oct, Sat-Sun Nov-Feb; U/S-Bahn Zoologischer Garten
This huge lake-side beer garden in Tiergarten park is a picturesque place to while away a warm summer night. For sustenance, there's Bavarian sausage, pretzels and pizza. And you can even rent a boat to take your sweetie for a spin.

DIEKMANN IM WEINHAUS HUTH
Map p334 *French*
☎ 2529 7524; Alte Potsdamer Strasse 5; mains €14-20; U/S-Bahn Potsdamer Platz
Oysters are a speciality at this elegant restaurant inside the only prewar Potsdamer Platz building. If you're not into slimy molluscs, you might start things off with a bowl of *Bouilli* (a savoury consommé), followed by *coq au vin* and truly decadent *crème brûlée*. The €10 weekday lunch, including one main course, mineral water and espresso, is great value.

EDD'S Map pp330-1 *Thai*
☎ 215 5294; Lützowstrasse 81; mains €8-16; ☾ dinner; U-Bahn Kurfürstenstrasse
Thai restaurants have proliferated like rabbits on Viagra in recent years, but Edd's, one of Berlin's oldest, is still king. The eponymous owner helms the kitchen most nights, churning out such palate-pleasers as twice-roasted duck and chicken steamed in banana leaves. Even the curries are culinary poetry. Reservations essential.

KAISERSAAL Map p334 *Franco-German*
☎ 2575 1454; Bellevuestrasse 1; mains €25-30; ☾ dinner; U/S-Bahn Potsdamer Platz
Emperor Wilhelm II used to dine in this magnificent neorococo hall when it was still part of the Hotel Esplanade, the grandest of the old Potsdamer Platz hotels. Now his life-size likeness looks out over patrons savouring the fantastic

creations of Mario Mauthner. This hot Austrian chef digs deep into his repertory to give dove, duck or dorado the gourmet treatment.

CHEAP EATS

ASIA PAVILLON Map p334 *Chinese*
Potsdamer Platz Arkaden; meals €3.50-9.50; ✆ 9am-8pm; U/S-Bahn Potsdamer Platz

Go ye forth and shop! But before you drop, stop by this bustling self-service Chinese kitchen, which doles out respectable fast food – hot, cheap and heaps of it. The tasty soups (around €2) are great for fighting off a cold.

SALOMON BAGELS Map p334 *Deli*
☎ 2529 7626; Potsdamer Platz Arkaden; dishes €2-4; ✆ 9am-8pm; U/S-Bahn Potsdamer Platz

The lowly bagel goes spiritual at this sleek shopping-mall café (the owners actually regard them as 'wisdom that's fit to eat'). Pair a plain bagel with some jam or Nutella, or go savoury with your favourite spread, from avocado to the classic cream cheese and lox. Soups and salads, too. There's a second branch in **Charlottenburg** (Map pp332-3; ☎ 881 8196; Joachimstaler Strasse 13; U-Bahn Kurfürstendamm).

CHARLOTTENBURG

Mitte may have the edge when it comes to trendiness and ambitious chefs pushing the culinary envelope but there's no doubt that some of the city's finest restaurants are still in Charlottenburg. Many places are well established and have a loyal following among the generally affluent, professional locals for whom eating out is a popular pastime. A clutch of interesting restaurants and cafés line Kurfürstendamm, Kantstrasse and their side streets. The most fashionable haunts cluster around Savignyplatz, although the residential streets around Sophie-Charlotte-Platz, south of Schloss Charlottenburg, yield great off-the-beaten-track discoveries.

ALT-LUXEMBURG

Map pp330-1 *Franco-German*
☎ 323 8730; Windscheidstrasse 31; mains €24-28, 4-/5-course meal €65/72; ✆ dinner Mon-Sat; U-Bahn Sophie-Charlotte-Platz

Like a good wine, this elegant but disarmingly unpretentious restaurant – a gourmet mainstay for more than two decades – only gets better with age. Owner-chef Karl Wannemacher's

Top Five Charlottenburg Eats
- **Alt-Luxemburg** (this page)
- **Cassambalis** (this page)
- **First Floor** (p170)
- **Jules Verne** (p179)
- **Mar y Sol** (p179)

signature dishes are foie gras and lobster, but he also does great things with vegetables and quality meats. Service is swift and attentive.

ARCHE NOAH Map pp332-3 *Kosher*
☎ 882 6138; Fasanenstrasse 79; mains €10-17, buffet €18; ✆ 11.30am-3.30pm & 6.30-11pm; U/S-Bahn Zoologischer Garten

Berlin's oldest certified kosher restaurant is a small and old-fashioned kind of place upstairs in the Jewish Community House. The menu features lots of traditional favourites such as kreplach, gefilte fish and beef brisket. Insiders book a table for Tuesday night's scrumptious buffet, a smorgasbord of 30 different tasty hot and cold dishes from Europe and the Middle East.

BORRIQUITO Map pp332-3 *Spanish*
☎ 312 9929; Wielandstrasse 6; mains €7-13; ✆ 7pm-5am; S-Bahn Savignyplatz

Don't be surprised if you show up at dinner time and find this place as empty as a politician's promise. Most nights, the 'little donkey' doesn't really kick up its hooves until midnight when fans of flamenco, sherry and classic Spanish cuisine (lots of meaty mains) move in for the fiesta, often with live guitar music.

CAFÉ WINTERGARTEN IM LITERATURHAUS Map pp332-3 *Café*
☎ 882 5414; Fasanenstrasse 23; mains €10-16; ✆ 9.30-1am; U-Bahn Uhlandstrasse

Book rats, artists and shoppers gather at this lovely Art Nouveau villa on one of Berlin's most exclusive streets. When the weather plays along, the idyllic garden is ideal for a light lunch or a leisurely afternoon of coffee and cake. In contrast, the black furniture and stucco ceilings of the interior ooze intellectual flair.

CASSAMBALIS Map pp332-3 *Mediterranean*
☎ 885 4747; Grolmanstrasse 35; mains €9-24; U-Bahn Uhlandstrasse

Owner Costas Cassambalis pairs passions for art and food in his congenial restaurant,

Cassambalis (p169)

popular with everyone from Charlottenburg literati to guests of the adjacent Hecker's Hotel (p246). Regulars swear by the grilled dorado and the tender beef roulade, although we were seriously impressed by the huge buffet (hot and cold dishes at lunch, antipasti at night). Reservations recommended.

DIE ZWÖLF APOSTEL Map pp332-3 *Italian*
☎ 312 1433; Bleibtreustrasse 49; pizza €9-12, mains €15-18; ⊙ 24hr; S-Bahn Savignyplatz
This eatery with its 'heavenly' décor of cherubs, frescoes and gaudy chandeliers brims with people lusting after excellent, if pricey, wood-fired pizzas named for the apostles. Divine intervention may be necessary to score a table on weekdays when the business lunch costs a mere €5. Also in **Mitte** (Map pp328-9; ☎ 201 0222; Georgenstrasse 2; S-Bahn Hackescher Markt).

ENGELBECKEN Map pp318-19 *Bavarian*
☎ 615 2810; Witzlebenstrasse 31; mains €8-16; ⊙ 4pm-1am Mon-Sat, noon-1am Sun; U-Bahn Sophie-Charlotte-Platz
It's no Munich beer hall but this corner restaurant with its big windows and scrubbed wooden tables serves what many say is Berlin's best Bavarian food. The menu features all the usual suspects such as *Weisswürste* with chewy pretzels, roast pork with dumplings and red cabbage, and apple strudel with custard. All meats are organic.

FIRST FLOOR Map pp332-3 *French*
☎ 2502 1020; 1st fl, Palace Hotel, Europa-Center, Budapester Strasse 45; mains €30-38; ⊙ closed Sat lunch; U/S-Bahn Zoologischer Garten
Michael Buchholz is a shooting star on Berlin's growing gourmet scene. Young and ambitious, he pairs first-rate ingredients and classic cooking techniques into such sophisticated dishes as Bresse chicken and filo-wrapped venison fillet. For gourmets on the run there's even a three-course business lunch (€40) designed to get you in and out in less than an hour.

GOOD FRIENDS Map pp332-3 *Chinese*
☎ 313 2659; Kantstrasse 30; mains €7-19; S-Bahn Savignyplatz
It's the dangling ducks in the window that offer the first hint this is not your run-of-the-mill Chinese restaurant. Good Friends is a bona fide Cantonese dining parlour where you can indulge in such delicacies as 'thousand-year-old egg with jelly fish' and 'sea cucumber with fish belly'. If this proves just a tad too challenging, you can always go with the *kung pao* chicken.

HARD ROCK CAFÉ Map pp332-3 *American*
☎ 884 620; Meinekestrasse 21; mains €8-16; U-Bahn Uhlandstrasse, Kurfürstendamm
This place gets a quick mention in case you're keen to add to your T-shirt collection or simply have a hankering for a great burger. Otherwise, it's the same predictable mix of rock memorabilia, loud music and fast service.

HITIT Map pp318-19 *Turkish*
☎ 322 4557; Knobelsdorffstrasse 35; mains €7.50-15; ⊙ dinner, plus lunch Sun; U-Bahn Sophie-Charlotte-Platz
Stone reliefs and fountains create a stylish and relaxed ambience in this popular Turkish restaurant off the tourist track. The combination of hot and cold appetisers is 'finger-lickin' good', though main courses of grilled lamb, as well as the meatless casseroles, are tasty choices too.

Top Five Breakfast Cafés
- Buddha Lounge (p188)
- Jules Verne (p179)
- Milagro (p165)
- Morgenland (p185)
- Tomasa (p183)

(Continued on page 179)

1 Contemporary music posters
2 Metropol (p118), Schöneberg
3 Marlene Dietrich exhibit, Filmmuseum Berlin (p102), Potsdamer
Platz 4 Kasbah (p165), Mitte

1 Leysieffer chocolate shop (p231), Charlottenburg 2 Tomasa (p183), Schöneberg 3 Newton (p194), Mitte 4 Food hall, KaDeWe (p232), Schöneberg

1 Mao Thai (p189), Prenzlauer
Berg 2 Reingold (p194), Mitte
3 Bocca di Bacco (p164), Mitte
4 Umspannwerk Ost (p187),
Friedrichshain

1 *Die Tagung (p197), Friedrich-shain* 2 *Staatsoper Unter den Linden (p210), Mitte* 3 *Country and western band, Kaffee Burger (p200), Mitte* 4 *Performance of Mrs Icarus, Die Schaubude (p213), Prenzlauer Berg*

1 Yosoy (p167), Mitte *2* Quasi-modo (p208), Charlottenburg
3 Kino International (p215), Mitte
4 Stadtbad Neukölln (p222)

1 *Galeries Lafayette (p227), Mitte*
2 *Arzu Import-Export (p234),*
Kreuzberg 3 *Türkenmarkt (p235),*
Kreuzberg 4 *Jugendmode – Fuck*
Fashion (p238), Prenzlauer Berg

1 Sterling Gold (p229), Mitte
2 Perfume bottles, Harry Lehmann
(p230), Charlottenburg **3** Propeller
Island City Lodge (p250), Wilmersdorf **4** Hertha BSC football club
paraphernalia, Karstadt Sport
(p231), Charlottenburg

1 Hecker's Hotel (p246), Charlottenburg 2 Suite with a view, Hotel Adlon Kempinski (p243), Mitte 3 Hotel-Pension Art Nouveau (p247), Charlottenburg 4 Pension mitArt (p244), Mitte

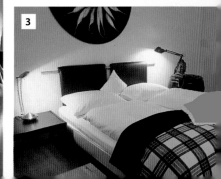

(Continued from page 170)

JULES VERNE Map pp332-3 *International*
☎ 3180 9410; Schlüterstrasse 61; breakfast €4-10, mains €5-15; ☺ 8-1am; S-Bahn Savignyplatz

Jules Verne was a well-travelled man, so it's only fitting that a restaurant named for him would feature a global menu. Feast on North African couscous, French *flammekuche* or Austrian schnitzel. The lavish breakfasts (served until 3pm) are named for such Verne novels as *20,000 Leagues Under the Sea* and *Around the World in 80 Days*.

LA CALETA Map pp332-3 *Spanish*
☎ 8862 7475; Wielandstrasse 26a; mains €10-18; ☺ dinner Mon-Sat; S-Bahn Savignyplatz

In Spanish, *caletas* are little bays where fish find refuge and that's just how owner Señor Bonfiglio would like his guests to feel when they visit his restaurant. In two beautiful dining rooms patrons enjoy food from around the Iberian peninsula. The salt-encrusted dorado is a speciality (€17), but La Caleta also makes a mean paella Valenciana (€13). Respectable wine list, too.

LA PETITE FRANCE Map pp318-19 *French*
☎ 325 8242; Knobelsdorffstrasse 27; mains €14-18; ☺ dinner Wed-Mon; U-Bahn Sophie-Charlotte-Platz

This place is so fantastically French you may actually mistake the nearby Funkturm for the Eiffel Tower, especially after imbibing too much of its excellent Côte du Lubéron. The food's delicious but not as fussily prepared and served as in your typical French restaurant. It's within walking distance of Schloss Charlottenburg.

MAR Y SOL Map pp332-3 *Spanish*
☎ 313 2593; Savignyplatz 5; tapas €2-4, mains €10-18; ☺ dinner; S-Bahn Savignyplatz

On a balmy night, grab a table on the tiled patio and feel transported to Seville while munching on *manchego* (sheep's milk cheese), chorizo, *jamón serrano* (cured ham), *gambas* (prawns), *albondigas* (meatballs) and other taste bud–tickling tapas. In winter the action moves inside the sprawling and elegant dining room. Reservations advised.

PARIS BAR Map pp332-3 *French*
☎ 313 8052; Kantstrasse 152; mains €13-25; U-Bahn Uhlandstrasse

This art-filled establishment has long been one of the top places for A-list celebrity spotting. David Bowie, Jack Nicholson and Madonna have all helped build this legendary haunt's reputation. Mere mortals don't get quite the same attention but that just gives you more time to concentrate on gawking. The food, after all, is just an afterthought.

STELLA ALPINA Map pp330-1 *Italian*
☎ 322 2805; Suarezstrasse 4; mains €6-16; U-Bahn Sophie-Charlotte-Platz

The humble pizza goes gourmet at this upmarket outpost that makes for a fine meal after a day of museum hopping around Schloss Charlottenburg. The friendly Italian servers will happily make a recommendation, although we're partial to the pizza Stella topped with spinach and Gorgonzola, salami and, as the *pièce de résistance*, a big shrimp. Good lunches, too.

WOOLLOOMOOLOO
Map pp320-1 *Australian*
☎ 3470 2777; Röntgenstrasse 7; mains €10-19; ☺ dinner; U-Bahn Richard-Wagner-Platz

Fancy a bit(e) of 'roo? Would you like it grilled, fried, paired with figs or headlining a salad? At Woolloomooloo, modern Oz cooking is as good as it gets outside of Down Under. Market-fresh ingredients, healthfully prepared and ripe with flavour, nicely complement a pint of Foster's or excellent Australian wine. The name, by the way, refers to a Sydney neighbourhood.

YVA-SUITE Map pp332-3 *European*
☎ 8872 5573; Schlüterstrasse 52; mains €9-18; ☺ 6pm-3am Sun-Thu, to 5am Fri-Sat; S-Bahn Savignyplatz

This hip bar-lounge-restaurant is a sophisticated retreat for the rich and fabulous. Nibble on European-inspired dishes in the seductively lit dining room, or choose from more than 1000 whiskeys in the bar. The place is named for YVA, a 1930s fashion photographer killed by the Nazis (see also Hotel Bogota, p247).

CHEAP EATS

PICCOLA TAORMINA Map pp332-3 *Italian*
☎ 881 4710; Uhlandstrasse 29; pizzas €3-12; ☺ 10-2am; U-Bahn Uhlandstrasse

Join the leagues of Ku'damm shoppers, Italian expats, families and office folk here for the habit-forming, wafer-thin pizzas generously topped with fresh mushrooms, pepperoni and other goodies. It's self-service, so grab your plate, find a seat in the labyrinth of Smurf-blue rooms and chow down while showered with Italo pop.

GOSCH Map pp332-3 *Fish*

☎ 8868 2800; Kurfürstendamm 212; sandwiches €2-3.50, mains €6-15; U-Bahn Uhlandstrasse

Only the brisk North Sea wind is missing from this stylish fish bistro, a clone of the original branch on the Frisian island of Sylt. Come here for a quick takeout sandwich or pick your *poisson* (fish) at the counter, then wait while it's being turned into a delicious meal. Also at **Potsdamer Platz** (Map p334; ☎ 2529 6820; Alte Potsdamer Strasse 1; U/S-Bahn Potsdamer Platz).

MARCHÉ Map pp332-3 *International*

☎ 882 7578; Kurfürstendamm 14-15; meals €5-10; ☺ Mon-Sat; U-Bahn Kurfürstendamm

If you need a break from Ku'damm shopping, lug your bags along to this casual self-service bistro, where you can pick from salad, vegetable, pasta and cake buffets or wait for a hot meal to be prepared to order. The food won't win any awards but it's fresh, clean and well-priced. Smoke-free areas and a playground are additional perks.

SCHWARZES CAFÉ Map pp332-3 *Café*

☎ 313 8038; Kantstrasse 148; dishes €4.50-9; ☺ 24h; U/S-Bahn Zoologischer Garten, Savignyplatz

Not many cafés have shown as much staying power as this classic, founded in 1978 by 15 women. For a while they charged men DM1 (€0.50) 'admission', with proceeds benefiting a women's shelter (a practice long since abandoned). It's great for a bite, a beer or breakfast no matter where the hands of the clock are.

WILMERSDORF

Wilmersdorf isn't a famous foodie destination but if you're hankering for a burger or nachos, look no further than Pariser Strasse. West of Ludwigkirchplatz, it boasts the greatest concentration of American diners and Tex-Mex cantinas anywhere in town. Restaurants east of the square, along Ludwigkirchstrasse, cater for the chic but more sedate Wilmersdorf crowd.

DIE QUADRIGA Map pp332-3 *French*

☎ 2140 5650; Eislebener Strasse 14, inside Brandenburger Hof; mains €20-35, tasting menus €55-90; ☺ dinner Mon-Fri; U-Bahn Augsburger Strasse

This intimate dining shrine is a highlight on any foodie quest. Chef Wolfgang Nagler whips up his classic, gimmick-free gourmet

Top Three Wilmersdorf Eats

- **Die Quadriga** (this page)
- **QBA** (this page)
- **Sushi Imbiss** (opposite)

cuisine (eg Bresse chicken, shrimp-stuffed calamari) that has even received the blessing of the Michelin crew. The setting is reminiscent of an elegant 1920s salon, complete with Frank Lloyd Wright chairs and live piano after 7pm. Reservations essential.

JIMMY'S ASIAN DINER

Map pp332-3 *American & Chinese*

☎ 882 3141; Pariser Strasse 41; mains €6.50-10; U-Bahn Spichernstrasse, Uhlandstrasse

Berlin's oldest diner has changed its colours from red to minty green and has expanded its menu to include *kung pao* chicken and other Asian offerings. Fortunately, nothing's changed about its big, juicy burgers that still deserve their cult status.

MANZINI Map pp332-3 *Italian*

☎ 885 7820; Ludwigkirchstrasse 11; breakfast €6-10, mains €10-17; ☺ 8-2am; U-Bahn Spichernstrasse

This elegant, tunnel-shaped restaurant with a vaguely Art Deco look has garnered a loyal following among the well-heeled locals. Settle into the snug leather banquettes to indulge in a leisurely breakfast or treat yourself to one of the creative dishes based on seasonal ingredients. The risottos are prepared to perfection.

QBA Map pp332-3 *Cuban*

☎ 8855 1754; Konstanzer Strasse 1; tapas €2-5.50, mains €7-14; ☺ dinner; U-Bahn Adenauerplatz

Fans spin lazily beneath smoke-stained ceilings, the furniture has seen better days and Fidel and Che stare down upon the action. QBA definitely lays on the Cuban clichés with a trowel but fortunately backs it up with some pretty rich fare, tasty cocktails and a respectable cigar selection. Also in **Mitte** (Map pp328-9; ☎ 2804 0505; Oranienburger Strasse 45; U-Bahn Oranienburger Tor).

ROUTE 66 Map pp332-3 *American*

☎ 883 16 02; Pariser Strasse 44; mains €5-12; ☺ 10-2am Sun-Thu, 10-4am Fri-Sat; U-Bahn Spichernstrasse

Named for the legendary US highway, Route 66 is almost a parody of an American '50s diner with sparkling vinyl booths, neon signage and vintage movie posters. It does burgers best but there are plenty of other classics – spare ribs to baked potato – to get you into that *American Graffiti* vibe. Fun factor: table-side miniature jukeboxes (€0.50 buys two songs).

SCARABEO Map pp332-3 *Egyptian*
☎ 885 0616; Ludwigkirchstrasse 6; mains €12-16; ☽ dinner; U-Bahn Spichernstrasse
The statues of Nefertiti and other Egyptian royals and gods may border on kitsch, but the food here is fit for a Pharaoh. Start things off with smoky *baba ghanoush* or *kibbe* (bulgur patties), then tantalise the palate with succulently spiced lamb or chicken. At weekends, belly dancers add another layer of exotic flair.

SUSHI IMBISS Map pp332-3 *Sushi*
☎ 881 2790; Pariser Strasse 44; nigiri €2-3, maki €3-8; ☽ noon-midnight Mon-Sat, 4-11pm Sun; U-Bahn Spichernstrasse, Uhlandstrasse
This squeaky-clean hole-in-the-wall claims to be Berlin's oldest sushi purveyor, in business since 1991. What really matters, though, is that the fishy morsels here are super-fresh, expertly cut and affordably priced. You can save by ordering combinations (€11.50 to €20).

CHEAP EATS

CURRY 195 Map pp332-3 *Sausage Kitchen*
☎ 881 8942; Kurfürstendamm 195; snacks €2-3.50; ☽ 11-5am; U-Bahn Uhlandstrasse
A much-loved institution, this sausage parlour satisfies the proletarian hunger pangs of deep-pocketed locals who have the option of washing down their franks with a bottle of Dom Perignon (€150). Also a popular hangout for off-duty chefs who often keep the place open until the wee hours.

SCHÖNEBERG
If you're not sure what you're hungry for, take the U-Bahn to Nollendorfplatz and start walking south. Chances are one of the two dozen or so places between the station and Hauptstrasse will lure you in. Don't expect gourmet cuisine; these are mostly easy-going, café-style places where you can fill up well without blowing your budget. There's a clutch of Indian eateries on Goltzstrasse, just south of Winterfeldtplatz, and some Greek places further south.

AUGENSCHMAUS
Map pp330-1 *International*
☎ 7889 0781; Vorbergstrasse 10; mains €5.50-11; U-Bahn Eisenacher Strasse
It's mostly neighbourhood folks who find their way to this brightly pigmented restaurant whose name translates as 'feast for the eyes'. The menu takes a trip around the world with red snapper in coconut, *coq au vin*, and stir-fried vegetables making appearances. In good weather the terrace is the place to be.

BAMBERGER REITER Map pp332-3 *Austrian*
☎ 218 4282; Regensburger Strasse 7; mains €18-30, menu €37-55; ☽ dinner Tue-Sat; U-Bahn Viktoria-Luise-Platz
This elegantly rustic restaurant has been one of Berlin's top culinary destinations since long before the Wall came down. Devotees swear by the Wiener schnitzel and the roast chicken but there are also some excellent less-obvious choices, including a killer wild-mushroom terrine and meatless spinach dumplings. Great wine list and lovely garden.

CAFÉ BERIO Map pp330-1 *Café*
☎ 216 1946; Maassenstrasse 7; breakfast €4-12, dishes €3-7; ☽ 8-1am; U-Bahn Nollendorfplatz
This two-level café serves cakes as sweet as the gooiest love letter along with classical music. In business for more than 50 years, its quasi-baroque décor and Viennese coffee house vibe has been a gay fave for a while now, although anyone is welcome.

CAFÉ EINSTEIN Map pp330-1 *Austrian*
☎ 261 5096; Kurfürstenstrasse 58; breakfast €4-13, mains €10-20; U-Bahn Nollendorfplatz
Schnitzels with noodles and warm apple strudels – you'll find them at this classic Viennese coffee house in a gorgeous villa with garden. Marble table tops, jumbo-sized mirrors and red upholstered banquettes add to the stylish look, although the staff and clientele can appear to be a bit on the snooty side.

Top Five Schöneberg Eats
- **Bamberger Reiter** (this page)
- **La Cocotte** (p182)
- **Storch** (p182)
- **Tomasa** (p183)
- **Witty's** (p184)

The villa, by the way, was once owned by Henny Porten, Germany's earliest superstar actress, who fled Nazi Germany after refusing to divorce her Jewish husband. Also in **Mitte** (Map pp328-9; ☎ 204 3632; Unter den Linden 42; U/S-Bahn Friedrichstrasse).

FEINBECKEREI Map pp330-1 — *Swabian*
☎ 784 5158; Vorbergstrasse 2; mains €5.50-10.50; 🕑 noon-2am; U-Bahn Kleistpark

This cosy place in an early-20th-century bakery specialises in food from the southern German region of Swabia. On a wintry night, hearty dishes such as *Maultaschen* (Swabian ravioli), *Kässpätzle* (Swabian macaroni and cheese) and *Zwiebelröstbraten* (roast pork with onions) fill the belly perfectly. The nicest seats are in the *Backstube* (bakery room) with its huge, historic, tiled bread oven.

HAKUIN Map pp330-1 — *Vegetarian*
☎ 218 2027; Martin-Luther-Strasse 1; mains €15-19; 🕑 dinner Tue-Sun, lunch Sun; U-Bahn Wittenbergplatz

No matter how hectic the day, as soon as you step inside this Zen Buddhist-run restaurant, stress evaporates as fast as light rain on summer asphalt. Dishes eschew meat, make ample use of organic ingredients and have such poetic names as Surabaya (an Indonesian rijsttafel) or Kabuki (a smorgasbord of Japanese delicacies). Smoking is not allowed. Reservations advised.

LA COCOTTE Map pp330-1 — *French*
☎ 7895 7658; Vorbergstrasse 10; mains €12-16; 🕑 dinner; U-Bahn Eisenacher Strasse

The look of the place and the food on the plates are so French you may have to pinch yourself to remember you're actually in Berlin. The menu is more country than *haute* with such flavour-intense dishes as *coq au vin* or smoked pork with champagne-cooked sauerkraut. It's all in a charming Art Nouveau building with small outdoor terrace. Reservations advised.

NEMESIS Map pp330-1 — *Greek*
☎ 781 1590; Hauptstrasse 154; mains €9-15; 🕑 dinner; U-Bahn Kleistpark

Although in a decidedly nontrendy section of Schöneberg, Nemesis packs them in nightly with finger-lickin' Greek food that feeds both the body and soul. Hearty helpings of grilled souvlaki or roast lamb are sure to get you through a wintry night, or go meat-free with the tasty vegetable casseroles.

OUSIES Map pp330-1 — *Greek*
☎ 216 7957; Grunewaldstrasse 16; dishes €2.60-7; 🕑 dinner; U-Bahn Eisenacher Strasse

This is not your typical Greek taverna but a so-called *ouzeria*, a sort of Greek-style tapas bar where you build your meal from small portions of hot and cold dishes. It's great for grazers and those wishing to keep their slim figure. Order the excellent sampler (€8) and you'll be as happy as Zorba himself. Reservations advised.

PAN Y TULIPAN Map pp330-1 — *Spanish*
☎ 2191 3014; Winterfeldtstrasse 40; dishes €1.80-13; U-Bahn Nollendorfplatz

An appetising aroma streaming from the open kitchen envelops you as soon as you step into this convivial café just off Winterfeldtplatz. The long menu features classic tapas plus a good selection of satisfying mains. Special lunches are only €5. On market days (Wednesday and Saturday), you may have to shoehorn your way inside.

PETITE EUROPE Map pp330-1 — *Italian*
☎ 781 2964; Langenscheidtstrasse 1; mains €4.50-10; 🕑 dinner; U-Bahn Kleistpark

Night after night, tables at this earthy little eatery fill up with patrons hungry for the home-made pastas and wood-fired pizzas. It probably won't be the best meal you'll have in Berlin but you're likely to remember this place for its charming, low-key ambience, friendly service and generous portions. Reservations won't hurt.

STORCH Map pp330-1 — *Alsatian French*
☎ 784 2059; Wartburgstrasse 54; flammekuche €8, mains €14-20; 🕑 dinner; U-Bahn Eisenacher Strasse

The wooden floors are worn from the legions of guests who have flocked here for casual meals of *flammekuche* (the Alsatian version of the thin-crust pizza) or more robust mains such as stuffed goose or wild-boar ragout. Owner Volker Hauptvogel – whose mellow demeanour belies his punk-rocker past – is often around to greet patrons with disarming charm.

TIM'S CANADIAN DELI Map pp330-1 — *Café*
☎ 2175 6960; Maassenstrasse 14; mains €5-17; 🕑 8-1am; U-Bahn Nollendorfplatz

When the sun's out, there are few better places for breakfast than this corner café's convivial outdoor tables with view of the Winterfeldtplatf. At other times, it's the veggie burgers, bagels, steaks and other feel-good food that keep the cash register ringing.

TOMASA Map pp332-3 *International*
☎ 213 2345; Motzstrasse 60; breakfast €5-15, mains €10-20; ⏰ 8-1am; U-Bahn Viktoria-Luise-Platz

It serves lunch and dinner, sure, but it's really the prospect of Tomasa's scrumptious breakfast that helps us get out of bed. The best deal is the individually served brunches, each one a different mosaic of both classic and innovative culinary temptations. Reservations are essential, especially on Sunday.

There's another branch in **Schöneberg** (Map pp330-1; ☎ 7895 8888; Salzburger Strasse 19; U-Bahn Bayerischer Platz) and one in **Charlottenburg** (Map pp332-3; ☎ 312 8310; Knesebeckstrasse 22, S-Bahn Savignyplatz).

TRATTORIA Á MUNTAGNOLA
Map pp330-1 *Italian*
☎ 211 6642; Fuggerstrasse 27; pizza €5.50-9.50, pasta €9.50-11.50, mains €15.50-20; ⏰ dinner; U-Bahn Viktoria-Luise-Platz, Wittenbergplatz

The owners hail from the deep Italian south, a rural region called Basilicata, whose sun-baked hills have produced a rustic cuisine with feisty flavours. The pizza is decent, the homemade pasta great, but it's the meat dishes – especially the braised lamb – that will make you come back for more. Kids welcome.

CHEAP EATS
BAHARAT FALAFEL
Map pp330-1 *Middle Eastern*
☎ 216 8301; Winterfeldtstrasse 37; dishes €2-5; ⏰ 11-2am; U-Bahn Nollendorfplatz

The humble falafel goes gourmet at this little takeout place where the proprietor greets customers with a big smile and the sultry sounds of Cesaria Evora waft through the lovingly decorated room. We also like the freshly pressed carrot juice – the ultimate vitamin kick.

EINHORN Map pp332-3 *Vegetarian*
☎ 218 6347; Wittenbergplatz 5-6; buffet items €1.20 per 100g, mains €5-7.50; ⏰ 11am-5pm Mon-Sat; U-Bahn Wittenbergplatz

This is a great refuelling stop for Ku'damm shoppers, with a delectable selection of fast, fresh and meatless fare. Help yourself from the appetising antipasto buffet or sit down in the bistro for a quick lunch of daily changing dishes, from *fusilli* with lemon-caper sauce to Moroccan vegetables with minty couscous. Also in **Charlottenburg** (Map pp332-3; ☎ 881 4241; Mommsenstrasse 2; S-Bahn Savignyplatz).

HISAR Map pp330-1 *Middle Eastern*
S-Bahnhof Yorckstrasse; dishes €2.50-5; ⏰ 10am-midnight; U/S-Bahn Yorckstrasse

It's in a strange location but Hisar is, handsdown, one of the best doner kebab stands in

Tomasa (above)

town. You'll be glad you made the pilgrimage along with scores of other fans.

RANI Map pp330-1 *Indian*
☎ 215 2673; Goltzstrasse 32; dishes €3.50-7;
🕑 11-1am; U-Bahn Nollendorfplatz
This self-service eatery stands out from the pack of Indian restaurants south of Winterfeldt-platz. Order at the counter, grab some cutlery, find a table, then start salivating like Pavlov's dogs in anticipation of big plates of basmati rice smothered with meat or vegetable curry. In fine weather the pavement tables are the coolest, as are the tangy lassis (yogurt drinks).

WITTY'S Map pp332-3 *Sausages*
☎ 853 7055; Wittenbergplatz; snacks €2-4;
🕑 11-1am; U-Bahn Wittenbergplatz
If there is such a thing as healthy fast food, you'll probably find it at this unassuming saus-age kitchen across from the palatial KaDeWe department store. Sink your teeth into one of Witty's certified organic sausages and discover why it enjoys a veritable cult following. The crispy French fries and home-made sauces (including mayonnaise, peanut and garlic) are great as well.

KREUZBERG

Berliners from all over town are rediscovering Kreuzberg, a multicultural cauldron endowed with an intriguing mosaic of flavours and flairs. Bohemian cafés rub shoulders with old-school German pubs; Middle Eastern snack bars are just around the corner from full-out gourmet temples. Bergmannstrasse, the main drag in the western half of the district, is lined with chic cafés and casual restaurants, whereas Oranienstrasse, its equivalent in eastern Kreuzberg, preserves some of the old anarchic vibe. Both are great streets for eating, drinking and partying.

ABENDMAHL Map pp325-7 *Vegetarian*
☎ 612 5170; Muskauer Strasse 9; mains €9-16;
🕑 dinner; U-Bahn Görlitzer Bahnhof
Vegetarians come to worship at the upmarket 'Last Supper', although fish also makes an appearance on the menu. Watched over by 'heavenly' kitsch, you'll be treated to such cleverly named creations as Hot Venus on Earth (pasta shells stuffed with spinach-ricotta mix) or Flaming Inferno (a Thai fish curry).

ALTES ZOLLHAUS
Map pp325-7 *Modern German*
☎ 692 3300; Carl-Herz-Ufer 30; 2-/3-/4-/5-course meals €25/33/37/39; 🕑 dinner Tue-Sat; U-Bahn Prinzenstrasse
A customs house in an earlier incarnation, this elegantly restored half-timbered jewel hugs an idyllic spot right on the Landwehrkanal. Offer-ing country charm galore, it is a perfect set-ting for the upmarket and innovative German cuisine, laced with Mediterranean touches, prepared by chef Günter Beyer. First-timers can't go wrong with the roast duck.

AMRIT Map pp325-7 *Indian*
☎ 612 5550; Oranienstrasse 203; mains €7-11;
U-Bahn Görlitzer Bahnhof
With its heavy pine tables and boldly pig-mented canvases, Amrit may be furnished like a Swedish living room but the food is first-rate Indian. Portions are ample, fragrant and steamy. Both this branch and the one in **Mitte** (Map pp328-9; ☎ 2888 4840; Oranienburger Strasse 45; U-Bahn Oranienburger Tor) get busy nightly; make reservations.

AUSTRIA Map pp325-7 *Austrian*
☎ 694 4440; Bergmannstrasse 30; mains €13-18;
🕑 dinner; U-Bahn Gneisenaustrasse
With its collection of deer antlers, Romy Sch-neider posters and rustic floors, this place looks like a hunting lodge designed in Hollywood. Clichés aside, the Wiener schnitzel – thin, ten-der, huge – is indeed worthy of an Oscar and best paired with a cool Kapsreiter beer.

BAR CENTRALE Map pp325-7 *Italian*
☎ 786 2989; Yorckstrasse 82; appetisers & pastas €9-12, mains €13-20; U-Bahn Mehringdamm
Creative Italian (not a pizza in sight) at abso-lutely honest prices is the name of the game at this attractive eatery, which, so he tells us, is a favourite of Berlin mayor Klaus Wowereit. Much of the chef's imagination goes into the antipasto menu, which may feature grilled

---

Top Five Kreuzberg Eats
- **Altes Zollhaus** (this page)
- **Austria** (this page)
- **Café Jacques** (opposite)
- **Le Cochon Bourgeois** (opposite)
- **Osteria No 1** (opposite)

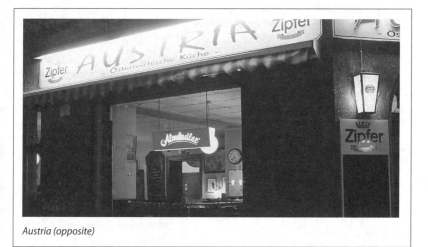
Austria (opposite)

scallops, shrimp in lobster sauce with rucola, or duck fillet with pine-nut sauce. Hungry yet?

CAFÉ JACQUES Map pp325-7 *Mediterranean*
☎ 694 1048; Maybachufer 8; mains €7-13; ✆ dinner; U-Bahn Schönleinstrasse

If browsing the Turkish market has given you hunger pangs, a visit to this darling neighbourhood café is in order. Behind a curtain of leafy plants awaits a blackboard menu full of Mediterranean supper choices, many with Middle Eastern accents. The couscous is excellent and the 'vegetarian fairytale platter' divine. Wash it all down with a bottle of the house red (€11).

CHANDRA KUMARI
Map pp325-7 *Sri Lankan*
☎ 694 1203; Gneisenaustrasse 4; mains €5-13; U-Bahn Mehringdamm

Blending a bouquet of exotic spices, the food here is so perky it may get you off your Prozac. Only organically grown vegetables and hormone-free meats make it into the richly flavoured curries and rice dishes. For a special indulgence, order the *Hochzeitsmenu* (a 'wedding menu', though without the tux and veil), a banquet for two costing €50.

LE COCHON BOURGEOIS
Map pp325-7 *French*
☎ 693 0101; Fichtestrasse 24; mains €16-22; ✆ dinner Tue-Sat; U-Bahn Südstern

Simple rooms, fresh flowers and solid but clever French cuisine are the ingredients for success at the 'Bourgeois Pig'. Chef Hannes Behrmann has captured the hearts and stomachs of leagues of faithful diners, including the occasional hotshot from politics, cinema or theatre. The menu changes daily but if roast lamb and *tarte tatin* are featured, go for it.

MORGENLAND Map pp325-7 *Café*
☎ 611 3183; Skalitzer Strasse 35; mains €5-12; ✆ 9.30-2am; U-Bahn Görlitzer Bahnhof

This eastern Kreuzberg café is a breakfast institution, especially on Sunday when everyone from red-eyed night owls to churchgoers invades for the table-bending brunch. At other times it's a relaxed café with pan-European food – pasta to lamb to fried fish.

NATURKOST SEEROSE
Map pp325-7 *Vegetarian*
☎ 6981 5927; Mehringdamm 47; dishes €3-7; ✆ 10am-10pm Mon-Sat, noon-9pm Sun; U-Bahn Mehringdamm

Vegetarians in the know flock to this little café, which tempts taste buds with delicious casseroles, soups, salads, pastas and freshly pressed juices. Order at the counter, then pay when you leave.

OSTERIA NO 1 Map pp325-7 *Italian*
☎ 786 9162; Kreuzbergstrasse 71; mains €7-16; U-Bahn Mehringdamm

In business for 25 years, this restaurant with its framed movie stills and white linen draped tables is a foodie's delight that appears on the radar screens of celebs such as Wim Wenders and Nastassia Kinski. Kids are welcome and there's even a playground for them in the palm-studded courtyard garden. Antipasti to pasta to meats and fish, it's all good.

SALE E TABACCHI Map pp325-7 *Italian*
☎ 2529 5003; Kochstrasse 18; mains €15-22; ✹ 9-2am Mon-Fri, 10am-2am Sat-Sun; U-Bahn Kochstrasse

With luck you might be privy to the latest gossip when patronising this buzzy bistro popular with journalists from the *taz* newspaper headquartered above. The chef likes to spin culinary creations around exquisite ingredients such as lobster tails, artichoke hearts and veal cutlets. Great antipasti, too, but service could be friendlier.

SUMO Map pp325-7 *Japanese*
☎ 6900 4963; Bergmannstrasse 89; mains €7-11; U-Bahn Gneisenaustrasse

With its sleek, stylish looks – black furniture, red walls, classy art – and top-notch Japanese food, it's no wonder that Sumo has long been a favourite among Kreuzberg foodies. Sushi in its infinite varieties is clearly the star of the show, but the giant bowls of udon-noodle soup and the teriyaki salmon or tuna are just as convincing.

WELTRESTAURANT MARKTHALLE
Map pp325-7 *German*
☎ 617 5502; Pücklerstrasse 34; mains €8-15; ✹ from 9-2am (at least); U-Bahn Görlitzer Bahnhof

Any time of day is good for dropping into this mellow· Kreuzberg pub with its century-old pedigree and new fame as a location for the 2003 Berlin cult flick *Herr Lehmann*. It draws a mixed clientele of ageing scenesters and earthy neighbourhood folk with its relaxed vibe and no-nonsense food. There's a nightclub in the basement on Friday and Saturday.

CHEAP EATS
GASTHAUS DIETRICH HERZ
Map pp325-7 *German*
☎ 693 7043; Marheinekeplatz 15; mains €6-9; ✹ 8am-midnight; U-Bahn Gneisenaustrasse

If you think a schnitzel is a schnitzel is a schnitzel (with apologies to Gertrude Stein), well, not quite. This old-school inn serves a dozen varieties (including the '*Braumeister*' with beer, onions and bacon, the '*Zigeuner*' with spicy tomato sauce, and the '*Jäger*' with mushrooms),

each costing a mere €6 and as big as baseball mitts. Breakfast (€3 to €5, including coffee) is a steal as well.

HABIBI Map pp325-7 *Middle Eastern*
☎ 6165 8346; Oranienstrasse 30; snacks €2.50-5; ✹ 10-3am; U-Bahn Kottbusser Tor

This small chain of snack bars is the granddaddy of Berlin's falafel and *shwarma* circuit. Its late hours make it a favourite spot to restore balance to the brain between bars. It also has two branches in **Schöneberg** (Map pp330-1; Winterfeldtplatz 24 and Akazienstrasse 9; U-Bahn Nollendorfplatz and Kleistpark).

SCHLOTZKY'S DELI
Map pp325-7 *American Deli*
☎ 2233 8899; Friedrichstrasse 200; sandwiches €3.50-5; ✹ 10am-7pm; U-Bahn Stadtmitte

It's touristy, sure, but the Berlin branch of this American franchise near Checkpoint Charlie makes fresh, honest-to-goodness sandwiches and offers soft drinks with free refills.

SESAM Map pp325-7 *Middle Eastern*
☎ 694 6801; Gneisenaustrasse 22; dishes €2-5; ✹ noon-3am; U-Bahn Gneisenaustrasse

In a neighbourhood swarming with falafel and *shwarma* joints, Sesam stands out from the pack. The papaya-coloured walls and blue tile mosaics are cheerful and welcoming, but it's the tasty trio of sauces (garlicky yogurt, yellow sweet and sour, and spicy red) accompanying all dishes that keeps this place humming until the wee hours.

TURKIYEM IMBISS
Map pp325-7 *Middle Eastern*
Schlesische Strasse 1; dishes €2.50-5; ✹ 10-3am; U-Bahn Schlesisches Tor

Right next to the U-Bahn station, this is another great *döner* place with big, yummy pita pockets bulging with perfectly spiced meat (the chicken is recommended) and fresh vegetables laced with a tangy sauce.

FRIEDRICHSHAIN
There's no question that Friedrichshain does bars best, but times are a-changing. The recent arrival of a handful of restaurants that can hold their own against many establishments in Mitte and Charlottenburg has ushered in a new era in

Top Three Friedrichshain Eats

- **Aotearoa** (this page)
- **Fritz Fischer** (this page)
- **Noi Quattro** (this page)

what was once a culinary badlands. Prices are still low, by comparison, although this may soon change as gentrification runs its unstoppable course.

AOTEAROA Map pp318-19 *New Zealand*

☎ 2977 0582; Weichselstrasse 26a; mains €7-15; ☽ 9-1am; U/S-Bahn Frankfurter Allee

Aotearoa – Land of the Long White Cloud – is what the Maori call New Zealand, a land where sheep far outnumber human beings. So it's no surprise that lamb looms large on the menu here, although the fish and chips, paired with a spicy hot sauce, also fill up the belly nicely. There's a children's corner upstairs.

FRITZ FISCHER

Map pp325-7 *Modern German*

☎ 520 072 202; Stralauer Allee 1; mains €13-20; ☽ dinner; U/S-Bahn Warschauer Strasse

Friedrichshain isn't known for its chic cuisine scene but exceptions such as Fritz Fischer, which shares a building with Universal Music, dispute that perception. Assets include a killer river-side location next to the Oberbaumbrücke, a cool angular interior and solid offerings of modern German fare. In summer it's a veritable beach party in the beer garden and on the terrace.

NOI QUATTRO Map pp322-4 *Italian*

☎ 2404 5622; Strausberger Platz 2; mains €9-18; U-Bahn Strausberger Platz

Top-notch *nuova cucina italiana* with a view of the 'worker's palaces' – where else but Berlin can you get this? Noi Quattro doesn't shine with fancy décor but instead puts a premium on quality ingredients and delightful, if occasionally out-there, creations: caramelised goat cheese, linguini with crayfish and kohlrabi and pheasant terrine with grappa grapes are typical menu items.

PAPAYA Map pp325-7 *Thai*

☎ 2977 1231; Krossener Strasse 11; mains €6-12; U/S-Bahn Warschauer Strasse

This bustling café is a favourite fuel stop for Friedrichshain scenesters ready to launch on an extended exploration of the many nearby pubs and cocktail bars. Nicely spiced, coconut-based *tom ka* soups, tangy *pad Thai* noodles, toothsome Thai basil chicken and other classics are all delicious hangover preventions.

PI-BAR Map pp325-7 *Vegetarian & Fish*

☎ 2936 7581; Gabriel-Max-Strasse 17; mains €7-17; ☽ 4pm-2am (at least), from 10am Sun; U/S-Bahn Warschauer Strasse

It didn't take long for the Pi-Bar crew to capture the hearts and tummies of locals and visiting Friedrichshain revellers. The cooks make wonderful casseroles, risottos and stir-fries plus such cool creations as mushrooms stuffed with spinach and shrimp and tossed in a gorgonzola sauce (€7.50). There's also a cocktail bar out back.

SHISHA Map pp325-7 *Middle Eastern*

☎ 2977 1995; Krossener Strasse 19; mains €6-10; ☽ 11-2am (at least); U/S-Bahn Warschauer Strasse

Yes, you *can* puff on a *shisha* (water pipe) in this cosy restaurant, although most people come here for the tasty food. Free sesame seed dip with pita bread arrives while you peruse the menu, which is especially strong on appetisers (the €9 platter is enough for two). The service can be a bit challenged when it's crowded.

TRIANGOLO Map pp325-7 *Italian*

☎ 9700 2520; Grünberger Strasse 69; mains €12-17; ☽ dinner Mon-Sat, lunch Sun; U/S-Bahn Warschauer Strasse

With its floor-to-ceiling windows, sleek black furniture and citrus-yellow walls, Triangolo looks almost too grown-up for grungy Friedrichshain. But times are changing and tables here are almost always filled with patrons keen on sampling such appealing Sardinian specialities as black calamari risotto or almond-encrusted dorado.

UMSPANNWERK OST

Map pp322-4 *Modern German*

☎ 4280 9497; Palisadenstrasse 48; mains €8-16; U-Bahn Weberwiese

This historic transformer station has been transformed into an industrial-chic restaurant. You can watch the kitchen staff prepare such dishes as marinated rack of lamb or black fettuccine with salmon in saffron sauce in an open kitchen. It's an intimately lit space with a long bar and upstairs gallery seating that offers bird's-eye views of the trendy crowd.

Eating – Friedrichshain

CHEAP EATS

NIL Map pp325-7 · *Sudanese*
☎ 2904 7713; Grünberger Strasse 52; ☽ noon-midnight; U/S-Bahn Warschauer Strasse
This friendly snack bar makes a nice change from the *döner* and falafel circuit. It helps if you're a peanut fan, for the humble pip shows up in all kinds of dishes, from soups to habit-forming sauces.

SAUERKRAUT UND BULGUR
Map pp322-4 · *Pan-European*
☎ 293 518; Strasse der Pariser Kommune 35; mains €3-10; ☽ 7.30-2am; S-Bahn Weberwiese
Sauerkraut and bulgur are the ingredients of a hearty Armenian soup, but at this casual eatery the name stands for the geographical range of the dishes it serves: Germany to the Middle East. Because it's part of the Pegasus Hostel, the clientele is as international as its menu and keeps the place busy from breakfast to midnight.

TIGRIS Map pp325-7 · *Middle Eastern*
☎ 2935 1212; Simon-Dach-Strasse 11; ☽ 11-1am; U/S-Bahn Warschauer Strasse
Tigris' tasty falafel and *shwarma* sandwiches are just what the doctor ordered as a hangover antidote. In summer, the pavement tables offer a great vantage point for people watching.

PRENZLAUER BERG

It's no longer a secret that there's plenty of good food to be had in this fashionable district, whose considerable charms peak in summer when tables crowd the pavement and an almost Mediterranean feel envelops the leafy streets. There's a cornucopia of tourist-friendly cafés and restaurants around Kollwitzplatz and the residential streets to its north. Prices drop in establishments north of Danziger Strasse, as does the average age of patrons. Helmholtzplatz, Schliemannstrasse and Lychener Strasse all yield some excellent possibilities in this part of the district.

BELLUNO Map pp322-4 · *Italian*
☎ 441 0548; Kollwitzstrasse 66; mains €6-10; ☽ 10-1am; U-Bahn Senefelderplatz
A little pizza, a little red wine, laughter and good company – what more does one need to feel good about life? In summer, grab a seat on the sunny pavement terrace and watch the world on parade. Dolce vita with a view of Kollwitzplatz.

BUDDHA LOUNGE Map pp322-4 · *Asian*
☎ 4471 6024; Stargarder Strasse 60; mains €10-13; ☽ dinner Mon-Fri, from 10am Sat-Sun; U/S-Bahn Schönhauser Allee
This nice little Asian restaurant-bar combo bursts at the seams on weekends when it dishes up a table-bending buffet of vegetarian sushi, chicken satay, Thai risotto and other tasty goodies. If you don't watch it, you risk leaving here with a belly as big as the eponymous Buddha that serenely watches over the pandemonium.

DIE DREI Map pp322-4 · *Californian*
☎ 4473 8471; Lychener Strasse 30; mains €11-16; ☽ dinner; U-Bahn Eberswalder Strasse
Bar, lounge and restaurant in one (hence the name, 'the three'), this snazzy place takes a serious stab at catapulting northern Prenzlauer Berg onto the foodie map. The menu is loaded with interesting items that pair healthy ingredients with low-fat cooking techniques. Grilled salmon with tangy *wasabi* mash (€13) is a typical entry. Even waist-watching Beverly Hills belles would approve. Also in **Charlottenburg** (Map pp332-3; ☎ 5471 0271; Savignyplatz 2; S-Bahn Savignyplatz).

FRIDA KAHLO Map pp322-4 · *Mexican*
☎ 445 7016; Lychener Strasse 37; breakfast €4-8, mains €10-15; ☽ 9.30-2am; U-Bahn Eberswalder Strasse
The look of this long-established neighbourhood haunt was supposedly inspired by the eponymous painter's house in Mexico City. The menu plays it pretty safe, although Mexican standards such as guacamole, enchiladas and fajitas get enough people salivating to keep the place jumping most nights. The Sunday brunch is legendary.

GUGELHOF Map pp322-4 · *Alsatian French*
☎ 442 9229; Knaackstrasse 37; mains €8-14; ☽ dinner Mon-Fri, 10am-midnight Sat-Sun; U-Bahn Senefelderplatz
Bill Clinton was here and Berlin mayor Klaus Wowereit likes the joint too. Gugelhof's food might be described as Alsatian soul food, with cheese fondue, *choucroute* (a sauerkraut-based dish) and *tarte flambé* being the menu headliners.

Top Five Prenzlauer Berg Eats

- **Gugelhof** (opposite)
- **Konnopke Imbiss** (p190)
- **Mao Thai** (this page)
- **Miro** (this page)
- **Trattoria Paparazzi** (this page)

MAO THAI Map pp322-4   *Thai-Chinese*
☎ 441 9261; Wörther Strasse 30; mains €10-18;
U-Bahn Senefelderplatz

The menu is as intriguing as the carved statu-
ettes and the original Asian art filling the two
floors of this classy restaurant. Even simple curries become extraordinary here, although the
chef truly shines when it comes to the duck
dishes. Artistic garnishes – radish birds, carrot
roses – never fail to bring smiles to the faces
of first-timers. Reservations advised.

It also runs another restaurant, **Kamala** (Map
pp328-9; ☎ 283 2797; Oranienburger Strasse
69; U-Bahn Oranienburger Strasse), in Mitte.

MIRO Map pp322-4   *Turkish*
☎ 4473 3013; Raumerstrasse 29; mains €8-15; S-Bahn
Offenbach Strasse

If you're a Turkish food virgin, this place is
perfect for losing your innocence. Miro, which
translates as 'hero', does indeed serve heroic
portions of delicious dishes from the eastern
province of Anatolia. The cooking has an accent on grilled or fried meats, although vegetable fiends will also find plenty to talk about.
Killer appetiser platter.

OFFENBACH STUBEN
Map pp322-4   *German*
☎ 445 8502; Stubbenkammerstrasse 8; mains €8-17;
☽ dinner; S-Bahn Prenzlauer Allee

Jacques Offenbach, *bon vivant* and composer of operettas, was the namesake of this
GDR relic, which gets its ample appeal from
truckloads of old theatre props. It's stuffy but
stylish, with cleverly named dishes inspired by
Offenbach's characters. Try Popolanis Magic,
a portion of juicy, herb-encrusted lamb with
baby carrots and potato gratin.

OSTWIND Map pp322-4   *Chinese*
☎ 441 5951; Husemannstrasse 13; mains €6.50-13;
☽ dinner, plus lunch Sun; U-Bahn Eberswalder Strasse

A long-time local favourite, this is a subterranean pastel maze where you can sit at regular

tables or in lotus pos[...]
booths. The food is cre[...]
quality and as authenti[...]
of the motherland. The [...]
speciality (€12/21 for one[...]

PASTERNAK Map pp322-4
☎ 441 3399; Knaackstrasse 22; ma[...]
Senefelderplatz

The décor here is as dramatic a[...]
Chekhov play, big sofas and lusty[...]
included. Russian nostalgia also ext[...]
food at this well-established restaur[...]
view of the landmark water tower. C[...]
goodies (borscht, *pelmeni*, beef str[...]
dominate the menu but the chef often[...]
in a few surprises for good measure.

SALSABIL Map pp322-4   *Ara[...]*
☎ 4403 3846; Raumerstrasse 14; mains €5-7;
☽ dinner; U-Bahn Eberswalder Strasse

This friendly and relaxed eatery is perfect for
winding down after a day of turf pounding.
The sweet apple aroma wafting from the water
pipes blends with the fragrant aroma of suc-
culent lamb, fluffy couscous and mysteriously
spiced vegetables. For the complete pasha
feel, surrender to the sumptuous languor of
the private alcoves with thick pillows and
low tables.

SODA Map pp322-4   *International*
☎ 4405 6071; Schönhauser Allee 36-39; mains €8-15;
U-Bahn Eberswalder Strasse

This sleek restaurant-bar-club combo amid
the red-brick romance of the Kulturbrauerei
features a menu that travels around the world.
You can play it safe with pizza, mahi-mahi and
ravioli or get into *Survivor* mode and order the
grasshopper curry with couscous. Enjoy…

TRATTORIA PAPARAZZI
Map pp322-4   *Italian*
☎ 440 7333; Husemannstrasse 35; mains €8-15;
☽ dinner; U-Bahn Eberswalder Strasse

When Doris Burneleit opened her first restaurant in 1987 in Köpenick, deep inside East
Berlin, she'd never been to Italy nor been
trained as a chef. Yet she proved to be such
a magician in the kitchen, even the Italian
ambassador couldn't resist. Now in Prenzlauer
Berg, she continues to pamper patrons with
feel-good pastas and such innovative dishes
as *malfatti* (cheese and spinach dumplings in
sage butter). Reservations recommended.

national
10,
atz

on pillows in raised
ative, above average in
as things get outside
Chinese fondue is a
two people).

ns €8-15; U-Bahn

Russian

the set of
chandeliers
ends to the
ant with a
dies but
ganoff)
tosses

bic

International
e 31; soups €4-6;
auer Allee

of liquidity' you can chill
.ile trying one of the dozen
The house version, an exotic
...an blend, is perfect for nursing a
or staving off the winter chills. Look
.ed lanterns scavenged from the now
t-defunct Café Kranzler. Self-service.

Eating
er Berg

KONNOPKE IMBISS

Map pp322-4 *Sausage Kitchen*

☎ 442 7765; Schönhauser Allee 44a; sausage €1-2;
🕑 5.30am-8pm Mon-Fri; U-Bahn Eberswalder Strasse

Times were tough when Max and Charlotte Konnopke opened their first sausage kitchen beneath the roaring U-Bahn tracks in 1930. Since then, the family has weathered war and the GDR to churn out millions of what many say is the best Currywurst in town. A true Berlin classic.

RICE QUEEN Map pp322-4 *Asian*

☎ 4404 5800; Danziger Strasse 13; mains €5-9;
🕑 dinner; U-Bahn Eberswalder Strasse

Cheerfully painted walls and modernist furniture form the backdrop for the creations of Rice Queen chef Garry Chan. His restless palate and bottomless imagination produce intriguing flavour bombs that draw inspiration from the cuisines of Malaysia, China, Thailand and Indonesia. The service here is charming, fast and attentive.

Entertainment

Entertainment

Berlin's status as a cultural capital doesn't just come from its strength in home-grown arts. The number, variety and accessibility of arts and entertainment options in the city puts it on a par with London or New York, and while it's famed mainly for its radical alternative scene and all-out nightlife, more highbrow pursuits such as opera, dance and theatre also thrive here. Berliners like to go out, and with so much choice it's hardly surprising that they're doing so ever more frequently.

Like most things in Berlin, the nature of the entertainments on offer varies from district to district. In the west, Charlottenburg and Tiergarten cater for an older, more affluent public, with plenty of chic bars and theatres; Wilmersdorf and Schöneberg are slightly less refined but have denser concentrations of venues; while Kreuzberg largely retains the punky, alternative feel that made it famous in the 1960s, with some of the city's rowdiest bars and clubs centred on Oranienstrasse.

On the eastern side of the city, Mitte is rapidly becoming a two-tier district. South of Oranienburger Tor you'll find the really exclusive haunts and cultural bastions such as the Deutsches Theater, attracting tourists, celebrities and better-heeled folk than even Tiergarten. Further north are the less elitist but equally fashionable haunts of the Berlin *Szene* (scene), as well as plenty of straightforwardly populist venues extending up into lively, experimental Prenzlauer Berg.

The real revelation for visitors at the moment, however, is Friedrichshain, once a grotty district favoured by backpackers for its cheapness. Right now this is the place to come for a long night out. Things are still cheap here by Berlin standards, but the area south of Frankfurter Allee has suddenly become the city's hottest nightlife zone, with new bars and clubs popping up like magic mushrooms. The original spirit of the district still survives around Rigaer Strasse, where hard-core squatters run some pretty anarchic bar-clubs. Most open whenever someone feels like it, and their existence is constantly threatened by police busts. **Fischladen** (Map pp322-4; Rigaer Strasse 83) and **Schizzotempel** (Map pp322-4; Rigaer Strasse 77) are among the longest survivors.

Cabaret at the Wintergarten Varieté (p211)

Perhaps the real distinguishing feature of the Berlin entertainment scene, however, is the inventive use of the most unlikely spaces – the years of raves, squats and illegal parties have had a visible influence, and sites as diverse as breweries, vaults, swimming pools, kebab shops and even old U-Bahn tunnels have been commandeered in the name of fun, adding that extra bit of character to a night out.

Listings

Zitty (€2.40) and *Tip* (€2.60) are the best of the listings magazines, full of insider tips and colourful articles. *Tip* tends to be more mainstream, while *Zitty* is younger and edgier. *Berlin Programm* (€1.60) and *Kultur Pur* (annual; €5) cover the arts in more detail. There are also dozens of free entertainment mags covering everything from nightlife to film and literature; try *030*, *Partysan* or *Fresh* for club and music news. The freebie *Siegessäule* is the Berlin Bible for all things gay and lesbian, and produces the biannual *Kompass* directory. *Sergej* magazine is strictly for men.

The above publications are in German, but you should be able to make sense of the listings even with a minimal command of the language.

Tickets & Reservations

Outlets selling tickets to cultural and sporting events are scattered all over the city; a 15% commission charge usually applies to ticket sales. Hekticket (below) sells half-price theatre tickets from 4pm on the day of the performance; choices are limited to what's officially left unsold that day.

Box Office Theaterkasse (Map pp330-1; ☎ 2101 6960; Nollendorfplatz 7, Schöneberg; U-Bahn Nollendorfplatz)

Hekticket Charlottenburg (Map pp332-3; ☎ 230 9930; www.hekticket.de; Hardenbergstrasse 29d, Charlottenburg; ☺ 10am-8pm Mon-Sat, 2-6pm Sun; U/S-Bahn Zoologischer Garten)

Hekticket Mitte (Map pp328-9; ☎ 2431 2431; www.hekticket.de; Karl-Liebknecht-Strasse 12, Mitte; ☺ noon-7pm Tue-Fri, 10am-8pm Sat; U/S-Bahn Alexanderplatz)

KOKA 36 (Map pp325-7; ☎ 6110 1313; www.koka36.de; Oranienstrasse 29, Kreuzberg; U-Bahn Kottbusser Tor)

Spectrum Theaterkasse Friedrichshain (☎ 427 9119; Ring-Center, Frankfurter Allee 111, Friedrichshain; U/S-Bahn Frankfurter Allee)

Spectrum Theaterkasse Mitte (Map pp328-9; ☎ 2463 8811; Berlin-Carré, Karl-Liebknecht-Strasse 13, Mitte; U/S-Bahn Alexanderplatz)

Theaterkasse Centrum (Map pp332-3; ☎ 882 7611, Meinekestrasse 25, Charlottenburg; U-Bahn Uhlandstrasse, Kurfürstendamm)

Theaterkasse Friedrichstrasse (Map pp328-9; ☎ 2840 8155; S-Bahnhof Friedrichstrasse, Mitte; ☺ 8am-8pm Mon-Fri, 10am-6pm Sat)

Gay & Lesbian Berlin

Berlin has the biggest, most active gay and lesbian scene in Germany, and can even rival Amsterdam, with exclusive and mixed facilities available for just about any activity. The scene concentrates in four districts: around Nollendorfplatz in Schöneberg; Oranienstrasse in Kreuzberg 36; along Mühlenstrasse in Friedrichshain; and around the northern end of Schönhauser Allee in Prenzlauer Berg. Check with **Mann-O-Meter** (Map pp330-1; ☎ 216 8008; Bülowstrasse 106, Schöneberg) and www.berlin.gay-web.de for the latest on the cruising scene, popular parties and the ins and outs of the lesbigay landscape.

Entertainment

DRINKING

No matter where you are in Berlin, you're never very far from a drinking hole of some kind. The cocktail boom has seen even more places spring up around town, most adopting a lounge style, often with DJs at night. Indeed, the main result of Friedrichshain's newfound popularity has been an explosion of new cocktail and lounge bars in areas around Simon-Dach-Strasse and Boxhagenener Platz, slowly smartening up the traditionally grungy local scene.

Unlike in UK-style pubs, table service is common and it's customary to keep a tab instead of paying each round separately. Most bars open in the early evening, between 5pm and 8pm, unless they serve food during the day. Happy hours are practically mandatory, usually falling between 5pm and 9pm; the website www.bartime.de has a handy search engine for dedicated discount drinkers.

Top Five Bars & Pubs

- Galerie Bremer (p196)
- Kurvenstar (this page)
- Prater (p198)
- Trompete (p195)
- Zur letzten Instanz (p199)

MITTE

925 LOUNGE BAR Map pp328-9
☎ 2018 7177; Taubenstrasse 19; ☽ 4pm-2am; U-Bahn Hausvogteiplatz
At first glance this red-hued cocktail joint doesn't look quite as upmarket as its Gendarmenmarkt colleagues, but take a closer look at the bar – it's supposedly made of solid silver, 70kg of it. If that doesn't faze you, you're probably in exactly the right place.

AMBULANCE BAR/SILBERSTEIN
Map pp328-9
☎ 281 2095; Oranienburger Strasse 27; ☽ from 4pm Mon-Fri, from 6pm Sat & Sun; S-Bahn Oranienburger Strasse
Two very different bars. The Ambulance Bar is more of a DJ space, with red lights, video screens and nightly lounge sounds, while artsy metal chairs and avant-garde sculptures feature in Silberstein, which also has a small sushi bar.

ERDBEER Map pp322-4
Max-Beer-Strasse 56; ☽ from 6pm; U-Bahn Rosa-Luxemburg-Platz
Strawberry by name, strawberry by nature – the red colour scheme and €7 pints of daiquiri make drinking here pretty sweet, and the lack of pretension separates it from many similar cocktail joints.

GREENWICH Map pp328-9
☎ 2909 5566; Gipsstrasse 5; U-Bahn Weinmeisterstrasse
Bars don't come much better upholstered than Greenwich, with padding on almost every surface (helpful when you're trying to elbow your way in or out at weekends). On quieter nights you can grab a stool and gaze into the long aquarium.

KURVENSTAR Map pp328-9
☎ 2472 3115; Kleine Präsidentenstrasse 4; ☽ Tue-Sat; S-Bahn Hackescher Markt
One of our all-time-favourite retro eye-candy parlours, the outré decor in this bar-restaurant-club seems to have been cannibalised from every 1960s and '70s cliché. The programme is equally cool, with soul-tinged music, dancing and food from around the world.

NEWTON Map pp328-9
☎ 2061 2990; Charlottenstrasse 57; ☽ 6pm-4am; U-Bahn Französische Strasse, Stadtmitte
The Helmut Newton nudes on the walls are about the only thing more chic and languorous than the glamorous Mitte bodies colonising this überstylish cocktail and cigar bar. Funnily enough, it was actually named after Sir Isaac.

O&G Map pp328-9
☎ 2576 2667; Oranienburger Strasse 48-49; U-Bahn Oranienburger Tor
Tasteful retro? Yes, it is possible – the pastel stripes and squares here could even be considered unironically cool. This was one of the first bars on the strip to open after the *Wende* (turning point), and while the interior's grown up a bit it still pulls in a friendly young crowd.

REINGOLD Map pp322-4
☎ 2838 7676; Novalisstrasse 11; U-Bahn Oranienburger Tor
The metal cladding outside is pretty forbidding but inside is a beautifully opulent 1930s

glamour lounge. Deep house and Latin sounds dominate the decks, and there are readings on Tuesday.

ROBERTA/HOTELBAR Map pp322-4
☎ 4432 8577; Zionskirchstrasse 5-7; ☾ 5pm-6am; U-Bahn Rosenthaler Platz

The narrow, tiled Roberta bar-bistro is pretty popular in its own right, with guest chefs and occasional DJs, but from Wednesday to Saturday it's little more than a warm-up bar for the smarter, roomier, clubbier Hotelbar in the basement.

RUTZ Map pp322-4
☎ 2462 8760; Chausseestrasse 8; ☾ Mon-Sat; U-Bahn Oranienburger Tor

Dedicated oenophiles should seek out this classy wine bar and restaurant, which stocks no fewer than 1001 quality varieties from all over the world. Glasses of the really good stuff can cost up to €11.50; staff will happily advise you on your options.

SEVEN LOUNGE Map pp322-4
☎ 2759 6979; Ackerstrasse 20; U-Bahn Rosenthaler Platz

Very comfy and very beige, this smart, slightly saucy lounge bar is owned by Mo Asumang, erstwhile host of an erotic TV show. It's also very convenient for the MTV studios, so look out for familiar faces.

TIERGARTEN
BAR AM LÜTZOWPLATZ Map pp330-1
☎ 262 6807; Lützowplatz 7; ☾ 2pm-4am; U-Bahn Nollendorfplatz

Apparently having a really long bar never goes out of style. This classic cocktail spot is still a firm fixture with the upper echelons of the Berlin scene. Since rival Trompete opened next door, happy hour has become happy seven hours (2pm to 9pm).

KUMPELNEST 3000 Map pp330-1
☎ 8891 7960; Lützowstrasse 23; ☾ 5pm-5am; U-Bahn Kurfürstenstrasse

You can't get much further removed from the studied elegance of Lützowplatz – the Kumpelnest was once a brothel and has been famed since the 1980s for its wild, inhibition-free nights, attracting a hugely varied public. Much of the original whorehouse décor remains intact.

TROMPETE Map pp330-1
☎ 2300 4794; Lützowplatz 9; ☾ from 6pm Thu, from 9pm Fri & Sat; U-Bahn Nollendorfplatz

It takes something pretty spectacular to eclipse the competition in Tiergarten, that is until Trompete arrived with a blast. It is owned by Tresor's Dimitri Hegemann and actor Ben Becker, and the latter's notoriety is enough to guarantee permanent crowds, especially as he appears to be the bar's best customer (though perhaps not its most talented singer). The varied events schedule is a bonus.

VICTORIA BAR Map pp330-1
☎ 2575 9977; Potsdamer Strasse 102; ☾ 6pm-2am; U-Bahn Kurfürstenstrasse

You might walk past this place without noticing it but, if so, you're missing out. Dedicated to 'serious drinking', proprietor Stefan Weber has won awards for his cocktail skills, and everything from the drinks to the décor is top quality. Just remember, perfection doesn't come cheap.

CHARLOTTENBURG
GAINSBOURG Map pp332-3
☎ 313 7464; Savignyplatz 5; S-Bahn Savignyplatz

This cramped, American-style bar speaks to a 30-something intellectual crowd, and might well have appealed to Serge himself. Relax in the warmly lit, relaxed atmosphere while sipping one of the award-winning (and copyrighted) cocktails.

LOUNGE 77 Map pp332-3
Knesebeckstrasse 77; ☾ Tue-Sun; S-Bahn Savignyplatz

Savignyplatz's affluent English speakers are the core clientele of this comfortable, swish but (relatively) unposey cocktail and champagne lounge, and half the bar staff seem to be American.

ZEITLOS Map pp332-3
☎ 323 1681; Schlüterstrasse 60; ☾ 7pm-3am; S-Bahn Savignyplatz

One of an extraordinary number of tropical-themed 'beach bars' around Berlin, boasting sand on the floor, fake bamboo and suitably nonspecific ethnic-style art. Popular with a cocktail-swilling young crowd who have probably never seen the real thing. There's another two identical branches nearby: **Sybelstrasse 16** (Map pp332-3) and **Franklinstrasse 10** (Map pp320-1).

WILMERSDORF

GALERIE BREMER Map pp332-3

☎ 881 4908; Fasanenstrasse 37; ☾ bar 8pm-2am
Mon-Sat; U-Bahn Spichernstrasse

Art lovers should make a beeline for this gallery-
bar – proprietor Rudolf van der Lak has been
in charge since 1955, serving up sophisticated
drinks and modernist art in equal measures.
It's named for his wife, artist Anja Bremer, who
returned from the USA in 1946 to start a gallery
and sadly died in 1985.

IL CALICE Map pp332-3

☎ 324 2308; Walter-Benjamin-Platz 4; ☾ noon-midnight Mon-Sat, 5pm-2am Sun; U-Bahn Adenauerplatz

It's technically a bar-restaurant but the stunning wine list completely eclipses the un-
spectacular food at this classy Italian place.
The terrace kiosk and family-friendly ethos
also undermine the elitist veneer.

LEIBNIZ BAR Map pp332-3

☎ 3276 4699; Leibnizstrasse 57; U-Bahn
Adenauerplatz

Run by Americans for Americans, but don't let
that put you off – with 240 cocktails on the
list, this cheery bar is a welcome break from
the posy trend spots. If you think you can take
it, spring the €10 for a Leibniz Killer.

SCHÖNEBERG

GREEN DOOR Map pp330-1

☎ 215 2515; Winterfeldtstrasse 50; U-Bahn
Nollendorfplatz

One of Berlin's classic cocktail bars, tended by
Stefan Weber until he left to found the Victoria
Bar (p195); current incumbent Heike Heyse is
equally highly rated. For that added feeling of
exclusivity, you have to ring the bell to get in.

HAFEN Map pp330-1

☎ 214 1118; Motzstrasse 19; U-Bahn Nollendorfplatz

Despite not offering cocktails, Hafen is usually full of gay yuppies fortifying themselves
before moving on to Tom's Bar (p202) for the
real action.

HAR DIE'S KNEIPE Map pp332-3

☎ 0172-302 3068; Ansbacher Strasse 29; ☾ noon-
3am; U-Bahn Wittenbergplatz

The successor to the much-loved Andreas
Kneipe has vowed to uphold its convivial
ambience and remains a good place to meet

locals, even in the day. It's staunchly gay, but
everyone's welcome.

MISTER HU Map pp330-1

☎ 217 2111; Goltzstrasse 39; U-Bahn Nollendorfplatz

The ill-conceived Stone Age decor is a bit off-
putting but Mister Hu still manages to be a
popular little chap, tempting a surprisingly hip
lot of drinkers to linger over cocktails until the
early hours of most mornings.

PRINZKNECHT Map pp332-3

☎ 2362 7444; Fuggerstrasse 33; ☾ from 3pm;
U-Bahn Wittenbergplatz

Next door to Connection (p202), this chic,
American-style gay bar displays bare brick
walls, chrome lamps and Georgia O'Keefe
posters. The clientele doesn't always live up
to the smart surroundings.

KREUZBERG

ANKERKLAUSE Map pp325-7

☎ 693 5649; Kottbusser Damm 104; U-Bahn
Kottbusser Tor

Low on aesthetics but high on energy, this
Kreuzberg favourite occupies an old harbour-
master's house above the Landwehrkanal.
Breakfast on the terrace, coffee after shopping
at the Turkish Market, drinks all night – this
place packs 'em in at all hours.

BARBIE BAR Map pp325-7

☎ 6959 8610; Mehringdamm 77; ☾ from 4pm;
U-Bahn Mehringdamm

Trash kitsch lovers of the world unite, for this
is your bar. Pink walls, doll parts on the walls
and Barbie swap nights make for a unique
experience. Perhaps unsurprisingly, it appeals
to a mixed gay clientele.

Barbie Bar (above)

GOLGATHA Map pp330-1
☎ 785 2453; Dudenstrasse 48-64; 🕐 Apr-Oct;
U/S-Bahn Yorckstrasse

This low-key beer garden in the Viktoriapark has been around forever and is still great for grilled snacks and cool drinks on a balmy night. A DJ springs into action after 10pm.

KONRAD TÖNZ Map pp325-7
☎ 612 3252; Falckensteinstrasse 30; 🕐 Tue-Sun;
U-Bahn Schlesisches Tor

Another long-standing classic, Konrad Tönz takes retro to extremes, with kitsch '70s furniture, panoramic wallpaper and possibly the last surviving mono DJ setup in Europe.

MÖBEL OLFE Map pp325-7
☎ 6165 9612; Reichenberger Strasse 177;
🕐 Tue-Sun; U-Bahn Kottbusser Tor

This sparsely decorated pub is good for at least a couple of hours after the regular places close, and thanks to the huge windows it's easy to see what's going on. The table football's always busy, the beer's always excellent and the crowd's mixed in every respect.

SCALA Map pp325-7
☎ 693 3662; Nostitzstrasse 38; 🕐 from 4pm Mon-Fri,
from noon Sat & Sun; U-Bahn Gneisenaustrasse

An essential stop for happy-hour crawlers: the classic cocktails here are all €4.50 from 6pm to midnight. If that leaves you feeling rich, invest in some of the art.

WALDOHREULE Map pp325-7
☎ 3974 2060; Köpenicker Strasse 194; U-Bahn
Schlesisches Tor

Named after a type of owl, this friendly bar is packed with a mixed bunch of students, regulars and session drinkers admiring the neat stacking furniture, the tiny dance floor or the ancient GDR headlines on the walls (ask someone to translate *Hoden-Entzündung*).

WÜRGEENGEL Map pp325-7
☎ 615 5560; Dresdener Strasse 122; U-Bahn
Kottbusser Tor

The 'Angel of Death' pays homage to the 1962 Luis Buñuel movie. Its dramatic blood-red velvet décor and unique tile ceiling are more reminiscent of a Belle Epoque brothel than a church, but plenty of people find it fittingly hard to leave. The cocktails are heavenly (sorry), and the place is crammed the second the adjacent Babylon cinema closes.

FRIEDRICHSHAIN

ABGEDREHT Map pp322-4
☎ 294 6808; Karl-Marx-Allee 140; U-Bahn Frankfurter
Tor

For a 'crazy' student theme pub, this place isn't half as annoying as you'd expect. The slapdash décor gives you plenty to look at (the tables are made from old sewing machines for a start), film and DJ nights bring in the punters and the Sunday buffet is a snip at €7.77.

ASTRO BAR Map pp325-7
☎ 2966 1615; Simon-Dach-Strasse 40; U/S-Bahn
Warschauer Strasse

Holding its own against the new arrivals, this hip bar time warps you back to the 'spacey' 1960s, with long-forgotten robot toys adorning the walls and nightly DJs after 10pm.

BLOONA Map pp325-7
☎ 0179-490 9514; Gärtnerstrasse 12; U-Bahn
Samariterstrasse

The best thing about this lounge bar/restaurant is the, um, unusual cocktails on offer – try a Hello Kitty, an absinthe caipirinha or a Bitch Wallbanger. The four-shot caipi (€5) packs quite a punch as well.

DACHKAMMER Map pp325-7
☎ 296 1673; Simon-Dach-Strasse 39; U/S-Bahn
Warschauer Strasse

Two concepts in one bar: downstairs you get the traditional, rustic pub look, with hearty snacks and stacks of magazines; trip upstairs for a cool 1950s flash back in the cocktail bar, or step out onto the balcony.

DIE TAGUNG Map pp325-7
☎ 292 8756; Wühlischstrasse 29; U/S-Bahn
Warschauer Strasse

GDR paraphernalia from flags to busts of Lenin and old advertisements let you wallow in Ostalgie. The former basement Cube Club has struck out on its own as Octopussy (p204), with a programme of alternative sounds.

FEUERMELDER Map pp325-7
Krossener Strasse 21; 🕐 from 3pm Mon-Sat, from
noon Sun; U/S-Bahn Warschauer Strasse

Punks, rockers and other leather-clad folk gather in this loud bar to knock back beers and play pinball, pool, table football or the ancient fruit machines. It's popular with members of Berlin's active antifascist movement.

Open All Hours

Most bars in Berlin give their closing times as 'open end', but in practice this generally means between 1am and 3am during the week, and maybe 5am at weekends. So what to do once you've been kicked out by homesick bar staff?

Help is at hand – there are still a handful of bars in Berlin that never close, keeping the great tradition of the 24-hour bender alive. And if none of these appeal, you can always just start drinking earlier...

Under Hackescher Markt S-Bahn, **am to pm** (Map pp328-9; Am Zwirngraben 2, Mitte) is the original 24/7 bar-club, and has a good claim to be the best, packing them in to '80s music all night. Also in a railway arch is the **Besen-Kammer-Bar** (Map pp328-9; ☎ 242 4083; S-Bahnhof Alexanderplatz, Mitte). It's unusually glum for a gay pub, but with infinite drinking time people do cheer up eventually.

On the other side of town, **Graffiti** (Map pp332-3; ☎ 8800 1764; Kurfürstendamm 69, Wilmersdorf; U-Bahn Adenauerplatz) is a fairly typical cocktail bar and restaurant. **Voltaire** (Map pp332-3; ☎ 324 5028; Stuttgarter Platz 14, Charlottenburg; S-Bahn Charlottenburg), on the other hand, calls itself a 'caravanserai' and serves unusual Arabic-type food as well as the usual drinks.

For lounge people, though, the late-night highlight has to be the 'Good Morning Vietnam' sessions at **Delicious Doughnuts** (p200), which start at 5am Thursdays and most weekends for the ideal morning wind-down.

Entertainment – Drinking

HABANA Map pp325-7
☎ 2694 8661; Grünberger Strasse 57; U-Bahn Frankfurter Tor
Habana is one of Berlin's smarter and more credible Cuban bars, with bright lighting, tiled design, excellent food and that all-important touch of genuine Latin class. Happy hour is from 3pm to 9pm, and again from 1am to 2am in case you missed it.

STEREO 33 Map pp325-7
☎ 9599 9433; Krossener Strasse 24; ☽ Mon-Sat; U/S-Bahn Warschauer Strasse
Linked with the super-posy Shark Bar in Kreuzberg, Stereo 33 is without a doubt the coolest bar in Friedrichshain, and attracts a suitably hip-to-it crowd of scenesters. The modern, minimalist design, well-schooled DJs and bargain sushi all add to the appeal.

SUPAMOLLI
☎ 2900 7294; Jessnerstrasse 41; ☽ 8pm-7am Tue-Sun; U-Bahn Frankfurter Tor
This one-time squatter haunt has morphed into a respectable pub (by Friedrichshain standards anyway) with an eclectic programme of live concerts, theatre and films.

PRENZLAUER BERG

DRUIDE Map pp322-4
☎ 4849 4777; Schönhauser Allee 42; U-Bahn Eberswalder Strasse
With 300 cocktails, 40 different types of absinthe (the largest number in Germany) and DJs at weekends, there's more than enough

to make you sink into the chintzy sofas in this downbeat bar.

FREIZEITHEIM Map pp322-4
☎ 0174-402 6444; Schönhauser Allee 157; ☽ Tue-Sun; U-Bahn Eberswalder Strasse
Next door to the nbi club (p205), there's a similarly retro but more colourful flavour here, with two floors of cocktails and proto-hippy décor. Thursday is glamorous lesbian night.

GRAND HOTEL Map pp322-4
☎ 4432 7963; Schliemannstrasse 37; ☽ 5pm-3am Mon-Sat, from 3pm Sun; U-Bahn Eberswalder Strasse
Not many bars could get away with looking like a hotel lobby but the Grand Hotel makes a virtue of it, creating a thoroughly five-star atmosphere (it even has a 'champagne of the day'). Don't worry about the huge, scary ventilation fans – they're just for decoration.

LA BODEGUITA DEL MEDIO Map pp322-4
☎ 4403 2760; Husemannstrasse 10; ☽ 6pm-2am Sun-Thu, 6pm-3am Fri & Sat; U-Bahn Eberswalder Strasse, Senefelderplatz
Founded in 1942 in Havana, Hemingway's favourite haunt branched out to Berlin in 1993, bringing Cuban food, cigars and serious rum and tequila drinking to a clamorous crowd.

PRATER Map pp322-4
☎ 448 5688; www.pratergarten.de; Kastanienallee 7-9; ☽ from 4pm Mon-Fri, from noon Sat, from 10am Sun; U-Bahn Eberswalder Strasse
Berlin's oldest beer garden is also one of the prettiest and is great for quaffing away

beneath the chestnut trees. The complex includes a small stage which is operated by the Volksbühne, a cocktail bar, an old-fashioned restaurant and the legendary Bastard@Prater club nights.

RAZZIA IN BUDAPEST Map pp322-4
☎ 4862 3620; Oderberger Strasse 38; U-Bahn Eberswalder Strasse
Prenzlauer Berg meets Kreuzberg: this totally hip joint trades retro sophistication for complete kitsch, with tasselled lamp shades, chaise longues and electro DJs. Don't ask what any of it has to do with Hungarian police raids.

SCHALL UND RAUCH Map pp322-4
☎ 443 3970; Gleimstrasse 23; ⌚ 9-2am; U/S-Bahn Schönhauser Allee
A bistro by day, this trendy gay place turns into a chic cocktail bar when the moon gets high, with award-winning design and a young, buff following. The Sunday brunch (€7) has cult status.

SCHWARZE PUMPE Map pp322-4
☎ 449 6939; Choriner Strasse 76; ⌚ 9-1am; U-Bahn Senefelderplatz
For a quiet drink away from the busy main streets, this place offers semitraditional pub

surrounds and all kinds of mining-related signs and objects to muse over (it's named after a coal town in the Niederlausitz region).

SONNTAGS CLUB Map pp322-4
☎ 449 7590; Greifenhagener Strasse 28; U-Bahn Schönhauser Allee
This friendly, relaxed, lesbigay café-bar project is open to all and holds frequent events. There is also a piano just begging to have its ivories tickled.

ULURU RESORT Map pp322-4
☎ 4404 9522; Rykestrasse 17; U-Bahn Senefelderplatz
Homesick Australians can drop into this friendly Aussie pub for live music, the occasional mini-barbie and a suitably boisterous atmosphere. You won't hear much German spoken here!

WOHNZIMMER Map pp322-4
☎ 445 5458; Lettestrasse 6; ⌚ 10-4am; U/S-Bahn Schönhauser Allee
The 'Living Room' is a bit big now to be part of someone's house, but the comfy and laid-back atmosphere still brings in the scene-conscious Prenzlberg set for coffee, cakes and cocktails. The back room retains suitably homey sofas and random décor.

Berlin Kneipen

Old-fashioned Berlin *Kneipen* (pubs) have their own tradition of hospitality, serving up cheap beer, vicious schnapps, hearty food and wry humour in rustic, smoke-filled surroundings. Occasionally you'll come across a real *Kiezkneipe*, one that natives from the neighbourhood – usually paunchy, working-class stiffs or pugnacious, mulleted ex-rockers – have staked out as their own private turf. OK, it's local colour, but as a stranger you'll probably have a better time elsewhere.

Dicke Wirtin (Map pp332-3; ☎ 312 4952; Carmerstrasse 9, Charlottenburg; ⌚ from noon; S-Bahn Savignyplatz) If the 'Fat Landlady' could speak she'd doubtless dismiss the chic haunts of nearby Savignyplatz as poncy – this is a *Kneipe par excellence*, only saved from local exclusiveness by its fashionable location and regular influxes of students seeking cheap food and booze.

E&M Leydicke (Map pp330-1; ☎ 216 2973; Mansteinstrasse 4, Schöneberg; ⌚ from 4pm; U/S-Bahn Yorckstrasse) Founded in 1877, this old-fashioned pub and wine merchant bottles its own flavoured schnapps and fruit wines on the premises.

Gambrinus (Map pp328-9; ☎ 282 6043; Linienstrasse 133, Mitte; ⌚ noon-4am Mon-Sat, 3pm-4am Sun; U-Bahn Oranienburger Tor) With its prime location this is inevitably a bit touristy but the regulars are real Berliners and the huge collection of photos documenting turn-of-the-century Mitte is a treat. In homage to the '80s, you can even buy Helmut Kohl wine.

Zur letzten Instanz (Map pp328-9; ☎ 242 5528; Waisenstrasse 14, Mitte; U-Bahn Klosterstrasse) As the legalese menu here suggests, the name of this historic pub – 'The Final Authority' – relates to the presence of the courtroom opposite, although how it came to be called this is another story (or two). The hostelry itself is as Berlin as Currywurst, cabaret and communism.

SOUTHERN DISTRICTS

LORETTA AM WANNSEE

☎ 803 5156; Kronprinzessinenweg 260; ⊙ 9am-midnight Oct-Mar, 9-1am Apr-Sep; S-Bahn Wannsee

This huge beer garden has more than 1000 seats, perfect for capping off a hot summer day's swimming in the lake.

LUISE

☎ 832 8487; Königin-Luise-Strasse 40-44;
⊙ 10-1am; U-Bahn Dahlem-Dorf

This is a legendary student haunt with space for 700 outside.

CLUBBING

Berlin is the club capital of Germany. Frankfurt, Munich and even Rostock may have their contenders but Berlin's reputation is founded on an unbeatable combination of quality, quantity and variety. Whether you're into house, techno, drum and bass, punk, Britpop, dancehall, easy-listening, ska, folk or ballroom, you can find a place to party almost any night of the week. To get the best from the scene peruse the listings magazines (you'll find at least 130 different events on any given Saturday) or sift through the myriad flyers in shops, cafés and bars.

Getting into clubs is easier in unpretentious Berlin than most European cities. Even in the few places with a dress code, imagination usually beats income, so you don't have to swathe yourself in labels. Wherever you're going, though, don't bother showing up before midnight, and don't worry about closing times!

MITTE

COOKIES Map pp328-9

Cnr Charlottenstrasse & Unter den Linden; ⊙ from midnight Tue & Thu; U/S-Bahn Friedrichstrasse

This semisecret midweek club and champagne bar is a favourite of Mitte's wildest scenesters and fashionable types, and reputedly has Berlin's toughest door policy.

COX ORANGE Map pp328-9

☎ 0160-9585 1766; Dircksenstrasse 40; ⊙ from 8pm Thu, from 10pm Fri & Sat; S-Bahn Hackescher Markt

This basement club caters for a more mature audience, with rock, funk and disco sounds from the 1960s to '90s. Less manic than the clubbers' clubs, it's a cool place to explore with a cocktail in each hand.

DELICIOUS DOUGHNUTS Map pp322-4

☎ 2809 9279; Rosenthaler Strasse 9; ⊙ from 10pm Thu-Sat; U-Bahn Weinmeisterstrasse

Another tasty slice of Mitte nightlife, Doughnuts is a lot more laid-back, as befits its cosy velvet-lounge look. It's a friendly place with a lively dance floor, table football and a tendency to stay open well into daylight hours.

GRÜNER SALON Map pp328-9

☎ 2859 8936; www.gruener-salon.de; Volksbühne, Rosa-Luxemburg-Platz; admission €3-15; ⊙ Tue, Thu-Sat; U-Bahn Rosa-Luxemburg-Platz

Smoky sophistication and nostalgia reign in Volksbühne's intimate 'Green Salon', an elegant throwback to the wicked 1920s. Its salsa, tango and swing nights are legendary and often preceded by dance lessons. *Chansons*, comedy, plays and readings draw a full house as well.

KAFFEE BURGER Map pp322-4

☎ 2804 6495; www.kaffeeburger.de; Torstrasse 60; admission €3-5; ⊙ from 7pm Sun-Thu, from 9pm Fri & Sat; U-Bahn Rosa-Luxemburg-Platz

A cornerstone of the alternative scene, Kaffee Burger and the adjacent Burger Bar are decked out in what appears to be original GDR '60s living-room furniture and wallpaper, flashing you straight back to mod nightclub times. The indie, rock and punk parties and gigs are often preceded by literature and poetry readings by groups such as the Surfpoeten; most importantly, however, this is the home of the legendary Russendisko (Russian disco).

KOPIERBAR Map pp322-4

☎ 2859 8116; www.kopier-bar.de; Rosenthaler Strasse 71; ⊙ 1-10pm Mon-Thu, from 1pm Fri, from 8pm Sat; U-Bahn Rosenthaler Platz

Cunningly disguised as a copy-shop, this is actually a record store, Internet café, lounge bar, nightclub and multimedia duplicating facility all in one. As well as Goa trance nights, there's a monthly lesbigay NDW event.

MUDD CLUB Map pp328-9

☎ 2759 4999; www.muddclub.de; Grosse Hamburger Strasse 17; ⊙ from 9.30pm Wed-Sun; S-Bahn Hackescher Markt

Named in homage to the legendary SoHo original, hub of the New York underground in the '70s and '80s. It's set back from the street and down a steep staircase but today's Berlin rock chicks and indie kids seem to have no problem finding their way in. Russian and Slavic acts feature heavily.

OXYMORON Map pp328-9

☎ 2839 1886; www.oxymoron-berlin.de; Rosenthaler Strasse 40-41; admission €5-10; ☼ club Fri & Sat; S-Bahn Hackescher Markt

Inside the Hackesche Höfe, this shape-shifting salon is a café-restaurant by day and a chic club after 11pm, with a variety of retro and electro nights on the menu and occasional 'extras' such as go-go dancers. Dress code is just on the smarter side of casual.

ROTER SALON Map pp328-9

☎ 2406 5806; www.roter-salon.de; Volksbühne, Rosa-Luxemburg-Platz; ☼ Mon & Tue, Thu-Sat; U-Bahn Rosa-Luxemburg-Platz

The Grüner Salon's red counterpart ditches the sophistication and goes for a more rowdy retro atmosphere, hosting readings, live concerts and dance parties (including a terrific northern soul all-nighter). Postpremiere bashes are especially well attended.

SAGE CLUB Map pp328-9

☎ 2787 6948; www.sage-club.de; Köpenicker Strasse 76; admission €4-10; ☼ Thu-Sun; U-Bahn Heinrich-Heine-Strasse

Berlin's premier house club is not as exclusive as it could be, though door policy can be pretty picky when it's busy. It's worth it just for the fire-belching dragon and amazing summer garden area (with pool); the euphoric music and good-looking public aren't bad either. Thursday is 'rock meets electronic beats' night.

SOPHIENCLUB Map pp328-9

☎ 282 4552; www.sophienclub.de; Sophienstrasse 6; admission €3-10; ☼ from 10pm Tue, Thu-Sat; U-Bahn Weinmeisterstrasse

Even after 20 years no-one could accuse this club of trendsetting but that's just fine with the virtually school-age crowds who gather here for regular doses of familiar '60s to '90s, funk, soul and Britpop tunes.

TRESOR/GLOBUS Map pp325-7

☎ 609 3702; www.tresorberlin.de; Leipziger Strasse 126a; admission €3-15; ☼ from 11pm Wed, Fri & Sat; U/S-Bahn Potsdamer Platz

House sounds dominate Globus, the ground floor of this legendary double-decker haunt.

Downstairs is Tresor, former department-store vault and standard-bearer of the techno revolution. Equally legendary Detroit DJ Jeff Mills packs the place out with his occasional residency. However, building developments on Leipziger Platz may soon overtake the location – check listings.

WMF Map pp322-4

☎ 2838 8850; www.wmfclub.de; Karl-Marx-Allee 34; admission €6-12; ☼ from 11pm Fri & Sat; U-Bahn Schillingstrasse

This peripatetic Berlin classic is now on its sixth location, a great spacious lounge in the former Moskau café, complete with '60s GDR design features. The music is mostly cutting-edge electro, though frequent special events provide plenty of variety. The regular appearances by remix gods Jazzanova, with guests, are essential and count among the best nights anywhere in Germany. Sunday is GayMF night.

XMF Map pp328-9

☎ 2758 2682; www.2be-club.de; Ziegelstrasse 23; ☼ from 11pm Fri & Sat; S-Bahn Oranienburger Strasse

Also known as 2BE, this was the WMF's (above) previous venue, though there's not much similarity. 2BE deals almost exclusively in hip-hop and dancehall nights, with the occasional big-name special event.

TIERGARTEN

DIE 2 Map pp320-1

☎ 3983 8969; www.die2-berlin.de; Rathenower Strasse 19; ☼ Wed-Sat; S-Bahn Westhafen

Lesbians of all ages and styles gather here for the disco nights and Thursday's more sedate cultural programme of exhibitions and readings. Fans of small dogs also meet here once a month (no, we're not kidding).

POLAR.TV Map pp320-1

☎ 2462 95320; www.polar.tv; Heidestrasse 73; ☼ from 11pm Wed & Sat; S-Bahn Lehrter Stadtbahnhof

Home to the No UFOs club, this cutting-edge venue in an old warehouse has a solid track record of pulling in energetic young crowds with the finest electro and techno sounds. Local boy Westbam is a regular sight behind the decks. In summer you can head outdoors, and there's also a slightly calmer sister club, **Sternradio** (Map pp328-9; ☎ 2462 95320; Alexanderplatz 5; U-Bahn Alexanderplatz).

CHARLOTTENBURG

ABRAXAS Map pp332-3

☎ 312 9493; Kantstrasse 134; admission €3-5; ☺ from 10pm Tue-Sat; S-Bahn Savignyplatz

It may look like a sex shop from the outside but inside this little club is a hotbed of salsoul, hip-hop and funk cuts. The dance floor is packed from about 1am and often the entire crowd seems to be on the pull.

SCHÖNEBERG

90 GRAD Map pp330-1

☎ 2300 5954; www.90grad.de; Dennewitzstrasse 37; admission €8-10; ☺ from 11pm Fri & Sat; U-Bahn Kurfürstenstrasse

Unimpressive from the outside, this squat black cube is actually as trendy as anything in Mitte, with a similarly elitist door policy and a backlist of celebrity visitors from George Clooney to Heidi Klum.

CONNECTION Map pp332-3

☎ 218 1432; www.connection-berlin.de; Fuggerstrasse 33; ☺ Fri & Sat; U-Bahn Wittenbergplatz

This well-established den is one of the most popular gay discos in town, renowned for its dense warren of underground darkrooms. Upstairs there are three floors of cruising action, a mirrored dance floor and blaring techno.

METROPOL Map pp330-1

☎ 2173 6811; www.metropol-berlin.de; Nollendorfplatz 5; ☺ Fri & Sat; U-Bahn Nollendorfplatz

Erwin Piscator's old theatre, its façade festooned with seductive nude sculptures, has seen many incarnations but is currently home to high-intensity gay nights.

TOM'S BAR Map pp330-1

☎ 213 4570; Motzstrasse 19; U-Bahn Nollendorfplatz

Serious gay pick-up place with an active cellar. If you're OFB ('out for business'), don't arrive here before midnight.

KREUZBERG

AQUALOUNGE Map pp325-7

www.aqua-lounge.net; Ohlauer Strasse 11; admission €2-11; ☺ from 10pm Sat; U-Bahn Görlitzer Bahnhof

Formerly 'Fish & Friends', this trend-conscious club is known for its picky door policy and entry prices are decided by throwing dice, but it's worth making an effort for – instead of a dance floor you get a king-sized swimming pool heated to a glorious 32°C, and you can even take a diving course before the party! Obviously the chance to pose in swimsuits brings out a lot of beautiful people.

DÖNER LOUNGE Map pp325-7

www.doenerlounge.de; Schlesische Strasse; ☺ Thu

We can't say too much about this one but if you happen to wander into the back room of a certain kebab shop, you'll find one of Berlin's best top-secret club tips.

PRIVATCLUB Map pp325-7

☎ 611 3302; www.monosound.de; Markthalle, Pücklerstrasse 34; ☺ Fri & Sat; U-Bahn Görlitzer Bahnhof

Down in the basement of the Weltrestaurant Markthalle (p186), an unshowy bunch of party people soak up the alternative soul, funk, easy,

---

Sex Clubs

The hedonism of the 1920s is back – anything goes in Berlin, and we mean *anything*. While full-on sex clubs are most common in the gay scene, there are also several mixed and/or straight places catering for consenting adults rather than overpaying voyeurs. The wildest parties take place once or twice a month and change venues often.

Club Culture Houze (Map pp325-7; ☎ 6170 9669; www.club-culture-houze.de; Görlitzer Strasse 71, Kreuzberg; ☺ Wed-Mon; U-Bahn Görlitzer Bahnhof) The CCH democratically caters for all tastes, persuasions and fetishes, with two mixed and four hard-core gay parties a week, plus a monthly lesbian event. Check listings *very* carefully before you set out.

Greifbar (Map pp322-4; ☎ 444 0828; Wichertstrasse 10, Prenzlauer Berg; S-Bahn Schönhauser Allee) This is a simple cruising den with a busy darkroom where you can retreat to Portakabins for some privacy. It draws a slightly older clientele of active gays aged around 30.

KitKat Club (☎ 7889 9704; www.kitkatclub.de; Bessemer Strasse 2-14, Schöneberg; admission €10-15; ☺ Thu-Sun; S-Bahn Papestrasse) The original Berlin den of decadence is still going strong, now in a new location with the main club downstairs and the separate Penthouse above it. Most parties are open to all comers, subject to the erotic dress code; Saturday's Penthouze and the Sunday-morning Piep Show are infamous.

trash pop and indie sounds in this kitsch but cool lounge. Occasional film nights and mid-week concerts spice up the regular weekend schedule.

SCHWUZ Map pp325-7

☎ 693 7025; www.schwuz.de; Mehringdamm 61; ☽ Wed, Fri & Sat; U-Bahn Mehringdamm

On Saturday Melitta Sundström turns into the warm-up bar for this mainstream dance club in the SchwuZ gay centre. Come here to check out the flamboyant drag queens and get sweaty on the two dance floors.

SO36 Map pp325-7

☎ 6140 1306; www.so36.de; Oranienstrasse 190; U-Bahn Kottbusser Tor

This place is Kreuzberg's punk heart, keeping the district's alternative ethos alive with its schedule of relentlessly offbeat live concerts and theme nights.

The lesbigay events here are consistently popular, particularly Gayhane, a monthly 'homoriental' party with Turkish and German pop, transvestites and belly dancing.

WATERGATE Map pp325-7

☎ 6128 0394; www.water-gate.de; Falckensteinstrasse 49a; admission €10; ☽ from 11pm Fri & Sat; U-Bahn Schlesisches Tor

One of Berlin's hottest recent arrivals, Watergate has a fantastic location with a downstairs lounge overlooking the Spree, opposite the colour-changing logo of the Universal Music building. It's quite possible to walk in at 8am and find people still here. Upstairs, the main floor has inherited the notorious hard-edged drum and bass nights from the WMF, and hosts more down-tempo, but equally high-quality, events on Saturday. The lounge occasionally opens on Thursday.

FRIEDRICHSHAIN

BLACK GIRLS COALITION Map pp318-19

☎ 6953 4300; Samariterstrasse 32; ☽ from 10pm Mon, Wed & Thu; U-Bahn Samariterstrasse

Don't be fooled by the word 'girls'; these are male wolves in expensive, very tight sheep's clothing. Fans may recognise proprietor Miss Paisley Dalton from her appearance on *Sex and the City*. For the many regulars who pack into this tiny space, however, it's all about the monthly Roots Night, Berlin's trashiest trannie party. Outrageous with a capital D-R-A-G.

Top Five Clubs

- **Kaffee Burger** (p200)
- **Maria am Ufer** (p204)
- **Sage Club** (p201)
- **Watergate** (this page)
- **WMF** (p201)

CASINO Map pp325-7

☎ 2900 9799; Mühlenstrasse 26-30; admission €10-14; ☽ Fri-Sun; U/S-Bahn Warschauer Strasse

Welcome to trance country, boys and girls – this is home-grown megastar Paul van Dyk's dance floor of choice, so queues are a dead cert on his monthly Vandit nights. At other times it's a bit easier to get in, and random reggae and even punk nights are creeping onto the programme. Sunday's early-evening lounge sessions are a good way to end your weekend (or start your week).

CONSULAT Map pp322-4

☎ 4208 0780; Karl-Marx-Allee 133-135; ☽ Tue-Sat; U-Bahn Frankfurter Tor

You wouldn't expect that a pointedly classy club/cocktail bar would last long in doggedly alternative Friedrichshain, but the Consulat somehow manages to find enough people willing to turn out, dress up and show off in the well-styled lounges.

DIE BUSCHE Map pp325-7

☎ 296 0800; www.diebusche.de; Mühlenstrasse 11-12; admission €3.50-5; ☽ 10pm-5am Wed & Sun, 10pm-6am Fri & Sat; U/S-Bahn Warschauer Strasse

The ghosts of communism have long been exorcised from what used to be the only gay disco in GDR-era Berlin but the place is still alive and kicking. Loud music, mirrored rooms, strong alcohol and a young, mixed clientele make up its raunchy dance parties.

LAUSCHANGRIFF Map pp322-4

☎ 4221 9626; www.lauschangriff-berlin.de; Rigaer Strasse 103; admission €2; ☽ from 10pm Fri-Mon; U-Bahn Frankfurter Tor

The name means 'bugging operation', though with the volumes generated the police could just stand outside to listen in! This former squat club is legit now anyway. Friday concentrates on hard electronic sounds, Saturday is world styles, Sunday is for readings and Monday is reggae chill night.

Entertainment – Clubbing

Parties

Some of the best club nights in Berlin are independent of the venues they use and may move around, although they'll usually have one home residency where they can be found every week or month. There is also a thriving illegal party scene, relying on word of mouth and often using buildings outside the central districts.

!K7 Flavour (☎ 202 0957; www.k7.com) Groundbreaking record label !K7 holds monthly nights showcasing its eclectic artists, currently at Watergate (p203).

Kachelklub (Map pp322-4; ☎ 449 4598; www.stadtbad-oderberger.de) With typical Berlin ingenuity, Prenzlauer Berg's old municipal bathhouse (Oderberger Str 57-59; U-Bahn Eberswalder Strasse) is occasionally used as a party venue to help fund its restoration. The main dance floor is actually in the central pool (luckily it's been drained).

Karrera Club (☎ 7895 8410; www.karreraclub.de) DJs Tim, Christian and Spencer must be the hardest-working vinyl spinners in Berlin, putting on indie and Britpop parties almost every night. Regular venues include Kaffee Burger, Mudd Club and the Sophienclub.

Sally's (☎ 6940 9663; www.sallys.net) Besides sponsoring all kinds of rock gigs, music mag *Uncle Sally's* runs its own bimonthly parties in the **Silver Wings club** (Map pp325-7; Columbiadamm 8, Tempelhof).

Yaam (☎ 615 1354; www.arena-berlin.de) The granddaddy of all summer parties, this Caribbean Sunday session outside the Berlin Arena (p208) has been running for years, with food, drink and dub-reggae music bizness. It's so popular it now has winter events in venues such as Casino and the MS Hoppetosse in the Arena.

MARIA AM UFER Map pp325-7

☎ 2123 8190; www.clubmaria.de; Stralauer Platz 33-34; admission €5-10; ☽ from 10pm Fri & Sat; S-Bahn Ostbahnhof

Since the demise of nearby Ostgut, Maria's musical supremacy is unchallenged – the DJs playing here are invariably among the best in their field, whether it's breakbeat, down-tempo, techno or some other strand of electronica. Live concerts often take place here weekdays, and Ostgut's André Galluzzi has brought over his legendary marathon sessions.

NARVA LOUNGE Map pp325-7

☎ 2935 1111; Warschauer Platz 18; admission €6-8; ☽ from 10pm Fri & Sat; U/S-Bahn Warschauer Strasse

With the Matrix next door going all mainstream, this swish place is the new hot spot under Warschauer Strasse station. Coloured projections make the most of the space, house, black and '80s classics keep the dance floor packed, and bright lights make sure you can see and be seen. Dress code may apply.

OCTOPUSSY

www.octopussy-club.de; Gürtelstrasse 36; admission €3-4; ☽ from 9pm Thu-Sat, from 2pm Sun; U/S-Bahn Frankfurter Allee

Formerly known as the Cube Club, this underwater-themed venue recently moved out of the basement at Die Tagung (see p197) to peddle alternative nights to a wider public.

ROSIS Map pp325-7

www.rosis-berlin.de; Revaler Strasse 29; admission €3-5; ☽ Thu-Sat; S-Bahn Ostkreuz

We're not sure if this derelict house was ever actually a squat but it catches the Friedrichshain vibe spot-on – dim lighting, dank concrete, totally random music policy (country, karaoke, soul, nu jazz, happy hardcore...) and, for entertainment, table football and a Scalextric-style racing track.

TRAFO Map pp325-7

www.trafo-berlin.de; Libauer Strasse 1; ☽ from 10pm Wed-Sat; U/S-Bahn Warschauer Strasse

Trafo is definitely the place to come if you like your music loud, noncommercial and indefinable: regular jungle, dancehall and disco nights rub shoulders with live punk'n'roll, tribal funk and psycho-hillbilly rock gigs. It's a bit like clubbing in a freight container, but you can't fault the state-of-the-art sound system.

PRENZLAUER BERG

ICON Map pp322-4

☎ 4849 2878; www.iconberlin.de; Cantianstrasse 15; admission €8-10; ☽ from 11pm Fri & Sat; U-Bahn Eberswalder Strasse

Along with Watergate, this cave-like space is Berlin's top location for seriously heavy-duty drum and bass – Recycle on Saturday is an eardrum-rinsing local institution. Friday is generally given over to hip-hop, dancehall or special events. The regular nights from left-field London label Ninja Tune should not be missed.

KNAACK Map pp322-4

☎ 442 7060; www.knaack-berlin.de; Greifswalder Strasse 224; tickets €5-18; ⏰ from 6pm Mon, from 9pm Wed, Fri & Sat; U-Bahn Senefelderplatz, tram 2/3/4

Part venue, part club, this place is known for its popular rock and punk concerts (it's even hosted '80s legends The Stranglers), but the regular five-floor parties are pretty good too.

NBI Map pp322-4

☎ 4405 1681; www.neueberlinerinitiative.de; Schönhauser Allee 157; ⏰ from 10pm; U-Bahn Senefelderplatz

For a new club, the décor here looks decidedly shabby, but that's all part of its slightly retro charm – sink into the large sofas, admire the egg boxes on the walls, and try some of the excellent *Schwarzbier* (dark beer) while DJs spin the latest house and electro tracks. The dance floor's essentially a space on the way to the bar, but no-one seems to mind.

SODA Map pp322-4

☎ 4431 5155; Kulturbrauerei, Schönhauser Allee 36; admission €3-10; ⏰ Thu-Mon; U-Bahn Eberswalder Strasse

This sophisticated club-lounge has a good mixed-music policy, with tango and salsa weekdays and weekends tending towards R&B and house grooves, plus the odd bit of reggae/dancehall and a regular '80s floor. Friday is ladies' night but in a spirit of nondiscrimination 'queens' get in free too!

CULTURAL CENTRES

Cultural centres are an integral part of Berlin's entertainment scene, providing a forum for all kinds of local and international performers and genres that would never make it onto the mainstream programmes. These multi-use venues often fill unusual spaces, taking over derelict and repurposed buildings, and impose few limits on their stages – on any given night you might find cinema, dance, live music, theatre, art, literature or even circus acts. Most also have bars, cafés and restaurants on site.

ACUD Map pp322-4

☎ 449 1067; www.acud.de; Veteranenstrasse 21, Mitte; U-Bahn Rosenthaler Platz

Set up in a derelict house, this alternative arts centre hosts plays, exhibitions, parties and a superb programme of lesser-known movies from around the world, shown in the original languages.

BEGINE Map pp330-1

☎ 215 1414; www.begine.de; Potsdamer Strasse 139, Schöneberg; U-Bahn Bülowstrasse

Things have calmed down considerably since this historic building was first occupied by militant female squatters. Now it's an entirely legal café and cultural centre for women, primarily lesbians, with an intellectual bent, putting on concerts, readings and films.

INSEL DER JUGEND

☎ 5360 8020; www.insel-berlin.com; Alt-Treptow 6, Treptow; S-Bahn Plänterwald

The Island of Youth is a former GDR youth club housed in a mock medieval castle on an island in the Spree. There's something for everybody, from workshops to live rock concerts, open-air cinema (June to September) and dance parties of all musical stripes. There's even a family café (on weekends) where parents can relax while the tots are being entertained with craft projects or puppet theatre.

KALKSCHEUNE Map pp328-9

☎ 5900 4340; www.kalkscheune.de; Johannisstrasse 2, Mitte; S-Bahn Oranienburger Strasse

You can't get much more eclectic than this – while it's not a centre per se, the Kalkscheune puts on as wide a variety of events as anywhere listed here. Favourites include ballroom dancing, live gigs, fashion shows, club and singles' nights, and one of Berlin's top Kabarett brunches.

KULTURBRAUEREI Map pp322-4

☎ 484 9444; www.kulturbrauerei-berlin.de; Schönhauser Allee 36, Prenzlauer Berg; U-Bahn Eberswalder Strasse

The former 19th-century Schultheiss brewery has been turned into a huge art, shopping and nightlife complex boasting a frightening range of venues, most well-known in their own right. These include a multiscreen cinema, pool hall, art gallery, two nightclubs, three live venues and two repertory theatres.

KUNSTHAUS TACHELES Map pp328-9

☎ 282 6185; www.tacheles.de; Oranienburger Strasse 54-56, Mitte; U-Bahn Oranienburger Tor

If you need proof that Mitte is being gentrified, look no further than the front of the Tacheles complex – a shiny, new and incongruously mainstream restaurant has sprung up in the centre of this dilapidated former department store. Luckily the post-apocalyptic squat spirit of the centre remains intact, and it's still a premier address for antimainstream cinema, dance, jazz, cabaret, readings, workshops, art, theatre and more. Look out for Bomb-o-drom nights, seriously hard techno with a political bent.

PFEFFERBERG Map pp322-4

☎ 4438 3342; www.pfefferberg.de; Schönhauser Allee 176, Prenzlauer Berg; U-Bahn Senefelderplatz

Also converted from a brewery, Pfefferberg is rougher, readier and more alternative than Kulturbrauerei, promoting a lot of cross-cultural and antifascist projects. The grounds were being renovated at the time of research.

PODEWIL Map pp328-9

☎ 247 496; www.podewil.de; Klosterstrasse 68-70, Mitte; U-Bahn Klosterstrasse

This place offers a mixed bag of film, dance, theatre and live music, as well as a café, all in a renovated mansion dating from 1704. There's also a full-time puppet theatre and a seasonal beer garden.

TRÄNENPALAST Map pp328-9

☎ 2061 0011; www.traenenpalast.de; Reichstagsufer 17, Mitte; U/S-Bahn Friedrichstrasse

In a retired border-crossing facility, the 'Palace of Tears' offers a variety of multicultural entertainment, from African jazz and Russian rock to Norwegian folk and Polish dance via German cabaret and the odd spot of 'comedy blues'.

UFA-FABRIK

☎ 755 030; www.ufafabrik.de; Viktoriastrasse 10-18, Tempelhof; U-Bahn Ullsteinstrasse

Housed in the former UFA studios, you'll find eclectic music, theatre, dance, cabaret and circus shows year-round, with performances on the outdoor stage from June to September.

URANIA Map pp330-1

☎ 218 9091; www.urania-berlin.de; An der Urania 17, Schöneberg; lectures €5; U-Bahn Nollendorfplatz

In contrast to the entertainment slant of most centres, the Urania is a cultural heavyweight

with a very serious intellectual agenda, holding lectures by international experts on a broad spectrum of disciplines. The 'Philosophical Café' is one of the more popular regular discussion events, and the film and theatre programme is also highly recommended.

LIVE MUSIC
CLASSICAL

Classical music fans have plenty to pick from just about any night of the week, except during the summer hiatus (usually July and August). A trip to the Philharmonie or the Konzerthaus is a special treat, although regular concert series are also organised in Berlin's castles (☎ 4360 5390 for information). Aficionados under 27 who are planning a longer stay, or making repeated visits, should look into the Classic Card (www.classiccard.de).

BERLINER PHILHARMONIE Map p334

☎ 2548 8132; www.berliner-philharmoniker.de; Herbert-von-Karajan-Strasse 1, Tiergarten; tickets €8-61; U/S-Bahn Potsdamer Platz

The Philharmonie is arguably the finest place in Berlin to hear classical music, thanks to its supreme acoustics. The current director is the flamboyant and controversial conductor Sir Simon Rattle; expect to pay anything up to €110 when he steps behind the baton with the Berliner Philharmoniker. The adjacent **Kammermusiksaal** (tickets €5-40) is a much smaller chamber-music venue with an annually appointed pianist in residence. There isn't a bad seat in either house.

BERLINER SYMPHONIKER

☎ 325 5562; www.berliner-symphoniker.de; Christstrasse 30, Charlottenburg; tickets €7-30

Founded in 1966, the Berliner Symphoniker has no permanent home and performs mainly in the Philharmonie and the Konzerthaus. Israeli conductor Lior Shambadal is the man in charge.

C BECHSTEIN CENTRUM Map pp332-3

☎ 3151 5200; www.bechstein.de; Stilwerk, Kantstrasse 17, Charlottenburg; tickets €16; S-Bahn Savignyplatz

Germany's most prestigious piano manufacturer holds concerts at its flagship store in the Stilwerk centre about eight times a year, inviting world-class musicians to showcase its instruments. Such is its reputation that a further series of concerts was held in major venues throughout the country (including the Philharmonie and Konzerthaus) for the firm's 150th anniversary in 2003.

DEUTSCHES SYMPHONIE-ORCHESTER

☎ 2029 8711; www.dso-berlin.de; Charlottenstrasse 56, Mitte; tickets €10-55

This orchestra, directed by Kent Nagano, started life as the RIAS Symphonie Orchester, founded in 1946 and financed by the USA until 1953. Like the Symphoniker, it has no permanent venue, performing regularly at the Philharmonie, the Konzerthaus, the Tempodrom and other major stages.

HOCHSCHULE FÜR MUSIK HANNS EISLER Map pp328-9

☎ 9026 9700; www.hfm-berlin.de; Charlottenstrasse 55, Mitte; U-Bahn Stadtmitte

This top-rated music academy maintains several orchestras, a choir and a big band, which collectively stage as many as 400 performances annually. Almost all events are free or low-cost.

KONZERTHAUS BERLIN Map pp328-9

☎ 203 090; www.konzerthaus.de; Gendarmenmarkt 2, Mitte; tickets €5-40; U-Bahn Stadtmitte/Französische Strasse

The lavish, Schinkel-designed Konzerthaus is one of Berlin's top classical venues. The 'house band' is the very well-known Berliner Sinfonie-Orchester, helmed by Eliahu Inbal. There are two auditoriums here, as well as a smaller music club which is used for literary and children's events.

UNIVERSITÄT DER KÜNSTE Map pp332-3

☎ 3185 2374; www.hdk-berlin.de; Hardenbergstrasse 33, Charlottenburg; U-Bahn Ernst-Reuter-Platz

The University of the Arts concert hall was under renovation at the time of research. It's usually busy in season, and things should be no different when it reopens as the Karajan-Konzertsaal. In the meantime, look out for benefit concerts.

JAZZ

Partly thanks to the recent Latin explosion, Berlin's jazz scene keeps going from strength to strength, with several fancy places in Charlottenburg balanced out by some pleasingly insalubrious joints further to the east.

Wherever you go, you're guaranteed a good mix of local and international performers presenting some very diverse interpretations of the core genre.

A-TRANE Map pp332-3

☎ 313 2550; www.a-trane.de; Bleibtreustrasse 1, Charlottenburg; admission €5-20; ⏰ 9pm-2am Mon-Thu & Sun, from 9pm Fri & Sat; S-Bahn Savignyplatz

This is everything a jazz club should be – intimate, loud and usually packed. The varied talent on display is invariably top-class and, despite the cosy tables, everyone is standing by the end of the evening. Entry is free Monday and Tuesday when local boy Andreas Schmidt is playing, and after 12.30am on Saturday for the late-night jam session.

B-FLAT Map pp328-9

☎ 283 3123; www.b-flat-berlin.de; Rosenthaler Strasse 13, Mitte; admission €4-10; ⏰ from 8pm; U-Bahn Weinmeisterstrasse

Latin flavours have crept into the programme but jazz still rules the roost at this increasingly versatile venue, with no shortage of noodly free form and stomping Cajun to complement the trad bottom line. Wednesday is acoustic night (free entry), while the film lounge takes over on Thursday.

FLÖZ Map pp330-1

☎ 861 1000; www.floez.com; Nassauische Strasse 37, Wilmersdorf; ⏰ from 8pm; U-Bahn Berliner Strasse

Modern jazz, folk and rock are on the musical menu at this fairly rough'n'ready, old-time cellar haunt, which is popular with an older clientele. Midweek events at Flöz are often free, with admission at other times costing around €5.

JUNCTION BAR Map pp325-7

☎ 694 6602; www.junction-bar.de; Gneisenaustrasse 18, Kreuzberg; admission €3-6; U-Bahn Gneisenaustrasse

Live music 365 days a year – check your lungs and your eardrums at the door before descending into this cellar, where you'll be confronted with a rowdy crowd drinking in everything from trad jazz to blues, fusion, hip-hop and crossover. Nightly DJs follow the bands. The upstairs café-bar is slightly more sedate.

Entertainment – Live Music

QUASIMODO Map pp332-3

☎ 312 8086; www.quasimodo.de; Kantstrasse 12a, Charlottenburg; admission €7.50-13; ☺ from 9pm; U/S-Bahn Zoologischer Garten

Underneath the Delphi cinema, Berlin's oldest jazz club attracts high-calibre national and international acts. Its petite size puts you close to the stage but the low ceiling, black walls and smoky air can be just a tad claustrophobic. The spacious upstairs café is a breath of fresh air if you need it.

SCHLOT Map pp322-4

☎ 448 2160; www.kunstfabrik-schlot.de; Chaus-seestrasse 18, Mitte; admission €5-10; U-Bahn Zinnowitzer Strasse

Schlot, which translates as 'chimney', is an unpretentious venue that opened immediately after reunification and quickly garnered a reputation for its fine jazz and cabaret. Managed by a pair of marathon runners, it has an interesting and eclectic mix of acts and styles presented in a spacious setting, which was extensively rebuilt in 2003-04.

SOULTRANE Map pp332-3

☎ 2309 9333; www.soultrane.de; Stilwerk, Kant-strasse 17, Charlottenburg; tickets from €15; ☺ 10am-7pm Mon, 10-2am Tue-Thu, from 10am Fri & Sat, 7pm-1am Sun; S-Bahn Savignyplatz

This smart dining and dancing place in the überstylish Stilwerk centre is actually a reasonable facsimile of an old-school jazz club, though the well-dressed crowd is far too well behaved. If you can't get into A-Trane, the Saturday night jam session and dance party that is held here is worth staying out for.

UMSPANNWERK OST Map pp322-4

☎ 4208 9323; Palisadenstrasse 48, Friedrichshain; ☺ from 11.30am; U-Bahn Weberwiese

Amazingly, this posh-looking house was originally built as an electricity substation around the turn of the 20th century, when considerable space was needed to house the huge transformers. Today it contains a restaurant and the Berliner Kriminal Theater (p213) as well as this atmospheric cellar jazz club.

VOLLMOND Map pp325-7

☎ 614 2912; Oranienstrasse 160, Kreuzberg; ☺ from 4.30pm Sun-Fri, from 6pm Sat; U-Bahn Kottbusser Tor

Real blues, R&B and jazz flow as freely as the beer in Vollmond, an earthy but satisfying music bar.

BIG VENUES

Any time that big international acts and megastars roll into town, they'll probably play at one of these large venues. Touring productions such as *Lord of the Dance* and the Cirque de Soleil also have extended runs here.

ARENA Map pp325-7

☎ 533 2030; www.arena-berlin.de; Eichenstrasse 4, Treptow; S-Bahn Treptower Park

On the south bank of the Spree, the midsized Berlin Arena is slightly out of the way but can otherwise hold its own against even larger venues, particularly when the open river-side area is being used. The adjacent **Glashaus** hosts smaller gigs and some theatre; the **Club der Visionäre** and **MS Hoppetosse** bars are also part of the complex.

COLUMBIAHALLE Map pp325-7

☎ 698 0980; www.columbiahalle.de; Columbiadamm 13-21, Tempelhof; U-Bahn Platz der Luftbrücke

Just opposite Tempelhof airport, this unfancy hall hosts everything from international name artists to punk festivals and metal gigs. Next door, the smaller **Columbia Fritz** is more geared towards party nights and offbeat events.

MAX-SCHMELING-HALLE Map pp322-4

☎ 443 045; www.max-schmeling-halle.de; Am Falk-platz, Prenzlauer Berg; U-Bahn Eberswalder Strasse

This 8500-seat hall, which was completed in 1997, is home to Berlin's professional basketball team and also hosts concerts, theatre and conferences.

OLYMPIASTADION

☎ 300 633; Olympischer Platz 3, Charlottenburg; U-Bahn Olympia-Stadion, S-Bahn Olympiastadion

Due to finally finish renovations in late 2004, the historic Olympic Stadium should be back at its best and hosting Berlin's biggest sports and music events.

TEMPODROM Map pp325-7

☎ 695 3385; www.tempodrom.de; Möckernstrasse 10, Kreuzberg; S-Bahn Anhalter Bahnhof

Housed in a huge tent-like structure on the grounds of the former Anhalter Bahnhof, the Tempodrom puts on a range of large concerts, performances, musicals, circuses and the like. The attached Liquidrom spa centre (p221) is another fun spot.

Tempodrom (opposite)

TIPI Map pp320-1

☎ 390 6650; www.tipi-das-zelt.de; Grosse Querallee, Tiergarten; tickets €18.50-42; bus 100

This large new tent venue between the Haus der Kulturen der Welt and the Chancellery stages a variety of mainstream musical and theatrical events. For an extra €30 you get a four-course meal.

VELODROM Map pp322-4

☎ 443 045; www.velomax.de; Paul-Heyse-Strasse 26, Lichtenberg; S-Bahn Landsberger Allee

Major cycling races and other top sporting and music events, as well as conferences, are held at this 11,000-seat hall, run by the same company as the Max-Schmeling-Halle.

WALDBÜHNE

☎ 810 750; Am Glockenturm, Charlottenburg; ☼ May-Sep; U-Bahn Olympia-Stadion, S-Bahn Pichelsberg

This huge open-air amphitheatre is a local favourite: 22,000 people can and do pack in to enjoy rock, pop and classical concerts (and Phil Collins). Movie nights are understandably popular too, although you get a better view in an IMAX.

OPERA & MUSICALS

With three controversially state-funded venues, opera has always been big in Berlin, and fans can catch some of the biggest and best performances in the country here – only Dresden's Semperoper (p270) has a better reputation. Bizarrely, though, this interest has never translated into a great public passion for musicals, and there's no equivalent of London's West End here. Lloyd Webber enthusiasts will have to take what they can get around the Ku'damm and Potsdamer Platz.

DEUTSCHE OPER Map pp330-1

☎ 343 8401; www.deutscheoperberlin.de; Bismarckstrasse 35, Charlottenburg; tickets €10-112; U-Bahn Deutsche Oper

Berlin's largest opera house may look a bit blockish but its musical supremacy is seldom questioned. Wagner is the house orchestra's forte – conductor Christian Thielemann is well-versed in his work, and Wagner abridger Loriot, better known as Germany's favourite humorist, was made an honorary member in 2002. All operas are performed in their original language.

KOMISCHE OPER Map pp328-9

☎ 4799 7400; www.komische-oper-berlin.de; Behrenstrasse 55-57, box office Unter den Linden 41, Mitte; tickets €8-93; S-Bahn Unter den Linden

Musical theatre, light opera, operetta and dance theatre are the mainstays at this opera house. There's less of an elite touch here: productions are drawn from many periods and all are sung in German.

MUSICAL THEATER AM POTSDAMER PLATZ Map p334

☎ 01805-114 131; Marlene-Dietrich-Platz 1, Tiergarten; tickets €42-110; U/S-Bahn Potsdamer Platz

This state-of-the-art theatre in DaimlerCity opened in June 1999 with the world premiere of *The Hunchback of Notre Dame*. Subsequent turns at this musical theatre have included *Cats* and the Blue Man Group. All performances are in German and run for several months before changing.

NEUKÖLLNER OPER Map pp325-7

☎ 688 9070; www.neukoellner-oper.de; Karl-Marx-Strasse 131-133, Neukölln; tickets €9-21; U-Bahn Karl-Marx-Strasse

This place is much more avant-garde than its heavily subsidised fellows. The actively anti-elitist repertory includes children's and experimental shows alongside rare operas by Mozart and Schubert. It's all staged with little money and much creativity in a refurbished prewar ballroom and attracts an unpretentious, surprisingly young audience.

STAATSOPER UNTER DEN LINDEN
Map pp328-9

☎ 2035 4438, tickets ☎ 2035 4555;
www.staatsoper-berlin.de; Unter den Linden 5-7,
Mitte; tickets €8-120; U-Bahn Französische Strasse

Berlin's oldest opera house looms proudly on Unter den Linden in a neoclassical temple of the arts. Felix Mendelssohn-Bartholdy once served here as music director. Current incumbent Daniel Barenboim places much emphasis on lavish productions of baroque operas and works by later composers. All operas are performed in the original language.

THEATER DES WESTENS Map pp332-3

☎ 319 030; www.theater-des-westens.de; Kantstrasse 12, Charlottenburg; tickets €27-85; U/S-Bahn Zoologischer Garten

This is Berlin's traditional venue for German-language productions of big-name musicals, hosting both touring and home-grown companies. It's a good stage but quality varies widely. The cheapest seats tend to have lousy views.

CABARET
With *Cabaret* the film/play doing a roaring trade abroad, cabaret the entertainment form has seldom been stronger in Berlin – there are plenty of venues dedicated to reviving the lively and lavish variety shows of the Golden Twenties. Programmes include dancers, singers, jugglers, acrobats among other entertainers, each performing a short number. For the full experience you can often dine at your table.

BAR JEDER VERNUNFT Map pp332-3

☎ 883 1582; www.bar-jeder-vernunft.de; Schaperstrasse 24, Wilmersdorf; tickets €14-30; U-Bahn Spichernstrasse, Uhlandstrasse

With an emphasis on entertainment rather than *varieté*, most performers visiting this wonderful, offbeat venue have cult followings and shows are often sold out in advance. Part of the draw is the exquisite Art Nouveau-style tent setting. Look out for appearances by Irmgard Knef and Désirée Nick.

CHAMÄLEON VARIETÉ Map pp328-9

☎ 282 7118; www.chamaeleon-variete.de;
Rosenthaler Strasse 40-41, Mitte; tickets €4-27;
☽ shows 8.30pm Mon-Sat, midnight Fri & Sat, 7pm
Sun; S-Bahn Hackescher Markt

This intimate venue in the Hackesche Höfe used to be a ballroom, and while the twirling couples are long gone, the troupes here do their best to bring back a bit of the glamour. Enjoy the show from your candle-lit coffee house table.

FRIEDRICHSTADTPALAST Map pp328-9

☎ 2326 2203; www.friedrichstadtpalast.de; Friedrichstrasse 107, Mitte; tickets €12-59; U-Bahn Oranienburger Tor

The Friedrichstadtpalast is the largest musical-revue theatre in Europe and often sells out all 2000 seats. The ambitious scale of the glam, ritzy, Vegas-style productions, which feature

Bar jeder Vernunft (above)

an 80-strong corps of leggy dancers supported by excellent in-house musicians, ensures an entertaining evening.

SCHEINBAR VARIETÉ Map pp330-1

☎ 784 5539; www.scheinbar.de; Monumentenstrasse 9, Schöneberg; tickets €6-11; ☼ shows 8.30pm; U/S-Bahn Yorckstrasse

To say Scheinbar is tiny is an understatement but the intimacy of the venue makes for good views of the stage and gives you a chance to chat to the performers after the show – most are newcomers hoping to get a break here before moving on to bigger venues such as the Wintergarten.

WINTERGARTEN VARIETÉ Map pp330-1

☎ 2500 8888; www.wintergarten-variete.de; Potsdamer Strasse 96, Tiergarten; tickets €18-53; U-Bahn Kurfürstenstrasse

This is the closest vaudeville has ever come to being cool. It's a classy venue, with lots of polished brass and velvet. Every night top magicians, clowns, acrobats and artistes from around the world appear beneath the starry ceiling. The line-up changes every few months and quality varies but it's worth a peek.

KABARETT

Cabaret should not be confused with Kabarett, which is satirical comedy featuring a team of *Kabarettisten* in a series of stand-up monologues or skits. The humour ranges from biting to surreal, and shows can be hilarious – if your German is up to it!

BERLINER KABARETT ANSTALT

Map pp325-7

☎ 202 2007; www.bka-luftschloss.de; Mehringdamm 32-34, Kreuzberg; tickets €5-26; U-Bahn Mehringdamm

Despite the name, Kabarett is only a small part of the programme at this double venue. The original BKA Theatre hosts comedy, plays, revues, dance, classical and jazz concerts, while the larger BKA Luftschloss (Map pp328-9; Schlossplatz, Mitte) tent also has live gigs and regular cheesy club nights.

DIE WÜHLMÄUSE

☎ 3067 3011; www.wuehlmaeuse.de; Pommernallee 2-4, Charlottenburg; tickets €11.50-32; U-Bahn Theodor-Heuss-Platz

'The Voles' is one of Berlin's most professional outfits, with a regular procession of quality acts.

DR SELTSAMS FRÜHSCHOPPEN

www.dr-seltsams-fruehschoppen.de; Kalkscheune, Johannisstrasse 2, Mitte; ☼ 1pm Sun; S-Bahn Oranienburger Strasse

'Dr Strangelove's Liquid Brunch' is a longtime fixture on the Kabarett scene, with seven satirists, including local celebrity Horst Evers, plus guests gathering to sup beer, crack political jokes and read (or sing) humorous texts. Find out who Roland Koch is before coming here! It's free but donations are requested.

QUATSCH COMEDY CLUB Map pp328-9

☎ 3087 85685; www.quatschcomedyclub.de; Friedrichstadtpalast, Friedrichstrasse 107, Mitte; tickets €13-20; ☼ shows 8.30pm

In the basement of the Friedrichstadtpalast, Quatsch is the Berlin equivalent of the London Comedy Store and even has its own TV show, fronted by übercamp host Thomas Hermanns. Expect to see some of Germany's top stand-up talent alongside new faces.

CASINOS

CASINO BERLIN Map pp328-9

☎ 2389 4144; www.casino-berlin.de; Park Inn Hotel, Alexanderplatz; admission €5, machines €1; ☼ 11-3am; U/S-Bahn Alexanderplatz

Way up on the 37th floor of this former GDR flagship hotel you can gamble away your trip money on all of the usual card and random-chance games. There's even a separate slot machine area on the ground floor for those prone to vertigo.

SPIELBANK BERLIN Map p334

☎ 255 990; www.spielbank-berlin.de; Marlene-Dietrich-Platz 1, Tiergarten; Casino Royal admission €5; ☼ 11.30-3am; U/S-Bahn Potsdamer Platz

The Spielbank claims to be Germany's largest casino, with tables and slot machines spread over three floors, and bingo most nights. The gaming areas are split into Casino Leger (casual) and Casino Royal (formal dress). Admission is to over 18s only throughout.

THEATRE

If you like your acting wooden and your hams overdone, you might want to look elsewhere – theatre is the mainstay of Berlin's cultural scene, and its reputation for quality productions is unrivalled in Germany.

With more than 100 stages and a particularly active collection of experimental outfits, there's no shortage of offerings to satisfy all possible tastes, and you won't even need to dress up for an evening out.

Many theatres are closed on Monday and from mid-July to late August. Box offices generally keep at least office hours on days without performances. Good seats are often available on the evening itself, with unclaimed tickets sold 30 minutes before curtain. It's also perfectly fine to buy spare tickets from other theatre goers, though you should make sure they're legit and watch out for scalpers. Some theatres offer discounts of up to 50% to students and seniors.

Friedrichstrasse and the Kurfürstendamm are Berlin's main drama drags; check listings magazines for smaller, experimental theatres around town.

MAJOR STAGES

BERLINER ENSEMBLE Map pp328-9
☎ 2840 8155; www.berliner-ensemble.de; Bertolt-Brecht-Platz 1, Mitte; tickets €4-32; U/S-Bahn Friedrichstrasse
Founded by Bertolt Brecht, this prestigious theatre was taken over by acclaimed Viennese director Claus Peymann in 1999 – you can expect plenty of modern Austrian writers to crop up alongside German classics and Shakespeare. The building itself is gorgeous, and cheap tickets are usually available.

DEUTSCHES THEATER Map pp328-9
☎ 2844 1225; www.deutschestheater.de; Schumannstrasse 13a, Mitte; tickets €4-42; U-Bahn Oranienburger Tor
This theatre has long prided itself on a rich tradition, counting Max Reinhardt among its former directors, but since reunification its pre-eminent reputation has waned – even the surprise appointment of Bernd Wilms from the smaller Maxim Gorki Theater has done little to shake up the repertoire. Wilms has, however, brought in plenty of fresh talent, who can also be seen at the smaller Kammerspiele (studio theatre) next door.

HEBBEL AM UFER Map pp325-7
☎ 2590 0427; www.hebbel-am-ufer.de; box office Hallesches Ufer 32, Kreuzberg; tickets €6-15; U-Bahn Hallesches Tor
In 2003 the Hebbel Theater (Stresemannstrasse 29) merged with the nearby Theater am Halle-sches Ufer (Hallesches Ufer 32) and Theater am Ufer (Tempelhofer Ufer 10) to create the HAU. With an emphasis on modern, experimental drama and dance on all three stages, the new entity is already a serious presence on the avant-garde scene, building on the Hebbel's superb reputation and unrivalled international contacts.

MAXIM GORKI THEATER Map pp328-9
☎ 2022 1115; Am Festungsgraben 2, Mitte; tickets €12-26; U/S-Bahn Friedrichstrasse
The smallest and least subsidised of the state-funded theatres, the Gorki stages a good mix of traditional and modern pieces – boss Volker Hesse is a fan of contemporary plays and collaborations with other innovative groups. Young directors and actors such as Ben Becker frequently take the stage here, and quality is uniformly high.

SCHAUBÜHNE AM LEHNINER PLATZ Map pp330-1
☎ 890 023; www.schaubuehne.de; Kurfürstendamm 153, Wilmersdorf; tickets €10-30; U-Bahn Adenauerplatz
The cutting edge lives in this former 1920s cinema, under the control of internationally acclaimed choreographer Sasha Waltz and director Thomas Ostermeier. Appointed to shake up a stagnating venue, the pair has staged everything from Buñuel to Büchner with equal flair.

The wide-ranging programme aims to compete with the Volksbühne far more than the Deutsches Theater.

VOLKSBÜHNE AM ROSA-LUXEMBURG-PLATZ Map pp328-9
☎ 247 6772; www.volksbuehne-berlin.de; Rosa-Luxemburg-Platz, Mitte; tickets €10-21; U-Bahn Rosa-Luxemburg-Platz
Nonconformist, radical and provocative: Volksbühne head Frank Castorf wouldn't have it any other way, and his young-gun guest directors tend to agree. The clued-up, trash-political-post-pop ethos pulls in a predominantly East Berlin, 18-to-35-year-old audience, and there are moments of genius amid the frequent controversy.

Smaller, even more off-beat performances take place over at the **Volksbühne am Prater** (Map pp322-4; Kastanienallee 7-9, Prenzlauer Berg).

ENGLISH-LANGUAGE THEATRE

FRIENDS OF ITALIAN OPERA Map pp325-7
☎ 691 1211; www.thefriends.de; Fidicinstrasse 40, Kreuzberg; adult/concession €14/8; U-Bahn Platz der Luftbrücke

Despite its name, you won't find any aria-shrieking tenors here – it's actually code for 'Mafia' and the venue is, in fact, Berlin's oldest English-language theatre. Resident troupes and visiting ensembles perform modern material almost nightly to the 60-seat auditorium. On Tuesday all tickets are €7.

SPECIALIST THEATRE

BAMAH JÜDISCHES THEATER
Map pp330-1
☎ 251 1096; www.bamah.de; Hohenzollerndamm 177, Wilmersdorf; tickets €22; U-Bahn Fehrbelliner Platz

Berlin's Jewish Theatre stages traditional and modern Jewish works and other relevant pieces to an appreciative audience.

BERLINER KRIMINAL THEATER
Map pp322-4
☎ 4799 7488; www.kriminaltheater.de; Palisadenstrasse 48, Friedrichshain; tickets €19-35; U-Bahn Weberwiese

Part of the Umspannwerk Ost building, the BKT is sadly not run by criminals – instead it specialises in whodunnits and other crime-related plays. Naturally *Die Mausefalle* (The Mousetrap) gets a frequent airing.

FREIE THEATERANSTALTEN Map pp318-19
☎ 325 5023; www.freietheateranstalten.de; Klausenerplatz 19, Charlottenburg; ⏱ 8.30pm Tue & Wed, Fri-Sun; S-Bahn Westend

The FT has been run almost single-handedly by founder, director and leading man Hermann van Harten since 1977. In the last 15 years he has put on more than 3000 performances of his own play *Ich bin's nicht, Adolf Hitler ist es gewesen* (It wasn't me, it was Hitler), confronting the issue of collective responsibility in an idiosyncratic but effective way.

THEATERDISCOUNTER Map pp328-9
☎ 4404 8561; www.theaterdiscounter.de; Packhalle, Monbijoustrasse 1, Mitte; S-Bahn Oranienburger Strasse

The central conceit here is 'theatre on the cheap' – everything is put in supermarket terminology, particularly on the budget website.

On the serious side, it's rapidly becoming a one-stop shop for brand-new experimental plays, and tickets are seldom more than €9.99.

UNSICHT-BAR Map pp322-4
☎ 2434 2500; www.unsicht-bar-berlin.de; Gormannstrasse 14; tickets €12-15; ⏱ from 6pm; U-Bahn Weinmeisterstrasse

This eat-in-the-dark restaurant (p167) also has a dark stage, with nightly readings, Kabarett, concerts and plays. The lights go on and the bar stays open after the performances. Reservations recommended.

CHILDREN'S & YOUTH THEATRE

CABUWAZI
☎ 530 0040; www.cabuwazi.de; Bouchéstrasse 75; adult €4.50-8, child €2.50-6

The mysterious name stands for 'Chaotisch-Bunter WanderZirkus' (Chaotic and Colourful Travelling Circus), a not-for-profit programme that trains kids aged 10 to 17 as circus artistes who then perform at venues around town. Call or check listings magazines for shows.

CARROUSEL
☎ 557 752; www.carrousel.de; Parkaue 29, Friedrichshain; adult/child €11/7; U/S-Bahn Frankfurter Allee

This theatre on the eastern side of town has an intelligent programme of classics and new plays catering for teenagers and adults, as well as a dedicated children's department.

GRIPS THEATER Map pp320-1
☎ 397 4740; www.grips-theater.de; Altonaer Strasse 22, Tiergarten; tickets €3.50-15; U-Bahn Hansaplatz

The best, and best-known, of Berlin's youth stages is the Grips, which does high-quality topical and critical plays for older children and teenagers. The regular productions of director Volker Ludwig's highly successful U-Bahn musical *Linie 1* are a real highlight.

Puppet Theatre
DIE SCHAUBUDE Map pp322-4
☎ 423 4314; www.schaubude.de; Greifswalder Strasse 81-84, Prenzlauer Berg; adult €5.50-12.50, child €3.60; S-Bahn Greifswalder Strasse

Not just for the little 'uns – the puppeteers here take their art seriously, and evening shows are generally aimed at adults.

Die Schaubude (p213)

PRENZLKASPER Map pp322-4

☎ 4430 8244; Dunckerstrasse 90, Prenzlauer Berg; tickets €4.50; U-Bahn Eberswalder Strasse

This miniature stage is tucked away off Danziger Strasse, with plenty to amuse infants and preteens.

PUPPENTHEATER FIRLEFANZ

Map pp328-9

☎ 283 3560; Sophienstrasse 10, Mitte; ☺ Wed, Fri-Sun; U-Bahn Weinmeisterstrasse

Traditional puppetry and marionettes play to crowds of all ages here.

DANCE

With the new Hebbel Am Ufer (p212) promoting experimental choreography and Sasha Waltz in charge of the Schaubühne (p212), Berlin's independent dance scene has never been stronger. Many theatres now include dance performances in their programmes; check the listings for upcoming events.

Over in the mainstream, classical ballet is performed at the Staatsoper Unter den Linden (p210) and the Deutsche Oper (p209), while the city's finest scantily clad showgirls strut their stuff at the Friedrichstadtpalast (p210).

DOCK 11 STUDIOS Map pp322-4

☎ 448 1222; www.dock11-berlin.de; Kastanienallee 79, Prenzlauer Berg; ☺ shows Wed-Sun; U-Bahn Eberswalder Strasse

As well as a programme of performances, Dock 11 runs courses and workshops during the week, teaching everything from ballet and street dance to Pilates and acrobatics.

SOPHIENSAELE Map pp328-9

☎ 2859 9360; www.sophiensaele.com; Sophienstrasse 18, Mitte; tickets €13; S-Bahn Hackescher Markt

Under the direction of Sasha Waltz, Sophiensaele became Berlin's number-one spot for experimental and avant-garde dance. Now Waltz is gone, the emphasis is edging back towards theatre and performance art, but you can still expect some exciting dance events.

TANZFABRIK BERLIN Map pp330-1

☎ 786 5861; www.tanzfabrik-berlin.de; Möckernstrasse 68, Kreuzberg; shows €10; U/S-Bahn Yorckstrasse

Like Dock 11, the 'Dance Factory' offers dance tuition as well as staging events.

CINEMAS

Going to the movies can be pricey in Berlin, with Saturday-night tickets at the multiplexes costing as much as €9. Almost all cinemas also add a sneaky *Überlängezuschlag* (overrun supplement) of €0.50 to €1 for films longer than 90 minutes. Seeing a show on a *Kinotag* (film day, usually Monday to Wednesday) or before 5pm can save up to €4. Smaller, independent neighbourhood theatres are usually cheaper and may offer student discounts. The big cinemas show mostly mainstream Hollywood movies dubbed into German. Many smaller screens show movies in their original language, denoted in listings by the acronym 'OF' (*Originalfassung*) or 'OV' (*Originalversion*); those shown with German subtitles are marked 'OmU' (*Original mit Untertiteln*).

People with young children should look out for the Spatzenkino (☎ 449 4750; www.spatzenkino.de) screenings organised by the Youth Culture Service in cinemas all over the city.

ARSENAL Map p334

☎ 2695 5100; Sony Center, Potsdamer Strasse 21, Tiergarten; adult/child €6/3; U/S-Bahn Potsdamer Platz

Nonmainstream movies from around the world, usually dubbed into English, can be seen at this excellent theatre in the Filmhaus.

BABYLON Map pp325-7

☎ 6160 9693; www.yorck.de; Dresdener Strasse 126, Kreuzberg; adult/concession €7.50/5.50; U-Bahn Kottbusser Tor

The popular Babylon is one of 13 Berlin cinemas making up the Yorcker family of broad-appeal art house screens, which also includes the **Central Cinema** (Map pp328-9) in Hackesche Höfe and the enormous **Delphi-Filmpalast** (Map pp332-3) on Kantstrasse.

CINEMAXX POTSDAMER PLATZ Map p334

☎ 4431 6316; www.cinemaxx.de; Voxstrasse 2, Tiergarten; adult/concession €7.30/4.50; U/S-Bahn Potsdamer Platz

This state-of-the-art megacomplex is the primary venue of the International Film Festival. Up to 20 movies are on the programme at any given time, and the big releases are often shown in the original language.

CINESTAR IM SONY CENTER Map p334

☎ 2606 6260; www.cinestar.de; Potsdamer Strasse 4, Tiergarten; adult/concession €6.90/4.50, IMAX €7.90/6.70; U/S-Bahn Potsdamer Platz

Yup, it's yet another huge multiplex on Potsdamer Platz. This one has both standard and IMAX screens, and is the venue of choice for most international premieres.

DISCOVERY CHANNEL IMAX THEATER Map p334

☎ 2592 7259; www.imax-berlin.de; Marlene-Dietrich-Platz 4, Tiergarten; adult €7-8, concession €5.50-6.70; U/S-Bahn Potsdamer Platz

This big domed cinema screens the usual IMAX films and documentaries about travel, space and wildlife, many in 3D. You can forget subtitles – for a €20 deposit you get your own radio receiver to hear the English version.

EISZEIT Map pp325-7

☎ 611 6016; Zeughofstrasse 20, Kreuzberg; tickets €6; U-Bahn Görlitzer Bahnhof

There's a daily changing programme of obscure, alternative and experimental film fare at this tiny but long-running picture house.

FILMKUNSTHAUS BABYLON Map pp328-9

☎ 242 5076; Rosa-Luxemburg-Strasse 30, Mitte; adult/concession €6.50/5.50; U-Bahn Rosa-Luxemburg-Platz

Not to be confused with the Kreuzberg Babylon, this is another fantastic world-cinema specialist with a very varied programme.

FSK Map pp325-7

☎ 614 2464; www.fsk-kino.de; Segitzdamm 2, Kreuzberg; tickets €6; U-Bahn Kottbusser Tor

Just off Oranienplatz, this high-calibre art house theatre shows plenty of European cinema.

INTIMES Map pp325-7

☎ 2966 4633; Niederbarnimstrasse 15, Friedrichshain; adult/child €6/2.50; U-Bahn Samariterstrasse

You certainly wouldn't expect Berlin's alternative district to be without an alternative cinema, and this art house screen is just the ticket. The vaguely Arabic cocktail bar is a further bonus.

KINO INTERNATIONAL Map pp322-4

☎ 2475 6011; Karl-Marx-Allee 33, Mitte; adult/concession €7.50/5.50; U-Bahn Schillingstrasse

The jewel in the Yorcker crown: with its long dangling Bohemian glass chandeliers, wainscoting, glitter curtain and parquetry floor, the Kino International is a show in itself. On Monday night, it goes 'MonGay' with homo-themed classics, imports and previews, while certain Saturdays are gay or lesbian party nights.

KLICK Map pp330-1

☎ 323 8437; www.klick-kino.de; Windscheidstrasse 19, Charlottenburg; tickets €6; S-Bahn Charlottenburg

As a slightly shabby, one-screen art house, Klick seems a bit out of place in smart Charlottenburg, but the film selection is generally pretty good.

KOSMOS Map pp322-4

☎ 422 0160; Karl-Marx-Allee 131a, Friedrichshain; tickets €6.80-7.50; U-Bahn Weberwiese

The squat Kosmos was the largest cinema in East Berlin when it was built in 1961 and is now a protected building. The programme is fairly straightforward mainstream with some good extras.

MOVIEMENTO Map pp325-7

☎ 692 4785; www.moviemento.de; Kottbusser Damm 22, Kreuzberg; adult/concession €6/5.50; U-Bahn Hermannplatz

This three-screen independent place shows a good range of nonblockbuster mainstream and German movies.

NEUE KANT Map pp332-3

☎ 319 9866; www.neuekantkinos.de; Kantstrasse 54, Charlottenburg; adult/child €7/3; U-Bahn Wilmersdorfer Strasse

Originally built in 1912, the original Kant-Kino was rescued from closure in 2001 by a group of industry professionals, including director Wim Wenders, and now screens a mix of popular and art house fare.

XENON Map pp330-1

☎ 782 8850; www.xenon-kino.de; Kolonnenstrasse
5-6, Schöneberg; tickets €6; U-Bahn Kleistpark

The city's second-oldest movie theatre shows
predominantly lesbigay flicks, with lots of imports. Watch out for Dykescreen, its occasional
lesbian film series.

SPORTS, HEALTH & FITNESS

Like most Germans, Berliners have a fairly
ambivalent attitude towards sport and
fitness – for every six-pack on display
there's at least one beer gut, and although
gyms, spas and particularly solariums do a
roaring trade, no-one seems to see much
contradiction in heading off for a *Currywurst* afterwards. That said, Berlin is generally quick to catch on to the latest exercise
trends, and the many sports on offer are
taken pretty seriously by participants and
spectators alike.

In terms of amenities, the city is as well-
equipped as you'd expect from a European
capital, although for larger and more
specialised facilities you'll need to head
outside the central districts. For comprehensive listings on just about every activity
imaginable, look for *Tip* magazine's annual
Fitness & Wellness Directory (€7.90).

WATCHING SPORT
American Football
BERLIN THUNDER

☎ 3006 4400; www.berlin-thunder.de; Olympia
Stadion; tickets €8-31.50

Pigskin-tossing may still come second to soccer in Germany but for increasing numbers
of converts Thunder is definitely the team
of choice – it has two World Bowl wins to its
name. The recent move into the Olympic Stadium saw crowd numbers shoot up by 23%.
Expect the best turnouts against national
rivals and 2003 titleholder Frankfurt Galaxy.

Athletics
BERLIN MARATHON

☎ 302 5370; www.berlin-marathon.com

Every September you have the opportunity
to watch or participate in Germany's principal

contribution to the marathon calendar. The
route starts at Charlottenburger Tor and fin-
ishes at the Gedächtniskirche. In 2003 Kenya's
Paul Tergat beat the world record here, so
expect some stiff competition.

ISTAF

☎ 3038 4444; Olympia Stadion

This international track-and-field meet is held
in early September, shortly before the Berlin
Marathon.

Basketball
ALBA BERLIN

☎ 300 9050; www.albaberlin.de; Max-Schmeling-
Halle, Prenzlauer Berg; tickets €6.50-47

Berlin's European-class basketball team,
founded in 1990, can usually be found topping
the table in any given season. Home games
mostly take place at 3pm Saturday.

Cycling
BERLINER SECHSTAGERENNEN

☎ 4430 4430; www.sechstagerennen-berlin.de;
Velodrom/Berlin Arena; tickets €26-40

Held in January, the Berlin Six-Day Event attracts more than 75,000 spectators for nearly a
week of serious two-wheeled action.

Horse Racing
GALOPPRENNBAHN HOPPEGARTEN

☎ 03342-389 313; Gotheallee 1, Dahlwitz-
Hoppegarten; tickets €4-12; ☽ races 1pm Sun
Apr-Oct; S-Bahn Hoppegarten

Built in 1867 northeast of the city, this is one
of the fanciest European racetracks.

TRABRENNBAHN KARLSHORST

☎ 5001 7121; Treskowallee 129, Lichtenberg; tickets
€1; ☽ races 6pm Wed; S-Bahn Karlshorst

This track dates to 1862 but was completely
destroyed in WWII. After the war, it was the only
trotting (trap-racing) course in the GDR. Occasional Friday and Sunday meets are also held.

TRABRENNBAHN MARIENDORF

☎ 740 1212; Mariendorfer Damm 222-298, Tempelhof; tickets €2.50 (Sun only); ☽ races 6pm Wed & Fri,
1.30pm Sun; U-Bahn Alt-Mariendorf

Founded in 1913, this is the trotting course
of choice for hobnobbing politicos and business folk.

Ice Hockey

A hugely popular sport in Berlin, which has two teams in the national Ice Hockey league. The arenas are small compared with most other sports, but the pyrotechnics and vocal crowds more than compensate – on the rare occasions that the two teams meet in inter-division games, the sparks can really fly.

BERLIN CAPITALS

☎ 3081 1829; www.berlin-capitals.de; Deutschland-halle, Messedamm 26, Charlottenburg; tickets €8.50-16.50; S-Bahn Eichkamp

Representing West Berlin, the Caps have a flashier rink and a better overall record than their eastern rivals, though recent seasons haven't seen them at their best.

EHC EISBÄREN

☎ 9718 4040; www.eisbaren.de; Sportforum Berlin, Steffenstrasse, Hohenschönhausen; tickets €15-30; S-Bahn Hohenschönhausen

Traditionally the underdog, the Ice Bears managed to top their division in the 2003–04 season and are rapidly becoming the team to watch. You may feel slightly out of place without a shirt, scarf or thorough knowledge of the relevant chants.

Soccer

Call it what you want, football is king in Germany, and Berlin makes no exception. The game proliferates at every level, with 341 official clubs ranging from grassroots amateurs to heavyweight professional teams.

DEUTSCHER FUSSBALL-BUND

☎ 896 9940; www.dfb.de; Humboldtstrasse 8a, Wilmersdorf

The DFB (German National Soccer Association) holds two national-championship finals in Berlin every year. The main event is the hugely popular *DFB-Pokalendspiel* (DFB Cup final), played at the Olympic Stadium; tickets are hard to come by and should be ordered months in advance. In January you can also catch the annual indoor-soccer championship in the Max-Schmeling-Halle.

HERTHA BSC

☎ 01805-189 200; www.herthabsc.de; Olympia Stadion; tickets €8-51

Berlin's long-standing and sporadically successful Bundesliga (National League) team is one of the country's most high-profile clubs and enjoys a loyal fan-base. Kick-off at Olympic Stadium is usually at 3.30pm Saturday.

The stadium is generally packed when big-name teams such as Bayern München come calling; otherwise, you should be able to get tickets without any trouble on game day.

UNION BERLIN

☎ 656 6880; www.fc-union-berlin.de; Stadion an der Alten Försterei, An der Wuhlheide, Köpenick; tickets €7.50-22; S-Bahn Köpenick

For die-hard fans, try a Union game – the former East's pride and joy is currently languishing at the bottom of the Bundesliga's second division but still holds the unswerving devotion of its supporters. The 18,000-seat stadium in working-class Köpenick is seldom lacking in atmosphere.

Tennis
LADIES GERMAN OPEN

☎ 0180-517 0517; www.mastercard-german-open.de; Rot-Weiss Tennis Club, Grunewald; tickets €16-55; S-Bahn Grunewald

This very popular event takes place every May near the Hundekehlesee lake, usually attracting high-ranking players (previous winners include Martina Hingis, Conchita Martinez and Justine Henin-Hardenne). The tournament has had financial problems, but the Berlin Senate has promised support to help keep it going. Tickets, especially for the later rounds, are tough to get.

Water Polo
WASSERFREUNDE SPANDAU 04

☎ 304 6866; www.spandau04.net; Deutsches Sportforum, Olympia Stadion; tickets €6; S-Bahn Olympiastadion

Want to follow a winning team? For the last 20 years Spandau 04 has dominated the German *Wasserball* league, as well as producing some outstanding swimming and diving performances. Try to catch a local derby (SG Neukölln are big rivals).

OUTDOOR ACTIVITIES
Cycling

The countryside surrounding central Berlin offers many lovely cycling routes. Check at major book shops for guides with detailed

Cycling along the Spree River

route descriptions, and see p279 for details on bike rentals and taking your bike on public transport.

ADFC BERLIN Map pp322-4
☎ 448 4724; Brunnenstrasse 28, Mitte; ☷ noon-8pm Mon-Fri, 10am-4pm Sat; U-Bahn Rosenthaler Platz
The Allgemeiner Deutscher Fahrradclub (General German Bicycle Club) is a great source of information for cyclists, publishing a *Radwegekarte* (cycle route) map (€7.80) that shows all bike routes in Berlin. Members receive automatic third-party insurance.

Golf
As you'd expect in a big city, the full-size traditional golf courses are outside Berlin, but there are a couple of smaller central ranges such as Airport-Golf-Berlin (☎ 4140 0300; Kurt-Schumacher-Damm 176, Reinickendorf; U-Bahn Jakob-Kaiser-Platz), with driving, chipping, pitching and putting greens, and the Golf-Zentrum Berlin-Mitte driving range (Map pp320-1; ☎ 2804 7070; Chausseestrasse 94-98; U-Bahn Schwarzkopffstrasse). In addition, two rather unorthodox clubs practise 'extreme golf' – check out Natural Born Golfers (www.naturalborngolfers.com) and Turbogolfer (www.turbogolfer.de). Membership fee for the latter is a case of beer!

Ice Skating
Every year around Christmas time temporary open-air ice rinks set up shop in public areas all over Berlin, often as part of the Christmas markets, with music, mulled wine and Santa hats everywhere. The most popular spots include Unter den Linden, Potsdamer Platz and Alexanderplatz; there are also plenty of less crowded rinks tucked away in corners such as Wilmersdorfer Strasse.

Skating on these surfaces is usually free, with skate hire available for around €2.50.

In-Line Skating & Skateboarding
In-line skating and skateboarding remain firm favourites with young Berliners, and there are plenty of outdoor ramps, pipes and parks scattered around the suburbs. Check out www.skate-spots.de for location. Some of the best are at the old Radrennbahn in Weissensee, Grazer Platz in Schöneberg, the Gartenschau in Marzahn and Räcknitzer Steig in Spandau.

The Technische Universität (TU) also has its own Inline-Skating Halle (Map pp320-1; ☎ 3142 7810; Franklinstrasse 5-7, Charlottenburg; €2).

Multisport

FREISPORTANLAGE AM SÜDPARK

☎ 361 5201; Am Südpark 51, Spandau; ☺ 10am-8pm May-Sep; S-Bahn Spandau, bus 131/134

A rare treat for outdoor sports fans, this 10,000-sq-metre facility is absolutely free and incorporates tennis, volleyball, basketball and beach volleyball courts, an in-line skating area and table tennis. For the less energetic, there's also a café and mini-golf (€2). It'll take a while to get there with public transport, so allow at least half a day for a visit.

Running

Berlin is a great place for running because of its many parks. Easily the most popular – largely because of its large size and central location – is the Tiergarten (Map pp320-1), although both the Volkspark Hasenheide (Map pp325-7) in Neukölln and the Grunewald in Wilmersdorf/Zehlendorf are also popular.

The trip around the scenic Schlachtensee here is 5km. If you prefer to run in historic surroundings, consider trying out the gardens of Schloss Charlottenburg (Map pp320-1), although seasoned joggers might feel under-challenged.

Swimming

One of the great summer delights in land-locked Berlin is its many lakes; swimming is allowed, but if you prefer some amenities try one of the public lake-side pools. Outdoor pools are usually open 8am to 8pm daily from May to September, depending on the weather. For details of indoor swimming centres see p222.

SOMMERBAD KREUZBERG

☎ 616 1080; Prinzenstrasse 113-119, Kreuzberg; U-Bahn Prinzenstrasse

This is the city's most central, multicultural and popular facility, also known as the Prinzenbad (Princes' Pool) and it's often crawling with hormone-crazed teenagers. There are two 50m pools, a slide and an FKK (nudist) section.

SOMMERBAD OLYMPIASTADION

☎ 3006 3440; Osttor, Olympischer Platz, Charlottenburg; U-Bahn Olympia-Stadion

Built for the 1936 Olympic Games, you can do your laps here in the 50m pool once used by the world's top athletes. You'll be watched by oversized sculptures and four gigantic clocks.

STRANDBAD HALENSEE

☎ 891 1703; Königsallee 5a/b, Wilmersdorf; S-Bahn Halensee

Well situated in a forest, this lakeside pool is popular with those who like to swim au naturel. It's occasionally closed for poor water quality.

STRANDBAD WANNSEE

☎ 803 5612; Wannseebadweg 25, Zehlendorf; S-Bahn Nikolassee

Claiming to be the largest lake-side pool in Europe, 'Berlin's Lido' has been in business since 1907 and its kilometres of sandy beach are about as crowded as the real thing. You can rent boats, take an exercise class, eat and drink at several restaurants or relax in giant wicker chairs like those typically found at German coastal resorts. The water quality is decent.

HEALTH & FITNESS
Gyms & Fitness Centres

Most Berlin gyms are membership-based, and many require you to sign a contract (often for 12 months), take an induction course, shell out a registration charge and pay monthly fees – hardly worth the hassle unless you're staying long-term. In less uptight places you can get a day pass for around €25; some also offer free trial workouts before joining. It won't hurt to ask. Opening times are generally around 8am to 11pm, with slightly shorter hours at weekends.

CONDITIONS Map pp332-3

☎ 892 1009; www.conditionsclub.de; Kurfürstendamm 156, Charlottenburg; U-Bahn Adenauerplatz

This women-only gym at the far end of the Ku'damm runs all the standard classes, plus a few interesting variants such as aqua-aerobics.

ELIXIA Map pp328-9

☎ 2063 5300; Behrenstrasse 48, Mitte; U-Bahn Französische Strasse

Elixia offers 2500 state-of-the-art sq metres in a central location, with extensive cardio training, free weights and spa areas. There are eight more branches around the city.

FITNESS COMPANY Map pp328-9

☎ 279 0770; www.fitcom.de; Panoramastrasse 1a, Mitte; U/S-Bahn Alexanderplatz

One of Germany's largest gym companies, Fitcom has another eight outlets spread around central and suburban Berlin, including a full health club and a business-oriented centre with pool. Another of its central clubs is located in **Neukölln** (Map pp325-7; ☎ 627 3963; Karl-Marx-Strasse 64-72; U-Bahn Hermannplatz).

GOLD'S GYM Map pp322-4

☎ 443 7940; www.goldsgymberlin.de; Immanuelkirchstrasse 3-4, Prenzlauer Berg; U-Bahn Senefelderplatz

Arnold Schwarzenegger's favourite gym hit Berlin in 1991; it currently has a weights room, aerobics classes, sauna and solariums.

HOLMES PLACE LIFESTYLE CLUB
Map pp328-9

☎ 2062 4949; www.holmesplace.de; Quartier 205, Friedrichstrasse 67-71, Mitte; U-Bahn Französische Strasse

The latest venture of this luxury British chain boasts an exclusive address and twice the space of its nearest Elixia rival, not to mention a body-boggling choice of classes.

JOPP FRAUEN FITNESS Map pp332-3

☎ 210 111; www.jopp.de; Tauentzienstrasse 13a, Charlottenburg; U-Bahn Kurfürstendamm, Zoologischer Garten

Owned by Fitness Company, there are six further branches of this multifaceted women-only facility around Berlin, including one in Mitte (Map pp328-9; ☎ 2434 9355; Karl-Liebknecht-Strasse 13, Mitte; U/S-Bahn Alexanderplatz), offering a wide variety of classes, equipment and spa features.

MOVEO Map pp325-7

☎ 6950 5254; Am Tempelhofer Berg 7d, Kreuzberg; classes €5-11; 🕑 5-11pm Mon-Fri, 10-11.30am & 3.30-7pm Sat, 10-11.30am & 4-7pm Sun; U-Bahn Platz der Luftbrücke

Various forms of yoga (including iyengar, asthanga, power-yoga) ensure physical and spiritual well-being at this low-key studio; some are even taught in English.

Ice Skating

As well as the open-air rinks that spring up around town every Christmas, Berlin has several well-maintained municipal indoor ice halls that are usually open from mid-October to early March. The cost is around €3.30/1.65 adult/child per session,

plus €2.60 to €3.60 to rent skates. Skating periods vary but most rinks have three a day, usually lasting three hours.

EISSTADION NEUKÖLLN

☎ 6280 4403; Oderstrasse 182, Neukölln; U-Bahn Hermannstrasse

Monday and Wednesday are 'Happy Days' here, with 50% discount on every session.

ERIKA-HESS-EISSTADION Map pp320-1

☎ 2009 45551; Müllerstrasse 185, Mitte; U-Bahn Reinickendorfer Strasse

Up towards Wedding, this is another good ice-skating rink.

HORST-DOHM-EISSTADION Map pp330-1

☎ 824 1012; Fritz-Wildung-Strasse 9, Wilmersdorf; U-Bahn Heidelberger Platz

The city's largest ice rink, with a 400m outer ring encircling a second skating area. Admission buys two hours of skating time.

Saunas & Spas

Germans are far from prudish and saunas are usually mixed and nude, so check your modesty at the reception desk. However, hours are set aside for women only, so call ahead. The cheapest saunas are those at public pools. Privately operated facilities usually have more amenities and may be luxurious.

Men should also note the distinction between 'normal' and men-only (ie gay) saunas, which tend to double as cruising venues.

APOLLO-CITY-SAUNA Map pp332-3

☎ 213 2424; Kurfürstenstrasse 101, Schöneberg; 🕑 1pm-7am Mon-Thu, 24hr Fri-Sun; U-Bahn Wittenbergplatz

This traditional gay sauna has steam rooms, cruising hallways and cabins. It's famous for its Slivovitz sauna infusions.

ARS VITALIS Map pp330-1

☎ 788 3563; www.ars-vitalis.de; Hauptstrasse 19, Schöneberg; day pass €25; U-Bahn Kleistpark

This combined gym and spa is one of Berlin's nicest sweat spots. If the huge range of classes (including jazz dance, yoga, t'ai chi and Pilates), separate ladies' area, three different types of sauna and a posse of trained masseurs aren't enough, in summer you can strike out onto the roof terrace.

GATE SAUNACLUB Map pp328-9

☎ 229 9430; Wilhelmstrasse 81, Mitte; entry €8-11;
🕙 11-7am Mon-Thu, 24hr Fri-Sun; U-Bahn
Mohrenstrasse

This is one of the biggest and most active gay saunas, just southeast of the Brandenburg Gate. As well as two floors of modern saunas and steam rooms, it has a bar, restaurant and video room.

HAMAM Map pp325-7

☎ 615 1464; Mariannenstrasse 6, Kreuzberg; three hours €12; 🕙 3-11pm Mon, noon-11pm Tue-Sun; U-Bahn Kottbusser Tor, Görlitzer Bahnhof

Ladies of all persuasions frequent Kreuzberg's women-only, Turkish-style bathhouse, part of the Schokofabrik centre, to relax in the steam room or enjoy the fitness and beauty services (who can resist a full-body peeling?).

LIQUIDROM Map pp325-7

☎ 7473 7171; Tempodrom, Möckernstrasse 10, Kreuzberg; 2hr admission €15; 🕙 10am-10pm Sun-Thu, 10am-midnight Fri & Sat, full moon 10am-2am; S-Bahn Anhalter Bahnhof

Soothing, sensual and slightly surreal, this is Berlin's ultimate chill-out zone: a futuristic indoor pool complete with 'liquid sound system' piping in anything from whale song to orchestral music. Soft, psychedelic projections complete the trippy experience, while the bar, sauna, steam room and Jacuzzi provide additional playgrounds.

SURYA VILLA Map pp322-4

☎ 4849 5780; www.ayurveda-wellnesszentrum.de; Rykestrasse 3, Prenzlauer Berg; full day €165;
🕙 10.30am-9pm; U-Bahn Eberswalder Strasse

With four floors of massages, baths, saunas, yoga, qi gong, meditation, health food and other treatments, this Ayurveda (holistic) centre is a real treat for the strained and stressed.

THERMEN AM EUROPA-CENTER

Map pp332-3

☎ 257 5760; www.thermen-berlin.de; Nürnberger Strasse 7, Schöneberg; one hour €9.20, day pass €17.90; U-Bahn Wittenbergplatz

If you're bored with your basic Swedish, check into this stylish facility near the Gedächtniskirche. It incorporates indoor and outdoor pools filled with salt-rich thermal waters, fitness rooms, beauty treatments, restaurants, a tanning terrace and nine saunas, with all kinds of added aromas to choose from.

Well Done

Wellness is a word you'll hear a lot around Berlin - it's a very fashionable German concept, somehow encompassing everything from fitness, sport and exercise to spas, tanning, health food, massage, meditation and alternative therapies. Be warned though, in some places 'wellness area' can just mean 'we have a vaguely functional sauna'.

TREIBHAUS SAUNA Map pp322-4

☎ 448 4503; Schönhauser Allee 132, Prenzlauer Berg; three hours €9.50; 🕙 1pm-7am Mon-Thu, 24hr Fri-Sun; U-Bahn Eberswalder Strasse

This is one of the nicest gay saunas in town; prices include a drink from the spacious bar.

Sports Centres

In the outer suburbs, you'll find several large sports centres combining pools, squash and tennis courts, fitness studios, saunas etc under one roof.

FEZ WUHLHEIDE

☎ 5307 1504; www.fez-berlin.de; An der Wuhlheide 197, Köpenick; entry €2, swimming €3.50; S-Bahn Wuhlheide

It's a bit far from the centre but Köpenick's FEZ has plenty to offer, with a BMX track, dance studio and various courses supplementing the usual fitness and swimming facilities. An added highlight is the virtual-space-station training, which you won't find in many gyms.

SPORT- UND ERHOLUNGSZENTRUM

Map pp322-4

☎ 4208 7920; Landsberger Allee 77, Friedrichshain; S-Bahn Landsberger Allee

Currently in the throes of a major renovation, parts of this huge complex are reopening gradually, with bowling lanes and sports hall already finished and fitness area to follow. Final completion of the swimming area is scheduled for 2007.

Sports Clubs

If you're looking to play any kind of team game, your only option will usually be to join a relevant club. The best way to find one is by checking local magazines and notice boards. There are also several clubs catering for particular 'interest groups'.

ROLLSTUHLSPORT
CHARLOTTENBURG Map pp318-19
☎ 753 7497; Neue Kantstrasse 23, Charlottenburg; ⏰ 4-9pm Mon & Tue, 4-8pm Thu; S-Bahn Witzleben
Wheelchair badminton and basketball are the main sports organised by this competitive club, and an increasing number of 'pedestrians' are sitting down to compete with the hardened regulars.

VORSPIEL Map pp330-1
☎ 4405 7740; www.vorspiel-berlin.de; Naumannstrasse 33, Schöneberg; ⏰ 5-8pm Tue, 10am-1pm Thu; S-Bahn Papestrasse
Berlin's lesbigay sports club is far from exclusive, running a huge range of different activities for players of all levels and preferences. As an added bonus, you get four free trial sessions before signing up. In time-honoured innuendo tradition, the name means 'foreplay'.

Swimming
Berlin has plenty of indoor pools in each district. Some may be closed on mornings when school groups take over; others are reserved for specific groups – women, men, nudists, seniors – at certain times of the week. Tickets for almost all municipal pools are €4/2.50 adult/concession (€2.50 before 8am and after 8pm).

Opening hours vary by day, pool and season. For full information, contact the BBB (☎ 01803-102 020; www.berlinerbae derbetriebe.de) or pick up a pamphlet at any pool.

For details of outdoor swimming pools and lakes see p219.

BAD AM SPREEWALDPLATZ
Map pp325-7
☎ 6953 5210; Wiener Strasse 59h, Kreuzberg; adult/concession €5/4, sauna €9/7; U-Bahn Görlitzer Bahnhof
This consistent local favourite has a wave pool, cascades, Jacuzzis and a slide in addition to a 25m lap pool.

BLUB BADEPARADIES
☎ 606 6060; Buschkrugallee 64, Neukölln; admission €10.70-13.30; ⏰ 10am-11pm; U-Bahn Grenzallee
A modern 'fun' pool with a whole lot of attractions, including wave pool, waterfall, 120m slide, saltwater pool, hot whirlpools, sauna landscape and restaurants.

STADTBAD CHARLOTTENBURG
Map pp320-1
Alte Halle ☎ 3438 3860, Neue Halle ☎ 3438 3865; Krumme Strasse 10; sauna €11; U-Bahn Bismarckstrasse
The Alte Halle (Old Hall) here is a protected monument, one of the few of its kind still in use – with its Art Nouveau ceiling and colourful tiles dating back to 1898, it definitely has museum character. On nude bathing nights, the 25m, 28°C pool and sauna attracts large numbers of gay men. The modern Neue Halle (New Hall) is more suited for serious swimmers and has a 50m lap pool.

STADTBAD MITTE Map pp322-4
☎ 3088 0910; Gartenstrasse 5; adult/concession €4/2.50; S-Bahn Nordbahnhof
Another one for fans of unusual architecture. The 50m lap pool here is in a renovated 1928 Bauhaus structure, and feels like swimming in a glass cube.

STADTBAD NEUKÖLLN Map pp325-7
☎ 6824 9812; Ganghoferstrasse 5; sauna adult/concession €14/11; U-Bahn Rathaus Neukölln
Called the most beautiful pool in Europe at its opening in 1914, this is one of Berlin's most impressive bathing temples, wowing swimmers with mosaics, frescoes, marble and brass. There are 25m and 20m pools. The sauna area also has a dry sauna, Russian-Roman bath and steam room.

Tennis & Squash
FITFUN Map pp332-3
☎ 312 5082; Uhlandstrasse 194, Charlottenburg; squash €6 per hour; U/S-Bahn Zoologischer Garten
For squash fans only, this is a good central option with 13 courts and a fully featured fitness setup.

TENNIS SQUASH FITNESS Map p133
☎ 333 4083; Galenstrasse 33, Spandau; U-Bahn Rathaus Spandau
Indoor tennis and squash courts, plus sauna, solarium and a fitness studio.

TSB CITY SPORTS Map pp330-1
☎ 873 9097; Brandenburgische Strasse 53, Wilmersdorf; U-Bahn Konstanzer Strasse
One of the largest and more central facilities. Prices vary according to court, time and day.

Shopping

Shopping

Shopping Areas

From penny-pinchers to power shoppers, anyone can buy just about anything in Berlin, but not usually in one place. Unlike, say, London with its Oxford St, or New York with its 5th Ave, shopping in the German capital is not concentrated in a central area. Each neighbourhood has its own approach for separating you from your cash, with a unique mix of stores calibrated to the tastes and pocketbooks of the local residents. This is why you'll find international designers in posh Charlottenburg, while funky Kreuzberg is filled with eclectic second-hand boutiques. In Mitte, ritzy Friedrichstrasse has cosmopolitan flair, while the cosy Scheunenviertel and Prenzlauer Berg are hotbeds of hip local designers. Schöneberg has the big KaDeWe department store but its side streets are lined with low-key speciality boutiques.

Berliners generally prefer patronising small establishments and can be fiercely loyal to the ones they like. Chain stores – which suck the juice out of shopping in so many cities – are mostly relegated to designated commercial strips, such as Kurfürstendamm, and to the shopping malls. The latter especially have popped up all over the city in recent years, usually conveniently located next to a U-Bahn or S-Bahn station. This is especially true in the outer districts but there are also some central areas, including the Potsdamer Platz Arkaden in Tiergarten and the Schönhauser Allee Arkaden in Prenzlauer Berg.

Shopping in Berlin is a relatively laid-back pastime but there are still plenty of unusual items to be found no matter if you're into the hottest club sounds, high-end porcelain or Eastern bloc memorabilia. The city supports a huge creative community that churns out unique outfits, shoes, hats, bags, home accessories etc. Many are handmade, one-of-a-kind and imbued with that urban, quasi-industrial Berlin edge. The city's contemporary art scene is huge and aficionados could easily spend an entire week gallery hopping and still not see everything. If you don't have a trust fund, give the flea markets a try (see the boxed text, opposite). It's worth taking a couple of hours raking through the muck if you dig up some prize you could only have found in Berlin.

For the full lowdown on how to best burn holes in your wallet, readers of German should consult the special shopping editions published by the listings magazines *Zitty*, *Tip* and *Prinz*, available at any newsagent.

Note that many stores, especially smaller ones, do not accept credit cards.

KaDeWe (p232)

The Urban Treasure Hunt

Flea markets are great places to engage in a spot of cultural archaeology. You never know what kind of treasure you'll dig up among the trash. Here's our shortlist of the best:

Flohmarkt am Arkonaplatz (Map pp322-4; Arkonaplatz, Prenzlauer Berg; 🕒 10am-4pm Sun; U-Bahn Bernauer Strasse) This flea market feeds the current retro frenzy, with lots of groovy furniture, accessories, clothing, vinyl and books from the 1960s and '70s. It teems with hip Berlin folks poking around for stylish finds and is also a good place for GDR-era souvenirs.

Flohmarkt am Boxhagener Platz (Map pp325-7; Boxhagener Platz, Friedrichshain; 🕒 9am-4pm Sun; U/S-Bahn Warschauer Strasse) This sizzling market is at risk of falling victim to its own success, as its small size can't keep up with its popularity. But for now it still brims with great finds for those who worship at the altar of retro or Ostalgie (nostalgia for East Germany). Coffee or breakfast at a neighbourhood café is part of the tradition.

Flohmarkt Moritzplatz (Map pp325-7; Moritzplatz, Kreuzberg; 🕒 8am-4pm Sat & Sun; U-Bahn Moritzplatz) Pretty junky but the rock-bottom prices regularly guarantee a good turn out of multicultural penny-pinchers. Keep an eye out for that perfect Berlin memento.

Flohmarkt Rathaus Schöneberg (Map pp330-1; John-F-Kennedy-Platz, Schöneberg; 🕒 9am-4pm Sat & Sun; U-Bahn Rathaus Schöneberg) Pro and amateur vendors mix it up at this neighbourhood market, where you can hone your bargaining skills. It's not the trendiest of markets but deals on used clothing and books are quite common.

Flohmarkt Strasse des 17 Juni (Map pp320-1; along Strasse des 17 Juni, west of S-Bahn station Tiergarten; 🕒 10am-5pm Sat & Sun) Berlin's biggest flea market is also a tourist favourite, making bargains as rare as tulips in Tonga. Still, with its great selection of Berlin memorabilia, plus grandma's jewellery and furniture, it's definitely a fun browse.

Hallentrödelmarkt Treptow (Map pp325-7; Eichenstrasse 4, Treptow; 🕒 10am-4pm Sat & Sun; U-Bahn Schlesisches Tor, S-Bahn Treptower Park) This indoor market has mountains of funky and trashy stuff requiring a well-trained 'shit detector' to dig up true treasure. You'll find everything from cool clothes to the proverbial kitchen sink, along with cheap new electronics and Chinese imports.

Trödelmarkt Museumsinsel (Map pp328-9; cnr Am Zeughaus & Am Kupfergraben, Mitte; 🕒 11am-5pm Sat & Sun; U/S-Bahn Friedrichstrasse) In the heart of historical Berlin, this flea market is easily the most scenic but naturally you won't find too many Berliners rummaging for treasure here. Antique book collectors have plenty of boxes to pick through and there's no shortage of furniture, bric-a-brac and Eastern bloc detritus.

Opening Hours

Thanks to a recent expansion of trading hours, stores are now permitted to welcome customers until 8pm from Monday to Saturday. In practice, though, only department stores, shops in major commercial districts, such as the Kurfürstendamm, and those in malls take full advantage of this change; these stores usually open at around 9.30am. Most of the smaller establishments keep flexible hours, opening sometime mid-morning and generally closing at 7pm on weekdays and 4pm on weekends.

MITTE

Mitte's shopping scene has exploded in recent years and now offers several interesting environments. You'll have no trouble maxing out your credit card along Friedrichstrasse, especially in the elegant Friedrichstadtpassagen, anchored by the Galeries Lafayette. The narrow lanes of the Scheunenviertel offer choice browsing for trendy fashions, especially along Alte Schönhauser Strasse and Neue Schönhauser Strasse and inside the Hackesche Höfe. Some of the city's most avant-garde art galleries hold forth along Auguststrasse. The Nikolaiviertel is the place to go for cutesy Berlin souvenirs, while Alexanderplatz is home to big mainstream stores.

AMPELMANN GALERIE SHOP

Map pp328-9   *Souvenirs & Gifts*
☎ 4404 8801; Hackesche Höfe, Court 5; 🕒 10am-8pm; S-Bahn Hackescher Markt
It took a vociferous grass-roots campaign to save the little Ampelmann, the endearing

Top Five Shopping Strips

- **Alte and Neue Schönhauser Strasse, Mitte** (p225) – the latest local trends hot off the sewing machine
- **Bergmannstrasse, Kreuzberg** (p233) – hip vintage duds, chic home accessories and groovy sounds
- **Friedrichstrasse, Mitte** (p225) – all the big international names united on one glamour strip
- **Kastanienallee and Oderberger Strasse, Prenzlauer Berg** (p236) – neat knick-knacks and fashion-forward outfits
- **Kurfürstendamm, Charlottenburg** (p229) – mainstream chains meet *haute couture*

traffic-light man who helped generations of East Germans safely cross the street. Now a beloved cult figure, his likeness fills an entire store's worth of T-shirts, towels, key rings, cookie cutters and many other products.

BERLIN STORY Map pp328-9   *Books*
☎ 2045 3842; Unter den Linden 10; bus 100
This central store has a mind-boggling assortment of Berlin-related maps, videos, magazines and books of all kinds (guides, history, architecture, cooking etc), many in English and other foreign languages.

BERLINER ANTIKMARKT
Map pp328-9   *Antiques & Collectables*
☎ 208 2655; Georgenstrasse 190-203; ☽ 11am-6pm Wed-Mon; U/S-Bahn Friedrichstrasse
Although it targets the cashed-up tourist, this indoor 'market' – really more a row of shops – is a fun place to rummage for jewellery, lamps, art, porcelain, military regalia and lots of other old-timey stuff.

BERLINER BONBONMACHEREI
Map pp328-9   *Food*
☎ 4405 5243; Oranienburger Strasse 32, Heckmann-Höfe; ☽ noon-8pm Wed-Sat; S-Bahn Oranienburger Strasse
The lost art of handmade sweets has been lovingly revived in this little basement store with its integrated show kitchen. Watch master candy-makers Katja and Hjalmar using antique equipment and traditional recipes to produce such tasty delights as tangy sour drops or green leaf-shaped *Maibl*ätter (May leaves), a local speciality.

BUTTENHEIM LEVIS STORE
Map pp328-9   *Clothing*
☎ 2759 4460; Neue Schönhauser Strasse 15; ☽ noon-8pm Mon-Fri, noon-5pm Sat; U-Bahn Weinmeisterstrasse
Fashion is fickle but some designs are timeless. Jeans, for instance, were invented in 1873 in San Francisco by Levi Strauss, a German immigrant hailing from the hamlet of Buttenheim. This retail space pays homage to the man and his product with its wide range of vintage styles and accessories to match.

CLAUDIA SKODA
Map pp328-9   *Berlin Designer Wear*
☎ 280 7211; Alte Schönhauser Strasse 35; ☽ noon-8pm Mon-Fri, 11am-6pm Sat; U-Bahn Weinmeisterstrasse
Berlin-born Claudia Skoda has been a major presence on the city's design scene since the 1970s, when she used to hang out with David Bowie and Iggy Pop. Her signature material is knitwear, sometimes in bold colours, which she turns into innovative yet eminently wearable outfits.

Clothing Sizes
Measurements approximate only, try before you buy

Women's Clothing

Aus/UK	8	10	12	14	16	18
Europe	36	38	40	42	44	46
Japan	5	7	9	11	13	15
USA	6	8	10	12	14	16

Women's Shoes

Aus/USA	5	6	7	8	9	10
Europe	35	36	37	38	39	40
France only	35	36	38	39	40	42
Japan	22	23	24	25	26	27
UK	3½	4½	5½	6½	7½	8½

Men's Clothing

Aus	92	96	100	104	108	112
Europe	46	48	50	52	54	56
Japan	S		M	M		L
UK/USA	35	36	37	38	39	40

Men's Shirts (Collar Sizes)

Aus/Japan	38	39	40	41	42	43
Europe	38	39	40	41	42	43
UK/USA	15	15½	16	16½	17	17½

Men's Shoes

Aus/UK	7	8	9	10	11	12
Europe	41	42	43	44½	46	47
Japan	26	27	27½	28	29	30
USA	7½	8½	9½	10½	11½	12½

Shopping – Mitte

DNS RECORDSTORE Map pp328-9 *Music*
☎ 247 9895; Alte Schönhauser Strasse 39-40;
🕲 11am-8pm Mon-Fri, 11am-6pm Sat; U-Bahn
Weinmeisterstrasse
This DJ favourite is one of the best-stocked stores for electronic club sounds from drum and bass and techno to trip-hop and acid, all nicely sorted in racks of vinyl. A handful of turntables are around if you're itching for a test-listen.

**DUSSMANN – DAS KULTURKAUF-
HAUS** Map pp328-9 *Music & Books*
☎ 2025 2400; Friedrichstrasse 90; 🕲 10am-10pm
Mon-Sat; U/S-Bahn Friedrichstrasse
It's easy to lose track of time as you browse through Dussmann's four floors of wall-to-wall books, DVDs and an astonishing selection of music CDs that leaves no genre unaccounted. Unique services such as rentals of reading glasses and CD players are a definite bonus, while the café, Internet terminals (€1 per 10 minutes) and a smattering of cultural events provide additional temptations to linger.

FISHBELLY Map pp328-9 *Lingerie*
☎ 2804 5180; Sophienstrasse 7a, Hackesche Höfe;
🕲 12.30-7pm Mon-Fri, noon-5pm Sat; S-Bahn
Hackescher Markt
Get your nocturnal niceties at Jutta Teschner's sleek lingerie shop, where the motto is 'sexy wear for sexy women'. From briefs to bustiers to baby dolls – you'll find big names (Christian Dior to Versace) alongside Teschner's own designs.

GALERIE EIGEN + ART
Map pp328-9 *Art Gallery*
☎ 280 6605; Auguststrasse 26; 🕲 11am-6pm
Tue-Sat; S-Bahn Oranienburger Strasse
Legendary art dealer Gerd Harry Lybke has a keen eye for new German talent, whom he often shepherds to international success. The gallery's roster includes Carsten and Olaf Nico-

lai, Jörg Herold and Uwe Kowski. Lybke also cofounded the popular Mitte art gallery walks, which regularly draw scores of connoisseurs and the merely curious.

GALERIE WOHNMASCHINE
Map pp328-9 *Art Gallery*
☎ 3087 2015; Tucholskystrasse 35; 🕲 11am-6pm
Tue-Sat; S-Bahn Oranienburger Strasse
Founded in a private living room in 1988, Wohnmaschine has long been one of the top galleries in this district. Named after an architectural concept by Le Corbusier, it represents top Berlin talent such as Florian Merkel and Anton Henning, along with a new generation of Japanese artists, including Rika Noguchi and Yoshihiro Suda.

GALERIES LAFAYETTE
Map pp328-9 *Department Store*
☎ 209 480; Friedrichstrasse 76; 🕲 10am-8pm
Mon-Sat; U-Bahn Französische Strasse
The Berlin branch of the exquisite French fashion emporium is worth a visit if only to admire Jean Nouvel's dramatic central light cone which shimmers in a rainbow of colours. From here it's three floors of designer wear and accessories, plus a gourmet food hall in the basement with to-die-for displays of cheeses, tarts, chocolates and other goodies.

JÜDISCHE GALERIE BERLIN
Map pp328-9 *Art Gallery*
☎ 282 8623; Oranienburger Strasse 31; 🕲 10am-
6.30pm Mon-Thu, 10am-5pm Fri, 11am-3pm Sun;
S-Bahn Oranienburger Strasse
This gallery next to the New Synagogue offers an excellent introduction to art produced by 20th-century Jewish artists. Although most are now Berlin-based, many actually hail from Russia and the former Soviet republics.

KOCHLUST Map pp328-9 *Books*
☎ 2463 8883; Alte Schönhauser Strasse 36-37;
🕲 noon-8pm Mon-Fri, 11am-4pm Sat; U-Bahn
Weinmeisterstrasse
If you've got a passion for cooking, Kochlust will likely quicken your pulse. Tiny but crammed to the rafters with cookbooks, it has recipes for every dish under the sun – apple pie to zebra steak. There's also a good assortment of chefs' bios, restaurant guides and culinary travel books. Sign up early if you want to take one of the store-run cooking classes.

LISA D Map pp328-9 *Berlin Designer Wear*
☎ 283 4354; Hackesche Höfe, courtyards 4 & 5;
⏰ noon-6.30pm Mon-Sat; S-Bahn Hackescher Markt

Lisa D is the pseudonym of Austrian-born fashion maven Elisabeth Prantner, one of Berlin's most boundary-pushing designers. Her clothes are veritable fashion adventures, reflecting her flair for the dramatic, which is especially evident at her twice-yearly fashion shows to introduce new collections. The store in courtyard No 5 has a slightly cheaper selection.

MEISSENER PORZELLAN
Map pp328-9 *Fine China*
☎ 2267 9028; Unter den Linden 39b; ⏰ 10am-8pm Mon-Fri, 10am-6pm Sat; U-Bahn Französische Strasse

Costly and highly collectable, Meissen porcelain is among the world's finest, with each piece masterfully handcrafted and hand-painted. On display here are elegant bowls, vases and teacups beside some bizarre figurines with 'bad-taste-award' aspirations: picture a harp-playing ape wearing a ball gown and a crazy smile. The cost: €1545. Good taste, it seems, is priceless.

MISS SIXTY Map pp328-9 *Clothing*
☎ 9700 5113; Neue Schönhauser Strasse 16;
⏰ 11.30am-8pm Mon-Fri, 10.30am-6pm Sat; U-Bahn Weinmeisterstrasse

Barbie would feel at home in the psychedelic flagship store of this retro label, whose girly and fun outfits celebrate 1960s glam. Heads are sure to turn when you're kitted out in their ultra-low denim hip-huggers, ruffled halter-tops or one-shoulder, tie-dye blouses. Also in **Charlottenburg** (Map pp332-3; ☎ 2360 9940; Tauentzienstrasse 15; U-Bahn Wittenbergplatz).

Quartier 206 (right)

NIX Map pp328-9 *Clothing & Accessories*
☎ 281 8044; Oranienburger Strasse 32, Heckmann-Höfe; ⏰ 11am-7pm Mon-Fri, noon-6pm Sat; S-Bahn Oranienburger Strasse

The name stands for New Individual X-tras, a line of feminine fashions by Berlin designer Barbara Gebhardt, who knows what busy women need: comfortable yet with-it outfits that transition well from the office to the party. She's also branched out to clothes for men and children, all sold at moderate prices.

O.K. Map pp328-9 *Souvenirs & Gifts*
☎ 2463 8746; Alte Schönhauser Strasse 36-37;
⏰ noon-8pm Mon-Fri, noon-4pm Sat; U-Bahn Weinmeisterstrasse

This is an import store with a twist. Instead of rattan chairs or African masks, O.K. stocks a potpourri of everyday items from around the world, mostly made from simple materials in developing nations. Recycled tyre ashtrays from Morocco, hand-painted tin watering cans from India and floral wrapping paper from Thailand all show that there's plenty of beauty in the ordinary.

QUARTIER 205 Map pp328-9 *Shopping Mall*
☎ 2094 5100; www.q205.com; Friedrichstrasse 67;
⏰ 10am-8pm Mon-Sat; U-Bahn Stadtmitte

Part of the exclusive Friedrichstadtpassagen, Quartier 205 lets you pick sleek Italian handbags from Da Vinci, a new pair of sunglasses from Brille 54, beautiful handmade South African candles from Kapula and fragrant blends of tea from Der Teeladen. John Chamberlain's *Tower of Clythe* anchors the ground floor with its pleasant food court.

QUARTIER 206 Map pp328-9 *Shopping Mall*
☎ 2094 3000; Friedrichstrasse 70; ⏰ 10am-8pm Mon-Sat; U-Bahn Französische Strasse

This stunning Art Deco symphony in glass and marble, designed by Henry Cobb and IM Pei, is a fitting shrine for luxury labels such as Gucci, Yves Saint Laurent, Cerruti and La Perla's barely-there lingerie. If you need a new bag to lug it home, drop in at Louis Vuitton. A stylish café and clusters of black leather armchairs are there in case you need a quick rest.

SATURN Map pp328-9 *Electronics & Music*
☎ 247 516; Alexanderplatz 8; ⏰ 10am-8pm Mon-Sat; U/S-Bahn Alexanderplatz

This huge electronics store has some of the lowest prices for mainstream CDs plus lots of discount offers. Most amazingly, you can listen to *any* CD by scanning its barcode into one of the listening stations dotted around the store. Also in the Potsdamer Platz Arkaden in **Tiergarten** (Map p334; ☎ 259 240; Alte Potsdamer Strasse 7; U/S-Bahn Potsdamer Platz).

STERLING GOLD
Map pp328-9   *Vintage Clothing*
☎ 2809 6500; Oranienburger Strasse 32, Heckmann-Höfe; noon-8pm Mon-Fri, noon-6pm Sat; S-Bahn Oranienburger Strasse
Unleash your inner princess when slipping into one of the superb vintage evening gowns, wedding outfits, prom frocks or cocktail dresses billowing from the racks of this gorgeous store. Everything's extremely classy and in good shape and there is even a dressmaker to do alterations for that perfect fit. One-night rentals are available too.

TAGEBAU
Map pp328-9   *Clothing & Accessories*
☎ 2839 0890; Rosenthaler Strasse 19; 11am-8pm Mon-Fri, 11am-6pm Sat; U-Bahn Weinmeisterstrasse
This warehouse-sized space with gallery flair is an innovative cooperative of young local designers. The cast of characters fluctuates but mainstays include Angela Klöck and her line of whimsical hats and Eva Sörensen, who's known for her delicate necklaces. It's also worth looking out for furniture, clothing and home accessories.

TENDERLOIN
Map pp328-9   *Clothing & Accessories*
☎ 4201 5785; Alte Schönhauser Strasse 30; noon-8pm Mon-Fri, 11am-6pm Sat; U-Bahn Weinmeisterstrasse
Not as funky as the San Francisco district after which it is named, Berlin's Tenderloin carries unisex streetwear, much of it in psychedelic colours last seen during the disco decade. Racks hold an interesting mix of local and international labels, including Friedrichshain-based Stoffrausch, and Skunk Funk from Spain. Great wig collection too.

WAAHNSINN BERLIN
Map pp328-9   *Vintage Clothing*
☎ 282 0029; Rosenthaler Strasse 17; noon-8pm Mon-Sat; U-Bahn Rosenthaler Platz
You'll need a wacky sense of aesthetics paired with a good dose of humour to put together

a winning outfit from this shop's outrageous vintage fashions and accessories. But at least you're guaranteed to be a standout on the party circuit. Home furnishings too.

YOSHIHARU ITO
Map pp328-9   *Men's Clothing*
☎ 4404 4490; Auguststrasse 19; noon-8pm Mon-Sat; S-Bahn Oranienburger Strasse
Classic cuts with an avant-garde club-wear edge are the hallmark of this Tokyo-trained couture designer. His clean-lined three-piece power-suits are currently all the rage among Berlin's brigade of young and hip urban professional men.

TIERGARTEN
You won't find many spending temptations in this district – *except* at Berlin's best shopping mall, right on bustling Potsdamer Platz.

POTSDAMER PLATZ ARKADEN
Map p334   *Shopping Mall*
☎ 255 9270; Alte Potsdamer Strasse; 10am-8pm Mon-Sat; U/S-Bahn Potsdamer Platz
This pleasant, American-style indoor mall brims with chain stores such as H&M, Mango, Esprit (all clothing), Mandarina Duck (handbags, luggage), Hugendubel (books) and Saturn (electronics and music). In between are smaller stores selling everything from eye-wear to cigars to tuxedos. The basement has Kaiser's and Aldi supermarkets and several fast-food outlets. There's a post office on the ground floor, while the 1st floor is anchored by Caffé & Gelato, a hugely popular Italian ice cream parlour.

CHARLOTTENBURG
Kurfürstendamm is the premier shopping mile in the western city. It's chock-a-block with multiple outlets of H&M, Mango, Zara and other international chains flogging mostly affordable fashions and accessories. The more exclusive shops, selling such things as *haute couture*, porcelain and Italian shoes, flank such side streets as Fasanenstrasse and Bleibtreustrasse. The area around Savignyplatz is also dotted with quality speciality stores, while on nearby Kantstrasse the focus is on interior design.

BERLINER ZINNFIGUREN

Map pp332-3   *Collectables*

☎ 315 7000; www.zinnfigur.com; Knesebeckstrasse 88; ⏲ 10am-6pm Mon-Fri, 10am-3pm Sat; U-Bahn Ernst-Reuter-Platz, S-Bahn Savignyplatz

Build up your own Prussian army – in miniature, that is – at this family-owned store, in business since 1934. More than 30,000 flat tin figurines, over half of them soldiers, neatly pose on shelves and in glass cases. Each little guy is hand cast and painted with historical accuracy and detail. There are also thousands of books and videos dealing with military history.

BOOKS IN BERLIN Map pp332-3   *Books*

☎ 313 1233; Goethestrasse 69; ⏲ noon-8pm Mon-Fri, 10am-4pm Sat; U-Bahn Ernst-Reuter-Platz

No matter whether you need to brush up on Beowulf or are lusting for the latest potboiler, you'll find them at this small but well-stocked repository of English literature from around the world. If you're not sure, the knowledgeable staff will happily help you wade through the selection or even custom-order titles.

GALERIE BROCKSTEDT

Map pp332-3   *Art Gallery*

☎ 885 0500; Mommsenstrasse 59; ⏲ 10am-6pm Tue-Fri, 10am-2pm Sat; S-Bahn Savignyplatz

This well-respected gallery has built a name for itself with art by modern masters, especially those working between the two world wars, including Otto Dix, George Grosz and Franz Radziwil. A secondary focus belongs to post-WWII realists, including Isabel Quintanilla and Francesco Lopez, and abstract German artists such as Willi Baumeister and Ernst Wilhelm Nay.

GALERIE MICHAEL SCHULTZ

Map pp332-3   *Art Gallery*

☎ 324 1591; Mommsenstrasse 34; ⏲ 11am-7pm Tue-Fri, 10am-4pm Sat; U-Bahn Adenauerplatz

This gallery showcases high-profile contemporary German painters and sculptors, including

Markus Lüpertz, Georg Baselitz, Jörg Immendorf and AR Penck. Armando and Luciano Castelli are among the smaller roster of international artists also represented here.

GLASKLAR Map pp332-3   *Glass*

☎ 313 1037; Knesebeckstrasse 13-14; ⏲ 11am-6.30pm Mon-Fri, 11am-4pm Sat; U-Bahn Ernst-Reuter-Platz

Glasses for wine, water, tea, grappa, champagne and martini. Thick glasses fit for a peasant and delicate ones suitable for a duke's dinner party. Glasklar has nothing but floor-to-ceiling shelves of beverage vessels in their infinite, timeless variety, complemented by a smallish assortment of vases, ashtrays, teapots and bowls. Prices start at less than €1.

HARRY LEHMANN Map pp332-3   *Perfume*

☎ 324 3582; Kantstrasse 106; ⏲ 9am-6.30pm Mon-Fri, 9am-2pm Sat; U-Bahn Wilmersdorfer Strasse

An endearing slice of 'Old Berlin', Harry Lehmann has been making perfumes from family recipes since 1926. The flowery scents, such as lavender blossom, jasmine and acacia, are kept in big-bellied glass jars and then filled into smaller flasks and sold by weight. The smallest costs €4.50. Note: it's inside another store selling silk flowers.

HAUTNAH Map pp332-3   *Erotica*

☎ 882 3434; Uhlandstrasse 170; ⏲ noon-8pm Mon-Fri, 11am-4pm Sat; U-Bahn Uhlandstrasse

Those who worship at the altar of hedonism should check out Hautnah's three floors, which are stocked with everything girls and boys with imagination might need for a naughty night. The assortment ranges from frilly feather boas to fantasy and fetish outfits, plus various sex toys and plenty of unprintable stuff.

HEIDI'S SPIELZEUGLADEN

Map pp332-3   *Toys*

☎ 323 7556; Kantstrasse 61; ⏲ 9.30am-6.30pm Mon-Fri, 9.30am-2pm Sat; U-Bahn Wilmersdorfer Strasse

In an age when kids know Nintendo long before learning the alphabet, Heidi's may seem like an anachronism. For nearly 30 years she has specialised in low-tech, quality toys, from wooden trains to sturdy stuffed animals to 'edutaining' children's books. Heidi's also has great doll houses, play kitchens and toy stores to help spur kids' imaginations and social skills.

Top Five Bookshops

- **Another Country** (p234)
- **Berlin Story** (p226)
- **Books in Berlin** (this page)
- **Hugendubel** (p231)
- **Marga Schoeller Bücherstube** (p231)

HUGENDUBEL Map pp332-3 *Books*
☎ 214 060; Tauentzienstrasse 13; ⌚ 10am-8pm
Mon-Sat; U-Bahn Kurfürstendamm

This excellent all-purpose nationwide chain has a sweeping selection of books, including Lonely Planet titles and novels in English. You can browse as long as you like or preview your purchase while comfortably ensconced in leather sofas or enjoying a latte at the in-store café. Also in **Mitte** (Map pp328-9; Friedrichstrasse 83; U-Bahn Französische Strasse) and **Tiergarten** (Map p334; Potsdamer Platz Arkaden; U/S-Bahn Potsdamer Platz).

KARSTADT SPORT
Map pp332-3 *Sports Gear*
☎ 880 240; Joachimstaler Strasse 5-6; ⌚ 10am-8pm
Mon-Sat; U/S-Bahn Zoologischer Garten

This multistorey department store has four floors of equipment and outfits for any sport – tennis to soccer to caving.

LEHMANN'S COLONIALWAREN
Map pp332-3 *Antiques & Collectables*
☎ 883 3942; Grolmanstrasse 46; ⌚ 2-6.30pm
Tue-Fri, 11am-2pm Sat; S-Bahn Savignyplatz

This store's curious assortment of colonial artefacts harkens back to a time when travelling meant Atlantic crossings on the *Queen Mary* or barging down the Nile. Heavy leather luggage, hatboxes, old globes, travel advertisements and books are all stylish vehicles for your own time-travel adventure.

LEYSIEFFER Map pp332-3 *Chocolates*
☎ 885 7480; Kurfürstendamm 218; ⌚ 10am-8pm
Mon-Sat; U-Bahn Uhlandstrasse

Leysieffer has been composing irresistible chocolates for nearly a century. Its champagne truffles, nougats, dark chocolates and other temptations, all artfully displayed at this busy flagship store, make nice gifts for the folks back home.

MARGA SCHOELLER BÜCHERSTUBE
Map pp332-3 *Books*
☎ 8862 9329; Knesebeckstrasse 33; ⌚ 9.30am-7pm
Mon-Wed, 9.30am-8pm Thu-Fri, 9.30am-4pm Sat;
U-Bahn Uhlandstrasse

Founded in 1929, this well-regarded bookstore has a long list of illustrious patrons, including Bertolt Brecht and Elias Canetti. The emphasis of its sophisticated assortment is on new and classic English literature, works by and about

women, and books about theatre and film. The super-helpful staff can order anything that's not in store. Check for book signings and readings.

NIKETOWN Map pp332-3 *Sports Gear*
☎ 250 70; Tauentzienstrasse 7b; ⌚ 10am-8pm
Mon-Sat; U-Bahn Wittenbergplatz

Two floors of chrome and glass constitute a suitable setting for Nike's hi-tech sports gear. No matter what gets you off that couch – be it soccer to golf to basketball – you'll look stylish in your little outfit with matching watch and sunglasses. What would the namesake Greek goddess think of that?

PAPETERIE HEINRICH KÜNNEMANN
Map pp332-3 *Pens & Stationery*
☎ 881 6363; Uhlandstrasse 28; ⌚ 10am-8pm
Mon-Sat; U-Bahn Uhlandstrasse

Penmanship may be a dying art in the age of emails and text messages, but this elegant store still caters for traditionalists. Choose from the full range of finely crafted fountain pens by famous makers, including Pelikan, Mont Blanc and Caran d'Ache. Stylish office accessories and stationery are also available.

PRINZ EISENHERZ Map pp332-3 *Books*
☎ 313 9936; Bleibtreustrasse 52; ⌚ 10am-8pm
Mon-Fri, 10am-4pm Sat; S-Bahn Savignyplatz

This is one of the best shops in town for international lesbigay literature, coffee-table books and magazines. Also stocks videos and CDs.

STEIFF IN BERLIN Map pp332-3 *Toys*
☎ 8872 1919; www.steiffinberlin.de;
Kurfürstendamm 220; ⌚ 10am-8pm Mon-Sat;
U-Bahn Uhlandstrasse

What do Happy the pig, Hoppel the bunny and Sniffy the hedgehog all have in common? They're all creations of this famous stuffed-animal company, founded in 1880 by Margarete Steiff. Meet the entire menagerie at this delightful store, which also has some highly collectable limited-edition animals.

STILWERK Map pp332-3 *Interior Design*
☎ 3151 5500; Kantstrasse 17; ⌚ 10am-8pm
Mon-Sat; S-Bahn Savignyplatz

At this four-floor emporium of good taste you'll find everything for home and hearth, from egg cups to lamps to full professional kitchens. Only the top names in international design are featured, including Bang & Olufsen,

Alessi, Ligne Roset, Leonardo and Gaggenau. There's also a restaurant, the jazz club Soultrane (p208), and the occasional piano concert.

WERTHEIM BEI HERTIE

Map pp332-3   *Department Store*
☎ 880 030; Kurfürstendamm 231; ☽ 10am-8pm Mon-Sat; U-Bahn Kurfürstendamm
Almost as huge as KaDeWe (p232) but considerably more down-to-earth, with prices to match, Wertheim is where Berliners shop. If hunger strikes, drop by the rooftop cafeteria, which has alfresco seating in good weather.

ZWEITAUSENDEINS Map pp332-3   *Music*
☎ 312 5017; Kantstrasse 41; ☽ 10am-7pm Mon-Wed, 10am-8pm Thu-Fri, 10am-4pm Sat; U-Bahn Wilmersdorfer Strasse
Penny-pinching music fans keep this Berlin outlet of a Frankfurt-based online store busy as a beehive. New books, CDs, DVDs and video are all sold at steeply discounted prices. You probably won't find the latest releases but the selection of classical, world, jazz and rock music is likely to yield some surprising finds.

SCHÖNEBERG

Schöneberg is home to KaDeWe, one of Europe's grandest department stores and a quintessential Berlin shopping experience. The district's true character, though, reveals itself south of Nollendorfplatz. The entire strip along Maassenstrasse to Winterfeldtplatz to Goltzstrasse and Akazienstrasse brims with unique and fun boutiques selling everything from shoes to flamenco frocks, jewellery and books.

BRUNO'S Map pp330-1   *Gay-themed Store*
☎ 2147 3293; Bülowstrasse 106; ☽ 10am-10pm Mon-Sat; U-Bahn Nollendorfplatz
This nicely decked-out store is the go-to place for gay-themed books, magazines and videos plus knick-knacks of all sorts. About one-third of the floor space is given over to erotic videos for sale and rent.

DORIS IMHOFF SCHMUCK & PERLEN

Map pp330-1   *Jewellery*
☎ 7871 6700; Akazienstrasse 26; ☽ 10.30am-8pm Mon-Fri, 10.30am-4pm Sat; U-Bahn Eisenacher Strasse
Gorgeous baubles at moderate prices fill about a dozen glass vitrines at this friendly little store

on bustling Akazienstrasse. Besides owner Doris' own creations, you'll be tempted by the streamlined designs of Thomas Sabo, the playful necklaces of Konplott's Miranda Konstantinidou or the dramatic pieces of Rodrigo Otazu. There's even an assortment of quality beads in case inspiration strikes.

GARAGE Map pp330-1   *Vintage Clothing*
☎ 211 2760; Ahornstrasse 2; ☽ 11am-7pm Mon-Wed, 11am-8pm Thu-Fri, 10am-4pm Sat; U-Bahn Nollendorfplatz
Bargains abound in this basement warehouse where you buy your clothing by weight (1kg costs €14). Quality is pretty uneven and many items are soiled or tattered, so prepare to spend some time picking your way through the racks and stacks.

KADEWE Map pp332-3   *Department Store*
☎ 212 10; Tauentzienstrasse 21-24; ☽ 10am-8pm Mon-Sat; U-Bahn Wittenbergplatz
Shopaholics will get their fix at this amazing, seven-floor department store. KaDeWe, which stands for Kaufhaus des Westens (Department Store of the West), is Europe's second-largest consumer temple, after Harrod's of London. If you're pushed for time, make a beeline for the gourmet food hall on the 6th floor – it's legendary.

KÖRPERNAH Map pp330-1   *Lingerie*
☎ 215 7471; Maassenstrasse 8; ☽ 10.30am-7.30pm Mon-Thu, 10.30am-8pm Fri, 10am-5pm Sat; U-Bahn Nollendorfplatz
This pretty little store has fabulously trendy, often provocative, but never sleazy, undergarments for him and her in all sizes. The winsome staff will help even the most body-conscious find a flattering fit. Labels include Woolford, Cotton Club and Huit for women, and Body Art, Boss and Homme for men.

LUCCICO Map pp330-1   *Shoes*
☎ 216 6517; Goltzstrasse 34; ☽ noon-8pm Mon-Fri, 11am-4pm Sat; U-Bahn Nollendorfplatz
'Shoes till death', promises Luccico, one of Berlin's most popular purveyors of fashionable Italian footwear. The slogan may be a tad ominous but, given the high quality, probably not entirely unfounded. Styles range from sleek boots to classic flats, sexy sling pumps to comfy flip-flops. Also in **Kreuzberg** (Map pp325-7; ☎ 691 3257; Bergmannstrasse 8; U-Bahn Gneisenaustrasse) and **Mitte** (Map pp328-9;

☎ 283 2372; Neue Schönhauser Strasse 18; U-Bahn Weinmeisterstrasse).

MR DEAD & MRS FREE Map pp330-1 *Music*
☎ 215 1449; Bülowstrasse 5; ☽ 11am-7pm Mon-Fri, 11am-4pm Sat; U-Bahn Nollendorfplatz
With a pedigree going back two decades, this legendary store has expanded from its original focus on UK and US imports to include the best of all genres – jazz, reggae, soul and even blues and folk. Most of it is on vinyl with a few CDs thrown into the mix.

RAHAUS WOHNEN
Map pp332-3 *Interior Design*
☎ 218 9393; Wittenbergplatz; ☽ 10am-8pm Mon-Sat; U-Bahn Wittenbergplatz
Okay, so that bold crimson couch may not fit into your suitcase, but this store is still worth a browse for its stylish, well-priced accessories. Many of the lamps, wine glasses, candlesticks and other items are exclusively designed for this small chain. The other three branches are all in Charlottenburg: **Rahaus Country & Rahaus Loft** (Map pp320-1; ☎ 3999 4834; Franklinstrasse 8-14) and **Rahaus Living** (Map pp332-3; ☎ 313 2100; Kantstrasse, cnr Uhlandstrasse).

SCHROPP Map pp330-1 *Books & Maps*
☎ 2355 7320; Potsdamer Strasse 129; ☽ 9.30am-7pm Mon-Fri, 10am-4pm Sat; U-Bahn Bülowstrasse
Schropp fits the entire world onto its two floors, each crammed with every conceivable map, travel guide, dictionary and globe. It's the perfect place for some quality armchair travelling or for planning your next trip.

TUMA BE! Map pp330-1 *Gifts & Accessories*
☎ 216 9414; Goltzstrasse 34; ☽ noon-6.30pm Mon-Fri, 11am-4pm Sat; U-Bahn Eisenacher Strasse
Owner Andrea Knörr has a knack for rooting out stylish accoutrements that go well with just about any home on her trips around Africa and Asia. Items such as elegant wooden fruit bowls, cleverly carved masks, iron candlesticks and jewellery are all sold at reasonable prices. The name, by the way, is Mali for 'the time has come'.

VAMPYR DE LUXE
Map pp330-1 *Clothing & Accessories*
☎ 217 2038; Goltzstrasse 39; ☽ noon-7pm Mon-Fri, noon-5pm Sat; U-Bahn Eisenacher Strasse, Nollendorfplatz
If you like to stay ahead of the fashion curve, pop into this hip haven chock-full of outfits and accessories from both emerging designers and established labels, many of them local and many one-of-a-kind. Vamp it up with handbags by Tita Berlin, sexy outfits for men by io, cool leather wear by stylesucks.com and sassy undies by Vive Maria.

WINTERFELDTMARKT
Map pp330-1 *Outdoor Market*
Winterfeldtplatz; ☽ 8am-2pm Wed, 8am-4pm Sat; U-Bahn Nollendorfplatz
A Schöneberg institution, this is a great place for stocking up on fresh produce, eggs, meat, flowers and other essentials for living *la dolce vita* in Berlin. There is also a smattering of vendors who sell candles, jewellery, scarves and other nonedible goods. Do as the locals do and cap it all off with coffee or breakfast in a nearby café.

Winterfeldtmarkt (above)

KREUZBERG

Kreuzberg has a predictably eclectic shopping scene. Bergmannstrasse, in the western district, offers a fun cocktail of vintage and progressive fashions, music and books, along with the historic Marheineke market hall. Eastern Kreuzberg's multicultural flair is best sampled along Kottbusser Damm and at the Turkish Market. Oranienstrasse is also worth a stroll, especially if you're into funky second-hand duds.

ANOTHER COUNTRY Map pp325-7 *Books*
☎ 6940 1150; Riemannstrasse 7; ⏰ 11am-8pm Mon-Fri, 11am-4pm Sat; U-Bahn Gneisenaustrasse

Another Country is the universe of its bearded and slightly eccentric British owner Alan Raphaeline. Knowledgeable and always up for a chinwag, he presides over a meticulously sorted library/store of used English-language books, including a vast science fiction collection. You can borrow or buy, join the book club, come for film screenings and poetry readings or simply hang out on the sofas.

ARZU IMPORT-EXPORT
Map pp325-7 *Souvenirs & Gifts*
☎ 693 8934; Maybachufer 1; ⏰ 11am-8pm Mon-Sat; U-Bahn Schönleinstrasse

Shisha bars, where you can guzzle your beer while sucking on a water pipe, are all the rage in Berlin these days. If you want to continue puffing away back home, this little store next to the Turkish Market offers a great selection of hookahs in different sizes and colours, ranging from €25 to €45.

BAGAGE Map pp325-7 *Bags*
☎ 693 8916; Bergmannstrasse 13; ⏰ 11am-8pm Mon-Fri, 10am-4pm Sat; U-Bahn Mehringdamm

At this hip store a bag isn't just a transporting tool, it's a fashion statement. Hundreds of the latest designs by labels such as Leonca, Tita Berlin, Kultbag and Luma sprawl across the floor and walls. Much of it has that industrial edge favoured by Berlin fashionables and is made from recycled rubber, air mattresses or even postal sacks.

BELLA CASA Map pp325-7 *Interior Design*
☎ 694 0784; Bergmannstrasse 101; ⏰ 11am-7pm Mon-Fri, 10am-4pm Sat; U-Bahn Mehringdamm

The name evokes Italy but Bella Casa's collection actually comes from the shores of North Africa and as far away as India. Its henna lamps, silk pillows, Moroccan tiles and Turkish *kilims* (rugs) will add a touch of fairy tale to your flat.

BELLA DONNA Map pp325-7 *Cosmetics*
☎ 6904 0333; Bergmannstrasse 103; ⏰ 10am-7pm Mon-Fri, 10am-4pm Sat; U-Bahn Mehringdamm

Bella Casa rubs shoulders with Bella Donna, a natural cosmetics store that carries a vast product palette from such well-respected Ger-

Top Five Music Stores
- DNS Recordstore (p227)
- Mr Dead & Mrs Free (p233)
- Scratch Records (p235)
- Space Hall (p235)
- Vopo Records (p238)

man makers as Dr Hauschka, Weleda, Lavera, Logona and Bioturm. In the little studio out the back you can get a deep-cleansing 90-minute facial for around €50.

BLINDENANSTALT BERLIN
Map pp325-7 *Housewares*
☎ 2588 6616; Oranienstrasse 26; ⏰ 9am-5pm Mon-Wed & Fri, 10am-5.30pm Thu; U-Bahn Kottbusser Tor, Görlitzer Bahnhof

Blind and sight-impaired craftspeople have been making traditional brooms and brushes by hand in this mini-factory for over 120 years. Recently, though, the repertory has been expanded to include stylish and extravagant designs as well as other products, including lamp shades and cat entry doors. The store is worth a visit for the original 1920s interior alone.

CHAPATI
Map pp325-7 *Clothing & Accessories*
☎ 2904 4023; Simon-Dach-Strasse 37; ⏰ 11am-7pm Mon-Sat; U/S-Bahn Warschauer Strasse

Silk, velvet, jacquard and other sensuous fabrics imported from India are wrought into flowing dresses, skirts and blouses at this exotic emporium with its Arabian Nights ambience. If you're not into that flower-power look, it also stocks plenty of lamps, pillows and bed throws with which to tart up your home. Other branches are in **Kreuzberg** (Map pp325-7; ☎ 6956 4423; Zossener Strasse 37; U-Bahn Gneisenaustrasse) and **Prenzlauer Berg** (Map pp322-4; ☎ 447 6507; Stargarder Strasse 2; U/S-Bahn Schönhauser Allee).

COLOURS KLEIDERMARKT
Map pp325-7 *Vintage Clothing*
☎ 694 3348; 1st floor, rear Bergmannstrasse 102; ⏰ 11am-7pm Mon-Wed, 11am-8pm Thu & Fri, 10am-4pm Sat; U-Bahn Mehringdamm

This huge loft has great vintage outfits going back to the days when Madonna was first singing about virgins, plus new street- and club-wear for today's hip young things. Most items are in great condition and fairly priced.

Good range of accessories too. It's in the back courtyard, upstairs on the right.

FRITZ Map pp325-7 *Jewellery*
☎ 615 1700; Dresdner Strasse 20; ☿ 10am-7pm Mon-Fri, 10am-3pm Sat; U-Bahn Kottbusser Tor
Manuel Fritz has a stunning way of rendering precious metals. Many of his innovative and very wearable designs are museum quality. They're offered for sale along with jewellery by other artists from throughout Germany. Wedding rings are a speciality.

HAMMETT Map pp325-7 *Books*
☎ 691 5834; Friesenstrasse 27; ☿ 10am-8pm Mon-Fri, 10am-4pm Sat; U-Bahn Gneisenaustrasse
Amateur sleuths won't be able to walk past this bookshop crammed to the rafters with classic and contemporary mysteries, detective and crime stories. Named after one of the genre's finest, Dashiell Hammett, it also has a good selection of English-language titles, hundreds of used books and a children's corner. Look out for book signings or readings.

MARHEINEKE MARKTHALLE
Map pp325-7 *Market Hall*
Marheinekeplatz; ☿ 7.30am-7pm Mon-Fri, 7.30am-2pm Sat; U-Bahn Gneisenaustrasse
This is one of Berlin's three surviving historic market halls and a popular shopping destination with locals. Browse through aisles where produce, cheeses and sausages are piled high, and others where stalls are stocked with everything imaginable – from hiking socks to yarn to liquorice. Prices are low but quality varies, so caveat emptor (buyer beware).

MOLOTOW
Map pp325-7 *Clothing & Accessories*
☎ 693 0818; Gneisenaustrasse 112; ☿ 2-8pm Mon-Fri, noon-4pm Sat; U-Bahn Mehringdamm
Molotow has given young Berlin designers a platform for their wares for nearly two dec-

ades. Outfits – for both men and women – range from the sedate to the outrageous and there's a whole range of accessories to complete the look. All in all, a fun place to dawdle.

SCRATCH RECORDS Map pp325-7 *Music*
☎ 6981 7591; Zossener Strasse 31; ☿ 11am-7pm Mon-Wed, 11am-8pm Thu & Fri, 11am-4pm Sat; U-Bahn Gneisenaustrasse
A small but choice selection of world music, R&B, soul-funk and jazz on vinyl and CD, much of it hard-to-find imports, forms the core of Scratch Records. The in-the-know staff will be only too happy to help you source a new favourite.

SPACE HALL
Map pp325-7 *Music*
☎ 694 7664; www.space-hall.de; Zossener Strasse 33; ☿ 11am-8pm Mon-Fri, 11am-4pm Sat; U-Bahn Gneisenaustrasse
Next door to Scratch Records, this store is nirvana for fans of electronica with everything from techno to drum and bass, breakbeat to trance, most of it for the turntable brigade. A dozen or so players stand by for easy pre-purchase listening.

TÜRKENMARKT
Map pp325-7 *Outdoor Market*
Maybachufer; ☿ noon-6.30pm Tue & Fri; U-Bahn Schönleinstrasse
Heaps of fruit and vegetables, mountains of bread loaves, buckets spilling over with olives, great selections of feta spreads and cheeses – Berlin's Turkish Market is as good as anything you'll find this side of Istanbul. Quality is high, prices are low and helpful smiles abound. Grab your loot and head west along the canal to carve out your picnic spot on the scenic Fraenkelufer.

FRIEDRICHSHAIN
The lower-echelon demographics of the Friedrichshain district don't yet support a major shopping scene but this is certainly bound to change sooner or later. The streets around Boxhagener Platz have seen an influx of pint-sized knick-knack and local designer stores, and the original 'workers' palaces' along Karl-Marx-Allee are also increasingly being enlivened by commercial activity.

Top Five 'Unique Berlin' Stores

- Berliner Bonbonmacherei (p226)
- Berliner Zinnfiguren (p230)
- Blindenanstalt Berlin (p234)
- Harry Lehmann (p230)
- Mondos Arts (p236)

Berlinomat (below)

BERLINOMAT

Map pp325-7   *Clothing & Accessories*

☎ 4208 1445; Frankfurter Allee 89; ☼ 11am-8pm
Mon-Fri, 10am-4pm Sat; U/S-Bahn Frankfurter Allee

This bright and airy store is great for getting a first-hand look at the latest trends in the flourishing Berlin design scene. More than 30 local designers working in furniture, fashion, jewellery and accessories display their latest collections under one roof. Look for cutting-edge necklaces and rings by Dreigold, furniture by Flip Sellin, and Hotinaf fashions by founders Jörg Wichmann and Theresa Meirer.

DAZU Map pp325-7   *Bags*

☎ 2966 7531, 0178 288 1822; www.ichichich-berlin.de;
Kopernikusstrasse 14; ☼ 4-8pm Thu-Fri, noon-4pm
Sat or by appointment; U/S-Bahn Warschauer Strasse

Lui Gerdes designs big, sturdy bags that trade under the ironic label 'Ichichich' (MeMeMe) and are sold in this little shop shared with hatmaker Helena Ahonen. Each bag is handmade, colourful and unique, although all are from the same basic material: truck tarpaulin. Ask about custom designs.

KARL-MARX-BUCHHANDLUNG

Map pp322-4   *Books*

☎ 292 3370; Karl-Marx-Allee 78; ☼ 11am-7pm
Mon-Fri, 10am-4pm Sat; U-Bahn Weberwiese

Anyone with a soft spot for the history of the workers' movement, the GDR, old Berlin or architecture should drop into this store in one of Friedrichshain's original 'workers' palaces'.

It's easy to get lost browsing through the vast assortment of used and new books.

MONDOS ARTS Map pp318-19   *Ostalgiana*

☎ 4201 0778; Schreinerstrasse 6; ☼ 10am-7pm
Mon-Fri, 11am-4pm Sat; U-Bahn Samariterstrasse

Cult and kitsch from the GDR is the bread and butter of this funky store named after the brand of condoms once sold behind the Iron Curtain. It's fun to have a look even if you didn't grow up crossing the road with the *Ampelmann* (traffic-light man), falling asleep to the *Sandmännchen* (little sandman) or listening to rock by the Puhdys.

RAUMDEKOLLETE

Map pp325-7   *Souvenirs & Gifts*

☎ 6676 3783; Kopernikusstrasse 21; ☼ 11am-7pm
Mon-Fri, 11am-4pm Sat; U/S-Bahn Warschauer Strasse

Close to Simon-Dach-Strasse, this store showcases the innovative creations of emerging Berlin artists and designers. Fun and spatial, elegant and stylish – you never know what's on the shelves this week, but you can be sure you won't find it on the high street back home. Prices are moderate.

PRENZLAUER BERG

This district's hippest shopping zone along Kastanienallee and Oderberger Strasse is home to avant-garde and street-wear fashions by local designers as well as a couple of worthwhile second-hand boutiques. Travelling one train stop further north will take you to the Schönhauser Allee Arkaden, a huge shopping mall that is orbited by mostly down-market outlets. The streets around Kollwitzplatz, with their potpourri of speciality stores selling everything from kitchenware to bath accessories, are also worth a stroll.

BELLY BUTTON

Map pp322-4   *Second-Hand Clothing*
☎ 2327 2234; Stargarder Strasse 10; ⏱ 11am-7pm Mon-Fri, 11am-4pm Sat; U/S-Bahn Schönhauser Allee
With its neat racks and shelves backed against lavender walls, Belly Button looks almost too sophisticated for a used-clothing store. Prices are moderate for labels ranging from H&M to Calvin Klein, and we found all items clean, in good condition and sorted by size. There's even a good selection of handbags and shoes.

CALYPSO Map pp322-4   *Shoes*
☎ 281 6165; Oderberger Strasse 61; ⏱ 3-8pm Mon-Fri, noon-4pm Sat; U-Bahn Eberswalder Strasse
This store is crammed with historic footwear for women. Step up to sort through a mountain of lace-up boots from the 1920s, stiletto heels from the '60s, platform shoes from the '70s and other must-have retro styles. Also in **Mitte** (Map pp328-9; ☎ 2854 5415; Rosenthaler Strasse 23; ⏱ noon-8pm Mon-Sat; S-Bahn Hackescher Markt).

CLAMOTTI Map pp322-4   *Women's Clothing*
☎ 445 9521; Stargarder Strasse 7; ⏱ 11am-7pm Mon-Fri, 10am-6pm Sat; U/S-Bahn Schönhauser Allee
'Real women have curves' might as well be the motto of Berlin designer Susi Feÿ, who's been making fun clothing from natural fabrics, mostly imported from Italy, since 1990. Catering for a grown-up clientele, her carefully tailored outfits look good even on less than 'perfect' bodies. Feÿ also custom-designs special-occasion dresses, including ball and wedding gowns.

COLEDAMPF'S CULTURCENTRUM

Map pp322-4   *Kitchenware*
☎ 4373 5225; Wörther Strasse 39; ⏱ 10am-8pm Mon-Fri, 10am-6pm Sat; U-Bahn Senefelderplatz
Cooking is one of life's great pleasures and can be even more fun if you have nice, good-quality utensils to work with. This store's vast assortment ranges from the functional to the frivolous. From shiny copper pans to ravioli

cutters, ice-tea glasses to espresso pots, you're sure to find something you can't live without. There's also a store in **Wilmersdorf** (Map pp332-3; ☎ 883 9191; Uhlandstrasse 54/55; ⏱ 10am-8pm Mon-Fri, 10am-4pm Sat; U-Bahn Spichernstrasse).

EAST BERLIN

Map pp322-4   *Clothing & Accessories*
☎ 534 4042; Kastanienallee 13; ⏱ 2-8pm Mon-Wed, noon-8pm Thu & Fri, 11am-8pm Sat; U-Bahn Eberswalder Strasse
Local design guru Cora Schwind has ditched her Coration label and now fills this fun store with trendy big-city clothes for the fashion conscious. Many sport the store's Ostalgie logo or abstract versions of Berlin landmarks such as the TV tower.

EISDIELER

Map pp322-4   *Clothing & Accessories*
☎ 285 7351; Kastanienallee 12; ⏱ noon-8pm Mon-Sat; U-Bahn Eberswalder Strasse
Not simply flavour of the month – the urban street-wear designed by this five-person co-op and sold in a former ice cream parlour has firmly established itself in the Berlin design world. Browse through racks of cool and comfortable jackets, shirts, pants and sweaters while being showered by electronica. Jewellery, shoes, bags and other accessories help you complete your Berlin look.

FALBALA Map pp322-4   *Vintage Clothing*
☎ 4405 1082; Knaackstrasse 43; ⏱ 1-6pm Mon-Fri, noon-3pm Sat; U-Bahn Senefelderplatz
Josefine Edle von Krepl, who used to edit a GDR women's magazine, has a passion for collecting vintage dresses from 1860 to 1970. Many of them are for sale in her welcoming little store, along with matching accessories. The quality and range are so high, that even film and TV costume designers stop by on occasion.

Top Five Vintage Emporia

- **Colours Kleidermarkt** (p234)
- **Falbala** (p237)
- **Sgt Peppers** (p238)
- **Sterling Gold** (p229)
- **Waahnsinn Berlin** (p229)

Shopping – Prenzlauer Berg

HASIPOP SHOP

Map pp322-4   *Clothing & Accessories*
☎ 4403 3491; Oderberger Strasse 39; ☽ noon-8pm
Mon-Fri, noon-4pm Sat; U-Bahn Eberswalder Strasse
You'll need a flair for the flashy and a sense of
humour to take a fancy to the clothes dreamed
up by the owner/designer team of Esther and
Claudia. Their cartoonish logo – a skull and
bones bunny – graces many of their shirts,
dresses and skirts, often in brazen pink or blues.
Lots of knick-knacks and accessories too.

JUGENDMODE – FUCK FASHION

Map pp322-4   *Clothing & Accessories*
☎ 4471 6932; Schönhauser Allee 72b; ☽ 10am-8pm
Mon-Fri, 10am-4pm Sat; U/S-Bahn Schönhauser Allee
Youthful hipsters flock to this store jam-packed
with the latest fashion must-haves. The last
time we checked, this included lingerie by
Pussy Deluxe, shoes by Onitsuka Tiger and
shirts by Dragonfly. A giant glass case holds
silver jewellery for every body part, eyebrows
to unmentionables, and there's also a huge assortment of bongs and various smoking paraphernalia. Also in **Charlottenburg** (Map pp332-3;
☎ 8871 0491; Joachimstaler Strasse 39/40;
U/S-Bahn Zoologischer Garten).

KOLLWITZ 45 Map pp322-4   *Interior Design*
☎ 4401 0413; Kollwitzstrasse 45; ☽ 11am-8pm
Mon-Fri, 11am-4pm Sat; U-Bahn Senefelder Platz
Katja Wilhelm and Stephan Dass are interior
designers who show off their talents and
good taste in this smallish showroom near
Kollwitzplatz. There's lots of neat stuff for
beautifying your home – cool candlesticks to
chrome ashtrays – plus stylish quality furniture,
lamps and textiles by exclusive makers, including Alias, Casa Milano and Wogg.

LUXUS INTERNATIONAL

Map pp322-4   *Gifts & Accessories*
☎ 4432 4877; Kastanienallee 101; ☽ 11am-8pm
Mon-Fri, 11am-4pm Sat; U-Bahn Eberswalder Strasse
There's no shortage of creative spirits in Berlin
but not many of them can afford to open their
own store. In comes Luxus International, which
rents them a shelf or two to display everything
from necklaces to handbags to ashtrays and
lamps. You never know what you'll find but
you can bet it's a Berlin original.

MONT K Map pp322-4   *Outdoor & Camping*
☎ 448 2590; Kastanienallee 83; ☽ 10am-8pm
Mon-Fri, 10am-4pm Sat; U-Bahn Eberswalder Strasse
If you're into climbing something other than
stairs – say, the Matterhorn or Kilimanjaro –
Mont K will set you up with everything from
backpacks to karabiners to crampons. The
young, in-the-know team is happy to divulge
an arsenal of peak-bagging tips.

SCHÖNHAUSER ALLEE ARKADEN

Map pp322-4   *Shopping Mall*
☎ 4471 1711; Schönhauser Allee 79-80; ☽ 8am-
8.30pm Mon-Fri, 8am-4.30pm Sat; U/S-Bahn Schönhauser Allee
This modern mall has revitalised the traditional
but once moribund shopping district along
Schönhauser Allee. It's nicely designed, with
more than 100 retailers, including the usual
chains, and a post office and supermarket.

SGT PEPPERS

Map pp322-4   *Vintage Clothing*
☎ 448 1121; Kastanienallee 91; ☽ 11am-7pm Mon-
Fri, 11am-4pm Sat; U-Bahn Eberswalder Strasse
The 1960s and '70s are alive and well at this
groovy retro store on fashion-forward Kastanienallee. Besides a colourful assortment of
shirts, dresses, slacks and jackets, there's also
new duds by the store's own label.

UHRANUS Map pp322-4   *Gifts & Accessories*
☎ 7072 8400; Kastanienallee 31; ☽ noon-8pm
Mon-Fri, noon-4pm Sat; U-Bahn Eberswalder Strasse
Diesel watches, Funk sunglasses and Roebuck
bags are among the must-have accessories at
Uhranus. There's also a small assortment of
furniture, vases and lamps, most of them with
a retro bent. There's a second branch, also in
Prenzlauer Berg (Map pp322-4; ☎ 442 4168; Sene-
felderstrasse 33; S-Bahn Prenzlauer Allee).

VOPO RECORDS Map pp322-4   *Music*
☎ 442 8004; Danziger Strasse 31; ☽ noon-8pm
Mon-Fri, 11am-4pm Sat; U-Bahn Eberswalder Strasse
Punk, metal and hardcore fans could get lost
for hours perusing the selection here, although
if you're into electronica, hip-hop and ska you
also stand a good chance of digging up some
choice finds. Prices are moderate and the try-
before-you-buy policy is a welcome asset.

Sleeping

Sleeping

No matter whether you have the budget of a pauper or a prince, with more than 68,000 beds you're likely to find a suitable place to lay your head in Berlin. Sleek new places crop up all the time, especially in sight-filled Mitte and party-intense Friedrichshain. Many older properties, especially in Charlottenburg and Wilmersdorf, have undergone thorough makeovers to improve standards and keep up with the competition.

Rooms or entire floors set aside for nonsmokers are becoming more common and most of the newer or renovated hotels have special rooms for the mobility-impaired.

Accommodation Styles

Berlin offers the full gamut of lodging options. Hotels can be anything from luxurious international chains to comfortable mid-level properties to basic private affairs. Especially popular are the so-called *Kunsthotels* (art hotels), which are designed by artists and/or liberally sprinkled with art.

Also common to Berlin are small family-run establishments called *Hotel-Pensions* or simply *Pensions*. The difference is minimal, although Hotel-Pensions usually have slightly better amenities and a staffed reception desk. What they lack in comfort, these places often make up for in charm, local colour and personal attention. Many occupy one or several floors of historic apartment buildings.

In older hotels and pensions, rooms usually vary considerably in size, décor and amenities. The cheapest rooms have only a washbasin or have been retrofitted with a shower cubicle but no private toilet; only the priciest have en suite bathrooms.

> ### Top Five Sleeps
>
> - **Best Boutique Hotel** – Alexander Plaza Berlin (p241)
> - **Best Hostel** – Circus Hostel Weinbergsweg (p244)
> - **Best Pension** – Hotel-Pension Art Nouveau (p247)
> - **Best Pool & Spa** – Grand Hyatt (p245)
> - **Best Suites** – Hecker's Hotel (p246)

Berlin's backpacker hostel scene has exploded in recent years and competition is fierce. The newest hostels all seem to outdo each other in comfort, décor and services. In addition to dorms, most now offer private rooms, often with en suite facilities, and even small apartments catering for couples and families.

Check-in & Check-out Times

Normal check-in time at hotels is 4pm and you're expected to vacate your room by 11am or noon. Late check-in is possible in most cases but you should notify the reception staff so they don't give your room to someone else. Arranging an arrival time (and sticking to it) is especially important when staying in the smaller, private places, which are not staffed around the clock. Once you've checked in, you'll get a set of house keys to allow you to come and go as you please.

Price Ranges

Berlin's room rates are low compared to many other European capitals. Recommendations in this book cover the entire price spectrum, with an emphasis on mid-range places, where a double room with private bathroom will cost you between €70 and €130. We've also included a few deserving high-end options – usually full-service international hotels or historical charmers – where rates can reach into the financial stratosphere. A selection of Berlin's best budget abodes is listed in a subcategory called 'Cheap Sleeps' at the end of each section.

Prices in this book are generally the official rates supplied by the properties. They do not take into account special promotional rates, which may become available at any given time. Most establishments offer winter discounts (except around the holidays) and business hotels often have weekend specials. It may also pay to check hotel websites (listed where available) for special deals and packages.

Prices are quoted per room and, unless noted, include breakfast, which is usually an all-you-can-eat buffet.

Reservations

It's always a good idea to make reservations but especially so from May to September, around major holidays (p285), during major events such as the Love Parade or the Berlin Marathon (see City Calendar, p9) and when big trade shows are in town.

Most properties accept reservations by phone, fax or, increasingly, the Internet. You can also book a room through **Berlin Tourismus Marketing** (☎ 250 025; also see Tourist Information, p291), the city's official tourist office. There's no charge for this service but agents can only make reservations at member hotels (which includes most listed in this book).

Long-Term Rentals

If you're planning to stay in Berlin for a month or longer, consider renting a room or an apartment through a *Mitwohnzentrale* (flat-sharing agency), which matches people willing to let their digs to those needing a temporary home. Accommodation can be anything from rooms in shared student flats to furnished apartments. Agencies to try include:

Erste Mitwohnzentrale (Map pp332-3; ☎ 324 3031; www.mitwohn.com; Sybelstrasse 53, Charlottenburg; U-Bahn Adenauerplatz)

HomeCompany (Map pp332-3; ☎ 194 45; www.homecompany.de; Joachimstaler Strasse 17, Charlottenburg; U-Bahn Kurfürstendamm)

Wohnagentur am Mehringdamm (Map pp325-7; ☎ 786 2003; www.wohnung-berlin.de; Mehringdamm 66, Kreuzberg; U-Bahn Mehringdamm)

MITTE

Mitte is the obvious choice for those wanting to be within walking distance of Berlin's major sights and burgeoning nightlife. No other district boasts a greater concentration of new or newly renovated hotels. The high-end international chains cluster on or around Gendarmenmarkt, whereas smaller and artsy establishments have opened up north of Unter den Linden, especially in or near the Scheunenviertel.

Top Five Rooms with a View

- **Hotel Adlon Kempinski** (p243)
- **Dorint Am Gendarmenmarkt** (p242)
- **Grand Hotel Esplanade** (p245)
- **Grand Hyatt** (p245)
- **Park Inn Berlin-Alexanderplatz** (p244)

ALEXANDER PLAZA BERLIN

Map pp328-9   *Hotel*

☎ 240 010; www.alexander-plaza.com; Rosenstrasse 1; s €140-195, d €150-205; S-Bahn Hackescher Markt

In this boutique hotel late-19th-century glamour meets new-millennium comforts. It's on a quiet side street close to blockbuster attractions and has a sleek, streamlined look. Rooms feature Vitra chairs, Tolomeo lamps and a fresh, bright colour scheme. The Wintergarten restaurant in the central courtyard serves breakfast and dinner. Gay-friendly.

ANDECHSER HOF Map pp322-4   *Hotel*

☎ 2809 7844; www.andechserhof.de; Ackerstrasse 155; s €55-70, d €70-90; U-Bahn Rosenthaler Platz

The young owners are pouring their hearts and cash into turning this little hotel into an oasis of charm. Rooms are available in three categories of comfort and spread over two buildings linked by a nice courtyard that's great for a summery breakfast. The nicest rooms are at the

241

back and feature sparkling new bathrooms and country-style furniture. Good restaurant, too (see Restaurant Kürbis, p166).

ARTIST RIVERSIDE HOTEL

Map pp328-9   *Hotel*
☎ 284 900; www.great-hotel.de; Friedrichstrasse 106; s €70-100, d €100-160, ste €200-280; U/S-Bahn Friedrichstrasse

Flea market finds, GDR kitsch and movie props decorate the attractive lobby lounge, which, like some of the 40 rooms, has a sweeping view of the Spree. The romantically inclined should book one of the huge and luxurious 'spa suites' – complete with waterbed and whirlpool bath – and order the in-room champagne breakfast (€19). It's within walking distance to theatres, shopping, eating and sightseeing. Gay-friendly.

Lamp in the lobby of Artist Riverside Hotel (above)

ART'OTEL BERLIN MITTE

Map pp328-9   *Hotel*
☎ 240 620; www.artotels.de; Wallstrasse 70-73; s €130-180, d €160-210; U-Bahn Märkisches Museum

Overlooking the Historical Harbour on the southern tip of Museum Island, this refined boutique hotel cleverly fuses an ultramodern wing with a rococo townhouse via a soaring atrium (now the breakfast room and restaurant). It offers serious eye-candy for fans of cutting-edge design and the art of Georg Baselitz, whose original works decorate lobby,

halls and rooms. Gay-friendly and suitable for most mobility-impaired travellers.

BOARDING HOUSE MITTE

Map pp328-9   *Serviced Apartments*
☎ 2838 8488; www.boardinghouse-mitte.com; Mulackstrasse 1; one-/two-room apartments from €120/135; U-Bahn Weinmeisterstrasse, Rosa-Luxemburg-Platz

You won't miss many comforts of home in these breezy apartments where a full kitchen and large closet are as much a part of the inventory as the direct-dial telephone, VCR and CD player. The split-level units have terrific views over the rooftops of the Scheunenviertel. Rates drop for stays of more than four days. Gay-friendly.

DIETRICH-BONHOEFFER-HAUS

Map pp328-9   *Hotel*
☎ 284 670; www.hotel-dbh.de; Ziegelstrasse 30; s €85-115, d €125-150; U/S-Bahn Friedrichstrasse, Oranienburger Tor

Named for the German theologian murdered by the Nazis, this church-affiliated hotel offers a central location, warm atmosphere and large, nicely furnished modern rooms. In December 1989, the first round-table meeting that paved the way for free elections in the GDR, and thus reunification, took place here. Guests from all religions are welcome.

DORINT AM GENDARMENMARKT

Map pp328-9   *Hotel*
☎ 203 750; www.dorint.de; Charlottenstrasse 50-52; s €222-272, d €274-324; U-Bahn Französische Strasse

With less than 100 rooms, this stylish property has the character of a boutique hotel, yet the amenities of a big 'hotel de luxe'. Noteworthy extras include voice mail and a stress-melting spa with Roman steam bath, sauna and colour therapy rooms. For unforgettable views, snag a room on one of the upper floors facing Gendarmenmarkt. This hotel can accommodate most wheelchair-bound guests.

FRAUENHOTEL INTERMEZZO

Map pp328-9   *Hotel-Pension*
☎ 2248 9096; www.hotelintermezzo.de; Gertrud-Kolmar-Strasse 5; s €45, d €70-80, breakfast €5.50; U-Bahn Potsdamer Platz, Mohrenstrasse

Run by a trio of young women, this man-free hotel puts you within a hop, skip and jump of Potsdamer Platz and Unter den Linden. Rooms are largish and have an uncluttered, Scandinavian look but most only have private shower and require sharing a toilet. Triples and quads are also available. Boys under 13 are allowed.

HONIGMOND GARDEN HOTEL

Map pp322-4 *Hotel*

☎ 2844 5577; www.honigmond-berlin.de; Invalidenstrasse 122; s €89-109, d €109-159; U-Bahn Zinnowitzer Strasse

Never mind the busy thoroughfare: this hotel, in a carefully restored 1845 building, is utterly enchanting. The pretty rooms are filled with hand-picked furniture and some have stucco ceilings, four-poster beds and polished wood floors. The most romantic rooms adjoin the rambling garden, a veritable island of tranquillity with a goldfish pond, fountain and old trees.

HOTEL ADLON KEMPINSKI

Map pp328-9 *Hotel*

☎ 2261 1111; www.hotel-adlon.de; Unter den Linden 77; s €300-600, d €350-650, breakfast €24; S-Bahn Unter den Linden

The Adlon is Berlin's most illustrious defender of the grand tradition. With front-row vistas of the Brandenburg Gate and a sumptuous 'restored-historical' ambience, this elegant full-service hotel leaves no desire unfulfilled. Rooms are wired for connectivity and even have 110V for American appliances. High celebrity quotient. This hotel caters well for the needs of the disabled.

Hotel Adlon Kempinski (above)

HOTEL GARNI GENDARM

Map pp328-9 *Hotel Garni*

☎ 206 0660; www.hotel-gendarm-berlin.de; Charlottenstrasse 61; s €99-199, d €119-199; U-Bahn Stadtmitte

This small hotel puts you smack dab in the poshest part of Mitte but its price tag is surprisingly modest. With its sleek white façade and stately entrance, the building perfectly blends with its historical surroundings but is, in fact, brand-new. Blue, white and yellow hues

give the rooms a fresh feel, and the two-room suites with kitchen are great for families.

HOTEL HACKESCHER MARKT

Map pp328-9 *Hotel*

☎ 280 030; www.hackescher-markt.com; Grosse Präsidentenstrasse 8; s €105-155, d €140-205, breakfast €15; S-Bahn Hackescher Markt

The historic-looking façade of this elegant hotel with its doesn't-get-more-central location belies the fact that it's actually only a few years old. This translates into stylish rooms dressed in English-country style paired with hi-tech touches, including heated bathroom floors. Get one facing the charming central courtyard to cut down on the noise level. Gay-friendly.

HOTEL HONIGMOND Map pp322-4 *Hotel*

☎ 284 4550; www.honigmond-berlin.de; Tieckstrasse 12; s €45-70, d €90-145, d shared facilities €65-85, breakfast not included; U-Bahn Oranienburger Tor

This 1st-floor guesthouse comes close to scoring a perfect 10 on our 'charm-meter'. Rabbits frolic in the garden, the downstairs restaurant (p165) is a neighbourhood favourite and the rooms are meticulously restored to their early-20th-century glory. There are even a few surprise luxury touches, such as crisp bed linen designed by Paloma Picasso.

HOTEL KASTANIENHOF

Map pp322-4 *Hotel*

☎ 443 050; www.hotel-kastanienhof-berlin.de; Kastanienallee 65; s €73-128, d €88-113, ste €118-128; U-Bahn Eberswalder Strasse, Rosenthaler Platz

Staff are quick with a smile at this popular place, an excellent jumping-off point for exploring either Mitte or Prenzlauer Berg on foot. Most rooms exude old-time charm and are spacious enough to accommodate a desk and/or small sitting area. Those in need of more elbow space should book one of the good-value suites or apartments.

HOTEL KUBRAT Map pp325-7 *Hotel*

☎ 201 1054; www.hotel-kubrat.de; Leipziger Strasse 21; s €82-112, d €95-128; U-Bahn Stadtmitte

This property may look hopelessly stuck in the disco decade, but the rooms are good-sized and the staff generally winsome. The larger rooms (eg No 405) have an extra sitting area, desks and full baths. Of course it helps if you like white furniture and pink satin bedspreads. Checkpoint Charlie and fancy Friedrichstrasse shopping are nearby.

HOTEL PRINZALBERT Map pp322-4 *Hotel*

☎ 590 029 420; www.prinzalbert-berlin.de; Veteranenstrasse 10; s €60-70, d €80-100; U-Bahn Rosenthaler Platz

It's just a small property above a stylish café-restaurant-bar, but the Prinzalbert has a lot to recommend it. It's close to excellent nightlife and overlooks the sweet little Weinbergpark, nice for an early-morning stroll. The immaculate rooms have modern, minimalist flair accented by platform beds, leather sofas and floor-to-ceiling windows (Nos 2 and 6 have park views). Gay-friendly.

KÜNSTLERHEIM LUISE Map pp328-9 *Hotel*

☎ 284 480; www.kuenstlerheim-luise.de; Luisenstrasse 19; s €82-95, d €121-139, breakfast €7; U/S-Bahn Friedrichstrasse

'A gallery with rooms', some pundits have called this unique place. And indeed, where else can you sleep in a bed built for giants (room No 107), in the company of astronaut suits (No 310) or inside a comic book (No 306)? Each room of this hotel reflects the vision of a different artist, right down to the choice of towels. Art is everywhere, from the lobby to the staircase to the restaurant with its famous wine selection. On a tight budget? Ask about the smaller, bathless rooms on the top floor. Gay-friendly.

MARITIM PROARTE BERLIN

Map pp328-9 *Hotel*

☎ 203 35; www.maritim.de; Friedrichstrasse 151; s €149-265, d €168-278; U/S-Bahn Friedrichstrasse

Thanks to a thorough renovation, progressive management and a stellar art collection, this 1970s hotel has completely shaken its GDR-era vibe and is now solidly rooted in the 21st century. The grand lobby with its cathedral ceiling leads to good-looking rooms with marble baths and designer furniture. About half the rooms are designated nonsmoking. Ask about specials. Gay-friendly.

PARK INN BERLIN-ALEXANDERPLATZ

Map pp328-9 *Hotel*

☎ 238 90; www.parkinn.com; Alexanderplatz; s €90-190, d €90-231; U/S-Bahn Alexanderplatz

After an extreme make-over, the hulking GDR-era Forum Hotel has been reincarnated as the Park Inn and flaunts its rejuvenated look with pride. It's a big, full-service house with up-market international flair and a contemporary aesthetic vaguely inspired by Asian design. Rooms have great views and feature rich

woods, thick carpets and granite washbasins. Leisure facilities include a sauna, solarium and casino. Gay-friendly.

PENSION MITART Map pp328-9 *Pension*

☎ 2839 0430; mitart@t-online.de; Friedrichstrasse 127; s €58-88, d €88-110; U-Bahn Oranienburger Tor

Modern-art fans who are on a budget should try snagging one of the five hip rooms in this combination guesthouse/gallery. It's on the 2nd floor of a typical 19th-century townhouse with high stucco ceilings that have been carefully restored to their former frill. Amenities are basic but you'll be surrounded by art, and the lavish organic breakfast buffet is a special treat indeed. Gay-friendly.

TAUNUS HOTEL Map pp328-9 *Hotel*

☎ 283 5254; www.hotel-taunus.de; Monbijouplatz 1; s €90-130, d €110-150; S-Bahn Hackescher Markt

In a converted textile factory, this small hotel puts you right into the thick of the Scheunenviertel. The 18 rooms are clean, if nothing special, although some enjoy views of the TV Tower or the Berliner Dom and the massage shower heads are an unexpected perk. Light sleepers are likely to find the adjacent tram terminus a drawback.

CHEAP SLEEPS

CIRCUS HOSTEL WEINBERGSWEG

Map pp322-4 *Hostel*

☎ 2839 1433; www.circus-hostel.de; Weinbergsweg 1a; 3-8-bed dm €15-20, s/d €32/48, linen €2, 2-/4-person apartment €75/130 with 2-night minimum, discounts Nov-Feb; U-Bahn Rosenthaler Platz

Beg, borrow and/or steal to secure a bed at this hostel, now in two excellent locations with easy access to sights and nightlife. Clean, cheerfully painted rooms, excellent showers,

Circus Hostel Weinbergsweg (above)

free lockers and competent and helpful staff are just a few factors that put these places at the top of the hostel heap.

The penthouse apartments with private facilities, a full kitchen and a terrace with killer views offer excellent value. The café downstairs serves up inexpensive breakfast, drinks and small meals, and the basement bar has different activities nightly. Good wheelchair access, too.

The **Circus Hostel Rosa-Luxemburg-Strasse** (Map pp328-9; ☎ 2839 1433; Rosa-Luxemburg-Strasse 39; U-Bahn Rosa-Luxemburg-Platz) has the same prices and similar facilities.

HOTEL-PENSION MERKUR

Map pp322-4 *Hotel-Pension*
☎ 282 8297; www.hotel-merkur-berlin.de;
Torstrasse 156; s €40-78, d €60-96; U-Bahn
Rosenthaler Platz
The friendly people running this little pension, in business since GDR days, know they're not offering you the Ritz, but they'll still try to make you feel comfortable. Breakfast, for instance, is not a buffet affair but delivered to your table along with a smile. Rooms are small and only those at the back have full private bathrooms.

MITTE'S BACKPACKER HOSTEL

Map pp322-4 *Hostel*
☎ 2839 0965; www.baxpax.de; Chausseestrasse 102; dm €15-18, s/d €30/46, d with bathroom €56, discounts Nov-Mar, except holidays; U-Bahn Zinnowitzer Strasse
Quite a bit of imagination has gone into the décor of this well-established hostel in a former hat factory. The best rooms are designed by artists and have unique themes. Choices include the Arabic Room, the Underwater Room and the Honeymoon Suite (lots of hearts but why the twin beds?). Other welcome features include a communal kitchen, bike rentals, Internet access, laundry and women-only dorms.

TIERGARTEN

You'll be mixing it up with moguls, movie stars and power mongers when staying in Tiergarten, which offers easy access to the government and embassy quarters. The ritziest accommodation options are on Potsdamer Platz.

HOTEL ALTBERLIN Map pp330-1 *Hotel*
☎ 260 670; info@altberlin.de; Potsdamer Strasse 67;
s €60-110, d €80-145; U-Bahn Kurfürstenstrasse
Unless you're a nostalgia buff, you might find the heavy oak furniture, chintzy lamps and thick carpets a bit overdone. Still, all rooms were fully modernised a few years ago and don't feel cramped. It's not on the trendiest of streets, but Potsdamer Platz and Unter den Linden are only a short U-Bahn ride away and the on-site restaurant specialises in German soul food.

GRAND HOTEL ESPLANADE

Map pp330-1 *Hotel*
☎ 254 780; www.esplanade.de; Lützowufer 15;
s €250-300, d €295-345; U-Bahn Nollendorfplatz
This ultradeluxe, postmodern outpost with its striking mirror-glass façade occupies a scenic stretch of canal close to the Embassy Quarter and Tiergarten Park. Inside, it's all edgy and streamlined with striking furniture, some of it designed by Le Corbusier and Marcel Breuer. Unwind after a day's work or sightseeing with a perfect cocktail at the oh-so-fashionable Harry's New York Bar.

GRAND HYATT Map p334 *Hotel*
☎ 2553 1234; www.berlin.grand.hyatt.com; Marlene-Dietrich-Platz 2; s €190-235, d €220-355; U/S-Bahn Potsdamer Platz
The moment you step into the Hyatt's Zen-inspired lobby, you know it's luxury all the way from here to the breathtaking rooftop pool and spa. In between are 342 sumptuous guest rooms, each fully wired for connectivity and sporting pragmatic and artistic touches, including heated marble bathroom floors and framed Bauhaus photographs. It's all in a building by Spanish maestro Josè Rafael Moneo. Gay-friendly.

MADISON POTSDAMER PLATZ

Map p334 *Suite Hotel*
☎ 590 050 000; www.madison-berlin.de;
Potsdamer Strasse 3; ste €130-490; U/S-Bahn
Potsdamer Platz
How 'suite' it is to be staying at this ultra-deluxe abode in its made-to-impress location right on Potsdamer Platz. Six types of suites, ranging from 40 to 110 sq metres, are available, each outfitted for maximum comfort and ideal working conditions in case you're here to ink that deal. Gay-friendly.

SORAT HOTEL SPREE-BOGEN

Map pp320-1   *Hotel*

☎ 399 200; www.sorat-hotels.de/spree-bogen; Alt-Moabit 99; s €128-230, d €170-260; U-Bahn Turmstrasse
This classy hotel occupies a heritage-listed ex-dairy and fuses postmodern chic with early-20th-century industrial architecture. It's a full-service affair hugging an idyllic stretch of the Spree, with the Federal Ministry of the Interior as an immediate neighbour. Sleek rooms brim with designer furniture and hi-tech gadgetry; the nicest enjoy river views.

CHARLOTTENBURG

It may no longer be the trendiest district but you'll generally find better value for money and more mid-priced options in Charlottenburg than anywhere else in the city. This is where traditional Old Berlin pensions in graceful, late-19th-century townhouses sit side by side with posh designer temples favoured by the international jet set. Excellent public transport puts you within easy reach of everything.

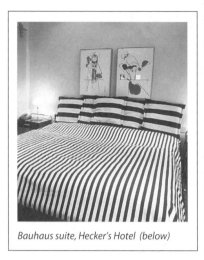

Bauhaus suite, Hecker's Hotel (below)

Top Five Time Warps

- **Hotel Askanischer Hof** (this page)
- **Hotel-Pension Dittberner** (p247)
- **Hotel-Pension Funk** (p248)
- **Hotel-Pension Nürnberger Eck** (p248)
- **Pension Kettler** (p249)

CHARLOTTENBURGER HOF

Map pp332-3   *Hotel*

☎ 329 070; www.charlottenburger-hof.de; Stuttgarter Platz 14; s €50-95, d €60-150, breakfast €6; U-Bahn Wilmersdorfer Strasse
Behind the bland façade awaits a youthful hotel that looks as if designed by Mondrian. The bright blues, reds and yellows throughout should help you get out of bed. Rooms are fairly frill-free, except for the flat-screen PC with free Internet access. A few extra euros buy a whirlpool bath or kitchenette. Gay-friendly.

CONCEPT HOTEL Map pp332-3   *Hotel*

☎ 884 260; www.concept-hotel.com; Grolmanstrasse 41/43; s €70-180, d €100-180; U-Bahn Uhlandstrasse
One hotel, two buildings. Rooms in the main wing are pretty dated, so if style matters book

one in the modern extension, where air-con and data ports are standard features. If you need a break from sightseeing, you could soak up some rays on the rooftop terrace or, in the absence of sunshine, hit the sauna and solarium (€8).

HECKER'S HOTEL Map pp332-3   *Hotel*

☎ 889 00; www.heckers-hotel.de; Grolmanstrasse 35; s €125-210, d €150-220, ste €350-485, breakfast €15; U-Bahn Uhlandstrasse
Close to the Ku'damm, this boutique hotel dazzles with class not glitz and has a guest book that includes artists, actors and *even* people with good taste. The Art Deco–inspired lobby-bar (which doubles as a breakfast room) gives way to spacious, elegant rooms, some with walk-in closets. The deluxe doubles are suitable for families, whereas the three themed suites (cool Bauhaus, cosy Tuscany and exotic Colonial) offer the ultimate in luxury and hi-tech gadgets, including a bathroom TV.

HOTEL ASKANISCHER HOF

Map pp332-3   *Hotel*

☎ 881 8033; www.askanischer-hof.de; Kurfürstendamm 53; s €95-110, d €117-145; U-Bahn Adenauerplatz
Ornately carved doors open up to good-sized rooms decked out in nostalgic 1920s style. It's a world of eclectic antique furniture, frilly window drapes, chandeliers and oriental carpets coupled with the usual range of modern comforts. Framed photographs of old-time German actors add a touch of glam.

Some rooms are set aside for nonsmokers. Gay-friendly.

HOTEL BLEIBTREU BERLIN

Map pp332-3 *Hotel*

☎ 884 740; www.bleibtreu.com; Bleibtreustrasse 31; s €157-237, d €182-262; U-Bahn Uhlandstrasse

In a pretty side street off Ku'damm, the Bleibtreu flaunts an edgy, urban feel tempered by the warmth of Italian design and natural materials. Rooms are small but stylish and they feature a fancy lighting system that can be controlled by remote. Each floor has a different flair and colour scheme. A flower shop, deli and restaurant are also onsite.

HOTEL BOGOTA Map pp332-3 *Hotel*

☎ 881 5001; www.hotelbogota.de; Schlüterstrasse 45; s/d €72/98, s/d shared facilities €44/69; U-Bahn Uhlandstrasse

Step back in time at this delightful hotel, which offers nostalgia with a smile at no-nonsense prices. Rooms ramble over four floors built around a light court usually filled with spherical music. Size and amenities vary greatly, so inspect before deciding. The communal areas are great for bumping into fellow travellers. Also check out the 4th-floor hall, the one-time studio of YVA, a famous 1930s fashion photographer and Helmut Newton mentor. Children stay free in their parents' room. Gay-friendly.

HOTEL CALIFORNIA GARNI

Map pp332-3 *Hotel*

☎ 880 120; www.hotel-california.de; Kurfürstendamm 35; s €99-170, d €119-180; U-Bahn Uhlandstrasse

Neither heaven nor hell (to borrow a line from the Eagles song), this private hotel tries for a cheerful west-coast feel with palm trees, movie-theme décor and a rainbow of colours. Shopaholics will get a buzz from browsing the many nearby boutiques and department stores, and great restaurants and theatres are just steps away as well. Gay-friendly.

HOTEL GATES Map pp332-3 *Hotel*

☎ 311 060; www.hotel-gates.com; Knesebeckstrasse 8-9; s €95-210, d €120-250, breakfast €10; U-Bahn Ernst-Reuter-Platz

If you're a serious surfer dude (of the Internet, that is), this is the place for you. Rates include unlimited, round-the-clock high-speed access on your in-room flat-screen PC. Room sizes vary but all are comfortable, if a tad functional. In its earlier incarnation as the

Hotel Windsor, stars including Marlon Brando and Claudia Cardinale used to shack up here. Gay-friendly.

HOTEL MEINEKE ARTE

Map pp332-3 *Hotel*

☎ 889 2120; www.hotel-meineke-berlin.de; Meinekestrasse 10; s/d €92/140; U-Bahn Kurfürstendamm, Uhlandstrasse

This 60-room hotel earns its 'arte' moniker with the works of Austrian artist Günter Edlinger, whose abstract oils and pastoral florals add splashes of colour to the rooms and hallways. Amenities include satellite TV, direct-dial phones with data ports and full bathrooms. Smoking is a no-no on the upper two floors.

HOTEL-PENSION ART NOUVEAU

Map pp332-3 *Hotel-Pension*

☎ 327 7440; www.hotelartnouveau.de; Leibnizstrasse 59; s/d/ste €95/110/160; U-Bahn Adenauerplatz

A rickety birdcage lift drops you off on the 4th floor, leading to one of Berlin's best pensions, offering a unique blend of youthful flair and tradition. The affable owners, both fluent in English, have made creative use of colour and furnished each room (all nonsmoking) with hand-picked antiques and heavenly beds. Bonuses: the sunny breakfast room and honour bar.

HOTEL-PENSION AUGUSTA

Map pp332-3 *Hotel-Pension*

☎ 883 5028; www.hotel-augusta.de; Fasanenstrasse 22; s €65-95, d €95-175; U-Bahn Uhlandstrasse

Right on ritzy Fasanenstrasse, the Augusta is a welcoming cocktail of class and comfort. Rooms here have undergone a rigorous face-lift and now sparkle in cheerful colours and décor ranging from romantic to modern. Some have balconies or cosy alcoves and one floor is reserved for nonsmokers. Ask about the brand-new suites.

HOTEL-PENSION DITTBERNER

Map pp332-3 *Hotel-Pension*

☎ 884 6950; www.hotel-dittberner.de; Wielandstrasse 26; s €67-87, d €93-118; U-Bahn Adenauerplatz

It's hard not to be charmed by this elegant 3rd-floor pension and its friendly owner, Frau Lange, who has presided over her realm since 1958. The soaring ceilings, plush rugs and arm-loads of original artwork ooze genuine Old Berlin flair. Even getting there aboard a creaky oak-and-brass lift is a 'trip' indeed.

HOTEL-PENSION FISCHER

Map pp332-3   *Hotel-Pension*
☎ 2191 5566; www.hotel-pension-fischer.de;
Nürnberger Strasse 24a; s €60-90, d €80-125; U-Bahn
Augsburger Strasse

The owners have seriously slicked up this place, bringing the décor and furniture into the new millennium. Seven of the 10 rooms now have their own shower and toilet. Those with shared facilities cost about €20 to €30 less.

HOTEL-PENSION FUNK

Map pp332-3   *Hotel-Pension*
☎ 882 7193; www.hotel-pensionfunk.de;
Fasanenstrasse 69; s €34-82, d €52-112; U-Bahn
Uhlandstrasse, Kurfürstendamm

Stucco ceilings, Art Nouveau windows, old-fashioned wallpaper and 1920s furniture are among the authentic retro touches of this romantic pension in the former apartment of Danish silent-movie star Asta Nielsen (1881–1972). The cheaper rooms share facilities. This place offers great value but it's not exactly a well-kept secret, so book early.

HOTEL-PENSION IMPERATOR

Map pp332-3   *Hotel-Pension*
☎ 881 4181; Meinekestrasse 5; s €40-70, d €60-105;
U-Bahn Kurfürstendamm

This quirky 2nd-floor pension, steps from the Ku'damm, shares a building with the Haitian

Pension Kettler (opposite)

Embassy and has an exceptionally nice lobby resplendent with gilded stucco and marble. The 11 large rooms blend antiques with modern furniture and are said to be popular with musicians, actors and other artistic types. Cheaper rooms share facilities.

HOTEL-PENSION NÜRNBERGER ECK

Map pp332-3   *Hotel-Pension*
☎ 235 1780; www.nuernberger-eck.de; Nürnberger
Strasse 24a; s/d €60/92, s/d shared bathroom €45/70;
U-Bahn Augsburger Strasse

For 1920s nostalgia, head along to this pint-sized, 1st-floor pension, which has welcomed guests since that roaring era of jazz and cabaret. Each of the eight rooms gracefully pairs modern facilities with period furniture and accessories. Original art, some left by former guests, decorates the public areas. Three rooms share bathrooms.

CHEAP SLEEPS
A&O HOSTEL AM ZOO

Map pp332-3   *Hostel*
☎ 297 7810, toll-free 0800-222 5722; www.aohostel
.com; Joachimstaler Strasse 1-3; dm with bathroom
€20-24, dm shared bathroom €15-17, breakfast €4, s/d
with bathroom & breakfast €70/72 , discounts Nov-Feb;
U/S-Bahn Zoologischer Garten

Right opposite Zoo station, this chipper, newish hostel is a convivial, international place with a big communal room and a fun bar right next to the train tracks for serious partying. Dorms and rooms are bright with neat laminate flooring, metal-frame beds and large lockable cabinets. Also in **Friedrichshain** (Map pp318-19; ☎ 2977 8114; Boxhagener Strasse 73; S-Bahn Ostkreuz) and **southern Mitte** (Map pp325-7; ☎ 2977 8115; Köpenicker Strasse 127-129; S-Bahn Ostbahnhof).

HERBERGE GROSSE Map pp330-1   *Pension*
☎ 324 8138; www.herbergegrosse.de; Kantstrasse
71, 4th fl; s €50-75, d €60-83, €12 surcharge for
one-night stays, breakfast €8; U-Bahn Wilmersdorfer
Strasse

With three rooms, this place is anything but *gross* (big) but its range of amenities certainly rivals large hotels: cable TV, VCR, direct-dial telephones, free PC and Internet use, bathrobes – and that's just for starters. Communal kitchen, guest laundry, bicycle rentals, free pick-ups from airports and train stations, art exhibits…you get the picture. Gay-friendly.

HOTEL-PENSION CASTELL

Map pp332-3 *Hotel-Pension*

☎ 882 7181; www.hotel-castell.de; Wielandstrasse 24; s €50-80, d €60-95; U-Bahn Adenauer Platz

Most rooms here are plain and the furniture is getting a bit long in the tooth, but all are clean and have their own shower and toilet. If you're after ambience, ask for the one with the beautiful Art Nouveau window. It's in a pretty residential street, close to the Ku'damm and the restaurants on Pariser Strasse.

HOTEL-PENSION KORFU II

Map pp332-3 *Hotel-Pension*

☎ 212 4790; www.hp-korfu.de; Rankestrasse 35; s €53-79, d €67-99, s/d shared bathrooms €33/47, breakfast €6; U-Bahn Kurfürstendamm

Opposite the Gedächtniskirche, this is a great bargain base for exploring Berlin. The pleasantly bright, carpeted rooms sport high ceilings, Scandinavian-style furniture and more amenities than one would expect for the price, including cable TV, telephone, hairdryer and in-room safe. There are also a few simpler rooms with shared bathrooms. Free Internet guest terminal.

HOTEL-PENSION MAJESTY

Map pp332-3 *Hotel-Pension*

☎ 323 2061; Mommsenstrasse 55; s/d €40/50, with shower €55/85; S-Bahn Savignyplatz

With a name like this and the swank residential address, you might expect a place with royal flourish. Well, not quite… Wallet-watching travellers, though, might still like the largish rooms, some with balcony, and the congenial proprietor, Michael Herzog. Rooms have phones and some have been retrofitted with showers.

PENSION KETTLER Map pp332-3 *Pension*

☎ 883 4949; Bleibtreustrasse 19; s €50-75, d €60-90; U-Bahn Uhlandstrasse

If you want quirk and true Berlin character, you'll find heaps of it at this little B&B. Its owner, Isolde Josipovici, has created a nostalgic retreat that will time warp you back about 100 years. Our favourite room oozes sexy boudoir charm with its grand sleigh bed and pink patterned wallpaper. Unique knick-knacks and original art abound throughout. The place's most memorable 'feature', though, is Frau Josipovici herself. A former model, she now works tirelessly to save Berlin's fountains and is well known as the city's *Brunnenfee* (Fountain Fairy).

WILMERSDORF

Wilmersdorf, just south of Charlottenburg, may be light on sights and have a rather sedate flair, but it's quiet, pretty and still reasonably close to where you truly want to be. For some odd reason, it's also home to the coolest of Berlin's proliferating art hotels, the Propeller Island City Lodge.

Top Five Artistic Havens

- Artist Riverside Hotel (p242)
- Art'otel Berlin Mitte (p242)
- Künstlerheim Luise (p244)
- Pension mitArt (p244)
- Propeller Island City Lodge (p250)

ALSTERHOF BERLIN Map pp332-3 *Hotel*

☎ 212 420; www.alsterhof.com; Augsburger Strasse 5; s €85-230, d €100-250; U-Bahn Augsburger Strasse, Wittenbergplatz

This modern hotel is well equipped for business travellers, families and couples on a quick city getaway. You'll find all the usual big-hotel trappings but the state-of-the-art 'wellness centre' with its top-notch work-out equipment, divine sauna (with light and sound installation) and aromatic steam bath deserves a special mention (€13 per day). Gay-friendly.

ART'OTEL CITY CENTER WEST

Map pp332-3 *Hotel*

☎ 887 7770; www.artotels.de; Lietzenburger Strasse 85; s €130-210, d €160-240; U-Bahn Adenauerplatz, Uhlandstrasse

This sleek and chic haven pays homage to the father of pop art, Andy Warhol. More than 200 originals turn the lobby, lounge and rooms into a veritable art gallery. The bar is great for a nightcap before retreating to the comforts of the cutting-edge rooms with white leather beds, designer lamps and such bold colour accents as a purple chair.

BRANDENBURGER HOF

Map pp332-3 *Hotel*

☎ 214 050; www.brandenburger-hof.com; Eislebener Strasse 14; s €165-285, d €240-320; U-Bahn Augsburger Strasse

Opposites attract – the timeworn adage certainly rings true in this ritzy abode. In an amazing feat of architectural alchemy, it smoothly blends a palatial 19th-century townhouse with the sexy edginess of 1920s New Objectivity. From the sleek rooms and sumptuous day spa to the Zen garden and Michelin-starred restaurant, this place is perfectly orchestrated indeed. Gay-friendly.

FRAUENHOTEL ARTEMISIA

Map pp332-3   *Hotel*

☎ 873 8905; www.frauenhotel-berlin.de; Branden-burgische Strasse 18; s €59-79, d €82-115; U-Bahn Konstanzer Strasse

Named for a 16th-century Italian woman artist, this stylish and quiet women-only retreat has individually decorated rooms with modern furniture, original art and bold, sunny fabrics. Two rooms share a bathroom; the others have their own. The rooftop terrace is great for breakfast, sunbathing and meeting fellow guests, as is the bar and art gallery. Gay-friendly.

HOTEL-PENSION WITTELSBACH

Map pp332-3   *Hotel-Pension*

☎ 864 9840; www.hotel-pension-wittelsbach.de; Wittelsbacherstrasse 22; s €66-92, d €92-128, ste €140-170, family rooms €80-130; U-Bahn Konstanzer Strasse

This hotel has a special floor designed with kids in mind. Rooms have their own themed playground (western fort, medieval castle, Snow White) and tots get to sleep in Porsche or Barbie beds. Some of it is a bit hokey but kids love it. Babysitters are available for €8 per hour. Quieter accommodation is found on the other floors.

PROPELLER ISLAND CITY LODGE

Map pp332-3   *Guesthouse*

☎ 891 9016 (8am-noon), 0163-256 5909 (noon-8pm); www.propeller-island.de; Albrecht-Achilles-Strasse 58; s/d €65-110, breakfast €7; U-Bahn Adenauerplatz

Hands down Berlin's most eccentric hotel, this is the brainchild of artist/musician Lars Stroschen, who designed and handcrafted every piece of furniture and accessory in the 30 rooms. The result is a series of unique, warped and wicked environments perfect for those with imagination and a sense of adventure. How about a night in the 'Flying Bed' room with slanted walls and a bed seemingly hovering above the floor? Or the one called 'Gallery' with a rotating round bed and upstairs viewing platform? Don't expect the usual amenities: this is no conventional hotel, it's a work of art. Gay-friendly.

Propeller Island City Lodge (this page)

CHEAP SLEEPS
HOTEL-PENSION MÜNCHEN

Map pp330-1   *Hotel-Pension*

☎ 857 9120; www.hotel-pension-muenchen-in-berlin.de; Güntzelstrasse 62; s €40-70, d €70-80, apt €75-105; U-Bahn Güntzelstrasse

This small and quiet pension is owned by artist Renate Prasse, whose drawings, paintings and sculptures add aesthetic touches to the entrance area and rooms. Furnishings are rather ordinary but the good range of modern amenities, including private bathrooms, cable TV and telephone, and the gracious hostess make this place a good bet.

SCHÖNEBERG

Lodging options are thin on the ground in this delightful but overwhelmingly residential area. It's a shame, really, because it's close to fabulous nightlife and shopping and extremely well served by public transport.

HOTEL AIR IN BERLIN Map pp332-3   *Hotel*

☎ 212 9920; www.hotelairinberlin.de; Ansbacher Strasse 6; s €70-125, d €85-150; U-Bahn Wittenbergplatz

You'd never know it from the frilly façade or grand entrance, but this hotel means 'business'. Rooms, although comfortable and well-equipped, are decked out in the kind of generic décor unlikely to offend anyone.

A little more imagination has gone into the family apartments, which can accommodate up to eight. Gay-friendly.

HOTEL ARTIM Map pp330-1 *Hotel*
☎ 210 0250; www.hotel-artim.de; Fuggerstrasse 20; s/d/ste €75/95/149; U-Bahn Wittenbergplatz
Conveniently located between Charlottenburg shopping and Schöneberg nightlife, the new-ish Artim has large, appealing rooms, most sheathed in a subdued primary colour scheme. It's popular with tour groups and families who find much to like about the good value, two-room suites sleeping up to five people. Gay-friendly and decent wheelchair access.

HOTEL-PENSION DELTA
Map pp330-1 *Hotel-Pension*
☎ 7809 6480; www.cca-hotels.de; Belziger Strasse 1; s €65-89, d €89-109; U-Bahn Kleistpark
This fine-looking property in an Art Nouveau building may not be in the trendiest part of town, but it's near plenty of interesting eateries and shops, not to mention the U-Bahn for quick getaways. Rooms have high ceilings, comfy beds and small desks. The breakfast buffet is so generous it may well tide you over to dinner.

CHEAP SLEEPS
ENJOY BED & BREAKFAST
Map pp330-1 *B&B*
☎ 2362 3610; www.ebab.de; Bülowstrasse 106; ⓧ reservations 4.30-9.30pm; s €20-30, d €35-50; U-Bahn Nollendorfplatz
This private room-referral service caters specifically for gays and lesbians. It is affiliated with the central information centre Mann-O-Meter. The website has all the details.

KREUZBERG
There's much to recommend Kreuzberg as a base of operation, especially the western half around Viktoriapark. For some reason, though, it has been almost completely bypassed by Berlin's growing new-hotel scene and only offers a few, if reliable, standbys.

HOTEL AM ANHALTER BAHNHOF
Map pp325-7 *Hotel*
☎ 251 0342; www.hotel-anhalter-bahnhof.de; Stresemannstrasse 36; s €50-75, d €75-105, tr €90-125, q €104-140; S-Bahn Anhalter Bahnhof

This older place is still a good destination thanks to its laid-back, multilingual staff and location close to Potsdamer Platz and the Jewish Museum. Rooms offer a variety of comfort levels; pricier ones with private bathrooms face away from the busy street. An innovative computerised system allows you to check in 24/7.

HOTEL RIEHMERS HOFGARTEN
Map pp325-7 *Hotel*
☎ 7809 8800; www.riehmers-hofgarten.de; Yorckstrasse 83; s €98-108, d €123-138, breakfast €14; U-Bahn Mehringdamm
In the nicest section of Kreuzberg, near Viktoriapark, this intimate 20-room hotel is inside a beautifully restored 1891 building complex with a lush inner courtyard certain to delight romantics. Custom-made classical-modern furniture graces the rooms and original contemporary art sets colour accents throughout. The ETA Hoffmann restaurant serves fine cuisine in an elegant setting.

CHEAP SLEEPS
GASTHAUS DIETRICH HERZ
Map pp325-7 *Pension*
☎ 691 7043; Marheinekeplatz 15; s €28-53, d €45-75; U-Bahn Gneisenaustrasse
It's nothing fancy but this place has, how shall we say…character. It's literally above the historic Marheineke market hall (bring ear plugs, the action starts around 7am) and schnitzel fumes may waft through your window from the affiliated downstairs restaurant (p186). This is one of the few places left with humble but authentic Old Berlin flair.

MEININGER CITY HOSTELS
Map pp325-7 *Hostel*
☎ 6663 6100; www.meininger12.com; Hallesches Ufer 30, Tempelhofer Ufer 10; dm €13.50, s/d/tr/q €49/66/78/ 100; U-Bahn Möckernbrücke
This small, well-run chain is part of the new generation of Berlin hostels offering modern rooms and a comfort level that rivals small hotels. All rooms have private shower and toilet and there's lots of free stuff, including an all-you-can-eat breakfast buffet, parking, linen, towels and lockers.

The Hallesches Ufer branch has a fun bar and rooftop terrace, great for kicking back and making new friends. The one at Tempelhofer Ufer, in a nearby historic building, is smaller and quieter. The original house in **Schöneberg**

(☎ 6663 6100; Meininger Strasse 10; U-Bahn Rathaus Schöneberg) is a bit cheaper, less central and caters primarily for youth groups.

FRIEDRICHSHAIN

Friedrichshain's gritty GDR aesthetic sets it apart from heavily gentrified Mitte and Prenzlauer Berg and, given its vibrant bar and café scene, makes for a fun and reasonably priced Berlin base. Nearly all hotels and hostels in this neighbourhood are newcomers.

EAST-SIDE HOTEL Map pp325-7 *Hotel*
☎ 293 833; www.eastsidehotel.de; Mühlenstrasse 6; s €60-100, d €70-110; U/S-Bahn Warschauer Strasse
The East-Side has ultramodern rooms that are a meditation in understatement. Singles all face the Spree River and East Side Gallery, the longest remaining stretch of the Wall, while the extra-big deluxe rooms feature generous marble bathrooms and a couch. Video and PC rentals are available.

GOLD HOTEL AM WISMARPLATZ
Map pp325-7 *Hotel*
☎ 293 3410; www.gold-hotel-berlin.de; Weserstrasse 24; s €53-68, d €73-103; U-Bahn Samariterstrasse
The flowery bedspreads and patterned furniture are in no danger of making it into the glossy style magazines, but the newly renovated rooms here are still quite comfortable. Quality mattresses and soundproof windows are standard features and the Friedrichshain party scene is a whisker away.

HOTEL 26 Map pp325-7 *Hotel*
☎ 297 7780; www.hotel26.de; Grünberger Strasse 26; s €59-69, d €69-79; U-Bahn Warschauer Strasse, Frankfurter Tor
If you've outgrown hostels but don't feel like dropping bundles of cash for shelter, this newish hotel may suit your expectations. It has largish, bright rooms with a modern look, private bathrooms and good amenities, including a desk and data ports in case you brought your laptop. The terraced garden café makes for a nice hang-out. Gay-friendly.

NH BERLIN-ALEXANDERPLATZ
Map pp322-4 *Hotel*
☎ 422 6130; nhberlinalexanderplatz@nh-hotels.com; Landsberger Allee 26-32; s €98-173, d €126-201; U/S-Bahn to Alexanderplatz, then tram 5, 6

Despite the name this large, full-service hotel is actually opposite the Volkspark Friedrichshain, a nice place for a wake-up jog. Rooms are fine-looking and comfortable, if a touch generic with their easy-on-the-eyes natural colour palette. Bonus facilities include a fitness centre with sauna and steam room.

UPSTALSBOOM HOTEL FRIEDRICHSHAIN Map pp325-7 *Hotel*
☎ 293 750; www.upstalsboom-berlin.de; Gubener Strasse 42; s €85-145, d €100-160; U/S-Bahn Warschauer Strasse
If this modern and well-kept hotel feels like a breath of fresh air, it may be because it's the Berlin branch of a small chain of German seaside resorts. Rooms are attractively furnished and come in four categories, the largest with kitchenette. Fitness fans can rent bicycles or hit the treadmill before retreating to the sparkling spa (all free).

CHEAP SLEEPS
HOTEL FRIEDRICHSHAIN
Map pp325-7 *Hotel/Hostel*
☎ 9700 2030; www.boardinghouse-berlin.com; Warschauer Strasse 57; s €40-70, d €80-95; ☺ reception staffed 9am-6pm; U/S-Bahn Warschauer Strasse
Friendliness, cleanliness and a quiet courtyard location are among the assets of this newish place. It's ideal for self-caterers who can fry an egg or whip up an entire gourmet meal in the modern kitchens (one on each floor). Rooms have twin beds, a desk and TV, but only the triples have en suite bathrooms. Excellent disabled access and gay-friendly.

ODYSSEE GLOBETROTTER HOSTEL
Map pp325-7 *Hostel*
☎ 2900 0081; www.globetrotterhostel.de; Grünberger Strasse 23; dm €13-19; s/d shared bathroom €35/45, d with shower €52, breakfast €3; U/S-Bahn Warschauer Strasse
This energetic hostel puts the 'fun' in funky and is a perfect base for those keen on making an in-depth study of Friedrichshain's nightlife. Rooms are artily decorated, clean and have lockers. Other perks include free linen, late checkout and a happening bar-lounge (yes, the parties are legendary). New: a big dorm with cooking facilities.

PEGASUS HOSTEL Map pp322-4 *Hostel*

☎ 297 7360; www.pegasushostel.de; Strasse der Pariser Kommune 35; dm €13-19 plus €2.50 for linen, s/d shared bathroom €30/46, d with bathroom €60, discounts Nov-Mar; U-Bahn Weberwiese

In a former girls' school, this large hostel has cheerful rooms and a beautiful backyard that's great for chilling and socialising, as are the well-equipped communal kitchen and on-site restaurant. The reception is open 24/7 and staff can help with everything from U-Bahn tickets to phonecards.

PRENZLAUER BERG

Prenzlauer Berg is one of Berlin's prettiest neighbourhoods, still central, yet quieter than Mitte, with handsome architecture and an excellent after-dark scene. It's hard to fathom why more hoteliers haven't yet capitalised on its considerable charms.

ACKSEL HAUS

Map pp322-4 *Serviced Apartments*

☎ 4433 7633; www.ackselhaus.de; Belforter Strasse 21; s €70-100, d €55-105; U-Bahn Senefelderplatz

This charismatic place on a pretty residential street has 10 comfortable rooms and apartments (most sleeping two, some up to four, with full kitchen). Each has unique décor in such subdued themes as 'exotic safari', 'frilly Tuscany' (with four-poster bed), or 'cool blue'. The nicest ones overlook the well-tended garden with cosy nooks for catching a nap on a lazy summer afternoon.

PENSION AMSTERDAM

Map pp322-4 *Pension*

☎ 448 0792; www.pension-amsterdam.de; Gleimstrasse 24; 1-/2-/3-/4-person occupancy €33.50/67/77/85, discounts for stays of more than three days; ☺ reception staffed after 3.30pm, 9am Sun; U-Bahn Schönhauser Allee

There's plenty to like about this contemporary guesthouse: the location on a lively street with good eating and partying; the big apartments with snazzy leather sofas, full kitchen and dining table perfect for entertaining; the rooms, some with romantic four-poster beds, and all with kitchenettes; the buzzy downstairs café with its eclectic, omnisexual clientele. Oh yes, free Internet, too.

EASTSIDE GAYLLERY

Map pp322-4 *Guesthouse*

☎ 4373 5484; www.eastside-gayllery.de; Schönhauser Allee 41; r per person from €36; ☺ check-in noon-8pm Mon-Sat or by arrangement; U-Bahn Eberswalder Strasse

This guesthouse for gays and lesbians consists of just a few functional rooms behind a gay shop. The scene's steps away and host Ulli will quickly fill you in on the local hang-outs. Ask for discounts Monday to Thursday.

HOTEL GREIFSWALD Map pp322-4 *Hotel*

☎ 443 5283; www.hotel-greifswald.de; Greifswalder Strasse 211; s €65-78, d €78-88; bus 100, tram 2, 3, 4

This small hotel in an historic building is tailor-made for those wanting to take full advantage of Berlin's lusty after-dark scene. There's a gentle and unhurried ambience about the place, where breakfast is available until a hangover-friendly 1pm. In the summer, you can even sit outside and sample the backyard charm that is unique to Berlin. Gay-friendly.

MYER'S HOTEL Map pp322-4 *Hotel*

☎ 440 140; www.myershotel.de; Metzer Strasse 26; s €80-135, d €100-165; U-Bahn Senefelder Platz

In a stately 19th-century building on a quiet street, yet close to Käthe-Kollwitzplatz, Myer's has classically furnished rooms sheathed in soothing colours and rich woods. Size and amenities vary but all have private bathroom, TV and telephone. The lobby bar, tearoom with bold red walls, garden and rooftop terrace are great for unwinding between sightseeing forays. Gay-friendly.

CHEAP SLEEPS

GENERATOR BERLIN Map pp322-4 *Hostel*

☎ 417 2400; www.the-generator.co.uk; Storkower Strasse 160; dm €12-16.50, s/tw/tr/q per person with bathroom €40/27/24/21, without €35/23/19/18; S-Bahn Landsberger Allee

This slick 854-bed hostel scores big with backpackers. It has clean, safe and spacious rooms with supercomfortable mattresses, free breakfast, in-room lockers, linen and towel, and a youthful, party atmosphere. The liberal use of psychedelic blue neon adds a cool techno touch, and the hip circular bar is great for striking up friendships. Its 'deep-east' location, though, means you'll be riding the train a lot.

LETTE 'M SLEEP Map pp322-4   *Hostel*

☎ 4473 3623, 0800-HOSTELS; www.backpackers.de; Lettestrasse 7; dm €15-19, d with shared bathroom €48, apt €66, discounts Oct–mid-May; U-Bahn Eberswalder Strasse

This is a hostel as hostels used to be: low-key, low-tech, welcoming, with a communal kitchen and cosy common room for meeting fellow backpackers. The location on trendy Helmholtzplatz puts you right in the middle of hip cafés and bars. Dorms sleep three to six and have sinks, lockers and a table. Some twin rooms come with refrigerator and stove. Free Internet access, and a beer garden in summer.

HOTEL TRANSIT LOFT

Map pp322-4   *Hotel & Hostel*

☎ 789 0470; www.transit-loft.de; Greifswalder Strasse 219, enter on Immanuelkirchstrasse; dm €19, s/d €59/69; bus 100, tram 2, 3, 4

Behind the yellow brick façade of an old factory awaits this thoroughly modern hybrid hostel/hotel. Natural light floods the rooms, which are functionally furnished and have private baths and high ceilings. This place has more 'adult' feel than some of the other hostels. The accommodation rates include a big breakfast buffet served until noon. Gay-friendly.

Excursions

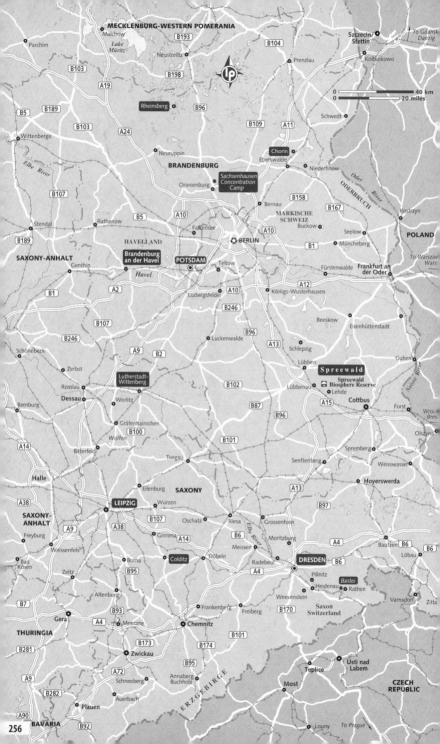

Excursions

Almost everything worth seeing around Berlin is in the surrounding state of Brandenburg, which boasts a wide range of undervisited attractions. Efficient rail links also mean that cities further afield, such as Lutherstadt-Wittenberg, Dresden and Leipzig, are within easy reach and make for good day or overnight trips.

PARKS & PALACES

Few places in Germany can compete with the pomp and splendour of historic **Potsdam** (p258), a superbly civilised break from the bustle of cutting-edge Berlin. Easily reached with local transport, it's definitely the number-one day trip for most visitors. Fans of the famous Schloss Sanssouci (Sanssouci Palace) can also head north to the smaller but equally charming Schloss at **Rheinsberg** (p265), an early example of its kind.

ARCHITECTURE

Despite the notoriously heavy bombing at the end of WWII, the centre of **Dresden** (p267) is still a treasure-trove of architectural gems, including the instantly recognisable Semperoper. Just walking around the Altstadt (old town) for a day should be enough to satisfy most building buffs. Further classical treats can be found in **Leipzig** (p272).

PILGRIMAGES

As the name suggests, **Lutherstadt-Wittenberg** (p266) is a magnet for devotees of the Great Reformer, Martin Luther. Anyone with an interest in religion or this period of history should find plenty to keep them busy here.

NIGHTLIFE

Why confine yourself to the Berlin scene? Wining and dining in **Leipzig** (p275) makes for equally lively nights, and few visitors fail to pop into the legendary Auerbachs Keller, Goethe's old local. For bar density, the Neustadt area of **Dresden** (p271) can also more than hold its own. Hook up with the gregarious student populations of either city and you'll quickly find a day trip turning into an all-nighter.

WETLANDS

One thing Brandenburg isn't short of is water, and **Spreewald** (p264) is a great place to get out onto the many miles of canals, rivers and marshes that make up much of the landscape around Berlin. Punt trips from the picturesque little towns of Lübben and Lübbenau are a popular highlight in summer. Elsewhere, **Brandenburg an der Havel** (p262), once a major river trade town and still a red-brick delight, is set on three islands and has plenty to offer visitors.

ACOUSTICS

There's no shortage of classical-music venues in Berlin, but the summer concerts at the ancient red-brick monastery in **Chorin** (p266) are known throughout Brandenburg for their exceptional atmosphere and sound quality. Well worth an evening out.

BRANDENBURG
POTSDAM

Potsdam, on the Havel River just beyond the southwestern tip of Greater Berlin, is the capital of Brandenburg state. In the 17th century, Elector Friedrich Wilhelm of Brandenburg made it his second residence. With the creation of the Kingdom of Prussia, Potsdam became a royal seat and garrison town. In the mid-18th century Friedrich II (Frederick the Great) built many of the marvellous palaces to which visitors flock today. In April 1945, Royal Air Force (RAF) bombers devastated the historic centre of Potsdam, including the City Palace on Am Alten Markt (Am Alten Square), but fortunately most other palaces escaped undamaged.

Potsdam's focal point is **Sanssouci Park**, a sprawling beast with crisscrossing trails strewn throughout; take along the free map provided by the tourist office or you'll find yourself up the wrong path at almost every turn. The various palaces are spaced fairly far apart – it's about 15km to complete the entire circuit. Sadly, cycling in the park is strictly *verboten* (forbidden).

Begin your park tour with Georg Wenzeslaus von Knobelsdorff's **Schloss Sanssouci** (1747), the celebrated rococo palace with glorious interiors. Only 2000 visitors a day are allowed entry (a rule laid down by Unesco), so tickets are usually sold out by 2.30pm, even in the quiet seasons – arrive early and avoid weekends and holidays. Tours run by the tourist office guarantee entry.

Our favourite rooms include the frilly rococo **Konzertsaal** (Concert Hall) and the bed chambers of the **Damenflügel** (Ladies' Wing), including a 'Voltaire slept here' chamber (don't ask what he was doing in the Ladies' Wing). Just opposite the palace is the **Historische Mühle** (Historical Windmill), which was designed to give the palace grounds a rustic appeal.

The palace is flanked by the twin **Neue Kammern** (New Chambers), which served as a guesthouse and orangery. They include the large **Ovidsaal**, with its gilded reliefs and green-and-white marble floor, and Meissen porcelain figurines in the last room to the west. Nearby, the **Bildergalerie** (Picture Gallery) was completed in 1764 as Germany's first purpose-built art museum. It contains a rich collection of 17th-century paintings by Rubens, Van Dyck, Caravaggio and others.

The Renaissance-style **Orangerie** (Orangery Palace), built in 1864 as a guesthouse for foreign royalty, is the largest of the Sanssouci palaces but hardly the most interesting. The six sumptuous rooms on display include the **Raphaelsaal**, featuring 19th-century copies of Italian Renaissance painter Raphael's work, and a **tower** that can be climbed for great views over the Neues Palais and the park. Part of the west wing is still used to keep sensitive plants alive in the cold, north German winter.

Two interesting buildings west of the Orangerie are the pagoda-like **Drachenhaus** (Dragon House, 1770), which houses a café-restaurant, and the rococo **Belvedere**, the only building in the park to suffer serious damage during WWII (but fully restored in 1999).

The late-baroque **Neues Palais** (New Palace), built in 1769 as the royal family's summer residence, is one of the most imposing buildings in the park and the one to see if your time is limited. The tour takes in about a dozen of the palace's 200 rooms, including the **Grottensaal** (Grotto Hall), a rococo delight with shells, fossils and baubles set into the walls and ceilings; the **Marmorsaal** (Marble Room), a large banquet hall of white Carrara marble with a wonderful ceiling fresco; the **Jagdkammer** (Hunting Chamber), which has lots of dead furry things and fine gold tracery on the walls; and several chambers fitted out from floor to ceiling in rich red damask. The **Schlosstheater** in the south wing has classical-music concerts at weekends. Opposite the Neues Palais is the **Communs**, which originally housed the palace servants and kitchens but is now part of Potsdam University.

Transport

Distance from Berlin 24km.
Direction Southwest.
Travel Time 33 minutes.
Train The S7 links central Berlin with Potsdam Hauptbahnhof (central train station) about every 10 minutes. Regional DB trains are faster but operate on a more limited schedule. You need a ticket covering zones A, B and C (€2.40).

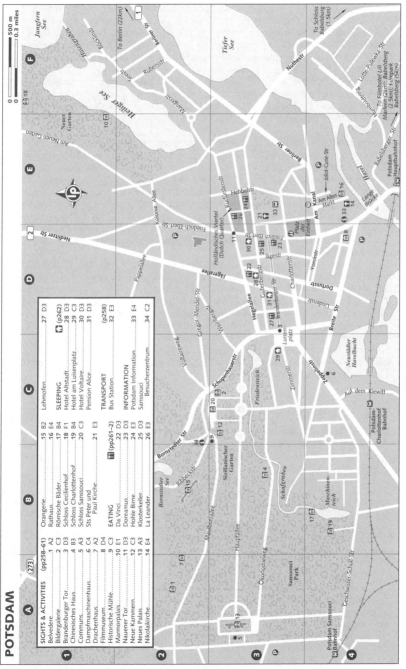

POTSDAM

SIGHTS & ACTIVITIES	(pp258-61)
Belvedere	1 A2
Bildergalerie	2 C3
Brandenburger Tor	3 D3
Chinesisches Haus	4 B3
Communs	5 A3
Dampfmaschinenhaus	6 C4
Drachenhaus	7 A2
Filmmuseum	8 D4
Historische Mühle	9 C3
Marmorpalais	10 E1
Nauener Tor	11 D3
Neue Kammern	12 C3
Neues Palais	13 A3
Nikolaikirche	14 E4
Orangerie	15 B2
Rathaus	16 E4
Römische Bäder	17 B4
Schloss Cecilienhof	18 F1
Schloss Charlottenhof	19 B4
Schloss Sanssouci	20 C3
Sts Peter und Paul Kirche	21 E3

EATING	(pp261-2)
Da Vinci	22 D3
Doreamus	23 D3
Hohle Birne	24 E3
Klosterkeller	25 D3
La Leander	26 E3
Lehmofen	27 D3

SLEEPING	(p262)
Hotel Altstadt	28 D3
Hotel am Luisenplatz	29 C3
Hotel Voltaire	30 D3
Pension Alice	31 D3

TRANSPORT	(p258)
Bus Station	32 E3

INFORMATION	
Potsdam Information	33 E4
Sanssouci Besucherzentrum	34 C2

259

Excursions – Potsdam

Towards the southern end of the park, **Schloss Charlottenhof** (1826) was Karl Friedrich Schinkel's main contribution to the park and is considered one of his finest works, but don't wait around if the queues are too long. The exterior (modelled after a Roman villa) is more interesting than the interior, especially the Doric portico and the bronze fountain to the east.

A short distance to the northeast, on the edge of the Maschinenteich (Machine Pond), the **Römische Bäder** (Roman Baths) were built in 1836 by a pupil of Schinkel but were never used. The floor mosaics and caryatids, inspired by the baths at Herculaneum, are impressive, and we also like the flounder spitting into a clamshell near the entrance.

Follow the path north along the west bank of the Schafgraben to Ökonomieweg, then head east, and you'll come to what many consider to be the pearl of the park: the **Chinesisches Haus** (Chinese Teahouse, 1757), a circular pavilion of gilded columns, palm trees and figures of Chinese musicians and animals. One of the monkeys is said to have the features of Voltaire!

Moving into the town itself, the baroque **Brandenburger Tor** (Brandenburg Gate, 1770), on Luisenplatz at the western end of the old town, is hardly on the scale of its namesake in Berlin but is actually older. From this square, pedestrian Brandenburger Strasse runs east to the **Sts Peter und Paul Kirche** (Church of Sts Peter and Paul, 1868).

Northwest of here, bounded by Friedrich-Ebert-Strasse, Hebbelstrasse, Kurfürstenstrasse and Gutenbergstrasse, the **Holländisches Viertel** (Dutch Quarter) has 134 gabled red-brick houses, built for Dutch workers who came to Potsdam in the 1730s at the invitation of Friedrich Wilhelm I. The homes have been prettily restored and now house galleries, cafés and restaurants. Further along Friedrich-Ebert-Strasse is the **Nauener Tor** (Nauen Gate, 1755), another monumental arch.

South of here, past the monumental Platz der Einheit, is the great neoclassical dome of Schinkel's **Nikolaikirche** (1850) on Am Alten Markt. On the eastern side of the square is Potsdam's old **Rathaus**, dating from 1753, which now contains several art galleries upstairs.

West of the Am Alten Markt on Breite Strasse and housed in the Marstall (1746), the former royal stables designed by Knobelsdorff, is the smallish **Filmmuseum**. It contains exhibits on the history of the UFA and DEFA studios in Babelsberg, Marlene Dietrich costumes and footage of Nazi-era and German Democratic Republic (GDR) films.

A short distance beyond the 'bay' of the Havel is the wonderful **Dampfmaschinenhaus** (pump house), a Moorish-style structure often called the *Moschee* (mosque), which was built in 1842 to house the palace waterworks.

Detour: Neuer Garten and Babelsberg

Venture out from the centre of Potsdam and you'll find the **Neuer Garten**, a winding lakeside park on the west bank of the Heiliger See – it's a fine place to relax after all the baroque-rococo and high art of Sanssouci. The **Marmorpalais** (Marble Palace; ☎ 0331-969 4246; adult/concession €2.50/1.50; ☯ 10am-5pm Tue-Sun Apr-Oct, 10am-4pm Sat & Sun Nov-Mar) on the lake, built in 1792 by Carl Gotthard Langhans, has been carefully restored.

Further north is **Schloss Cecilienhof** (☎ 0331-969 4244; tour adult/concession €4/3; ☯ 9am-5pm Tue-Sun), a rustic, English-style country manor contrasting with the extravagant rococo palaces and pavilions of Sanssouci. Cecilienhof was the site of the 1945 Potsdam Conference, where captured German territory was reassigned to Poland, and large photos of the participants – Stalin, Truman and Churchill – are displayed inside. The conference room can be visited on a guided tour.

Schinkel's neo-Gothic **Schloss Babelsberg** (☎ 0331-969 4250; adult/concession €5/4; ☯ 10am-5pm Tue-Fri Apr-Oct, 10am-4pm Sat & Sun Nov-Mar) is near the lakes. You can stroll in the pleasant park past the great architect's **Flatowturm** (☎ 0331-969 4249; adult/concession €2/1.50; ☯ 10am-5pm Sat & Sun 1 Apr-15 Oct).

Filmpark Babelsberg (☎ 0331-212 755; www.filmpark.de; Grossbeerenstrasse; adult/concession/child €15/14/9; ☯ 10am-6pm 15 Mar-2 Nov), Germany's one-time response to Hollywood, is also located east of the city centre. Filming still goes on here, though the main reason to visit is the theme park that's sprung up on the grounds. New attractions are added yearly. You can also watch animals being trained as actors and tour the warped, expressionistic **Caligari Hall**. There's a **guided tram ride** (in German) around the backlot that offers a peek at the sound stages and production studios, as well as the props and costumes room. To get to the park, take the S7 to Babelsberg and then bus No 690 or 698 to Ahornstrasse. Alternatively, get off the S-Bahn at Griebnitzsee and take bus No 696 to the Drewitz stop.

Caligari Hall, Filmpark Babelsberg (opposite)

Information

Potsdam Information (☎ 0331-275 580; www.potsdam tourismus.de; Neuer Markt 1; ✌ 9am-7pm Mon-Fri & 10am-6pm Sat & Sun Apr-Oct, 10am-6pm Mon-Fri & 10am-2pm Sat & Sun Nov-Mar)

Sights

Sights within **Sanssouci Park** (admission free; ✌ dawn to dusk):

Belvedere (admission free; ✌ Apr-Oct)

Bildergalerie (☎ 0331-969 4202; tours adult/concession €3/2.50; ✌ 10am-5pm Tue-Sun 15 May-15 Oct)

Chinesisches Haus (☎ 0331-969 4222; admission €1; ✌ 10am-5pm Tue-Sun 15 May-15 Oct)

Damenflügel (Schloss Sanssouci; adult/concession €2/1.50; ✌ 10am-5pm Tue-Sun 15 May-15 Oct)

Historische Mühle (☎ 0331-969 4202; adult/concession €1.50/0.50; ✌ 10am-6pm daily Apr-Oct, 10am-6pm Sat & Sun Nov-Mar)

Neue Kammern (tours adult/concession €3/2.50; ✌ 10am-5pm Tue-Sun 15 May-15 Oct, 10am-5pm Sat & Sun Apr-14 May)

Neues Palais (☎ 0331-969 4255; adult/concession €5/4; ✌ 10am-5pm Sat-Thu)

Orangerie (☎ 0331-969 4280; tours adult/concession €3/2.50, tower €1; ✌ 10am-5pm Tue-Sun 15 May-15 Oct)

Römische Bäder (adult/concession €2/1.50; ✌ 10am-5pm Tue-Sun 15 May-15 Oct)

Schloss Charlottenhof (☎ 0331-969 4228; tours adult/concession €4/3; ✌ 10am-5pm Tue-Sun 15 May-15 Oct)

Schloss Sanssouci (☎ 0331-969 4190; tours adult/concession €8/5; ✌ 9am-5pm Tue-Sun Apr-Oct, 9am-4pm Tue-Sun Nov-Mar)

Other sights:

Dampfmaschinenhaus (☎ 0331-969 4248; cnr Breite Strasse & Zeppelinstrasse; admission & tour adult/concession €2/1.50; ✌ 10am-5pm Sat & Sun 15 May-15 Oct)

Filmmuseum (☎ 0331-271 8112; Breite Strasse; admission adult/concession €2/1, films €4.50/3.50; ✌ 10am-6pm)

Nikolaikirche (Alter Markt; ✌ 2-5pm Mon, 10am-5pm Tue-Sat, noon-5pm Sun)

Rathaus (Alter Markt; ✌ 2-7pm Tue-Sun)

Eating

Da Vinci (☎ 0331-280 5189; Dortusstrasse 4; pasta €6.50-11, mains €13-19) Classy and popular Italian restaurant, often enlivened by musicians.

Doreamus (☎ 0331-201 5860; Brandenburger Strasse 30/31; mains €7.80-13.50) Some of the finest views you'll get over the Altstadt, with decent food to boot.

Hohle Birne (☎ 0331-280 0715; Mittelstrasse 19; mains €6-13) Earthy but tasty German cuisine, plus a huge beer and wine menu. The name (literally 'hollow pear') is a local insult!

Klosterkeller (☎ 0331-291 218; Friedrich-Ebert-Strasse 94; mains €9.45-12.75) Touristy but fun restaurant, wine bar, beer garden and cocktail bar serving traditional regional dishes.

La Leander (☎ 0331-270 6576; Benkertstrasse 1; light meals €3.50-4.75) Dutch Quarter café with a loyal gay following.

Lehmofen (☎ 0331-280 1712; Hermann-Elflein-Strasse 10; mains €10-17) Worlds away from your average doner-kebab shop, serving up tasty and authentic Turkish dishes.

Sleeping

Filmhotel Lili Marleen (☎ 0331-743 200; Grossbeerenstrasse 75; s €49-65, d €65-90) You're near Babelsberg here, though the posters on the walls treacherously salute Hollywood.

Hotel Altstadt (☎ 0331-284 990; Dortusstrasse 9/10; s €60-72, d €80-90) The Altstadt offers a good range of

rooms and has plenty of extra services, which makes it a decent bet.

Hotel am Luisenplatz (☎ 0331-971 900; Luisenplatz 5; s €79-109, d €119-139) Cosy four-star hotel with big rooms and some balconies overlooking the Brandenburger Tor.

Hotel Voltaire (☎ 0331-231 70; Friedrich-Ebert-Strasse 88; s €79-158, d €92-181) Posh address opposite the Dutch Quarter, with two restaurants, a roof terrace and the customary 'wellness area'.

Pension Alice (☎ 0331-292 304; Lindenstrasse 16; s/d €25/50) Potsdam's most central budget option, with a few quirky rooms above a busy café.

SACHSENHAUSEN CONCENTRATION CAMP

In 1936 the Nazis opened a 'model' concentration camp for men in a disused brewery in Sachsenhausen, near the town of Oranienburg. By 1945 about 220,000 men from 22 countries had passed through the gates – labelled, as at Auschwitz, *Arbeit Macht Frei* (Work Sets You Free). About 100,000 were murdered here, their remains consumed by the fires of the horribly efficient ovens.

After the war, the Soviets and the communist leaders of the new GDR set up Speziallager No 7 (Special Camp No 7). An estimated 60,000 people were interned here between 1945 and 1950, and up to 12,000 are believed to have died. There's a mass grave of victims at the camp and another one 1.5km to the north.

The Sachsenhausen Memorial and Museum consists of several parts. Even before you enter you'll see a memorial to the 6000 prisoners who died on the *Todesmarsch* (Death March) of April 1945, when the Nazis tried to drive the camp's 33,000 inmates to the Baltic in advance of the Red Army.

About 100m inside the camp is a mass grave of 300 prisoners who died in the infirmary after liberation in April 1945. Further on is the camp commandant's house and the so-called Green Monster, where SS troops were trained in the finer arts of camp maintenance. At the end of the road is the Neues Museum (New Museum), which has excellent exhibits. East of the museum are Barracks 38 and 39, reconstructions of typical huts housing most of the 6000 Jewish prisoners brought to Sachsenhausen after Kristallnacht (November 1938). North of here is the prison, where particularly brutal punishment was meted out to prisoners. Inside the prison yard is a memorial to the homosexuals who died here, one of the few monuments you'll see anywhere to these 'forgotten victims' (there's another at Berlin's Nollendorfplatz U-Bahn station, p118).

To get to the Lagermuseum (Camp Museum), with moth-eaten and dusty exhibits on both Nazi and GDR camps, walk north along the parade ground, past the site of the gallows. The museum is in the building on the right, which was once the camp kitchen. In the former laundry room opposite, a gruesome film of the camp after liberation is shown throughout the day.

Left of the tall, ugly monument (1961) erected by the GDR in memory of political prisoners interned here is the crematorium and Station Z extermination site, a pit for shooting prisoners in the neck with a wooden 'catch' where bullets could be retrieved and recycled. A memorial hall on the site of the gas chamber provides a fitting visual metaphor for the 'glorious' Third Reich and the 'workers' paradise' of the GDR: subsiding slowly, the paving stones are cracked and the roof is toppling over an area containing, we're told, 'considerable remains from corpses incinerated in the crematorium'.

Sights

Sachsenhausen Memorial and Museum (☎ 03301-200 200; admission free; ⏰ 8.30am-6pm Tue-Sun Apr-Sep, to 4.30pm Oct-Mar)

Transport

Distance from Berlin 35km.
Direction North.
Travel Time One hour.
Train The easiest way to get here is the frequent S1 to Oranienburg (€6.45). There are also RB trains from Berlin-Lichtenberg (€6, 30 minutes). From Oranienburg it's an easy 20-minute walk.

BRANDENBURG AN DER HAVEL

Brandenburg is the oldest town in the March of Brandenburg, with a history going back to at least the 6th century. It was an important bishopric from the early Middle Ages and the seat of the Brandenburg margraves until they moved to Berlin in the 15th century. Severe damage suffered during WWII as well as GDR neglect is gradually being repaired, and the baroque churches and waterside setting make for a refreshing day trip or overnight stay.

Brandenburg is split into three sections by the Havel River, the Beetzsee and their canals. The Neustadt occupies an island in the centre; the Dominsel is to the north; and the Altstadt, on the mainland, is to the west.

Begin a stroll at the Romanesque **Dom St Peter und Paul** (Cathedral of St Peter and Paul), on the northern edge of Dominsel. Begun in 1165 by Premonstratensian monks and completed in 1240, this red-brick edifice contains the wonderfully decorated **Bunte Kapelle** (Coloured Chapel), with a vaulted and painted ceiling; the carved 14th-century **Böhmischer Altar** (Bohemian Altar) in the south transept;

Transport

Distance from Berlin 60km.
Direction Southwest.
Travel Time One hour.
Train Frequent regional trains link Brandenburg with Berlin-Zoo (€5.70) and Potsdam (€4.50).

a fantastic baroque **organ** (1723), which was restored in 1999; and the **Dommuseum**.

From the cathedral, walk south on St Petri to Mühlendamm. Just before you cross the Havel to the Neustadt, look left and you'll see the **Hauptpegel**, the 'city water gauge', which was erected to measure the river's height. On the other side is the **Mühlentorturm** (Mill Gate Tower), which marked the border between Dominsel and Neustadt in the days when they were separate towns.

Molkenmarkt, the continuation of Mühlendamm, runs parallel to Neustädtischer Markt and leads to the **Pfarrkirche St Katharinen** (Parish Church of St Catherine). This Gothic brick church was originally two chapels, the first dating from 1395. See if you can spot your favourite New Testament characters on the 'Meadow of Heaven' painted ceiling.

To reach the Altstadt, walk up the pedestrianised Hauptstrasse and then west over the Jahrtausendbrücke (Millennium Bridge). Passing the **glockenspiel** (Ritterstrasse 64; ⌚ rung hourly 9am-7pm), you reach the **Stadtmuseum im Frey-Haus**. It's a local history museum with much emphasis on the EP Lehmann factory, which produced cute mechanical toys and pottery.

Information

Tourist Information (☎ 03381-585 858; www.stadt-brandenburg.de; Steinstrasse 66/67; ⌚ 8.30am-7pm Mon-Fri & 10am-3pm Sat & Sun May-Oct, 10am-6pm Mon-Fri & 10am-2pm Sat Nov-Apr)

Sights

Dom St Peter und Paul (☎ 03381-112 221; Burghof 9; admission free; ⌚ 10am-4pm Mon-Fri, 10am-5pm Sat, 11am-5pm Sun, Wed 10am-noon Jun-Sep)

Dommuseum (☎ 03381-200 325; Dom St Peter und Paul; admission adult/concession €3/2)

Pfarrkirche St Katharinen (admission free; ⌚ 10am-4pm Mon-Sat, 1-4pm Sun)

Stadtmuseum im Frey-Haus (☎ 03381-522 048; Ritterstrasse 96; admission adult/concession €3/1.50; ⌚ 9am-5pm Tue-Fri, 10am-5pm Sat & Sun)

Eating

Bismarck Terrassen (☎ 03381-300 939; Bergstrasse 20; mains from €5.80, set menus from €7.50) Dine on the city's most elegant French-German food amid a festival of Bismarck memorabilia.

Kultur-Café (☎ 03381-6660; www.kultur-labor.de; Ritterstrasse 69; mains €6-11) Part of the busy Kulturlabor cultural centre, it has a great balcony overlooking the Havel and the Jahrtausendbrücke.

Marienberg (☎ 03381-794 960; Am Marienberg 1; mains €6.50-12.50) Huge beer garden and restaurant in the Stadtpark, it has recently been restored. Come here for Brandenburg's newly inaugurated Oktoberfest.

Sleeping

Pension Zum Birnbaum (☎ 03381-527 500; Mittelstrasse 1; s €34-41, d €48-62) Well placed for the station and the Neustadt, with an assortment of good-value rooms.

Sorat Hotel Brandenburg (☎ 03381-5970; Altstädtischer Markt 1; s €94-120, d €110-136) Brandenburg's main top-end choice and the only place in town with wheelchair access. Champagne breakfast and sauna use are included.

SPREEWALD

The rivers, canals and streams of the 287-sq-km 'Spree Forest' are the closest thing Berlin has to a back garden. Visitors come here in droves to punt on more than 400km of waterways, hike countless nature trails and fish in the region that was declared a biosphere reserve by Unesco in 1990. The Spreewald is also home to most of Germany's indigenous Sorbian minority, who call the region the Blota. The region is renowned throughout Germany for its gherkins.

Transport

Distance from Berlin 80km.
Direction Southeast.
Travel Time One hour.
Bus There are frequent buses between Lübben and Lübbenau on weekdays, but it's much quicker to catch a train.
Train Regional trains serve Lübben and Lübbenau every one to two hours from Berlin–Ostbahnhof (€12.80) en route to Cottbus.

There's an ongoing debate among Berliners over **Lübben** (Lubin in Sorbian) and its neighbour **Lübbenau** (Lubnjow), 13km away: which is the more historic and picturesque 'Spreewald capital'? For our money, Lübben, a tidy and attractive town at the centre of the drier Unterspreewald (Lower Spreewald), just pips Lübbenau. It feels more like a 'real' town and has a history going back at least two centuries further than its neighbour. That said, you'll find a visit to either town has its merits.

In Lübben the compact **Schloss** is worth a visit but the real highlight is a (free) wander through the gardens of the **Schlossinsel**, an artificial archipelago with gardens concealing cafés, jetties and all kinds of play areas.

Lübbenau, in the Oberspreewald (Upper Spreewald), is just as pretty but has more of a model-village air, despite being considerably bigger. The secluded Altstadt is almost invariably crammed with tourists trying to get out onto the canals on *Kähne* (punt boats), which were once the only way to get around in these parts. If you want to join them, head for the **Grosser Hafen** (large harbour) or **Kleiner Hafen** (small harbour). You can rent boats from €3.50 per hour.

Spreewald Walks

The Spreewald has hiking and walking trails to suit everyone – local tourist offices sell a good range of useful maps.

From Lübbenau, walkers can follow a **nature trail** (30 minutes) west to Lehde, the 'Venice of the Spreewald', with its wonderful **Freilandmuseum** (☎ 03542-2944; admission adult/concession €3/2; 10am-6pm Apr–15 Sep, 10am-5pm 16 Sep–Oct) boasting traditional Sorbian thatched houses and farm buildings.

Another walking option is the **Leiper Weg**, which starts near the Grosser Hafen. Part of the E10 European Walking Trail from the Baltic to the Adriatic, the route leads southwest to Leipe, which has been accessible only by boat since 1936.

Information

Spreewaldinformation/Tourismus Lübben (☎ 03546-3090; www.luebben.de; Hafen 1, Ernst-von-Houwald-Damm 15; 10am-6pm)

Touristinformation Lübbenau (☎ 03542-668; www.spreewald-online.de; Ehm-Welk-Strasse 15; 9am-6pm Mon-Fri, 9am-1pm Sat)

Sights

Grosser Hafen (☎ 03542-2225; Dammstrasse 77a, Lübbenau)

Kleiner Hafen (☎ 03542-403 710; Spreestrasse 10a, Lübbenau)

Schloss Lübben (☎ 03546-874 78; Ernst-von-Houwald-Damm 14, Lübben; admission adult/concession €4/2; 10am-6pm Tue-Sun May-Sep, 10am-4pm Wed-Fri & 1-5pm Sat & Sun Oct-Apr)

Eating

Bubak (☎ 03546-186 144; Ernst-von-Houwald-Damm 9, Lübben; mains €6.40-15.30) Bubak is a characterful roadside restaurant that has been named after a local bogeyman. It even comes complete with a singing proprietor.

Dodge City Saloon (☎ 03546-4051; Bergstrasse 1, Lübben; mains €6.50-20) Possibly the least-likely location for a Wild West theme restaurant ever.

Strubel's (☎ 03542-2798; Dammstrasse 3, Lübbenau; mains €6.50-13.90) Try Strubel's for fresh Spree eel, pike and perch.

Sleeping

Hotel Schloss Lübbenau (☎ 03542-8730; Schlossbezirk 6, Lübbenau; s €62-82, d €104-134) Check into your local castle for all the class you can handle.

Hotel Spreeufer (☎ 03546-272 60; Hinter der Mauer 4, Lübben; per person €30-45) The Spreeufer is a smart, friendly hotel near the river.

RHEINSBERG

Rheinsberg, a delightful town hugging the shore of the Grienericksee, has much to offer visitors: a charming Renaissance palace, walks in the lovely Schlosspark, plenty of boating and some top-notch restaurants.

The first moated castle here was built in the early Middle Ages to protect the March of Brandenburg's northern border from the marauders of Mecklenburg. However, the present **Schloss Rheinsberg** only began to take shape in 1566, when its owner, Achim von Bredow, had it reconstructed in the Renaissance style.

Transport

Distance from Berlin 50km.
Direction Northwest.
Travel Time One hour.
Bus Two buses per day make the trip between Rheinsberg and Oranienburg.
Train Rheinsberg is no longer served by direct trains from central Berlin; head north from Berlin–Spandau or Oranienburg (€8.10) and change at Herzberg.

Friedrich Wilhelm I purchased the castle in 1734 for his 22-year-old son, Crown Prince Friedrich (the future Frederick the Great), and spent a fair wedge expanding the palace and cleaning up the town. The prince, who spent four years here studying and preparing for the throne, later said this period was the happiest of his life. He personally oversaw much of the remodelling of the palace, and some say this was his 'test', on a minor scale, for the much grander Sanssouci (1747) in Potsdam.

A tour of the palace takes in about two dozen, mostly empty, rooms on the 1st floor, including the oldest ones: the **Hall of Mirrors**, where young Friedrich held flute contests; the **Tower Chamber**, which he recreated in the Berlin Schloss in 1745; and the **Bacchus Room**, with a ceiling painting of a worn-looking Ganymede. Among our favourites are the **Lacquer Room**, with its chinoiserie, **Prince Heinrich's bedchamber**, which sports an exquisite trompe l'oeil ceiling, and the rococo **Shell Room**.

The ground floor of the north wing contains a small **Gedenkstätte** (museum), which is dedicated to the life and work of writer Kurt Tucholsky (1890–1935). He wrote a popular novel called *Rheinsberg – ein Tagebuch für Verliebte* (Rheinsberg – a Lovers' Diary) in which young swain Wolfgang traipses through the Schloss with his beloved Claire in tow, putting the palace (and Rheinsberg itself) firmly on the literary map.

Information

Infoladen (☎ 033931-395 10; Rhinpassage, Rhinstrasse 19; 🕑 10am-6pm Mon-Sat, 10am-4pm Sun) Private tourist office.

Tourist Information (☎ 033931-2059; www.rheinsberg .de; Kavalierhaus, Markt; 🕑 10am-5pm Mon-Sat, 10am-4pm Sun)

Sights

Schloss Rheinsberg (☎ 033931-7260; admission adult/concession €4/3, tour €5/4; 🕑 9.30am-5pm Tue-Sun Apr-Oct, 10am-4pm Tue-Sun Nov-Mar)

Tucholsky Gedenkstätte (Schloss Rheinsberg; admission adult/concession €2/1; 🕑 9.30am-5pm Tue-Sun Apr-Oct, 10am-4pm Tue-Sun Nov-Mar)

Eating

Cafe Tucholsky (☎ 033931-343 70; Kurt-Tucholsky-Strasse 30a; mains €5.25-10.45) Smart café opposite the yacht club that has live music most summer weekends.

Zum Alten Fritz (☎ 033931-2086; Schlossstrasse 11; mains €6-13.90) Excellent north-German specialities and fish.

Zum Fischerhof (☎ 033931-2625; Uferpromenade; mains €6-14.50; 🕑 Wed-Mon Apr-Oct) An authentic local *Raucherei* (smokehouse), serving up fish straight off the boat.

Sleeping

Haus Rheinsberg (☎ 033931-3440; Donnersmarckweg 1; s €45-65, d €85-105) One of the few hotels in Germany that's specially designed for disabled guests.

Seehof (☎ 033931-4030; Seestrasse 18; s €65-85, d €75-120) Bright, modern rooms and superb food.

CHORIN

The tiny town of Chorin is not exactly a tourist hub, but plenty of people do make the day trip from Berlin to visit the renowned **Kloster Chorin** (Chorin Monastery), one of the finest red-brick Gothic structures in northern Germany.

Some 500 Cistercian monks laboured over six decades starting from 1273 to erect their monastery and church on a granite base (a practice copied by the Franciscans at the Nikolaikirche and Marienkirche in Berlin). The monastery was secularised in 1542 and fell into disrepair after the Thirty Years' War. Renovation has gone on in a somewhat haphazard fashion since the early 19th century.

The entrance to the monastery is through the ornate western façade and leads to the central cloister and ambulatory. To the north is the early-Gothic **Klosterkirche**, with its wonderful carved portals and long lancet windows.

The celebrated **Choriner Musiksommer** (Chorin Summer of Music) concerts take place in the monastery cloister on Saturdays and Sundays from June to August; expect to hear some top talent. At 4pm some Sundays from late May to August there are chamber music concerts in the church, which is said to have near-perfect acoustics.

If you want to walk from the station, you can reach the monastery in less than 30 minutes via a pretty, marked trail that goes through the woods.

Sights

Choriner Musiksommer (☎ 03334-657 310; Schickel-strasse 5, Eberswalde-Finow)

Kloster Chorin (☎ 033366-703 77; Amt Chorin 11a; admission adult/child €2.50/1.50, parking €2.50; ⊗ 9am-6pm Apr-Oct, 9am-4pm Nov-Mar)

Transport

Distance from Berlin 60km.
Direction Northeast.
Travel Time 50 minutes.
Train Chorin is served by regional trains from Berlin–Ostbahnhof (€6.90) about every two hours. Kloster Chorin is 3km southeast of the train station by road.

SAXONY-ANHALT

LUTHERSTADT-WITTENBERG

As the crucible of the Reformation, where Protestant Christians first split from the Roman Catholic Church, Wittenberg is among Saxony-Anhalt's most popular destinations. Religious pilgrims, scholars, fans of Joseph Fiennes (who starred in *Luther*) and the merely curious all swarm here to follow in the footsteps of Martin Luther, whose campaigning zeal changed the face of Europe and the course of history. Quaint and picturesque, Wittenberg can be seen in a day. The town is busiest in June, during the Luther's Wedding festival, and on 31 October, the anniversary of the publication of Luther's 95 Theses.

If you only visit one of the various museums in Germany devoted to the father of the Reformation, make it the **Lutherhaus**. The exhibition here, in Luther's one-time home, was revamped in 2003 to the tune of €17.5 million, and even those with no previous interest in the subject will be drawn in by its combination of accessible narrative, personal artefacts, Cranach paintings and interactive multimedia displays. There's also an original room furnished by Luther in 1535, decorated with a bit of royal graffiti from Russian Tsar Peter the Great in 1702.

The **Luthereiche** (Luther's Oak), the spot where the preacher burned the 1520 papal bull threatening his excommunication, is on the corner of Lutherstrasse and Am Bahnhof. The oak itself is only about 100 years old.

Legend has it that it was the door of the **Schlosskirche** (Castle Church) where Luther, on 31 October 1517, nailed his 95 Theses confronting the Catholic Church. There's no hard evidence this happened, especially as the door in question was destroyed by fire in 1760. In its place, however, stands an impressive bronze **memorial** (1858) inscribed with the theses in Latin. Inside the church is Luther's tombstone, opposite that of his friend and fellow reformer Philipp Melanchthon.

If the Schlosskirche was the billboard used to advertise the forthcoming Reformation, its sister **Stadtkirche St Marien** (City Church of St Marien) was where the ecumenical revolution began, with the world's first Protestant worship services in 1521. It was also here that Luther preached his famous Lectern sermons in 1522 and three years later married ex-nun Katharina von Bora. The centrepiece is the large **altar**, designed jointly by Lucas Cranach the Elder and his son. The side facing the nave shows Luther, Melanchthon and other Reformation figures, as well as Cranach himself, in biblical contexts. Behind it, on the lower rung, you'll see a seemingly defaced painting of heaven and hell. Medieval students etched their initials into the painting's divine half if they passed their final exams – and into purgatory if they failed.

Wittenberg's Martin Luther Gymnasium is usually called the **Hundertwasser School**, because the famous Viennese artist and architect Freidenreichs Hundertwasser designed its current look. In 2000 he helped remodel a series of East German concrete blocks into one of his signature buildings, with organic curves, brightly coloured elements, touches of gold, mosque-like cupolas and rooftop vegetation. The school is a 20-minute walk northeast of the town centre. It's possible to view the exterior any time, but tours wait for at least four participants before they start. Unbelievably, at the time of writing, this fantastically well-equipped, modern high school was threatened with closure.

Alongside the Lutherhaus, the former homes of two other Reformation stalwarts are now museums. The **Galerie im Cranachhaus** is devoted to artist Lucas Cranach the Elder, while the rather text-heavy **Melanchthon Haus** discusses the life of university lecturer and humanist Philipp Melanchthon. An expert in ancient languages, Melanchthon helped Luther translate the Bible into German from Greek and Hebrew, and in the process became the preacher's friend and his most eloquent advocate.

Transport

Distance from Berlin 100km.
Direction Southwest.
Travel Time 1½ hours.
Train Wittenberg is on the direct RE line from Berlin-Ostbahnhof (€16.20) and Schönefeld airport. Be sure to board for 'Lutherstadt–Wittenberg' – there's also a Wittenberge west of Berlin.

Information

Wittenberg-Information (☎ 03491-498 610; www.wittenberg.de; Schlossplatz 2; 9am-6pm Mon-Fri, 10am-3pm Sat, 11am-4pm Sun)

Sights

Galerie im Cranachhaus (☎ 03491-420 1911; Markt 4; admission adult/concession €3/2; 10am-5pm Mon-Sat, 1-5pm Sun)

Hundertwasser School (☎ 03491-881 131; Strasse der Völkerfreundschaft 130; tours €1; 1.30-5pm Tue-Fri, 10am-4pm Sat & Sun)

Lutherhaus (☎ 03491-420 30; Collegienstrasse 54; admission adult/concession €5/3; 9am-6pm daily Apr-Oct, 10am-5pm Tue-Sun Nov-Mar)

Melanchthon Haus (☎ 03491-403 279; Collegienstrasse 60; admission adult/concession €2.50/1.50; 9am-6pm Tue-Sun Apr-Oct, 9am-5pm Tue-Sun Nov-Mar)

Schlosskirche (admission free; 10am-5pm Mon-Sat, 11.30am-5pm Sun)

Stadtkirche St Marien (admission free; 9am-5pm Mon-Sat, 11.30am-5pm Sun)

Eating

Café Hundertwasserschule (☎ 03491-410 685; Markt 15; mains €4-14) Health-conscious modern café complete with no-smoking policy, vegetarian options and fresh juices.

Tante Emmas Bier-und Caféhaus (☎ 03491-419 757; Markt 9; mains €8.50-14) German country-kitchen-style eatery, with traditional cuisine to match.

Zur Schlossfreiheit (☎ 03491-402 980; Coswigerstrasse 24; mains €6.50-10.50) Cosy, dark-wood surrounds and slightly different fare, including *Lutherschmaus* (duck in peppery sultana sauce).

Sleeping

Best Western Stadtpalais (☎ 03491-4250; Collegienstrasse 56/57; s €90-100, d €110-120) Asian touches distinguish this place from its stable mates, though the standard of accommodation is typically high.

Brauhaus Wittenberg (☎ 03491-433 130; Im Beyerhof, Markt 6; s/d €50/70) For a room with a brew, try this busy central hotel/restaurant.

Stadthotel Wittenberg Schwarzer Baer (☎ 03491-420 4344; Schlossstrasse 2; s/d €55/70) Clean, modern rooms and just enough olde-worlde charm to keep it atmospheric.

SAXONY

DRESDEN

In the 18th century the Saxon capital was famous throughout Europe as the 'Florence of the north', a centre of artistic activity presided over by Augustus the Strong and his son Augustus III. Since February 1945, however, Dresden has been synonymous with the controversial Allied bombing campaign that devastated the city, killing 35,000 people in attacks that had scant strategic justification. The resurrection and restoration of Dresden as a cultural bastion is founded to some degree on this historical resonance, giving the city's great baroque buildings a weighty gravitas all their own.

Reminders of Dresden's golden age are a big attraction, but outside the historic Altstadt, modern life has firmly asserted itself – the Neustadt has one of the densest concentrations of nightlife in Germany, and Dresden's many students are never short of ideas for entertainment.

This sprawling city invariably wins the affection of visitors. With major restoration work going on for its 800th anniversary in 2006 and a bid for European Capital of Culture 2010 in the offing, the next few years should see Dresden garner even more fans.

The **Altmarkt** area is Dresden's historic centre and the starting point for most visitors, though it still hasn't fully recovered from the bombings. Many restaurants have set up street-side tables, and when markets aren't operating it's nice to sit outside and gaze across the square. The spanking-new **Altmarkt Galerie** shopping centre is also excellent.

From the square, proceed east to the rebuilt **Kreuzkirche** (1792). Originally the Nikolaikirche, the church was renamed for a *Kreuz* (cross) found floating in the Elbe River by fishermen. The church is famous for its 400-strong boys' choir, the Kreuzchor.

Opposite the Altmarkt is the obnoxiously squat **Kulturpalast**, which hosts a huge range of concerts and performances year-round. Pass through Galeriestrasse, to the right, and you'll reach the **Neumarkt** – no longer a market these days – with the **Frauenkirche** (Church of Our Lady; 1726–43) wrapped in scaffolding at its eastern end. Built under the direction of baroque architect George Bähr, the Frauenkirche is one of Dresden's most beloved symbols. Until the end of WWII it was Germany's greatest Protestant church; the bombing raids of 13 February 1945 flattened it, and the communists decided to leave the rubble as a war memorial. After reunification, the movement to rebuild the church prevailed and a huge archaeological dig began in 1992. Reassembly is scheduled for completion in 2006, but funding has been so generous that it's likely to finish early!

From the Frauenkirche, turn up Rampstrasse and veer northeast to the **Brühlscher Garten**, the lovely green park east of the main terrace. In front stands the **Albertinum**, which houses many of Dresden's art treasures, including the **New Masters Gallery**, with renowned 19th- and 20th-century paintings from leading French and German Impressionists, and the **Skulpturensammlung**, which includes classical and Egyptian works. Here, too, is one of the world's finest collections of jewel-studded precious objects, the **Grünes Gewölbe** (Green Vault).

West of the Albertinum is the **Brühlsche Terrasse**, a spectacular promenade that's been

Barges and ferries on the famous Elbe River

DRESDEN

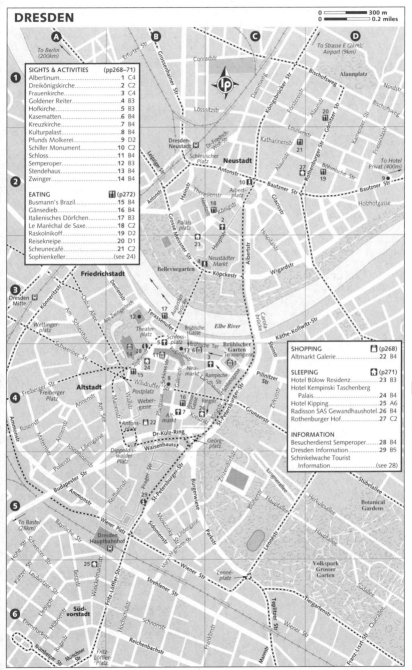

0 ——— 300 m
0 ——— 0.2 miles

SIGHTS & ACTIVITIES	(pp268–71)
Albertinum	1 C4
Dreikönigskirche	2 C2
Frauenkirche	3 C4
Goldener Reiter	4 B3
Hofkirche	5 B3
Kasematten	6 B4
Kreuzkirche	7 B4
Kulturpalast	8 B4
Pfunds Molkerei	9 D2
Schiller Monument	10 C2
Schloss	11 B4
Semperoper	12 B3
Stendehaus	13 B4
Zwinger	14 B4

EATING	(p272)
Busmann's Brazil	15 B4
Gänsedieb	16 B4
Italienisches Dörfchen	17 B3
Le Maréchal de Saxe	18 C2
Raskolnikoff	19 D2
Reisekneipe	20 D1
Scheunecafé	21 C2
Sophienkeller	(see 24)

SHOPPING	(p268)
Altmarkt Galerie	22 B4

SLEEPING	(p271)
Hotel Bülow Residenz	23 B3
Hotel Kempinski Taschenberg Palais	24 B4
Hotel Kipping	25 A6
Radisson SAS Gewandhaushotel	26 B4
Rothenburger Hof	27 C2

INFORMATION	
Besucherdienst Semperoper	28 B4
Dresden Information	29 B5
Schinkelwache Tourist Information	(see 28)

Excursions – Dresden

269

called the 'Balcony of Europe', with a pavement nearly 15m above the southern embankment of the Elbe. In summer it's a must for strolling, with expansive views of the river and the opposite bank. Beneath the promenade is the Renaissance brick bastion known as the **Kasematten**, which has a museum showing how the fortress was used.

Further along, off the Neumarkt, you'll find the fabulous **Augustusstrasse**, with its 102m-long *Procession of Princes* mural depicted on the outer wall of the former **Stendehaus** (Royal Stables). The scene, a long row of royalty on horses, was first painted in 1876 by Wullhelm Walther and then transferred to some 24,000 Meissen porcelain tiles. Join the crowds standing and squinting across the street.

Augustusstrasse leads directly to **Schlossplatz** and the baroque Catholic **Hofkirche** (1755), which contains the heart of Augustus the Strong. Just south of the church is the neo-Renaissance **Schloss**, which is being reconstructed as a museum. Restoration of the palace is scheduled, perhaps a bit optimistically, to finish in 2006.

On the western side of the Hofkirche is **Theaterplatz**, with Dresden's dramatic and long-suffering **Semperoper**. The original opera house on the site opened in 1841 but burned down less than three decades later. Rebuilt in 1878, it was pummelled in WWII and reopened only in 1985 after the communists invested millions in restoring this neo-Renaissance jewel. The 2002 floods closed it down yet again, albeit only briefly, and repairs were ongoing at the time of research. Thanks to a recent beer commercial, the Semperoper is probably one of the best-known buildings in Germany.

From the opera house, proceed south a few metres to reach the sprawling baroque **Zwinger** (1728). An open-air gallery and several charming portals frame its lovely, fountain-studded courtyard. Conceived by star architect Matthäus Daniel Pöppelmann for royal tournaments and festivals, the exterior has some fine examples of baroque sculpture, and the courtyard is a popular summer venue. Atop the western pavilion stands a tense-looking Atlas; opposite is a cutesy carillon of 40 Meissen porcelain bells, which chime on the hour.

The palace also houses six museums. The most important are the **Old Masters Gallery**, featuring masterpieces like Raphael's *Sistine Madonna*, and the **Rüstkammer** (armoury), with its superb collection of ceremonial weapons. An adult/concession combined ticket for the two places costs €6/3.50. The dazzling **Porcelain Collection** is another highlight, with plenty of Meissen classics. Old instruments, globes and timepieces are displayed in the **Mathematics and Physics Salon**; the **Naturhistorische Sammlungen** (Natural History Museum) and the **Museum of Minerology and Geology** are found in the Unterm Kronentor part of the fortress.

Crossing the Elbe, you enter the **Neustadt**, actually an old part of Dresden largely untouched by the wartime bombings. After reunification this became the centre of the city's alternative scene, but as entire street blocks are renovated it's losing some of its Bohemian feel. **Königstrasse**, which runs roughly parallel and to the west of Hauptstrasse, is developing into a swish shopping district.

The **Goldener Reiter statue** (1736) of Augustus the Strong stands at the northern end of the Augustusbrücke. This leads to the

Zwinger (above)

pleasant pedestrian mall of **Hauptstrasse**. Moving north you'll come to the newly renovated **Dreikönigskirche**, the parish church designed by Pöppelmann. It houses some lovely Renaissance artworks, including the *Dance of Death* frieze, which once hung in the Schloss.

On **Albertplatz** two lovely fountains flank the walkway down the centre, representing turbulent and still waters. North of the circle is an evocative marble **Schiller monument** and a fountain sourced from an artesian well, where Dresdeners still get water for their coffee. East of here is 'the world's most beautiful dairy shop', **Pfunds Molkerei**, a riot of hand-painted tiles and enamelled sculpture. Founded by the Pfund brothers in 1880, the dairy claims to have invented condensed milk. It was nationalised by the GDR in 1972 and fell into disrepair before restoration in 1995. The shop sells replica tiles, wines, cheeses and, of course, milk, and there's a café-restaurant upstairs.

Detour: Bastei

The open fields and rolling hills surrounding the **Bastei**, on the Elbe, 28km southeast of Dresden, give little clue as to the drama within. One of the most breathtaking spots in the whole of Germany, it features towering outcrops 305m high and unparalleled views of the surrounding forests, cliffs and mountains, not to mention a magnificent sightline right along the river itself. Look out for the wooden figure perched on top of the Monk's Peak.

The crags are linked by a series of footbridges that encompass **Neue Felsenburg** (☎ 03501-581 00; admission adult/concession €1.50/0.50; ☺ 9am-6pm), the 13th-century remains of a Saxon outpost. Centred on the **Basteibrücke** (Bastei Bridge) this fortress was the site of a medieval catapult; a replica stone-thrower and artefacts from the period are displayed in the terrain.

There's a marked path leading down to the river-side resort of Rathen, with the lovely **Felsenbühne** (open-air theatre; ☎ 035024-7770) halfway up.

The GDR-era **Berghotel Bastei** (☎ 035024-7790; s €41-44, d €33-56) is the only hotel in the park, boasting comfy rooms and superb views, plus extras like bowling and a sauna.

The nearest train station is Rathen, from where it's a steep 25-minute walk to the top. By bus, take No 236/23T which is frequent from Pirna train station (€1.50). There's also an open-topped double-decker bus, the **Bastei-Kraxler**, which serves Königstein, Hohnstein and Bad Schandau. If you're driving, follow the signs from Pirna, 12km southeast of Dresden.

Information

Besucherdienst Semperoper (☎ 0351-491 10; Schinkelwache, Theaterplatz 2; ☺ 10am-6pm Mon-Fri, 10am-1pm Sat) Information, tickets and tours.

Dresden Information (☎ 0351-4919 2100; www.dresden -tourist.de; Prager Strasse 21; ☺ 9.30am-6pm Mon-Fri, 9.30am-4pm Sat)

Schinkelwache Tourist Information (☎ 0351-491 1705; Theaterplatz 2; ☺ 10am-6pm Mon-Fri, 10am-4pm Sat & Sun)

Sights

Albertinum (☎ 0351-491 4619; combined museum ticket adult/child €6/3.50; ☺ 10am-6pm Fri-Wed)

Dreikönigskirche (☎ 0351-812 4102; admission to tower adult/concession €1.50/1; ☺ 10am-6pm Mon-Sat & 11.30am-6pm Sun Apr-Oct, 10am-4.30pm Mon-Sat & 11.30am-4.30pm Sun Nov-Feb)

Frauenkirche (☎ 0351-439 3934; admission free, donations appreciated; ☺ tours hourly 10am-4pm)

Hofkirche (☎ 0351-484 4712; admission free; ☺ 9am-5pm Mon-Thu, 1-5pm Fri, 10.30am-4pm Sat & noon-4pm Sun May-Oct, 10.30am-5pm Sat Nov-Apr)

Kasematten (☎ 0351-491 4786; admission adult/child €3.10/2; ☺ 10am-5pm)

Kreuzkirche (☺ 10am-6pm Mon-Sat, 11am-6pm Sun Apr-Oct, 10am-4pm Mon-Sat, 11am-4pm Sun Nov-Mar; concerts 6pm Sat)

Kulturpalast (☎ 0351-486 60; Schlossstrasse 2)

Mathematics and Physics Salon (☎ 0351-491 4622; Zwinger; admission adult/concession €2/1.50)

Museum of Minerology and Geology (☎ 0351-495 2503; Zwinger; admission adult/concession €3/1.50)

Naturhistorische Sammlungen (☎ 0351-892 6326; Zwinger; admission adult/concession €2.05/1.02)

Old Masters Gallery (☎ 0351-491 4619; Zwinger; admission adult/concession €3/2)

Pfunds Molkerei (☎ 0351-816 20; Bautzner Strasse 79; admission adult/concession €3/2)

Porcelain Collection (☎ 0351-491 4622; Zwinger; admission adult/concession €5.50/3.50)

Rüstkammer (☎ 0351-491 4619; admission adult/concession €3/2)

Semperoper (☎ 0351-491 1496; tours adult/concession €5/3)

Zwinger (Theaterplatz 1; ☺ 10am-6pm Tue-Sun)

Eating

Busmann's Brazil (☎ 0351-862 1200; Kleine Brüdergasse 5; mains €9.60-21.20) Brazilian culture beyond the *caipirinha* (a Brazilian cocktail), with such strange delicacies as frogfish and rattlesnake (€40.90).

Gänsedieb (☎ 0351-485 0905; Weisse Gasse 1; mains €6.50-10.80) Goose dishes are the pick of the menu in this inventive café-restaurant.

Italienisches Dörfchen (☎ 0351-498 160; Theaterplatz 3; mains €5-20) Four restaurants, stylish surroundings and varied cuisine, from bargain barbecue to swish Italian and Saxon.

Le Maréchal de Saxe (☎ 0351-810 5880; Königstrasse 5; mains €8.70-14) Upscale restaurant in a smart area, offering 18th-century Saxon-court cuisine.

Raskolnikoff (☎ 0351-804 5706; Böhmische Strasse 34; mains €5.20-7) Good-value light meals on a bohemian eastern European tip.

Reisekneipe (☎ 0351-889 4111; Görlitzer Strasse 15) Exotic and massively popular bar. Hardened globetrotters give talks every Wednesday.

Scheunecafé (☎ 0351-802 6619; Alaunstrasse 36-40; mains €6.40-10.10) Indian food in an alternative-rock venue with regular crowds in the beer garden.

Sophienkeller (☎ 0351-497 260; Taschenberg 3; mains €9-16.50) Tourist-oriented, but the costumed wenches serve up good local specialities and wines.

Sleeping

Hotel Bülow Residenz (☎ 0351-800 30; Rähnitzstrasse 19; s/d €170/210) A real gem on a quiet street near Palaisplatz. The house restaurant is rated one of the best in Saxony.

Hotel Kempinski Taschenberg Palais (☎ 0351-491 20; Taschenberg 3; s €255-340, d €285-370) Restored 18th-century mansion with views over the Zwinger, incredibly quiet corridors and Bulgari toiletries.

Hotel Kipping (☎ 0351-478 500; Winckelmannstrasse 6; s €70-95, d €85-115) Family-run, family-friendly hotel with fervent reader recommendations.

Hotel Privat (☎ 0351-811 770; Forststrasse 22; s €46-61, d €62-82) One of Germany's few entirely non-smoking hotels.

Radisson SAS Gewandhaushotel (☎ 0351-494 90; Ringstrasse 1; r €135-200) Top choice for class and personal service.

Rothenburger Hof (☎ 0351-812 60; Rothenburger Strasse 15-17; s/d €95/130) Clean, bright atmosphere and lots of beauty treatments.

LEIPZIG

Leipzig became known as the Stadt der Helden (City of Heroes) for its leading role in the 1989 democratic revolution. Residents organised protests against the communist regime in May of that year; by October, hundreds of thousands were taking to the streets, placing candles outside Stasi headquarters and attending peace services at Nikolaikirche (St Nicholas Church). By the time the secret police started pulping their files, Leipzigers were partying in the streets, and they haven't stopped – from late winter, street-side cafés begin opening their terraces, and countless bars keep the beat going through the night.

Leipzig has some of the finest classical music and opera in the country, and its art and literary scenes are flourishing. It was once home to Bach, Wagner and Mendelssohn, and to Goethe, who studied here. Today the big news for Leipzig is its strong Olympic bid for 2012, which would rocket the city to international stardom. Right now Leipzig is arguably the most dynamic city in eastern Germany and great things are expected here in the next few years.

Leipzig's centre lies within a ring road that outlines the town's medieval fortifications. To reach the centre from the railway station, cross Willy-Brandt-Platz and continue south along Nikolaistrasse for about five minutes; the central **Markt** is a couple of blocks southwest. Here, the Renaissance **Altes Rathaus** (1556), one of Germany's most stunning town halls, houses the **City History Museum**.

Move south across the street to enter the orange, baroque **Apelshaus** (1606–07), with its lovely bay windows. It's now a contemporary shopping mall known as the Königshaus Passage, but in its heyday overnight guests included Peter the Great and Napoleon. The Passage leads directly into the **Mädlerpassage**, which must be one of the world's most beautiful shopping centres. A mix of neo-Renaissance and Art Nouveau, it opened as

Transport

Distance from Berlin 160km.
Direction Southwest.
Travel Time 1½ hours.
Car Leipzig lies just south of the A14 and east of the A9 Berlin–Nuremberg road. It's best to leave your vehicle in one of the parking lots outside the Altstadt.
Train Regular regional trains link Leipzig and Berlin–Ostbahnhof (€33.20).

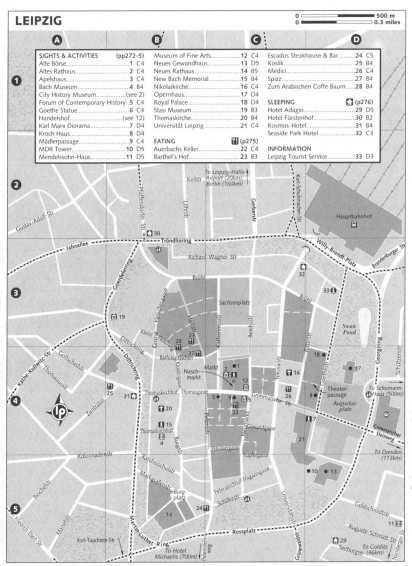

LEIPZIG

0 — 500 m
0 — 0.3 miles

SIGHTS & ACTIVITIES	(pp272-5)	Museum of Fine Arts	12 C4	Escados Steakhouse & Bar	24 C5
Alte Börse	1 C4	Neues Gewandhaus	13 D5	Koslik	25 B4
Altes Rathaus	2 C4	Neues Rathaus	14 B5	Medici	26 C4
Apelshaus	3 C4	New Bach Memorial	15 B4	Spizz	27 B4
Bach Museum	4 B4	Nikolaikirche	16 C4	Zum Arabischen Coffe Baum	28 B4
City History Museum	(see 2)	Opernhaus	17 D4		
Forum of Contemporary History	5 C4	Royal Palace	18 D4	SLEEPING	(p276)
Goethe Statue	6 C4	Stasi Museum	19 B3	Hotel Adagio	29 D5
Handelshof	(see 12)	Thomaskirche	20 B4	Hotel Fürstenhof	30 B2
Karl Marx Diorama	7 D4	Universität Leipzig	21 C4	Kosmos-Hotel	31 B4
Kroch Haus	8 D4			Seaside Park Hotel	32 C3
Mädlerpassage	9 C4	EATING	(p275)		
MDR Tower	10 D5	Auerbachs Keller	22 C4	INFORMATION	
Mendelssohn-Haus	11 D5	Barthel's Hof	23 B3	Leipzig Tourist Service	33 D3

Excursions – Leipzig

a trade hall in 1914 and was renovated at great expense in the early 1990s. Today it's home to shops, restaurants, cafés and, most notably, **Auerbachs Keller** (see Eating, p275). There are statues of Faust, Mephistopheles and some students at the northern exit; according to tradition you should touch Faust's foot for good luck.

Next to this exit, the haunting and uplifting **Forum of Contemporary History** depicts the history of the GDR from division and dictatorship to resistance and demise. Watching videos of families stifling tears as the Berlin Wall was built between them, it's hard not to feel moved by the Gentle Revolution that started right here in Leipzig.

Turn north out of the Mädlerpassage and you'll reach the **Naschmarkt** (snack market) which is dominated by the **Alte Börse** (1687), an ornate former trading house. In front is a statue of **Goethe** (1903), who studied law at Leipzig University. Today, the Alte Börse is a cultural centre, with concerts, plays and readings throughout the year, and the courtyard is a wonderful place for a drink on sunny afternoons. On your right is the **Handelshof**, the old trade hall, which temporarily houses the **Museum of Fine Arts** (due to move to Sachsenplatz in late 2004).

Northeast of here is the **Nikolaikirche** (1165). Begun in Romanesque style, it was enlarged and converted to late Gothic, and has an amazing classical interior. The church was the chief meeting point for peaceful demonstrators from May 1989, shortly before the GDR imploded. The church still runs 'Swords to Ploughshares' services, which are peace-oriented sermons with a political edge, on Mondays at 5pm.

Carry on east through the Theaterpassage to reach **Augustusplatz**, Leipzig's cultural-nerve centre. The glass structures (actually lifts to the underground car park) glow at night, lending the concrete slabs some much-needed warmth. Pivot left and you'll see the neoclassical **Royal Palace**, which is now a university building.

To the north is the functional **Opernhaus** (opera house, 1956–60), which has a **statue of Richard Wagner** out the back. To the west, the 11-storey **Kroch Haus** was Leipzig's first 'sky-scraper' and now houses part of the university's art collection. At the southern end of the square are the modern, heroic **Neues Gewandhaus** (1981), home to the city's classical and jazz concerts, and the **MDR tower** (1970; lift €1.50), occupied by the Mitteldeutscher Rundfunk broadcasting company. A new concert hall is currently under construction at its base.

On the west side of the square, at the entrance to Universität Leipzig (Leipzig University), is a revolting bronze **diorama** that depicts Karl Marx. The red steel A-frame around it is the **monument** to St Paul's Church (Paulinerkirche), which stood on this site. Leipzigers have never quite forgiven the church's destruction during WWII.

New Bach Memorial (below)

Heading west around the ring road, you confront the impressive 108m-high tower of the baroque **Neues Rathaus**. Although the building's origins date back to the 16th century, its current manifestation was completed in 1905. Recently renovated, the interior makes it one of the finest municipal buildings in Germany, with a grand staircase straight out of a Donald Trump dream.

From Burgplatz, walk up Burgstrasse to find the **Thomaskirche** (St Thomas Church; 1212), which contains the tomb of composer Johann Sebastian Bach. The church was extended and converted to Gothic style in 1496, and was the site of the baptisms of Richard Wagner, Karl Liebknecht and all of Bach's offspring. Bach worked here as a cantor from 1723 until his death in 1750. Outside the church is the **New Bach Memorial** (1908), showing the composer standing against an organ, with his left-hand jacket pocket turned inside out (with 20 children from two marriages, the great composer always claimed to be broke).

Opposite the church, in a baroque house, is the **Bach Museum**, which focuses on the composer's life in Leipzig. The Matthäus Passion, Johannes Passion, Weihnachts Oratorium and the h-Moll Messe, among others, were written here.

Musical Footnotes

Besides Bach, two other important composers have museums dedicated to them in Leipzig: Felix Mendelssohn Bartholdy, who lived (and died) in the **Mendelssohn-Haus** (☎ 0341-127 0294; Gold-schmidtstrasse 12; ☽ 10am-6pm); and Robert Schumann, who spent the first four years of his marriage to Leipzig pianist Clara Wieck in the **Schumann-Haus** (☎ 0341-393 9620; Inselstrasse 18; ☽ 2-5pm Wed-Sat).

Detour: Colditz

In the secluded Zwickauer Mulde valley, 46km south of Leipzig, lies the sleepy town of Colditz and its impressive (though run-down) fortress. The Renaissance structure was used by Augustus the Strong as a hunting lodge in the 17th century and it became a mental hospital in the 1800s. In WWII the Nazis converted it into a high-security prison, known as Oflag IVc (Officer's Camp IVc).

Its inmates, mostly Allied officers who had already escaped other prisons, proved this was a mistake. Between 1939 and 1945 there were more than 300 escape attempts, earning Colditz the reputation as a 'bad boys' camp. In all, 31 men managed to flee, aided by ingenious self-made gadgetry, such as a glider made of wood and bed sheets. Most astounding, though, is the 44m-long tunnel that French officers dug between 1941 and 1942 before the Germans caught them.

A number of prisoners turned writers after the war, and their tales have spawned more than 70 books, several films and at least one BBC TV series. Today the fortress houses a small but fascinating **Escape Museum** (☎ 034381-449 87; admission adult/concession €3/2; 🕑 10am-5pm).

Bus Nos 931 and 690 run to Colditz from Leipzig. You can also take a train to Bad Lausick and catch bus No 613. The town is at the junction of the B107 and B176 between Leipzig and Chemnitz.

Back on the ring road, the chilling **Stasi Museum** is in the former headquarters of the East German secret police, a building known as the Runde Ecke (Round Corner). At the front are photographs of demonstrations in October and November 1989; inside are exhibits on propaganda, preposterous disguises, surveillance photos and, in the back, mounds of papier-mâché created when officers shredded and soaked secret documents before the fall of the GDR.

Information

Leipzig Tourist Service (☎ 0341-710 4260; www.leipzig .de; Richard-Wagner-Strasse 1; 🕑 9am-7pm Mon-Fri, 9am-4pm Sat, 9am-2pm Sun)

Sights

Alte Börse (☎ 0341-961 0368; 🕑 tours by appointment 5pm Mon-Fri)

Bach Museum (☎ 0341-964 110; Thomaskirchhof 16; admission adult/concession €3/2; 🕑 10am-5pm)

City History Museum (☎ 0341-965 130; Markt 1; admission adult/child €2.50/2; 🕑 10am-6pm Tue-Sun)

Forum of Contemporary History (☎ 0341-222 20; Grimmaische Strasse 6; 🕑 9am-6pm Tue-Fri, 10am-6pm Sat & Sun)

Museum of Fine Arts (☎ 0341-216 990; Grimmaische Strasse 1-7; admission adult/concession €2.50/1; 🕑 10am-6pm Tue, Thu-Sun, 1-8pm Wed)

Neues Gewandhaus (☎ 0341-127 00; Augustusplatz 8)

Neues Rathaus (☎ 0341-1230; Nikolaiplatz; admission free; 🕑 6.45am-4.30pm Mon-Fri)

Nikolaikirche (☎ 0341-960 5270; Nikolaiplatz; admission free; 🕑 10am-6pm)

Opernhaus (☎ 0341-126 1261; Augustusplatz)

Stasi Museum (☎ 0341-961 2443; Dittrichring 24; admission free; 🕑 10am-6pm)

Thomaskirche (☎ 0341-212 4676; Thomaskirchhof; admission free; 🕑 9am-6pm)

Eating

Auerbachs Keller (☎ 0341-216 100; Mädlerpassage; mains €10.50-20.60) One of Germany's classic restaurants, founded in 1525 and featured in Goethe's *Faust – Part I*. Ludicrously popular with locals and tourists alike.

Barthel's Hof (☎ 0341-141 310; Hainstrasse 1; mains €8-14) Has fantastic buffets (€8.30-11.99) and quirky Saxon dishes such as *Heubraten* (lamb roasted on hay).

Escados Steakhouse & Bar (☎ 0341-960 7127; Martin-Luther-Ring 2; mains €8.50-18.40) Tropical meets classical, with palm trees, columns and lots of Argentine beef.

Koslik (☎ 0341-998 5993; cnr Gottschedstrasse & Zentralstrasse; mains €5.60-13) Stylish interior and excellent mixed cuisine, from Italian standards to duck *à l'orange*.

Medici (☎ 0341-211 3878; Nikolaikirchhof 5; mains €19.50-23) Impossibly classy Italian, widely regarded as one of the best restaurants in Leipzig.

Spizz (☎ 0341-960 8043; Markt 9) One of the coolest bars in town, with excellent live jazz and a dance floor.

Zum Arabischen Coffe Baum (☎ 0341-965 1321; Kleine Fleischergasse 4; mains €7.50-15) Leipzig's oldest café; excellent meals over three floors, plus a coffee museum.

Sleeping

Hotel Adagio (☎ 0341-216 699; Seeburgstrasse 96; s/d €67/79) Small, stylish private hotel in a quiet area, smartly decked out in black and white.

Hotel Fürstenhof (☎ 0341-1400; Tröndlinring 8; s €125-270, d €151-300) Ultra-luxurious grand hotel with a 200-year tradition and more mod cons than you can imagine.

Hotel Michaelis (☎ 0341-267 80; Paul-Gruner-Strasse 44; s €70-95, d €85-125) Superior three-star townhouse with well-equipped rooms.

Kosmos-Hotel (☎ 0341-233 4422; Gottschedstrasse 1; s/d €35/60) Unique theatre-inspired hotel with individually styled rooms – wake up next to Marilyn Monroe or in one of a dozen equally fantastical surrounds.

Seaside Park Hotel (☎ 0341-985 20; Richard-Wagner-Strasse 7; s €105-125, d €126-140) Nice Art Nouveau house in the town centre, with a commendable restaurant.

Directory

Directory

TRANSPORT

AIR

Lufthansa and all major European national carriers offer direct flights to Berlin, but if you're travelling from overseas you will most likely have to change carriers in another European city such as Frankfurt, Munich, Amsterdam, London etc. Berlin is also a major destination for the new crop of low-cost carriers that has sprung up throughout Europe in the recent years.

When making your flight booking, the Internet can be your best friend for ferreting out bargain fares. Discount online agencies such as www.travelocity.com and www.expedia.com should be your first stop, but also check the airlines' own websites for promotional fares, which may have to be booked online. This is especially important with most of the low-frills carriers, which only sell to travellers directly and don't even show up in the computerised systems used by travel agencies.

Airlines

EUROPEAN CARRIERS

Air Berlin (☎ 01805-737 800; www.air-berlin.com)

Air France (☎ 01805-830 830; www.airfrance.fr)

Alitalia (☎ 01805-074 747; www.alitalia.it)

British Airways (☎ 01805-266 522; www.britishairways.co.uk)

Deutsche BA (☎ 01805-359 3222; www.flydba.com)

duo (☎ 0711-490 813 040; www.duo.com)

easyJet (☎ 01803-654 321; www.easyjet.com)

Germania Express (☎ 01805-737 100; www.gexx.com)

Iberia (☎ 01803-000 613; www.iberia.es)

KLM (☎ 01805-254 750; www.klm.com)

Lufthansa (☎ 01803-803 803; www.lufthansa.com)

Ryan Air (☎ 0190-170 100; www.ryanair.com)

SAS (☎ 01803-234 023; www.scandinavian.net)

Swiss (☎ 01803-000 334; www.swiss.com)

Volare Airlines (☎ 0800-101 4169; www.volareweb.com)

OVERSEAS CARRIERS

Air Canada (☎ 01805-024 7226; www.aircanada.ca)

Air New Zealand (☎ 0800-5494 5494; www.airnz.co.nz)

American Airlines (☎ 0180-324 2324; www.aa.com)

Continental (☎ 0180-321 2610; www.continental.com)

Delta Airlines (☎ 01803-337 880; www.delta.com)

Qantas Airways (☎ 01805-250 620; www.quantas.com.au)

United Airlines (☎ 069-5007 0387; www.ual.com)

US Airways (☎ 01803-000 609; www.usairways.com)

ONLINE TICKETING

Recommended online ticketing agents:

Australia (www.travel.com.au)

Canada (www.expedia.ca; www.travelocity.ca)

France (www.anyway.fr; www.lastminute.fr; www.nouvelles-frontieres.fr)

Italy (www.cts.it)

New Zealand (www.travel.co.nz)

Spain (www.barceloviajes.com; www.nouvelles-frontieres.es)

UK & Ireland (www.b-t-w.co.uk; www.ebookers.com; www.flightcentre.co.uk; www.northsouthtravel.co.uk; www.questravel.com; www.statravel.co.uk; www.trailfinders.co.uk; www.travelbag.co.uk)

USA (www.cheaptickets.com; www.expedia.com; www.lowestfare.com; www.orbitz.com; www.sta.com; www.travelocity.com)

Airports

Berlin has three airports; the general information number for all of them is ☎ 0180-500 0186 (www.berlin-airport.de).

The busiest airport is Tegel (TXL), about 8km northwest of the city centre, which primarily serves destinations within Germany and western Europe.

Schönefeld (SXF), some 22km southeast of the city centre, handles mostly flights to/from eastern Europe, the Americas, Asia and Africa. It is also a popular airport with low-frills carriers such as easyJet and Ryan Air. Both airports have left-luggage offices (⏰ 5.30am-10pm), ATMs, currency exchange desks and postal facilities.

The third airport is the central but tiny Tempelhof (THF) in southern Kreuzberg, but it is expected to close in 2005.

TEGEL

Tegel airport (Map pp318-19) is connected to Mitte by the JetExpressBus TXL (€4.10, 30 minutes), which makes stops at such strategic places as Unter den Linden and Alexanderplatz. If you're making your way to Charlottenburg or northern Wilmersdorf, you're better off hopping aboard bus Nos X9 or 109 (€2, 30 minutes).

Tegel is not directly served by the U-Bahn. The nearest station is Jakob-Kaiser-Platz (U7), which is on the route of bus No 109. Alternatively, you could take bus No 128 from the airport to the Kurt-Schumacher-Platz station, with onward services on the U6.

A taxi between Tegel and either Zoo station or Mitte costs about €20.

SCHÖNEFELD

Schönefeld airport (Map pp318-19) is served twice hourly by the AirportExpress train, with departures from Zoo station (30 minutes), Friedrichstrasse (23 minutes), Alexanderplatz (20 minutes) and Ostbahnhof (15 minutes). You'll need a standard AB zone ticket (€2; see Tickets & Fares, p280).

An alternative is the much slower S9 (€2, 50 minutes). The Schönefeld train station is located about 300m from the terminal, to which it is linked by a free shuttle bus every 10 minutes. Bus No 171 links the terminal directly with the U-Bahn station Rudow (U7) with connections to central Berlin. A taxi between Schönefeld and central Berlin costs between €25 and €35.

TEMPELHOF

Tempelhof airport (Map pp325-7) can be easily reached on the U6 (get off at Platz der Luftbrücke) or by bus No 119 from Kurfürstendamm via Kreuzberg. A taxi to Bahnhof Zoo or Mitte costs about €15.

BICYCLE

The German bicycle club **ADFC** (Map pp322-4; ☎ 448 4724; www.adfc-berlin.de; Brunnenstrasse 28; ☒ noon-8pm Mon-Fri, 10am-4pm Sat) publishes an excellent guide showing all the bike routes throughout Berlin. It's available at their office/shop and also in bookshops and bike stores.

Bicycles are allowed all day in designated areas on U-Bahn trains and trams, but not on buses. The cost is an additional €1.40. Taking your bike on a Deutsche Bahn train costs €3 on RE (RegionalExpress) and RB (Regional-

bahn) trains and €8 on long-distance IC, ICE and IR trains.

Hire

Several agencies rent bicycles with costs ranging from €10 to €25 per day and €35 to €85 per week, depending on the model. A minimum deposit of €50 and/or ID is required. The largest outfit is **Fahrradstation** (☎ 0180-510 8000), which has several centrally located branches.

Fahrradstation (Map pp328-9; ☎ 2859 9661; Augustusstrasse 29a; ☒ 10am-7pm Mon-Fri, 10am-3pm Sat; U-Bahn Weinmeisterstrasse)

Fahrradstation (Map pp328-9; ☎ 2045 4500; Friedrichstrasse 141/142; ☒ 8am-8pm Mon-Fri, 10am-4pm Sat & Sun; U-/S-Bahn Friedrichstrasse)

Fahrradstation (Map pp328-9; ☎ 2838 4848; Hof VII, Hackesche Höfe; ☒ 10am-7pm Mon-Fri, 10am-4pm Sat; S-Bahn Hackescher Markt)

Fahrradstation (Map pp325-7; ☎ 215 1566; Bergmannstrasse 9; ☒ 10am-7pm, 10am-3pm Sat; U-Bahn Mehringdamm)

Fahrradservice Kohnke (Map pp328-9; ☎ 447 6666; Friedrichstrasse 133; ☒ 9am-midnight Mon-Fri; U-/S-Bahn Friedrichstrasse)

Pedal Power (Map pp325-7; ☎ 5515 3270; Grossbeerenstrasse 53; ☒ 10am-7pm Mon-Fri, 10am-2pm Sat; U-Bahn Mehringdamm) Specialises in tandems (per day/week €20/79).

Prenzlberger Orange Bikes (Map pp322-4; ☎ 442 8122; Kollwitzstrasse 35; ☒ 2.30pm-7pm Mon-Fri, 1pm-7pm Sat, 6pm-7pm Sun; U-Bahn Senefelderplatz) No bike hire on Sunday; hours are for return only.

BUS

Berlin's central bus station, **ZOB** (Map pp318-19; Masurenallee 4-6), is about 4km west of Zoo station, right by the Funkturm radio tower in western Charlottenburg. The closest U-Bahn stop is Kaiserdamm (U2, U12). Tickets are available from the **ZOB Reisebüro** (information ☎ 301 8028, reservations ☎ 301 0380; ☒ 6.30am-9pm), although many travel agencies in town also sell them. The main operator is **BerlinLinienBus** (☎ 0180-154 6436, in Berlin ☎ 860 960; www.berlinlinienbus.de) with departures for destinations throughout Europe. **Gulliver's** (☎ 311 0211; www.gullivers.de) also has an extensive route system. Both companies offer discounts to students and people under 26 and over 60.

See Local Transport (p280) for details about Berlin's local bus network.

CAR & MOTORCYCLE

Driving

Berlin is less congested than other capitals, making getting around by car comparatively easy, but we still don't recommend it. The public transport system is wonderfully efficient, easy to comprehend and generally a much faster, comfortable and environmentally friendly way of getting around. If you're driving, keep in mind that finding parking can be a nightmare, or at least an expensive proposition with public garages charging a cool €1 to €2 per hour.

Rental

There aren't many reasons you'll want to rent a car in Berlin, but in case you really need one, you'll find branches of all the major international chains at the airports, major train stations and throughout town. Contact the following central reservation numbers for the branch nearest you:

Avis (☎ 01805-557 755; www.avis.com)

Budget (☎ 01805-244 388; www.budget.com)

Europcar (☎ 01805-8000; www.europcar.com)

Hertz (☎ 0800-816 1712; www.hertz.com)

Although you can make a booking with the reservation agent, it may be worth checking directly with the local branch for special deals the central agent doesn't know about.

You may also do better by renting from a local outfit. One of the most popular and reliable is **Robben & Wientjes** (Map pp325-7; in Kreuzberg ☎ 616 770; Prinzenstrasse 90-91; U-Bahn Moritzplatz; Map pp322-4; in Prenzlauer Berg ☎ 421 036; Prenzlauer Allee 96; U-Bahn Prenzlauer Allee).

There are a couple of reliable motorcycle rental outfits in case you get that 'Harley Hunger' urge. Prices range from €50 to €130 per day, depending on the model:

Classic Bike Harley-Davidson (Map pp325-7; ☎ 616 7930; Skalitzer Strasse 127/8; U-Bahn Kottbusser Tor)

V2-Moto (Map pp325-7; ☎ 6128 0490; Skalitzer Strasse 69; U-Bahn Schlesisches Tor)

LOCAL TRANSPORT

Berlin's public transport system is composed of services provided by **Berliner Verkehrsbetriebe** (BVG; 24hr information ☎ 194 49) and **Deutsche Bahn** (DB; ☎ 11861). BVG operates the U-Bahn, buses, trams and ferries, while DB is in charge of the S-Bahn, Regionalbahn (RB) and Regional-express (RE).

The **BVG information kiosk** (Map pp332-3; Hardenbergplatz; ☼ 6am-10pm) outside Zoo station has free route network maps and also sells tickets. For information on S-Bahn, RE and RB connections, visit the Reisezentrum office inside any train station.

Tickets & Fares

Berlin's metropolitan area is divided into three tariff zones – A, B and C. Tickets are valid in at least two zones, AB or BC, or in all three zones, ABC. Unless you're venturing to Potsdam or the very outer suburbs, you'll only need the AB ticket. The Group Day Pass is valid for up to five people travelling together. Kids aged under six travel free. Children aged six to 14 qualify for reduced (Ermässigt) rates.

Ticket type	AB	BC	ABC
Single	2	2.25	2.60
Day Pass	5.60	5.70	6
Group Day Pass (up to 5 people)	14	14.30	15
7-Day Pass	23.40	24	29

Buying & Using Tickets

Bus drivers sell single tickets and day passes (Tageskartes), but tickets for U-/S-Bahn trains and other multiple, weekly or monthly tickets must be purchased before boarding from orange vending machines (with instructions in English) in U-/S-Bahn stations or from the BVG information kiosk. Tickets must be stamped (validated) at station platform entrances or at bus stops before boarding. If an inspector catches you without a ticket (or even an unvalidated one), you will have to pay an on-the-spot €40 fine. Once the domain of retired gentlemen, inspectors now come in all ages, races and genders. To stop potential impostors, all inspectors carry a BVG identity card with their photograph.

Buses & Trams

Berlin's buses are rather slow, but being ensconced on the upper level of a double-decker is an inexpensive way to do some relaxed sightseeing (see the boxed text opposite).

Bus stops are marked with a large `H' (for Haltestelle) and the name of the stop. The next stop is usually announced via a loudspeaker or displayed on a digital board. Push the button on the handrails if you want to get off.

Night buses operate from around midnight until 6am, running at roughly 30-minute intervals. Normal fares apply.

Trams only operate in the eastern districts.

S-Bahn & Regional Trains

S-Bahn trains make fewer stops than U-Bahns and are therefore handy for longer distances, but they don't run as frequently. They operate from around 4am to 12.30am and throughout the night on Friday, Saturday and public holidays.

Destinations further afield are served by RB and RE trains. You'll need an ABC or Deutsche Bahn rail ticket to use these trains.

See Train (below) for information on long-distance travel within Germany and Europe.

U-Bahn

The most efficient way to travel around Berlin is by U-Bahn, which operates from 4am until just after midnight, except at weekends and holidays when it continues through the night on all lines (aside from the U1, U4 and U12). The next station is announced on most of the U-Bahn trains and is also displayed at the end of carriages on some newer trains.

TAXI

You'll find taxi ranks at the airports, major train stations and throughout the city. Flag fall is €2.50, then it's €1.50 per kilometre up to 7km and €1 for each kilometre after that. You can order a taxi on ☎ 194 10, ☎ 0800-8001 1554 or ☎ 0800-026 1026.

For short trips, you can use the €3 flat rate, which entitles you to ride for 2km. It is *only* available if you flag down a moving taxi and request this special rate before the driver has activated the regular meter.

Velotaxis

A nonpolluting alternative for short hops is a **velotaxi** (☎ 0151-122 8000; www.velotaxi.de), a comfortable two-seater pedicab, aided by an electric engine, which you can simply flag down. They operate from April to October from noon to 8.30pm along four routes: Kurfürstendamm, Unter den Linden, Potsdamer Platz and Tiergarten. The cost is €2.50 per person for the first kilometre, then €1 for each additional kilometre. Half-hour tours are €7.50 per person.

TRAIN

Germany's rail system is operated almost entirely by the **Deutsche Bahn** (DB; reservations & information ☎ 118 61, toll-free automated timetable ☎ 0800-150 7090; www.bahn.de).

Until completion of the main central station at Lehrter Bahnhof (currently projected for 2006), **Bahnhof Zoo** (Zoo Station; Map pp332-3) and **Ostbahnhof** (Map pp325-7) are Berlin's two major train stations for national and international long-distance service; most trains stop at both. Stations have great infrastructure with left-luggage offices, coin lockers, car rental agencies, currency exchange offices and various shops and restaurants.

Berlin is well connected by train to other German cities, as well as to eastern European destinations, including Prague, Budapest and Warsaw. Coming from other international cities will most likely involve at least one change of train.

Tickets can be bought from agents inside the large *Reisezentrum* (travel centre) and, for shorter distances, from vending machines.

Directory – Transport

Buying tickets on board (cash only) incurs a surcharge of €2 to €7.50. For trips over 101km, you can also buy tickets online (www.bahn.de) up to one hour before departure at no surcharge; you'll need a major credit card and a print-out of your ticket to present to the conductor.

Seat reservations for long-distance travel are highly recommended, especially if you're travelling on a Friday or Sunday afternoon, during holiday periods or in summer. The fee is a flat €2.60, regardless of the number of seats booked, and reservations can be made as late as a few minutes before departure.

PRACTICALITIES

ACCOMMODATION

Accommodation listings in the Sleeping chapter (pp240-54) are organised by district, and then in alphabetical order. Most of our recommendations are mid-range options, which generally offer the best value for money. Expect clean, comfortable and decent-sized rooms with at least a modicum of style, a private bathroom, TV and telephone. Our selection also includes a few top-end hotels, which have an international standard of amenities and perhaps a scenic location, special décor or historical ambience. Budget places (listed under Cheap Sleeps at the end of each sleeping section) are simple establishments where bathrooms are usually shared.

Berlin is busiest between May and September, with the thinnest flow of visitors arriving between November and March (except around the year-end holidays) when rates may drop and special deals abound. Prices generally soar during busy trade shows like the ITB (International Tourism Fair) in early March, mega-events like the Love Parade in July or major holidays, especially New Year's Eve.

For additional details refer to the introductory sections of the Sleeping chapter (p240).

BUSINESS

With the world's third-largest economy, Germany has long been one of Europe's most important addresses for doing business. Although Berlin is still eclipsed by Frankfurt as the country's commercial and financial centre, it is slowly gaining in esteem with such international corporations as Sony and Universal Music, which have moved their European headquarters here.

Berlin's new generation of hotels, especially the high-end international chains, cater well for the needs of business travellers. Rooms are usually wired for connectivity, and various services, including PC and fax machine rentals and photocopying, are widely available. Some properties even have full business centres with meeting rooms or can arrange secretarial services. Berlin has a high concentration of English speakers, making getting down to business a great deal easier.

The commercial division of your country's embassy in Berlin can be a great help in sourcing reliable translators or other service providers. Another good place to turn for help is the **Industrie- und Handelskammer Berlin** (Chamber of Industry & Commerce; ☎ 315 1000; www.berlin.ihk.de; Fasanenstrasse 85).

All major international courier services operate in Berlin. To schedule a pick-up, call **FedEx** (☎ 0800-123 0800), **UPS** (☎ 0800-882 6630) or **DHL** (☎ 0800-225 5345).

Business Centres

If you need your own office to ink that deal, you can rent one through the companies listed below. Each provides the full range of turnkey business operations, including furnished offices and conference rooms, secretarial services, convention organisation, and telecom needs such as video conferencing. Offices are usually high-end and in prestigious locations.

MWB Business Exchange (Map p334; ☎ 2589 4000; info.de@mwbex.com; Potsdamer Platz 11, Tiergarten)

Regus Berlin (☎ 206 590; www.regus.com; Friedrichstrasse 95, Kreuzberg) Check the website or *Yellow Pages* for additional Berlin branches.

Worldwide Business Centres (Map pp328-9; ☎ 2431 0211; www.wwbcnetwork.com; Rosenstrasse 2, Mitte) Check the website or *Yellow Pages* for additional Berlin branches.

Business Hours

With the recent relaxation of shop trading hours, stores can open from 6am to 8pm Monday to Saturday. Actual hours vary widely. Stores in malls and major shopping streets such as the Kurfürstendamm are usually open from 9.30am to 8pm, but small boutiques and stores in the outer districts often close at 6pm or 7pm weekdays and at 4pm on Saturday. Train stations, petrol stations and the supermarkets listed in the Eating chapter (p163) are good places for stocking up after hours.

Banking hours are from 8.30am to 4pm Monday to Friday with most staying open until 5.30pm or 6.30pm on Thursday. Post office hours vary widely, although 9am to 6pm Monday to Friday and 9am to 1pm on Saturday is fairly typical for branches in the central city (also see Post, p289).

Travel agencies and other service-oriented businesses are usually open from 9am to 6pm weekdays and till 1pm or 2pm on Saturday. Government offices, on the other hand, close for the weekend as early as 1pm on Friday. Many of the major museums are closed on Monday but stay open late one evening a week.

For restaurant hours, see the Eating chapter (p161). Most bars open in the early evening, between 5pm and 8pm, although some now lure the after-work crowd with Happy Hour starting as early as 3pm or 4pm. With no compulsory closing hours, they tend to stay open until at least 1am. Clubs don't really get going before 11pm or midnight and often keep buzzing until sunrise.

CHILDREN

Travelling to Berlin with the tots in tow is not a problem, especially if you don't keep the schedule overly packed and involve the kids in the day-to-day planning. Lonely Planet's *Travel with Children*, by Cathy Lanigan, offers a wealth of tips and tricks on the subject.

There's certainly no shortage of things to see and do around Berlin, from wonderful zoos to kid-oriented museums to magic and puppet shows. Parks and imaginative playgrounds abound in all neighbourhoods, but especially in Prenzlauer Berg and Schöneberg, the districts most popular with young families. On hot summer days, a few hours spent at a public outdoor pool or on a lakeside beach will go a long way towards keeping toddlers' tempers cool. For more ideas, see the boxed text p119.

Baby food, infant formulas, soy and cow's milk, disposable nappies (diapers) and the like are widely available in chemists (drugstores) and supermarkets. Breastfeeding in public is practised, although most women are discreet about it.

Children's discounts are widely available for everything from museum admissions to bus fares and hotel accommodation. The definition of a 'child' varies, however; some places consider anyone under age 18 eligible for discounts, while others put the cut-off at age six.

Babysitting

Aufgepasst (☎ 851 3723; www.aufgepasst.de) English-speaking babysitters, nannies and daycare.

Biene Maja (☎ 344 3973; www.babysitteragentur -berlin.de)

Kinder-Hotel (Map pp322-4; ☎ 4171 6928; www.kinderinsel.de; Eichendorffstrasse 17, Mitte; U-Bahn Zinnowitzer Strasse) Children-only hotel with 24-hour daycare in 12 languages.

CLIMATE

Berlin has a moderately cool and humid climate and is generally comfortable to visit any time of year. The weather tends to be the most pleasant in summer, which is rarely suffocatingly hot (usually around 25°C), the occasional freak heat wave notwithstanding. Spring is beautiful but can be slow to arrive, even if jackets are sometimes stripped off as early as April. Early autumn brings the added bonus of bright foliage and sunshine, which can keep outdoor cafés open through October. Predictably, December to February are the coldest months. When fierce winds blow in from Russia, it gets mighty chilly, with subzero temperatures but clear, cloudless skies. Rain is a possibility any time of year.

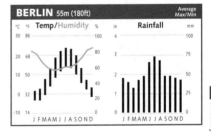

CUSTOMS

Articles that you take to Germany for your personal use may be imported free of duty and tax, with some conditions. The following restrictions apply to duty-free goods purchased in a non-EU country (imagine the poor bureaucrats who have to come up with these regulations):

Alcohol 1L of alcohol above 22%, or 2L of alcohol less than 22% and 2L of wine (if over age 17).

Coffee & Tea 500g or 200g of extracts (if over age 15).

Perfume 50g of perfume and 0.25L of eau de toilette.

Tobacco 200 cigarettes, 100 cigarillos, 50 cigars or 250g of loose tobacco (if over age 17).

Additional products Up to the value of €175.

Directory – Practicalities

DISABLED TRAVELLERS

There's been a definite improvement in Berlin when it comes to catering for the needs of the disabled (Behinderte), especially the wheel-chair-bound. You'll find access ramps and/or lifts in many public buildings, including train stations, museums, theatres and cinemas. For specifics, check **Mobidat** (www.mobidat.net in German), a databank evaluating 18,000 public places – hotels, restaurants, department stores, museums etc – for accessibility to the mobility-impaired. If your wheelchair breaks down, call ☎ 0180-111 4747 for 24-hour assistance.

Newer hotels can offer rooms for disabled guests with extra-wide doors and spacious bathrooms. Individual listings in the Sleeping chapter mention hotels classified on Mobidat as wheelchair-friendly. Your best bet, though, may be the **Hotel MIT-Mensch** (☎ 509 6930; www.mit-mensch.com; Ehrlichstrasse 48; s €47-57, d €72-93; S-Bahn: Karlshorst), which is run by and for people in wheelchairs.

Getting around Berlin on public transport is possible but requires some planning. Four out of five buses and just over half of all trams have special ramps or lifts that enable the wheelchair-bound to get on and off without help. Look for the blue wheelchair symbol on the vehicles.

Getting into U-Bahn and S-Bahn trains isn't as difficult as getting onto the platform itself. Only 31% of U-Bahn stations –compared to 70% of S-Bahn stations – have lifts and ramps. To assist blind passengers, stations are being equipped with grooved platform borders for better orientation. Upcoming station names are announced via loudspeakers on nearly all public transport vehicles.

For full details, call **BVG** (☎ 19419) around the clock. You can also find complete mobility information in English on their website (www.bvg.de) under Service/Mobility Aid.

DISCOUNT CARDS

Cutting the costs while exploring Berlin is as easy as locating the TV Tower in the city's skyline. If you're a student, never leave home without an **International Student Identity Card** (ISIC; www.isiccard.com), which entitles you to discounts on movie and theatre tickets, travel insurance, and reduced admission to museums and other sights. If you're under 26 but not a student, get an **International Youth Travel Card** (IYTC) or the **Euro<26 youth card** (www.euro26.org), which offer similar savings and benefits. All these cards are issued by student unions, hostelling organisations and youth-oriented travel agencies.

The following Berlin-specific discount cards will help you stretch your travel euros even further, regardless of age:

Berlin WelcomeCard (€21) Entitles one adult and up to three children under 14 to 72 hours of public transport within the Berlin-Potsdam area and free or discounted admission to museums, shows, attractions, sightseeing tours and boat cruises. It's available at the BTM tourist offices (p291) and many hotels.

SchauLust Museen Berlin (adult/child €10/5) An unbeatable deal for museum lovers, this pass is valid for three consecutive days and gives unlimited admission to 60 Berlin museums, including blockbusters such as the Pergamon and the Egyptian. Sold at the BTM tourist offices (p291) and any participating museum.

SMB Museum Passes (adult/child one day €10/5, three days €12/6) Good for unlimited admission to all museums run by the Staatliche Museen zu Berlin (State Museums Berlin), denoted 'SMB' throughout this book. Available at any SMB museum.

ELECTRICITY

Standard voltage throughout Germany is 220V, 50 Hz AC. Plugs are the Continental type with two round pins. Your 220V appliances may be plugged into a German outlet with an adaptor, but their 110V cousins (eg from North America) require a transformer. Most shavers and laptops are designed to work on both 110V and 220V.

EMBASSIES & CONSULATES

Australia (Map pp328-9; ☎ 880 0800; www.Australian-embassy.de; Wallstrasse 76-78; U-Bahn Märkisches Museum)

Canada (Map pp328-9; ☎ 203 120; www.kanada-info.de; Friedrichstrasse 95; U-/S-Bahn Friedrichstrasse; U-/S-Bahn Potsdamer Platz) Scheduled to move to the Leipziger Platz in 2005.

Czech Republic (Map pp328-9; ☎ 226 380; www.mzv.cz/berlin; Wilhelmstrasse 44; U-Bahn Mohrenstrasse)

France (Map pp328-9; ☎ 590 039 000; www.botschaft-frankreich.de; Pariser Platz 5; S-Bahn Unter den Linden)

Ireland (Map pp325-7; ☎ 220 720; www.botschaft-irland.de; Friedrichstrasse 200; U-Bahn Kochstrasse)

Italy (Map p334; ☎ 254 400; www.botschaft-italien.de; Hiroshimastrasse 1; bus No 200)

Japan (Map p334; ☎ 210 940; www.botschaft-japan.de; Hiroshimastrasse 6; bus No 200)

The Netherlands (Map pp328-9; ☎ 209 560; www.dutch-embassy.de; Friedrichstrasse 95; U-/S-Bahn Friedrichstrasse)

New Zealand (Map pp328-9; ☎ 206 210; www.nzembassy.com; Friedrichstrasse 60; U-Bahn Stadtmitte)

Poland (☎ 223 130; www.botschaft-polen.de; Lassenstrasse 19-21; S-Bahn Grunewald)

Russia (Map pp328-9; ☎ 229 1110; www.russische
-botschaft.de; Unter den Linden 63-65; S-Bahn Unter den
Linden)

South Africa (Map p334; ☎ 220 730; www.suedafrika
.org; Tiergartenstrasse 18; bus No 200)

Switzerland (Map pp320-1; ☎ 390 4000; www.botschaft
-schweiz.de; Otto-von-Bismarck-Allee 4a; bus No 100)

United Kingdom (Map pp328-9; ☎ 204 570; www.britische
botschaft.de; Wilhelmstrasse 70; S-Bahn Unter den Linden)

USA (Map pp328-9; ☎ 238 5174; www.us-botschaft.de;
Neustädtische Kirchstrasse 4-5; U-/S-Bahn Friedrichstrasse)

USA Consulate (☎ 832 9233; Clayallee 170; U-Bahn
Oskar-Helene-Heim)

EMERGENCY

In the event of an emergency, call the **police**
(☎ 110) or **fire department/ambulance** (☎ 112).
Other useful phone numbers and addresses
include:

BVG Public Transport Lost & Found (Map pp330-1;
☎ 2562 3040; Potsdamer Strasse 180/182; ☺ 9am-6pm
Mon-Thu, 9am-2pm Fri; U-Bahn Kleistpark)

Drug Hotline (☎ 192 37)

Emergency Dental Referrals (☎ 8900 4333;
☺ after 8pm Mon-Fri, 24hr Sat & Sun)

International Helpline (☎ 4401 0607 in English;
☺ 6pm-midnight) Volunteer-run, anonymous help for
people in any crisis situation.

Medical Emergencies (☎ 310 031; ☺ 10am-12.30am
Mon-Fri, 8am-12.30am Sat & Sun) Provides medical
advice and dispatches doctors for 24-hour house calls.

Municipal Lost & Found (Map pp325-7; ☎ 756 00; Platz
der Lufbrücke 6, Tempelhof airport; ☺ 7.30am-2.30pm
Mon, 8.30am-4pm Tue, 1pm-7pm Thu, 7.30am-noon Fri;
U-Bahn Platz der Luftbrücke)

Police Headquarters (Map pp325-7; ☎ 6995; Platz der
Lufbrücke 6, Tempelhof airport; U-Bahn Platz der Luftbrücke)

Rape Crisis Hotline (☎ 251 2828)

Wheelchair Breakdown Service (☎ 0180-111 4747)

GAY & LESBIAN TRAVELLERS

Berlin's legendary liberalism has spawned one
of the world's biggest gay and lesbian scenes.
Anything goes in 'Homopolis' – and we mean
anything, from the highbrow to the hands-on,
the bourgeois to the bizarre, the mainstream
to the flamboyant.

Berlin's emergence as a gay mecca was kick-
started by sexual scientist Magnus Hirschfeld
who, in 1897, founded the Scientific Humanitarian Committee in the city, which paved the

way for gay liberation. The 1920s were especially
wild and wacky, a demimonde that drew and
inspired writers like Christopher Isherwood until
the Nazis put an end to the it in 1933. Postwar
recovery came slowly, but by the 1970s the
scene was firmly re-established, at least in the
western city. Since 2001, Berlin has been governed by an openly gay mayor, Klaus Wowereit,
who outed himself by saying 'I'm gay, and that's
a good thing', which has since become a popular slogan in the community.

As befits Berlin's decentralised nature, the
city has no dedicated gay ghetto, although
established bar and club scenes exist along
Motzstrasse and Fuggerstrasse in Schöneberg;
Schönhauser Allee and Gleimstrasse in Prenzlauer Berg; Oranienstrasse in Kreuzberg and
Mühlenstrasse in Friedrichshain. In early June,
huge crowds turn out in Schöneberg for the
Schwul-Lesbisches Strassenfest (Gay-Lesbian
Street Fair), which basically serves as a warm-up
for Christopher Street Day later that month.

Your best source for listings and news is the
free **Siegessäule** (www.siegessaeule.de), which
also publishes the handy English/German booklet **Out in Berlin** (www.out-in-berlin.de). *Sergej* is
another magazine, although it caters strictly for
men. *Zitty* and *030* also have listings.

For advice and information, gay men can
turn to **Mann-O-Meter** (Map pp330-1; ☎ 216
8008; Bülowstrasse 106; U-Bahn Nollendorfplatz) or the **Schwulenberatung** (Gay Advice Hotline; ☎ 194 46). For gay women there is the
Lesbenberatung (Lesbian Advice Hotline; ☎ 215
2000).

HOLIDAYS

Berlin observes nine religious and three secular holidays. Shops, banks, government offices
and post offices are closed on these days.

Germans are big fans of mini-vacations built
around public holidays – especially those in
spring – meaning that the city is likely to be
more crowded and lodging can be at a prime
cost on those dates.

For a list of festivals and special events in
Berlin, see the City Calendar p9.

Public Holidays

New Year's Day 1 January

Easter (Good Friday, Easter Sunday & Easter Monday)
March/April

Ascension Day 40 days after Easter

Labour Day 1 May

Whit/Pentecost Sunday & Monday May/June

Day of German Unity 3 October

Christmas Eve 24 December

Christmas Day 25 December

Boxing Day 26 December

School Holidays

Berlin kids get one week off in early February, two weeks around Easter, six weeks in summer, two weeks in early October and one week around Christmas and New Year. Exact dates vary each year.

INTERNET ACCESS

Surfing the Internet and checking your emails is no problem while in Berlin; internet cafés abound (see the list on below) and all hostels and many hotels offer Internet terminals for their guests. Hotel Gates (p247) and the Charlottenburger Hof (p246) are among those offering in-room PCs. Most public libraries offer free Internet access but connections tend to be slow and queues long.

If you're travelling with your own laptop, you'll find that many of the newer and recently renovated hotels in Berlin have the technology that lets you plug in from the comfort of your own room. However, you will most likely need to bring an adapter for the German-style telephone plug (available in electronics stores in Berlin, such as Saturn, or from your home country).

Lines are usually analogue but data ports and high-speed digital connections are becoming increasingly common. Be aware of potential problems you might encounter. If your hotel has digital phones but no data ports, you will need a digital-to-analog converter or risk frying your modem. Older properties still have hardwired telephones (ie wired into the walls), which cannot be unplugged. The only way to get around this problem is by using an acoustic coupler.

Sometimes your modem will not be able to recognise the dial tone. If you're using a PC, you can fix this by doing the following: open My Computer, go to Dial-Up Networking, right-click on your connection and select Properties, click Configure on the General tab, click the Connection tab and uncheck 'Wait for dial tone before dialling', then click 'OK' twice.

For more information on travelling with a portable computer and gadgets you might need to help you get online, see www.teleadapt.com or www.roadwarrior.com.

Internet Cafés

@Internet (Map pp325-7; ☎ 2977 6270; 1st fl Main Hall, Ostbahnhof, Friedrichshain; per hr €1; 🕑 10am-10pm; S-Bahn Ostbahnhof)

Al Hamra (Map pp322-4; ☎ 4285 0095; Raumerstrasse 16, Prenzlauer Berg; per 15 min €1; 🕑 10am-late; S-Bahn Prenzlauer Allee) Surfing goes exotic with water pipes and cocktails.

Alpha Café (Map pp322-4; ☎ 447 9067; Dunckerstrasse 72, Prenzlauer Berg; per 20 min €1; 🕑 noon-midnight; S-Bahn Prenzlauer Allee)

easyEverything (Map pp332-3; Kurfürstendamm 224, Charlottenburg; per hr €2; 🕑 6.30am-2am; U-Bahn Kurfürstendamm)

Netz Galaxie (Map pp332-3; ☎ 7870 6446; Joachimstaler Strasse 19, Charlottenburg; per hr €1; 🕑 11am-2am; U-Bahn Kurfürstendamm)

Surf & Sushi (Map pp328-9; ☎ 2838 4898; Oranienburger Strasse 17, Mitte; per 30 min €2.50; 🕑 noon-late Mon-Sat; 1pm-late Sun; S-Bahn Hackescher Markt, Oranienburger Strasse)

LEGAL MATTERS

German police are well trained, fairly 'enlightened' and usually treat tourists with respect. Most can speak some English. By German law you must carry some form of photographic identification, such as your passport, national identity card or driving licence.

Reporting theft to the police is usually a simple, if occasionally time-consuming, matter. Remember that the first thing to do is show some form of identification.

The legal drinking age is 16, and the legal driving age is 18. Penalties for drinking and driving are stiff. The permissible blood-alcohol limit is 0.05%; drivers caught exceeding this amount are subject to big fines, a confiscated licence and even jail time.

The sensible thing is to avoid illegal drugs entirely, as penalties can be harsh. Although treated as a minor offence, the possession of even small quantities of cannabis for personal use remains illegal, and getting caught may result in a court appearance. In practice, the courts often waive prosecution if it's a first offence involving only a small amount of cannabis. The definition of 'small', however, is up to the judge, so there are no guarantees. Most other drugs are treated more seriously.

If you are arrested, you have the right to make a phone call and are presumed innocent until proven guilty. For a referral to a lawyer, contact your embassy.

Directory – Practicalities

MAPS

The maps in this book should suffice in most cases, although the foldout map available for €1 from the BTM tourist offices (p291) might be a useful supplement.

For detailed explorations of outlying suburbs, you might need a larger city map such as those by ADAC, the RV Verlag Euro City or Falkplan. These are widely available at petrol stations, bookshops, newsagents and tourist offices and cost between €4.50 and €7.50.

MEDICAL SERVICES

The standard of healthcare is excellent in Germany, and with nearly 9000 doctors and dentists in Berlin alone you're never far from medical help. The US and UK consulates are among those who can provide you with lists of English-speaking doctors. Also see Emergency, p285.

If you are a citizen of the EU, an E111 form, available from health centres or, in the UK, post offices, covers you for most medical emergencies, although not for emergency repatriation home. Non-EU citizens should check if a similar reciprocal agreement exists between their country and Germany, or if their policy at home provides worldwide healthcare coverage.

If you need to buy travel health insurance, be sure to get a policy that also covers emergency flights back home. While some plans pay doctors or hospitals directly, note that many healthcare providers may still demand payment from non-locals at the time of service. Except in emergencies, call around for a doctor willing to accept your insurance.

There are no vaccinations required to visit Germany.

Emergency Rooms

Hospitals are plentiful throughout Berlin, but the following are university-affiliated and have large 24-hour emergency rooms:

Uniklinikum Benjamin Franklin (☎ 855 50, emergencies ☎ 8445 3015; Hindenburgdamm 30; S-Bahn Botanischer Garten) In the Steglitz district in southern Berlin.

Uniklinikum Charité (Map pp320-1; ☎ 280 20, emergencies ☎ 2802 4766; Schumannstrasse 20-21; U-Bahn Oranienburger Tor, S-Bahn Lehrter Stadtbahnhof) The most central of the major hospitals.

Virchow Klinikum (Map pp320-1; ☎ 450 50, emergencies ☎ 4505 2000; Augustenburger Platz 1; U-Bahn Amrumer Strasse) In the Wedding district in northern Berlin.

Zahnklinik Medeco (Dental Clinic) (Map p334; ☎ 2309 5960; Stresemannstrasse 121; ⏰ 7am-midnight; U-/S-Bahn Potsdamer Platz) Call or check the *Yellow Pages* for branches.

METRIC SYSTEM

Germany uses the metric system; there's a conversion table on the inside front cover of this book. Germans indicate decimals with commas and thousands with points (ie 10,000.00 is 10.000,00).

Clothing sizes – especially for women's clothing – are quite different from those in North America (NA) and Great Britain (UK). Women's size 8 in NA (size 10 in the UK) equals size 36 in Germany. Sizes then increase in increments of two, making German size 38 an NA 10 (UK 12) and so on.

MONEY

Since 1 January 2002, euro notes and coins have been Germany's official currency. One euro is divided into 100 cents. There are notes of 5, 10, 20, 50, 100, 200 and 500 euros and eight different coins of 1, 2, 5, 10, 20 and 50 cents and 1 and 2 euro.

Cash is still king in Germany, so you can't really avoid having at least some notes and coins, say €100 or so, on you at all times. Plan to pay in cash almost everywhere (see Credit Cards, p288 for likely exceptions).

ATMs

Automatic teller machines, found at most bank branches throughout Berlin, are convenient for obtaining cash from a bank account back home by using a debit (ATM) card. Most are linked to international network systems such as Cirrus, Plus, Star and Maestro. Check fees and availability of services with your bank before you leave.

Many ATMs also spit out cash if you use a credit card. This method tends to be more expensive because, in addition to a service fee, you'll be charged interest immediately (ie there's no grace period as with purchases).

For exact fees, check with your bank or credit card company.

Changing Money

The exchange services listed here usually offer some of the better rates, but you can also change money at most banks, post offices and airports. Remember that banks only exchange foreign notes and not coins.

American Express (Map pp328-9; ☎ 2045 5721; Friedrichstrasse 172; ☑ 9am-7pm Mon-Fri, 10am-1pm Sat; U-Bahn Französische Strasse)

Cash Express (Map pp328-9; ☎ 2045 5096; Bahnhof Friedrichstrasse; ☑ 7am-8pm Mon-Fri, 8am-8pm Sat & Sun; U-/S-Bahn Friedrichstrasse)

Reisebank (Map pp325-7; ☎ 881 7117; Hardenbergplatz, Bahnhof Zoo; ☑ 7.30am-10pm; U-/S-Bahn Zoologischer Garten)

Reisebank (Map pp325-7; ☎ 296 4393; Ostbahnhof; ☑ 7am-10pm Mon-Fri, 8am-8pm Sat & Sun; S-Bahn Ostbahnhof)

Thomas Cook/Travelex (Map pp328-9; ☎ 2016 5916; Friedrichstrasse 56; ☑ 9am-6.30pm Mon-Fri, 9.30am-1pm Sat; U-/S-Bahn Friedrichstrasse)

Credit Cards

Germany is still a largely cash-based society. Although major credit cards are becoming more widely accepted in central Berlin, it's best not to assume that you'll be able to use one – inquire first. Even so, credit cards are vital in emergencies and also useful for renting a car, booking a train or for other sorts of booking over the phone or Internet. Following is a list of phone numbers to report lost or stolen cards:

American Express (☎ 01805-840 840)

MasterCard (☎ 0800-819 1040)

Visa (☎ 0800-811 8440)

Exchange Rates

An unstable world economy, wars and other factors have caused the value of the euro to fluctuate rather severely, especially against the US dollar. The exchange-rate table on the inside front cover of this book can only offer some guidelines. For current rates, check with your bank or online at www.xe.com/ucc or www.oanda.com.

International Transfers

Western Union and MoneyGram both offer fast international cash transfers through agent banks such as Reisebank and American Express (see Changing Money for branch information, p287). Cash sent becomes available within minutes. Commissions are paid by the person initiating the transfer; how much varies from country to country but it is usually in the 10% to 15% range.

Travellers Cheques

Travellers cheques, which can be replaced if lost or stolen, are hardly accepted anywhere in Berlin, even if denominated in euro. Usually they must be cashed at a bank or exchange outlet (bring a passport). Cheques issued by American Express can be cashed free of charge at American Express offices. Always keep a record of the cheque numbers separate from the cheques themselves.

NEWSPAPERS & MAGAZINES

Berliners are news junkies who support five daily local newspapers, including the mainstream *Der Tagesspiegel* and *Berliner Morgenpost*, the left-leaning *Berliner Zeitung* and *taz*, and the sensationalist *BZ*. *Zitty*, *Tip* and *Prinz*, in that order, are the dominant listings magazines, although the freebie *030* is popular as well. The free *Siegessäule* is required reading for Berlin's large gay and lesbian community. For the complete low-down on all these publications, see Media (p17) and Listings (p193).

Most neighbourhoods have newsstands selling not only all of these German titles but also a healthy selection of international ones, including the major European dailies, *USA Today* and the *International Herald Tribune*. The latter comes with a handy eight-page supplement of translated articles from the *Frankfurter Allgemeine Zeitung*, one of Germany's most respected dailies. Most places also stock *Newsweek*, the international edition of *Time* and *The Economist*. For anything less mainstream, swing by any large train station, which have large newsstands with everything from *Cosmo* to *National Geographic*.

Most of Berlin's cafés have piles of publications for their patrons to enjoy while nursing their coffee or beer.

PHARMACIES

German chemists (drugstores) do not sell any kind of medication, not even aspirin. Even for over-the-counter *(Rezeptfrei)* medications for minor health concerns, such as flu or a stomach upset, you need to go to a pharmacy *(Apotheke)*. For more serious conditions, you will need to bring a prescription *(Rezept)* from a licensed physician. If you need medication after hours, call ☎ 31 00 31. The names and addresses of pharmacies open after hours (these rotate) are posted in every pharmacy window. Alternatively, call ☎ 011 41.

POST

The German postal service is efficient and post offices abound throughout Berlin. The branch at **Joachimstaler Strasse 7** (Map pp332-3; U-/S-Bahn Zoologischer Garten) is open from 8am to midnight (from 10am Sunday). For regular post office hours, see Business Hours p282.

Mail can be sent poste restante to any branch (select one, then find out the exact address) as long as it is marked *Postlagernd*. There's no charge, but you must show your passport or other photo ID when picking up mail. Post offices will hold mail for two weeks.

Within Germany and the EU, standard-sized postcards cost €0.45, a 20g letter is €0.55 and a 50g letter is €1. Postcards to North America and Australasia cost €1, a 20g airmail letter is €1.55 and a 50g airmail letter is €2. A surcharge applies if the postcard or letter is oversized. German postal workers can be very finicky about this and may measure any letter that looks even remotely non-standard.

Letters sent within Germany take one to two days for delivery; those addressed to destinations within Europe or to North America take four to six days, and to Australasia five to seven days.

RADIO

Berlin's radio dial is crowded with stations. Some of the most popular stations mix chart music with inane talk and ads, such as the youth-oriented Fritz at 102.6, the techno-driven Kiss at 98.8 or Radio Energy at 103.4. The BBC broadcasts at 90.2. Among the more sophisticated stations is Radio Eins (95.8), which alternates pop music with cultural and political reports and interviews. Radio Multi-kulti (106.8) is a feast for world music fans and also has regular programming in various foreign languages. Jazz fiends should check out Jazzradio at 101.9, while classical music rules on Klassik-Radio at 101.3. InfoRadio at 93.1 has an all-news format, including live interviews.

SAFETY

By all accounts, Berlin is among the safest and most tolerant of European cities. Walking alone at night is not usually dangerous, although there's always safety in numbers as in any urban environment.

Despite some bad press, racial attacks are quite rare in Berlin. Having said that, although people of any skin colour are usually safe in the central districts, prejudice towards foreigners and gays is more likely to rear its ugly head in the outlying eastern districts such as Marzahn and Lichtenberg, which are scarred by high unemployment and post-reunification depression. No matter the colour of your skin, if you see any 'white skins' (skinheads wearing jackboots with white boot laces), run the other way – and fast.

Drugs should be avoided for obvious reasons, but particularly because a lot of the stuff is distributed by Mafia-like organisations and is often dangerously impure.

Most U-/S-Bahn stations are equipped with electronic information and emergency devices labelled 'SOS/Notruf/Information' and are indicated by a large red bell. If you require emergency assistance, simply push the 'SOS' button. The information button allows you to speak directly with the stationmaster.

TAX & REFUNDS

Most German goods and services include a value-added tax (VAT), called Mehrwertsteuer (or MwSt), of 16%. If your permanent residence is outside the EU, you can have up to 12.7% refunded if you take goods home with you within three months of purchase. The only hitch is that this scheme is only good at stores displaying the 'tax free shopping' sign.

At the time of purchase (€25 minimum), you must request a global refund cheque from the sales staff. When you get to the airport, show your goods and receipts to a customs official *before* checking in for your flight (with the exception of Frankfurt, where you check in yourself but not your luggage, then go to customs, then check in your luggage). The customs official will stamp your global refund cheques, which you can then take straight to the cash refund office and walk away with a wad of money. Alternatively, you can mail your cheques to the address provided in the envelope for a refund via credit card or bank cheque. For full details, see www.globalrefund.com.

TELEPHONE

Most public pay phones only work with Deutsche Telecom (DT) phonecards, available in denominations of €5, €10 and €20 from post offices, newsagents and tourist offices.

To call a Berlin number from abroad, dial your country's international access code, then 49 (Germany's country code), then 30 (area code without initial 0), followed by the local number. Germany's international access code is 00. For directory assistance in English, dial ☎ 11837 (€0.20 connecting fee plus €1 per minute, ☷ 6am-11pm).

Numbers starting with 0800 are toll free, 01801 numbers are charged at 4.6 cents per minute, 01803 at 9 cents and 01805 at 12 cents. Calls to numbers starting with 01802 cost a flat 6.2 cents, while those to 01804 numbers cost a flat 24 cents. Most 0190 numbers cost 62 cents per minute. Direct-dialled calls made from hotel rooms are often charged at a premium.

If you have access to a private phone, you can benefit from cheap rates by using a call-by-call access code offered by a bewildering number of providers such as **Arcor** (☎ 01070) and **Freenet** (☎ 01015). An excellent website for wading through the tariff jungle and ferreting out the best rates is www.billigertele fonieren.de.

Faxes can be sent and received at most hotels, photocopy shops and Internet cafés.

Mobile Phones

Americans call it a 'cell phone', Brits use a 'mobile' and Germans are addicted to their 'handy'. Germany uses GSM 900/1800, which is compatible with the rest of Europe and Australia, but not with the North American GSM 1900 or the totally different system in Japan. Multiband GSM phones that work on both sides of the Atlantic are becoming increasingly common.

If yours isn't one of these, the simplest solution may be to buy a GSM prepaid 'handy' at a German telecom store, such as those run by **T-Online** (☎ 0800-330 6699; www.t-mobile.de) or **Debitel** (☎ 0180-583 3444; www.debitel -center.de), found on practically every major street corner. All sell mobiles for less than €100, which includes some prepaid minutes and a rechargeable SIM chip for buying additional airtime. Most throw in free voicemail as well. There are no contracts or billing hassles and you don't have to be a resident to buy one. On the downside, per minute rates are higher than with a contract, but different plans are available to suit your particular needs.

Note: in Germany calls to a handy are more expensive than those to a stationary number.

Phonecards

Deutsche Telekom phonecards are OK for local calls, but for calling long-distance or internationally, you'll usually get better rates with prepaid phonecards commonly sold at news kiosks and discount telephone call shops.

With these phonecards, calls can be made from any phone by first dialling a toll-free access number, followed by a PIN listed on the card, followed by the number. Most cards also work with pay phones but usually at a surcharge.

Beware of cards with hidden charges such as an 'activation fee' or a per-call connection fee. Those sold at Reisebank outlets (see Changing Money, p287) offer some of the best prices around. At the time of writing, calls within Germany and to many countries, including the UK, US and Australia, cost only €0.06 cents per minute.

TELEVISION

Many budget and all mid-range and top-end hotel rooms have a television set, and most will be hooked up to a cable connection or a satellite dish, providing access to at least 15 channels. English-language channels broadcasting within Germany include CNN, BBC World, CNBC and MSNBC.

Germany has two national public channels, the ARD (Allgemeiner Rundfunk Deutschland, commonly known as Erstes Deutsches Fernsehen) and the ZDF (Zweites Deutsches Fernsehen). The Berlin channels B1 and ORB (Ostdeutscher Rundfunk Brandenburg) are regional public stations. Generally, public television programming is a fairly highbrow cocktail of political coverage, discussion forums and foreign films. Advertising is limited to the two hours between 6pm and 8pm.

Private cable TV offers the familiar array of sitcoms and soap operas (including many dubbed US shows), chat and game shows and, of course, feature films of all genres. DSF and EuroSport are dedicated sports channels, and MTV and its German equivalent VIVA can also be viewed. Commercial breaks are frequent on these stations.

TIME

Throughout Germany, clocks are set to Central European Time (GMT/UTC plus one hour). Daylight-saving time comes into effect at 2am on the last Sunday in March and ends on the last Sunday in October. Without taking daylight-saving times into account, when it's noon in Berlin, it's 11am in London, 6am in New York, 3am in San Francisco, 8pm in Tokyo, 9pm in Sydney and 11pm in Auckland. The use of the 24-hour clock (eg 6.30pm is 18.30) is common.

Directory – Practicalities

TIPPING

Restaurant bills always include a service charge *(Bedienung)*, but most people add 5% or 10% unless the service was abhorrent (see Tipping, p163). At hotels, bellhops are given about €1 per bag and it's also nice to leave a few euros for the room cleaners. Tip bartenders about 5% and taxi drivers around 10%.

TOURIST INFORMATION

Berlin Tourismus Marketing (BTM; www.berlin-tourist-information.de) operates three tourist offices, and a **call centre** (☎ 250 025; ☺ 8am-7pm Mon-Fri, 9am-6pm Sat & Sun) whose multilingual staff can answer general questions and make hotel and event bookings. When not staffed, you can listen to recorded information or order brochures.

BTM Tourist Office Brandenburg Gate (Map pp320-1; Pariser Platz, south wing; ☺ 10am-6pm; S-Bahn Unter den Linden, bus No 100, 200)

BTM Tourist Office Europa-Center (Map pp332-3; Budapester Strasse 45; ☺ 10am-7pm Mon-Sat, 10am-6pm Sun; U-/S-Bahn Zoologischer Garten)

BTM Tourist Office TV Tower (Map pp328-9; Alexanderplatz; ☺ 10am-6pm; U-/S-Bahn Alexanderplatz)

Euraide (Map pp332-3; ☎ ; www.euraide.de; Bahnhof Zoo; ☎ 8.30am-noon Mon-Sat, 1pm-4.30pm Mon-Fri; U-/S-Bahn Zoologischer Garten) Inside Zoo station, behind the Reisezentrum, this helpful office provides advice and information on trains, lodging, tours and other travel-related subjects in English.

VISAS

EU nationals and those from certain other European countries, including Switzerland, require only a passport or their national identity card to enter and stay in Germany. Citizens of Australia, Canada, Israel, Japan, New Zealand and the US are among those countries that are exempt from visa status and require only a valid passport if entering as tourists for a maximum stay of three months.

Nationals from most other countries need a so-called Schengen Visa, named for the Luxembourg town where the treaty to abolish intra-EU border checkpoints and passport controls was signed in 1995. With a Schengen Visa, you may enter any one of the 15 member countries and then travel freely to all the others. These countries are: Austria, Belgium, Denmark, Finland, France, Germany, Iceland, Italy, Greece, Luxembourg, The Netherlands, Norway, Portugal, Spain and Sweden. You must apply for the Schengen Visa with the embassy or consulate of the country that is your primary destination. It is valid for stays up to 90 days. Legal residency in any Schengen country makes a visa unnecessary, regardless of your nationality. For full details, see www.eurovisa.info.

Visa applications are usually processed within two to 10 days, but it's always best to start the process as early as possible. You'll need a valid passport and must demonstrate that you have sufficient funds to finance your stay. Visa fees vary by country.

Make sure your passport is valid until well after your trip. If it's just about to expire, renew it before you go. This may not be easy to do overseas, and some countries insist your passport remain valid for a minimum period (usually three months) after your arrival.

WOMEN TRAVELLERS

Berlin is generally a safe place for women, but naturally this doesn't mean you can let your guard down and entrust your life to every stranger. Simply use the same common sense as you would at home. Getting hassled in the streets happens infrequently and is usually limited to wolf-whistles and unwanted stares. In crowded situations, ie on public transport or at events, groping is a rare possibility.

It's perfectly acceptable to go alone to cafés, restaurants and bars and clubs, although how comfortable you feel doing so depends entirely on you. If you don't want company, most men will respect a firm but polite 'no thank you'. If you feel threatened, protesting loudly will often make the offender slink away with embarrassment – or will at least spur other people to come to your defence.

If you'd like to meet Germans, you may find that it's actually not so easily done – as a whole, they tend to be a rather reserved and cliquish bunch. This shouldn't stop you from striking up a conversation, though, since most will quite happily respond and even be extra-helpful once they find out you're a traveller. Women don't need to be afraid of taking the first step, even with men. Unless you're overtly coquettish, it most likely won't be interpreted as a sexual advance.

Women's centres are great for meeting other women in a pleasant and low-key setting. Try Kreuzberg's **Schokofabrik** (Map pp325-7; office ☎ 615 2999, café ☎ 615 1561; Naunynstrasse 72; café ☺ from 5pm; U-Bahn Görlitzer Bahnhof), which operates a friendly café and a Turkish-style spa called a hamam (p221).

Physical attack is very unlikely but, of course, it does happen. If you are assaulted, call the **police** (☎ 110) immediately or, if you're too traumatised to do so, contact the **Rape Crisis Hotline** (☎ 251 2828) or the **Women's Crisis Hotline** (☎ 615 4243). Note that neither is staffed around the clock, but don't be discouraged, try again later.

WORK

Non-EU citizens cannot work legally in Germany without a residence permit *(Aufenthalt-serlaubnis)* and a work permit *(Arbeitserlaubnis)*. EU citizens don't need a work permit but they must have a residence permit, although obtaining one is a mere formality. Since regulations change from time to time, it's best to contact the German embassy in your country for the latest information.

Because of its high unemployment, finding work in Berlin can be a full-time job in itself. A good place to start is at the local employment offices *(Arbeitamt)*, which maintain job banks of vacancies. The classified sections of the daily papers are another source, as are private placement and temp agencies.

Work as an au pair is relatively easy to find and can be done legally, even by non-EU citizens. There's no need to speak fluent German, although most families require at least rudimentary language skills. A useful guide is *The Au Pair and Nanny's Guide to Working Abroad* by Susan Griffith & Sharon Legg.

You may be able to find work teaching English at language schools or privately. Hourly rates vary dramatically – from a low of €15 per hour rising to about €40 per hour for qualified professionals in large cities. Local newspapers are the best way to advertise, but notice boards at universities, photocopy shops or local supermarkets are also places to hang out your linguistic shingle.

Citizens of Australia, New Zealand and Canada between the ages of 18 and 30 may apply for a Working Holiday Visa, which entitles them to work in Germany for up to 90 days in a 12-month period. Contact the German embassies in those countries for details.

Language

Language

It's true – anyone can speak another language. Don't worry if you haven't studied languages before or that you studied a language at school for years and can't remember any of it. It doesn't even matter if you failed English grammar. After all, that's never affected your ability to speak English! And this is the key to picking up a language in another country. You just need to start speaking.

Learn a few key phrases before you go. Write them on pieces of paper and stick them on the fridge, by the bed or even on the computer – anywhere that you'll see them often.

You'll find that locals appreciate travellers trying their language, no matter how muddled you may think you sound. So don't just stand there, say something! If you want to learn more German than we've included here, pick up a copy of Lonely Planet's user-friendly *German Phrasebook*.

SOCIAL
Meeting People
Hello.
Guten Tag.
Goodbye.
Auf Wiedersehen.
Please.
Bitte.
Thank you (very much).
Danke (schön).
Yes/No.
Ja/Nein.
Do you speak English?
Sprechen Sie Englisch?
Do you understand (me)?
Verstehen Sie (mich)?
Yes, I understand (you).
Ja, ich verstehe (Sie).
No, I don't understand (you).
Nein, ich verstehe (Sie) nicht.

Could you please ...?
Könnten Sie ...?
  repeat that
  das bitte wiederholen
  speak more slowly
  bitte langsamer sprechen
  write it down
  das bitte aufschreiben

Going Out
What's on ...?
Was ist ... los?
  locally
  hier
  this weekend
  dieses Wochenende

today
heute
tonight
heute Abend

Where are the ...?
Wo sind die ...?
  clubs
  Klubs
  gay venues
  Schwulen- und Lesbenkneipen
  restaurants
  Restaurants
  pubs
  Kneipen

Is there a local entertainment guide?
Gibt es einen Veranstaltung skalender?

PRACTICAL
Numbers & Amounts

1	ains
2	zwei
3	drei
4	vier
5	fünf
6	sechs
7	sieben
8	acht
9	neun
10	zehn
11	elf
12	zwölf
13	dreizehn
14	vierzehn
15	fünfzehn

16	sechzehn
17	siebzehn
18	achtzehn
19	neunzehn
20	zwanzig
21	einundzwanzig
22	zweiundzwanzig
30	dreizig
40	vierzig
50	fünfzig
60	sechzig
70	siebzig
80	achtzig
90	neunzig
100	hundert
1000	tausend

Days

Monday	Montag
Tuesday	Dienstag
Wednesday	Mittwoch
Thursday	Donnerstag
Friday	Freitag
Saturday	Samstag
Sunday	Sonntag

Banking

I'd like to ...
Ich möchte ...
  cash a cheque
  einen Scheck einlösen
  change money
  Geld umtauschen
  change some travellers cheques
  Reiseschecks einlösen

Where's the nearest ...?
Wo ist der/die nächste ...? m/f
  automatic teller machine
  Geldautomat
  foreign exchange office
  Geldwechselstube

Post

I want to send a ...
Ich möchte ... senden.

fax	ein Fax
parcel	ein Paket
postcard	eine Postkarte

I want to buy a/an...
Ich möchte ... kaufen.

aerogram	ein Aerogramm
envelope	einen Umschlag
stamp	eine Briefmarke

Phones & Mobiles

I want to make a ...
Ich möchte ...
  call (to Singapore)
  (nach Singapur) telefonieren
  reverse-charge/collect call (to Singapore)
  ein R-Gespräch (nach Singapur) führen

I want to buy a phonecard.
Ich möchte eine Telefonkarte kaufen.

Where can I find a/an ...?
Ich hätte gern ...
I'd like a/an ...
Ich hätte gern ...
  adaptor plug
  einen Adapter für die steckdose
  charger for my phone
  ein Ladegerät für mein Handy
  mobile/cell phone for hire
  ein Miethandy
  prepaid mobile/cell phone
  ein Handy mit Prepaidkarte
  SIM card for your network
  eine SIM-Karte für Ihr Netz

Internet

Where's the local Internet café?
Wo ist hier ein Internet-Café?

I'd like to ...
Ich möchte ...
  check my email
  meine E-Mails checken
  get Internet access
  Internetzugang haben

Transport

What time does the ... leave?
Wann fährt ... ab?

boat	das Boot
bus	der Bus
train	der Zug

What time does the plane leave?
Wann fliegt das Flugzeug ab?

What time's the ... bus?
Wann fährt der ... Bus?

first	erste
last	letzte
next	nächste

Where's the nearest metro station?
Wo ist der nächste U-Bahnhof?

Are you free? (taxi)
Sind Sie frei?
Please put the meter on.
Schalten Sie bitte den Taxameter ein.
How much is it to ...?
Was kostet es bis ...?
Please take me to (this address).
Bitte bringen Sie mich zu (dieser Adresse).

FOOD

breakfast	Frühstück
lunch	Mittagessen
dinner	Abendessen
snack	Snack
eat	essen
drink	trinken

Can you recommend a ...?
Können Sie ... empfehlen?

bar/pub	eine Kneipe
café	ein Café
coffee bar	eine Espressobar
restaurant	ein Restaurant
local speciality	eine örtliche Spezialität

What's that called?
Wie heisst das?
Is service included in the bill?
Ist die Bedienung inbegriffen?

For more detailed information on food and dining out, see the Eating chapter, p162.

EMERGENCIES

It's an emergency!
Es ist ein Notfall!
Call the police!
Rufen Sie die Polizei!
Call a doctor/an ambulance!
Rufen Sie einen Artzt/Krankenwagen!
Could you please help me/us?
Könnten Sie mir/ uns bitte helfen?
Where's the police station?
Wo ist das Polizeirevier?

HEALTH

Where's the nearest ...?
Wo ist der/die/das nächste ...?

(night) chemist	(Nacht)Apotheke
dentist	Zahnarzt
doctor	Arzt
hospital	Krankenhaus

I need a doctor (who speaks English).
Ich brauche einen Arzt (der Englisch spricht).

Symptoms

I have (a) ...
Ich habe ...

diarrhoea	Durchfall
fever	Fieber
headache	Kopfschmerzen
pain	Schmerzen

Glossary

You may encounter the following terms and abbreviations while in Berlin.

Abfahrt – departure (trains and buses)
Altstadt – old town
Ankunft – arrival (trains and buses)
Ärztlicher Notdienst – emergency medical service
Ausgang, Ausfahrt – exit

Bahnhof (Bf) – train station
Bahnpolizei – train station police
Bahnsteig – train station platform
Bedienung – service, service charge
Behinderte – disabled persons
Berg – mountain
Bezirk – district
Bibliothek – library
BRD – Bundesrepublik Deutschland (abbreviated in English as FRG – Federal Republic of Germany); see also *DDR*
Brücke – bridge
Brunnen – fountain or well

Bundestag – lower house of the West German Parliament
CDU – Christliche Demokratische Union (Christian Democratic Union), centre-right party
DB – Deutsche Bahn (German railway)
DDR – Deutsche Demokratische Republik (abbreviated in English as GDR – German Democratic Republic); the name for the former East Germany; see also *BRD*
Denkmal – memorial, monument
Deutsches Reich – German Empire 1871–1918
Dom – cathedral
Drittes Reich – Third Reich; Nazi Germany 1933–45

Eingang – entrance
Eintritt – admission
ermässigt – reduced (as in admission fee)

Fahrplan – timetable
Fahrrad – bicycle
FDP – Freie Demokratische Partei (Free Democratic Party), centre party
Feuerwehr – fire brigade
Flohmarkt – flea market

Flughafen – airport
FRG – Federal Republic of Germany; see also *BRD*

Gasse – lane or alley
Gästehaus, Gasthaus – guesthouse
Gaststätte – informal restaurant
GDR – German Democratic Republic (the former East Germany); see also *DDR*
Gedenkstätte – memorial site
Gepäckaufbewahrung – left-luggage office
Gestapo – Geheime Staatspolizei (Nazi secret police)
Gründerzeit – literally 'foundation time'; early years of German Empire, roughly 1871–90

Hafen – harbour, port
Haltestelle – bus stop
Hauptbahnhof (Hbf) – main train station
Heilige Römische Reich – Holy Roman Empire; 8th century to 1806
Hochdeutsch – literally 'High German'; standard spoken and written German, developed from a regional Saxon dialect
Hof (Höfe) – courtyard(s)
Hotel garni – a hotel without a restaurant where you are only served breakfast

Imbiss – snack bar, takeaway stand
Insel – island

Jugendstil – Art Nouveau

Kaffee und Kuchen – literally 'coffee and cake'; traditional afternoon coffee break
Kaiser – emperor; derived from 'Caesar'
Kapelle – chapel
Karte – ticket
Kartenvorverkauf – ticket booking office
Kino – cinema
König – king
Konzentrationslager (KZ) – concentration camp
Kristallnacht – literally 'Night of Broken Glass'; Nazi-organised pogrom against Jewish businesses and institutions on 9 November 1938
Kunst – art
Kurfürst – prince elector

Land (Länder) – state(s)
Lesbe(n) – lesbian(s)

Mehrwertsteuer (MWST) – value-added tax
Mietskaserne(n) – tenement(s) built around successive courtyards

Notdienst – emergency service

Ossis – literally 'Easties'; nickname for East Germans
Ostalgie – word fusion of Ost and Nostalgie, meaning nostalgia for East Germany

Palais – small palace
Palast – palace
Parkhaus – car park
Passage – shopping arcade
PDS – Partei des Demokratischen Sozialismus (Party of Democratic Socialism)
Pfand – deposit levied on most beverage containers
Platz – square

Rathaus – town hall
Reich – empire
Reisezentrum – travel centre in train or bus stations
Rezept – prescription
rezeptfrei – describes over-the-counter medications

SA – Sturmabteilung; the Nazi Party militia
Saal (Säle) – hall(s), large room(s)
Sammlung – collection
Schiff – ship
Schiffahrt – literally 'boat way'; shipping, navigation
Schloss – palace
schwul – gay (adj)
Schwuler, Schwule (pl) – gay (n)
SED – Sozialistische Einheitspartei Deutschland (Socialist Unity Party of Germany); only existing party in the GDR
See – lake
SPD – Sozialdemokratische Partei Deutschlands (Social Democratic Party of Germany)
SS – Schutzstaffel; organisation within the Nazi party that supplied Hitler's bodyguards, as well as concentration camp guards and the Waffen-SS troops in WWII
Stasi – GDR secret police (from Ministerium für Staatssicherheit, or Ministry of State Security)
Strasse (often abbreviated to Str) – street
Szene – scene (ie where the action is)

Tageskarte – daily menu; or day ticket on public transport
Telefonkarte – phonecard
Tor – gate
Trabant – GDR-era car boasting a two-stroke engine
Trödel – junk, bric-a-brac
Turm – tower

Übergang – transit point
Ufer – bank

verboten – forbidden
Viertel – quarter, neighbourhood

Wald – forest
Weg – way, path
Weihnachtsmarkt – Christmas market
Wende – 'change' or 'turning point' of 1989, ie the collapse of the GDR and the resulting German reunification
Wessis – literally 'Westies'; nickname for West Germans

Zeitung – newspaper

Language

Behind the Scenes

THE LONELY PLANET STORY

The story begins with a classic travel adventure: Tony and Maureen Wheeler's 1972 journey across Europe and Asia to Australia. There was no useful information about the overland trail then, so Tony and Maureen published the first Lonely Planet guidebook to meet a growing need.

From a kitchen table, Lonely Planet has grown to become the largest independent travel publisher in the world, with offices in Melbourne (Australia), Oakland (USA), London (UK) and Paris (France).

Today Lonely Planet guidebooks cover the globe. There is an ever-growing list of books and information in a variety of media. Some things haven't changed. The main aim is still to make it possible for adventurous travellers to get out there – to explore and better understand the world.

At Lonely Planet we believe travellers can make a positive contribution to the countries they visit – if they respect their host communities and spend their money wisely.

THIS BOOK

This 4th edition of *Berlin* was researched and written by Andrea Schulte-Peevers and Tom Parkinson. Andrea also wrote the 2nd and 3rd editions; the 1st edition was written by Andrea and David Peevers. This guide was commissioned in Lonely Planet's London office and produced in Melbourne: The project team included:

Commissioning Editor Judith Bamber
Coordinating Editors Danielle North & Gabbi Wilson
Coordinating Cartographer Natasha Velleley
Coordinating Layout Designer Pablo Gastar
Assisting Editors & Proofreaders Andrew Bain, Dan Caleo, Miriam Cannell, Katie Evans, Carly Hall, Margedd Heliosz, Evan Jones, Brooke Lyons, Lucy Monie & Katrina Webb
Assisting Cartographers Jack Gavran, Birgit Jordan, Valentina Kremenchutskaya & Sarah Sloane
Cover Designer Annika Roojun
Series Designer Nic Lehman
Series Design Concept Nic Lehman & Andrew Weatherill
Managing Cartographers Mark Griffiths & Adrian Persoglia
Managing Editors Kerryn Burgess & Danielle North
Layout Managers Adriana Mammarella & Kate McDonald
Mapping Development Paul Piaia
Project Manager Rachel Imeson
Language Content Coordinator Quentin Frayne
Regional Publishing Manager Amanda Canning
Series Publishing Manager Gabrielle Green

Cover photographs Dome of the Reichstag, Liubi Images/Photolibrary.com (top); Berlin sculpture, Chad Ehlers/Stone (bottom); Gilded lady atop the Siegessäule, Tiergarten, Richard Nebesky/Lonely Planet Images (back).

Internal photographs by Richard Nebesky/Lonely Planet Images, except for the following: p8, p20 Lee Foster/Lonely Planet Images; p67 (#2) Neil Setchfield/Lonely Planet Images; p87 Jon Davison/Lonely Planet Images; p154, p261, p268 Andrea Schulte-Peevers/Lonely Planet Images; p192 David Peevers/Lonely Planet Images; p270 Jeremy Gray/Lonely Planet Images; p274 John Borthwick/Lonely Planet Images. All images are the copyright of the photographers unless otherwise indicated. Many of the images in this guide are available for licensing from Lonely Planet Images: www.lonelyplanetimages.com.

ACKNOWLEDGMENTS

Many thanks to Berliner Verkehrsbetriebe (BVG) for the use of their S+U-Bahn-Netz Tarifbereich Berlin map.

THANKS
ANDREA SCHULTE-PEEVERS

Heaps of thanks to my husband David, who's had more dates with the TV than with me throughout much of this project. Thanks for the pep talks, the dinners, the love. In Berlin, special thanks are due to my friends Kerstin and Marco Göllrich, who so generously opened their beautiful new home to me and tolerated my endless complaints about the gruelling Berlin weather. Natasha Kompatzki of Berlin Tourismus Marketing deserves a special nod for her efforts in keeping me current about the inner workings of the city for the past, oh, eight years or so. Finally, a big round of thanks to the small army of Lonely Planet wizards who make books like these happen.

TOM PARKINSON

Huge thanks to the two Beckers, Anne and Annika (no relation), for putting me up, sorting me out and showing me around some unfamiliar corners of Berlin nightlife. B52s are on me next time out. Big thanks to Marko as well, for not complaining every time I dragged his girlfriend around clubs till 7am. I'm also grateful to Katja Kutsch at K7 and, in the UK, Jill at Mingo PR for their help with the Music section. Cheers to the many people who kept me company and fed me tips on my way round the scene: Sonia, Enrico, Sandra, Tom, Stevie, Robert and Patrick; Manu (it doesn't matter!); Mr and Mrs Becker; Stefan Karl and friends; Kiara, Beck and Kalle; Oliver and friends; Taka, Mark, Pierre and Jan at the Eule; and of course Nina K. Finally, a sincere if confused thank you to the kindly döner kebab man who presented me with a bread roll on my way home one morning. Only in Berlin.

OUR READERS

Many thanks to the travellers who used the last edition and wrote to us with helpful hints, useful advice and interesting anecdotes. Your names follow:

Ian Andersen, Tom Bailess, Medelien Bierema, Ienke Bosch, Bob Box, Ellen den Braber, David Bush, Rita Campos, Eric Carlson, Robert Codling, Abby Dowling, Kitty Frijters, Alan Garvie, Michael Giongo,

SEND US YOUR FEEDBACK

We love to hear from travellers – your comments keep us on our toes and help make our books better. Our well-travelled team reads every word on what you loved or loathed about this book. Although we cannot reply individually to postal submissions, we always guarantee that your feedback goes straight to the appropriate authors, in time for the next edition. Each person who sends us information is thanked in the next edition – and the most useful submissions are rewarded with a free book.

To send us your updates – and find out about LP events, newsletters and travel news – visit our award-winning website: www.lonelyplanet.com.

Note: We may edit, reproduce and incorporate your comments in Lonely Planet products such as guide-books, websites and digital products, so let us know if you don't want your comments reproduced or your name acknowledged. For a copy of our privacy policy visit www.lonelyplanet.com/privacy.

Maria Giouzeli, Andrew Harper, Frederik Helbo, Kees Hendrikse, Rebecca Johannsen, Gerald Kellett, Clarence Kent, Christoph Knop, Olaf Kosel, Sami Kureishy, James Leitzell, James Lewis, B MacWhirter, Bruce Mansell, Gordon and Lorraine Maze, Vivienne Neary, Robin O'Donoghue, Jennifer Patriquin, Jerry Peek, Nigel Peters, Jean-Renaud Ratti, Danyo Romijn, Mary Saldanha, Julia Scheunemann, Louise Stapley, Anne Tait, Conor Waring, Wayne Weidmann.

Notes

Notes

Notes

Index

See also separate indexes for Eating (p312), Shopping (p313) and Sleeping (p313).

000 map pages
000 photographs

Index

000 map pages
000 photographs

MAP LEGEND

ROUTES

Tollway	One-Way Street
Freeway	Unsealed Road
Primary Road	Mall/Steps
Secondary Road	Tunnel
Tertiary Road	Walking Tour
Lane	Walking Tour Detour
Under Construction	Walking Trail
Track	Walking Path

TRANSPORT

Ferry	Rail
Bus Route	Rail (Underground)
S-Bahn	Rail (Fast Track)
U-Bahn	Tram

HYDROGRAPHY

River, Creek	Canal
Intermittent River	Water

BOUNDARIES

International	Regional, Suburb
State, Provincial	Ancient Wall

AREA FEATURES

Airport	Cemetery, Other
Area of Interest	Forest
Building, Featured	Land
Building, Information	Mall
Building, Other	Park
Building, Transport	Sports
Cemetery, Christian	Urban

POPULATION

✪ CAPITAL (NATIONAL)	◉ CAPITAL (STATE)
● Large City	● Medium City
● Small City	● Town, Village

SYMBOLS

Sights/Activities
- Christian
- Jewish
- Monument
- Museum, Gallery
- Point of Interest
- Ruin
- Swimming Pool
- Zoo

Eating
- Eating

Drinking
- Drinking

Entertainment
- Entertainment

Shopping
- Shopping

Sleeping
- Sleeping

Transport
- Airport, Airfield
- Bus Station

Information
- Bank, ATM
- Embassy/Consulate
- Hospital, Medical
- Information
- Internet Facilities
- Police Station
- Post Office, GPO
- Toilets

Geographic
- River Flow

Map Section

BERLIN TRANSIT

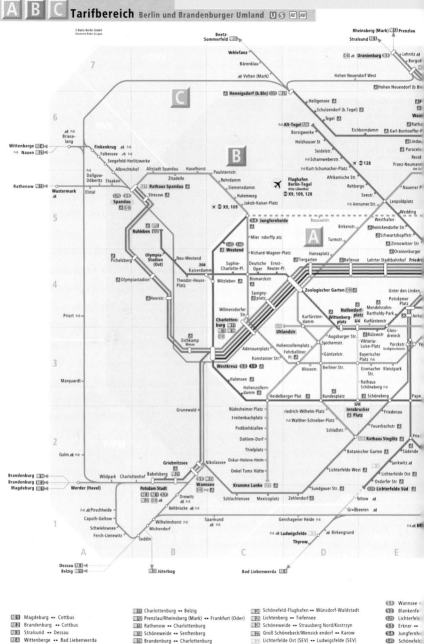

RE1	Magdeburg ↔ Cottbus
RE2	Brandenburg ↔ Cottbus
RE3	Stralsund ↔ Dessau
RE4	Wittenberge ↔ Bad Liebenwerda
RE5	Stalsund ↔ Hoyerswerda/Dresden
RE6	Schewdt (Oder) ↔ Berlin-Lichtenberg

RB11	Charlottenburg ↔ Belzig
RB12	Prenzlau/Rheinsberg (Mark) ↔ Frankfurt (Oder)
RB11	Rathenow ↔ Charlottenburg
RB14	Schöneweide ↔ Senftenberg
RB16	Brandenburg ↔ Charlottenburg
RB21	Hennigsdorf/ Nauen ↔ Griebnitzsee
RB22	Potsdam Stadt ↔ Eberswalde

RB24	Schönefeld-Flughafen ↔ Wünsdorf-Waldstadt
RB25	Lichtenberg ↔ Tiefensee
RB26	Schöneweide ↔ Strausberg Nord/Kostrzyn
RB27	Groß Schönebeck/Wensick endorf ↔ Karow
	Lichterfelde Ost (SEV) ↔ Ludwigsfelde (SEV)
RB33	Wannsee ↔ Jüterbog
RB55	Beetz-Sommerfeld ↔ Birkenwerder

S1	Wannsee
S2	Blankenfe
S25	Lichterfe
S3	Erkner ↔
S4	Jungfern
S45	Schönefel
	Königs Wu
S5	Strausber

BERLIN TRANSIT

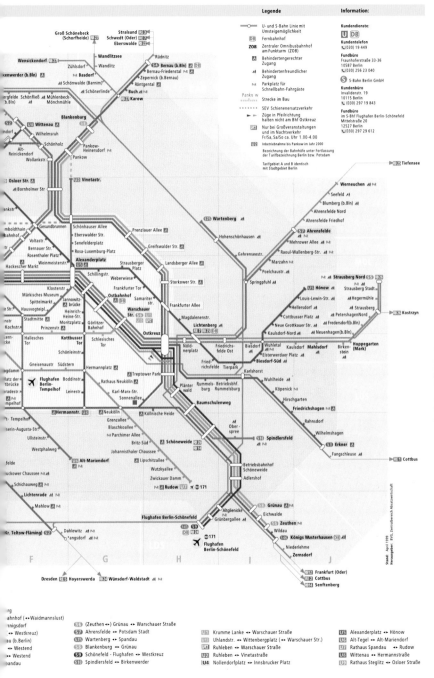

SIGHTS & ACTIVITIES	(pp75–148)
Belvedere...1 A3	
Bröhan Museum...................................2 A3	
Friedhof Stubenrauchstrasse	
(Grave of Marlene Dietrich).......3 B6	
Mausoleum..4 A3	
Museum für Vor-und	
Frühgeschichte..............................5 A3	
Sammlung Berggruen..........................6 A3	
Schloss Charlottenburg.......................7 A3	

EATING	(pp170–9)
Engelbecken...8 A4	
Hitit...9 A4	

La Petite France...................................10 A4

ENTERTAINMENT	(pp191–222)
Black Girls Coalition..........................11 H3	
Freie Theateranstalten.......................12 A3	

SHOPPING	(p236)
Mondos Arts.......................................13 H3	

INFORMATION
East of Eden International Bookshop..14 H3

OTHER
Rollstuhlsport Charlottenburg...........15 A4

NORTHERN CHARLOTTENBURG & NORTHERN TIERGARTEN

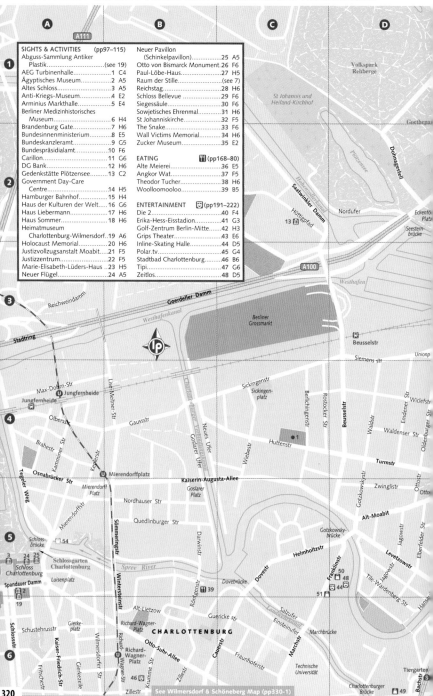

See Wilmersdorf & Schöneberg Map (pp330-1)

500 m
0.3 miles

SHOPPING (pp229–32)
Flohmarkt Strasse des 17 Juni..49 D6
Rahaus Country.....................50 D5
Rahaus Loft..........................51 C5

SLEEPING (p246)
Sorat Hotel Spree-Bogen.........52 E5

TRANSPORT (pp278–82)
Tour Boat Landing.................53 G6
Tour Boat Landing.................54 A5

INFORMATION
BTM Tourist Office..............(see 7)
Future US Embassy...............55 H6
Swiss Embassy......................56 H5
Uniklinikum Charité..............57 H5
Virchow Klinikum.................58 E2

321

NORTHERN MITTE & PRENZLAUER BERG

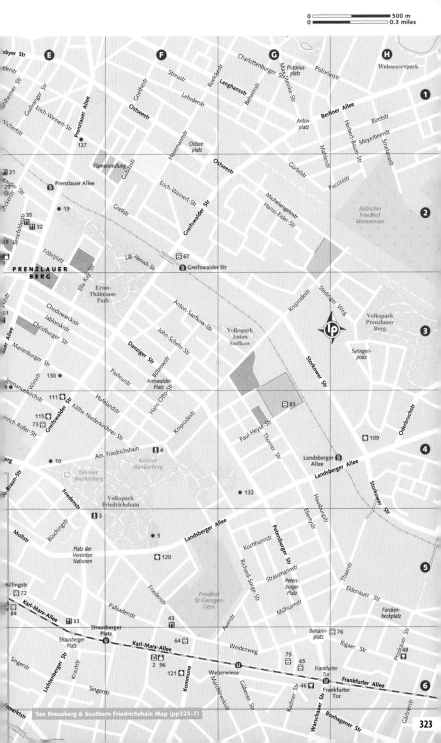

E **F** **G** **H**

sbyer Str

hlheiner Str

Gudvanger Str
Erich-Weinert-Str
Nichertstr

Prenzlauer Allee

Goethestr

Streustr

Lehrderstr

Langhansstr

Roelckestr

Charlottenburger Str

Max-Steinke-Str

Pistorius-
platz

Pistoriusstr

Weissenseepark

1

Ostseestr

Berliner Allee

Anton-
platz

Herbert-Baum-Str

Mahlerstr

Bizetstr

Meyerbeerstr

Smetanastr

gauger Str
@hchenstr
@2g

127

Flamensiedlung

Gubitzstr

Hosemannstr

Ostsee-
platz

Ostseestr

Gürtelstr

Puccinistr

S Prenzlauer Allee

19

Grellstr

Erich-Weinert-Str

Greifswalder Str

Michelangelostr

Hans-Eisler-Str

Jüdischer
Friedhof
Weissensee

2

35
32

Senefeldstr

Fröbelplatz

Ella-Kay-Str

Lilli-Henoch-Str

67

Greifswalder Str

S Greifswalder Str

28

**PRENZLAUER
BERG**

Ernst-
Thälmann-
Park

Kniprodestr

Stedinger Weg

Volkspark
Prenzlauer
Berg

3

rtstr

uer Allee

Marienburger Str

Immanuelkirchstr

8

Chodowieckistr
Jablonskistr
Christburger Str

Danziger Str

Anton-Saefkow-Str

John-Schehr-Str

Pasteurstr

Bötzowstr

Arnswalder
Platz

Volkspark
Anton
Saefkow

Storkower Str

Syringen-
platz

Osterbuchtstr

130

111

115
73

Greifswalder Str

inrich-Roller-Str

Hufelandstr

Käthe-Niederkirchner-Str

Hans-Otto-Str

Kniprodestr

83

Paul-Heyse-Str

Thorner Str

109

Storkower Str

4

erg

10

Am Friedrichshain

4

Kleiner
Bunkerberg

Landsberger
Allee **S**

Landsberger Allee

o-Braun-Str

Grosser
Bunkerberg

Volkspark
Friedrichshain

Friedenstr

132

5

Mollstr

Büschingstr

3

5

Landsberger Allee

Kochhannstr

Richard-Sorge-Str

Petersburger Str

Hausburgstr

Ebertystr

Thaerstr

Eldenaer Str

Forcken-
beckplatz

hillingstr

72

Karl-Marx-Allee

84

33

Platz der
Vereinten
Nationen

120

Friedenstr

Palisadenstr

Friedhof
St-Georgen-
Gem.

Auerstr

Strassmannstr

Peters-
burger
Platz

Mühsamstr

Bersarin-
platz

76

Rigaer Str

Proskauer Str

48

5

Strausberger
Platz **U**

Strausberger
Platz

43

64

Karl-Marx-Allee

Weidenweg

75

65

Frankfurter
Tor **U**

Frankfurter Allee

6

Singerstr

Lichtenberger Str

Krautstr

Singerstr

2 96

121 **Kommune**

Weberwiese

Marchlewskistr

Güterstr

Kadiner Str

46

Wühschauer Str

Frankfurter
Tor

Boxhagener Str

Gärtnerstr

tzmarktstr

See Kreuzberg & Southern Friedrichshain Map (pp325-7)

323

NORTHERN MITTE & PRENZLAUER BERG (pp322-3)

KREUZBERG

TEMPELHOF

See Mitte Map (pp328-9)

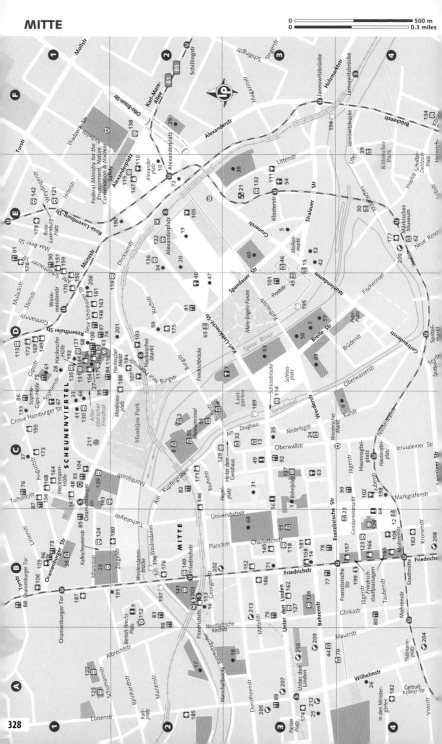

MITTE

WILMERSDORF & SCHÖNEBERG

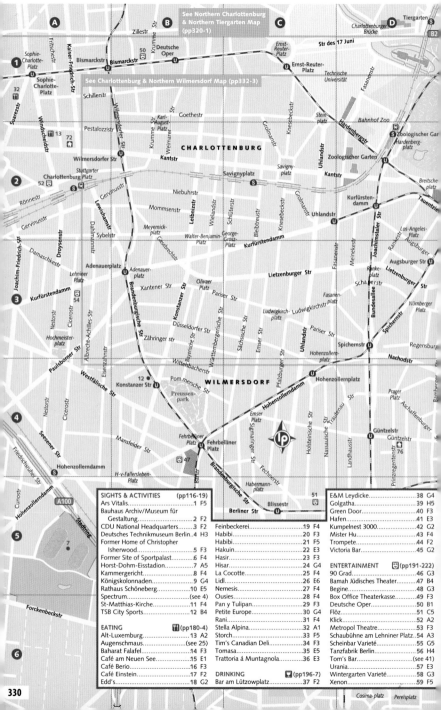

Cosima-platz   Perelsplatz

0   500 m
0   0.3 miles

TRANSPORT	(pp278-81)
Mitfahr2000	78 G4
Tour Boat Landing	79 E2

INFORMATION

BVG Public Transport Lost & Found	80 F4
Copyhaus I	81 F4
Copyhaus II	82 F4
Kopier Blitz	83 F5
Lesberberatung	84 G4
Mann-O-Meter	(see 70)
Mexican Embassy	85 F2
Nordic Embassies	86 F1
Pro Business	87 F3

OTHER

Vorspiel	88 G5

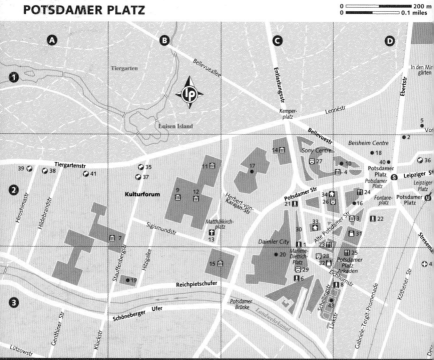